FROMMER'S DOLLARWISE CRUISES

MARYLYN SPRINGER
DONALD A. SCHULTZ

P.37 - Barbados
p. 40 - Nassau Bahamas
p 61 - Martinique
p 67 - St. Maarten
p.73 St. Thomas

1989–1990 Edition

Copyright © 1985, 1987, 1989
by Simon & Schuster, Inc.

All rights reserved
including the right of reproduction
in whole or in part in any form

Published by Prentice Hall Trade Division
A division of Simon & Schuster, Inc.
Gulf + Western Building
One Gulf + Western Plaza
New York, NY 10023

ISBN 0-13-048596-9

ISSN 0899-3343

Manufactured in the United States of America
Text Design: Levavi & Levavi

CONTENTS

Introduction DOLLARWISE CRUISES   1
    1. The Reason Why   2
    2. Return with Us to Days of Yesteryear   3
    3. A Cruise Revolution   6
    4. Cruise Information Sources   7
    5. How to Read This Book   11
    6. Frommer's™ Dollarwise® Travel Club—How to Save Money on All Your Travels   12

I. WHICH WAY TO THE GLACIER?/BEACH?: PORTS OF CALL   17
    1. Alaska/Northwest Passage   19
    2. Caribbean Islands   29
    3. Mexican Riviera/Yucatán Peninsula   79
    4. Mississippi and Ohio Rivers   89
    5. Bermuda/Northeast Passage/Inland Waterways   93
    6. Panama Canal   101
    7. South America   102

II. RITES OF PASSAGE: HOW MUCH WILL IT COST?   108
    1. Help from Travel Agents   109
    2. Comparing Costs   109
    3. Seasonal Sailing   111
    4. More Budgetwise Tips   111
    5. Fly-Free and Air/Sea Programs   113
    6. When Is a Bargain Worth the Price?   114
    7. Tipping   114
    8. Shore Excursions   115
    9. Fun and Games and Other Expenses   117

III. IS THAT YOUR SHIP COMING IN?: SELECTING YOUR CRUISE   119
    1. Price   120
    2. Entertainment   120
    3. Crew Nationality   120
    4. Ports   121
    5. Fellow Passengers and Other Special People   122
    6. Long vs. Short Cruises   123

IV. YOUR HOME IS YOUR CABIN: CHOOSING QUARTERS   125
    1. How It Will Look   126
    2. Cabin Location   130
    3. Sharing a Cabin   131

V. CHOOSING A SHIP: CRUISES FROM A TO Z   133
    1. Admiral Cruise Line   133
       Azure Seas
       Emerald Seas
       Future Seas
       Stardancer
    2. American Canadian Caribbean Line   141
       Caribbean Prince
       New Shoreham II
    3. American Cruise Lines   144
       Charleston
       New Orleans
       Savannah
    4. American Hawaii Cruises   148
       Constitution
       Independence
    5. Bermuda Star Line   151
       Bermuda Queen
       Bermuda Star
       Veracruz
    6. Carnival Cruise Lines   155
       Carnivale
       Celebration
       Festivale
       Holiday
       Jubilee

  Mardi Gras
  Tropicale
 7. **Chandris Fantasy Cruises 167**
  Amerikanis
  The Azur
  Britanis
  Galileo
  Romanza
  The Victoria
 8. **Clipper Cruise Line 173**
  Nantucket Clipper
  Newport Clipper
  Yorktown Clipper
 9. **Commodore Cruise Line 175**
  Caribe I
10. **Costa Cruises 178**
  CarlaCosta
  CostaRiviera
  Daphne
11. **Crown Cruise Line 185**
  Viking Princess
12. **Cunard Line 186**
  Cunard Countess
  Cunard Princess
  QE2
  Sagafjord
  Sea Goddess I
  Sea Goddess II
  Vistafjord
13. **Delta Queen Steamboat Co. 202**
  Delta Queen
  Mississippi Queen
14. **Discovery Cruises 207**
  Discovery I
15. **Dolphin Cruise Line 208**
  Dolphin
16. **Epirotiki Lines 211**
  World Renaissance
  Pegasus
17. **Exploration Cruise Lines 218**
  Colonial Explorer
  Explorer Starship
  Glacier Bay Explorer

     Great Rivers Explorer
     Majestic Tahiti Explorer
     North Star
     Pacific Northwest Explorer
18. **Holland America Line/Westours** 222
     Atlantic
     Nieuw Amsterdam
     Noordam
     Rotterdam
     Westerdam
19. **Norwegian Cruise Line** 237
     Norway
     Seaward
     Skyward
     Southward
     Starward
     Sunward II
20. **Ocean Cruise Lines** 250
     Ocean Islander
     Ocean Pearl
     Ocean Princess
21. **Premier Cruise Lines** 256
     Starship Oceanic
     Starship Royale
22. **P&O/Princess Cruises** 261
     Island Princess
     Pacific Princess
     Royal Princess
     Sea Princess
     Sun Princess
23. **Regency Cruises** 271
     Regent Sea
     Regent Star
     Regent Sun
24. **Royal Caribbean Cruise Line** 278
     Nordic Prince
     Song of America
     Song of Norway
     Sovereign of the Seas
     Sun Viking
25. **Royal Cruise Line** 291
     Crown Odyssey
     Golden Odyssey

26. **Royal Viking Line** 295
    Royal Viking Sea
    Royal Viking Sky
    Royal Viking Sun
27. **SeaEscape** 301
    Scandinavian Saga
    Scandinavian Sky
    Scandinavian Star
    Scandinavian Sun
28. **Sitmar Cruises** 303
    FairMajesty
    Fairsea
    Fairsky
    Fairwind
29. **Sun Line Cruises** 310
    Stella Oceanis
    Stella Solaris
30. **Windstar Sail Cruises** 314
    Wind Song
    Wind Spirit
    Wind Star
31. **World Explorer Cruises** 317
    Universe

VI. FARE WEATHERING: BOOKING YOUR TICKET 320
1. **Working with a Travel Agent** 320
2. **Booking Your Ticket** 321
3. **Cancellations** 323
4. **Dining, Mail, Special Plans** 324
5. **Documentation** 324

VII. SURELY YOU DIDN'T FORGET THE . . . : WHAT TO PACK 326
1. **Shoes** 327
2. **Daytime Wear** 327
3. **Jewelry** 327
4. **Evening Wear** 328
5. **Rain and Glacier Wear** 330
6. **Laundry Facilities** 331
7. **Other Things to Pack** 331

VIII. GET ME TO THE PORT ON TIME: BON VOYAGE 333
1. **Miami/Port of Miami** 334
2. **Fort Lauderdale/Port Everglades** 336

    3. Cape Canaveral/Port Canaveral   338
    4. Tampa Bay/Port of Tampa and Port of St. Petersburg   340
    5. San Juan/Port of San Juan   342
    6. New York/New York City Passenger Ship Terminal   343
    7. New Orleans/Wharves   344
    8. Los Angeles/Port of Los Angeles   346
    9. San Francisco/Port of San Francisco   347
   10. Vancouver/Port of Vancouver   349
   11. Getting Your Luggage Aboard   351
   12. Bon Voyage Parties   351
   13. Exploring the Ship   352

IX. LOOK OUT SCALE, HERE IT COMES: DINING AT SEA   354
    1. Morning to Night   354
    2. Selecting a Table and a Time   356
    3. Drinking, Romancing, and Behaving Yourself   358
    4. Special Occasions   363

X. SMALL SAILORS: CHILDREN AT SEA   364
    1. What Will It Cost?   364
    2. Kids and Cabins   365
    3. Keeping Them Busy   365
    4. Kid Food   366
    5. Ashore with the Small Fry   366
    6 Is It Worth It?   367

XI. ONE CAN BE FUN: SINGLES AT SEA   368
    1. Will You Be Lonely?   368
    2. Paying the Price   369
    3. Delivery from Dining Traumas   370
    4. Shipboard Friends . . . and Romances   371

XII. MAL DE MER: IT'S NOT THE SIZE OF THE SHIP, IT'S THE MOTION OF THE OCEAN   373
    1. Cures and Preventions   373
    2. Is There a Doctor in the House?   375
    3. Special Problems   376

XIII. SEA TALK: SOUNDING LIKE A SAILOR   378
    1. Ahoy, Buoy, Get That Hand off the Fantail   378
    2. Ship Designations   384
    3. Counting Stripes: Calling a Captain a Captain   384

XIV. IS IT POSSIBLE A WEEK IS ONLY SEVEN DAYS?: HOME AGAIN   **386**
   1. Packing Up   387
   2. Customs   387
   3. Getting Your Luggage and Getting Off   389

XV. TAKING A SLOW BOAT: FREIGHTER TRAVEL   **391**

XVI. WHAT'S GOING WHERE: SHIP SCHEDULES   **395**
   1. Alaska   396
   2. The Bahamas   397
   3. Bermuda   397
   4. Cruises to Nowhere   397
   5. Caribbean   397
   6. Hawaii / Tahiti / The Orient / Southeast Asia / South Pacific   398
   7. Mexico   398
   8. Mediterranean Sea and Europe   399
   9. Mississippi River   400
   10. Northeastern U.S. / Canada / Chesapeake Bay / Inland Waterways   400
   11. Panama Canal   400
   12. South America   400
   13. Transatlantic and World Cruises   401
   14. Caribbean Island-by-Island Port Calls   402

Appendix MATCHING SHIPS AND LINES   408
   INDEX   411

MAPS & ILLUSTRATIONS

Alaskan/Northwest Passage Ports of Call 21
Caribbean, Mexican, & South American Ports of Call 30–31
Ports of Call on the Mississippi & Ohio Rivers 90
Northeast Passage Ports of Call 97
Lower New England Ports of Call 99
East Coast/Inland Waterways Ports of Call 100
Deck Plans 128–129
A Sample Newspaper/Activities Sheet 329
A Sample Menu 360–361

A DISCLAIMER:
Although every effort was made to ensure the accuracy of the prices and travel information appearing in this book, it should be kept in mind that prices do fluctuate in the course of time, and that information does change under the impact of the varied and volatile factors that affect the travel industry.

INTRODUCTION

DOLLARWISE CRUISES

▫ ▫ ▫

1. THE REASON WHY
2. RETURN WITH US TO DAYS OF YESTERYEAR
3. A CRUISE REVOLUTION
4. CRUISE INFORMATION SOURCES
5. HOW TO READ THIS BOOK
6. FROMMER'S™ DOLLARWISE® TRAVEL CLUB

Black velvet nights that slide as smoothly off the memory as vintage cognac. . . . Diamond days, bright and brilliant and everlasting.

Ah, cruises. Instant imagery, of . . . flashbulbs and champagne corks popping . . . confetti in your hair and stars in your eyes . . . chandeliers glittering, brass shining, and teak deck gleaming . . . white-gloved stewards pouring tea . . . organdy dresses fluttering in the sea breeze, dancing in the starlight.

Across the water comes the deep, unmistakable bellow of the ship's great whistle, signaling departure to the silvery beaches of the Caribbean Sea, the icy-blue depths of massive Alaskan glaciers, the pastel loveliness of the Mexican Riviera.

Can all this be yours?

Can it be you dining on seven-course dinners, leaning on the rail as emerald isles slip by and a silver wake streams out behind you slashing through sapphire waters like a river of shooting stars?

Can it be you dancing, dining, and dreaming the shimmering days away?

Of course it can be you, and to prove it, hear this: last year 1.6 million other dreamers just like you found their dream boat—and sailed away on it.

These days, thanks to the power of competition, this heady world, once the milieu only of the powerful and full-pocketed, is available to the slimmest of wallets.

Now travelers everywhere are discovering the magic of multicourse meals followed by block-long midnight buffets, of 24-hour room service, high tea, mornings by the pool, afternoon naps, saunas and spas, rum punch at sunset, skeet shooting and deck tennis, dancing until dawn, glaciers by moonlight and beaches glittering in the sun.

The cruise vacation has become so popular that it has spawned an explosion of new cruise ships, which in the next few years will have added 10,000 berths to the present fleet! Never in recent history have the shipbuilders of Europe and America been so busy, and never have so many fleets grown so fast.

So popular has the cruise vacation become, in fact, that cruise lines themselves are calling it the "Cruise Revolution."

1. THE REASON WHY

"So what's all the fuss about?" you ask. Why are people taking to the sea in unprecedented numbers, dropping out of land vacations like human lemmings to sign up for floating resorts?

Why? Well, because it's entertaining, amusing, casual, formal, simple, complex, energetic, lazy, and most of all because it's rich in experience and cheaper in bankbook than ever.

In fact, in a recent poll of some happy cruisers the reasons they cited for taking to the high seas were:

- It's lazy and relaxing.
- There are no travel frustrations.
- It's an escape from the telephone and stress.
- It makes you feel like a millionaire.
- The sea is beautiful and fascinating.
- There's a feeling of shared adventure.
- It's fun for couples.
- It's comfortable for singles.
- You get good value for your money, whether you pay a lot—or a little—for your cabin.
- There's something to do every minute.
- There's lots of evening entertainment.
- Kids like cruises.
- You meet new friends.
- It's romantic and "alone" for honeymooners.
- Everyone's in a good mood.
- There's an activity to suit everyone.
- You discover new places.

There's a revolt afoot, all right, but in this cruise revolution the guerrillas are shooting mai-tais, lobbing nothing more lethal than a volleyball, and killing only ennui.

So why not? Don't you deserve it?

Surely, you know what we mean. You've been living, or should we say, surviving, in the age of the nouveau poor, the decade of no decadence.

Year after drab and dreary year you've togged out in crummy cutoffs and shoveled down Quickdraw hamburgers. You've endured airplanes packed so tightly you once drank the cola of the guy next to you. You've made do with resorts that selected their employees from Surly Anonymous and their décor from Pink Plastic, Inc.

Ah, but in your soul . . . in your *soul,* life was elegant. In your imagination the tuna casserole was filet of sole Véronique. In your dreams that week's vacation you spent painting the house was seven days on deck with a cold daiquiri and a warm companion.

Yes, we've all survived these last couple of years, decades maybe, telling ourselves that when the time was right, we'd certainly owe it to ourselves.

Well . . . the time is right.

2. RETURN WITH US TO DAYS OF YESTERYEAR

For those of us born *sans* silver spoon the time could not be *righter*. Supply and demand are for once making something less expensive than ever before—and that something is a cruise.

Less expensive they may be, but less expansive they most certainly are not. On one of today's floating resorts you can live every bit as royally as merchant princes of old, reliving in lovely formal evenings (or lovely informal ones) all the glitz and glamour that has for so long been associated with sea voyages.

Ah, the history of it all.

Beautiful women with glittering diamonds and fluttering fans, dashing gentlemen in tuxedos and wing collars . . . wealth and power, posturing and pampering and posh . . . a month or so of bracing sea air, physician-prescribed, of course . . . royalty and the regal, coquettes and crowned heads, Hollywood and the highborn, mixing ever-so-elegantly on ships designed to provide a suitably glittering backdrop for the glitterati.

Those were the days, my friend—days of fine wine and daily roses, days in which transoceanic cruises elevated travel from mere mundane movement to an art form, posh and elegant days that offered the fortunate few an opportunity to change scenery without sacrificing servitude—a truly moveable feast.

POSH IS BORN: Indeed that very word "posh" is a seaborn creation: Port Out Starboard Home, P & O Cruise Lines' designation for the choicest cabins on months-long voyages that once were a required course in the University of Life Above-Stairs.

Elegant cruising got its start for the most mundane of reasons: money. Shipping magnates, looking for a way to make money from transoceanic cargo liners during slow winter seasons, dreamed up a plan to send *people* on the ship. One of the first such voyages occurred as long ago as 1891, although P & O, the world's oldest line, had begun excursions from England as far back as 1844 in wooden paddlesteamers.

Back then, more than a century ago when ships were the only way to cross the vast expanses of water that separate continents, it took weeks and weeks to get across the Atlantic.

Communication has inspired many a tumultuous change in the history of mankind and communication played a vital part in the cruise industry too Among the first goads to creation of speedy sailing ships was, of all things, mail.

An early entrepreneur by the name of Samuel Cunard (sound familiar?) took the first steps toward a fortune—and an enduring name—when he talked the British government into letting him carry mail to the U.S. aboard a small but quick (for those days) ship called the *Britannia*, an 1,800-ton wooden paddlesteamer that crossed the Atlantic in just 14 days and eight hours!

SEA SPAS: Britons and Americans have always had a strong competitive streak, no less evident on the high seas where speed soon became the goal of every ship operator. So important were these sea races, in fact, that a prize, the Blue Riband, was awarded for 80 years (from the 1880s to 1960) to the fastest ship afloat.

Emigrants and adventurers began to join the mail aboard these early mail boats, and soon the passenger race was on. Edward Collins, an American entrepreneur with five ships in his fleet, won over some of Cunard's business with amenities like steam heat, bathrooms, even a barbershop.

At the end of the 1800s people were beginning to be almost as infatuated with fitness as we are today, and spas of all kinds appeared. Floating spas called cruise ships became, for some, the solution to everything from gout to a broken heart. Many were the tears shed by a heartbroken lass as her parents dragged her aboard a sailing ship to remove her from the attentions of an ineligible suitor.

Sea cure enthusiasts were followed by adventurers and the socially alert in search of the status-broadening experiences of a European Grand Tour.

Ships' architects met the demands of those early travelers with huge ballrooms lighted by equally huge chandeliers filled with candles and trimmed with fireplaces. Cabin stewards attended both passengers and their servants as they sailed with considerable fanfare on month-long voyages across the oceans.

Among the showiest vessels of those days was a black 1881 luxury liner named the *City of Rome*. It sported a massive bust of the emperor Hadrian as a figurehead, and boasted rooms trimmed in ebony and gold!

It was inevitable, of course, that we hoi-polloi would follow in those wellshod footsteps, anxious to share what was fast becoming the status symbol of the century: the transoceanic cruise. It is just as inevitable that this swirling of socially pure waters would lead to the creation of proper places for all: first class, second class, tourist class, and sometimes even third class.

Class, however, hardly mattered to adventuresome students and Europaphiles who were intent on viewing *la vie parisienne* and didn't much care how they got there.

EVERYBODY INTO THE POOL: In the late 1800s many nationalities got into the shipping act, each replicating much of their national ambience on board their flagships.

By the early 1900s French, German, British, Scandinavian, Italian, and Dutch shipping magnates had launched such famous vessels as the *Deutschland*, Holland America's *Nieuw Amsterdam* and *Rotterdam*, Cunard's *Caronia* and *Carmania*. Britain also produced the *Lusitania* and the *Mauretania*, which surprised the cruising world with such goodies as private bathrooms and some of the most elegant furnishings afloat.

Competition often breeds imitation, and it certainly did so aboard cruise ships, which set about to outdo each other until ships began to look like extravagant floating mansions: columned swimming pools, goldleaf moldings in the dining room, silk hangings, jewel-like colors verging on the gaudy, fine china, elegant silver services—all the baroque and show-biz glitziness that characterized those times.

When war broke out in 1914, the New York-Europe waters were awash with transatlantic liners from many nations. War, however, is not particularly conducive to high-flying good times. It certainly didn't do much for the shipping industry, except reduce the competition. A number of liners were damaged or destroyed by mines or U-boats in the North Sea, a circumstance that dampened voyagers' enthusiasm for ocean travel.

After the war, many lines returned to the passenger business. Ships that were to become legendary included the *Aquitania*, the *Mauretania*, Italy's *Conte di Savoia*, the *Île de France*, Germany's *Bremen* and *Europa*, the *Normandie*, complete with regulation-size tennis court, and later the most famous of them all, the *Queen Mary* and *Queen Elizabeth*, constructed in the 1930s.

WET MARTINIS: During the 1920s transatlantic service flagged for a while, but regained some spirit, shall we say, from a strange source: Prohibition.

Ships flying foreign flags could still carry liquor, and did so happily. Passengers in search of a snort poured onto ships, which by now were becoming egalitarian, aiming their appeal at many income brackets.

These voyages, dubbed "booze cruises," had quite a leveling influence on the formerly upper-crust world of cruises. Soon shipping companies were sending their vessels out for quickie cruises on which swingers of all ages and incomes mingled reasonably happily together for a few days at sea.

Cunard's *Berengaria,* a 50,000-ton ship, became known as the "Bargain Area" for its cheap gin-soused cruises on which fares began at $50.

It was not long before the barriers fell. First class, second class, tourist class, and all the other classes became one class—and that is the way they remain today on almost all cruising ships. (Cunard's massive *QE2* remains a haughty exception to that rule.)

Historians agree that never before or since the 1930s have cruises and cruise ships been as grandly elegant as they were in those outdo-each-other days. Cole Porter took his piano on a 1935 cruise to Fiji where he wrote "Begin the Beguine," and the 83,000-ton *Normandie* of the French Line sailed to Rio (*sans* air conditioning), the largest ship ever to cross the equator. Some of her passengers had grand pianos in their suites too!

Where, you may be wondering, were the Americans in all this? In a word, nowhere. Rimmed as we are by water, you'd think Americans would take to the seas like dolphins, but it was not to be so.

As the years rolled by, Americans made many an attempt to run successful shipping operations and did create a massive vessel called the *United States,* but that ship, along with the U.S.-flagged *Constitution, Independence, Brasil,* and *Argentina,* hit rocky financial waters. Two of those, the *Constitution* and *Independence,* have been restored and are now sailing Hawaiian waters, while the *United States* remains in Virginia, her restoration a dream as yet unfulfilled.

Time is the leveler of all things, including cruise ships, many of which have gone to junkyards or watery graves. Some, like the *Queen Mary,* have been salvaged. You can still see her, majestic as ever, permanently docked in Long Beach, California, where she serves as a floating hotel. Her sister, the first *Queen Elizabeth,* sank in Hong Kong harbor where she was to have become a floating university.

Some craft still afloat today were built in the 1940s as troop carriers, or in the 1950s when cruising experienced another resurgence of interest. Carnival Cruise Lines has refurbished some 1950s vessels, as has Costa Cruises, Eastern/Western Cruise Lines, Paquet Cruises, Bahama Line, and American Hawaii Cruises.

It's quite amazing how much difference a thorough restoration can make too, so don't reject a line or liner on age alone. Older ships are often more spacious, and retain nostalgic design elements that will give you a wonderful insight into the way we were in long-gone sailing days.

AIRING TROUBLES:
Then, of course, was born that pedestrian, and altogether common, creation known as the aeroplane.

Suddenly, all was sacrificed for haste. One must mingle with the masses, survive coffee, tea, and mediocrity, and endure while the posh of pomp was eroded by the need for speed.

When Orville and Wilbur Wright appeared on the scene, little did anyone expect their creation to have an impact on anything, let alone on the world of sailing ships. That was exactly what was to happen, however, as Americans took to the air and abandoned ships. Fascination with jets and rapid transoceanic travel dealt the cruise industry a mighty blow.

But there is backlash in many things, in this case helped along by some clever marketing. In the 1970s that tidal wave of change from sea to air was to ebb, and for the strangest of reasons: television. In some fertile mind was born a program called "The Love Boat." Fantasy sailed on that craft. Romance reigned supreme and endings were inevitably happy. "Love Boat's" simplicity, its aura of glamour and entertainment, captured first the American imagination and then the American travel dollar. Space on popular ships was suddenly booked months in advance and the world's major shipyards were booming.

3. A CRUISE REVOLUTION

Of course, it wasn't a television show alone that fanned the spark that was to become a four-alarm blaze of interest in cruises. Something more mundane but infinitely more persuasive provided the final dénouement: money.

As the economy has shrunk in recent years and the cruise industry has burst its seams, competition for travel dollars spawned price wars and marketing maneuvers that made previous revolutions look like a tea party.

To lure travelers of all vacation beliefs and bank accounts to try this floating life of fun, sun, good food, and good times, cruise lines began offering all the inducements a group of very creative minds could dream up: free air fare from practically anywhere . . . third and fourth travelers at a laughable (or at least affordable) rate, sometimes even free . . . saunas fancier than a condominium, gymnasiums better equipped than the Y, fitness programs, walkathons, and jogging tracks . . . entertainment showy as a Broadway chorus line and variable as Las Vegas . . . stops in the most famous of world ports and intriguing lesser-known destinations.

Meanwhile, air travel to many destinations was becoming increasingly expensive. Resort vacations that looked like bargains turned out to be something less than thrifty when service charges, restaurant bills, bar tabs, and often even energy add-ons were added to the accounting.

It wasn't long before those who have to watch their vacation pennies discovered that cruises offer something few land resorts can boast: transportation, accommodations, meals, and entertainment of all kinds—all for a single prepaid price. No more surprises at checkout time. No more trying to figure taxi bills and car rentals, cover charges and tips, city tours and lunches. No more frantic calls to the credit-card company asking for, please, just another $200. On cruises, the world discovered that you *can* leave home without it!

That alone was a feature irresistible to many travelers—but there was more. Now you could go from place to place in the comfort of a floating home staffed with plenty of smiling help: no more airport battles, no more luggage-wrestling, no more lines at the checkout desk. No longer was the fun limited to being there —now the fun was getting there too!

So there you were, goggle-eyed in exotic ports, places you'd always dreamed of seeing, and you'd done nothing more strenuous on your way there than lift another martini.

All that—and competitive bargains tossed in for wonderful measure—have the cruise business booming. Some people discover they love this so much that they return over and over again, often to the same cruise ship, which has become an old friend. We once met a really ship-lovesick lady who had sailed 25 times on the same ship and got stars in her eyes at the very mention of the vessel. On upper-crust lines like Royal Viking, as many as 50% of the travelers are repeat passengers!

Don't be a late-comer to the trend. Toss out all your doubts and go now before the world discovers what bargains are out there waiting for them. That won't take long, either, if cruise executives' predictions are to be believed.

On a visit to the Port of Miami any Saturday, you may very well think the world has *already* discovered the wonder of a cruise. It isn't true, however—only about 5% of the population has ever sailed away into the sunset—but cruise lines are running hard after that other 95%! Get there before the crowd.

4. CRUISE INFORMATION SOURCES

As alluring as the world of cruise ships may seem to you, deep in your psyche there lurks a little voice crying, "But how will I pick a ship? How will I book a ticket? I don't know anything about all this."

Well, rest easy. There is someone near you who does know all about this—a travel agent. Never before in history has this career group been so important to the traveler.

TRAVEL AGENTS: When every airline charged the same amount and went to the same places at the same time, and there were only a few cruise lines to choose among, well, who really needed a travel agent? Just call up, order your ticket, and *voilà!* finished.

No more. As everything in our world grows, you have more and more choices—but also more and more decisions.

Travel agents can help you narrow those decisions down to manageable limits, and can arm you with brochures so you can read and dream at home until you're convinced.

SAFETY AT SEA: If you're concerned about safety at sea, you can perhaps rest easier knowing that your bureaucracy is at work. Since the mid-1960s all passenger ships calling at U.S. ports must meet stringent safety requirements outlined by the Safety of Life at Sea Act.

Frequent inspections by U.S. Coast Guard officials make sure that ships don't slip in their attention to safety factors. They take a very careful look at electrical connections, safety equipment, fire doors, fire equipment.

Those safety factors include such things as the boat drills in which you will participate soon after you board the ship. As silly as you may feel when you're messing about with a clumsy Mae West, you are learning survival methods, so pay attention.

Crew members have regular fire drills too, and fire-safety regulations aboard ships are stringent and carefully enforced by the captain and crew as well as by Coast Guard inspectors. If a ship doesn't meet the approval of Coast Guard inspectors, it can be prohibited from sailing until the problems are corrected. This has happened in several highly publicized cases in recent years.

Modern cruise ships are considered as near to fireproof as anything can be. Special nonflammable materials are used in construction of the ships, and elaborate safety equipment is on board.

Until 1986 the U.S. Public Health Service conducted inspections of cruise-ship kitchens twice a year, regularly terrorizing chefs who complained that infractions that would go unnoticed in a home or restaurant kitchen could cause a ship to fail an inspection. Often their claims seemed rather well founded, as most ships afloat sooner or later failed. Health inspection failures earned reams of negative publicity, and in one case that publicity is credited with putting a cruise line right out of business.

All that publicity had a positive end, however. Cruise lines desperate to avoid seeing their names in negative headlines set up their own sanitation crews, complete with one officer assigned the responsibility of successful sanitation inspections—and the blame if something went wrong. Shortly, nothing did.

Ships began to police themselves with such skill, the Public Health Service says, that the service decided there was no longer any need to maintain a full staff assigned to cruise-ship inspections.

A spokesperson for the Center for Disease Control says that the center began the inspection program in 1975 after a number of outbreaks of gastrointestinal disease on cruise ships. At that time not one ship could pass the inspection, the spokesperson said. "Since then we've seen a steady improvement and now two-thirds of the ships inspected routinely pass," the spokesperson said. Those that do not pass are usually those not stopping regularly at U.S. ports, the center says.

Despite cessation of regular inspections by the center, inspections do still occur. Most of those are on new ships, reconstructed or refurbished ships, and ships that are not in compliance with inspections standards.

You can get a copy of Public Health Service inspection reports, which also keep you updated on the outbreak of diseases in various parts of the world, by writing to the U.S. Public Health Service, Center for Disease Control, Atlanta, GA 30333. Ask for the "Weekly Summary of Health Information for International Travel."

CRUISE BROCHURES / DECK PLANS: Brochures from the cruise lines you are contemplating sailing are not only the loveliest wish-books in town but they're also quite useful in helping you decide which love boat you will sail on.

Write or call a travel agent or the cruise line (many of them have toll-free numbers) and ask them to send you brochures outlining their ships and upcoming cruises. Be sure to tell them you want to see a deck plan of the ship (not every cruise line has deck plans in every cruise brochure, although most do).

When you get the plan, read it carefully, particularly the back page where all the details of booking and sailing are outlined.

Just as you've become inured to beautiful travel brochures of all kinds, learn to overlook some of the more Madison Avenue aspects of the brochures. If a brochure doesn't show a typical cabin but pictures dozens of lovely scenes from the ports it visits, perhaps you should wonder why and ask some careful questions about accommodations and on-board facilities.

If you're traveling with children, look carefully to see if there are any special facilities for the youngsters. Much as you love them, it's nice to have the little darlings busy somewhere *else* part of the day, at least. There's also the possibility that you don't *want* to be on a ship that happily caters to the little ones.

You will not be surprised to discover that the most elegant and luxurious ships have matching brochures. Class will tell. If you look carefully and judge with your now-jaundiced eye, you will see plenty in even the glossiest of paper productions.

If you like sports, you will want to see what kinds of facilities there are on board. If you are interested in the finest dining, note how the line discusses its dining possibilities. They'll give all the selections fancy names of course, but if it boils down to some pretty simple culinary options and you're a gourmet (self-styled at least), you may want to search until you've found some really special kitchens.

As you're mulling over the cabins and price selections, keep an eye on where the cabin is located and be sure to look at the decks above and below it, as well as nearby public rooms. Right down the hall from the disco is great if you're a nightowl but howling horrible if you're not.

Port calls are important to most cruise passengers, so when you're looking at the brochure, take special note of the length of time in each port. Subtract a couple of hours from the length of time the ship appears to be in port to allow for docking and casting-off procedures. Brief port calls—say, less than five hours—can be very unsatisfactory. You'll find yourself spending much of your time looking at your watch and calculating how soon you ought to head back to the ship.

Some people care nothing at all about port calls and don't even bother to get off the ship. If you're one of those passengers, perhaps you should think about finding a cruise ship that spends most of its time at sea with port calls kept to a minimum.

If you like lots of service, you'll do well to take a look at the ratio of crew to passengers. If you like lots of space, deck or interior, you'll want to take a close look at the number of public rooms.

If a ship carries about 1,000 passengers, as many do, but has only one dining room and one main lounge, you can expect to find yourself lining up to share the facilities with others. Ships are good at spreading passengers out so you don't feel crowded, but if you're determined to have lots of roaming room, pick a ship with plenty of lounges, nightclubs, bars, and sitting rooms, plus high tonnage and low passenger figures.

Deck plans will also tell you some things about the size of your cabin, although not as much as you might like. Adjust to the possibility that unless you spend a great deal of money, your cabin will not be much bigger than about half the size of an average bedroom. You'll have room to change your clothes, sit around, and read, but you won't be dancing and throwing a party for half a dozen friends in there, unless they're *very* good friends.

If the cabins all seem to be the same size but some are higher priced than others, believe your eyes. Many modern ships have cabins that resemble each other more closely than peas in a pod so that all you are buying in the upper price brackets is proximity to public rooms. On those, book early and book cheap.

If you see some sizes or shapes you find interesting, call the line and ask for approximate cabin sizes. Subtract from that the size of the bathroom and figure how much space the beds will take. Then you'll have an idea how much walking space you'll find. If you can afford it, a separate sitting area, even if it's only a couple of chairs and a table, is nice. Rooms with beds that fold up out of the way give you moving-around space too.

You can't tell much about ambience from a cruise brochure, but you can tell something. If more mention is made of informality than of formality, you'll find fewer formal evenings and a more devil-may-care attitude among the passengers aboard.

Price is an indicator, as it always is. Certainly there are good bargains, but you get what you pay for on cruise ships too. High-priced ships will treat you to the best of food, service, ambience, ports, and entertainment, while lower-priced craft will cut back on some or all of those features.

BOOKS TO READ: If you're sailing the Panama Canal, David McCullough's *Path Between the Seas* will give you a deeper appreciation of the wonder of that journey.

A difficult book to find, but one that beautifully describes man's love of and life with the sea, is Robert Wilder's *Wind from the Carolinas*. It details the story of early American Tory settlers who emigrated to the Bahamas rather than abandon their loyalty to the British king. Once there, their interplay with Bahamian residents makes an intriguing tale, made even more interesting by descriptions of the beautiful seas you too will meet in the Caribbean.

Peter Freuchen's *Book of the Seven Seas* will tell you absolutely everything you could want to know about the watery wonderland around you. You can spend fascinating hours out on deck or curled up in the ship's library with this one, reading about tides, winds, waves, great voyages like the *Kon Tiki*, sea battles, food from the sea, jewels plucked from the oceans, famous sea people, navigation —you name it, it's in there.

Joshua Slocum, a famous, famous seaman who once sailed around the world on a tiny boat, wrote about his experiences in *Sailing Around the World* and *The Voyage of the Liverdale.*

Ernest Hemingway spent much of his time living on or around the sea, penning one of his most famous novels, *The Old Man and the Sea*, while living and fishing in Florida.

A strange tale of the sea comes to us from Samuel Taylor Coleridge, who wrote a haunting poem called "The Rime of the Ancient Mariner."

Innocents Abroad is typically Mark Twain-ian with some interesting observations on his ship's passage across the sea. Anything Twain wrote makes atmospheric pre-Mississippi River cruise reading too.

Other books that will give you a wonderful look at the fascinating history of the great cruise liners include: *Beau Voyage: Life Aboard the Last Great Ships*, by John M. Brinnin; *The Sway of the Grand Saloon: A Social History of the North Atlantic*, by John M. Brinnin; and *The Liners: A History of the North Atlantic Crossing*, by Terry Coleman.

A book called *The Great Luxury Liners, 1927-1954: A Photographic Record* (Dover Publications) offers some interesting photographs of famous cruise liners, as does Melvin Maddock's *The Great Liners.*

Sail, Steam and Splendour: A Picture History of Life Aboard the Trans-Atlantic Lines (Times Books) gives you still another fascinating look at luxury afloat.

For more extensive information on ports, you might pick up copies of Frommer's guides to the region you'll be visiting. Among those Frommer titles available are *Dollarwise Caribbean; Dollarwise Bermuda & The Bahamas; Dollarwise Canada; Dollarwise Florida; Dollarwise California & Las Vegas; Mexico on $20 a Day; Dollarwise Southeast & New Orleans;* and *South America on $30 a Day.*

If you're planning a cruise along the coastal or inland waterways of the eastern seaboard, state tourism offices and chambers of commerce in the states you'll be visiting can provide you with scads of reading material on the history and culture of those states. State tourism offices are a branch of that state government and can usually be reached at the state capital. Your local chamber of commerce will be able to provide you with an address and telephone number.

FILMS TO SEE: Enchantment is the business of movies, and in this day of the video cassette recorder for every home you can bring that enchantment right into your living room, if you like. If you want to get yourself—or someone else— bewitched by the beauties that can be yours aboard a cruise ship bound for some exotic port, here's some of the movies you might want to see before you sail:

In *Shall We Dance*, Fred Astaire and Ginger Rogers glide with their usual savoir-faire, but this time their gliding takes place on a cruise ship.

Bette Davis and Paul Henreid share some momentous on-board moments in *Now Voyager*, and Jean Arthur and Charles Boyer save each other from their respective fates in *History Is Made at Night.*

Those with a taste for adventure—and folks not given to the screaming squeamies—should have a look at *Titanic, The Last Voyage, The Poseidon Adventure, Ship of Fools*, and *A Night to Remember.*

To laugh yourself silly, watch the Marx Brothers and a crowd squeezing into a small cabin in *A Night at the Opera* or clowning around in *Monkey Business.*

Mystery has become a bestselling theme cruise aboard many cruise ships, and perhaps with good reason: several films focus on murder and mayhem afloat.

Among those are *Journey into Fear* with Orson Welles. Hercule Poirot performs his feats of machination in *Death on the Nile,* and Humphrey Bogart and Sidney Greenstreet trace each other down aboard a ship headed *Across the Pacific.*

There's probably no subject more subjective than good movies, so we welcome your contributions to our list of movie floaters.

CRUISE ENTHUSIASTS: The **Cruise Passengers Club International** produces an annual "Rating Report" that can be helpful in selecting a ship. The address of the group is P.O. Box 9, Cynwyd, PA 19004, and the report costs $10.

Cruise Travel magazine is a publication based in, of all places, Evanston, Illinois, proving once again that cruise enthusiasts come from all parts of the nation. Their inland-midland location doesn't stop editor Robert Meyers and publisher Norman Jacobs from producing a glossy and intriguing monthly magazine featuring a cruise, ship, and port of the month, plus some interesting looks at a wide variety of cruise topics ranging from paintings of the great liners to no-smoking policies on ships. Subscriptions are $12 a year. Contact Cruise Travel Magazine, P.O. Box 10139, Des Moines, IA 50340 (tel. 314/491-6440).

A club of cruise history buffs exists too. It's called the **Steamship Historical Society of America,** H. C. Hall Building, 345 Blackstone Blvd., Providence, RI 02906 (tel. 401/274-08045). The club maintains a marine library at the University of Baltimore, publishes a quarterly magazine, and has local clubs in many locations throughout the U.S. Membership dues, including the magazine, are $20.

OTHER SAILORS: Some of the best insider information on cruise ships come from other insiders! Those who have sailed on a vessel can—and will gladly—tell you a gread deal about food, service, décor, and ambience aboard. During a recent plane journey, we casually mentioned the word "cruise" to a lovely lady nearby and were treated all the way to Houston to some interesting observations about ships and cruises, including this one:

"I always check the *Farmer's Almanac* before we go on a cruise," she said.

"For the weather?" we asked innocently.

"No, to see when there's a full moon," she replied. "You haven't lived until you've sat on the deck of a cruise ship with the breeze blowing gently and a huge, pale full moon rising on the horizon. It's . . . well, you'll see."

5. HOW TO READ THIS BOOK

Welcome to the land of "When all else fails, read the instructions."

We sincerely hope that you have no trouble finding your way through 31 cruise lines and more than 100 cruise ships, but if you do, you've now come to the right place.

First, all ships discussed in this guide are listed in the Contents under their cruise line.

Second, if you, like most people, select a ship because it goes to some fascinating port of call that's always lingered in your get-me-out-of-here dreams, you'll discover that in Chapter I we lure you into some dreamy ports, then list the ships that call at those ports.

Third, in Chapter V all those floating hotels are discussed in detail, and their itineraries listed by season—where they spend their summer, fall, winter, and spring

Fourth, in Chapter XVI we've divided the world into favorite cruising grounds (Mexico, Caribbean, Alaska, etc.) and compiled a list of the ships most frequently seen there. As an easy cross check for you, at the end of Chapter XVI is

12 □ DOLLARWISE GUIDE TO CRUISES

another list of popular Caribbean islands, island by island, detailing the ships that visit each island.

Finally, at the back of the book, in an Appendix, each ship is listed alphabetically, followed by the name of the line that operates it. That's so you can easily look up the ship in the Contents, and then turn to the right pages to read about it.

One quick disclaimer here: do keep in mind that as more cruise ships are built, the competition gets fiercer. When that happens, there's good news and bad news. The good news is that you get great bargains on cruises as cruise lines fight each other for customers by offering discounts, super-savers, twofers, every kind of deal except—so far—a peanut fare. The bad news is that cruise lines move their ships around more frequently in an attempt to get out of a crowded market like Alaska or the Caribbean by luring passengers to some exotic and heretofore rarely visited port, Tahiti, for instance. That means that at any given moment a cruise line can just up and change its itinerary, publish a glossy new brochure, and sail its ship off to someplace new. Moral: These itineraries are not written in stone.

Keep an eye on your Sunday newspaper's travel-section ads to see what's happening. Keep in touch with your travel agent who knows what's going to happen long before it does. And keep dreaming.

6. FROMMER'S™ DOLLARWISE® TRAVEL CLUB— HOW TO SAVE MONEY ON ALL YOUR TRAVELS

In this book we'll be looking at how to get your money's worth in but there is a "device" for saving money and determining value on *all* your trips. It's the popular, international Frommer's Dollarwise Travel Club, now in its 27th successful year of operation. The club was formed at the urging of numerous readers of the $-A-Day and Dollarwise Guides, who felt that such an organization could provide continuing travel information and a sense of community to value-minded travelers in all parts of the world. And so it does!

In keeping with the budget concept, the annual membership fee is low and is immediately exceeded by the value of your benefits. Upon receipt of $18 (U.S. residents), or $20 U.S. by check drawn on a U.S. bank or via international postal money order in U.S. funds (Canadian, Mexican, and other foreign residents) to cover one year's membership, we will send all new members the following items.

(1) Any *two* of the following books

Please designate in your letter which two you wish to receive:

Frommer's™ $-A-Day® Guides
Europe on $30 a Day
Australia on $30 a Day
Eastern Europe on $25 a Day
England on $40 a Day
Greece (including Istanbul and Turkey's Aegean Coast) on $30 a Day
Hawaii on $50 a Day
India on $25 a Day
Ireland on $30 a Day
Israel on $30 & $35 a Day
Mexico (plus Belize and Guatemala) on $25 a Day
New York on $50 a Day
New Zealand on $40 a Day
Scandinavia on $50 a Day
Scotland and Wales on $40 a Day
South America on $30 a Day

Spain and Morocco (plus the Canary Is.) on $40 a Day
Turkey on $25 a Day
Washington, D.C., & Historic Virginia on $40 a Day

Frommer's™ Dollarwise® Guides
Austria and Hungary
Belgium, Holland, & Luxembourg
Bermuda and The Bahamas
Brazil (avail. Nov. 1988)
Canada
Caribbean
Egypt
England and Scotland
France
Germany
Italy
Japan and Hong Kong
Portugal, Madeira, and the Azores
South Pacific
Switzerland and Liechtenstein
Alaska
California and Las Vegas
Florida
Mid-Atlantic States
New England
New York State
Northwest
Skiing USA—East
Skiing USA—West
Southeast and New Orleans
Southwest
Texas
USA (avail. Feb. 1989)

(Dollarwise Guides discuss accommodations and facilities in all price ranges, with emphasis on the medium-priced.)

Frommer's™ Touring Guides
Australia
Egypt
Florence
London
Paris
Thailand
Venice

(These new, color illustrated guides include walking tours, cultural and historic sites, and other vital travel information.)

Gault Millau
Chicago (avail. Feb. 1989)
France (avail. Feb. 1989)
Italy (avail. Feb. 1989)
Los Angeles
New England (avail. Feb. 1989)
New York

San Francisco
Washington, D.C.
(Irreverent, savvy, and comprehensive, each of these renowned guides candidly reviews over 1,000 restaurants, hotels, shops, nightspots, museums, and sights.)

Serious Shopper's Guides
Italy
London
Los Angeles
Paris
(Practical and comprehensive, each of these handsomely illustrated guides lists hundreds of stores, selling everything from antiques to wine, conveniently organized alphabetically by category.)

A Shopper's Guide to the Caribbean
(Two experienced Caribbean hands guide you through this shopper's paradise, offering witty insights and helpful tips on the wares and emporia of more than 25 islands.)

Beat the High Cost of Travel
(This practical guide details how to save money on absolutely all travel items—accommodations, transportation, dining, sightseeing, shopping, taxes, and more. Includes special budget information for seniors, students, singles, and families.)

Bed & Breakfast—North America
(This guide contains a directory of over 150 organizations that offer bed & breakfast referrals and reservations throughout North America. The scenic attractions, and major schools and universities near the homes of each are also listed.)

Dollarwise Cruises
(This complete guide covers all the basics of cruising—ports of call, costs, fly-cruise package bargains, cabin selection booking, embarkation and debarkation and describes in detail over 60 or so ships cruising the waters of Alaska, the Caribbean, Mexico, Hawaii, Panama, Canada, and the United States.)

Dollarwise Skiing Europe
(Describes top ski resorts in Austria, France, Italy, and Switzerland. Illustrated with maps of each resort area. Includes supplement on Argentinian resorts.)

Guide to Honeymoon Destinations
(A special guide for that most romantic trip of your life, with full details on planning and choosing the destination that will be just right in the U.S. [California, New England, Hawaii, Florida, New York, South Carolina, etc.], Canada, Mexico, and the Caribbean.)

Marilyn Wood's Wonderful Weekends
(This very selective guide covers the best mini-vacation destinations within a 200-mile radius of New York City. It describes special country inns and other accommodations, restaurants, picnic spots, sights, and activities—all the information needed for a two- or three-day stay.)

Manhattan's Outdoor Sculpture
(A total guide, fully illustrated with black and white photos, to more than 300 sculptures and monuments that grace Manhattan's plazas, parks, and other public spaces.)

Motorist's Phrase Book
(A practical phrase book in French, German, and Spanish designed specifically for the English-speaking motorist touring abroad.)

Paris Rendez-Vous
(An amusing and *au courant* guide to the best meeting places in Paris, organized for hour-to-hour use: from power breakfasts and fun brunches, through tea at four or cocktails at five, to romantic dinners and dancing 'til dawn.)

Swap and Go—Home Exchanging Made Easy
(Two veteran home exchangers explain in detail all the money-saving benefits of a home exchange, and then describe precisely how to do it. Also includes information on home rentals and many tips on low-cost travel.)

The Candy Apple: New York for Kids
(A spirited guide to the wonders of the Big Apple by a savvy New York grandmother with a kid's-eye view to fun. Indispensable for visitors and residents alike.)

The New World of Travel
(From America's #1 travel expert, Arthur Frommer, an annual sourcebook with the hottest news and latest trends that's guaranteed to change the way you travel —and save you hundreds of dollars. Jam-packed with alternative new modes of travel that will lead you to vacations that cater to the mind, the spirit, and a sense of thrift.)

Travel Diary and Record Book
(A 96-page diary for personal travel notes plus a section for such vital data as passport and traveler's check numbers, itinerary, postcard list, special people and places to visit, and a reference section with temperature and conversion charts, and world maps with distance zones.)

Where to Stay USA
(By the Council on International Educational Exchange, this extraordinary guide is the first to list accommodations in all 50 states that cost anywhere from $3 to $30 per night.)

(2) Any one of Frommer's™ City Guides
   Amsterdam
   Athens
   Atlantic City and Cape May
   Boston
   Cancún, Cozumel, and the Yucatán
   Dublin and Ireland
   Hawaii
   Las Vegas
   Lisbon, Madrid, and Costa del Sol
   London

Los Angeles
Mexico City and Acapulco
Minneapolis and St. Paul
Montreal and Quebec City
New Orleans
New York
Orlando, Disney World, and EPCOT
Paris
Philadelphia
Rio (avail. Nov. 1988)
Rome
San Francisco
Santa Fe and Taos (avail. Dec. 1988)
Sydney (avail. Nov. 1988)
Washington, D.C.

(Pocket-size guides to hotels, restaurants, nightspots, and sightseeing attractions covering all price ranges.)

(3) A one-year subscription to *The Dollarwise®* Traveler

This quarterly eight-page tabloid newspaper keeps you up to date on fast-breaking developments in low-cost travel in all parts of the world bringing you the latest money-saving information—the kind of information you'd have to pay $35 a year to obtain elsewhere. This consumer-conscious publication also features columns of special interest to readers: **Hospitality Exchange** (members all over the world who are willing to provide hospitality to other members as they pass through their home cities); **Share-a-Trip** (offers and requests from members for travel companions who can share costs and help avoid the burdensome single supplement); and **Readers Ask . . . Readers Reply** (travel questions from members to which other members reply with authentic firsthand information).

(4) Your personal membership card

Membership entitles you to purchase through the club all Frommer publications for a third to a half off their regular retail prices during the term of your membership.

So why not join this hardy band of international budgeteers and participate in its exchange of travel information and hospitality? Simply send your name and address, together with your annual membership fee of $18 (U.S. residents) or $20 U.S. (Canadian, Mexican, and other foreign residents), by check drawn on a U.S. bank or via international postal money order in U.S. funds to: Frommer's Dollarwise Travel Club, Inc., Gulf + Western Building, One Gulf + Western Plaza, New York, NY 10023. And please remember to specify which *two* of the books in section (1) and which one in section (2) you wish to receive in your initial package of members' benefits. Or, if you prefer, use order form at the end of the book and enclose $18 or $20 in U.S. currency.

Once you are a member, there is no obligation to buy additional books. No books will be mailed to you without your specific order.

CHAPTER I

WHICH WAY TO THE GLACIER?/BEACH?: PORTS OF CALL

□ □ □

1. ALASKA / NORTHWEST PASSAGE
2. CARIBBEAN ISLANDS
3. MEXICAN RIVIERA / YUCATÁN PENINSULA
4. MISSISSIPPI AND OHIO RIVERS
5. BERMUDA / NORTHEAST PASSAGE / INLAND WATERWAYS
6. PANAMA CANAL
7. SOUTH AMERICA

Oh, the glories of the seaborne life: moonlight and roses, violins and vichyssoise, balmy breezes, salt air, saunas, and white-glove service. . . .

Piffle, says one cruise executive, none of that is what sells cruises. What sells cruises, the man insists, are ports, ports, and ports.

And who can deny the seductive lure of a silvery beach trimmed with fluttering palms swaying in the trade winds? Or of a blue-white glacier rising from a sapphire sea? Or of pink pastel architecture, smoking volcanoes, exotic perfumes, lilting accents, and sloe-eyed beauties?

Who among us hasn't dreamed of being whisked away to a tiny secluded cove where warm waters lap across your toes and the only sound around is a bee buzzing about its business?

As intriguing as is the idea of lazy days and action-packed nights, one still dreams of finally getting somewhere, of setting foot on strange, exotic foreign lands that look nothing at all like home.

That change of scenery is what travel is all about, and why ship lines are in business—to take you somewhere, offering you as much fun in the getting there as in the being there.

Once you do get there, you can explore in two ways: on your own or on a group tour called a shore excursion. A day or so before you are due to arrive in a port, the cruise director or shore excursion director will deliver a little—or a long—spiel outlining points of interest in the upcoming port. That talk is certain to include a detailed description of the ship's shore excursions. Shore tours are arranged by the cruise line, which buys tours from local tour operators. An office on board, usually called the shore excursion office or tour desk, then sells the land tour to you. You can also buy and pay for these tours from a travel agent when you book your ticket.

After the cruise director describes the upcoming port, what there is to see and do there, the planned shore excursions and how much they cost, you can trot over to the shore excursion office on the ship and buy your tickets. Port tours often are also outlined in the daily activity sheet "newspaper" delivered to your room or in brochures you'll find in your cabin.

Naturally, you do not *have* to go on a shore excursion. After you've heard the cruise director's port description, you may decide you're not particularly interested in spending two or three hours driving around in a bus or visiting ruins or snorkeling or any of the other amusements offered on that shore excursion.

You dream instead of staking a claim to a piece of beach, buying yourself an emerald or scrimshaw creation, or just roaming through historic streets and "discovering" this lovely spot on your own.

If that's the way you feel, do it. Nowhere is it written that you must take a shore excursion or even that you must visit a port just because the ship and most of the other passengers are doing so. You can stay right on the ship if you like.

If you are one of those who decides to see the port on your own and/or who doesn't like organized activities, you can just get up in the morning (or afternoon), eat breakfast, and walk off the ship anytime you like.

You may, however, decide a shore excursion is worth it. These tours often do give you a good overall view of the port, usually with knowledgeable commentary that provides a good introduction to the area.

If you decide to take a port tour, you will gather at an appointed hour at a designated spot and off you all will go on your tour. Most tours are only two or three hours long with several sipping stops included. Since you are usually in port for about eight hours, tours leave you several hours to shop and roam about on your own.

Opinions on the value of shore excursions vary greatly. For our money, any archeological or historic site is much better—and more easily—visited on a shore excursion. Unless you are a historian or archeologist, you won't understand what you're seeing without the commentary of a knowledgeable guide.

On the other hand, some Caribbean island tours offer *such* an overview that you'd do just as well to hire a taxi driver to point out the sights—which sometimes are few indeed. Often you can team up with a couple of other passengers so the taxi tour costs you the same or less than a shore excursion.

Taxi hours have this added advantage: you can call it quits whenever you get bored or tired, and you can stop for as long as you like anywhere you like.

You can also rent a car or motorscooter almost anywhere these days. Motorscooters are particularly popular in the Bahamas and in some Caribbean islands where the land is flat and easily negotiated on these putt-putts. Like taxis, rental vehicles offer you freedom to come and go as you please, to find a secluded beach or to drive up into the mountains for a crow's-nest look at the ship and the city.

On the negative side, rental cars often take time to rent, unless (sometimes even if) you've ordered and paid for the car in advance. You have to find the office, fill out papers, and budget time to return the car and get back to the ship.

If you're going to be in port for a day or more (Acapulco, for instance), you may enjoy the freedom of a rental car, but if you're only visiting for six or eight hours, you may end up spending two of them at the car-rental agency. That's particularly true in the Caribbean where absolutely nothing moves fast.

Ideally, you will have made those rental plans in advance with the advice and smoothing influence of a travel agent. If you haven't, you can just ask a taxi driver to take you to the nearest rental-car company, where you will plunk down your money or your credit card and drive off into the noonday sun.

So here you are, standing at the gangplank ready to set your sights ashore.

Once you walk down the gangplank or clamber out of the tender and hit terra firma, you will usually find yourself facing a horde of taxi drivers, all beaming happily—and hopefully. They will offer to take you on a private tour of the island/port/city/country/whatever and are happy to bargain over the price. If you don't want to go on *any* kind of tour, just say no thanks and keep on walking.

"Walk where?" you ask. Well, before you leave the ship, ask at the shore excursion office or the information desk for a map showing the port you're visiting. Most lines include a map of the day's port on the back of your daily activities sheet.

In many ports you will dock right in the middle of town so you can just get off the ship and follow the crowd to begin shopping or exploring. Or you can hire a cab to take you to the nearest (or best) beach. Most ports are pretty small places in which you soon will know your way around as well as any island native.

You shoppers might also remember that if you're planning to purchase liquor or other weighty items, many stores will deliver your purchases to the ship. Cruise lines have such faith in the delivery system, they will guarantee you replacement of any delivery that doesn't show up as expected. That very rarely happens. It is certainly worth the risk not to be carrying five pounds of liquor bottles in the heat of the Caribbean sun. You will need to order and pay for your liquor early, however, so the store has time to see to the delivery. Make that your first stop. All this liquor-carrying discussion, by the way, refers primarily to St. Thomas, the Caribbean's number one liquor port.

See, now wasn't that easy? Here you are aboard your floating resort visiting every corner of the world from the souks of Morocco to the sands of Hawaii, the icebergs of Alaska or the bathtub-warm waters of the Caribbean, the dramatic cliffs of Acapulco or the tranquil shores of the Mississippi.

Have you got the picture?

You, dipping a tentative toe into sea water so clear you can spot fish swimming by. . . .

You, sipping something tall and cool in the shadow of a gazebo under a spray of scarlet blossoms spread across the sky like floral fireworks. . . .

You, gazing in awe at a huge moon rising over a diamond-studded glacier. . . .

What are we waiting for? Hear that haunting foghorn booming out across the water, calling for all aboard who are coming aboard?

Quick, let's go! Let's see what there is to sea.

1. ALASKA/NORTHWEST PASSAGE

Waterfalls crashing over soaring cliffs . . . snow-capped peaks misty in the moonlight . . . pine-clad slopes, stark-white glaciers.

Alaska—an Arctic Circle wonderland at the top of the world, the kingdom, and the subject, of nature.

To sail past this dropjaw-awesome scenery is the dream of many a cruise enthusiast. An understandable dream it is too, for here you will see mammoth, eons-old glaciers soaring in great white peaks—and hear them too, as they crack with a great thunderous roar into pieces called pups.

On Alaska cruises, passengers spend every possible second up on deck just staring at the magnificence nature has created here in the farthest reaches of the globe. It's no wonder either, for this is humbling scenery, overpowering in grandeur.

Alaska seems so foreign a port and is so powerful an experience that people often forget it's now an American state, the 49th, and has been since January 3, 1959.

It wouldn't have been were it not for the oft-maligned William Seward, secretary of state in the cabinets of Abraham Lincoln and Andrew Johnson. Seward negotiated the purchase of this mammoth slab of land and islands from Russia in 1867, and won himself a place in history—but not before his contemporaries derisively labeled the land "Seward's Icebox."

Named for the Aleut word for "great land," Alaska is about one-fifth the size of the rest of the United States put together. This massive state stretches over 586,400 square miles, yet has a population of only about 300,000. That's almost two square miles for every person—no crowding here!

So vast is this land that, like the continental states, it stretches across four time zones. Juneau and most of the Yukon Territory are on Pacific Standard Time (the same as California, and three hours behind the East Coast). Anchorage (and most of the rest of the state) is on Alaska Standard Time (two hours behind California, and five hours behind the East Coast). And the Aleutian Islands project out so far into the ocean that they cause a major zigzag in the International Date Line.

As far northwest in the U.S. as you can go, Alaska includes the Aleutian Islands and the Alexander Archipelago, and cuddles up to the Bering Sea, the Pacific Ocean, and the Arctic Ocean. Its coastline is longer than the coastlines of the 48 continental states put together, 33,000 miles long.

Inside its boundaries you will find ten major rivers and 3,000,000 (!) lakes, plus 19 mountains higher than 14,000 feet and half the world's glaciers.

Similar in dramatic scenery to the fjords of Scandinavia, Alaska also shares that midnight sun and the starry wonder of the northern lights glowing on the horizon.

There might still be practically no one here were it not for the gold rush, all those cunning little mink and ermine running around waiting to drape a lucky shoulder, and the Alaskan Pipeline, which still employs many at high salaries in which cold-blooded types would find warm comfort.

Summer months are Alaska's high season, but even at that time of year weather can be tricky, so take your rainhat and sweaters on this cruise—but don't bother packing suntan oil.

Alaskans speak English, of course, although many still speak native languages, including Tlingit, Tsimshian, Haida, Aleut, and several Eskimo and Athabascan dialects. Most natives are bilingual but older folks tend to stick to their native language.

Tlingit (pronounced *Klink*-it) is a tribe you will hear much about in the favorite Alaska cruising region stretching from Ketchikan through Misty Fjords to Wrangell, Sitka, Juneau, and into Glacier Bay. Tlingit means "from-place-of-tidal-waters-people," and refers to the tribe that inhabited this long, narrow island section Alaskans call their "panhandle."

Rustic as it may be, Alaska is sometimes pricey. Expect to pay top dollar for what you eat, drink, and buy. Car rentals are not low either: you'll pay $200 a week for a subcompact up to $330 for a full-size car.

PORTS OF CALL: ALASKA □ 21

ALASKAN/NORTHWEST PASSAGE PORTS OF CALL

Crafts are beautiful and most unusual, stemming as they do from the handwork of the native Indian tribes. Ivory, totem pole souvenirs, jade, hematite (often called Alaska black diamonds), Russian dolls (one doll nested inside another), and Russian enameling crafts are good, although not cheap, buys. Everything you buy is duty free of course—this is the U.S.

Some other good buys here: woven cedar baskets, fur parkas, mukluks, caps and gloves, Alaska gold-nugget jewelry, soapstone carvings, and rare Chickat blankets.

If you're an art collector, you'll see some very unusual artwork and crafts in this region. Bone up a bit with a book or two on Alaska and northern Indian artwork before you go so you'll have an idea what you're looking at and where to look for what.

The capital of Alaska is Juneau, a city of about 6,050, in the southeastern part of the state.

Don't expect to find slick discos and feathered dancing girls up in these parts. Entertainment here runs more toward get-together bars, tall-story telling, historic reenactments, and on really ripping occasions, perhaps the flash of a cancan girl's garter. Nightlife tends to end about 10 p.m.

Through Alaska runs the Alaska Hwy., a road stretching from Dawson Creek in Canada's British Columbia, through the Yukon of gold rush fame, to Fairbanks, Alaska. Built in 1942, the road is 1,527 miles long and is better known as the Alcan Hwy.

Alaska's best-known landmark is Mount McKinley, which rises to 20,270 feet—the highest peak in the Alaska Range and the highest point in North America as well.

Southwest Alaska is a big peninsula that stretches between the Bering Sea and the Pacific, while the southeastern part of the state, the most popular cruise region, runs right alongside Canada's British Columbia and is a conglomerate of dozens of small and large islands, and misty fjords.

So you can keep your own Alaska sights-I-have-seen scoreboard, here are **the ten most popular Alaska attractions:** the Inside Passage, the Mendenhall Glacier, Glacier Bay, Ketchikan totems, the Portage Glacier, Denali National Park / Mount McKinley, Sitka's Russian Orthodox Cathedral and Dancers, Skagway's Gold Rush Historic District, the Trans-Alaska Pipeline, and the University of Alaska Museum in Fairbanks.

Despite its frigid image, the parts of Alaska you'll be touring on a cruise ship are quite pleasant in summer, ranging from an average high of 41° to 47° Fahrenheit in April to average temperatures of 63° to 72° in July, 53° to 55° in September. Juneau and the southern coast, warmed by the Japan Current, has winters like New York and summers like San Francisco.

Let's take a look at some of the ports you may be visiting on a cruise from San Francisco, Los Angeles, or Vancouver to Alaska.

Vancouver, British Columbia

Population: 1,200,000.
Climate: mild.
Currency: Canadian dollar.
Tourist Information: Greater Vancouver Travel Information Center, 562 Burrard St., Vancouver, BC V6 C2 V6 (tel. 604/683-2000).
Public Transportation: bus, taxi.
Car Rentals: Tilden, 1058 Alberni St. (tel. 685-6111); Budget, 450 W. Georgia St. (tel. 588-0261); Avis, 757 Hornby St. (tel. 682-1621); Hertz, 898 Burrard St. (tel. 688-2411).

Shopping Specialties: Northwest Indian crafts, jade carvings, Eskimo handwork. Try Images (779 Burrard St.) or Tempo (1107 Robson St.) for Cowichan sweaters, fur gloves, moccasins, and toques featuring native designs; and Nikka Traders (643 Howe St; tel. 684-5374) for frozen, canned, or smoked salmon (if you're flying from here, they'll deliver it to the airport).

Restaurants: Schnitzel House, 1060 Robson St. (tel. 682-1210); Pyrogy Inn, 1536 Robson St. (tel. 684-2816); in Gastown, try Brother Jon's, 1 Water St. (tel. 685-3285) or Leo's Seafood, 170 Water St. (tel. 682-1235).

Many cruises depart from this lovely Canadian seaside city. Its proximity to the beauties of the glaciers means that you can see much of the most beautiful parts of the Alaskan coastline on a less-expensive seven-day cruise. Cruises from San Francisco or Los Angeles take longer, 10 to 12 days generally, and spend several days of that time getting to this area. Vancouver is usually a stop on these longer tours.

Founded in the mid-1800s, Vancouver offers you beautiful vistas everywhere you look—mountains, sea, gardens, harbor, tiny inlets.

Just 25 miles from the U.S. border, Vancouver is the third-largest city in Canada, after Montréal and Toronto. You'll find another ranking here too: the biggest Chinatown in North America, after San Francisco. And there are lots of European influences here as well, as you can see from some of those restaurant selections.

The hit of the town and one of its most interesting sights is an area known as **Gastown.** Once a crumbling slum, Gastown was put back together again by concerned residents who restored its crooked alleys, cleaned it all up, and presented it to the world as an intriguing conglomeration of boutiques, galleries, and dining spots.

Named after Capt. George Vancouver, who took a small settlement here from the Spanish in 1790, the city was nothing more than a tiny way station until a character named John Deighton arrived with dog, Indian mistress, and whisky in tow. Egged on by promises of the whisky, local workers helped him build a saloon to dispense still more of the stuff. Others followed and, *voilà!* Vancouver. Deighton's loquaciousness earned him the name "Gassy Jack" and his area of town was later to become known as Gastown.

Ships Calling Here: *Cunard Princess, Daphne, Fair Majesty, Fairsea, Island Princess, Nieuw Amsterdam, Noordam, Regent Star, Rotterdam, Royal Princess, Royal Viking Sea, Sagafjord, Sea Princess, Stardancer, Sun Princess,* and *Universe.*

Misty Fjords

On your way up the coastline you'll cruise Misty Fjords National Monument, a place as beautiful as its name suggests. It is often misty too, but the mists lift early, burned away by the sunlight, and you see before you a stirring sight: deep blue waters and glistening white glaciers. Wildlife abounds here, so keep an eye out for a moose.

Ketchikan

Population: 10,000.

Tourist Information: Ketchikan Visitors Bureau, 131 Front St., Ketchikan, AK 99901 (tel. 907/225-6166).

Car Rentals: Avis, Gravina Island (tel. 225-4515).

Shopping Specialties: totem souvenirs.

Restaurants: Gilmore Hotel, 326 Front St. (tel. 225-9423).

Ketchikan likes to call itself the "Salmon Capital of the World" and proves it by offering you a look at salmon hatcheries—or at a grilled salmon platter.

Located on Revillagigedo Island in the Alexander Archipelago, Ketchikan was a supply point for miners in the 1890s gold rush and hasn't changed a great deal since those days. It is in fact still a distribution center for lumbering, fur farming, and mining, as well as a major center for the salmon industry.

This waterfront city is famous for its totems too, and at **Totem Bight Park** you can explore an excellent replica of a Tlingit community house and an intriguing display of totem poles. You can even learn to "read" them! **Totem Heritage Cultural Center** features Alaska's largest collection of original totems and an exhibit of rare Tlingit and Haida Indian artifacts. In case you're wondering what totems are all about, you're not alone. No one knows the origin of totemism, an ancient religion in which people consider themselves direct descendants of an animal or bird. Clans may also consider themselves related to a clan totem and take their name from that totem.

Water plays a very important role in this city whose name meant "salmon creek" in an Indian dialect. At the picturesque waterfront are three harbors, boats of all sizes and descriptions, docks, a seaplane base, and a ferry terminal. All the activity there makes for some intriguing photographs.

While you're here, don't miss **Creek Street.** Certainly none of the early gold bugs did! Once the red-light district of the city, it featured no fewer than 20 houses of . . . well, you know. Today the rainbow-hued dwellings built on pilings over a meandering stream contain an interesting Dolly's House Museum, plus galleries and shops.

Ships Calling Here: *Cunard Princess, Daphne, Explorer Starship, Fair Majesty, Fairsea, Glacier Bay Explorer, Great Rivers Explorer, Island Princess, Nieuw Amsterdam, Noordam, North Star, Pacific Northwest Explorer, Regent Star, Rotterdam, Royal Viking Sea, Sagafjord, Sea Princess, Stardancer, Sun Princess,* and *Universe.*

Metlakatla

You may cruise by this island village, the only Indian reservation in Alaska and once the site of a religious colony. Today Metlakatla is a fishing village inhabited by Tsmishian Indians.

Sitka

Population: 4,000.

Tourist Information: Greater Sitka Chamber of Commerce, Centennial Building, Harbor Drive, Sitka, AK 99835 (tel. 907/747-8604).

Car Rentals: Avis, Potlatch Motel, 713 Katliam St. (tel. 747-8611).

Shopping Specialties: totems, Tlingit crafts.

Restaurants: Sheffield Sitka Hotel, Katlin (tel. 747-6166).

Alaskan history lives on in this small town that has seen many a tourist, from early Indian tribes to Russian settlers and today's cruise passengers. Much of the state's earliest history centered on this village, which was for a time the capital of Alaska. In 1741 the Russians recorded their discovery of Alaska here, and it was here that proprietorship of Alaska was transferred from Russia to the United States in 1867.

Founded in 1799 by adventurer Alexander Baranov (who called it New Archangel), the town was destroyed by Indians in 1802, but intrepid settlers rebuilt. Ages ago the Tlingit Indians called this lovely mountain-ringed village home, and one of their clans, the Kiksadi, made it their ancestral home.

On a roam about the village, you'll find a picturesque harbor packed with small boats and colorful people—downright photographically inspirational. A landmark of Sitka is **St. Michael's Cathedral,** a handsome Russian Orthodox church containing glittering goldleaf adorning ornate chandeliers and carved moldings. This landmark church houses an extensive collection of icons and priceless religious artifacts, all carefully preserved, gleaming reminders of Sitka's past as a Russian colony when the city was known as the "Paris of the Pacific."

There are more reminders of this city's Russian heritage in the winsome forms of lovely, lively dancers called the **New Archangel Russian Dancers.** Dressed in floral babushkas, bright boots, and swirling skirts, these energetic lasses perform folk dances from various regions. You can sometimes see them at the docks, but usually at the Centennial Building where admission is $4 per person.

In the first three weeks of June each year Sitka celebrates a **summer music festival,** highly acclaimed by critics. Classical soloists appear in the Centennial Building, where they perform before a backdrop of glass that offers a spectacular view of the mountain and ocean scenery outside. Concerts are usually scheduled for Tuesday, Friday, and Saturday, and rehearsals are open.

The **Sheldon Jackson Museum** was built in 1895 by noted Alaskan traveler Dr. Sheldon Jackson to house his collection of native art, artifacts, and historical items. Even way back then he figured out a way to make it as fireproof as possible, and today the museum is listed in the National Register of Historic Places.

If you're lucky enough to be in town in the last days of June, you can watch some of the nation's fanciest footwork rolling up a storm in the **All-Alaska Logging Championships,** which come complete with 17 events including the world championships in the Hooktender's Race and Team Splicing.

Sitka Historical National Park was the site of a fierce fight by the Tlingit tribes against the Russians, but is now home to Indian craftsmen who will show you how they carve wood into both tiny and monumental treasures.

Ships Calling Here: *Glacier Bay Explorer, Great Rivers Explorer, Nieuw Amsterdam, Noordam, North Star, Pacific Northwest Explorer, Regent Star, Rotterdam, Royal Viking Sea, Sagafjord,* and *Universe.*

Juneau

Population: 7,000.

Tourist Information: Juneau Information Center, Davis Log Cabin, 3rd Street at Seward, Juneau, AK 99801 (tel. 907/586-2284).

Car Rentals: Avis, Juneau Municipal Airport, RR5 (tel. 789-9450); Hertz, Juneau Municipal Airport (tel. 789-9494).

Restaurants: Alaskan Hotel & Bar (featuring a turn-of-the-century oak bar), S. Franklin (tel. 586-1000); Cape Fox Sheffield Hotel, S. Franklin (tel. 586-6900); Red Dog Saloon, S. Franklin (tel. 586-6303).

This interesting city is the capital of Alaska, created lock, stock, and barrel during the 1880s rush for gold and named after Joe Juneau, the happy-go-spending prospector who first discovered gold in the state. If there is an unlovely view in Juneau, we certainly haven't seen it. Mountains, glaciers, and the sea are everywhere you look, providing views at once tranquilizing and stimulating.

Narrow streets and quiet, contemplative walkways give parts of this city a European flavor much loved by visitors and residents alike.

The **Mendenhall Glacier** is a top Juneau sight, just a short ride from downtown Juneau. (Now what other state capital do you know that can boast a glacier just a stone's throw away?) A river of ice a mile long and a mile and a half wide, the huge Mendenhall Glacier is part of the Juneau Icefield. Mendenhall is backing off at the rate of about 50 feet a year, so in another couple of eons you'll have to go farther out of town to see it. Gray Line of Juneau (tel. 907/586-3773) has package tours of the city and the glacier.

At the **Alaska State Museum** you can see a life-size diorama and some fascinating exhibits of the history, native cultures, wildlife, and wilderness of Alaska. You'll also get some background on the Eskimo, Aleut, Athapascan, and Tlingit cultures about which you'll be hearing much in this part of the world.

Two interesting religious sites here are the **Shrine of St. Therese** and the **Chapel-by-the-Lake.** Juneau's **St. Nicholas Russian Orthodox Church** offers another interesting look at the Russian influence that survives in Alaska.

If you like ski resorts, take a look at **Eaglecrest,** and if you like to look at animals in the wild, journey from Juneau by air or boat to **Admiralty Island,** a national monument wilderness where brown bears pad happily about and eagles soar. Tlingit and Haida Indians perform some of their intriguing tribal dances here.

Alaska tourists perform tribal rituals of a sort at the famed **Red Dog Saloon,** a must-stop spot of rusticity and whoop-it-up rib-tickling good times. Don't miss it.

Highrollers can take a seaplane at the waterfront and fly off to **Taku Lodge,** where you'll dine in a log cabin on grilled fresh salmon, biscuits, baked beans, and beer that doesn't need a refrigerator—they just stick it in a glacier.

A popular treat now in Juneau is celebrating 15 years of open fire and sourdough. Called the **Gold Creek Salmon Bake,** the event is an evening activity departing at 6 p.m. from the Baranof Hotel (tel. 586-1424) and offering (at $17 for adults, $8 for children) all you can eat of Alaska salmon barbecued over an open fire, salads, and sourdough bread, plus exploration of an abandoned gold mine and a chance to pan for some of your own.

Ships Calling Here: *Cunard Princess, Daphne, Explorer Starship, Fair Majesty Fairsea, Glacier Bay Explorer, Great Rivers Explorer, Island Princess, Nieuw Amsterdam, Noordam, North Star, Pacific Northwest Explorer, Regent Star, Rotterdam, Royal Princess, Royal Viking Sea, Sagafjord, Sea Princess, Stardancer, Sun Princess,* and *Universe.*

Skagway

Population: 2,000.

Tourist Information: Skagway Convention and Visitors Bureau, 7 Spring St., (P.O. Box 415), Skagway, AK 99840 (tel. 907/983-2297).

Shopping Specialties: gold rush souvenirs, gold nuggets.

Restaurants: Golden North Hotel (tel. 983-2294); Klondike Hotel (tel. 983-2291).

You may not be able to buy happiness with gold, but you can certainly get a good start on it with a couple of sizable nuggets. At least that's the way they figured it in Skagway's good old days when, without the pursuit of shiny yellow, there wouldn't have been a Skagway.

Located at the foot of White Pass, Skagway was the gateway to the Klondike, so in 1897 you stood out of the way or the roaring tide of gold seekers ran you down. In those days, thousands of gold bugs tore into this tiny town, turning it into a booming metropolis with a population of 20,000—19,900 or so of them moving in during two years of the gold boom.

Tents went up, then cabins, then all the accoutrements of life: hotels, gambling houses and other houses, dance halls, saloons.

You can still see many of those rugged-but-ready structures today, carefully preserved by residents proud of their rough-and-tumble heritage. In fact, most of the downtown section of Skagway has been designated a **National Historic Park**.

Buildings with false fronts and boardwalks line the street. Over at City Hall you can roam through the **Trail of '98 Museum** and get an idea what it must have been like to be one of those early pioneers (admission is $2; open from 8 a.m. to 8 p.m.).

Just outside of town, the **Gold Rush Cemetery**, about a two-mile flat walk from the ferry terminal, was the end of the line for many a brawling, claim-contesting gold enthusiast, including two local legends, gangster Frank Reid and gambler Soapy Smith, who were victims of each other in an 1898 gunfight.

In summer the city re-creates its past with a historical comic drama that's as hysterical as it is historical.

Getting the flavor of Alaska requires a visit to a saloon, whether or not you imbibe there. In Skagway the saloon to visit is the **Red Onion**, which has been around since 1898 when it was the village's most popular brothel. Back in those lusty days, you could tell which girls were available by the row of dolls above the bar—some sitting up, some lying down.

Finally, in 1988 a new attraction was added here: the **White Pass & Yukon Railway**, was completed in 1900, has reopened and now takes cruise passengers on three-hour journeys through some spectacular scenery along the Trail of '98.

A simple walking tour is the best way to see this town—just don't forget your camera.

You can also take a conducted motorcoach sightseeing tour of **Klondike Gold Rush National Park** and the historical district of Skagway from the Klondike Hotel. Alaska Hyway Tours, P.O. Box 536-DT, Skagway, AK 99840 (tel. 907/983-2241), has details.

Skagway city limits include part of Klondike Gold Rush National Historical Park, which commemorates the gold rush trail of '98. Roads from both Skagway and nearby Haines join the Alaska Hwy.

Ships Calling Here: *Cunard Princess, Daphne, Explorer Starship, Fair Majesty, Fairsea, Glacier Bay Explorer, Great Rivers Explorer, Island Princess, North Star, Pacific Northwest Explorer, Regent Star, Royal Viking Sea, Sagafjord, Sea Princess, Stardancer, Sun Princess,* and *Universe.*

Cruising Glacier Bay

Highlight of every Alaska cruise is the trip through a small part of the 11,400 square miles of **Glacier Bay National Monument,** where 16 towering ice mountains spill into the bay and its inlets. This is fjord country at its finest, with downright spectacular scenery that cannot be done justice by mere words.

As you sip a mid-morning mulled wine, your ship sails back 4,000 years into the Ice Age. Towering walls of ice glitter around you and icebergs bob in the water.

Great masses of ice break from the glaciers occasionally, accompanied by deep rumblings and thunderous cracks. It's called "calving," and the broken-off bits of ice that surge into the sea are called "pups." Two hundred years ago the land here was covered by ice that has receded to leave behind slopes covered in thick forests of spruce, alder, willow, and mosses.

In the 50 miles of sea here you may spot humpback and killer whales, porpoises, sunning seals, black and brown bear, and on the slopes, mountain goats and the bald eagle, one of 200 species of birds. Under the water, trout, salmon, and halibut thrive, many of them likely to end up on your plate at dinner.

Glaciers are formed by heavy snowfall that accumulates, packs, and fuses into ice masses. Advance or retreat of glaciers is measured at the terminus of a glacier where the ice is melting and accumulating at the same time. Two hundred years ago ice 4,000 feet deep and 20 miles wide walled the entrance to Glacier Bay, but by about a hundred years ago it had retreated nearly 50 miles to be replaced by the huge forests you see today. Glacier Bay's ice sheet is in fact shrinking at a pace so rapid that scientists are mired in controversy over the future of this glacial region.

By prearrangement, a naturalist comes on board every cruise ship cruising Glacier Bay and tells you a little about the evolutionary processes you see going on here. You'll get a good overview of the natural phenomenon you are witnessing from these naturalists, who love and respect the land they serve. Their talks are a highlight of the cruise.

Anchorage

Population: 48,000

Tourist Information: Anchorage Convention and Visitors Bureau, 201 East Third Ave., Anchorage, AK 99501 (tel. 907/276-4118).

Public Transportation: bus, train, ferry, taxi.

Car Rentals: Avis, 5th and B Streets (tel. 277-4567); Hertz, International Airport (tel. 243-3308).

Shopping Specialties: hand-knit garments made by Eskimos from wools combed from the Arctic musk ox at Oomingmak Musk Ox Producers' Co-op, 604 H St. (tel. 272-9225).

Restaurants: Sheraton Anchorage Hotel, Calista Square, 401 E. Sixth Ave. (tel. 276-8700); Hotel Captain Cook, 5th and K Streets (tel. 276-6000); and Samovar Inn, 720 Gambell St. (tel. 277-1511).

If you think you've been down at sea level long enough, get up in the world on a chair-lift ride 2,000 feet up to the **Skyride Restaurant** at Alyeska Resort, Girdwood (tel. 783-2222). Located about 40 miles southeast of Anchorage, the resort features night skiing in winter, hotel and condominium accommodations, a ski school, the works. In summer you can ride up to the restaurant in 45 minutes as a view of eight surrounding glaciers spreads out beneath your feet.

Largest city in Alaska, Anchorage is reached by train on a three-hour ride from the port at Whittier. Once there, you'll find quite a cosmopolitan city with all the restaurants, hotels, nightlife, and beautiful homes you'd expect to see in a major metropolis.

Founded in 1915 as the headquarters of the Alaska Railroad, the city is an important defense point for the U.S. and also is a center for commerce and communications in Alaska. About 48,000 people live here, many of them employed by fisheries, sawmills, and highway- or pipeline-related activities.

On the last Saturday in June the city welcomes summer with music, songs, dance, games, food, and plenty of fun at the annual **Alaska Fest** in Palmer State Fairgrounds.

An interesting springtime excursion from Anchorage takes you to a **gold-mining area** older than the Klondike, where you can pan for gold. It's 3½ miles up Crow Creek Road.

At the **Alaska Zoo,** Mile 2 O'Malley Rd. (tel. 344-8012), you can see orphaned native animals.

You can have a good time at an Alaska **show and sourdough buffet,** now in its 15th season here. Alaska's "ambassador," Larry Beck, recites poetry, sings songs, tells stories, and offers you a look at things Alaskan at a dinner and show. Phone 278-9225 for reservations.

Anchorage also sports a civic operation and concert association, a historical and fine-arts museum outlining the history of man in Alaska from prehistory to

PORTS OF CALL: CARIBBEAN ISLANDS □ 29

the present (free), a Scottish pipe band, a Bach festival, and a dinner theater. You can even go up above the glaciers in a hot air balloon!

If you didn't pan for gold at Juneau or Skagway, here's your chance: **Crow Creek Mine,** 123 Hightower Rd., Girdwood (tel. 783-2915), harks back to 1898 and is in the National Register of Historic Places. It's open to visitors who come here to pan ore or, for those lacking panning enthusiasm, to purchase it in the mine's shop. All the panning equipment is furnished free, so why not give it a try? Finders keepers. . . .

Not far from Anchorage is the best known of the many national parks in the state. **Denali National Park and Preserve,** one of the most dramatic national parks in North America, is 5.6 million acres of wilderness surrounding **Mount McKinley,** the tallest mountain in the world (the Himalayas start at higher elevations). You can reach the park from Anchorage by train, plane, bus, or car and stay right in the park at a hotel operated by the park service. Most people visit the region on a guided tour and one of the top Alaska tour operators is Westours (which also owns Holland America Cruise Lines). To see what the company has to offer, contact them, toll free, at 800/426-0327.

If you're planning to stay in Anchorage for a few days, major hotels there include the **Sheraton Anchorage,** Calista Square, 401 E. Sixth Ave., Anchorage, AK 99501 (tel. 907/276-8700, or toll free 800/325-3535); **Best Western Golden Lion,** 1000 E. 36th Ave., Anchorage, AK 99504 (tel. 907/278-4561, or toll free 800/528-1234); or **Hotel Captain Cook,** a 600-room hotel with swimming pool, at 5th and K Streets, Anchorage, AK 99501 (tel. 907/276-6000, or toll free 800/323-7500)—where double rates are in the $100 to $150 range. A budget choice is **Arctic Inn Motel,** 842 W. International Airport Rd., Anchorage, AK 99502 (tel. 907/561-1328), where rates are less than $50 double daily.

Ships Calling Here: *Cunard Princess, Explorer Starship, FairMajesty, Fairsea, Island Princess, Regent Star, Sagafjord,* and *Universe.*

2. CARIBBEAN ISLANDS

Welcome to perpetual summer. In the frosty throes of February and the miserable days of March, these islands, stretching more than 2,000 miles southward, are dressed in toasty golden sand and bathed in warm waters. Trade winds stream across the islands maintaining eternal June and seasons pass with nary a whimper of falling leaves or changing temperatures.

Here in these islands are what many call the world's most beautiful seas, clear as a teardrop, sluicing over beaches described in equivalent superlatives. Tiny bays hugged by craggy cliffs . . . great sweeps of silver, pink, gold, or black sand . . . secluded coves meant for lovers of beaches and of each other—all those are the rule here, no exceptions.

Just as each new beach you happen upon is surprisingly different from the last strip of silica you roamed, these islands are as culturally diverse as a history of imperialistic battling can make them. On some islands, Trinidad and Tobago, for instance, you'll find a dozen or more nationalities ranging from Indian to Chinese, Venezuelan, French, Spanish, English, and Lebanese.

On each island are the remnants, or the still-strong presence, of France, Holland, Denmark, England, Sweden, Spain, and sometimes a combination of several or all of the above. St. Maarten / St. Martin is so culturally divided it has two names! Settled by Dutch and French crewmen left behind by a Spanish ship, the island's first colonists couldn't reach the folks back home to find out which nation should rule, so they just split it up themselves, your half and my half.

Descendants of the thousands of slaves imported here from Africa to become the lowliest of citizens, working vast sugar, tobacco, and banana planta-

CARIBBEAN, MEXICAN & SOUTH AMERICAN PORTS OF CALL

PORTS OF CALL: CARIBBEAN ISLANDS □ 31

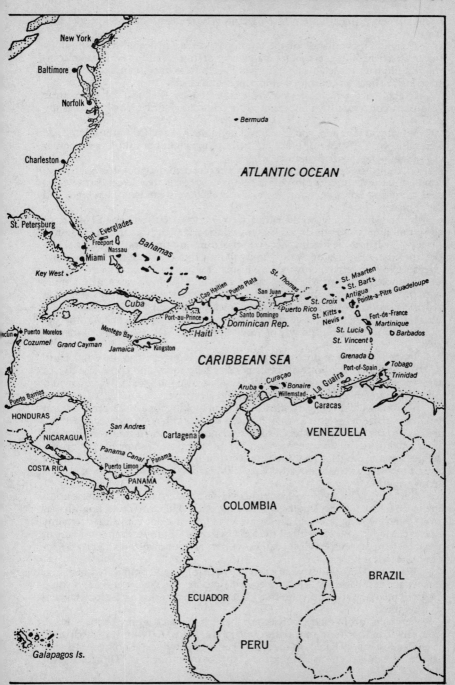

tions, are now prime ministers and governors, bureaucrats, business people, and bar owners.

Not all of these islands are the somnolent sands they were when Columbus first visited here 500 years ago. Jet-plane-loads of tourists and an era of rapid communication have turned sandy spots like Puerto Rico into sophisticated centers sporting the latest in couture, cosmopolitan and chic.

Others have remained virtually untouched by the tides of time, their colonial architecture lovingly restored or crumbling softly, slowly into sandy oblivion.

When you visit here you'll be traveling in the wake of Columbus, Ponce de León, Balboa, DeSoto, Admiral Lord Nelson, plus humble sailors and marauding pirates—not all of them men either!

All came here seeking treasure, but many returned disappointed not to have found it. Little did they dream that in centuries to come their descendants would find treasure—not in gold nuggets and shining jewels, but in golden sands and sapphire seas.

If you listen closely, on the ramparts of Puerto Rico's towering El Morro or the crumbling bricks of a dozen less imposing forts silently guarding the waters here, you will hear the roaring, fiery boom of cannons, the cries of battling warriors, the clash of sword on sword. You will hear the sounds of the past echoing over silence now broken only by the whisper of waves or the whirr of a wing.

In these lands you will meet broad grins and laughing eyes, share a smile with people who have known adversity and banished it with determination. You will meet proud people who work hard to overlook a slight and respond like 100-watt lightbulbs to your recognition of their pride. Give to these people quiet appreciation for their land and way of life and you'll get back a welcome fit for royalty.

Indeed royalty was once commonplace here, but these days there are plenty of poor peasants. Yes, you will meet poverty here today and come face-to-face with those who have nothing at all. While you may be shocked by it, you would do well to remember that much in this world is relative.

Yes, you will find beggars, mostly children looking for a quick handout, and yes, they can be persistent. There is no need for overkill, however. A simple "no, thanks" to the inevitable offer of song or dance or wilting flower is sufficiently discouraging. Maintain your pace and pay no attention. If someone performs a service for you, even if it's only holding a goat still or proffering a smile while you snap a picture, have a coin ready. They'll expect it—and we all have to make a living, right?

On many islands you will also discover that understanding often has nothing to do with common language. French, Spanish, Dutch, a lilting English that may sound nothing like your language, and a melting-pot patois that certainly doesn't, will hit your ear with all the foreign flavor of Europe. Fear not. Many of the local people speak English nearly as perfect as your own and all know a sign language that is universal.

Belay any fears you have of currency exchange and complicated banking. American greenbacks are happily accepted almost everywhere you go, and you'll be given plenty of advice on currency exchange in those ports where local currency is required.

Fear stems from many sources, not the least of which is pure physical dread. You can abandon those terrors in these gentle lands . . . with this disclaimer: even Paradise was plagued, so the same prudence you'd use at home seems wise advice. As one close to us advises: the 11th Commandment is "Thou Shalt Not Tempt."

Come to these islands prepared to luxuriate in the warm glow of hot sun and warm people. Come here ready for strange flavors and odd sights, weird sounds and exotic perfumes. Come here to see a way of life that is at once familiar and foreign. Come for all of this and you won't be disappointed.

There's a softness about life here, a blunting of the edges that envelopes you like a velvet cloak, that soothes your fears and strokes your battered psyche.

Stretch out on the warm silver sand of a few of these sleepy lagoons, drink in the quiet, and stealthily the islanders' soon-come-mon attitude will capture you and seep into your soul. Soon you, too, will forget to look at your watch, will shrug off the inevitability of rough road and slow boat.

In the lazing timelessness of these eons-old islets you will discover a newfound acceptance of things you cannot change, a peaceful coexistence with unseen forces that have shaped all this—and surely must have a masterplan for you too.

Where to Find It in the Caribbean

There's no question about it: the Caribbean is the single most popular cruise destination in the world. There is also no question that this is one of the most diverse parts of the world, with islands alike only in their unceasing sunshine and balmy trade winds. When you sail into the Caribbean, you step at each stop into different languages, different customs, different architecture, eye-popping colors juxtaposed upon each other.

If there is anywhere in the world that the history of man's exploration into the unknown is evident, it's here in these islands explored by Columbus, pirated by Sir Francis Drake, looted by Blackbeard, and loved in by Alexander Hamilton and Admiral Lord Nelson.

As marvelous as is the image conjured up by mere mention of a Caribbean isle, few of us know much about what is to be found on these islands. To help you decide which cruise will take you to the island of your dreams, here's a look at the diversions to be found in the Caribbean, followed by the islands on which those diversions can most easily be found.

Mall-ies of the World Arise—Chic Shoppes: Antigua, the Bahamas, Barbados, Curaçao, Martinique, St. Maarten, and the U.S. Virgin Islands (St. Thomas and St. Croix).

Biggest Water Hazard of Them All—Challenging Golf Courses: Antigua, the Bahamas, Barbados, the Cayman Islands, the Dominican Republic, Guadeloupe, Jamaica, Martinique, Montserrat, Puerto Rico, St. Kitts, St. Lucia, St. Martin, St. Vincent, Tobago, and the U.S. Virgin Islands (St. Thomas and St. Croix).

Hamilton Slept Here—Historic Sites: Antigua, the Bahamas, Barbados, Curaçao, the Dominican Republic, Grenada, Jamaica, Puerto Rico, St. Eustatius, St. Lucia, St. Vincent, and the U.S. Virgin Islands.

Wow!—Spectacular Scenery and Nature Hikes: Barbados, the Cayman Islands (Cayman Brac), Dominica, Grenada, Guadeloupe, Jamaica, Martinique, Montserrat, Puerto Rico, Saba, St. Kitts and Nevis, St. Eustatius, St. Vincent, Tobago, and the U.S. Virgin Islands.

Snake Eyes—Island Casinos: Antigua, Aruba, the Bahamas, Bonaire, Curaçao, the Dominican Republic, Guadeloupe, Haiti, Martinique, Puerto Rico, St. Kitts, St. Maarten, and St. Vincent.

"I Vant to Be Alone"—Tranquility Spots and Miles of Beaches: Anguilla, the British Virgin Islands, the Bahamas Family Islands, Dominica, the Cruise Lines' Private Islands, Grenada, Grenadines, Montserrat, Nevis, Saba, St. Barts, St. Eustatius, and Tobago.

Disneyland of the Deep—Scuba-Diving Spots: The Bahamas, Bonaire, the Cayman islands, Jamaica, Saba, St. Lucia, and the U.S. Virgin Islands.

Antigua (and Barbuda)
Size: 108 square miles.
Capital and Port City: St. John's (pop. 30,000).
Population: 73,000 (1,200 of these on Barbuda).
Language: English.
Average Temperatures: 78° F in winter, 83° F in summer.
Currency: Eastern Caribbean ("bee wee") dollar (E.C.$).
Public Transportation: taxis (buses not recommended).
Tourist Information: Antigua & Barbuda Department of Tourism, High Street and Corn Alley, St. John's (tel. 809/462-0029).
Car Rentals: Antigua Car Rentals, Barrymore Hotel, Fort Road, near St. John's (tel. 2-1055). Note that you must have a valid U.S. driver's license, but also must purchase an Antigua driver's license (price: E.C.$10) at the police station, High Street, St. John's; at the Inland Revenue Office, High Street, St. John's, over the post office; or at the car-rental agent.
Shopping Specialties: The main duty-free shops are on Redcliffe and Long Streets. Best buys are batiks, hand-painted island fashions, shell jewelry, polished stone jewelry, black coral, Sea Island cotton. A favorite gift is a Warri Board, a seed game brought from Africa played on a board with 14 holes.
Restaurants: Pimms, Cap Juluca (tel. 497-6666 or 497-6779); The Warden's Place, The Valley (tel. 497-2930); Old House Restaurant and Bar, George Hill Road (tel. 497-2228); Lucy's Harbour View, George Hill (tel. 497-2253).

Long before Columbus trained a glass on Antigua in 1493 and named it after the Santa Maria la Antigua Church in Seville, Spain, Carib and Arawak Indians had found its shores hospitable. They left calling cards of shell tools and stone artifacts that you can still see today.

Antigua is the largest of the Leeward Islands. From its shores shallow hills rise to a height of 1,330 feet at Boggy Peak. The few interior roads twist and turn among the hills, defying estimated driving times. But it's the beaches that lure travelers to Antigua's shores—365 separate coral beaches, one for each day of the year. And those are just on the Caribbean side—there are more on the Atlantic!

Barbuda's circle of reefs harbors a rainbow of fish and lobster, many of which end their days as the main course in local restaurants.

The British first settled Antigua in 1632, and by 1704, huge, protected English Harbour, proclaimed one of the safest in the world, had become home port to the British fleet. When the American Revolution loomed, English ships fanned out through the Caribbean to engage potential predators to British colonies—the French, Dutch, and Spanish. From the Dockyard here Admiral Nelson set off to court and marry Fanny Nisbet, who lived on nearby Nevis. In more recent times Princess Margaret and Anthony Armstrong-Jones honeymooned at Clarence House, and in 1977 Queen Elizabeth and Prince Philip visited.

Not many years after America won its independence, activity at English Harbour began to decline. Antigua's importance as a naval center plummetted when, in 1789, copper sheathing was discovered to deter worms and barnacles from ship's bottoms. Careening and cleaning hulls at naval outposts like this one was greatly reduced. The Industrial Revolution and the arrival of steamships in the 19th century issued the coup de grâce. English Harbour and the doors of Nelson's Dockyard formally closed in 1889, but in 1951 restoration of this historic harbor began.

In St. John's you'll see the cobblestone sidewalks and weather-beaten wooden houses that characterize this large, neatly laid-out town. Your ship will tie up on the right side of Deep-water Pier, less than a mile from the two towers of St. John's Cathedral. Drift down to the lower end of Market Street to the **open-air market.** Nowhere on Antigua can you drink in more of the local color that so typifies this exotic land. Fruits, vegetables, livestock, and colorful West Indian dresses battle for attention. It's a photographer's dream.

Seek out the landmark that has guided ships into St. John's for 300 years: **St. John's Cathedral,** at Church Lane between Long and Newgate Streets, the capital's most spectacular and famous structure, built in 1683. At the south entrance gates, erected in 1789, take a look at the figures of St. John the Baptist and St. John the Divine. Legend has it that these figures were redeemed from a Napoleonic ship and brought to Antigua by a British man-of-war.

Tours of the **Antigua Rum Distillery** at the Harbour can be arranged by the Tourist Office.

Take an excursion bus across the island to explore **English Harbour** and **Nelson's Dockyard.** Its docks and warehouses were built at great cost in human life. In the 18th century, 175,000 British soldiers are thought to have died fighting pirates, the French, the Dutch, and the Spanish, and from fatigue and disease contracted while erecting fortifications and docking facilities in the Caribbean.

Restoration of the Dockyard's port and historic buildings began in the 1950s. Accuracy of architectural detail has been a guiding principle, but now, in place of vast stores needed to supply a naval fleet, the warehouses and storehouses shelter shops, restaurants, and even an inn. To "do" the Dockyard, plan the better part of a day, so you can prowl Fort Berkeley and nearby Clarence House.

Clarence House, built in 1787, is filled with lovely furnishings and is the governor's weekend home, but open to the public at other times. A gatekeeper will guide you through the mansion.

General Shirley, governor of the Leewards in 1781, fortified the hills guarding English Harbour and the remnants of those fortifications remain, although they're now largely in ruins. Completed in 1731, **Fort Berkeley** is at the entrance to English Harbour. Walk the footpath from the Dockyard gate to get a good look at it.

Ships Calling Here: *Amerikanis, Atlantic, Caribbean Prince, Crown Odyssey, Cunard Countess, Daphne, Fair Majesty, Fairsky, Nantucket Clipper, New Shoreham, Nordic Prince, Pacific Princess, Sagafjord, Sea Goddess I, Song of Norway, Stella Oceanis, Starward,* and *Vistafjord.*

Aruba

Capital and Port City: Oranjestad.
Size: 20 miles long by 6 miles wide.
Population: 66,000.
Climate: median temperature 83°F.
Language: Dutch, English, Papiamento.
Currency: Aruban florin guilder.
Tourist Information: Aruba Tourist Bureau, 2 A. Schuttestraat, Oranjestad (tel. 23777).
Public Transportation: bus, unmetered taxi (prices posted).
Shopping Specialties: Duty-free shops for quality imports, no sales tax. The main shopping street is Nassaustraat: New Amsterdam Store for general and gift items, Spritzer & Fuhrmann for china, glass luxury items. Best buys: perfume, liquor, linens, jewelry, watches, cameras, designer clothes, crystal, china.
Restaurants: Italian, French, Indonesian, American, and Chinese cuisines

available. Try Papiamento, 7 Wihelminastraat, for elegant atmosphere and continental food; Bali, a floating houseboat docked at Schooner Harbor off Lloyd Smith Boulevard (tel. 2131), for Indonesian rijsttafel.

Trade-wind-sculptured divi-divi trees lean to the winds, their upper branches trailing like a mermaid's hair. Below the cliffs, thundering waves beat against a coral rock shore sending magnificent plumes of spray skyward. This is Aruba, where the pounding, turbulent Atlantic has pierced the coral cliffs, carving out the Caribbean's highest, most dramatic natural bridge.

So violent is this constant oceanic rage, so unsettling in its effect, so eerie in its mood, that one forgets this is quiet Aruba, a sleepy land whose opposite shoreline sports acres of white sands and gently lapping waves.

Located just 15 miles from Venezuela's coast, this long, skinny island is dry and sunny year round. On the low hills a variety of cacti, set among odd and sometimes wild rock formations, play extravagant contrast to island houses painted in soft pastels and rising demurely from flower gardens peeking from behind cactus fences.

Away to the south, this desert-like island rises to its highest point, Mount Yamanota, a 617-foot cone-shaped hill. On the coast a few miles away is Aruba's second city, St. Nicholaas, which sprang to life when Standard Oil of New Jersey built a refinery here in 1929.

Although Aruba's 66,000 people trace roots to 40 nationalities, about half count Arawak Indian among their ancestry. These gentle, smiling people were slender and handsome, and Arubans have retained these traits. Unlike the fierce Carib Indians, the Arawaks were a peaceful people living in small settlements and in the many caves on the island's north and east shores.

Here, where the desolate land drops sharply into a turbulent sea, excavations are unearthing ancient clay pottery of fine craftsmanship and artistic design. Hieroglyphs painted on cave walls and ceilings, and on great granite rocks that dot the near-moonscape scenery, remain a mystery.

Spanish Capt. Alonso de Ojeda first saw Aruba in the last year of the 15th century, but the 16th century was not a good one for the Spanish. Wars with the Dutch and the British defeat of the Spanish Armada in 1588 weakened Spain, permitting the determined, adventurous Dutch to take possession of Aruba in 1636.

A highlight of Aruban history: Gold was discovered in 1824 and mined for 89 years. Occasionally a fat nugget is still found and gold fever again rages over the island. Riches also came to the island when, in 1929, Standard Oil built a refinery near St. Nicholaas. But as the company turned to automation, even that "black gold" failed Arubans.

It wasn't until the 1970s that Aruba discovered its newest industry—tourism—and in recent years modern hotels and casinos have risen to meet the demand of steadily increasing numbers of visitors.

In Oranjestad, wander along an unusual marketplace: **Schooner Harbor,** an open boatman's market where sloops and ships of all kinds sell their wares from decks and stalls. This is the place to feel the throb of inter-island commercial life, and it doesn't take much to imagine what life must have been like here 200 years ago.

On the edge of town, explore **Fort Zoutman,** an 18th-century fort named after a Dutch rear admiral.

Then stroll over to **William III Tower:** the lighthouse lamp was first lit in 1867 on the king's birthday. Industrialists may want to pop over to Ranchostraat to see a gigantic lime kiln, reputedly the largest in the Caribbean.

To get a lasting impression of the real Oranjestad, keep looking up. Storefronts and shops along the streets have changed a bit over the years, but second stories still reflect **Dutch architecture.**

If you've always wanted to see an archeological excavation, the **Arawak hieroglyphs** in the cave at Fontein make a fascinating expedition. Combine this excursion with a stop at a natural **coral bridge** before heading back through the middle of the island to see the strange natural rock formations at Ayo and Casibari. Some of these diorite boulders are the size of buildings and remain a puzzle to geologists.

If a stroll along the powdery sand beaches and a view of swanky hotels is more your style, catch a bus in downtown Oranjestad across from the Tourist Office and ride out to **Eagle** and **Palm Beaches.**

Sizable gold-nugget finds around Bushiribana on the east coast and Balashi on the south Caribbean coast still generate rashes of **gold fever.** Drive over to see these smelters. Look around. Who knows?

No golf here, but tennis players will find courts, and horses are available for equestrians.

Ships Calling Here: *Britanis, Crown Odyssey, Ocean Princess, Sagafjord,* and *Vistafjord.*

Barbados

Capital and Port City: Bridgetown (pop. 97,000).
Size: 166 square miles.
Island Population: 247,000.
Climate: 75° to 85°F year round.
Language: English.
Currency: Barbados dollar.
Tourist Information: Barbados Board of Tourism, Prescod Boulevard and Harbour Road, Bridgetown (tel. 809/986-6516).
Public Transportation: bus, taxi.
Car Rentals: Note that your U.S. driver's license must be validated at the police desk at the airport or at car-rental agencies; fee: $5 (U.S.). For a rental, try Johnson Car Rental, Upper Collymore Rock, St. Michael (tel. 426-4205).
Dress: shorts for beach wear only.
Shopping Specialties: jewelry, china, crystal, rum (Mount Gay Rum has been produced since 1809), cashmere, Thai silks, French and Italian handbags. The duty-free shops are on Broad and Swan Streets. The three largest retailers—Harrison's, Da Costa & Musson, and Cave Shepherd Ltd.—are located on Broad Street. Try Pelican Village at Deep Water Harbour for straw goods and local handcrafts.
Food Specialties: flying fish, squid, lobster, crane chub, sea eggs (sea urchin roe), pepper-pot, suckling pig, and such fruits as soursop and pawpaws.
Restaurants: Le Bistro, Henry Street, Prince William (tel. 427-5161); Flying Fish, at Fairchild and Bay Streets (tel. 426-4537); Waterfront Café, near the Careenage (tel. 427-0093).

Only 100 miles east of the Lesser Antilles, Barbados floats like a green cloud on the horizon of an azure sea. It is as east as you can get in the Caribbean: waves born off Africa 7,000 miles away surge across the Atlantic to crash on Barbados's eastern shores, while on the island's other coast serene beaches bake in the sun and the blue Caribbean laps the palm-lined shores like a lazy river.

Over eons these tropical seas, rich in marine life, built the island layer upon coral layer, ringed its shores with wide beaches, and in time laid down the soil that was to bring abundance to the land. From the shores, rolling hills climb to the interior of this tiny island to reach Barbados's highest point, Mount Hillaby, 1,105 feet above the sea.

Exotic tropical vegetation clothes the land: tamarinds and breadfruit and palm trees. Scarlet bougainvilleas, fragrant frangipani, flaming poinsettias, and starry stephanotis splash rainbow colors across the landscape. Such exquisite natural beauty is mirrored in pastel houses and cottages perched high on the rolling hillsides, flaunting colors as striking as the flowers.

Britannia ruled the waves and guided the destiny of this tiny island, only 14 miles wide and 21 miles long, for more than 300 years, until 1966 when the island gained independence. Three centuries of that influence has left an indelible imprint of British formality and courtesy. Yet the warm, hospitable nature of the island and its people remains distinctively Barbadian—they call it a Bajan welcome. Literacy rates here are the highest in the Caribbean.

When the British first landed in 1625, Barbados was already old. Arawak Indians, the first known Caribbean island-hoppers, had long before followed the stars up from South America, sailing here in canoes. There is evidence that Barbados was a regular port of call until the end of the 16th century, when for reasons lost in time, no more was seen of this tribe.

No one knows the origin of the name Barbados, but 16th-century Portuguese maps refer to Los Barbados, the beards. Legend says that when the Portuguese landed in 1536, a species of fig tree growing on the island reminded them of *barbas,* or beards.

British colonists introduced and tended a wide variety of crops, but sugarcane offered the greatest profits. By 1645 large plantations had sprung up around the island. You can still see them today, restored and refurbished. One of the more famous is Drax Hall, built by Sir William Drax, one of the earliest sugar barons.

That cane still grows green on rolling hills and sways in the trade winds. An economy based on it flourishes. Sugar—and time—has been sweet to Barbados.

The famed, the fortunate, and the infamous have left their footprints in Barbados's golden sands. George Washington not only slept here, he stayed here for many months of his 20th year in 1751. On the corner of Bay Street and Chelsea Road is a house known as the George Washington House.

Queen Elizabeth II and Prince Philip visited in 1966 at Villa Nova, a gracious stone house built in 1834 as a sugar plantation house, later owned by British Prime Minister Anthony Eden. Beautiful gardens sweep out from the house toward valleys and the sea beyond.

One of Barbados's swashbuckling visitors was Captain Bligh of the good ship *Bounty*. That harsh captain, a regular Johnny Appleseed of the Caribbean, is said to have planted the first breadfruit tree here, but several other islands make the same claim.

To get the most from your Barbados visit, first savor some Barbados flavor. At the **Careenage** look for the Barbadian Harbour Patrol, who wear starched middy blouses reminiscent of Lord Nelson's jacktars. In sailing days ships like Nelson's came into Barbados to scrape their hulls. This meant laying the ship over on its side—careened—in shallow water. When the tide went out, the exposed side of the hull bottom was scraped to remove barnacles built up in months of sailing.

Today you'll see inter-island schooners and motor vessels unloading cargoes of bananas, plantains, and mangoes onto waiting carts and baskets—a photogenic sight.

Nearby is **Trafalgar Square** and **Chamberlain Bridge.** The square dates from 1874, but Admiral Lord Nelson's statue here was erected in 1815, about 25 years before London's famed monument to the victor of Trafalgar. Nelson and his fleet visited here on June 4, 1805, a few months before the battle and his death. On the north side of the square, public buildings, like the **House of Assembly,** are architecturally fascinating. The east wing has intriguing window paintings of British monarchs from James I to Elizabeth I.

In Bridgetown's Queen's Park you'll see an oddity: a **baobab tree** more than 61 feet in circumference reputed to be 1,000 years old. The baobab is native only to Africa and no one knows how this one got to Barbados.

Government House, at the corner of Belmont and Pine Roads, is a stately house built in 1680 of coral stone, the official residence of the queen's representative. Visitors are welcome to view this beautiful example of New World architecture and its gardens.

Barbados Museum, about 1½ miles down Hwy. 7, is housed in the old Military Detention Barracks, erected in 1853. Cells and warders' quarters have been made into galleries. The museum is a microcosm of Barbados past and present. A fine collection of archeological finds, including conch-shell tools used by the Arawak and Carib Indians, are on display and you can see silver, china, glass, and furniture typical of plantation days. Open Monday through Saturday from 9 a.m. to 6 p.m.

To get a glimpse of Barbados's plantation life and natural phenomena, drive out on the island. Although distances are small, the island speed limit is 30 miles per hour. All driving times given below are approximate, and assume a starting point of Trafalgar Square.

Harrison's Cave, in St. Thomas Parish, is about a 45-minute drive. You can tour this subterranean cavern by tram on an hour-long trip that visits the 150-foot-long Great Hall; two cascades, called Twin Falls, which plunge to the cave's floor and disappear; Mirror Lake; and the Rotunda Room, a stunning chamber 250 feet long and 100 feet high composed of cream and white formations that glitter like crystal.

Drax Hall, in St. George Parish, about an hour from town, is one of the oldest recorded buildings and operating sugar plantations on the island, and is still in the possession of the Drax family. Of particular interest is a Jacobean-design archway carved of mastic wood no longer found here. Remember, too, as you drive around the island, and see its old plantations, that transporting sugar to the docks in the 17th century was a problem. Camels were the Bajun solution! They were imported here to carry bagged sugar to ships waiting in the harbor.

St. Nicholas Abbey, in St. Peter Parish, is about a 90-minute drive. Built about 1650, the abbey, although never an "abbey," is one of the oldest sugar plantation Great Houses still standing in the Caribbean. It is also one of only three Jacobean houses remaining in the Americas. The house contains antique English and Barbadian furniture, some early porcelain, and a fine collection of Wedgwood portrait medallions. Still a working sugar plantation, it's open Monday through Friday from 10 a.m. to 3:30 p.m.

Mullins Mill, in St. Peter Parish, about 90 minutes from town, is shown on a 1717 map of the island. The house itself is one of the most fascinating on the island as it's built around the plantation's old mill wall. The house was rebuilt and restored in 1964.

Barbados recently inaugurated another new attraction, the **Changing of the Guard** and afternoon band concerts, starring the *Royal Barbados* Defence Force. These stirring events are staged periodically, usually in February and March. Tourism officials will know if one's scheduled when you're going to be in port.

In 1988 the island also opened a new **Cruise Passenger Center** on the beach at Carlisle Bay. It comes complete with stores, a swimming pool, watersports facilities, restaurants, and a Bajan rum shop.

In winter and spring the Barbados National Trust sponsors an **Open House**

Program with visits to some of the island's historic houses. At last check, the visits were taking place on Wednesday afternoon and featured a new house each week. Included among the historic structures on the tours are the 1830 Welches Plantation House and Yard, the Palladian Heron Bay styled after a 16th-century Italian villa, and several with intriguing names: Chummery, Koh-I-Noor, Beachy Head. The trust also sponsors Sunday-morning **hikes around the island,** although you need to be docked here by 6 a.m. to take part in these.

Ships Calling Here: *The Azur, Crown Odyssey, Cunard Countess, Daphne, Explorer Starship, Fair Majesty, Fairsky, Festivale, Nordic Prince, Ocean Islander, Pacific Princess, Royal Viking Sky, Royal Viking Sun, Sagafjord, Sea Goddess I, Song of Norway, Stella Oceanis, Starward, Vistafjord,* and *Wind Star.*

The Bahamas (Nassau and Freeport)

Capital and Port Cities: Nassau, New Providence; Freeport/Lucaya, Grand Bahama.

Size: New Providence—21 miles long by 7 miles wide (pop. 130,000). Grand Bahama—73 miles long by 4 to 8 miles wide (pop. 30,000).

Country Population: 230,000.

Language: English.

Currency: Bahamian dollar: $1 = $1 U.S.; the U.S. dollar is accepted everywhere.

Tourist Information: Nassau—Bahamas Tourist Office, Nassau Court on the east side of Rawson Square (tel. 809/322-7500). Freeport/Lucaya—in the International Bazaar (tel. 809/352-8044).

Public Transportation: Nassau—horse-drawn surreys, jitney bus, taxi. Freeport/Lucaya—taxi, jitney bus.

Car Rentals: Hertz, Sheraton British Colonial, Bay Street (tel. 53716); Avis, same as above (tel. 22889); motor scooters at Nassau Bicycle Co., West Bay Street (tel. 22787).

Shopping Specialties: Nassau—the straw market for all conceivable straw goods, woodcarvings, seashell jewelry, and other native crafts (expect to bargain); in other shops, a variety of imported goods from English crystal to coral jewelry, silver, china, cameras, cashmeres, and wools. Freeport/Lucaya—try the International Bazaar with dozens of shops showcasing the architecture and culture of more than 25 countries.

Food Specialties: conch chowder, conch fritters, and turtle pie.

Restaurants: Nassau—Green Shutters Restaurant, 48 Parliament St. (tel. 55702), and the Parliament Terrace Café, 20 Parliament St. (tel. 22836). Freeport/Lucaya—Sir Winston Churchill Pub, on the Mall at the International Bazaar (tel. 352-8866); Pub on the Mall, Ranfurly Circus (tel. 352-5110); the Stoned Crab, Taino Beach, Lucaya (tel. 373-1442); Britannia Pub, King's Road on Bell Channel (tel. 373-5919).

Nightlife: Nassau—casinos: at Paradise Island, and at Cable Beach Hotel and Casino at Cable Beach; for clubs: Ronnie's Rebel Room, West Bay Street (tel. 34481), for the native show, and the Peanuts Taylor Drumbeat Club, West Bay Street (tel. 24233), for fire dancers, calypso bands, glass eaters, and limbo. Freeport/Lucaya—El Casino, Princess Hotel (tel. 352-7811), for a revue nightly in addition to the casino, and Uncle Bill's Club Rolls-Royce, on Queen's Highway for American and Caribbean disco.

With the possible exception of its first settlers, the Arawak Indians, Bahamians have always banked on other people's money. Pirates like Henry Morgan, Blackbeard, Mary Read, and Anne Bonney sought refuge in these numerous islands from men-o-war. It took nearly a century to dislodge them, a feat finally accomplished by the first Bahamian governor, Woodes Rogers, nearly 100 years after the British settled here in 1629.

Next in the line of privateers came American Civil War-era blockade runners, followed in the 1920s by bootleggers running demon rum into the States. Each time, the Bahamas made money as her hotels burgeoned with these neo-swashbucklers partying it up at the Royal Victoria and the British Colonial.

Finally, island citizens, seeing the profits in privateering, went into the shipwrecking business themselves, earning scads of dollars by luring ships onto the rocks and shoals that surround the islands. Even today modern smugglers find the thousands of reefs, cays, and coves a useful cover for nefarious activities.

A vast and far-flung country, the 700+ Bahamian islands and 2,400 cays speckle 100,000 square miles of territorial waters of Atlantic Ocean. The islands and cays (pronounced "keys") are low and flat, actually the flattened tops of huge submarine mountains rising from the depths of the Atlantic Ocean.

Today the islands are a mecca whose muzzein is the sun calling faithful sun-worshippers here from all over the world. Lying less than 100 miles from Florida's east coast, the Bahamas are among the most developed islands in the tropics.

Nassau is the nation's capital and offers sophisticated hotels with both native and chic nighttime entertainment in town and on Paradise Island, just a bridge away, while Freeport/Lucaya on Grand Bahama Island is more of the same. Resort complexes, duty-free shops, golf courses, tennis courts, international bazaars, casinos, nightclubs, and hundreds of restaurants cater to every whim of modern man.

British Crown Colony days ended in 1964 when the Bahamas were granted internal self-government. Five years later their constitution was in place, and on July 10, 1973, the islands became the world's 143rd sovereign nation. But two centuries of British rule have left such legacies of pomp and ceremony as the changing of the governor's palace guard, the uniforms of traffic police, and the powdered wigs in courts of law.

Nassau is the country's capital. It is a proud and historic city, both old and sparkling new. The waterfront architecture of Bay Street and Woodes Rogers Walk hasn't changed all that much in the last 200 years, but a successful tourist economy has changed many things. Resorts have brought new land- and cityscapes, and in the process given the people a new sense of worth and a new focus. Nassau today is a city alive and bustling, its citizens aware that they are forging a destiny as a country catering to the vacationing needs of the world.

Both the famous and the infamous have visited here. In the Senate Building on Parliament Square, Queen Elizabeth II delivered her Silver Jubilee throne speech in 1977, a big event in Bahamian history. Winston Churchill stayed at lovely old Graycliff Mansion, now a small but plush hotel and restaurant, more than 60 years ago. And in their time, Howard Hughes and the Shah of Iran have enjoyed the indolent life of these shores.

Visiting the island is easy. You dock right in the middle of things at **Prince George Wharf,** where your ship ties up just a step away from **Rawson Square,** Bay Street, and the center of town. From there you can roam the shops of busy Bay Street and visit the famed **straw market.**

"You can make anything out of straw if you just put your mind to it" is the conviction of the craftspeople in this sprawling expanse. Reputedly the largest in the world, the straw market has been relocated from its former Rawson Square location and is now just a few blocks west on Bay Street to the right of the pier. From miniature animals to placemats, dolls, handbags, baskets, replicas of the horse and surrey, and a thousand other items await your selection, including the work of some of the best woodcarvers in the country. Here you can bargain and dicker to your heart's content.

When the straw market moved, the historical value of the square was revealed. Now you can imagine the activities that must once have taken place in this old slave market, the large open building on the north end of the square. The building dates back to the early 1800s to just before abolition.

Just up from Rawson Square across Bay Street is **Parliament Square.** The House of Assembly, Supreme Court, and the Library all front on this venerable old square under the watchful eyes of the statue of a young Queen Victoria, who sits placidly in the midst of these public buildings dating from 1812.

As you explore Nassau, seek out George Street, where you'll find **Government House,** an imposing structure with a pretty pink façade and green lawns rolling up to wide double doors. Once the governor's residence, this mansion atop a hill called Mount Fitzwilliam is where the Duke and Duchess of Windsor lived during the World War II years when he was governor. As imposing as its setting, the 12-foot statue of Christopher Columbus holds the commanding position in the center of the grand stairway. The **Changing of the Guard ceremony** takes place here on alternate Saturdays at 10 a.m.

Walking south on Elizabeth Avenue, you meet an unusual sight: the **Queen's Staircase,** 65 stone steps hand-hewn by slaves who carved them out of the solid limestone in the 18th century. They lead to crumbling Fort Fincastle and were carved as an escape route for troops stationed at the fort.

At the top of the Queen's Staircase is the 165-foot-tall **Water Tower,** offering the best panoramic view of Nassau, the harbor, and Paradise Island. Elevator up to enjoy a long view of the harbor.

Largest and most interesting of Nassau's fortifications is **Fort Charlotte,** built in 1789 and named after King George III's consort. Of particular interest are the many dungeons, underground passages, and the waxworks.

Next to Fort Charlotte is **Ardastra Gardens,** where flamingos steal the show as they parade from 11 a.m. to 4 p.m., walking and marching in unison.

Paradise Beach, a glorious strip of palm-fringed sand, is the best known of several island beaches. Get there on a ferryboat from the dock for $1 (U.S.) or by cab across the bridge ($2 plus cab fare). At Versailles Gardens here, statuary adorns the long row of terraces leading to the **French Cloister,** originally built in Montrejeau, France, near Lourdes, by Augustinian monks in the 14th century. It was disassembled and shipped here in pieces for reconstruction more than 600 years later.

The main sight in **Freeport/Lucaya** is the **International Bazaar.** More than 25 of the world's cultures display their architecture and wares in this world-famous bazaar. Built in 1967, this is the city's major sightseeing attraction.

Another favorite stopping spot is the **Garden of the Groves,** about seven miles from the International Bazaar. It's an 11-acre botanical garden, both tropical and subtropical, with waterfalls and ponds. The tranquil gardens are home to 10,000 plants and trees.

Out on East Settlers Way is the 100-acre **Rand Memorial Nature Center,** a place of unspoiled forest and trails. A 90-minute guided walk with a naturalist through this protected Bahamian forest is a top-flight chance to photograph Bahamian wildlife.

Ships Calling Here: *Britanis, Carnivale, Dolphin, Emerald Seas, Fair Majesty, Fairsky, Galileo, Homeric, Jubilee, Mardi Gras, Noordam, Rotterdam, Sagafjord, Scandinavian Star, Scandinavian Sun, Starship Oceanic, Starship Royale, Sunward II,* and *Vistafjord.*

Cayman Islands

Capital and Port City: George Town, Grand Cayman.
Population: 15,000.
Size: 22 miles long by 8 miles wide.
Climate: 73° to 88°F year round.
Language: English.
Currency: Cayman Islands dollar.
Tourist Information: Government Administration Building, Elgin Avenue (tel. 809/949-4844).
Public Transportation: bus, taxi.
Car Rentals: Ace Rent-a-Car, North Church Street (tel. 949-4158); Avis, Cayman Airport; and Coconut Car Rentals, Airport Road (tel. 949-4037). A driving permit costs $3. See Caribbean Motors, North Church Street (tel. 949-4051), for mopeds and motorcycles.
Shopping Specialties: Duty-free shops for bone china, British woolens, antique silver, cameras, French perfumes, Irish linens, Waterford crystal, Swedish cutlery, sculptured and black coral jewelry.
Restaurants: The Lobster Pot, North Church Street (tel. 949-2711); the Almond Tree, North Carolina Street (tel. 949-2893).

Some 500 miles due south of Miami lies a tri-island country that is one of the more unusual in the Caribbean, but for a strange reason—money!

The low-lying coral limestone Cayman Islands contain luxuriant foliage of mangroves, sea grapes, palms, breadfruit, mangoes, oranges, limes, grapefruit, and almonds, but what has put them on the map is an offshore banking-secrecy law that has lured thousands of corporations and monied types here.

Grand Cayman, largest of the three islands in the group, is only 22 miles long by 8 miles wide. Little Cayman and Cayman Brac lie 80 miles northwest of Grand Cayman.

Columbus recorded in his ship's log on May 10, 1503, on his fourth and last voyage, that he passed between two of the Cayman Islands, which he called Las Tortugas (the turtles) for the large numbers of turtles in the water and on the beaches.

The Caymans have a long history as a freebooter's haven. Henry Morgan and Blackbeard are believed to have cached some loot on Cayman Brac, and to have hidden out here while waiting to snag a gold-laden Spanish ship on its run up the gold route.

Most of this British Crown Colony's 15,000 people live in and around George Town, the port and capital on Grand Cayman. Most of them are descendants of soldiers AWOL from Cromwell's army in Jamaica or shipwrecked sailors. Although the early settlers brought a few slaves from Jamaica and elsewhere, they did not develop a plantation economy here so only a few islanders are of West Indian or African descent. Today's Caymanian speaks with a lilting Welsh accent overlaid with a trace of Scottish brogue intermixed with plenty of American slang.

This speck of an island is famous throughout the Western Hemisphere as a banking center. After tax law changes in 1966, Grand Cayman became known as an offshore tax haven, and at last count had registered 16,500 companies and 400 banks! All that on a vestpocket island.

Those who come with money (or without it) will delight in wide, often-deserted beaches with plenty of nearby wrecks to explore—and on slow evenings you can always visit your money, or somebody else's. Just looking at the hundreds of brass "company" plaques can be quite an amusement.

With a claimed 200-foot water visibility and 300 known shipwrecks, the Caymans are world renowned as a **diving** capital. Seven Mile Beach, with its sugar-white sand, is one of the most beautiful **beaches** in the Americas.

Outside of that silica, there's not a great deal to see or do in George Town: the village is easily explored in an afternoon. After you've checked out the **Clock Monument** to King George V, you might wander over to the **post office** on Edward Street to see one of the oldest government buildings in the Americas still in use today.

Out on the island, the **Cayman Turtle Farm** is interesting and has some handsome tortoise products on sale. For more of the same, catch a bus near the Buy-Rite Market on Panton Avenue and go out to Northwest Point. Here are more than 60,000 of the green beauties growing from a few ounces (at hatching time) to 600 pounds or more. Their life cycle is spent in tanks from 30 to 70 feet in diameter. Islanders now make a profitable venture of raising turtles, primarily for food.

Pedro's Castle, a few miles outside of Bodden Town, is the oldest standing building in the Caymans. Originally called St. James Castle, the building was erected by slave labor and today houses a restaurant.

And while you're on the island, **go to Hell!** Everyone does. It's a tiny village with an even tinier post office where you can have your postcards postmarked . . . well, Hell.

Ships Calling Here: *Cunard Princess, Fair Majesty, Fairsky, Regent Sea, Seaward, Skyward, Song of America, Stella Solaris, Sun Viking,* and *Westerdam.*

Curaçao

Capital and Port City: Willemstad (pop. 40,000).
Size: 38 miles long by 7½ miles wide; 180 square miles.
Island Population: 165,000.
Climate: 82°F on the average day.
Language: Dutch, English, Spanish, Papiamento.
Currency: Netherlands Antillean guilder. Both U.S. and Canadian money circulate freely.
Tourist Information: Curaçao Tourist Board, Schouwburgweg, z/n (tel. 677122), with several offices in Willemstad.
Public Transportation: bus, taxi (fares set).
Car Rentals: Hertz, Kiosk Wilhelminaplein (tel. 613686); Avis, Plesman Airport National, Plesman Airport (tel. 613924); Budget, at the airport (tel. 83420); National Car Rental, at the airport (tel. 83489) and main office (tel. 80373); also several local firms.
Dress: shorts at pool and beach only.
Shopping Specialties: The main shopping area is in the Punda section along Heerenstraat and Breedestraat. Best bets: Swiss watches, French perfumes, English china, Irish crystal, jewelry, Italian and French designer clothes, Norwegian ceramics, silver, English cashmere; for luxury items, Spritzer & Fuhrmann is on Breedestraat. Try the floating Obra di Man handcrafts center for gift items of local handcrafts.
Food Specialties: conch stew, red snapper in Créole sauce, fried plantains, keshi yena (a Dutch edam cheese stuffed with meat or fish and spices), rijsttafel (Indonesian-style banquet, with up to 24 dishes), erwtensoep (a thick, savory pea soup).
Restaurants: French, Italian, Swiss, Indonesian, and South American cuisines available. Try Fort Nassau, near Point Juliana overlooking the harbor (tel. 613086), or Indonesia Restaurant, 3 Mercuriusstraat (tel. 70917), to sample In-

donesian rijsttafel. The Wine Cellar, Cathedral Square (tel. 612178), is a local favorite; Kokkeltje's, Gomezplein (tel. 81120), is a casual, friendly downtown stop for lunch.

Old World and New blend in the Dutch-colonized islands creating a sophisticated and cosmopolitan collage. Nowhere is this more in evidence than on lovely pastel Curaçao. Expatriates from no fewer than 79 nations make their home on this antique, sun-bleached island that lies just 35 miles off the Venezuelan coast. Reason for the polyglot? In 1915 Royal Dutch/Shell built a refinery near Willemstad to process crude oil from Venezuela, bringing hundreds of workers.

Willemstad, the island's capital and for centuries the Dutch seat of government for the Netherlands Antilles, was named after King William II in 1647, only 13 years after the first Dutch settlement here. Red-tiled, stepped roofs of Dutch colonial houses face bright pastel façades of 17th- and 18th-century homes on clean, orderly streets.

Out on the island, windmills and plantation houses stud the landscape. Some of these *landhuizen* date back to Curaçao's settlement in 1634. They perch on the hilltops much as they did 300 years ago, and many are still in use as private homes today.

Arawak Indians were the first Curaçao settlers, and gave the tribal name to the island. The design and decoration of their pottery, the craftsmanship of their tools, and the artistry of the hieroglyphs decorating the walls and ceilings of their caves can still be seen in 14 locations on the **island**.

A long spine of an island, Curaçao stretches 38 miles to the north and is 2 to 7½ miles wide. Three-armed cacti and spiney aloe plants sprout from a sere landscape that is a study in browns, russets, and cactus greens.

Cooling trade winds blow steadily, bending the divi-divi trees at the waist. Flat arid countryside sweeps up toward the western end of the island where Mount Christoffel rises 1,300 feet. Over it all, the sun welcomes and warms visitors who roost contentedly along miles of beaches.

A long trading history and a generous infusion of Dutch hospitality have created a population attuned to sharing the delights of their homeland.

From the ship's deck as you enter the harbor you'll catch a good view of Willemstad's 200-year-old storybook waterfront buildings and narrow immaculate streets. These red-tiled, stepped roofs impart the old-world atmosphere for which Curaçao is famous.

Ships dock just a few minutes' walk from downtown and the curious **Queen Emma Pontoon Bridge,** a floating pedestrian bridge that joins the two halves of Curaçao. First built in 1888, the bridge still swings open 20 to 30 times a day for ships. From its center you get a lovely look at an architectural rainbow of the lavenders, pinks, ultramarines, and yellows that adorn the stately old buildings fronting the harbor.

Next stop should be the 300-year-old **Mikve-Israel Emanuel Synagogue,** on Columbusstraat at Kerkstraat, one of the oldest synagogues in the Western Hemisphere. Consecrated on the eve of Passover in 1732, it is today one of the better examples of Dutch colonial architecture. The complex now covers a square block in Willemstad's business district. In the 18th century it was sanctuary to Spanish and Portuguese Jews seeking refuge.

Take 45 minutes to see a good historical show at **De Tempel Theatre,** a restored landmark on Wilhelminaplein at the waterfront. Built in 1867, the theater projects Curaçao's past and present on a 38-foot screen.

A "must see" are the **Floating Schooner Markets,** at the north end of Handelskade. Here, scores of schooners from all over the Caribbean and South

America tie up to offer their colorful wares. Tropical fruits, exotic spices, and vegetables piled high make wonderfully colorful photographs.

Fort Amsterdam, at Breedestraat and Handelskade, is the center for both church and state: the fort encloses the Governor's Palace, the 1769 Dutch Reformed church, and the seat of the Netherlands Antilles government.

In the Otrabanda section, the **Curaçao Museum** on Van Leeuwenhoekstraat is a former military hospital, built in 1853, that now houses historic artifacts of island's history.

On the road north to Westpunt is one of the oldest buildings on the island, the **Jan Kock House,** constructed in 1650 and now a private home, restaurant, and museum. Many of the furnishings date to the 18th century. To add even more interest, the house is said to be haunted.

Chobolobo Mansion, a 17th-century *landhuiz,* offers Curaçao orange-flavored liqueur for sip and sale, as well as a tour of the house. The liqueur is a distillate of dried peel of a strain of orange found only in Curaçao!

Christoffel Natural Park is a 4,500-acre preserve with rare orchids growing near the upper reaches of the mountain. There are also four caves containing Arawak petroglyphs.

Golfers will find tees here, and there are courts for tennis, horses for riding. Water sports? Of course!

Ships Calling Here: *CarlaCosta, Crown Odyssey, Explorer Starship, Rotterdam,* and *The Victoria.*

Dominica

Capital and Port City: Roseau.
Size: 29 miles long by 15 miles wide.
Population: 81,000.
Climate: 75° to 90°F year round (cooler in the mountains); dry January to June on the west coast, rainy in the mountainous areas.
Language: English, French patois.
Currency: Eastern Caribbean ("beewee") dollar (E.C.$).
Tourist Information: Tourist Information Bureau, 37 Cork St., Roseau (tel. 809/445-2351).
Public Transportation: unmetered taxis, minibuses, trucks.
Car Rentals: none.
Shopping Specialties: vertivert grass mats, soaps made from fresh coconut oil.
Restaurants: Anchorage, two miles south of Roseau (tel. 445-2638); La Robe, 23 Cork St. (tel. 445-2896).

Until the story of Grenada hit the international press, there wasn't one person in 100 who could tell you where or what Dominica was, let alone pronounce it right (it's Dough-men-*eek*-ah). Then the island's feisty prime minister, Eugenia Charles, somehow managed to convince U.S. President Ronald Reagan that conditions in Grenada were threatening all the Caribbean, and *voilà!* instant notoriety for her and for this tiny island.

As the story goes, Dominica was named by Columbus who discovered it on a Sunday in 1493, naming it Sunday Island. Like so many islands in this region, Dominica was the scene of many battles for possession between the British and French, finally paying a ransom to get the French to go home.

In 1978 the country acquired its independence, but it's far from financially stable. A severe hurricane that devastated tourist facilities in 1979 dashed the island's tourism dreams, at least for a time.

Despite its difficulties, Dominica is one of the loveliest and most unspoiled islands in the Caribbean. The only remaining Carib Indians, a tribe that once populated all these islands and after which the Caribbean Sea was named, still live here. Nearly 3,000 of them dwell on a reservation in the northeast sector of the island, where they live much as they always did, weaving baskets and vertivert grass mats, even making dugout canoes.

Morne Trois Pitons National Park is an ancient rain forest, a deep green jungle lying at the foot of peaks that have inspired some to call Dominica the Switzerland of the Caribbean. You'll get a look at wild orchids and a rare species of parrot, hear a waterfall roaring, and see some of the island's 365 rivers, one for every day of the year, as they rush to the sea. Hiking can be quite an experience in Dominica, but it's only for the hardy and only with a guide.

At the island's **Sulfur Springs** you can see the offshoot of underground volcanic activity, and at **Trafalgar Falls** you can visit the world's second-largest boiling lake, splattering gray mud in fat bubbles. Again the region is difficult to visit, but it can be done with some determination and a guide.

Shopping will probably be the best bet for most people visiting the island. Native handcrafts are available at several stores, including Dominica Handcrafts, on Hanover Street; Caribana Handcraft, on Cork Street; Island Craft Co-operative and Bernard's, both on King George V Street; Tropicrafts, on Turkey Lane; and Bon Marché, on Old Street.

You'll see the island's few dining spots as you roam about: Mouse Hole, La Robe Créole, Guiyave, Ti Kai, Vena's Garden Bar and Restaurant.

You'll find natural swimming pools in some of the rivers, and underwater in the ocean is a wide variety of sponges, some of them fluorescent. Divers will find particularly good **skindiving** areas at coral reefs off the west coast from Castle Comfort to Scottshead, and at Cabrits, where remains of sunken ships can be seen.

Ships Calling Here: *The Azur* and *New Shoreham*.

Dominican Republic

Capital and Port Cities: Santo Domingo (pop. 1,300,000); Puerto Plata (pop. 45,000).

Size: 20,000 square miles.

Climate: 75° to 80°F in winter, 80° to 90°F in summer.

Language: Spanish; English widely spoken in the resort areas.

Currency: Dominican peso (RD).

Tourist Information: Dominican Ministry of Tourism, Avenida George Washington, Santo Domingo (tel. 809/682-8181); Ministry of Tourism, Long Beach, Puerto Plata (tel. 809/586-3676).

Public Transportation: buses, taxis (not metered, so determine the cost to your destination in advance).

Car Rentals: Santo Domingo—Hertz, Avenida Independencia 454, (tel. 685-1251); Puerto Plata—Hertz, Puerto Plata International Airport (tel. 687-0454).

Shopping Specialties: Best buys: native handcrafted jewelry, especially amber and larimar (a variety of turquoise), rum, coffee, hand-knits, ceramics, mahogany rocking chairs, and wicker. In Santo Domingo, El Conde Street is the main shopping street. In Puerto Plata, at the Factory Gift Shop, 23 Duarte, master jeweler Ramón Ortiz fashions larimar, amber, and rare black coral into works of art in gold and silver settings.

Food Specialties: chicharrones (pieces of chicken, fried green bananas, and spices), plátanos (a kind of banana), sancocho (a meat-and-vegetable stew).

Restaurants: Puerto Plata—Hotel Castilla, just off the main square at 34

John F. Kennedy St. (tel. 586-2559); Portofino, Avenida Hermanas Mirabel; Montemar, Avenida Circunvalación del Norte (tel. 586-2800).

For nearly a century Spain dominated the Caribbean and the New World through Hispaniola, the island shared by the Dominican Republic and Haiti. Columbus first landed on the coral-edged northwest coast of the island on December 5, 1492. Less than a year later he established the first European settlement in the New World on the south coast. In time this settlement would become Santo Domingo, Spain's gateway to colonization of the Caribbean, South America, and Mexico.

But Spain's fortunes ebbed, and with them went those of Hispaniola, the oldest country in the Western Hemisphere. Its palaces and forts became a siege site for buccaneers, privateers, and the fractious monarchs of Europe. In 1697 Spain agreed to France's demand for the western third of the island, today's Haiti. But the squabbling persisted well into this century until the United States felt called upon to institute a military occupation to secure peace for the country and, no less important, to provide security for American shores.

In 1966 a president and legislature were democratically elected and the economy began stabilizing. Today the Dominican Republic, which boasts some of the most spectacular but least developed terrain in the Caribbean, is capitalizing on it through tourism. All the elements are here: lush tropical forests grow right down to soft golden beaches; and the highest mountain range in the Caribbean moderates the tropical temperatures. The upward sweep of **Pico Duarte** stops at 10,417 feet, the tallest mountain in the West Indies, and the **Valley of the Cibao**—the rich sugarcane country—winds its way through the island.

At the center of this new republic is the jewel of the Caribbean that started it all, **Santo Domingo,** port city and capital of the Dominican Republic. Founded by Columbus's brother, Bartholomew, in 1496, the restored colonial Old Town is the bustling heart of this city of contrasts. Art galleries, museums, parks, restaurants, shops, hospitals, fortresses, a university—all these were "firsts" in the New World. And the first cathedral, Cathedral de Santa Maria la Menor, is said to hold the remains of Christopher Columbus.

On the north coast at Puerto Plata, Columbus's first landing site, a gigantic statue of Christ rises atop **Isabel de Torres**, the 2,575-foot mountain named for Spain's queen. Arms wide, it welcomes the world to the Dominican Republic's shores. Frequently hidden by dawn's mists, the statue shares the spectacular view of the Amber Coast and the surrounding botanical gardens with many visitors who get up here on a stately cable-car ride.

Green forested mountains swoop down to an indigo sea and crescent harbor. Nestled between the mountain's foot and the bay is **Puerto Plata,** a historic city whose streets are cobbled with ballast stones from treasure galleons that swapped their stones for gold and silver to take back to Ferdinand and Isabella. Columbus intended this city to be the first settlement of the New World, but fate intervened when gold was found on the south coast and Santo Domingo went on to become the leading city of the New World.

Puerto Plata, founded in 1502 by Nicolas de Ovando, means Port of Silver. Located 130 miles northwest of Santo Domingo, the city was named by Columbus, who saw silver reflections in the mists on the mountaintop. The cruise-ship pier is just a few steps from the center of town. **Fort San Felipe** is at the harbor end of the Malecon, the road that rims the sea and leads to a beautiful beach, Playa Dorado. Built in 1540 as defense against fierce and sometimes cannibalistic Carib Indians and marauding bands of English privateers, the fort guarded a city that was the last stop of the Spanish treasure galleons before they breasted the Atlantic for Spain and so was of keen interest to privateers.

In Santo Domingo, the **Alcazar de Colón** is a restored castle originally built by Columbus's son, Diego, in 1514. Located at the end of Las Damas Street, it's built of solid coral rock and furnished as it might have been when he and his bride, Dona Maria de Toledo, lived here.

La Atarazana was once a military depot and is now a hive of shops and small restaurants. Although the construction is mostly new, the effect is 16th century.

Casa de Bastidas, on Calle Las Damas, a former mayor's home, is now a museum for sunken ships' treasures.

The **Cathedral of Santa Maria la Menor** is early 16th-century Romanesque in style and is said to contain the bones of Columbus, although no one knows for sure just where the adventurer is really buried. You can visit what Dominicans claim are Columbus's caskets—there are three, lead inside crystal inside bronze—on your tour of the church.

Best buy on the island is **amber,** the semiprecious stone that is actually petrified resin. It is found only on this island in all the Caribbean, and in few other places in the world. The most valuable specimens of amber contain the remains of tiny insects or animals trapped for eternity in the clear golden resin.

Larimar, often called Dominican turquoise, is a semiprecious stone, pale blue in color. It was first uncovered by a Santo Domingo jeweler who named it after his daughter, Larissa, and the sea (*mar* in Spanish). Both stones are set into beautiful valuable jewelry by island craftsmen. Amber that has a red or blue hue is considered the rarest and most valuable, but other lighter colors are equally lovely.

Mahogany rocking chairs also are a favorite local buy—President John F. Kennedy ordered some of these comfortable chairs.

Ships Calling Here: *Caribe I, Crown Odyssey, Sagafjord,* and *Vistafjord.*

Grenada

Capital and Port City: St. George's (pop. 9,500).
Size: 21 miles long by 12 miles wide; 133 square miles.
Country Population (three islands): 85,000.
Climate: 83°F annual average, with low humidity.
Language: English.
Currency: Eastern Caribbean ("beewee") dollar.
Tourist Information: Grenada Tourist Office, Church Street, past the Careenage behind the public library, St. George's (tel. 2001).
Public Transportation: taxis (not metered, so agree on a price first); buses not recommended.
Car Rentals: Juliana Aird Agency, St. John's Street, St. George's (tel. 2504).
Shopping Specialties: spices (fresh bay leaves, nutmeg, ginger, ground coriander, pepper, cinnamon sticks, among others), all in neat baskets; duty-free shops; the Straw Market, on Granby Street at Market Square; Yellow Poui (Sendall Tunnel exit) for a good selection of local art; Charles of Grenada (Cross and Melville Streets) for a wide selection of English woolen imports, and Granby Stores (Granby Street) for crystal, Wedgwood, china, and watches.
Food Specialties: lambi (conch) dishes, callaloo soup, West Indian dishes, seafood.
Restaurants: Rudolf's, at the Careenage (tel. 2241); The Nutmeg, at the Careenage (tel. 2539); Red Crab, L'Anse aux Épines (tel. 4424).

Call it Gre-*nay*-ada (*not* Gren-nah-da), and recall that this was the mouse that roared for the U.S. in 1983 when President Ronald Reagan ordered troops onto the island to wrest it from what that administration called a threat to the peace of the Caribbean.

After a brief flurry of fighting and some internal struggling, the leftists who had controlled the island were ousted. Within weeks little Grenada, long an outpost of civilization, was the place everyone wanted to go. Cruise ships hat had been coming here for years returned to the island soon after the battling halted.

Grenada is a spectacularly beautiful island, where fertile valleys nestle amid green-clad mountains. The island's rugged volcanic interior is a jungle of palms, oleander, bougainvillea, purple and red hibiscus, crimson anthurium, bananas, breadfruit, birdsong, and ferns. Green mountains swoop to the sea, carving a dramatic coastline of coves, cliffs, and beaches.

Its stunning beauty is enhanced by attractive hotels and a local cuisine that is hard to beat. Known as the Spice Island, Grenada is fragrant with clove, cocoa, cinnamon, ginger, and vanilla—12 different spices in all—including nutmeg, of which it is the world's largest producer.

Located 100 miles north of Venezuela, Grenada was settled in 1650 by the French, who established a peace of sorts with the Carib Indians. But peace didn't last long and the struggle soon resumed. Finally the Caribs, pushed to the cliffs at Sauteurs in the north, rather than submit to enslavement, cast their women and children into the sea, and in a mass suicide leap threw themselves from the cliff onto the jagged rocks.

Columbus's log says he first sighted Grenada in 1498, on his third voyage, but passed it by. Later, its strategic location as a gateway to the Caribbean and South America made it a focus for Europe's monarchs, and it has changed hands many times over the centuries.

A sugar-producing colony, first under France and finally, after 1783, under Britain, the island gained independence in March 1979. Then the People's Revolutionary Government, which often flirted with Cuban influences, was established and the island became a part of the British Commonwealth. Today Grenada is the chief island of a three-island independent nation that includes Grenada, Carriacou, and Petit Martinique.

St. George's, the capital, is a hilly port city that flows around a horseshoe bay. Houses of yellow, blue, and pink, their red-tiled roofs a stark contrast to a backdrop of dark-green mountains, rim the bay. In the city's center, clusters of quaint, bright-roofed buildings of Georgian architecture line steep, narrow streets reminiscent of the Italian town of Portofino.

In St. George's, stop by old **Fort George.** This French-built fort has subterranean passageways and old guard rooms and cells open to visitors, but the fort is now police headquarters.

At the island's **Botanical Gardens and Zoo,** tropical flora is well labeled. There's a lovely vista from **Fort Frederick,** built by the French in 1779.

Out on the island, **Annandale Falls** offers a cascade that tumbles 50 feet into a basin in a tropical wonderland.

At **Dougaldston Estate** you can see most of the island's spices in their natural form, and at Grand Étang Lake you can visit a **rain forest** at 1,800 feet. Cobalt-blue waters here flow over 13 acres.

Carib's Leap, in the north at Sauteurs, is the great cliff from which the Caribs leaped to their death rather than face enslavement.

At Gouyave, a **spice factory** welcomes visitors and is a fascinating stop; and at sweeping Grand Anse Beach you'll see what many consider one of the **most beautiful beaches** in the West Indies. Beach lovers will freak over **Point Saline** too: here, two beaches, one gleaming white and one volcanic jet black, meet.

Ships Calling Here: *Caribbean Prince, CarlaCosta, Crown Odyssey, Cunard Countess, New Shoreham, Rotterdam, Sagafjord, Skyward, Stella Oceanis, The Victoria, Vistafjord,* and *Wind Star.*

Guadeloupe (and Îles-des-Saintes)
Capital and Port City: Pôinte-à-Pitre.
Size: 687 square miles on two main islands.
Population: 300,000.
Climate: 70° to 80°F year round; most rain during September to November.
Language: French, Créole.
Currency: French franc.
Tourist Information: Office du Tourisme, 5 Square de la Banque, Pointe-à-Pitre (tel. 82-09-30).
Dress: beach wear and scanty clothes not considered proper for urban areas.
Documentation: A visa, now required to enter the country, may be obtained in advance at a French consulate, or at the Guadaloupe airport upon presentation of a passport, or other proof of U.S. or Canadian citizenship plus a photograph.
Public Transportation: buses, taxis (unmetered, so agree on a price in advance).
Car Rentals: Avis, Hotel PLM Azur Marissol (tel. 90-84-44); National-Europcar, Aéroport du Raizet (tel. 82-50-51); Jumbo Car, Aéroport du Raizet (tel. 83-60-74); Hertz, route de la Gabarre (tel. 82-00-14).
Shopping Specialties: exotic spices, voodoo dolls, lovely shell jewelry, perfumes.
Food Specialties: Créole and French cuisines; curries, stuffed crab.
Restaurants: Auberge de la Vieille Tour, in Gosier (tel. 84-23-23); La Plantation, in the Bas du Fort Marina (tel. 50-84-83); La Canne à Sucre, 17 rue Jean-Jaurès, Pointe-à-Pitre (tel. 82-10-19); Le Baoule, Gosier (tel. 84-33-95); Le Bananier, Gosier (tel. 84-34-85). On Îles-des-Saintes—Café de la Marine, waterfront, Bourge, Terre de Haut (tel. 99-53-78); Auberge des Anacardiers, La Savane, Terre de Haut (tel. 99-50-99).

If your thoughts sometimes turn to a tiny cove with warm waters lapping at your toes and a sailboat skittering by on the horizon, your thoughts may be turning to Guadeloupe. If your thoughts turn to a monokini or less, you're definitely thinking of Guadeloupe.

Little known to most U.S. travelers, this cluster of five islands is a fantasyland for those who seek beautiful, unchallenging scenery, back-to-nature magic, and some wonderfully spicy Créole cooking.

Not as sophisticated as its fast-lane neighbor Martinique, Guadeloupe seems to snooze in the sun, its beauty running rampant but unassisted around it.

Still, there's more than a touch of the insouciant in Guadeloupe, as there always has been: when Martinique was adjusting happily to French rule, Guadeloupe was aligning itself with the enemy English. Paris did not take kindly to that and shipped out an enforcement squad that erected guillotines and promptly dispatched 4,000 Guadeloupeans.

In topography Guadeloupe is much like its sister island right down to a matching volcano, Soufrière. It's actually two islands, Grand-Terre and Basse-Terre, separated by a bridged channel.

Here you can explore lovely waterfalls and deep tropical forests, banana plantations and, of course, beautiful beaches. Known to the Arawaks as Karukera, "island of the beautiful waters," Guadeloupe was named by Columbus in 1493 when he dubbed it Santa Maria de Guadelupe de Estramaduros, after a saint in his homeland.

French settlers led by two Martinique men established a colony here in 1635. On and off, Guadeloupe belonged to the British, finally returning once and for all to the French in 1815.

Until 1946 the island was a dependency of Martinique, when it became a département (something like a state) of France.

Pointe-à-Pitre, the port city, is a bustling city with a picturesque **covered marketplace** filled with exotic fruits, spices, and vegetables—and often some pretty exotic people too. Both market and nearby port can be good stops for photographers. You can pick up some of the best in Caribbean spices here: vanilla, nutmeg, bois d'Inde peppercorns, cinnamon bark, cloves.

Martinique has better buys and a far wider selection of china, crystal, and the like, but on Guadeloupe you'll find good bargains on imports from France—perfumes, Dior, Lalique, Baccarat, Hermès, and the like. Shops usually give big discounts on prices if you're buying with traveler's checks in dollars or in U.S. cash. Shops are generally closed from noon to 2 p.m. and on Saturday afternoon and Sunday. Your ship's presence in port may change that, however.

Among the **shops,** of interest are: Les 7 Barils des 7 Pêches, 6 rue Frébault, for liquor; Vendôme, 7 rue Frébault, for fashions; Elstel, near the Ecotel at Gosier, for appliquéed wall hangings. Island-made favorites include pointed straw hats of split bamboo, which can make interesting planters, and native voodoo (*voudou*, in French) dolls.

Dining is elevated to a sport here. There are dozens of restaurants large and small, all serving fiery-hot Créole food or gentler French concoctions. Even tiny snack shops on the beaches can be trusted to produce some memorable goodies.

As for **beaches:** one of the best island beaches is La Plage du Souffleur at Port Louis; another is Plage du Grande Anse, a mile of curving sand with a grove of palms and sea grapes and a small restaurant, Karakoli.

Two very dramatic spots on a drive around the island are **Anse Bertrand,** about five miles from Port Louis, and **Pointe de la Grande Vigie,** about 280 feet above the sea and reached by four miles of gravel road. You can see Antigua from this vantage point.

About four miles south you'll find **Porte d'Enfer,** where waves crash against narrow cliffs at a spot called the "gateway to hell."

On Basse-Terre you'll pass tranquil, scenic **Deshaies,** home of a Club Med. About three miles away is a beautiful beach called **Grand Anse,** shaded by trees swaying in the breezes. This is a popular diving beach too. At Mahaut, four miles from Pointe Noire, you travel through a **rain forest** and past two hills called Les Deux Mamelles (the two breasts). Jacques Cousteau spends time at nearby Îlet du Pigeon.

Farther along the road you reach **Basse-Terre,** the main government enclave for the islands, but best known as the home of **Soufrière,** the smoking **volcano,** dormant now. Banana trees and tropical jungle cover the sides of the 4,800-foot-high volcano, which you reach by a road from St-Claude, an upper-crust suburb. You can travel to the 3,300-foot mark where you can feel the heat of the volcano beneath your feet and watch steam puffing out of fumaroles.

Continue your drive along the coastline to Trois-Rivières where you can still see **Arawak rock carvings** and on to Chutes du Carbet, three pretty **waterfalls,** but you'll have to do some long and determined climbing to find them.

If you are by now hot and tired, you can take it off—all off—on one of the island's beaches where **nude swimming** is, if not encouraged, quietly (although probably not literally) overlooked. Among the spots for al fresco bathing on Basse-Terre are beaches near hotels like the Club Med, or the Plage de Clugny between Ste-Rose and Deshaies; on Grande-Terre, Caravelle Beach and hotel beaches.

Snorkeling and scuba-diving are wonderful here, and you can arrange trips through the tourist office, Club Med, or Pigeon Island.

Fishing, boating, and waterskiing are also readily arranged, as are tennis and horseback riding. If you're ready to try out your land legs after a few days at sea, plan a hike through the trails of the Parc Naturel in Basse-Terre.

Ships Calling Here: *Cunard Countess, New Shoreham,* and *Sagafjord.*

Haiti

Capital and Port City: Port-au-Prince.
Size: 10,714 square miles.
Population: 5,000,000.
Climate: 70° to 80° F year round; about 20° cooler in the mountains.
Language: Créole, French.
Currency: Haitian gourd, but the U.S. dollar is accepted everywhere.
Tourist Information: Office National du Tourisme, Avenue Marie-Jeanne, Port-au-Prince (tel. 2-17-29).
Dress: avoid revealing shorts and abbreviated outfits.
Documents: proof of U.S. or Canadian citizenship required.
Public Transportation: taxis (unmetered, but the government sets the rates; ask cost in advance, and bargain if you wish), colorful tap-tap buses.
Car Rentals: Avis, Duvalier Airport (tel. 7-1325); Hertz, Delmas 27 (tel. 6-1132); Chatelain Tours, rue Geffrard, in Pétionville (tel. 2-4469).
Shopping Specialties: oil paintings, woodcarvings, Haitian cotton fabrics, straw baskets.
Food Specialties: Créole and French cuisine, tropical fruits.
Restaurants: Belvedere, Kenscott Road (tel. 7-1115), and La Lanterne, 14 rue Borno (tel. 7-0479), both in Pétionville.

Mountains rise to the sky in a blue haze, golden sands stretch for miles along glittering blue waters, and colorful blossoms run riot across the land. Haiti is a place of haunting beauty, but a place shocking and often depressing for travelers unprepared to stare poverty in the eye. It is indeed sad to see a land of such natural beauty and such cheerful, artistically talented people so unable to overcome the economic malaise that has long plagued this tiny nation.

Once a French colony, Haiti occupies the western third of the island of Hispaniola, sharing it with the Dominican Republic. It became the first independent black republic in the world when in 1801 its black slaves, led by Toussaint L'Overture, adopted a constitution and named a governor. Napoleon sent 25,000 men and 70 warships to bring the Haitians back in line, but they were unsuccessful and a year later the French signed an armistice and removed their troops. Independence was proclaimed on January 1, 1804.

Haiti's two victorious generals, Jean-Jacques Dessalines and Alexandre Pétion, ruled for a time, followed by the rise to power of Henri Cristophe, who crowned himself emperor and ordered the creation of a mountaintop citadel at Cap-Haïtien. You can still visit that sky-high fortress that was said to have taken the lives of 20,000 men during the decade of its construction. You get there atop a small but footsure donkey led by energetic and equally footsure youngsters.

Recently, Royal Caribbean Cruise Line developed a section of the island called **Labadee,** turning its lovely white beaches into a kind of private club for their passengers. It makes for quite an unusual stop, and one that has proven very popular with passengers. No other line calls there.

Separated from the rest of Haiti by a mountain range, the peninsula on which Labadee is located offers snorkeling at Nellie's Beach, Barefoot Beach, and Hideaway Beach. There's swimming at Columbus Cove Beach, where water cycles and inflatable rafts offer a watery diversion.

To get to the beach, passengers board the *Niña,* the *Pinta,* or the *Santa Maria,* which shuttle back and forth between the ship and Columbus Cove Beach. Once there, passengers can explore the ruins of Nellie's Beach and Fort Belli, remnants of the island's turbulent history, conjuring up visions of everything from Columbus at the helm to the rough-and-ready pirates who succeeded him.

On the beach, passengers enter walkathons, play at volleyball, water-balloon toss games, tug-of-war contests, ring tosses, and horseshoe tournaments. Those inclined toward sloth indulge their proclivity in a hammock, lounge chair, or on long stretches of empty beach. Lunch is served at Café Labadee, an open-air, thatch-roofed dining hall that comes complete with steel-drum band and buffet lunch brought from the ship. Drinks are served at Dragon's Breath Pub on Dragon's Tail Beach and are purchased with Labadollars provided by the line. RCCL even had the foresight to create a crafts market where you can buy Haitian products, from artwork to clothing and mahogany carvings, using U.S. dollars or credit cards.

While Labadee is located on an island that has had a particularly turbulent history of late, it is far removed from Haiti's major cities and has rapidly become the second most popular port in all RCCL's many itineraries.

Haiti has been beset by political problems for many generations and there seems to be no end to that in sight. Lines that regularly or occasionally call at this fascinating island, however, cancel that stop if there's any kind of difficulty, real or perceived.

On this mountainous third of the island of Hispaniola, **Port-au-Prince** is the principal city, a teeming metropolis that is not large in land area but is gigantic in population, all of which seems to be crammed into the narrow downtown streets of Port-au-Prince.

For beautiful views you'll want to ride up into the mountains where you'll find the resort village of **Pétionville,** home of a number of small, pretty hotels, restaurants, and boutiques, and the wealthiest residents of the country.

Still higher on the mountain is **Kenscoff,** a small village in which you can visit the Mountain Maid shop, a Baptist-supported crafts center featuring some of the finest examples of Haitian woodcarvings, pottery, paintings, embroidery, and cottons. Kenscoff is the end of the road, by the way, and you'll see some beautiful views on your way there.

Haiti is a bargain hunter's paradise. Here you can buy massive woodcarvings for a few dollars and brightly colored Haitian oil paintings by local artists, some of whom have become famous for their primitive styles. To get a look at the best of what's available, stop by the **Musée d'Art Haïtien du College St-Pierre** (the Museum of Haitian Art) in downtown Port-au-Prince at Place des Héroes, Champs de Mars. Dewitt Peters, an early collector of Haitian art and the operator of Centre d'Art, helped oversee the compilation of this collection. A boutique here at the museum offers some of the finest handcrafted items in Haiti at very reasonable prices.

The **Centre d'Art** should also be a stop on any art enthusiast's list too. Peters, an artist himself, discovered and encouraged many Haitian artists who are today famous, and his Centre d'Art features the best in Haitian artwork. It's at 56 rue Roy.

With the rise to prominence of Haitian artist Philome Obin and others, every Haitian who can hold a paintbrush seems to have taken to the easel. You'll see hundreds, perhaps thousands, of these colorful paintings being sold everywhere you go. While most are not likely to become collector's items (unless you have an excellent eye for art), all of them are very colorful reminders of a visit here.

Well-known shops at which you may buy some of the better examples of Haitian artwork of all kinds include Nader's, Issa's, and Claire's Galleries downtown; Red Carpet, Panaméricaine, Rainbow Art Display, and National Art Galleries in Pétionville.

A shop called El Cano is quite near the docks (taxi drivers will know it) and features gorgeous rugs, pillow covers, and fabrics, all made from nubby Haitian cotton and woven by a cooperative of workers. Carvings and straw work here are of high quality too, but the very best offerings are heavy cotton products in striking contemporary colors and patterns. The Salvation Army handcraft shop, off Delmas Road near the airport, has some quality items too.

You can bargain, bargain, and bargain in Haiti, securing yourself some bargains in the process. Offer the seller about half of the original price and work up very slowly. When you hear the word "finish," you know you've gotten about the best price you're going to get.

We recommend a visit to the **Iron Market** in Port-au-Prince only to our enemies. If you're very brave and don't mind being importuned from all sides and crushed in a mass of buyers and sellers, go . . . and good luck. It's an interesting place to walk through briefly, but you'll be very glad to get out of it and into a less frenetic shop. It's called the Iron Market, by the way, because it's built of ornate ironwork.

If you have read Graham Greene's intriguing novel about Haiti, *The Comedians,* and would like to meet the character who provided the inspiration for Greene's Petit Pierre gossipmonger, look for him at the not-to-be-missed Olaffson Hotel. Here you can have a lovely elegant lunch inside or out, and see the best of Haiti's impressive **gingerbread wood-trimmed architecture** all in one fell swoop. The Olaffson also was a central "character" in the novel, and has been the vacation home of an impressive array of celebrities. The hotel is surrounded by jungley growth and is one of the most interesting sights in the city.

Petit Pierre's real name is Aubelin Joliecoeur and just after Haiti's 1986 revolution he was named minister of tourism. If you see him—he always wears a spotless three-piece white suit and carries a walking stick—just go over and introduce yourself and he'll happily take you to visit his home and art gallery where he has an impressive, if high-priced, collection of Haitian art. He's the epitome of an old-world gentleman, right down to kissing the hand of any ladies present, and is as much a "sight" in Haiti as any tourist attraction. He also knows everything that's going on practically before it occurs.

Cathedral St-Trinité is an interesting stop and features a painting of Christ the way Haitians see him: as a black man.

If you take a city tour of Port-au-Prince or drive around on your own, you'll see the gleaming white **National Palace,** former home of former President Jean-Claude Duvalier, better known as Baby Doc (his father, a man greatly feared for both his political and his voodoo power, was called Papa Doc). In front of the palace is a bronze statue called **The Marron,** which represents a slave holding a conch shell that was used to sound the call to arms for the revolution of 1791.

Swimmers and divers can dabble at **Sand Cay Reef** or at **Le Grand Banc,** whose shallow waters are visited by a catamaran sailboat called the *Yellowbird,* docked at Beau Rivage Marina. It's a 90-minute ride to Sand Cay Reef on boats that depart from docks at the International Casino.

Rum lovers can sample to oblivion at the **Jane Barbancourt Distillery,** where some of the world's most unusual, indeed collector, rum is made. Haitian rum is a high-quality product much admired by rum drinkers. In addition to the basic aged rum, you can also buy hibiscus, mango, mint, coconut, cashew, and a dozen other flavors of rum. Samples are served to you in a lovely setting reminiscent of an 18th-century distillery.

Cap-Haïtien, a town of about 30,000 on the northwest tip of Haiti, is a much smaller and quieter town out in the Haitian countryside. French pirates once lived on the nearby island of Tortuga, and raided so often that the French finally ended up controlling the mainland. In the 1700s Cap-Haïtien was a fancy place for wealthy planters who drove around the streets in gilded carriages and built furbelowed mansions. You can still see some of them here today, although they don't exhibit much of their former grandeur.

Don't miss a trip to **La Citadelle,** whose 12-foot-thick walls took ten years to build and could house 10,000 people, with 40 rooms allocated to the "royal" family alone. (Cristophe-created "royalty" was unusual: Henri created some unique royal names, Prince Lemonade for instance.) As seen from above, the fortress, from which no shot was ever fired, forms the outline of a pistol, with the longest side measuring more than 450 yards. In the center is Cristophe's tomb—he killed himself with a silver bullet.

Below the Citadelle, which bristles with cannons and has a room containing 45,000 cannon balls, are the ruins of the **Palais de Sans Souci,** a palace designed to rival Versailles. From what is left you can tell that once it was really something, but it was badly damaged by an earthquake. Historians say that it was three stories high with silk curtains on every one of the 23 windows on each floor, panels of inlaid mosaic or polished mahogany on the walls, and gilded mirrors reflecting fabulous tapestries. Cristophe even had streams diverted to help keep the palace cool in summer, an early air conditioner.

La Badie and Cormier Plage are two lovely swimming and snorkeling spots in Cap-Haïtien, which has some fascinating hoteliers who run lovely and often historic operations. One hotel here, the Roi Cristophe, built in 1724, was once the property of Pauline Bonaparte, Napoleon's reportedly nymphomaniacal sister.

As you may have gathered, Haiti is a most unusual place, changing like a chameleon to fit the circumstances. One of its most unusual aspects is the practice of **voodoo,** a religion that adapted itself easily to Catholicism and other religions but has never relinquished its importance in Haitian life. Derived from the word "voudoun," meaning spirits, voodoo is designed to keep the individual in harmony with a raft of spirits, or loas. Head of the temple is the hougan priest or the mambo priestess, who oversees complicated ceremonies that can be as brief as an hour or as long as a week or more. Offerings are made to a loa, and symbols are drawn on the ground to lure the spirits. Drums beat as initiates prepare their bodies for possession by the loa. Voodoo ceremonies are held for tourists, but at night you can often hear the beat of real voodoo drums high in the hills.

Ships Calling Here: *Song of America, Sovereign of the Seas, Sun Viking,* and *Vistafjord.*

St. Kitts, Nevis, and Anguilla

Capital and Port Cities: Basseterre, St. Kitts; Charlestown, Nevis.
Size: St. Kitts—65 square miles. Nevis—36 square miles.
Country Population: 48,000.
Climate: 68° to 80°F year round, with low humidity.
Language: English.
Currency: Eastern Caribbean ("beewee") dollar.
Tourist Information: St. Kitts/Nevis/Anguilla Tourist Board, Church Street, Basseterre (tel. 809/465-4040).

Public Transportation: taxi (point-to-point rates are fixed by the government), ferry (between Charlestown and Basseterre, daily).

Car Rentals: Sunshine Car Rentals, Lesmike Auto, Cayon Road (tel. 465-2193). A local driver's license must be obtained from the Traffic Office, Pall Mall (tel. 2642); fee: E.C. $10.

Shopping Specialties: in Basseterre's duty-free shops—batik prints, coppercraft, rum, colorful cottons with embroidered designs.

Food Specialties: roast suckling pig, turtle steaks, crab backs, curried lobster, pawpaw, christophine, breadfruit, plantain, guavas, mammy apples, soursop, pixilated pork.

Restaurants: Ocean Terrace Inn, Harbor Street, Basseterre (tel. 465-2754); Rawlins Plantation, Mount Pleasant (tel. 465-6221); Golden Lemon, Dieppe Bay (tel. 465-7260).

Life is slow and quiet on these two beach-trimmed islands, moving slowly along much as it always has since Columbus stopped by here for a visit 500 years ago.

It was 389 years after Columbus spotted and named St. Kitts for his patron saint, St. Christopher, that St. Kitts/Nevis achieved its freedom. In 1623 the first successful English colony in the West Indies was established on St. Kitts and in 1983 the island acquired independence from the United Kingdom.

St. Kitts, with a 65-square-mile area, has a central mountain mass rising 3,792 feet at Mount Misery, and a narrow peninsula to the southeast, where you'll find salt pounds and the island's best beaches. Although the British were there first, the French navy also landed a force. After a four-year tug-o-war the two forces decided to divide the island and unite against the intruding Spaniards and the uncontainable Carib Indians. The British finally won the island in 1783.

Nevis, with only 36 square miles, rises from the sea as a single dominant volcanic peak, reaching a height of 3,542 feet, its summit usually encircled with clouds. Just two miles off St. Kitt's south coast, Nevis was settled in 1628. This small island had two big events: British Admiral Nelson married Fannie Nisbet in an island church, and Alexander Hamilton was born here.

In 1967 **Anguilla** broke away from the Associated State of St. Kitts–Nevis–Anguilla, and since that time has enjoyed separate administration and a continuing relationship with Britain. Its 5,000 people live on a tiny island measuring 16 miles long and barely 4 miles wide.

At **Basseterre** on St. Kitts, in **Pall Mall Square** you'll still see the sectioning lines that in the 18th century delineated special areas for slaves and freemen. Other interesting sights include: antique **St. George's Anglican Church,** on Church and Cayon Streets, first built in 1670 and rebuilt in 1867; and **Brimstone Hill Fortress,** a mighty fort once known as "The Gibraltar of the West Indies," and surrendered to the French in 1782 but returned a year later to the English.

You can descend into a dormant **volcano** on St. Kitts and visit a museum outlining that steamer's history. The way down descends from the top of the crater at 2,600 feet into the crater itself, but you have to hold onto roots and vines to get there. (Perhaps you might skip this adventure.)

At **Charleston,** on Nevis, you can visit the birthplace of American patriot **Alexander Hamilton,** on the waterfront, and the Hamilton Estate, once owned by Hamilton's father, above the town. Lovers should stop at **St. John's Church,** in Fig Tree Village, for a look at the marriage record of Lord Horatio Nelson and Fanny Nisbet of Nevis, who were married here all those many years ago. Their marriage certificate still reposes in the church register.

Ships Calling Here: *The Azur, Caribbean Prince, Explorer Starship, Nantucket Clipper, Sagafjord, Stella Oceanis,* and *Vistafjord.*

Jamaica

Capital and Port Cities: Kingston, Montego Bay, Ocho Rios.
Size: 4,411 square miles.
Population: 3,300,000.
Language: English.
Currency: Jamaican dollar (required).
Tourist Information: Jamaica Tourist Board, Cornwall Beach, Montego Bay (tel. 809/952-4425).
Public Transportation: bus, taxi, mini-van.
Car Rentals: Hertz, Montego Bay, Casa Montego Arcade, Kent Avenue (tel. 952-4471).
Shopping Specialties: straw goods, woodcarvings, coffee, batiks.
Restaurants: The Ruins, DaCosta Drive (tel. 974-2442), and Half Moon Hotel, Ocho Rios Road (tel. 953-2211), in Montego Bay; the Plantation Inn, in Ocho Rios (tel. 974-2501); Trident Villas, Frenchmen's Cove (tel. 993-2602), and De Montevin Lodge Private Hotel, 21 Fort George St. (tel. 993-2604), in Port Antonio; Richmond Hill Inn, Richmond Hill, Montego Bay (tel. 952-3859).

Deep green forests, silvery beaches, sparkling waters, jungle-sided mountains, cascading waterfalls, meandering rivers, antique plantations—that is Jamaica, a jewel of the Caribbean, breathtakingly beautiful and endlessly surprising.

Most cruise ships stop at only one of the three major Jamaican ports. More's the pity, for each of the three has its own brand of magic, the kind of siren's call that has been luring travelers here for generations.

It started eons ago with the Arawak Indians, who named the place Xaymaca, a word for wood and water. There are of course plenty of both here, which is why the next visitor of note was Columbus, who stopped by in 1494 and presumably raved on about it so convincingly that a bevy of Spaniards came and remained here for 161 years.

Towering over the island are the **Blue Mountains,** some of which rise as high as 7,400 feet. On the slopes, banana groves spread over vast acres and sugarcane waves in the wind. Mango and lime trees add splashes of green, and nutmeg drops casually to plop unceremoniously but amazingly at your feet. In the mountains are born 126 rivers, some of them cascading down to the sea over gentle waterfalls and in meandering streams. Amid all the green are violent splashes of color from magenta bougainvillea, bright-yellow alameda, and rose hibiscus.

Sugar turned Jamaica from a little outpost to a massive plantation. When the British invaded the island in 1655, Jamaica's economy depended on the continued success of sugar, whose production was controlled from plantation homes called Great Houses. In 1673 there were just 57 of these massive estates, but 65 years later there were more than 400 of them! Sugar planters accumulated the wealth of kings but abolition of slavery in 1838 spelled an end to plantation life.

An independent state since 1962, Jamaica is a laughing, loving place of gentle, proud people whose charming British lilt is a delight to the ear and whose humor is quick and bubbly. From their melting-pot ancestry that included Spanish, English, African, and Indian—traders, slaves, settlers, pirates, and merchant kings—the island has developed some distinctive music and dance that has recently become the rage in international circles. Jamaica's national dance company, which performs in Kingston and occasionally elsewhere on the island and in the U.S., draws SRO crowds. Reggae, a uniquely Jamaican sound, has taken both European and U.S. music circles by storm.

From this polyglot background has come some very interesting English too. You'll hear some strange words and sounds, and if you're lucky you'll be able to listen to some hilarious folk stories, each with its carefully constructed moral expressed in riotous Jamaican slang. Ask someone to tell you a "duppy" (ghost) story and you'll see what we mean.

While you're here, you'll want to try some Jamaican food and sample some of the island's exotic tropical fruit. Lobsters are wonderful; akee looks like scrambled eggs and is served with codfish; escaveche is marinated fish; curried mutton and goat are favorites; callaloo is something like spinach; and jerk pork is barbecued pork grilled over wood fires; breadfruit, jack fruit, and cho-cho defy description but taste exotic, and jelly coconuts are to die for, especially when filled with rum punch. In Montego Bay, try patties at a bakery. Tia Maria is made here in Jamaica from coffee beans, and the local beer is Red Stripe.

Kingston, the island's capital city and home of an outstanding art gallery, was once the haunt of English buccaneers who harassed the Spanish from Port Royal with such success that the town came to be considered the richest and most wicked city in the world in its day. Capt. Sir Henry Morgan, an unrepentant pirate, was even made governor of the island!

But while Kingston is the island's governmental capital, **Montego Bay** is its tourist capital. Here life flows at a lively pace on pretty Cornwall or Doctor's Beach, and in the city itself, which offers plenty of shops and sidewalk vendors to keep you occupied.

In town, a brick **Georgian town house** at 16 Church St. has been restored to its original splendor, and in Charles Square you can see a small building once used to incarcerate runaway slaves.

To get a look at life as lived in the sugar plantation days, take a shore excursion or taxi to **Sign Great House,** seven miles outside town, where smiling helpers will take you on a well-informed guided tour of the plantation house.

Rose Hall Great House has quite a reputation in Jamaica (or rather, its owner does). Built in the 1750s at a cost of £30,000 sterling (and that was a ton of money in those days!), the house became the home of the island's most notorious female, Annie Palmer, made famous in a novel by H. G. deLisser called *White Witch of Rose Hall*. She was said to have taken slaves as lovers and killed them off when a new one appeared on the scene. Annie treated her several husbands similarly, and was supposed to have played with the fire of voodoo as well. Nasty Annie met a violent end much like that of her several paramours. Now restored, Rose Hall can be visited daily from 9 a.m. to 5 p.m. It's gorgeous.

Greenwood Great House occupies a pretty hillside location 14 miles east of Montego Bay and is open from 10 a.m. to 6 p.m. daily. Once the home of a relative of Elizabeth Barrett Browning's, the house was recently restored and opened to public view. You'll see some lovely music boxes and elegant furnishings, and in the back room, some good-looking ironwood carvings are sold.

While you're here, treat yourself to a long, lazy float down the Martha Brae River—on a raft! **Rafting** begins about three miles from Falmouth, and is a great adventure. You'll love it.

Cornwall and **Doctor's Beaches** have been a favorite haunt of the famous and infamous for years. Lovely strips of sand with dressing cabañas, they're in or close to the city, and at Cornwall there's an interesting underwater marine park.

City Centre is the center for shopping, but you'll find plenty of interesting shops along the streets and in the straw market.

If you're docking in **Ocho Rios,** you'll pull up to some of the loveliest sand in the Caribbean. Off on both sides of the ship you'll see beautiful beaches just begging you to kick off your shoes and your inhibitions.

As you walk off the ship on the pier, you're just steps away from the city's **straw market,** an open-air group of stalls where sellers with their babies, dogs, and assorted hangers-on patiently weave straw creations and just as patiently ask you to buy. You'll find some interesting baskets in unusual shapes and plenty of small gifts for the folks back at the office.

Farther afield in Ocho Rios, a "must-do" trip is to **Dunn's River Falls.** Here a river tumbles to the sea, falling in gentle splashes over boulders that tumbled down eons ago. Wear your swimsuit, for you first descend to the sea; then, accompanied by a guide, clamber back up the "steps" of the falls, holding hands with other climbers. It's not a strenuous climb, although it's a merry, slippery trip. There's no need to know how to swim. All you need is a ready laugh and a desire to be a splashing child again.

On the way here you'll pass through **Fern Gully,** once a riverbed, now a fascinating rain forest filled with huge wild ferns and trees.

Some shore tours visit **Prospect Plantation,** for botany fans the best way to see and learn about the flora and fauna of the island. Tours by open jitney take you through this still-working plantation where you can watch a skilled climber shinny up a banana tree. You'll see coconuts, cocoa, coffee, sugarcane plants, and some beautiful views stretching as far as Cuba, more than 90 miles away. Horseback tours also are available along the **White River.**

Shaw Park Gardens is another favorite shore excursion stop. It's a beautiful garden set into a cliff, with representatives of hundreds of different plants, each carefully explained and described by a young guide.

Not far from Ocho Rios, above Oracabessa, stands Firefly, the **home of Sir Noël Coward,** in which everything has been kept just as he left it in the days when he entertained Britain's Queen Mother, among others. You can visit it daily.

Brimmer Hall Estate, near Port Maria, is a working plantation too, and offers a similar experience to that of Prospect Plantation. Here you can also sit around the pool and sample some interesting beverage concoctions or shop in a **souvenir gallery.**

A wonderful way to while away some exotic hours is over lunch, dinner, or bottomless rum punches at **The Ruins,** a perfectly gorgeous restaurant incorporating a waterfall that's actually a tiny spur of Dunn's River Falls. At night the restaurant is lighted by torches; by day it's a study in tinkling waterfalls, spreading greenery, and shady bowers.

Port Antonio is a dramatic harbor where great cliffs rise from the sea. A small town, Port Antonio is better for sightseeing than for shopping, although there's an interesting native market where straw goods and famed Jamaican Blue Mountain coffee can be purchased quite inexpensively—especially if you take time to bargain.

Far and away the number one favorite activity in Port Antonio is **rafting on the Rio Grande River.** Once the method used to transport bananas from the plantation down to the ships, the rafts were "discovered" by swashbuckling actor Errol Flynn, who lived here and hired rafts to amuse his friends. The rafts are about 30 feet long and 3 feet wide, and are poled down the river by rafting experts, some of whom have been working here for 20 years or more. There's usually a stop about midway in the three-hour trip to keep you supplied with the potables necessary to continue the journey. If you go on your own, you'll drive or take a taxi to Rafter's Rest at Burlington on St. Margaret's Bay and someone will take your car to the termination point of your cruise.

On a drive around this lovely little village you'll get a chance to visit **Somer-**

set Falls, about ten miles west of Port Antonio. It's a seductive spot that makes you want to curl up with a cool drink and just watch as the falls cascade down a gorge through a rain forest and into a deep rock pool.

Another popular stop is the **Caves of Nonsuch** and the **Gardens of Athenry,** a working banana plantation where a cave full of stalagmites and stalactites once shielded Arawak Indians who lived in the area. From the gardens there are beautiful views from an open-air lounge out across this lush island.

One final stop is the **Blue Lagoon,** near Frenchman's Cove Hotel. A lovely, tranquil spot meant for lazy contemplation of life's mysteries—with some serious thought to how you can quit everything and spend the rest of your life here!—the Blue Lagoon also offers scuba-diving and waterskiing. A mineral spring here is said to be good for rheumatism. Whatever the truth of that, the Blue Lagoon is good for the soul.

Ships Calling Here: *Britanis, Crown Odyssey, Cunard Princess, Fair Majesty, Fairsky, Regent Sea, Sagafjord, Seaward, Skyward, Song of America, Stella Solaris, Sun Viking, Vistafjord,* and *Westerdam.*

Martinique

Capital and Port City: Fort-de-France.
Size: 50 miles long by 19 miles wide.
Population: 100,000.
Government: Martinique is not a colony but a département of France, so all residents are citizens of France.
Climate: 70° to 80°F year round, with some rain June through September.
Language: French, Créole.
Currency: French franc.
Tourist Information: Office du Tourisme, Bord de Mer, B.P. 520, Fort-de-France (tel. 63-79-60).
Documentation: A visa, now required to enter the country, may be obtained in advance at a French consulate, or at the Martinique airport upon presentation of a passport, or other proof of U.S. or Canadian citizenship plus a photograph.
Public Transportation: taxis (unmetered, so agree on a price first), native buses, launch to Trois-Îlets.
Car Rentals: Hertz, 24 rue Ernest-Deproge (tel. 60-64-64); Avis, 4 rue Ernest-Deproge (tel. 70-11-60); Budget, 30 rue Ernest-Deproge (tel. 63-69-00).
Shopping Specialties: pottery, straw items, Martinican dolls, wood-carvings.
Food Specialties: French and spicy Créole cuisines; crab, turtle, conch, octopus, curries, blaff (fish stew).
Restaurants: La Grand'Voile, Pointe Simon (tel. 71-29-29); D'Esnambuc, 1 rue de la Liberté (tel. 71-45-51); La Lafayette, Hôtel Lafayette, 5 rue de la Liberté (tel. 63-24-09); La Biguine, 11 route de la Folie (tel. 71-40-07).

Martinique is the Paris of the Caribbean, a sunny volcanic islet that celebrates joie de vivre in lifestyle and culture.

Looming over the island is the fierce Mont Pélée volcano, which erupted in 1902 to kill 40,000 inhabitants in a fiery display of nature's violence. On the slopes of this 4,656-foot-high peak, deep-green rain forests thrive.

Martinique's most famous export was the Empress Josephine, consort to Napoleon, who hailed from the nearby island of Trois-Îlets. Another famous French royalty groupie, Madame de Maintenon, mistress of Louis XIV, also came from Martinique. Some say those two are testimony to the outstanding beauty of Martinique women, and go so far as to claim that the island shelters the most beautiful femmes of the Caribbean. Here beauty is indeed in the eye of the beholder, for topless beaches are common.

Discovered by Columbus, Martinique was settled by the French in 1635. Sugarcane plantations and rum distilleries have kept the island thriving over the years, and now tourism is doing its part.

This is an island of mountains, from its highest, **Mont Pélée**, to the 3,960-foot **Carbet Peak**. On the southern part of the island the land rises to about 1,500 feet. Along the edges of the sea, tiny coves provide intimate swimming spots, and beautiful bays are a photographer's dream.

You'll see fabulous flowers everywhere, adding splashes of color to the pastel loveliness of sleepy villages. Tropical birds of all kinds, including hummingbirds, live here, flitting happily among shrubs that may shield a mongoose, imported here decades ago to rid the island of snakes. Mongoose-snake competitions are still a favorite sport on the island, but baseball is the national passion.

In Fort-de-France you'll find yourself strolling the island equivalent of New Orleans or Key West: ornate iron grillwork, tropical flowers, café au lait, great French and Créole cooking. If by now you're thinking it might be nice to skip a ship meal in favor of shoreside flavors, this is the place to do that.

Be prepared for some healthy hiking here—most of the streets climb steep hills—with some beautiful views as a reward.

In town you'll see a white marble statue of Josephine in a park called **La Savane,** and nearby at the Palais de Justice a statuary tribute to Victor Schoelcher, who worked to free the slaves a century ago.

If you'd like to see more Josephine mementos, take a 20-minute drive or a ferry to **Trois-Îlets,** where an estate about a mile out of town features a collection that includes the empress's bed, a letter from Napoleon, and some other remnants of her time. It's called La Pagerie, and is open daily except Monday from 9 a.m. to 5:30 p.m.

St. Louis Roman Catholic Cathedral was built in 1875 of iron and is certainly an unusual church. Stop by and you'll see what we mean. Overlooking the town is **Sacré-Coeur de Balata Cathedral,** a copy of Montmartre's Sacré-Coeur in Paris.

Fort St-Louis is the guardian of the port and stands on a cliff overlooking it. Once called Fort Royal, the fortress was the scene of fierce battles among the Dutch, French, and English as the island changed ownership in the 17th and 18th centuries. A sound-and-light show takes place there each night, and there's a restaurant inside the fort, Le Lotus. Two other bastions, **Fort Tartenson** and **Fort Desaix,** offer plenty of exploration possibilities for fortress fans.

One very colorful spot you're sure to notice as you stroll the narrow byways here is **Library Schoelcher,** which features a red-and-blue portal in fancy furbelows, lotus-petal columns, and turquoise tiles. All of it was imported from Paris where it was part of the Paris Exposition of 1889.

History buffs should head for the **Musée Départementale de la Martinique,** where you'll see remnants of the early Arawak and Carib Indian tribes who once inhabited this and many other Caribbean islands.

If you'd like to be more active, there is horseback riding, waterskiing, scuba-diving, golf, tennis, and sailing. You can even try some airborne sightseeing, offered by Heli Antilles International and arranged at the Hotel Bakoua.

An "Aquascope" **glass-bottom boat** with gull-wing sides has taken up residence here and will take you on tours of the fish and coral, which you view through the craft's windows.

You can hardly go wrong on restaurants here—they all offer good French cooking or Frenchmen cooking Spanish or Caribbean style. Don't panic if the restaurant looks like a roadside shack; the food's good and life is casual here.

PORTS OF CALL: CARIBBEAN ISLANDS □ 63

A local **market** at Quai Desnambuc features local handcrafts and souvenirs, and in the **shops** you'll find some of the best of French imports—Vuitton, Limoges, Lalique—at prices often well below what you'd pay at home. Among the more interesting shops are Les Puces, 26 and 28 rue Victor-Hugo, two old mansions filled with antiques; Chantilly, on rue Victor-Hugo, for fashions; Gigi, 53 rue Lazare-Carnot; Au Printemps, rues Schoelcher and Antoine-Siger, a branch of the Paris department store although more modest; and Prisunic, on rue Lamartine, a cheaper version of Au Printemps.

For **island crafts,** try Calypso at Pointe du Bout, which is a bit out of town but has beautiful handcrafts and batik-ed silks; or the Caribbean Art Center, facing La Savane in town, where some of the best in island craftsmanship is displayed and sold. Rum's a good buy too, and comes in some unusual colors and types. Try a bottle of Bally from Boutique du Rhum, 41 rue Victor-Hugo (upstairs from the tea house below).

If you're going out on the island to explore, you'll see some plush hotels at Pointe du Bout; beautiful Diamond Beach with its grove of palms and towering **Diamond Rock; Savane de Petrifications,** a "forest" of petrified rock; Mont Pélée, and in **St-Pierre,** the town destroyed by the lava flow, the **Musée Volcanologique,** featuring relics dug from this Caribbean Pompeii.

Ships Calling Here: *The Azur, CarlaCosta, Crown Odyssey, Cunard Countess, Daphne, Explorer Starship, Fair Majesty, Fairsky, Festivale, Island Princess, New Shoreham, Nordic Prince, Ocean Islander, Ocean Princess, Pacific Princess, Rotterdam, Royal Viking Sky, Royal Viking Sun, Sagafjord, Sea Goddess I, Song of Norway, Starward, Stella Oceanis, The Victoria, Vistafjord,* and *Wind Star.*

Puerto Rico

Capital and Port City: San Juan (pop. 1,000,000).
Size: 100 miles long by 35 miles wide (about half the size of New Jersey).
Population: 3,000,000.
Climate: 70° to 80° F year round; rain forest in interior.
Language: Spanish, but many also speak English in the urban areas.
Currency: U.S. dollar.
Tourist Information: Puerto Rico Tourism Co., 301 Calle San Justo, about a block from the pier in San Juan (tel. 809/721-2400).
Documents: proof of citizenship required for non-U.S. citizens.
Public Transportation: taxis (metered), buses, jitneys (called publicos).
Car Rentals: Hertz, 1365 Ashford Ave. (tel. 725-2027 or 725-5537); other major companies as well.
Shopping Specialties: chic clothing and shoes, jewelry, antiques, carved wooden santos (saints), china, silver, crystal, rum (you can take back to the States as much Puerto Rican rum as you want, duty free).
Food Specialties: rice and beans, ropa vieja, picadillo, arroz con pollo, paella, tostones, fried bananas, pork; plus a variety of international cuisines.
Restaurants: Los Galanes, 65 San Francisco St. (tel. 722-4008); Mallorquina, 207 San Justo (tel. 722-3261) for casual, historic dining; Butterfly People, 152 Fortaleza (tel. 723-2432).

Puerto Rico is at once ancient and modern, its lovely old historic district surrounded by the most modern of cities.

You'll dock right at the entrance to Old San Juan, the city's oldest quarter and its most interesting shopping area. The best way to see the old city is on foot, but wear your most comfortable shoes as you'll be doing some serious, but wonderfully rewarding, **hiking.**

And, yes, Christopher Columbus was here *too*. (As you travel the Caribbean you begin to think Columbus must have commuted! He seems to have been everywhere, but then getting everywhere in the Caribbean isn't all that difficult as you're discovering aboard your very own *Niña, Pinta,* or *Santa Maria.*) On his second voyage to the New World in 1493 that man happened upon an island he called San Juan in honor of St. John the Baptist. Ponce de León (of Florida's "fountain of youth" fame) was the first governor of the island, which later was called Puerto Rico or "rich port."

Trade winds cool cosmopolitan Puerto Rico year round so it's never blazing hot. In fact in the mountains out on the island temperatures are as perfect as can be all year long.

Out on the island are deep, damp tropical rain forests, arid deserts, beautiful deserted beaches lined with swaying palms, even a phosphorescent bay filled with tiny organisms that glow in the dark when you swim there!

To get a look at lovely **Old San Juan,** begin with a stop at the tourist office, just up the street from the docks at 301 Calle San Justo. Called the Puerto Rico Tourism Co., the tourist office can supply you with a copy of "Que Pasa," which tells you everything that is going on in Puerto Rico and outlines a walking tour of the city. Here are some of the most interesting sights:

Nearest to the pier is **La Fortaleza,** on Calle (*calle* is "street" in Spanish) Fortaleza, the first castle built here by the Spanish in 1533. Now the home of the island's governor, it is one of the oldest executive mansions in this hemisphere. Tours in English are every half hour from 9 to 11:30 a.m. and 1:30 to 4 p.m. It's beautifully lighted at night.

San Juan Gate, Calle San Francisco and Calle Recinto Oeste, is more than 300 years old and was the main entry to San Juan in the 18th century.

City Hall, on Calle San Francisco, was completed in 1789 and has guided tours Monday through Friday from 8 a.m. to 4:15 p.m.

San Juan Cathedral, Calle Cristo and Caleta San Juan, was begun 400 years ago but suffered damage from 16th-century looters and storms. Ponce de León was buried here after he died from an arrow wound received in Florida.

Casa Blanca, on Calle Sol, was home to the descendants of Ponce de León for generations, although never to the governor and explorer himself. It now offers a fascinating look at life and homes of the 16th and 17th centuries. Tours are given daily from 9 a.m. to noon and 1:30 to 4:30 p.m.

Casa de los Contrafuertes, on Calle San Sebastian, is a museum of pharmaceuticals and has a sensational collection of "santos," saints carved in native woods and now one of the great Puerto Rican collectibles. It's open from 9 a.m. to noon and 1 to 4:30 p.m. daily (except Monday and Thursday).

Pablo Casals, the renowned cellist, was a Puerto Rican, and his work and memorabilia are displayed in the **Pablo Casals Museum,** a tiny 16th-century house, lovely in its own right. Open from 9 a.m. to noon and 1 to 4 p.m. Tuesday through Saturday, from noon to 5 p.m. on Sunday.

Dominican Convent, Calle Norzagaray, was begun in 1523 by Dominican friars and was often a refuge for San Juan residents attacked by Carib Indians. It is now the Institute of Puerto Rican Culture.

City walls 20 feet thick at the bottom, about half as thick at the top, protected the town against invaders and pirates. You can see the remains of these impressive walls between San Cristobal and El Morro Fortresses.

If you like forts, you're going to adore San Juan. No fewer than three well-preserved fortresses guard this island harbor. By name they are San Cristobal Fort on Calle Norzagaray, Fort San Jeronimo at the entrance to Condado Bay near the Caribe Hilton Hotel, and the granddaddy of them all, **El Morro,** on Calle Norzagaray. The most spectacular is El Morro, which looms above the harbor atop a vertical cliff. Ordered built in 1539, it was originally a single round tower, which you can still see inside the main part of the fort. In those days it was called the Castle of San Felipe, and from its walls were fired the cannons that drove away Sir Francis Drake in 1595. Guided tours are conducted at 9:30 and 11 a.m. and at 2 and 3:30 p.m., but you can wander around on your own and figure most of it out yourself. In the small museum inside the fort, all the major battles that took place are described in English and Spanish.

From the ramparts here you get a spectacular view of the glittering waters that surround the island and of Old San Juan. There's even a dungeon for your peering pleasure. If you're tired from your explorations, outside the wall massive lawns shaded by an impressive row of casuarina trees stretch to the sea—a lovely place to rest, picnic, even nap a bit.

As you walk through the old town, you will see ornate wrought-iron balconies above you, pretty painted doors with fancy brass hardware, and houses in all colors of the rainbow. Scarlet bougainvillea and deep-green vines climb the old walls, and tiny flower-filled window boxes add splashes of unexpected color.

You'll find intriguing **shops** by the dozens, so many it would be impossible to outline them all here, but we've picked out a few of our favorites. For hammocks, hanging woven chairs, all kinds of string, cord, or yarn things to sit and lie in, the Gentle Swing, 156 Calle Cristo, is wonderful. A hammock chair you hang from the ceiling is possibly the most comfortable seat you'll ever sit in, and costs about $50. It was invented by the Taino Indians in pre-Columbian times!

Butterfly People, 152 Fortaleza, offers the most interesting creations in the Caribbean. Two Americans with the unusual names of Drakir and Attendaire Purington buy the most gorgeous butterflies you've ever seen from special farms in New Guinea and South America, treat them with chemicals to preserve the color, and frame them in Lucite boxes. These are not just pinned-up butterflies but signed and numbered artworks in which the shimmering iridescent creatures seem to be suspended in flight, their wings glowing like jewels, never looking quite the same twice. This hand-work is expensive, but it's worth every dime if you're in search of mementoes more meaningful than an ashtray labeled San Juan. Butterfly People is housed in a lovely old building with a pretty courtyard and an enchanting small restaurant.

Collection d'Aqui, 204 Fortaleza, has fine, quality Puerto Rican handcrafts including pottery, metalwork, and woodcarvings.

Crazy Alice, 196 Fortaleza, has a shop packed with everything from Panama hats to papier-mâché fruit. Reinhold, at 201 Cristo St., is an old-line jewelry store.

You don't pay duty on purchases you take back to the mainland because Puerto Rico is part of the U.S. You also may find bargains as impressive here as in the Virgin Islands, and the shops are every bit as chic.

Sports enthusiasts will find golf, tennis, riding, and water sports of all kinds in and around San Juan. Details are available at the Puerto Rico Tourism Co. and in the "Qué Pasa" publication.

Ships often remain overnight in San Juan so passengers can take in the lively **San Juan nightlife.** Shore excursions generally are a choice between a flashy flamenco show at the Condado Plaza and a cabaret at El San Juan Hotel. Both are top-notch entertainment. Some top discos include Juliana's in the Caribe Hilton Hotel and Isadora's in the Condado Plaza.

Casinos are active in San Juan at several major hotels.

Authentic folklore entertainment is provided by a group of folk dancers who perform in the **LeLoLai Festival** at large hotels on the island. To discover where and when the show is playing, call 722-1513 or 723-3135.

Ships Calling Here: *The Azur, Caribe I, CarlaCosta, Celebration, Crown Odyssey, Cunard Countess, Daphne, Explorer Starship, Festivale, Island Princess, Noordam, Ocean Islander, Pacific Princess, Sagafjord, Skyward, Song of Norway, Sovereign of the Seas, Starward, The Victoria, Vistafjord,* and *Westerdam.*

St. Lucia

Capital and Port City: Castries.
Size: 27 miles long by 14 miles wide.
Population: 120,000.
Language: English, Créole.
Currency: Eastern Caribbean ("beewee") dollar (E.C.$).
Tourist Information: Tourist Office, Castries (tel. 452-2479).
Documents: passport required.
Public Transportation: unmetered taxis (verify whether price is quoted in U.S. or "beewee" dollars), jitney buses.
Car Rentals: St. Lucia Car Rental, Caribleu Hotel, Cap Estate (tel. 452-8551). Note that driving is on the left, and that a local license must be obtained from the Traffic Department, on Bridge Street in Castries (tel. 452-2455).
Shopping Specialties: sea island cottons, silkscreened fabrics, chic cottons, flour-bag clothing, shell jewelry, island perfumes.
Food Specialties: West Indian cuisine, curries.
Restaurants: Green Parrot, Le Morne Fortune (tel. 452-3399); Rain, Columbus Square (tel. 454-3022); The Still, Soufrière (tel. 454-7224).

You've heard of active volcanoes and quiescent volcanoes and now you're going to hear about a drive-in volcano! Yes sir, step right up and drive into the volcano, but sorry, you can't drive out the other side with a grilled burger. Another of the Caribbean's Mount Soufrières, St. Lucia's volcano is one of those bleak moon-landing landscapes steaming and fuming its way into the future.

You can drive a car right into it, parking and walking between sulfur springs and whooshing jets of steam. It makes a big stink, literally and figuratively, but this **Mount Soufrière** has never yet followed up its steaming threats.

Millions of years old, the volcano has two sisters, or brothers if you will, called **Petit Piton** and **Gros Piton,** both volcanic cones rising more than 2,400 feet, shooting right up out of the sea and visible for miles around. You'll probably see them first while you're still at sea.

All this area is a huge rain forest in which the annual rainfall is something like 150 inches.

Nobody is quite sure who happened upon St. Lucia, which is about 20 miles from Martinique, but it was settled by some St. Kitts colonists in 1605. Over the years it was a favorite battleground for the French and English, and actually changed hands 14 times! In 1967 the island became part of the British Commonwealth.

Here we've been talking about it all this time and you don't even know how to say it: it's pronounced St. *Loo*-sha. The island's capital, **Castries,** was named for an early French secretary of state to the colonies.

Although it has a long history, the capital city has been destroyed by fire several times so there's not much left of the early colonial architecture. Among the things you'll want to look at here are the Saturday-morning **market,** and **Morne Fortune** ("Good Luck Hill"), an 18th-century barracks with its "Four Apostles" cannons and a lovely view of the harbor.

From the fort you can spot **Pigeon Island,** where pirates and British sailors gathered in days past. It's no wonder they picked this meeting spot: there are lovely beaches here.

Marigot Bay may just look a little familiar too, but it's not an attack of déjà vu. Rex Harrison's *Dr. Doolittle* was filmed here, and Sophia Loren came here to star in a movie called *Fire Power*. Admiral Rodney hid his ships under palm leaves here and lay in wait for the French frigates. You'll see some of those same palms along the shoreline.

As you can see, it won't take you long to get a look at most of the sights. Then you can get down to what is serious business on St. Lucia: swimming, snorkeling, scuba-diving, tennis, golf, horseback riding, sailing, windsurfing, and deep-sea fishing.

Ships Calling Here: *Cunard Countess, Daphne, Explorer Starship, New Shoreham, Ocean Islander, Sagafjord, Sea Goddess I, Skyward,* and *Vistafjord.*

St. Maarten / St. Martin (and St. Barthélemy)

Capitals and Port Cities: Philipsburg, St. Maarten; Marigot, St. Martin.
Size: about 7 miles long by 6 miles wide.
Population: 21,000.
Climate: 70° to 80° F year round.
Languages: Dutch, French, French patois (called Papiamento).
Currency: St. Maarten—Netherlands Antillean guilder. St. Martin—French franc.
Tourist Information: St. Maarten—St. Maarten Tourist Bureau, De Ruyterplein, Front Street, Philipsburg (tel. 2337); St. Martin—Bureau du Tourisme, waterfront, Marigot (tel. 87-53-26).
Documents: proof of U.S. or Canadian citizenship required.
Public Transportation: taxis (unmetered, but the governments set the rates; agree on a price in advance for special tours), buses.
Car Rentals: Avis, Le Pirate Hôtel, Marigot (tel. 87-78-37); Hertz, Cape Bay Road (tel. 5995); plus local companies. For mopeds, try Carter's Rental, Bush Road, Cul-de-Sac, Philipsburg (tel. 2621).
Shopping Specialties: St. Maarten—Indonesian batiks, Delftware, Dutch dolls. St. Martin—chic French designer clothes, jewelry, perfumes.
Food Specialties: conch stew, lobster, Javanese peppersteak.
Restaurants: Philipsburg—West Indian Tavern, Front Street (tel. 22965); Le Pavillon, Simson Bay Village Beach (tel. 44254); Oyster Pond Hotel, Oyster Pond (tel. 22206). Marigot—Le Poisson d'Or, rue de la Liberté (tel. 87-50-33); Jean Dupont, Marina Port la Royale (tel. 87-71-13); La Maison sur le Port, at the port (tel. 87-56-38). St. Barthélemy—Castelets, Morne Lurin, Gustavia (tel. 27-61-73).

This is the split-personality island, half Dutch, half French. Legend has it that it got that way when the Dutch and French settlers here each picked a "citizen of sound wind" and had him walk around the island. Where the two met became the border.

That French walker must have been of very sound wind for he carved out the bigger slice of the island, about 21 of the 37 square miles, while the Dutch stroller was certainly of sound mind; he (or she) saw to it that the lovely harbor of **Philipsburg** was included in the Dutch sector.

That's why today you are likely to land on the Dutch side, called Sint Maarten, but it's no trick at all to hop a local bus and hie yourself off to the French side, St. Martin (pronounced on this French side San Mar-*tan*). Sint or St., the island is believed to have been named by Columbus in honor of the saint whose saint's day it was when he landed here.

Admittedly, that legend is more tale than truth. After Columbus sailed up and officially discovered the islands, Dutch and French settlers moved in and might have clashed if they had not gotten together to write a "mont des accords" agreement that established the two territories as separate but equal—and friendly—sectors.

Often a hideaway for pirates who found its horseshoe-shaped bays as accessible as modern sailing craft do, this craggy, hilly island for years sported tobacco and sugar plantations run by Dutch and French settlers who were so close they weren't sure which nationality they were!

You can move from side to side here with no concern for Customs or red tape, and we certainly suggest that you do so. Both sides of the island have beautiful beaches, 32 of them in all, and both sides have scads of interesting shops.

You may be relieved to know that you'll have few sightseeing obligations here. Very little remains of the plantation era and there are no archeological sights of note on the island.

Shoppers, however, will be busy. This island is a veritable treasure trove of duty-free goodies ranging from beautiful batik-ed cloth from Indonesia (try Java Wraps) to jewels of all kinds and the best of Dutch imports, things like Delft Blue ware and Dutch dolls. In the village of Grand Case live many painters whose work makes a handsome souvenir of your visit here. You'll find the buys on Front and Back Streets in Philipsburg.

When you cross over to **Marigot** on the French side of this mountainous island dotted with salt ponds, you'll find some beautifully stuffed string bikinis romping on the sands, often topless. You'll also find some beautiful beaches obviously designed by nature especially for you beachsitters.

Snorkelers and scuba-divers can visit some of the clearest waters in the Caribbean and poke around the 1801 British man-o-war wreck, the *Prostellyte,* complete with cannons and anchor.

Tennis and golf are available, as are waterskiing, boating, and fishing. Ask at the Tourist Office in Philipsburg for details on how to organize these activities.

There are casinos here for gambling fans.

Lobster lovers should head for the West Indian Tavern, Front Street, an intriguing spot that occupies the site of a 150-year-old synagogue and has as much local color as it does rainbow-hued décor. Le Pavillon and Oyster Pond Hotel are other pleasant spots. In Marigot, try Le Poisson d'Or or La Maison sur le Port.

Few cruise ships visit **St. Barthélemy** (pronounced Bar-tell-*emmy*), more's the pity. This island, most often called St. Bart's, has been a retreat for millionaires for generations and nobody ever said *they* don't know how to live!

Populated since the early 1600s, St. Bart's was owned by the French until they turned the island over to Sweden, which ruled for 100 years or so after exchanging trading rights in Gothenburg for possession of this sunny spot. Britain was in charge for a time, but in 1878 the island was returned to France and is today a satellite of Guadeloupe.

David Rockefeller and Edmond de Rothschild occupied some plush real estate here, lured by the beauty of the tiny island's beaches and its intriguing Breton and Norman fishermen who still speak with those accents and dress in costumes of France's northeastern countryside. You can still see some of that Swedish ancestry too, in blonde, blue-eyed residents.

You can get here from St. Maarten on a 145-foot motor yacht that makes the hour-long journey to the tiny harbor at St. Bart's Tuesday through Saturday at 9 a.m., returning at 3:30 p.m.

You'll land in **Gustavia,** testimony to the island's Swedish connections, where there are shops and taxis that can take you on an island tour or to one of the pretty beaches here. If you're hungry, try La Crémaillère.

You can get some good buys here on imported French perfumes and the like. Everything's sold without duty, so often the prices are lower than they are in France (not a wide range of choices, however). A St. Bart's straw hat is a must.

All the usual water sports, plus tennis and horseback riding, are offered.

Ships Calling Here: *Caribbean Prince, Celebration, Crown Odyssey, Cunard Countess, Daphne, Explorer Starship, Festivale, Island Princess, Nantucket Clipper, Nordic Prince, Norway, Pacific Princess, Sagafjord, Sea Goddess I, Skyward, Song of Norway, Starward, Stella Oceanis, Vistafjord, Westerdam,* and *Wind Spirit.*

St. Vincent (and the Grenadines)
Capital and Port City: Kingstown
Size: 18 miles long by 12 miles wide.
Population: 120,000.
Climate: 70° to 80° F year round.
Language: English.
Currency: Eastern Caribbean ("beewee") dollar (E.C.$).
Tourist Information: Department of Tourism, Kingstown (tel. 809/457-1502).
Documents: proof of U.S. or Canadian citizenship required.
Public Transportation: taxi, ferry.
Car Rentals: Star Garage, Grenville Street, Kingstown (tel. 61743).
Shopping Specialties: sea island cotton fabrics, native pottery, weavings, jewelry, wall hangings, baskets.
Food Specialties: seafood, tropical fruits.
Restaurants: Cobblestone Inn, Kingstown (tel. 456-1937); Pink Dolphin, Villa Beach (tel. 458-4238).

Throngs of tourists have not yet hit the serene beaches of St. Vincent, but throngs of other less-welcome visitors have stopped by here over the years to wreak a little havoc. Carib Indians were living here peacefully until they made the mistake of taking sides in the constant feuding between France and England. In 1795 French revolutionaries allied with the Caribs burned some British plantations, but lost the war and the Caribs were deported to British Honduras, where their descendants remain.

Since then the island has been allied to the British and is now a British Commonwealth country. You can still hear some French in these islands, however, although the primary language is English. Spanish is not heard at all, even though the first visitor here was Columbus, stopping by to plant the flag as he explored this part of the Caribbean on his third voyage to these waters.

As part of the Windward Islands, St. Vincent and the Grenadines—which include Mustique, Bequia, Cannouan, Mayreau, Union Island, Palm Island, and Petit St. Vincent—are cooled by trade winds that keep the temperature a steady gorgeous here all year long.

Tiny as **St. Vincent** is, it's a study in varied terrain ranging from valleys to peaks, waterfalls to silvery beaches, lush jungles to coral reefs—even a volcano and a crater lake 4,000 feet high. It's even sometimes called the "Tahiti of the Caribbean" for the groves of breadfruit trees that grow here. Legend has it that Captain Bligh of *Mutiny on the Bounty* fame (or infamy) brought them here on his return from Tahiti.

A volcanic island, St. Vincent is a sailor's heaven. You will see many a mariner here, some of them natives sailing produce off to other islands, some of them yachting fans here for the day or the week or the month.

Among the sights everyone will be looking at are **Fort Charlotte,** which isn't much of a fort anymore but does have a beautiful view of the sea from an aerie more than 600 feet above it, and **St. Mary's Catholic Church,** an improbable mélange of architectural styles that's both weird and wonderful.

The **Botanic Gardens,** about a mile from downtown, is the oldest such garden in the West Indies and will give you a look at some of the spices you use in your cooking while they're still on the trees.

Budding archeologists will want to take a close look at **Carib Rock,** one of the Caribbean's most outstanding petroglyphs, dating to A.D. 600. A human face stares back at you from the rock. There's an **Archeological Museum** in the Botanic Gardens too.

Barrouallie is a **whaling village** and for the Caribbean that's *unusual!* Whales are hunted here with harpoons, but don't worry too much about saving the whales. So few are seen here that it's a very big moment when one is actually spotted, let alone harpooned. Barrouallie also has a Carib stone altar.

A waterfall called the **Falls of Baleine** is accessible by boat, so check at the tourist office for arrangements if you want to see it.

A drive down the **Windward Highway** along the Atlantic coast is a study in crashing waves and rocky shoreline, accented by arrowroot, coconut, and banana plantations.

You'll see massive **La Soufrière** volcano in the distance. It's accessible to hikers, but makes a full day's journey and you will need a guide—ask at the Department of Tourism. The volcano erupted in 1979 sending a shot of steam 20,000 feet in the air. An earlier eruption in 1902 killed 2,000 people and created Rabacca Dry River, a lava flow, and an eruption in 1972 created Crater Lake, actually an island of lava rock.

Queen's Drive around Kingstown is another breathtaking series of beautiful views, and lush, green **Mesopotamia Valley** offers a panoramic view unexcelled anywhere in the Caribbean. Dominated by Grand Bonhomme at 3,181 feet, the valley is rich with plantations, and rivers and streams tumble to the sea over the rocks of Yambou Gorge.

Sports fans can take to the tennis courts, the golf course, go snorkeling and scuba-diving or fishing. Sailing buffs can rent a boat from Caribbean Sailing Yachts at the Blue Lagoon. Horseback riding and windsurfing are also available.

Shopping choices are sparse in St. Vincent, although you can buy some pretty sea island cotton fabrics and even have something made to order. The St. Vincent Handicraft Centre has interesting native crafts.

South of St. Vincent, the **Grenadines** stretch along in the ocean like a ribbon trailing from a package. Called the Grenadines because they are on the route to Grenada, these tiny islands are really sleepy places you can visit by boat or air if you're in the area long enough.

Bequia is a rare but wonderful stop. Stretched out before you here is a palm-fringed bay that stepped right out of a postcard. Tiny shops, a post office with a hole cut in the wall for a mail slot, a couple of friendly sipping spots and casual restaurants are stretched alongside a half mile of quiet roadway by the beach.

Don't plan anything energetic in this soporific atmosphere. Wander among shops that feature a bit of scrimshaw in tribute to the whales that sometimes are visible here, lots of pretty batiks, some skillfully hand-painted shirts, some unusual hand-painted postcards.

Seek out the island's two model shipbuilders, who can take a photograph and measurements of a boat and build a gorgeous handcrafted to-scale model of it in any size you like. You can't miss their shop as you stroll through town and most days you'll also see them working beside the sea, shaded by palms, cooled by sea breezes. So talented are they that Queen Elizabeth has a model of her blue royal yacht *Britannia* on display in the yacht's dining room.

For our money, one of the most enchantingly tropical islands in the Caribbean, Bequia is a beaut.

A few cruise ships stop at **Mustique,** a seductive enough spot to have lured Princess Margaret, a regular visitor who managed to find herself in a scandal even way out here. Another visitor, at the other end of the royalty spectrum, was Mick Jagger.

Here you'll find golden beaches, sand roads lined with a sentinel array of palms marching alongside, waters striated in what surely must be all the shades of blue invented, and one single resort, Cotton House.

You're on your own here, gloriously . . . and that's what it's all about, after all.

Ships Calling Here: *The Azur, Explorer Starship, Island Princess, New Shoreham, Ocean Islander, Sagafjord, Sea Goddess I, Stella Oceanis, Vistafjord,* and *Wind Star.*

Trinidad and Tobago

Capital and Port City: Port-of-Spain.
Size: 50 miles long by 38 miles wide.
Population: 1,100,000.
Climate: 70° to 80°F year round, with some rain June through September.
Language: English, plus Hindi, French patois, Spanish, Chinese, Urdu.
Currency: Trinidad/Tobago dollar.
Tourist Information: Trinidad and Tobago Tourist Board, 122-24 Frederick St., Port-of-Spain (tel. 62-31932).
Documents: passport required.
Public Transportation: unmetered taxis (ask if the fare is quoted in TT$ or U.S.$), pirate taxis (route taxis, which pick up and drop off passengers as they go, and are cheaper), buses.
Car Rentals: Hub Travel, 44 New St. (tel. 625-3011); Mike's Taxi, 37 Industry Lane (tel. 624-1590). Note that driving is on the left.
Shopping Specialties: Steel drums, banana leaf weavings, Oriental imports, cascadura jewelry, straw and fiber goods, Indian saris.
Food Specialties: Indian roti and curries, callaloo soup, stuffed crab backs.
Restaurants: Port-of-Spain—Mangal's, 13 Queen's Park East (tel. 624-4639); Copper Kettle Grill, 66-68 Edward St. (tel. 625-4381); Chez Véronique, 117A Henry St. (tel. 623-8249).

These islands are the home of the steel drum, so expect to hear plenty of that intriguing calypso music while you're here. Steel drums, which Trinidadians claim are the only new instrument invented in this century, were originally made from the tops of steel oil drums. So good are these Trinidadian drummers and calypso balladeers that they almost always win the annual Caribbean Islands' calypso competition.

Trinidad and Tobago are harmonious in other ways as well. As the melting pot of the Caribbean, these two islands are inhabited by the wildest variety of nationalities of any nation in the region. Among those who call these oil-producing islands home are Americans, Europeans, East Indians, Venezuelans, Syrians, Lebanese, Chinese, Hindustanis, Javanese, Créoles, descendants of slaves and of early Indian settlers. Christian, Hindu, and Muslim live side by side, and the language is . . . well, even pronouncing the name of the language is difficult so you can imagine what the tongue itself is like. It's called Trinibagianese, but English is widely spoken as well.

Located just ten miles off the coast of South America, Trinidad has a government perpetually feuding (verbally) with others in the Caribbean, but that shouldn't affect your enjoyment of a stop here.

You can explore **Port-of-Spain,** the capital, on foot beginning at **Queen's Park Savannah,** once a plantation until it was destroyed by fire in 1808. You'll hear the chimes from pink-and-blue **Queen's Royal College** on Maraval Road, which is also home to a gingerbready house that's quite a sight indeed.

Whitehall Mansion, home of the prime minister, is a Moorish-style building, while the home of the German Stollmeyers, built in 1905, is a Caribbean German castle. These three and some others you'll see in a row here are called the **"magnificent seven."** (It won't take you long to figure out why.)

If you'd like to see what Carnival is like here—and it's *really* something—you can ogle some of the costumes at the **National Museum and Art Gallery.**

The main shopping street is Woodford Square, where you will see the **Red House,** built in 1906. It houses the governmental activities of the islands.

On one side of the Cathedral of the Immaculate Conception is a street leading to the **Central Market,** on Beecham Hwy., where the spices for which Trinidad is famous are sold—very picturesque.

Is there a Caribbean island without a botanic garden? There may be, but it isn't Trinidad, which has a 70-acre **Botanic Garden,** including an orchid house and coca bushes. In the garden is the official residence of the president of the islands.

Fort fans get yet another chance here, at **Fort George,** which occupies a peak 1,100 feet above the city and was built in 1804. It's about ten miles out of town, a long trip in these parts.

Birdlovers will enjoy the **Caroni Bird Sanctuary,** where flocks of scarlet ibis settle each evening, or the **Asa Wright Nature Center,** where all kinds of exotic tropical flyers nest, including the only accessible colony of cave-dwelling guacharo birds.

Most cruise passengers are driven along the **Skyline Highway,** a seven-mile trek across a pass called "The Saddle" that runs between two valleys. You'll pass through Santa Cruz Valley, where huge stands of bamboo tower over you, and go back along Beecham Hwy. This route is the way to **Maracas Beach,** the best beach near the city.

Sports enthusiasts can play tennis, go fishing, try hunting alligators or wild hogs, shoot a round of golf, or attend the horseraces. Water sports are, of course, readily available, as are horseback riding and cricket matches.

Shoppers are in for a treat: this is one of the biggest and most elaborate **shopping** areas in the Caribbean. You'll find exotic treasures from all points of the globe here—saris, crystal, silver, china, Swiss clocks, gold jewelry, sisal items, woodwork, ivory and brass, Irish linens.

Local items made from dried banana leaves are available from the Trinidad and Tobago Blind Welfare Association, 118 Duke St., and a Trinidad and Tobago Handicraft Cooperative, on King's Wharf, sells small steel drums, hammocks, carved wooden items, and straw creations.

Tobago, Trinidad's sister island, is 27 miles long and 7½ miles wide. You can get to this former sugar empire, 20 miles from Trinidad, by air. So rich and powerful were those who once lived here that an expression "rich as a Tobago planter" was a favorite saying.

Unlike Trinidad, this is a quiet island, a frequent retreat for Trinidadians. Water sports, including pretty beaches and very good scuba and snorkeling waters, are the primary reasons for a stop here.

Trinidad, trivia lovers, is also the home of **Angostura Bitters,** dreamed up by a Venezuelan doctor who brought his still closely guarded secret here.

PORTS OF CALL: CARIBBEAN ISLANDS □ 73

Ships Calling Here: Ocean Islander, Ocean Princess, Stella Oceanis, and Wind Star.

U.S. Virgin Islands

Capital and Port City: Charlotte Amalie (pronounced Ah-*moll*-ya).
Islands: St. Thomas, St. Croix, St. John, plus about 50 smaller islands.
Size: St. Thomas—32 square miles. St. Croix—82 square miles. St. John—19 square miles.
Population: 70,000.
Language: English.
Currency: U.S. dollar.
Tourist Information: U.S. Virgin Islands Office of Tourism, Department of Commerce Bldg., Back Street, Charlotte Amalie, USVI 00801 (tel. 809/774-8784).
Public Transportation: taxi ($3 per person from dock to town).
Car Rentals: Hertz, Truman Airport (tel. 774-1879). Mopeds and scooters are also available for rent.
Shopping Specialties: duty-free imports of all kinds—jewelry, gold, cameras, liquor, silver, wools, china, watches, perfumes, etc.
Restaurants: St. Thomas—L'Escargot, on Creque's Alley; Greenhouse, on the waterfront (tel. 774-0533). St. Croix—Sprat Hall, two miles north of town, a former Great House famous for island cooking (tel. 772-0305); Barb McConnell's, 45 Queen St. (reservations are a must; tel. 772-3309). St. John—The Out, an alfresco café, Islandia at Mongoose Junction (tel. 776-6644); Rick's Hilltop, behind the public school (tel. 776-6341).

Got your wallet and credit card warmed up? Welcome to St. Thomas, St. Croix, and St. John, the duty-free shopping mall of the Caribbean. Cruise passengers can hardly wait to get down the gangplank to begin spending that cash on birthday presents for Peter, Christmas gifts for Aunt Maude, and a little something for everyone they know. Indeed St. Thomas and St. Croix make the pursuit of purchases very easy. There are, we are convinced, more shops here than people.

If you're not a shopper, rest easy. There are plenty of beautiful—no, gorgeous—beaches here, and some interesting sailing trips too. We can't imagine the hardy soul who could pass up at least a look at the bargains, but if you're dedicated to sun and surf, you'll be just as ecstatic as the shoppers in the crowd.

Let's take a look at the islands separately, because each has a quite distinct personality.

First, a little historical background. Here's Columbus again! That man certainly did get around, and is said to have gotten around here in 1493 when he was so moved by the beauty of these emerald isles he named them after the virgins of St. Ursula, a group of beautiful women who were martyred while protecting a princess in the early days of Christianity.

Part of the Antilles island chain that extends from south of Florida 1,500 miles east and south in a huge arc that divides the Caribbean from the Atlantic Ocean, the Virgin Islands are the tops of a submerged mountain range. All these islands and many more besides are called the Antilles, a name derived from a mythical continent believed to have existed in the Atlantic. (Could this be mysterious Atlantis?)

Along the north side of this arc of islands are the large islands of Cuba, Jamaica, Hispaniola, and Puerto Rico, called the Greater Antilles. East of Puerto Rico, stretching in a shallow croissant shape through 1,000 miles, are smaller islands called the Lesser Antilles, among them the Virgin Islands.

Just sailing among these islands is a treat. You may occasionally see a dolphin splashing and you'll often be within shouting distance of tree-covered, sand-rimmed islands—although there probably won't be anyone on them to shout back!

It won't take you long to decide you'd like to abandon ship here to take up residence on one of the skittery little sailboats darting about St. Thomas's harbor or sling your hammock on a deserted island and play Robinson Crusoe.

On St. Thomas, cliffs drop into the sea creating tiny coves with crescents of sand, one of which has been named one of the world's most beautiful beaches by people with the enviable job of judging such things.

Although you can fairly drown in gold chains here these days, Columbus is said to have given these islands short shrift because the Indians who lived here told him there was no gold. For decades after their discovery the Virgin Islands lay languishing in the sun, just as they had before Columbus happened along.

Danes, perhaps in search of some of the Virgin Islands' never-ending sunshine, sailed over in 1665 to colonize the islands, but the settlers did not fare well. Their ship was destroyed by two storms, a fire almost blew up their powder stores, their settlement was sacked twice by English pirates, diseases decimated their tiny colony, and finally a hurricane whipped through, after which they gave up.

Later, after the Danes and the English made a deal permitting the Danes to settle in St. Thomas, colonial life improved. In 1672 a little cluster of colonists built Fort Christian and began what was to be a long association with these islands.

Danes are a shrewd lot, no less so these settlers, who soon made a deal with marauding pirates, offering them refuge and a stronghold. Pirate booty was sold and traded openly in the streets, which rather discouraged legitimate shipping from pulling into port here. Slave traders took up the slack at the docks, however, and were an important economic force on the island for more than a century. Slaves brought here worked on huge sugar plantations that created many a millionaire.

While a few of the planters were Danes, they were by now joined by a polyglot of people from Holland, England, France, Ireland, Germany, and Sweden. Language was always a problem, so many residents scrapped multilingualism for Créole, a combination of many languages including African slave dialects.

Créole was even taught in schools, but eventually English won out over the other languages and is now the only language spoken here. Most streets, however, retain Danish names and the "Gade" appellation, Danish for "street." English as spoken here is distinctly West Indian, so expect to hear some very odd colloquialisms.

In the intervening years **St. Thomas** had its economic peaks and valleys, perhaps a little heavier on valleys than on peaks. By the time World War I broke out, Denmark had come to look upon these islands as a liability, while the United States eyed them as back-door protection against any moves Germany might make. Intent on securing this security real estate, the U.S. bought the islands from the Danes, who had ruled for more than 200 years, for $25 million in gold. A condition of sale saw to it that the islands retained their duty-free, free-port status. When air transportation increased after World War II and Cuban doors were closed, St. Thomas and St. Croix boomed once again.

To get a look at some of this history, go on a walking tour of downtown **Charlotte Amalie,** about a mile from the docks. All the shops you will see there are housed in what were once pirate warehouses, later used to offload legitimate goods. These storage spots were crumbling into ruin until a few years ago when an enterprising island developer revamped them and leased them to shopkeepers.

If you wander down the tiny alleyway to the right of A. H. Riise Alley as you face the town, you can still see one of the rails and flat cars used to roll goods from the waterfront to the warehouses.

Sir Francis Drake, Edward "Blackbeard" Teech, Henry Morgan, and their bands of pirates strode through the narrow streets and alleyways of St. Thomas, and galleons unloaded gold booty right where your ship is docked. They saw the same colorful native marketplaces and rough sailing craft along the waterfront that you see today, although they didn't have a handy little pocket camera to record it all!

As you stand at the waterfront just opposite King's Wharf, you'll see the distinctive structures of the island's **Legislative Building,** with its graceful staircase that echoes the elegant architecture of a century ago. Built in 1814, the building is the center of the island's political life.

Emancipation Park, a small square surrounded by tooting cars and the busy waterfront, commemorates July 3, 1848, when a courageous, or perhaps frightened, governor, prompted by a slave revolt on St. Croix, signed a slave emancipation order. He was recalled in shame, suspected by the Danes of orchestrating the revolt to make emancipation possible! In the park is a replica of America's Liberty Bell and a stand of old lignum vitae, a wood so hard it's often called 'iron wood.'

You can't miss waterfront **Fort Christian**—it's brick-red. It has served as governor's mansion, church, police headquarters, jail, and now Virgin Islands Museum, but never as an active fort.

Frederick Lutheran Church, just across Norre Gade from the Grand Hotel, was built in 1793 and has hardly changed in the nearly 200 years since its construction. Right behind it, **Hotel 1829,** once the home of a sea captain, is a delightful example of island architecture with its open-air second-floor terrace and central courtyard.

Nearby you'll find the **99 Steps,** one of the world's more perfect examples of the havoc a bureaucracy can create: Danish engineers who had never seen mountainous St. Thomas decreed that the city should be laid out in a neat grid, but the only way to accomplish that was to build steps into nearly every hillside—*voilà!* 99 steps. Bricks used to build them came from Denmark as ship ballast.

At the top of the steps is **Crown House,** built in 1750 and one of the few Danish mansions left on St. Thomas. It was home to island governors and still contains a Versailles crystal chandelier, a hand-carved four-poster, and beautiful domed ceilings.

The present governor lives at the bottom of the steps in **Government House,** the center of Virgin Islands life since the time of the American Civil War. Paintings by Camille Pissarro, one of the founders of French impressionist art and a St. Thomian born and bred, are on display here. Pissarro lived at 14 Dronningens Gade, which now houses shops just as it did when Pissarro's father ran a shop there. Pissarro himself began his art career here on St. Thomas sketching native scenes. He left when he was 22.

On Raadet's Gade near Dronningen's Gade is a **synagogue** first built in 1796 and reconstructed in 1833. The painter Pissaro, a sephardic Jew whose real name was Jacob Pizarro, probably attended this temple, the second-oldest Caribbean synagogue.

Some other sightseeing stops:

Coral World, an underwater observatory, is an interesting place in which you actually go beneath the water, descending an enclosed staircase 15 feet into the center of a coral reef where you look through windows at the flora and fauna of the deep.

Bluebeard's Castle is now a hotel, but was inhabited in the 17th century by Bluebeard and his wife who, legend has it, invited Bluebeard's six girlfriends to tea and poisoned them! Beats talking.

Blackbeard's Tower is the second stone tower you see looming over the city.

Drake's Seat is a stone bench from which you will have a dramatic view across **Magens Bay,** rated by *National Geographic* as one of the world's six most beautiful beaches. Drake is supposed to have reviewed his fleet from this aerie as it hid there prior to an attack on San Juan in 1595.

Most shore tours or taxi tours visit **Mountain Top,** a dramatic observation point that also thoughtfully offers you legendary banana daiquiris to keep you going as you stroll through boutiques and shops selling perfumes, jewelry, liquor.

Jim Tillett, a dedicated art supporter, runs a batik fabric operation at Estate Tutu to help native artisans perfect a craft. Attractive fabrics and clothing made from them, along with native art, are for sale here.

As for the **downtown shops:** well, we're not about to try and tell you where to shop! There are hundreds of boutiques and tiny shops in St. Thomas, each lovelier and more intriguing than the last and each seeming to offer a better bargain. We will go this far, however: among the more unusual shops in town are Java Wraps, at Palm Passage, specializing in Indonesian batik-ed fabrics in beautiful jewel tones; Colombian Emeralds; St. Thomas Fragrance & Cosmetic Factory, for unusual island flower scents like frangipani and ginger; Animal Crackers, for kid stuff; and Guitar Lady, for island instruments like steel drums, bongos, and mandolins.

Among the good buys in these islands are table linens, emeralds and some other precious gems, liquor, crocheted and embroidered clothing from China, as well as the usual duty-free items. Amber and larimar, the rare and unusual semi-precious stones of the Dominican Republic, are not as good a buy here as they are in their native land, but if you're not stopping at that island you might take a look at the stones here. They are among the few things from the Caribbean that are native to the islands.

Liquor is a favorite buy on this island, not only for the low prices you'll pay here—about half the Stateside price—but for the kindly eye Customs will turn on you when you bring it all back. You're permitted to bring back to the U.S., duty free, five fifths (a gallon) of liquor each, plus a bottle of local rum or other locally made liqueur. At the low prices available here, many people return with more than their allotted quota, figuring that even after they've paid a small duty charge on the excess they'll be getting a bargain.

If you're planning a big shopping trip to the Virgin Islands—and remember, you can bring back $800 worth of duty-free goods for each person, even children, in your party—you would do well to check the prices at home before you sail so you know when a bargain is a bargain.

Sadly, few ships stop at the other two populated Virgin Islands, St. John and St. Croix, although St. Croix has lured a few more in recent years and the upper-crust *Sea Goddess I* sometimes uses this lovely island as its winter base in the Caribbean.

On **St. Croix,** life and the land move at a much more stately pace. You will see gently undulating hills here, many of them crowned with the remnants of windmills once used to irrigate the sugar plantations. There are two primary settlements on the island, **Frederiksted** on the west and **Christiansted,** once the capital of the Danish West Indies, on the east. Each offers a full array of duty-free shops and each has its charms.

So well preserved are some of the 18th-century buildings here that they have been designated National Historic Sites. Among these buildings are the

Steeple Building, now a museum of St. Croix history; **Fort Christiansvaern,** complete with bastions, dungeons, and war relics; the **West India and Guinea Co.** warehouse; the **Customs House,** now the library; the **Old Scale House,** used to weigh rum barrels; elegant **Government House,** whose ballroom chandeliers were the gift of the king of Denmark; and the building where American patriot Alexander Hamilton worked as a boy.

Outside of town, beautifully restored 200-year-old **Whim Great House** encapsulizes all the fascinating history of this island into a moated mansion house filled with intriguing antiques. Outside on the lawns you can see a reconstructed windmill, remnants of an old refinery and the steam equipment used to create sugar and rum. It's fascinating.

At **St. George Botanical Gardens** lovely blooms play counterpoint to moldering relics of cane-growing and Arawak days. There's an interesting gift shop here too.

Frederiksted has another of those red Danish forts and lots of frilly, gingerbread-trimmed houses. There are two great places for lunch: Barb McConnell's, 45 King St. (tel. 772-3309), and Sprat Hall, just outside of town on Rte. 63 (tel. 772-0305), the island's oldest plantation house, where pumpkin fritters and soursop pie are on the menu. Call for reservations at either.

Take the road called **Scenic Route** up 900 feet to the observation point above Davis Bay, then drive through the rain forest.

For golfers there are two golf courses, one of them a Robert Trent Jones design called Fountain Valley. Tennis and horseback riding are available, and of course water sports are everywhere.

Once in a great while a cruise ship stops at **St. John,** home of beautiful scenery and **Virgin Islands National Park,** the only national park in the Caribbean. But even if yours doesn't, you can go there on day-long shore excursions to the island or on your own by catching the ferryboat from Red Hook docks. A taxi will take you there, and it's just a ten-minute sail.

St. John's fabulous park, which includes an **underwater park** where you can visit sunken wrecks, spreads over 9,500 acres, covering most of the center of St. John. It was given to the government by Laurance Rockefeller, who is also responsible for the construction nearby of the famous jet-set haven, Caneel Bay Plantation.

In the park you can explore the crumbling remains of an old Danish sugar **plantation,** hike or go horseback riding, visit a delightful **waterfall,** and see carvings left by prehistoric Indians, not even to mention superb beaches. Orchids are as common as toadstools here, and ferns come in the giant economy size. Virgin forests mix with wooded areas more than 150 years old, enclosing more than 260 kinds of plants.

Ships Calling Here: *The Azur, Caribe I, Caribbean Prince, CarlaCosta, Celebration, Colonial Explorer, CostaRiviera, Crown Odyssey, Cunard Countess, Daphne, Explorer Starship, Fair Majesty, Fairsky, Festivale Island Princess, Nantucket Clipper, Newport Clipper, Noordam, Nordic Prince, Norway, Pacific Princess, Rotterdam, Royal Viking Sky, Royal Viking Sun, Sagafjord, Sea Goddess I, Skyward, Song of Norway, Sovereign of the Seas, Starward, Stella Oceanis, Vistafjord, Westerdam, Wind Spirit,* and *Yorktown Clipper.*

British Virgin Islands
Capital: Road Town, Tortola.
Population: 11,000.
Language: English.
Currency: U.S. dollar.

Tourist Information: British Virgin Islands Tourist Board, Road Town, Tortola (tel. 809/494-3134).
Public Transportation: ferries, a few taxis (agree on a fare in advance).
Car Rentals: on Tortola—Dennis Alphonso (tel. 4-3137); De Castro Honda (tel. 4-2182). Note that driving is on the left, and a temporary local driver's license must be obtained at the police station in Road Town (fee: $2.50).
Shopping Specialties: straw products, shells.
Food Specialties: roti, fungi, seafood.
Restaurants: Tortola—Prospect Reef, Road Town (tel. 494-3311); Sugar Mill Estate, Apple Bay (tel. 495-4440). Peter Island—Peter Island Yacht Club (tel. 494-2561).

From the hills of St. Thomas and St. John you can see 36 of the eastern Virgin Islands, a Crown Colony of Great Britain known as the British Virgin Islands, or BVI to devotees.

Tortola, about the same size as St. John, is the main island, 12 miles long and 3 miles wide. Wooded peaks rise to more than 1,700 feet at Mount Sage and the terrain is rugged. Picturesque **Road Town** is just a small village, but it's the biggest spot on the island.

Other inhabited islands in the group include Virgin Gorda, Jost Van Dyke, and Peter Island. One more, Anegada, has big, beautiful reefs off of which lie more than 500 wrecks, some reputedly hiding treasure. Seek and perhaps ye shall find. Everyone at Peter Island knows where the treasure is: it's home in the bank or in Switzerland. A posh resort, Peter Island is a well-loved retreat for well-heeled jet-setters.

As cruise ships go farther afield to find interesting spots to take their passengers, these small islands are becoming what some people in the industry irreverently call "barbecue ports." What they mean is that when the ship anchors off one of these tiny islands, passengers go ashore to swim, sun, wander about a bit, and later partake of a barbecue or shore picnic, with lots of rum punch and beer. Then it's back on the boat and off again to the next stop.

One could hardly think of lovelier, more lusciously remote places for these picnic treats than the British Virgin Islands, each of which looks exactly like the place you'd dream up as an I-want-to-get-away-from-all-this-and-go-live-on-some-deserted-island spot.

If you'd like a few names to add to that fantasy, try these uninhabited, or hardly inhabited, British Virgin islands: Beef, Salt, Dead Man's Chest, Ginger, and Fallen Jerusalem. Tortola, by the way, means "dove of peace," and Virgin Gorda is a "fat virgin"!

These islands have been in the possession of the British for many, many years, although poor soil and limited rainfall have kept them from supporting major plantations. When sugar declined as a profitable crop and slavery was abolished, plantation agriculture was abandoned and most of the British residents left, leaving ex-slaves behind to eke a living from the land.

What to do here has much to do with sun, sand, and surf, and little to do with historical markers.

The Baths, on Virgin Gorda, formed by mammoth granite boulders and carved by wind and waves, make lovely labyrinthine swimming holes. The scenery is superb, sand beaches sparkle, and tropical rain forests cover some of the islands. Charter boats will take you sailing or fishing. You can get there by plane from Beef Island off Tortola, or on a boat called Speedy's Adventures.

Mount Sage is a national park 1,780 feet high overlooking tiny islands. Head west from Road Town to see "the Dungeon," the island's oldest fort, built in 1640. A rare wild West Indian cherry tree grows here.

A few boutiques on Tortola offer treasures, but this is not a duty-free port, although British items are not taxed. Shell jewelry made here is one of the more interesting buys, and hand-printed fabric from Caribbean Hand Prints is pretty.

Small shops can fit you out with **diving** equipment or you can participate in a diving shore excursion with shipmates. Most ships have them. A sunken wreck, the R.M.S. *Rhone*, off the west end of Salt Island, was called "the world's most fantastic ship wreck dive" by *Skin Diver* magazine. Aquatic Centers in Road Town (tel. 4-2858) can take you there.

Sailboats are available for rent too. Try the Moorings (tel. 4-2332).

On Jost Van Dyke, stop for a drink at Foxy's—everybody does. On Tortola, Sir Francis Drake Pub is a hangout, and Cell 5 is a good, very casual spot. The Ample Hamper can provision a picnic.

On Virgin Gorda, Little Dix Bay is a very posh and lovely place with an excellent dining room, Biris Creek is dramatically located atop a cliff, and the Bitter End Yacht Club lures the sailing crowd.

Ships Calling Here: *Caribbean Prince, Colonial Explorer, Cunard Countess, Explorer Starship, Nantucket Clipper, Newport Clipper, Noordam, Sagafjord, Sea Goddess I, Stella Oceanis, Vistafjord, Wind Spirit,* and *Yorktown Clipper.*

3. MEXICAN RIVIERA / YUCATÁN PENINSULA

Acapulco. Puerto Vallarta. Names that conjure up images of tanned bodies, daring high divers, a balcony perch for a mariachi serenade, legendary silvery beaches gleaming in the sunlight, moonlit nonstop evenings of dancing and laughter with days to match.

Mexico is as modern as a jet ski and as ancient as 10,000 years of history can make it. It's as changeable as the chameleons that sun themselves on remote rocks and as everlasting as the surf that breaks ceaselessly on its sandy shores.

Come here with preconceived ideas of its people and its way of life and you will find those conceptions fulfilled. But come here with an open heart and this land will steal into it, weaving a golden web of memories that will remain with you forever, returning at unexpected moments to shed a glow of delight on the gloomiest day.

It has been ever so in this mysterious land that stretches across the Texas, Arizona, New Mexico, and California borders, through desert into mountains and finally to the Pacific Ocean on one side, the Gulf of Mexico on the other.

Countless ages ago early sunseekers crossed the Bering Straits and wandered far down to these southern reaches, hunting what moved and gathering what didn't. Later, the ancestors of these early settlers began planting some of the crops they gathered and creating pots in which to store them. Pots dating as far back as 2400 B.C., nearly 4,400 years ago, have been discovered here.

More than 3,000 years ago in the Preclassic Period from about 2000 B.C. to A.D. 300 a tribe called the Olmecs, who were the first known people to use a 365-day calendar, lived near today's Veracruz. Here they created mammoth 40-ton basalt sculptures that remain a mystery: How were they cut and carved with only primitive implements, and why? What are they?

In a few thousand years the pastoral life of these early people had been supplanted by ancient cities. From A.D. 300 to 900 in the Classic Period, Maya tribes moved into prominence, creating outstanding scientific and artistic achievements ranging from complex calendars that could predict astronomical activity to arithmetic calculations that made the first known use of the mathematical concept of "zero."

Other cultures joined the Olmecs and the Mayans: the Toltecs, the Zapotecs, the Totonacs, each adding to the artistic and cultural history of this land.

Historians call the period from A.D. 900 to 1520 the Postclassic Period. During it the joy-filled, fun-loving life disappeared, replaced by war, migration, and social dissolution.

In the 1300s the warlike Aztecs ascended to supremacy near Mexico City, building a city huge for its time and creating a society rich in gold and material goods.

By the time the Spaniards arrived in the early 1500s the Aztec state was ruled by the Montezuma we've all heard so much about (although his name is said to be correctly spelled Moctezuma). When he tried to bribe them to leave, he only succeeded in tantalizing them, and finally was tortured by Cortés for information about his fabulous store of gold.

These Spaniards conquered Mexico and were soon followed by priests who brought Christianity here in the form of Franciscan and Augustinian friars. Silver and gold from this land turned Spain into the most formidable power in Europe.

Led by a priest, Fr. Miguel Hidalgo, the man now honored as the father of modern Mexico, the nation gained its independence in 1821. Turmoil reigned for several years during which, among other odd incidents, the Hapsburg Archduke Maximilian ruled Mexico during three years of civil war.

Benito Juárez, another important figure in Mexican history, led the nation through some troubled times. He was followed from 1877 to 1911 by the legendary Porfírio Díaz whose dictatorship spawned the rise of another legendary figure, Pancho Villa, whose real name was Doroteo Arango. In the final ten years before the fall of Porfírio Díaz the nation fought a battle called the Mexican Revolution, a historic period that laid the foundation for the progress that was to come.

Today the 30 United Mexican States are guided by an elected president and a bicameral legislature quite similar to that of the U.S.

If there is one thing most travelers have heard about Mexico, it is tales of a malady known variously as *turistas,* "Aztec Two-Step," and/or "Montezuma's Revenge." To avoid this unpleasant memory of Mexico, which takes the form of diarrhea, nausea, vomiting, and fever, it is wise, doctors say, to skip uncooked vegetables, unbottled water, and ice. If you do succumb anyway, take it easy for a day and avoid food; drink lots of liquids for 24 hours. Ship doctors often suggest Kaopectate or Pepto-Bismol.

Tropical weather prevails on the west coast, which is protected from fierce *nortes* (northern) winds by high mountains, except in Mazatlán, which is often chillier than other regions. On the east coast along the gulf, the unprotected shoreline can have temperature drops as great as 40°F in an hour, although the Yucatán Peninsula is usually spared by the warming effect of gulf waters. Rainy season in Mexico is May through September, with June and September the worst for water.

Living here are nearly 60 million people, spread out across a land that encompasses 760,373 square miles—nearly three times as large as Texas. Most people here speak Spanish, but there are also more than 50 different Indian dialects spoken in the country. In all but the most remote spots, however, everyone will know enough English and hand signals to exchange messages with you.

Mexican currency is the peso. Note that the dollar sign ($) is also used in Mexico to indicate peso amounts, so a sign that says "$75" means 75 pesos . . . usually.

Mexico City is the capital of this vast and varied land, but everywhere you go the shopping is wonderful. Specialties you can buy at very, very reasonable prices include pottery, cotton clothing, colorful glass, baskets, serapes, huaraches, rebozos, straw hats, embroidered dresses, silver, brass and copper, hammocks, tequila and mescal, and men's Guayabera shirts. Bargaining is expected and enjoyed.

To get around in Mexico you can rent cars, bicycles, motorbikes, and mopeds in most large cities, but you'll probably have to depend on taxicabs and local buses in the smaller towns. It's wise to work out the price of a trip to everyone's understanding before you get into the cab in all but the largest cities, and sometimes even there. Bargaining is quite permissible, particularly if you're in search of a regional tour.

Car-rental companies in Mexico include Avis, Hertz, Dollar, and Budget, plus local companies, which may be cheaper.

You can get scads of information about Mexico by contacting the **Mexican National Tourist Council,** which has offices in 17 cities in the U.S. and Canada from Atlanta to Chicago, New Orleans, and San Francisco.

Although it is wealthy in natural resources ranging from silver and gold to the black gold of oil, Mexico still suffers from an inequitable distribution of wealth that creates a wide social gap between the have-a-lots and the have-nothing-at-alls. Poverty is commonplace, but so is pride. You'll find a few, but not many, beggars, plenty of insistent urchin entrepreneurs, and determined salesmen of all ages. Treat them all gently, without rancor, and you'll both be the better for it.

Enseñada

Population: 10,000

Tourist Information: Tourist Office, via Oriente 1, Canalización Río Tiajuana, Baja California Norte (tel. 31013).

Public Transportation: taxis, buses.

Car Rentals: Scorpio Rent-a-Car, Alvarado 95-2 (tel. 83275); Hertz, Calle Alvarado Local 4 (tel. 83776).

Shopping Specialties: straw baskets, brass, silver shells, piñatas.

Restaurants: Casa Mar, Boulevard Costero y Blancarte 499 (tel. 70667); Restaurant Casa Argentina, 213 Balboa (no phone).

Enseñada is part of Baja California, a long, witch's-finger peninsula of land that points the way to Acapulco and the Mexican Riviera. A favorite weekend "quickie" trip for Southern Californians, this village just 67 miles south of the border is quintessentially Mexican, with tourist touches.

As the start of the sand strip Mexicans like to call their Riviera, Enseñada has been luring visitors since 1542 when adventurer Juan Rodriguez Cabrillo first stopped by here. No one stayed long in those days for a good reason: they couldn't find water.

Today there's plenty of water, both fresh from underground and salty from the Pacific Ocean that borders the long peninsula. A quiet spot, Enseñada is proud of its crescent-shaped strip of gleaming white sand. Its harbor, dotted with colorful sailing craft, is a pretty place too.

You can visit the old **Santo Tomas Winery,** and if you have time, go on an excursion to the picturesque Baja countryside.

There's not a great deal to do here, nor rafts of things to buy, but it's a lovely place to wander around, savor the flavor of Mexico, and get in some serious beach sitting.

Ships Calling Here: *Azure Seas* and *Southward.*

Cabo San Lucas

Most cruise ships include this on their list of ports of call, adding "cruising by" when you look closely at the itinerary. Tide and water conditions sometimes preclude a stop here, and really the area is quite as lovely a sight from offshore as it is if you anchored here.

Located on the very tip of the Baja Peninsula where the waters of the Pacific and the Gulf of Baja California mingle, Cabo San Lucas is a study in green sea and white sand. Springing up from the desert-like sands hereabout are some intriguing homes and hotels, glittering white in the sunshine. Mexico's tourist interests are trying hard to make this a popular tourist attraction, and are succeeding to the extent that certainly thousands more people know where the place is, thanks to the cruise industry.

Keep an eye out for **Los Arcos,** arches created by the rush of water against stone.

For those who do actually pull into port here, the **open-air market** is a lure for shoppers. Woodcarvings and silver are good buys (look for a "925" or a spread-eagle hallmark to indicate pure sterling). Other treasures: wool blankets in soft colors, ceramics, hand-woven embroidered blouses, lacquered goods, leather, onyx carvings, *rebozo* shawls, and weavings. Bargain and keep bargaining. If you can hold out long enough, prices tend to drop very quickly when the ship's departure time draws nigh.

If all goes well and the timing is right, you may also get a look at sea lions cavorting on the rocks.

Ships Calling Here: *Bermuda Star, Fairsea, Fairwind, North Star, Stardancer, Stella Solaris, Sun Princess,* and *Tropicale.*

Mazatlán

Population: 200,000.

Tourist Information: Mazatlán Tourism Office, Paseo Claussen, off Zaragoza (tel. 14966).

Public Transportation: buses, taxis.

Car and Moped Rentals: Hotel Playa Mazatlán, Avenida del Mar (tel. 34754), for bicycle, moped, and sailboat rentals. Hertz, Hotel de Cima (tel. 16303).

Shopping Specialties: local handcrafts at the Arts and Crafts Center, on Avenida del Mar about two miles north of town near the Hotel Playa Mazatlán.

Restaurants: El Shrimp Bucket, in the Hotel La Siesta, Boulevard Olas Altas II (tel. 16350); Camino Real Hotel, about ten miles from the docks, for banana coladas (tel. 32456).

Mazatlán is a typical seaside village, quintessentially Mexican Riviera. People here live for the sea, on the sea, and sometimes, it would seem, in the sea!

Sabalo Beach, at the northern end of town, is considered the best beach by locals. You can get there from the main square downtown, the Basilica, on the Basilica-Sabalo bus for just a few pesos.

You can also get around in rather grand rickshaw style on a contraption called a *pulmonia,* which is an open-air, motorized vehicle that carries three people. Bargain a little to get a good price on a ride around town or out to Sabalo. What a way to go!

If you'd like to get a closer look at this lovely bay, you can sail it on a double-decker boat. The **Fiesta Yacht Cruise** leaves daily from the south beach near the lighthouse, and tickets are available at hotels. On a three-hour cruise, bilingual guides tell you about the bay while musicians serenade you. There's a short swim stop at a small island too.

Top-flight **fishing** has long been one of the lures of Mazatlán, and remains a popular sport hereabouts. You can catch some whoppers here, including marlin, for which you can fish year round. If you'd like to rent a fishing boat, look for the lighthouse on the south side of town and you'll find the boats moored at the bottom of the hill. A trip, including equipment, will cost a few hundred dollars a day, but if you can round up a group you can share expenses. A fishing license is necessary, and can be obtained by writing Unifleet, Box 1035, Mazatlán, Sinaloa, México, or calling 15121 in Mazatlán for information.

Shoppers should make a beeline for the **Arts and Crafts Center,** where you'll find a beehive of shops inside and out, up and down: pottery, straw, leather, papier-mâché, dolls, brass, glass, embroidery. This is the Mexican Riviera's shopping spot, and bearable even for shopper companions: they serve free beer and margaritas at the beverage bar. If the shops there are jammed with cruise passengers, wander a few blocks to Las Gaviotas Designer's Bazaar for stylish cottons.

You can rent diving and snorkeling equipment at a number of small shops in the area too. Or watch someone else do the diving at **El Mirador,** where daredevil divers plunge 40 feet into the surf.

On a shore tour here you'll want to see the lovely **Malecon,** or seaside walk along the Olas Altas beach area, watch the cliff divers at Glorieta's Rocky Promontory, or visit beaches at the north end of town. Las Gaviotas Beach is a pleasant spot too.

In winter there are **bullfights** on Sunday, and the rest of the year there are some rousing rodeos.

Ships Calling Here: *Fairsea, Fairwind, Stardancer, Sun Princess,* and *Tropicale.*

Puerto Vallarta

Population: 60,000.
Tourist Information: Tourist Office, Libertad 152 at Morelos (tel. 20242).
Public Transportation: taxis.
Car Rentals: Avis, Carrerter al Aéropuerto (tel. 21412); Hertz, Hotel Oceana, 538 Avenida Presidente Díaz Ordaz (tel. 20024).
Shopping Specialties: chic clothing and accessories, art, embroidered clothing. Main shopping areas are Isla del Río Cuale in town, along the Malecon.
Restaurants: Lobster House, 254 Lázaro Cárdenas (tel. 20676); La Iguana, 167 Lázaro Cárdenas (tel. 20105); Camino Real Hotel, Mismaloya Beach (tel. 20004); Hotel Ocean (one-time sunset-bar favorite of John Wayne), Malecon (tel. 245545).

You can have it all in this city, which may be why practically every west coast cruise ship stops here: old-world elegance and charm, fast-paced city excitement, terrific lobster and shrimp, even the setting for the film *Night of the Iguana,* during which Elizabeth Taylor and Richard Burton became a hot gossip item.

Snuggled in beneath the tropical Sierra Madres mountains with the glittering Bay of Banderas stretching out before it, Puerto Vallarta is a photographer's paradise: scarlet bougainvillea glowing against whitewashed walls . . . a Malecon oceanside walkway rimming the bay . . . in the air the scent of jasmine.

Most everything in Puerto Vallarta is within walking distance since the town is hardly more than five or six blocks wide.

Beaches along the Malecon are lovely, but most bathers head across the Cuale River about a half mile south to the **Playa del Sol.** If you get hungry on a day's beach outing, you can buy a piece of fish grilled on a stick for next to nothing from one of the small boys who grill and sell them on the sand.

Boats depart from the Hotel Delfin just off Olas Altas at 10 a.m. (except

Saturday) to take you to **Yelapa Beach,** and return about 4:30 p.m. There's a band on board and a free bar.

Most visitors take to the streets here, however, roaming about the cobbled lanes, photographing donkey carts, admiring from a hill the panorama of Banderas Bay and the red-tiled roofs of town.

Hiking, tennis, golf, and horseback riding are popular pastimes, the details of which can be secured from the cruise director. Amuse yourself with a parasailing adventure or try burro polo on the sands.

Sights to see include the **Church of Guadalupe** with its crown-shaped spire, the **Municipal Marketplace,** the Handcrafts Center, the **Malecon,** Vallarta Water Sports Center and the Marina, and **Children's Island,** a cluster of shops and amusements on an island in the Cuale River. History buffs will enjoy the nearby village of **Yelapa,** where artifacts of this land's native Indians are preserved; nice beaches and great lobster feasts there too. Posh villas here are located in an area called "Gringo Gulch."

Ships Calling Here: *Crown Odyssey, Fairsea, Fairwind, North Star, Stardancer, Sun Princess,* and *Tropicale.*

Manzanillo

Population: 36,000.

Tourist Information: Tourism Department, 111 Avenida Juárez at the corner of 21 de Marzo (tel. 22090), open from 9 a.m. to 3 p.m. daily (except Sunday).

Public Transportation: taxis (unmetered, bargain in advance), buses (called camionetas).

Car Rentals: Auto Rentas de México cruceiro las Brisas S-N (tel. 21495); Hertz, Hotel de Cima, Avenida del Mar (tel. 16303).

Restaurants: Hotel Colonial, 100 Calle México 100 (tel. 21080); La Chiripa, Costa Azul between Manzanillo and the Santiago Peninsula (tel. 20722).

Once a harbor for the Spanish fleet, Manzanillo has come a long way from those 17th-century beginnings—it was recently a movie star! To be a bit more accurate about that, it was Bo Derek who was the star (*10* was the name of the movie), but part of the film was made here at the posh Las Hadas resort.

Until cruise ships began calling at this port, it was, like many other Mexican stops, just a quiet fishing village and a resort visited mostly by Mexican tourists. Now you'll be welcomed here with the bong of a great bronze bell.

Manzanillo's lure is a seven-mile curve of beach with the lovely name **Playa Azul** (it means "Blue Beach" in Spanish) that ends right at Santiago Peninsula. You'll find two lovely lagoons near Manzanillo, one right behind the city and the other behind the beach.

Downtown, the plaza (**zócalo**) is the center of life as it always is in Mexican and Spanish cities, but it's separated from the waterfront by railroad and ship yards.

Fishing and swimming are the major attractions of this port. You'll find **charter boats** for the former along the waterfront and a beach for the latter at San Pedrito, close to the downtown area. At **San Pedrito** the ocean is shallow for a long, long way out, which makes it a great splashing place for kids and nonswimmers. Serious ocean enthusiasts may prefer **La Audiencia Beach,** on the way to Santiago.

A note on taxicabs: They don't have meters, so make your deal before you close the door. You'll find a cab stand in the plaza and plenty of cabs waiting to take cruise-ship passengers anywhere they might like to go. A ride out to Las Hadas, Rincon de las Hadas, across the bay from town, a celebrity hangout (tel. 30000), makes a nice trip and its Moorish domes and minarets are quite a sight, not even to mention its yellow sand streaked with black.

If you're here on a Sunday night, you'll find a small dance band playing at the downtown breakwater called the Rompeolas.

Most evenings you'll also find carriages waiting to take you on a sunset ride along the sea boulevard.

Ships Calling Here: *North Star.*

Zihuatanejo / Ixtapa

Population: 18,000.

Tourist Information: Tourism Office, Paseo del Pesador (tel. 42207), open from 9 a.m. to 1 p.m. and 4 to 6 p.m. weekdays, half day on Saturday (closed Sunday).

Public Transportation: taxis, buses.

Car Rentals: Avis, Juan Alvarez 10 (tel. 42275); Hertz, Holiday Inn, Boulevard Ixtapa (tel. 42306).

Shopping Specialties: carvings, woven rugs.

Restaurants: Restaurant Don Juan, Vicente Guerrero y Ejido (tel. 43210); La Mesa del Capitán Nicolas, 18 Bravo (tel. 42027); El Pescadór, right along the waterside (tel. 42113); Villa del Sol, at the waterside (tel. 42231).

If you can pronounce these two spots you're already well ahead of most of your fellow passengers. So let's have a stab at it: Zihuatanejo is pronounced See-wah-tan-*nay*-ho, and Ixtapa is *Iks*-tah-pa.

These two small villages are, like many others along this coast, in the throes of development by a government anxious to lure tourists beyond the usual Acapulco–Taxco–Mexico City stops.

Nestled at the base of Mexico's Sierra Madre del Sur, **Zihuatanejo** is quiet, simple, peaceful, unchallenging. Until a few years ago there wasn't even a paved road here and they turned the lights out at 11 p.m.! People touting the spot like to say that this little village is what Acapulco was like before the onslaught. When you see a sloe-eyed burro clomping down the avenue, you'll believe it.

Certainly we wouldn't quarrel with that description. This is indeed a tranquil village with all the ambience of "Fantasy Island." Slip into something simple, stretch out on a beach, buy a coconut from a local vendor, and stare out over the coral reefs.

If you're more energetic, roam into the central market square (zócalo) or catch a boat over to the beach at La Ropa or Las Gatas, where you can repose in the shelter of a thatched hut.

Coconut plantations stretch out around the town and craftsmen offer carvings and woven rugs.

Zihuatanejo's **beach** is an entrancing spot, curving around a small bay where sailboats with colorful sails zip in and out among the fishing boats.

Ixtapa was discovered by computer! Government computers, put to the task of finding the perfect resort location, chose this beach-trimmed spot, and shortly thereafter the government created this resort about eight miles north of Zihuatanejo. The famous and the infamous visit here, so who knows what "name" you'll get to see?

You can get there on a bus from the market in Zihuatanejo or by taxi. As you enter the village, you go over a small rise in the ground from which you see this lovely bay stretched out before you like a silver-blue carpet. Waves roll over the sands, palms sway gracefully along the edges of the beach—paradise found!

Ships Calling Here: *Crown Odyssey, North Star, Stella Solaris,* and *Sun Princess.*

Acapulco
Population: 600,000.
Tourist Information: Department of Tourism, Costera Miguel Alemán 187 (tel. 22170) and at Río do Cameron (tel. 22246).
Public Transportation: buses.
Car Rentals: Hertz, 1945 Costera Miguel Alemán (tel. 56942); other major companies.
Shopping Specialties: pottery, silver, embroidery, haute couture.
Restaurants: Sanborn's, Costaera Miguel Alemán (tel. 26167); Carlos 'n Charlie's, Costera Miguel Alemán (tel. 41944); Miramar, in La Vista shopping center (tel. 41444); El Parador, in La Vista shopping center (tel. 40022).

Acapulco is as chic and trendy as the other Mexican Riviera ports are simple and old-fashioned. Here you'll see slick grande dames and dons turned out in clothes that may be casual but don't have casual price tags.

Life is casual here too, starting late and often ending about the time most people are just starting! Daytime to Acapulco dwellers is what you have to get through before the fun begins.

Beach lovers will find plenty in this handsome, busy city to keep them occupied. So many beaches are there, in fact, that Acapulco dwellers have **favorite beaches** they visit only in the morning, others for afternoon, and others for sunset, 23 of them in all!

Here are some of them, moving from west to east around the bay: Playa Langosta, Caleta, Caletilla, Terraplen, Clavelito, Carabali and Hornos, Paradiso, Condesa and Icacos and Guitarron, not far from the showplace hotel Las Brisas where some *rooms* have their own swimming pools!

Of all those, **Playa Langosta** is our choice. It's a small sheltered cove near La Quebrada, and if you're lucky you won't find many other people there. (Just don't stay on it too long or you'll look like the boiled langosta for which the beach is named.) Caleta and Caletilla are similarly tranquil spots popular with families.

You can also try **parasailing** here, go to the **bullfights,** ride a balloon-strewn buggy down Main Street at night, try **jet skis.** You'll find golf courses and tennis courts, sailing, fishing, and all the usual resort activities. Ask at the purser's desk for specific recommendations.

An open beach called **Revolcadero** has an intriguing woodsy lagoon, and **La Pie de la Cuesta,** although it's about eight miles from town, is simply not to be missed at sunset. You rock in a hammock, preferably with a companion and a coconut full of rum, and watch the sun flame into the sea.

Jillions of **cruises** operate from the pier called Bono Batani just west of the zócalo, offering everything from glass-bottom boat rides to moonlight cruises with dancing.

This is the easiest way to see it all, unless you want to rent a car, which is fun but means contending with traffic and parking.

At the very moment the first foot falls on the soil of Acapulco, the arms of the city's **"walking boutiques"** open. These itinerant sellers of everything from onyx beads to embroidery wheedle and haggle and lure and laugh. It can be wonderful fun if you love a good bargaining session.

Shoppers should have a field day in this city where the competition for "chicest of them all" is fierce and ongoing. A very, very fashionable port, Acapulco has some equally fashionable places to shop. Top of the lot is **La Vista,** a swanky spot that leads you down winding garden paths to the doors of Gucci and the like.

Vividly-colored papier-mâché creatures, gauzy hot-weather fashions, and abalone jewelry are among the treasures at colorful **Plaza de Artesanías,** a handcraft center, while Woolworth's and Sanborn's are favored by nonhagglers. Galería Victor, Rudic Art Gallery, and Cypango Art Gallery, all in the posh resort-hotel area, are the top spots for serious artwork.

Early in the evening you might consider a stroll up to the Mirador Hotel at the top of the hill at the end of La Quebrada, where you can plunk down at the bar to watch the sunset and then stay on for a good view of the famed **high divers** of Acapulco.

In case you have somehow missed hearing about this event: each night every hour from 8:15 or so to 11:30 p.m. an intrepid diver who suffers not at all from acrophobia steps out onto a spotlit ledge just below the Mirador's terraces, raises his arms dramatically, and plunges with much fanfare and applause into the sea—130 feet below! With a prayer before and some pesos from onlookers after, he accepts congratulations and returns again the following evening. Occasionally some up-and-coming adventurers try their luck too.

Mirador's La Perla Supper Club has music and good food with a minimum levied in the restaurant, but if you've seen enough here and are ready to see what all the **Acapulco nightlife** fuss is about, head for the Costera Alemán area. Here you'll find UBQ (at 115 Costera Alemán), an up-market spot frequented by the highest of society (or trying to be); Baby Q, not far down the street (it comes complete with Jacuzzi); or Carlos's Chili 'n' Dance Hall 'n' Bar 'n' Grill, whoop-de-doo spot.

Nightlife changes about as rapidly as the faces in this tourist haven, so some or all of those may have different names or not be around anymore by the time you get there. Ask around, though—everyone will have an opinion on the best sipping and soirée spots.

Mexico's **Ballet Folklorico** entertainment appears at one of the large hotels nearly every night of the week. Don't miss it.

Ships Calling Here: *Crown Odyssey, Fairwind, North Star, Stella Solaris,* and *Sun Princess.*

Cancún
Population: 70,000.
Tourist Information: Tourist Office, 13b Avenida Tulum (tel. 30123).
Public Transportation: buses, taxis (agree on the fare in advance).
Car Rentals: Hertz, Calle Guava, 25 Manzana (tel. 30938); local companies. Bicycles and motorbikes also available for rent.
Restaurants: Chocko's and Tere, Claveles 7 (tel. 41394), for mariachis, cowboys, and guitarists; La Longosta Feliz del Carib, Tulum 33c (tel. 43316).

Cancún has sprung up out of the sands like a glittering mushroom. Chosen by computer as a lively spot for a government-backed resort development, this island in the sun has proven the computers right. It's skyrocketed to fame in recent years and is now the favored destination for ships cruising in gulf waters as well as for jet-set travelers.

Soft, fine, even delicate, sand is a feature of the beaches here, and the Caribbean waters on this side of the world are just as devastatingly blue as they are in the eastern sector of the Caribbean Sea.

Cancún is in the heart of a historian's paradise. Ruins, comparatively recently discovered and still not fully explored or excavated, are everywhere. The most accessible, and some say the most spectacular, of these is **Chichén-Itzá**. Getting there is not everyone's cup of tea—until they get there and discover what a wonder they are beholding. Every ship that sails to the region features a shore excursion to the ruins, about a three-hour bus trip away (and three hours back too). Grueling as that may be, it's well worth it, for this site is one of the wonders of this ancient world. More on that in a moment.

Some cruise ships sailing in the area are considerate enough to stop at Playa del Carmen, a small beach village about 44 miles from Cancún—and 44 miles closer to the ruins.

Once you reach Chichén-Itzá you'll see why we think it worth the journey. Here is the Aztec pyramid you've seen in many a history book and perhaps seen reproduced on the deck of Norwegian Caribbean Line's *Skyward*.

Originally a Mayan city, Chichén-Itzá became part of the Toltec Empire in A.D. 987. Their leader, Kukulcán, built a sprawling city, part Toltec in style, part Mayan Puuc (a word taken from the hills in southwestern Yucatán) architecture.

The most outstanding feature of the ruins is the 75-foot stepped **El Castillo temple**, which features a stair for each of the 365 days of the year. This temple is evidence that the Toltecs had a firm grasp on the concept of the passage of time and calendars. It also has 52 panels on each side representing the 52 years of the Mayan calendar, and 18 terraces (nine on each side of the stairways) to represent the 18 months of their calendar.

To prove they really knew what they were doing: if you watch the sun set here on March 21, the spring equinox, you'll see the serpent head carving at the base of the stairs descend into the earth as the sun moves slowly down each stair, signaling to the Mayas the start of the corn-planting season.

At the top of the **Temple of the Warriors** is a Chacmool, the reclining figure so often reproduced as a symbol of Mayan culture—you've probably seen the figure with a pot of flowers sunk into its middle.

On the north side of the plaza you'll see a pathway leading to a huge sacred well, called a cenote. Sacrifices of young women often took place here, and excavations have dredged up scores of bones and gold objects.

Don't miss the **ballcourt**, the largest in Central America, with two stone rings through which the ball was thrown. Cheering your favorite player on must have been quite an experience here: if you stand at one end of the long court and speak in a normal tone, you can be heard at the other end.

Tulúm, another fascinating archeological site, is about an hour's drive from Cancún. Spread over several acres and walled on three sides, this "walled city" (which is what Tulúm translates to in English) is the only remains of a Mayan coastal town. Here you'll find the crumbling remnants of 56 structures, the best known of which is El Castillo or Temple of Kukulkán, a small temple-crowned pyramid on a bluff overlooking the Caribbean 40 feet below.

Constructed in the 10th century, Tulúm was built to serve as a fortress city overlooking the Caribbean. At one time 600 people lived here, according to an early Spanish bishop, in houses set up on platforms along the street. Tulúm was inhabited until about 70 years after the Spanish conquest, when it was abandoned.

Although these ruins can't compare with the drama and magnificence of Chichén-Itzá, if you use a little imagination and look carefully at what you see, you'll be rewarded. Note the red stucco that still remains in places, and imagine what this spot must have looked like when all the buildings here were painted in the same bright red!

Take a look at the Mayan city walls constructed of limestone, and don't miss the interesting frescoes dating from the 13th century inside the Temple of the Frescoes. Sadly, these are difficult to see in the dark temple, so if you're especially interested in getting a good look at them, bring a flashlight along. Look carefully on the cornice of the building and you'll spot a Mayan god staring down at you.

Ships Calling Here: *Skyward,* and *Seaward.*

Cozumél
Population: 5,000.
Tourist Information: Tourist Office, Calle 1 Sur, near the plaza.
Public Transportation: taxis, buses.
Car Rentals: Hertz, Hotel Cozumel Caribe (tel. 20100), and smaller companies. Bicycles and motorbikes are also available for rent.
Shopping Specialties: coral, local handcrafts.
Restaurants: Restaurant El Portal, Avenidas Juárez and Rafael Melgar (tel. 20227); Sheraton Sol Caribe, Playa Paradaíso at the port (tel. 20700); Pepes Grill, Avenida Melgar 220 (tel. 20213).

Cozumél is to Cancún as private plane is to Concorde: not as flashy or as publicized, but it gets you there just the same and with less huzzah.

Life in Cozumél is quiet, elegant, serene. While the jet-setters are outstatusing each other over in Cancún, people at Cozumél are using their energy to explore the sea, this island, and their own place in the world.

Sailing, snorkeling, scuba-diving, swimming, and elegant restaurants are the ingredients of your day here. You can plunk yourself down in a little bistro and watch the world go by or grab your snorkel and fins and watch the underwater world swim by on three-mile-long **Palancar Reef.**

You can get to Tulúm on a ferryboat or with a shore excursion, or take off on a Robinson Crusoe adventure complete with beach picnic.

There's something tranquil and determinedly unrushed about this seaside resort that may tempt you to get off and just let the world sail on without you.

Ships Calling Here: *Bermuda Queen, Britanis, Cunard Princess, Fair Majesty, Fairsea, Fairsky, Galileo, Holiday, New Shoreham, Nieuw Amsterdam, Regent Sea, Royal Princess, Royal Viking Sun, Sagafjord, Scandinavian Saga, Seaward, Skyward, Song of America, Sun Viking,* and *Veracruz.*

4. MISSISSIPPI AND OHIO RIVERS

Hum a couple of bars of "Up the Lazy River" and you have an immediate idea what life is like as you meander slowly through the waters of the mighty Mississippi. Life on the banks is as serene and intriguing as life on this busy river, which has provided the nation with folklore and fancy for generations. Tom Sawyer and Huck Finn are the river's two most famous sailors; New Orleans, Natchez, Memphis, and St. Louis some of its most famous ports.

On a cruise upriver or down, you will step back into the world of Panama-hatted, derringer-carrying riverboat gamblers whose dashing good looks turned hearts to jelly and aces to their advantage. Sonorous tones of a rumbling calliope welcome you aboard gleaming white paddlewheelers that chug merrily up and down the river like floating white wedding cakes. In an instant you are no longer part of this world but are time-warped back to the days of cotton plantations and hoop skirts, flirty fans and flighty ladies whose soft drawls hid iron wills.

Things haven't changed all that much along this 2,047-mile-long river. Life still moves slowly in many cities along its banks and people still talk softly. You'll settle into the tranquility the minute you step aboard a Mississippi River cruiser, and soon you, too, will be drawling an occasional "*y'all.*"

In **New Orleans** you'll hear the wail of a clarinet and the hoofbeats of a carriage horse echoing through the narrow streets.

Upriver you'll visit **Houmas House,** star of that spooky film, *Hush, Hush, Sweet Charlotte.* A Greek Revival mansion, Houmas House can trace its history to 1840 when it was the center of life for workers on 20,000 acres of sugar plantation, the most productive plantation in the nation. Owned by a quick-thinking Irishman, Houmas House was saved from destruction in the Civil War when its owner claimed that as a British citizen he—and the house—were immune from the Americans' troubles. Postwar changes took their toll on this plantation as on many others, and little by little it declined until, in 1940, a New Orleans doctor restored it to its former glory.

At **Baton Rouge,** 230 miles upriver, you'll see more of those hauntingly lovely plantation houses, and at the Louisiana Rural Life Museum you'll get a look at the working side of plantation life. Here you can visit a reconstructed plantation settlement complete with workers' cabins, blacksmith shop, and sugar house, the world plantation workers knew so well.

Named after a red post (a *baton rouge*) that was constructed to divide two

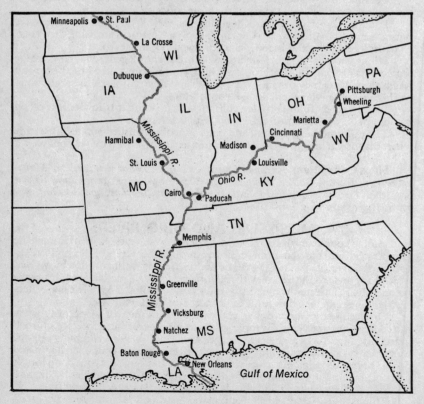

Indian settlements here, Baton Rouge was founded in 1719 and was the center of fighting in Revolutionary and Civil War days. These days you'll stroll down wide boulevards lined with former plantation homes so carefully restored that you can imagine yourself dancing in a candlelit ballroom or placing your afternoon calling card carefully on the butler's silver tray.

Don't miss the Old State Capitol, reconstructed in 1882 after it was destroyed by Union troops during the war. It's one of the most unusual architectural creations in the South.

If you like rubbing elbows with money, even if it's historic money, you'll love **St. Francisville.** Here lived nearly half the nation's 19th-century cotton millionaires, ensconced in the splendor of glamorous plantations like exquisite Rosedown Plantation and Gardens. In its parlors you'll see priceless furnishings brought here from France in 1835, gilded chandeliers, looping drapes, glittering crystal. At a similar plantation house, The Myrtles, you may even meet the ghost said to roam the massive halls and veranda.

In those elegant old days when King Cotton was growing up, **Natchez** was too, which accounts for the presence here of still more classic antebellum mansions. Spared by Gen. Ulysses S. Grant when he marched through the city during the Civil War, Natchez today sports some of the finest examples of antebellum architecture remaining in America.

You can ooh and ahh—and believe us, you will!—over more than 200 massive plantation houses and gorgeous gardens that have made this city's semi-annual Natchez Pilgrimage festivals one of the most popular of all U.S. tours. On one of these you may visit Stanton Hall where hoop-skirted damsels will escort you graciously through the high-ceilinged, antique-laden rooms of this block-long plantation house. On the floors of a Georgian manor called Rosalie you can still see the scars left by the spurs of Union officers who strode through these hallways. At D'Evereux you will attend in your imagination one of the elaborate balls whose elegance earned the hostess here the title of grandest partygiver in the city.

If you're here in spring, sniff: the heady scent of thousands of the city's famed magnolias fills the air.

More than 400 miles upriver is **Vicksburg,** where the sound of booming cannons seems still to haunt this tragic ground on which so many Americans fought each other. As it was surrounded for more than three months during the siege of 1863, Vicksburg natives refuse still to celebrate the Fourth of July, the day their ancestors surrendered to the Union army.

In the Old Court House Museum are grim reminders of the past in small memorabilia that somehow seem to carry a more poignant message than battlefields and history books can provide: Confederate money, old war uniforms, receipts from slave sales, faded photographs—the tiny human touches so often lost in stories of the national tragedy that was the Civil War.

Its strategic location on the river and in the heart of cotton country made **Memphis** by 1873 the world's largest cotton market. Located 736 miles upriver but still part of the area known as the lower Mississippi River, Memphis remains a cotton center. Its Cotton Exchange handles more than four million bales annually. You can visit the Exchange here, then go out and have a look at how the product that has made it famous grows and is worked in the fields.

A musical haven for generations, Memphis's Beale Street was home to blues musician W. C. Handy, while farther out of town another musician lived in considerable splendor—Elvis Presley, who lived at Graceland mansion.

Moving on upriver, you'll visit the now-quiet town of **Cairo,** Illinois, a city that once rivaled Chicago as a commercial center. As center of the steamboat trade, Cairo declined rapidly after the Illinois Central Railroad was built in the mid-1800s. You can still see wisps of the city's intriguing past, however, in the lovely restoration of Magnolia Manor and in Holiday Park.

When you reach the often-photographed Gateway Arch of **St. Louis** you're on the upper Mississippi River and at the old gateway to the West. There is much to see and do in this city, ranging from a visit to the largest brewery in the world, Anheuser-Busch, to a look at some of the trophies given aviator Charles Lindbergh who, you may recall, named his history-making aircraft *The Spirit of St. Louis* in honor of his St. Louis backers.

When the West was about to be won, pioneers gathered here to prepare for the trek onward through the wilderness. Traders, trappers, gamblers, dancehall girls, and all sorts in between made this a thriving city that remains to this day unexpectedly tolerant of the wide variety of adventurers who find their way here.

Another 300 miles up the upper Mississippi will bring you to **Hannibal,** Missouri, Mark Twain's boyhood home and the land that inspired his amusing tales of life on and about the river he loved. When you spot the first picket fence, you'll giggle at the memories of those young pranksters you once knew so well they seemed almost family: Tom Sawyer, Huck Finn, and Becky Thatcher. Mark Twain was born Samuel Clemens but acquired his unusual name when he worked as a riverboat pilot on a sternwheeler bound for New Orleans.

Water seems to affect the fate of many a Hannibal resident: this is also the birthplace of a lady known as *The Unsinkable Molly Brown* (her real name was Margaret Tobin).

Upriver you'll dock at **Burlington,** Iowa, but be sure to cross the river for a look at **Nauvoo,** Illinois, temporary home for Joseph Smith and his group of Mormon settlers. A dispute with the rest of the community here sent them on their way west, but before they left they constructed some interesting homes and buildings that have been restored by their descendants. Sip a glass of local wine while you're here in this vineyard capital of Illinois.

Next stop upriver is **Dubuque,** Iowa, nearly 600 miles into the upper Mississippi River. A vaudeville opera house built in 1910 is still in use here and is now listed on the National Register of Historic Places. You'll see more delightful 19th-century architecture in **Galena,** Illinois, a short bus ride away.

Victorian architecture begins to turn up regularly in this upper half of the Mississippi. You can see some interesting examples of it at Villa Louis in **Prairie du Chien,** Wisconsin, a quiet town near the confluence of the Mississippi and Wisconsin Rivers. Villa Louis was built by a representative of John Jacob Astor, the fur millionaire, who moved here in the 1800s to act as Astor's agent. Indian tribes lived in this area 10,000 years ago and the Hopewell culture settlement here features huge burial mounds 2,000 years old.

Logging and furs were important industries here in the early 19th century when the river was used to float logs downstream. Steamboats like the one you're traveling on were an important part of that history. You can learn something about their role in life on the Mississippi at the Wabasha Museum at **Wabasha,** Minnesota, where you can also visit Suilman Antique Museum and an antique hotel, the Anderson House, which opened in 1856. Wabasha is also a cheese-manufacturing center, so you can visit a cheesery and nibble some samples.

Finally you come to **Minneapolis / St. Paul,** the twin cities 839 miles up the river and as far north as you can go on it. To head north or west from here, people once had to travel by ox cart, and the traffic even in those days was terrific! Points of interest in this city include the renowned Guthrie Theater, Minnehaha Falls, and Fort Snelling, which dates back to 1825. Both these cities played a vital part in the opening of the Northwest Territory.

On some cruises you can branch off the Mississippi and head up the Ohio

River all the way to **Pittsburgh,** where three rivers (the Allegheny, Monongehela, and Ohio) merge. On the way you will travel up 1,000 miles of the Ohio River, home of the first steamboat, which was built in Pittsburgh in 1811 and named the *City of New Orleans.*

On this river mileage counting begins at Pittsburgh and rises as you move toward the river's confluence with the Mississippi at Cairo, Illinois. Stops on the Ohio include **Evansville** and **New Harmony,** Indiana, established in the early 1800s and once a major shipping center for coal. This is Abraham Lincoln Country, where the former president spent much of his early life. New Harmony gets its name from the Lutheran colony that settled here hoping to create a perfect community. Certainly they built a lovely one, and many of the early homes have been restored by proud homeowners.

An annual "Run for the Roses," that famed Kentucky Derby that pits the best of the nation's thoroughbreds against each other in the most famous horserace in the nation, brought fame to **Louisville.** You can even cruise here for the race on a special four-night Cincinnati-to-Cincinnati Kentucky Derby Cruise that includes seats at the Derby plus a call at Madison.

In **Louisville,** 603 miles up the Ohio from Pittsburgh, you can see memorabilia of past races at Churchill Downs Museum and get a look at one of the few remaining examples of Thomas Jefferson designs at the Manor House.

Eclectic architecture is a much-loved feature of **Madison,** Indiana, a town established in 1810 and once the largest city in the state. You'll see all styles of architecture here, from Federalist to an Italianate villa with all the best-known American styles in between. Many of the homes are open for tours.

A new itinerary takes you up the Tennessee River to **Chattanooga.** Chattanooga Choo-Choo! Need we say more?

Once upon a time a gentleman who knew how to combine a closed mouth and some open doors lived in **Ripley,** Ohio. He was the Rev. John Rankin, one of the leaders of a liberation movement that became known as the Underground Railroad. Rankin is said to have provided a railroad "station" in his home or the homes of his friends for more than 2,000 escaped slaves headed north to freedom, and you can still visit his house. One guest there was Harriett Beecher Stowe, who heard the story of one slave's escape and wrote about it in a novel that was to exacerbrate an already explosive situation—*Uncle Tom's Cabin.*

Ripley is now also home to Arabian stallions, many of which are bred here, carrying on the town's long history as a breeding ground of fine horses.

As you near the end of your Ohio River cruise, you will dock in downtown **Gallipolis** (pronounced Gala-*police*), Ohio, a French settlement that can still show you the first log cabin built here. If you look in the phone book, you'll still see plenty of French names, belonging to descendants of those early settlers, some of whom once played host to the Marquis de Lafayette. While you're here, stop in at "Our House," a brick riverside mansion and a tavern filled with intriguing antique furniture and unusual china, and don't miss the bevy of beautiful 19th-century homes surrounding Gallipolis City Park.

Ships Calling at Ports Along the Mississippi and Its Tributaries: *Delta Queen, Mississippi Queen,* and *New Orleans.*

5. BERMUDA / NORTHEAST PASSAGE / INLAND WATERWAYS

In summer there are a few ships sailing in these northern waters, calling at Bermuda, one of the most popular ports, and at small islands off the U.S. East Coast, places like Newport, Nantucket, Block Island, and Martha's Vineyard.

A fleet of small cruise ships carrying 100 passengers or less also visits ports along the Hudson River, up through Canada's Thousand Islands and into Québec.

Bermuda

Capital and Port City: Hamilton.
Size: 20 miles long by 1 mile wide.
Nickname: "The Onion Patch."
Population: 70,000.
Language: English.
Currency: U.S. dollar.
Tourist Information: Bermuda Department of Tourism, Global House, 43 Church St., Hamilton (tel. 809/292-0023); also offices in New York, Atlanta, Boston, Chicago, and Toronto.
Public Transportation: buses, taxis, horse-drawn carriages, ferries.
Car Rentals: none. Moped rental: J. B. Astwood Cycles, Front Street (tel. 292-2245).
Shopping Specialties: British imports, including china, crystal, wools.
Restaurants: Hamilton—Plantation, Bailiff Bay, Hamilton Parish (tel. 293-1188); Penthouse, Punch Street (tel. 295-3410). St. George—Fort William, Government Hill (tel. 297-0904).
Pubs: Rum Runners, Front Street, Hamilton (tel. 292-4737); Henry VIII, Southampton (tel. 298-0908); Country Squire, Somerset (tel. 294-0105); Village Inn, Somerset (tel. 298-9401).

Bermuda is an artist's palette of rainbow colors mixed with abandon and applied with glee. Vivid scarlet and magenta blossoms cascade down the walls of frilly but stately homes painted buttercup yellow, mint green, and sky blue. Even the sand is pink!

Human plumage matches nature's. You'll see men in some of the most outrageously colored trousers and shorts ever invented, and women that match, sometimes literally. To make matters even stranger, many of those men are garbed in knee socks and knee-length shorts so popular they bear the name of this island: Bermuda shorts. Atop these knee-ticklers they're wearing button-down shirts, ties, and suit jackets. This predilection for unusual outfits sometimes seems to us to be a perverse reaction to the formality that continues to pervade this island settled 300 years ago by the British and still possessed of much British formality.

Britain's oldest colony, Bermuda approaches the U.S. geographically about where Bermuda shorts touch the body—a little south of halfway. Located about 600 miles east of Savannah, Georgia, this 21-square-mile island is about 775 miles southeast of New York.

That means that in winter Bermuda is quite a bit cooler than its neighbors in the Caribbean, hence the summer cruise season. Ships call at Bermuda between May and October when the average temperatures range from 74° to 85° Fahrenheit and lows average 66° to 75°.

Quaint British customs live on in Bermuda, which still has a bell-ringing town crier, afternoon tea, snappy British accents—and rent of one peppercorn paid each April for use of the State House.

Lovely beaches are of course the lure here, so be sure to take a look at a couple of these strips of sand, scenically tucked in among cliffs and craggy rocks or stretched out with nothing to see but the glittering ocean beyond.

A glass-bottom boat ride out to the **Sea Gardens** is an intriguing trip, and the **Maritime Museum** at the Naval Keep Yard on Ireland Island features whaling mementos and antique boats, plus doubloons and jewels from a sunken treasure ship.

Life is not cheap on Bermuda, and few of the "bargains" are as much of a bargain as they may once have been. You'd be wise to check the prices at home before investing here. Some things are a good buy and some aren't. If you're buying liquor, you need to order it from the store "in bond" at least 24 hours before departure to take advantage of the greatest bargains.

Bermuda is actually the largest of 300 islands hereabouts, only 20 of which are inhabited.

Go exploring on this island that Mark Twain once called "the biggest small place in the world." You'll want to see the **Crystal** or **Leamington caves,** where you can wander through glittering stalagmites and stalactites, and the **Blue Grotto Dolphins,** where trained dolphins perform five times a day in a natural limestone grotto. Good walkers might try a climb up the 185 steps leading to the top of **Gibbs Hill Lighthouse,** now more than 100 years old.

In **Hamilton,** the capital city, you'll dock on Front Street right in the heart of the downtown shops, where you'll find Shetland and cashmere sweaters, Harris tweeds from Ireland, leather goods, bone china, crystal, Irish linens and glass, antique silver, French perfume. And, naturally, Bermuda shorts.

To experience the Britishness of the island, visit **Sessions House,** where the Bermudian Parliament and wigged Supreme Court justices convene. A block away, City Hall features a landmark *Sea Venture* weather vane.

Golf and tennis are available on the island, and horseback riding is a favorite sport, as are sailing and water sports too, of course. You can even don one of those Jules Verne-ish diving suits and walk on the floor of the ocean with diver Bronson Hartley—and you don't even have to know how to swim.

You won't find any rental cars in Bermuda, but if you want to explore you can rent a motorbike to scoot about the island. A hilly but not mountainous speck in the Atlantic, Bermuda is said to be the flat top of a submerged mountain.

The former capital of the island and a charmer of a spot, **St. George's** seems to us far more intriguing than Hamilton. Here along **Somers' Wharf** old warehouses have been converted into a cluster of small boutiques intertwined with narrow alleyways. These branches of Hamilton stores are much less crowded than their counterparts in the capital city.

Here the island's history lives on in churches, graveyards, museums. In **King's Square** you can be photographed in pillory and stocks, and in the **Print Shop** you can see a working model of a 17th-century press.

To get a look at an old English church, visit cedar-lined **St. Peter's,** the oldest Anglican church in the Western Hemisphere.

At the **Carriage Museum** you can see the style to which earlier settlers were accustomed—and the elegant transport they used (until cars came to the island in 1945).

Nearby, at the **President Henry Tucker House,** you can hear some interesting Revolutionary War stories from a different point of view and see some exquisite furniture and portraits. In St. George's you can also see the **Deliverance,** a replica of the ship built in 1609 by 150 passengers of the shipwrecked *Sea Venture*. Until these early British settlers arrived, the island had been visited by the Spanish but never inhabited.

Wander narrow old lanes with names like One Gun Alley or Shinbone Alley and visit elegantly restored homes and small pubs like the Country Squire.

Many ships stay overnight in this harbor, so if you're looking for a place to party at night, try any of the larger hotels of the Clay House Inn for steel-band entertainment, Robin Hood for folk music, the Club, the Hotel Sonesta's Electric Rainbow, and Infinity for dancing.

Something for trivia buffs: Bermuda was once the world's premier producer of Bermuda onions, and in tribute to that history Bermuda's residents are sometimes called "onions." We think it might be best, however, to know your new Bermuda friends quite well before you hang that moniker on them.

Ships Calling Here: *Amerikanis, Bermuda Queen,* and *Nordic Prince.*

Northeast Passage

Although this is a bit of a manufactured name, it aptly describes the route some cruise ships take along the northeast coastline up the St. Lawrence and Saguenay Rivers.

History buffs will adore this section of the nation, which retains all the best of its years as the home of sea captains and whalers.

On a cruise in this area you'll want to find yourself a good seat on deck and just watch the scenery float by your chair. Emerald islands, deep-blue waters, fancy furbelowed old houses capture your senses and your imagination. It's not at all difficult to imagine yourself hurling a harpoon or spinning the polished wheel of a sailing ship, a nor'wester beating spray into your eyes as you trim the sails and head home.

On a stately steam through this region you'll pass by **Martha's Vineyard,** Massachusetts, a major whaling center in the 18th and 19th centuries, and home to many sea captains and ship owners who built elaborate and beautiful mansions here.

Other whalers lived on nearby **Nantucket,** another frequent port of call on Northeast Passage voyages. At the Whaling Museum you can get a close look at the life led by those fearless souls who went in search of ambergris and whale oil. You can read about the island in Herman Melville's novel *Moby-Dick,* the story of a whale of a whale.

Newport dates from colonial times, but really "made it" when the super-rich (and even some of the merely wealthy) of the late 19th and early 20th centuries built summer cottages here—some of these "cottages" had 30 or more rooms! A number of these old homes are open to view. But Newport was perhaps best known as the site of an annual jazz festival, and for almost a century and a half (until 1983 when the Australians triumphantly carried off the trophy) as the home of the America's Cup yachting races that were held offshore every four years.

Boston was, of course, a pretty important place to the first settlers in America when they arrived in 1623. The city has recently done wonders with its waterfront, which is now one of the loveliest harbors in the nation. True sailors will want to get a look at the restored U.S.S. *Constitution,* "Old Ironsides," at the waterfront, and historians will want to walk the 1½-mile Freedom Trail that outlines some of America's earliest and most lump-in-the-throat history.

Waves crash off the rocky coast of Maine today just as they have for generations, and much else here is just as it was a hundred or more years ago. You can visit some of that changeless Maine seaside at **Bar Harbor** on Mount Desert Island off the east coast. Once the retreat of the very, very rich, Bar Harbor remains the summer getaway spot for some of the nation's fortune-eers.

Sailing in this area has the added benefit of an abundance of huge fresh Maine lobsters and fat succulent clams. No doubt you'll find some of these on the menu aboard, but if you don't, make it your business to get ashore and chow down.

Looming over **Halifax,** the capital of Nova Scotia, is the massive Citadel fortress, once the largest British fortress in this hemisphere. Don't hit the deck if you hear a giant cannon booming as you sail into harbor—it's fired each day at noon!

PORTS OF CALL: NORTHEAST U.S. COAST □ 97

From a perch up in the Citadel you'll have a lovely view of the harbor below, and while you're here, visit some of the 100-year-old structures that have been carefully preserved. Halifax's Public Gardens on Spring Garden Road were planned in 1753.

Those Britons really do know a good thing when they see it, and they saw it at **Prince Edward Island.** Many Northeast Passage cruises visit the capital city of Charlottetown where Fort Edward rises over the harbor. Just 145 miles long and 40 miles wide, the island is home to 120,000 people. They can trace their ancestry back to French explorers like Jacques Cartier who sailed here in 1523, British troops who took over in 1758, and American Loyalists who fled to the island when revolution threatened.

Anne of Green Gables, a delightful story, lives on at Green Gables in Cavendish, on the island's north shore.

On the **Gaspé Peninsula** tall pines shade streams where salmon spawned when French explorer Champlain first landed here. Called Land's End by the Indian tribe that lived here then, this rough and rocky land is a place of awesome beauty teeming with wildlife. Dotted with small fishing villages, this peninsula produces the Canadian peat moss so loved by gardeners throughout North America, and provides much of the salmon, cod, and shrimp that end up on North American tables.

Dramatic views of bare cliffs and hundreds of miles of deep green forests surround you as you sail past this rugged land.

As you steam up the **Saguenay River,** giant granite cliffs tower above you rising more than 1,000 feet into the sky. Whales come to feed at the confluence of the Saguenay and the **St. Lawrence River,** and the sight of their massive bodies surging through the water is downright breathtaking. People have been sailing this river for hundreds of years, some in search of the furry creatures that live along its shores and some, like the early explorers, in search of the land itself. They were not disappointed in the majestic beauty of this scenic wonderland, and you won't be either.

We've always been fascinated by walled cities, so you can be sure that we were intrigued by the fortifications of **Québec City.** But then everyone is fascinated with Québec City for one reason or another! As romantic as New Orleans, this antique village has kept to the French lifestyle first introduced here by explorer Samuel de Champlain who founded Québec City in 1608. Here you wander through a beautifully restored historic center that will set you right back into the 17th century when this village looked much as it does now.

Stand in front of the famed Château Frontenac Hotel, shut your eyes, listen to the clop of the horse-drawn carriages called calèches, and you'll be transported to days of yore.

History of many decades comes to life in this city of which the Québecois are so proud: Roosevelt and Churchill planned World War II tactics here; North America's oldest church, Notre-Dame des Victoires, dating back to 1688, is here; and way up above the waterway on Dufferin Terrace, Champlain built a fortress more than 350 years ago.

You'll run out of energy long before you run out of restored homes, beautiful architecture, and intriguing sights to explore.

Finally you reach **Montréal,** home of some of the finest cooks in Canada, even in North America. It gets cold up here in winter so you'll find much of this city's life underground, where shops, restaurants, boutiques, and amusements of all kinds abound.

The most historically interesting spot in this huge city, now the second-largest French-speaking city in the world, is the Place d'Armes, a central square where you can sit in a small sidewalk café and drink history with your café au lait. Roam the streets nearby to get a look at some beautifully restored old homes and typically Québecois architecture.

Not many cruise ships visit this appealing northeastern region of the hemisphere, but those that do offer their passengers a look at some of the loveliest landscapes and most intriguing lifestyles, past or present, of any region of the world.

Ships Calling Here: *Bermuda Star, Caribbean Prince, Charleston, Crown Odyssey, Fairsky, Fairwind, Nantucket Clipper, Newport Clipper, New Shoreham II, Royal Viking Sun, Sagafjord, Savannah,* and *Yorktown Clipper.*

Inland Waterways

As cruise lines begin to look farther and farther afield for new ports to visit, many areas of the country that have rarely or never been visited by a cruise ship are putting their best pier forward to attract sailing tourists.

A few small cruise ships, usually carrying fewer than 100 passengers, are U.S.-registered ships and are thus permitted to sail between these American ports. Among the lines making calls at places like Savannah, Yorktown, Williamsburg, and Charleston are American Cruise Lines, American Canadian Caribbean Line, and Clipper Cruise Line.

Those inland-waterway sailings most often occur on cruises called "positioning" cruises, which are created as a means of setting the ship from its winter schedule in the Caribbean, for instance, north to its summer schedule in the northeast.

To get there, the ship usually heads north in the spring through Florida's Intracoastal waterway. In the fall the itinerary is reversed. Stops along the way often include posh **Palm Beach,** home of the Kennedy clan and scads of other millionaires, and historic **St. Augustine,** the nation's oldest city. Occasionally ships also stop at **Titusville,** gateway to the space shots at the Kennedy Space Center and of course to inland Orlando, home of the world's most famous mouse, and at tiny **Vero Beach,** a pretty seaside city much loved by Floridians for its casual informality and beautiful beaches.

Then it's on to **Savannah** where on a day-long stop you can visit that city's cobblestone streets and stately plantations. From there the next stop may be **St.**

100 □ **DOLLARWISE GUIDE TO CRUISES**

Simons Island, a jet-set playground, then on to **Beaufort** where restored Greek Revival antebellum homes provide a fascinating look into the glamour of the Old South.

At **Charleston** you'll dock near the city's famous Battery and visit Fort Sumter where the first shot of the Civil War was fired. At nearby **Hilton Head,** the largest sea island south of New Jersey, miles of beaches beckon.

Ships head inland again at the Chesapeake Bay visiting the much-touted new **Baltimore** Inner Harbor waterfront revitalization project. Then it's on to **Yorktown** and **Williamsburg** where Revolutionary War history comes to life.

At **Crisfield** you can gorge on those famous Chesapeake Bay oysters and crabs. In **Oxford** the days of pirates Stede Connet and Blackbeard Teach come alive as you visit places these buccaneers swaggered while their ships were being built and outfitted.

Nearby **St. Michaels** earned itself a place in history when its citizens hung lanterns in the treetops to deceive the raiding British fleet, which shot its cannonballs at the lights and missed the town! In a stop at **Annapolis,** Maryland's capital, you can visit the U.S. Naval Academy, where those swabbies toss their caps in the air each graduation day, and roam this lovely old city which was the site for the final declaration of the end of the American Revolution.

Ships Calling Here: *Charleston, Fairsky, Nantucket Clipper, Newport Clipper, New Orleans, Savannah,* and *Yorktown Clipper.*

6. PANAMA CANAL

There may be no single cruise experience more memorable—or more frequently related—than a passage through the Panama Canal. In eight amazing hours you move from the Atlantic to the Pacific (or vice versa), traversing a man-made body of water often fondly called the "big ditch."

Opened in 1914, the Panama Canal took 10 years to build and 400 years to get started. Way back in the early 1500s Spain's King Carlos V ordered his minions to begin looking into a way to cut through the narrow neck of land that prohibited Spanish sailors from extending their explorations to the Pacific Ocean by sea.

Sailing from the Atlantic to the Pacific (but not from east to west; check a map—it's northwest to southeast), your ship will enter the channel in Limón Bay at **Colón.** During the passage across the isthmus heading for the Bay of Panamá at Balboa on the Pacific, you will cover 40¼ miles of water with a minimum depth of 41 feet.

At Gatun you enter the first of a series of six locks, huge chambers each 1,000 by 110 feet, where millions of gallons of water surge in to lift your ship a total of 85 feet above sea level, so that it can move into **Lake Gatun,** a 21-mile-long man-made lake. This basin is one of the largest artificial bodies of water on earth, covering 166 square miles. Ships that sail on what are called "double transits" of the canal—that is, into the canal, through a portion of it, but returning the same way—turn around in this massive basin.

Beyond the lake your ship navigates the narrow **Gaillard Cut,** an awesome eight-mile channel blasted through the solid rock of the Continental Divide (the cut is named for the engineer who presided over the creation of the canal).

On all sides throughout this journey you can see birds of flaming plumage flying through deep-green jungles sparked with the splashy colors of tropical flowers.

Finally, after your passage through **Miraflores Lake** and the **Miraflores and Pedro Miguel Locks,** you reach the Pacific Ocean at **Balboa.**

As beautiful and awe-inspiring as it all is, there is a sobering side to this magnificence. Hundreds of men lost their lives to malaria, yellow fever, and other diseases during the canal's construction. In the long run, one of the most beneficial offshoots of the canal may well have been the study of these diseases and their eventual eradication or control.

In recent years several cruise lines have begun calling on Panama's **San Blas Islands,** a breeze-swept, palm-fringed cluster of more than 360 coral islands off the northeast Caribbean coast of Panama. These islands, also known as the Mulatas Islands, are home to the Cuna Indians whose number one industry is an elaborate artistic creation called *mola* embroidery. A reverse applique, *mola* is turned into skirts, scarfs, shawls, wall hangings, blouses, and heaven knows what else, each featuring one to a dozen or more patterns.

Not only the creations are interesting: the people themselves have a rather mysterious background and are believed to be a mixture of Norse and Indian blood dating back many, many years before Columbus arrived here in 1501. Other theories say that these unusual people—women wear rings in their noses and smoke pipes—are pure-blooded descendants of aborigines of Caribbean Indian origin. Certainly, until very recently it was tribal custom to mete out a death sentence to a San Blas woman who married a man of another race.

Ships Calling Here: *Britanis, Crown Odyssey, Explorer Starship, Great Rivers Explorer, Regent Sea, Regent Star, Regent Sun,* and *Stella Solaris.*

7. SOUTH AMERICA

Huge as it is, South America is still a mystery to most North Americans who haven't yet discovered the many and varied enchantments of this vast southern neighbor.

Most cruise passengers don't get to see much of this huge continent either. Those lucky souls on world cruises will get a look at South America, but only a few harbors are regular ports of call on shorter voyages from the U.S. Among those are Caracas in Venezuela and Cartagena in Colombia, both of which are easy stops for ships making voyages through the Panama Canal.

One company, Sun Line Cruises, is now also featuring several voyages to the east coast of South America, exploring the remote Orinoco River and sailing down to Rio for the annual Carnival. Just reading the company's brochure for these cruises is a trip you make without leaving your chair!

Epirotiki Lines spent one season sailing its *World Renaissance* from Guadeloupe up the Amazon River to Manaus and liked it so well they repeated the experience in subsequent winters.

What fascinating cruises these are! In 11 days you wander down the river from Manaus, a rubber barons' stronghold deep in the Amazon jungles, past remote enclaves where villagers paddle out in hand-hewn dugout canoes to wave at the huge ship that towers over them like Atlas looking down on the world, its whistles booming out across the jungle.

Sun Line Cruises' *Stella Solaris* also travels the river.

In 1988 the popularity of South American ports increased and a number of lines scheduled long voyages around part or all of that massive continent. Most stopped in at Rio de Janeiro, sometimes during that city's famous Lenten-season Carnival festival, and at Buenos Aires and Montevideo.

Among the lines that schedule trips to a number of different ports in South America are Chandris Fantasy Cruises' *Britanis,* which scheduled a 47-day cruise around the continent; Cunard Lines' *QE2,* which planned a 60-day trip around the continent; Epirotiki Lines' *Pegasus,* which often travels between Rio de Janeiro and Buenos Aires; Royal Viking Lines' *Royal Viking Sky,* which often visits that hemisphere; and Sun Line Cruises' *Stella Solaris,* which heads for the west coast of the continent in the winter of 1989 to begin a continent-circling cruise in the Galápagos Islands. All those cruises are sold in shorter segments to make them more affordable in both time and money.

Let's take a look at some of the most popular South American ports visited on voyages leaving from the U.S.

Caracas / La Guaira, Venezuela

Population: 900,000.
Climate: 70° to 80° F year round.
Language: Spanish.
Currency: Venezuelan bolívar.
Tourist Information: Corporación de Turismo Venezuela, Centro Capriles, Piso 7, Plaza Venezuela (tel. 572-4196).
Documents: valid passport required.
Public Transportation: taxis, buses.
Car Rentals: Hertz, Edificio Hertz, Avenida Principal del Bosque (tel. 571-7901).
Shopping Specialties: straw bags, hammocks, semiprecious stones, ponchos, sculpture.
Food Specialties: pabellon (a beef-bean casserole); multinational cuisine.
Restaurants: Coq d'Or, Calle Real y Sabana Grande 90, Bolívar Shopping Gallery (tel. 579-9444); Sorrento, Avenida Manscal, Francisco Solano 42 (tel. 579-7983).

Venezuela's capital city, this thriving oil metropolis is visited by a number of cruise ships sailing deep into the Caribbean or to the Panama Canal.

You'll dock at La Guaira, a shabby spot that's really nothing but the port—and *that's* not a particularly lovely place. You can catch a local bus to town or hire a taxi driver to drive you around the city and show you the sights. Most speak fair English and are pleasant, smiling souls anxious to tote you around and keep you happy. Fix your price before you begin your tour, however.

Drivers and shore excursions alike will take you to a glass factory that does some ordinary bibelots and some very attractive ones. You can see the glass objects being created by glassblowers.

Looming over the city is **Mount Ávila,** a 7,000-foot peak that in the past offered a cable ride to the summit. It hasn't been working for years, however, so don't count on riding it during your visit.

Founded in 1567, Caracas was named after a patron saint Santiago de León de Caracas, but no longer exhibits much of its original colonial architecture. About as close as you can come is the home of South American hero and liberator Simón Bolívar. Called **Casa Natal,** it's next door to the **Bolivarian Museum,** which outlines South American history from its conquest by the Spanish to its colonial period, and finally its independence.

Bolívar, born here in Caracas, is the city's favorite son, so you will see statues of him and hear his name in many places in the city, one of the more interesting of which is **Plaza Bolívar,** the traditional center of Caracas.

At the **Colonial Art Museum** you'll find a restored mansion filled with art and objects from the Spanish era. Top that with a visit to **Quinta Caracas,** where artists are at work in the gracious antique patio.

You'll see just the opposite kind of architecture at **University City,** where 50,000 students attend classes—very contemporary styling here. Nearby you can roam through 175 acres of **Botanical Gardens** replete with orchids and a flurry of exotic tropical plants.

While there are not masses of things to see in Caracas, a drive through this city, with a stop at the central plaza, is pleasant. Ask the driver to show you the posh suburb that is home to some of the oil entrepreneurs, and drive through the bustling and modern downtown past miles of beautiful parkland on the outskirts of the city.

Beaches in the area include Marina Grande, Playa Sheraton, Macuto Beach, and Los Angeles Beach.

Shoppers will want to check out the jammed **shopping area** on the Sabana Grande stretching from the Plaza Venezuela along Avenida Lincoln to the **Centro Comercial Chacaito.** Gold and natural pearls from Margarita Island are good buys, as are hand-woven rugs made by Guajiro Indians. Piñatas are popular, as are high-fashion couture items.

Ships Calling Here: *Atlantic, CarlaCosta, Cunard Countess, Ocean Islander, Ocean Princess, Rotterdam,* and *The Victoria.*

Cartagena, Colombia
Population: 500,000.
Climate: 70° to 90°F year round.
Language: Spanish.
Currency: Colombian peso.
Tourist Information: Corporación Nacional del Turismo, Palace of the Inquisition, Plaza Bolívar (tel. 44921).
Documents: valid passport required.
Public Transportation: buses, taxis.
Car Rentals: Hertz, Hotel Capilla del Mar, 8–59 la Cartagena (tel. 42921).
Shopping Specialties: wall hangings, ceramics, ruanas, pre-Columbian artifacts and reproductions, coffee, emeralds, and aguardiente liquor (a great buy).
Restaurants: Capilla del Mar, Avenida Chile (tel. 42921); Pavillon de France, San Martín at Calle 8 (tel. 41504).

Walled cities seem romantic and mysterious, and none in the Caribbean is more intriguing than Cartagena, whose walls rose 300 years ago to protect the city from pirate raids.

Cartegena's a walking city best seen on foot, so we'll outline a couple of walking tours for you.

Begin at the **Tower of the Clock,** called La Boca de Reloj in Spanish, one of the city's landmarks and a favorite meeting place. This clock tower is at the city's main gate called La Boca del Puente (which actually has three gates). Inside is the Plaza de Los Coches, where, if you turn left at the gate, in a block or so you'll come across the old Customs House. There's a statue of Columbus there.

A little farther along you reach the **Church of San Pedro Claver,** which honors a priest who cared for African slaves imported to Cartagena by the Spanish.

Let's hope you haven't attended too many midnight buffets—some of the streets here are so narrow they're barely wide enough for one. See if you can squeeze through Calle de Boloco, for instance.

In the **Parque Bolívar** you'll see two-story houses with fancy balconies. At one end of the plaza is the **Palace of the Inquisition,** site of the Tourist Office, and at the other end is a basilica, a mosque-like structure. There's a 300-year-old sundial here too.

On Calle Santo Domingo is the **Santo Domingo Church and Convent,** a 16th-century creation housing a statue of the Virgin Mary with a crown of gold and emeralds. Nearby is the **Plaza de La Merced,** on Calle Factoría. From the wall here you'll see a beautiful view of the bay. Follow the wall and you're back on Avenida Venezuela near Boca del Puente.

Once there were two walls in this city, an outer and an inner wall. The inner, gone now, was designed to separate the wealthy from the hoi-polloi.

The outer city was called the **Getsemani Barrio,** and if you begin at the Tower of the Clock near the docks your first stop will be the **Parque Centenario,** where the independence fighters are commemorated. On Calle Larga, the main street in this part of the city, is a yellow bridge, the Roman Bridge, which crosses to the **island of Manga,** once a fort.

There you can see **San Felipe Fortress,** a mammoth fort rising 135 feet above sea level and completed in 1657 after 18 years of construction. Don't cross the Roman Bridge. Instead follow the outer wall to the left along Calle Lomba to another bridge, Paseo Heredia, where you will see a monument to a Colombian poet Luís Lopez de Mesa, who described the city as a pair of comfortable old shoes. Across the Paseo Heredia bridge is San Felipe Fortress, with some interesting underground tunnels and a good handcraft shop.

Among the other sights of interest in the city are **San Fernando Castle,** built 200 years ago and complete with dungeons; **Fort San José,** with 21 cannons plus valves to control waves and tides; **Fort San Sebastian,** completed in 1743; **Bovedas,** the dungeons, which feature 22 shell-proof cells from the 18th century that now house boutiques; **La Popa Monastery,** on a promontory overlooking the city and used for more than 375 years, now as a chapel and monastery.

Beaches in Cartagena feature dark sand, but the sun's just the same as elsewhere in the Caribbean. For snorkeling and diving, the Islas del Rosario are just off the coast.

If you're dining ashore, try the local seafood, particularly pargo (red snapper).

Colombia produces more **emeralds** than any other country in the world, so if you're in the market for an emerald, this is the place to look. Emerald quality depends on the depth of color—the darker the better, without blue or yellow hues. Crystallization marks are not a flaw but an expected part of a good emerald, and part of what makes it glow with what connoisseurs call green fire.

Pre-Columbian pottery, some of it 2,000 years old, is also a popular purchase in Colombia, although it would be wise to deal with only the most reputable dealers.

Ships Calling Here: *Britanis, Crown Odyssey, Regent Sea, Regent Star, Regent Sun, Royal Viking Sky,* and *Royal Viking Sun.*

The Amazon River

Population: Sparse along the river, varying in cities.
Climate: 70° to 90° F year round; rainy season January to May.
Language: Portuguese.
Currency: Brazilian cruzado.
Tourist Information: Contact the Brazilian embassy or consulate nearest you before you go.
Documents: passport and Brazilian visa required.
Public Transportation: taxis, buses.
Car Rentals: not readily available.
Shopping Specialties: primitive bows and arrows, beautiful big ceramic urns copied after ancient artwork, semiprecious jewels, wall hangings, straw objects, coffee, colorful hammocks, handmade brass and silver jewelry.
Restaurants: Not recommended except in major hotels like the Tropical in Manaus or the Hilton in Belém.

Your amazing Amazon journey may begin at Guadeloupe and end at Manaus, Brazil, or go the other way around. Either way you go, it's 11 days of oo-ing and ah-ing at the ethereal beauty of mountainous green islets trimmed in fairytale-blue waters, and at the mysterious depths of mile after endless mile of jungles where parrots squawk and monkeys chatter.

Either way you go—flying to Manaus or Guadeloupe to join the cruise—you get a look at **Manaus,** a city built 1,000 miles up the Amazon on the shores of the Río Negro. Rubber trees proliferated here on vast plantations that made millions for their owners, who became known as rubber barons. In 1896 they used $2 million to build an opera house designed to lure the most famous stars of the day to this remote city. It worked. All the top stars made their way deep into the jungle to sing here on the stage of **Teatro Amazonas,** a pretty pastel building lined with mahogany floors, crystal chandeliers, and all the best that money could buy.

Elsewhere in town are some of the best things modern money can buy—Brazilian **gemstones.** Inaccurately called semiprecious stones, these glittering aquamarines, amethysts, blue topaz, citrine (the list goes on and on) are sold at H. Stern in the Tropic Hotel, the best-known jeweler in South America. Prices are much, much lower than elsewhere in the world, perhaps no more than $50 or $60 for a huge unset amethyst.

As you begin your journey down 1,000 miles of this rarely explored river, you stop at a remote jungle village called **Boca do Valeria.** As you roam about, jungle residents who live alongside the river peer shyly at you through doorways. Often the ship's staff distributes some clothes and toys, the ship's doctor sees to aches and pains of the people living there, and passengers buy primitive bows and arrows that make oddly poignant souvenirs.

Next stop is **Santarém,** a bustling riverside town where you can buy one particularly intriguing souvenir for the most aggressive guy on your Christmas list: a stuffed piranha. Look for those, plus lacy straw bags and belts, snakeskin bracelets, and carvings, at Loja Regional Muraquita de João Mileo, 131 Avenida Senador Lameira Bittencourt, or at Regional a Tapicia, at 69B on that same street. Crew members can point the way.

Along the waterfront you'll see a riot of color—hundreds of rainbow-hued **hammocks** on display and on sale for prices under $20, one of the best buys in South America. Trimmed in dangling hand-crocheted fringe and often featuring hand-embroidered details as well, these showpieces are on sale in fancy U.S. catalogs for as much as ten times that price.

Then it's on to a lovely white untrammeled beach called **Alter do Chao,** where you splash about in crystalline water and walk miles of deserted beach, peeking through the underbrush at a lake in the interior of the island. A few intrepid sales types sit in the shade, lackadaisically selling little coconut-fiber dolls or trinkets. Look for the most fascinating bottles we've ever seen—they're covered with a clay-like substance formed into gargoyle, nightmare-closet faces trimmed in bits of fur and snakeskin.

Breves is a small town with wide, wide boulevards and crumbling old Spanish-style mansions. Passengers go ashore to roam the quiet streets and get a look at Brazil's exotic hardwoods—rosewood, mahogany—milled at riverside factories.

Finally, for its last Amazon stop the ship drops anchor in **Belém,** a bustling city with a fascinating zoological park and archeological museum chronicling the highlights of this ancient culture. Belém is the gateway to the billion-acre Amazon Basin and a charming town filled with century-old buildings built by the profits from huge rubber plantations. Anna Pavlova once danced in the city's pastel Teatro da Paz here.

A "don't miss" is the city's **Emilio Goeldi Museum,** an archeologically oriented museum surrounded by a fascinating botanical garden and small zoo where you may meet the first *real* sloth of your life. In the museum you can learn much about the cultural background of this ancient and mysterious jungle, get a look at the gemstones that are almost as common as rock in Brazil, and learn a little about the people, birds, and animals that have inhabited this remote region for millennia.

At the city's waterfront, a guide will take you through a maze called the **Vero-Peso Market,** where strange herbs are sold for home remedies, fruit is piled in colorful photographer's dream heaps, bags of Brazilian coffee are hawked by youngsters, and one herb-seller even drags a snake out of a bottle and lets it twine around her wrist, an ad perhaps for her snake-oil preparations.

A Belém must-stop for shoppers is the **Companhia Paraense de Turismo Paratúr,** Praça (Plaza) Kennedy S / N (tel. 23-3796 or 23-1646). Known simply as Paratúr (pronounced Par-ah-*tour*), it's just a few blocks from the port out the main gate (any taxi driver or port guard can direct you there). Once there you can sip something cool in a pleasant garden, go inside for a look at priceless ceramics on display—and buy some just like them. Urns about four feet tall are particularly dramatic pieces, incised with copies of ancient designs. They cost $50 to $100 and can't be matched in a U.S. interior design shop for five times that amount. For a few dollars more the shop will pack one up and deliver it to the ship (they won't send them through the mail, however). Paratúr also has smaller ceramic pieces, some interesting jewelry, and a few—but only a very few—gemstones, at bargain prices. Black ceramic pieces sold here are beautiful too.

On shore tours or on your own, have a look at the city's **castle / fort,** which contains a picturesque restaurant with views over the town. There are several handsome cathedrals in the city too.

Afternoon shore tours also often include a riverboat trip **into the jungle.** That may not sound like much after all those days on a ship, but it's a great chance to see a Brazil nut doing what comes naturally and feel a little like an Amazon explorer. These river cruisers are small double-decker boats that stop at an island where you walk through the jungle to the other side to meet your riverboat, which has chugged around to meet you. Those who never met a walk they liked can stay on the boat.

Ships Calling Here: *Fairsky, Fairwind, Ocean Princess,* and *World Renaissance.*

Chapter II

RITES OF PASSAGE: HOW MUCH WILL IT COST?

▫ ▫ ▫

1. HELP FROM TRAVEL AGENTS
2. COMPARING COSTS
3. SEASONAL SAILING
4. MORE BUDGETWISE TIPS
5. FLY-FREE AND AIR/SEA PROGRAMS
6. WHEN IS A BARGAIN WORTH THE PRICE?
7. TIPPING
8. SHORE EXCURSIONS
9. FUN AND GAMES AND OTHER EXPENSES

Sooner or later comes the moment of truth! What is it going to cost? Well, there's good news tonight: You can afford it!

Ship trips that once were the private preserve of royalty and the rich are now the playground of Mr. and Ms. Middle America. These days that "cruise revolution" so optimistically hyped by cruise lines draws its recruits from young singles, middle-aged marrieds, retirees, children, and every age and income bracket in between.

Part of that, it must be admitted, is a spin-off of the baby boom, which has left us with a population curve that bulges, literally and figuratively, in its early 30s. With masses of the population now falling in that 30 to 40 age bracket, the cruise industry is using all its considerable wiles to appeal to the pleasures and the pocketbooks of a wide range of travelers.

So somewhere, on some ship, there is a cabin that will fit your budget. Everything that comes afterward—all the mid-morning bouillon, afternoon tea, gorging midnight buffet, and showgirl entertainment—will cost you not one penny!

Yes, it's indeed wonderful to be living in this age of fierce competition and oversupply. No matter how your eyes glaze over when someone mentions the law of supply and demand, in this instance that law is working for you. Those supply and demand principles are what have made cruises affordable even down into the lowest reaches of nonrich pockets.

To explain it in a few words, there are now so many ships, and so many more under construction, that cutthroat competition for your dollars is pushing prices hard—down.

Even better for you, ship lines are not only fighting each other, they are also battling hotels, resorts, destinations, and all kinds of other leisure lures determined to convince you to spend your money on them.

Because all of those other forms of vacation entertainment are better known to most people than cruises, cruise lines must try just that much harder to tempt you into trying their fascinating kind of vacation. One way they do that is with very affordable prices and plenty of special promotions.

That desire to lure travelers away from the traditional two weeks in a heart-shaped Poconos bathtub has led to a proliferation of special money-saving deals that will warm the cockles of your bankbook. In recent memory there have been special offers for the third or fourth passenger sharing a cabin, deals for those over 40, specials for kids, specials for singles, specials for book-at-the-last-minute travelers, even let-us-choose-your-ship-and-save-you-money offers.

Every one of those deals offers you a chance to live like royalty for a day or a few weeks at a price even your gnomish banker would approve.

One of the keys to this money-saving business is your fertile brain, which ought to be reading the travel pages of the local newspaper in search of cruise bargains.

1. HELP FROM TRAVEL AGENTS

Another, and equally (perhaps most) important, key is a travel agent. If you don't have one, get one. Never in history have these people been more wonderful —and necessary—to have around than they are now as prices and special promotions proliferate.

Agents spend many hours, most of them in their so-called free time, attending endless industry seminars at which cruise companies promote their products and their prices. Travel agents are dedicated to absorption of huge quantities of information—after all, that's their business. Best of all (and here comes a lovely word), they'll offer you the benefit of all that knowledge for *free*. Agents are paid, of course, but not by you. Cruise lines pay them a percentage of your fare as a commission, just the way you pay a real estate agent for selling your house.

In their offices are brochures from all the cruise lines. In their heads are reams of detailed information about ships and prices, seasons and ports.

You may also save yourself money by reading newspaper ads run by travel agencies. If an agent says a special rate is available on a ship but doesn't quote the price, call. You may find that the agent has secured a price so low it couldn't be advertised without undercutting published rates.

Your first step in figuring out what a cruise will cost, however, is to decide how much you have to spend. Now that sounds pretty basic, but it's surprising how many people reject the whole idea of a cruise because they equate a cruise vacation with megabucks. It just ain't so anymore.

2. COMPARING COSTS

No one can help you find a cruise in your price bracket until you know what that bracket is. Once you know the top figure you can afford to spend, then you can begin the fun part—perusing the options.

That's when you'll discover fantasyland.

If you have $16,000 you can go around the world. If you have $1,000 you can visit the Caribbean or Alaska or Canada or Mexico. If you have only a few hundred dollars you can spend three or four days on a cruise at least.

In the cruise business, prices can range from the sublime to the ridiculous (well, they'd be ridiculous for *us,* but perhaps not for you). As you begin to see what you get for your dollar, however, you'll discover that what you spend on a cruise is about what you'd spend on any similar vacation. In fact you'll often discover that you spend *less* for a cruise and get a great deal more for your money.

One of the best-loved selling points of the cruise industry is that a cruise vacation—with all its ports, nonstop food, and entertainment—is the world's only prepaid vacation. As Madison Avenue as that sounds, it's quite true that you can compute your cruise vacation almost down to the last penny and you won't find a host of small hidden extras cropping up to haunt you.

To get a handle on cruise costs, and to convince yourself what a bargain you can get on a cruise, learn how to compute the average cost per day, or *per diem* as they say in Latin.

To do that, take a look at the brochure of the ship you're interested in and find the cost of the cabin you think will be a suitable nest for you. If port charges are levied, you'll find a notation of the amount in the brochure. Look for it so you're not surprised to discover another $25 or more tacked onto your ticket price.

Now add port charges to cabin fees. Next look in that same brochure for information on air fare add-ons from the city in which you live. Add those air fares, if any, to the total and tack on about $7 a day for tips. Here's how these computations look:

7-day Caribbean cruise	$1,600 per person
Port charges	$ 25 per person
Tips	$ 49 per person for the cruise
	$1,674

Divide that $1,674 per person total by seven (the number of days of the cruise) and you'll find that you're paying about $240 per person daily, double occupancy. That figure includes flights, ship transportation, all meals, all ports of call, entertainment, and tips for the duration of the voyage.

You'll need to add on those things you must add on to any vacation: gifts for Aunt Millie and Mom, drinks and tips for the bartender, taxis or buses you take in port, photographs you buy from the ship's photographer, postcards.

There is one more cost and it's an important one: shore excursions. For those, you need to figure about $20 a person in each port, although you need not take the planned shore excursions. If you do decide to take one of the ship's tours ashore, you can find out from your travel agent or the cruise line what those excursions cost and pay for them when you book your cruise. Thus again there will be no surprises.

To satisfy your penurious soul, make the same kind of computation for any other kind of vacation you might have in mind, adding the costs of transportation, seven nights at a hotel, seven nights of entertainment, meals for seven days, and tips (and don't forget all those doormen, bellmen, and maids). Divide your total cost by seven and compare.

If you're bringing children along on your cruise or traveling with friends, you'll find that the rate per person decreases, thanks to the discounts offered for third and fourth passengers sharing a cabin.

You can see that if you're on a strict budget you can figure the price of a cruise vacation right down to the last Indian-head penny. Cruise lines are quite up-front about prices, and they don't toss in a raft of extra hidden fees. Just read the brochure carefully and you'll be able to tally the total cost of your vacation right there at the kitchen table.

3. SEASONAL SAILING

If you've ever traveled to places where sunshine lives all year round, you've discovered there's a definite on-season and a just-as-definite off-season. When you begin to look at the prices of cruises, you find that the best cruise bargains occur in the off-seasons.

When are those? Well, in the Caribbean and Mexico, peak season is the dead of winter when everyone wants to escape the cold, and off-season is from about April through October.

Alaska cruises are cheapest before the weather begins to heat up or when it starts to cool down, roughly early in June and late September.

Best prices on cruises in the northeastern part of the United States and Canada are also at the beginning and the end of the sailing season, say, in June, September, and October.

If you want to cruise the Mississippi River, you'll pay the highest prices in the summer months when everyone else has the same idea. Cool fall and winter months are ideal for budget-watchers.

If you want to travel in the highest-priced season, don't despair. Even then, many fares can be as little as $100 higher per person.

4. MORE BUDGETWISE TIPS

FLEXIBILITY: You can also often save money if you can be flexible. Norwegian Cruise Line, for instance, offers a deal on which they pick the ship, you pick the sailing date. If ports aren't of primary interest to you and you're willing to let the cruise line decide which ship they'll send you on, you can save money with this deal.

No one in the cruise business is going to like this advice, but it's true: if you want to take the risk of waiting until the last minute to book your cruise, you can often walk right up to the booking desk with cash in hand and tell them how much you're willing to pay. Because the cheapest cabins are among the first to sell, those less costly accommodations are likely to be sold out well in advance of sailing. That means you may be able to get a very nice cabin in a higher price category for the minimum price. Cruise lines want to fill those ships, and not all lines are scrupulous about how they do it. On the other hand, not all lines will go for this bluff, so be prepared for a rebuff.

DISCOUNTS: In these days of fierce competition and severe overcapacity, discounting of cruise fares has become the number one moan in the cruise industry. What that means to *you* is that the prices you see in this book are almost surely higher than the prices you will actually have to pay if you take the time to do a little shopping and/or a little research. Even cruise line brochures rarely tell the whole story anymore. Yes, those prices listed in the brochures are the official prices, but almost no one pays them these days, thanks to the advent of discounting.

Discounts now come in so many forms it's difficult even for *us* to know them all—and we look at cruise-ship promotional material every day of our lives, including Sunday. We have not yet seen, but we are expecting any day, a cruise-ship peanut fare. It's likely they'll call it the macadamia-nut fare to shine it up a bit, but whatever they call it, you can be sure there will be a continuing increase in cruise-line discounting of published fares.

Some attribute this adoration for price cutting to the entry into the cruise industry of many former airline executives who learned the value of price slashing amid the sound and fury of airline deregulation. Others say the industry is just responding to the market, which is now crowded, going on jam-packed, with cruise ships, cruise ships, and soon to be more, cruise ships.

Whatever the cause of this slashing competition, for you it's a boon de voyage indeed.

Now you can get a discount if you book six months ahead of sailing; you can get a discount for booking three months ahead of sailing; you can get discounts for booking before a specified date, say January 1 or June 30, and when those dates run out, new discounts go into effect immediately or the old ones are extended.

Then there are Sea Saver and "C" Saver fares, granted to you if you let the line choose which of its ships you sail on. There are free air fares, free land packages, credits for on-board purchases, discounts for repeat passengers, discounts on selected sailings.

There are even discounts for people living in certain parts of the country in which one cruise line or another is trying to stimulate business. You'll see those prices advertised in your local newspapers, although you probably won't know that the discounted price is not also being offered in a neighboring state.

Travel agencies, particularly very large nationwide agencies, that agree to sell large blocks of space aboard a certain line are able to make deals on lower fares and pass some of the saving on to you.

And then there are discounts provided to last-minute-clubs and clearinghouses committed to selling cabins that would go unsold. Most of these book thousands of cruise passengers each year and so are able to secure, far in advance, many cabins on many sailing dates aboard several—or many—cruise ships. By doing that, they get good deals and are able to pass some of their discounts on to you.

One of the better-known cruise clearinghouses is **South Florida Cruises**, a Fort Lauderdale–based company that can be reached, toll free, at 800/327-SHIP. This company says that by allowing individuals to buy at its group rates, it can save its clients $300 to $1,500 on a ticket. There are no membership fees.

Other companies in the discount travel business include **Worldwide Discount Travel** in Miami Beach (tel. 305/534-2082); **Moment's Notice** in New York (tel. 212/253-7824); a Culver City, California, company called **Spur of the Moment** (tel. 213/838-9329, or toll free 800/343-1991); and **Stand-Buys**, a Southfield, Michigan–based company (tel. toll free 800/621-5839). All have annual membership fees in the $35 to $50 range.

Those companies deal primarily in short-term sales, rarely selling any cruise more than two or three months in advance, and often selling a cruise right up to the day it departs. So if you're a last-minute buyer—and have a good idea what you're buying after reading this book!—one of these companies may be the answer to your fiscal prayers.

These agencies, however, are not prepared to spend a lot of time giving you detailed information on cabins and cruises. They are order-takers, and often even have recorded messages outlining the price of a cruise without telling you the ship. If you are about to take your first cruise, you are likely to need more information than this kind of organization can offer you.

Your best bet is to shop around, ask lots of questions, and look into the offerings of a new kind of travel agency, known in the industry as cruise-only agencies, meaning they specialize in cruises and usually sell nothing else. These agencies almost always make their cruise-only status clear in their names—things like Sail Away, Cruise with Yva, any moniker with the word "cruise" prominent in it.

Any large agency of this kind is likely to have at least one sailing available every week at money-saving group rates.

In these competitive times even small agencies, the kind of friendly local places in which you may have been doing business for years, also are tapping into the bargains offered to very large agencies and/or banding together to form their own groups of allied agencies so they can get price breaks.

These days, the clearinghouses and other kinds of travel agencies are becoming specialists. You would do well to ask if the one with which you are dealing specializes in cruises to any certain part of the world, say, the Caribbean or Mediterranean, or in cruises of a certain length, seven-day cruises being the most popular.

There even is a movement afoot to create Frequent Cruiser Clubs, whose members are bent on obtaining the same kinds of giveaway breaks frequent flyers now enjoy.

Finally, there are travel clubs, products of the pre-regulation days when the way to get a cheap airline fare was to charter a plane. These clubs don't meet like the Rotary. Instead they keep you in contact with their bargains through newsletters, and like any club, they have annual dues.

Among the clubs that have been operating in recent years are the **Freighter Travel Club of America**, P.O. Box 12693, Salem, OR 97309; **Trav-L-Tips Cruise & Freighter Travel Assn.**, P.O. Box 188, Flushing, NY 11358; and **World Ocean & Cruise Liner Society**, P.O. Box 92, Stamford, CT 06904.

5. FLY-FREE AND AIR/SEA PROGRAMS

Far and away the best thing that has happened to pennywise cruisers, and to the cruise industry in general, is something called "fly free."

Born in this era of lively competition, **fly-free programs** were devised by cruise lines to lure Californians, for example, to Miami for a cruise on a Miami-based ship, and vice versa—that is, to lure Miamians and New Yorkers to the West Coast to a cruise line based there. In what seemed like minutes these kinds of programs expanded to include Omaha, Des Moines, Toledo, Dallas, Raleigh, Louisville, Savannah, Pittsburgh, Podunk, and your hometown.

Air/sea programs sometimes refer to getting on at one port and flying home from another, with air travel in only one direction. Usually, however, they are programs that include air fare in both directions. These fly-free or air/sea programs fly under all sorts of names too, but you won't have any trouble recognizing them in the brochure, which will spell out the deal in detail.

Now we all know there has been no free lunch for many a blue moon. Cruise companies are not going to break their banks to provide you with free or almost-free air fares. So somewhere along the line those costs are covered. Very large cruise lines, however, move such volumes of people that they are able to make some excellent deals with airlines. You get the benefit of their clout and of their subsidies. So let's not question how those air fares are subsidized. Let's just take advantage of the all-in prices now available to you wherever you live.

Not all lines are offering fly-free programs, but every line we know provides some kind of package that helps you reduce your air fare. These programs are called **air/sea packages**. They offer you air fare and often airport-to-ship transfers for a rate you add on to the price of your cruise. Sometimes they're also called "air add-on rates."

Whatever you call them, they're an excellent bargain, enabling you to go on cruises originating at ports thousands of miles from your home. Once again there are no hidden extras, so you can figure your costs ahead of time.

We've mentioned that point about "hidden extras" so many times that perhaps we just ought to remind you of the time you went off to that sun spot for a vacation. Remember how you thought you had figured the cost of everything right down to the crystal swan for Grandma, when all of a sudden someone totaled up your bill with a 10% government tax and a 15% fuel surcharge and $5 a day for a chaise longue, and a $20 cover charge in the nightclub, not to mention the three-drink minimum? Whoops, there went $50 a day you hadn't figured on, and/or there went the old credit-card limit.

Absence of just such dismays is the very best part of a cruise vacation, as cruise sellers will be quick to tell you.

6. WHEN IS A BARGAIN WORTH THE PRICE?

While you're mulling over all those glossy brochures full of romantic pictures of tempting ports and moonlit moments, keep in mind that the old saw about getting what you pay for is most often spoken in moments of serious displeasure.

Ships are as different as people. Each one is designed especially to appeal to a certain market, and it behooves you to know what kind of market that is. In our outline of the ships and the lines (coming up in Chapter V) we have tried to indicate what you can expect of the line and your fellow passengers.

In general, cruise lines charging very low prices will attract passengers in concomitant social, economic, and educational levels. Often those ships are among the older ships afloat as well. Entertainment is nonstop and geared toward beer-drinking competitions, pillow fights, bawdy contests.

Lines with prices in the middle bracket generally feature less raucous entertainment, although every bit as much of it. Overused as in the term "laid-back," this is one place it cannot be topped. Activities are simply more laid-back, quieter, more sedate. On these ships your fellow passengers will be a bit older and more sophisticated, probably in a middle to upper income bracket.

Ships that charge the highest prices are, of course, luxury cruisers aiming their appeal at sophisticated, well-traveled, high-income voyagers with time and money to spend. Life is more formal aboard and the masquerade party, if there is one, is more likely to star historical characters than male hula dancers dressed in beer cans. Afternoon tea is actually attended and enjoyed. Activities are generally quite genteel, with an emphasis on elaborate candlelit dinners, lectures, showy evening entertainment, casinos.

Each of the three has its own kind of appeal, but only you can know which will be of most interest to you.

7. TIPPING

Here comes that dreaded subject. One day near the end of your cruise, your cruise director will drop his voice a level or two and intone: "Now, ladies and gentlemen, on this matter of tipping. . . ." You begin to squirm. But fear not. It's really much easier than you think.

Every cruise ship distributes cruise information brochures on board, and one of them is sure to contain what the line considers the basic tip for your cabin steward, and your dining room waiter and busboy. On some lines the business of tipping seems to have become just that: a business Some cruise directors are downright tacky in their outline of what to tip their fellow workers and so pushy as to make you want to keelhaul them all the way back to port. This is a rarity, however, and we feel sure the line would like to know if its cruise director is offensive in his handling of the delicate matter of tipping.

Most lines recommend a minimum of $3 per person a day for the cabin steward, $3 a day per person for the dining room steward (your waiter) and $1 a day for the busboy. A few lines recommend tips totaling $6 a day.

Greek lines traditionally ask you to collect all your tips together at the end of the voyage and turn them in to a central source, from which they are evenly distributed to the crew.

On the *QE2,* recommended daily tips are $12 per person divided between the cabin steward and the waiter for passengers in upper-price levels. If you're traveling in a middle-bracket cabin, the recommended daily tip is $10 (same split), and for those in the lowest-priced cabins, $8 per person daily.

If the maître d'hôtel in the dining room has been particularly pleasant and/or attentive to some special request, you could slip him something appropriate to the situation.

Wine stewards, or sommeliers as they are often called, and bartenders on the ship are generally tipped 15% of the bill each time you order wine in the dining room or a drink at the bar, just as you would on land. You can tip them at the conclusion of the voyage, too, if you like.

Those are the basic recommended tips. If a cabin or dining room steward has been particularly wonderful—and they are often awesomely courteous, friendly, and out-of-their-way helpful—you can, of course, tip more lavishly.

Now, wasn't that painless?

Small as it may seem, a brief letter in praise of a particularly outstanding employee is a wonderful gesture that will earn you a lifelong friend and may earn that friend a promotion. Cruise lines put much stock in letters and comments from passengers, so if you want to give a newfound friend a lasting remembrance in addition to your financial one, send that letter or mention the name of that outstanding worker on your end-of-cruise comment sheet.

One more thing: Ignore all this tipping advice on Holland America Line/Westours. This chic and forward-thinking cruise line has a no-tipping-required policy, for which we offer them a 21-gun salute and a series of enthusiastic hip-hip-hoorays.

Still one more thing: Never, never, but absolutely *never* ever offer the captain or any of the ship's officers a tip. That is gauche beyond words.

8. SHORE EXCURSIONS

Happy as you are sailing along in your little 30,000-ton cocoon, sooner or later you will hear the chains rattling and clanking as the ship's anchor drops into the sea. Land ho, maties.

You will not arrive unprepared. First, you will have this guide to every port we could think of; and second, you will have heard a when-we-dock-tomorrow lecture from the cruise director.

Some of those presentations are so detailed that they become a mini-marketplace. On one ship we sailed, the presentation lasted well over an hour and included 5 minutes of local history and 55 minutes of shopping advice. You could, however, hardly call it *good* shopping advice since nearly every store in that port was recommended, and some were pushed with such fervor we began to wonder if this was a paid advertisement.

We regret to say that many cruise lines do a poor job of preparing you for the ports you are to visit. Most cruise directors certainly seem to know where every shop is located, but they know—or at least they tell passengers—very little about the history and cultural background of ports.

That generalization is particularly true of Caribbean cruises, less true on Alaskan voyages where some quite interesting wildlife talks are presented by a naturalist. His presence there is required by the park through which the ship cruises, however, so perhaps cruise lines should get less credit for these outstanding presentations.

You will also find, particularly on Caribbean cruises, some very enthusiastic sales of shore excursions. These are sometimes worthwhile, but more often, sadly, are not.

As a rule of thumb, if the shore excursion goes to a particular place of interest—Dunn's River Falls in Jamaica, for instance—go along. Hiring a taxi to get you there will probably cost nearly as much or more, and will be less convenient.

Otherwise, your enjoyment of a shore excursion will depend on how much you hope to get from it. Most do a very superficial job, ferrying you around the highlights with a few minutes here and a few minutes there.

If you're a shopping fanatic, you'll probably want to skip most shore excursions since they often leave you only a short time for shopping and/or take you to one store where you vie with a busload of other travelers for the attention of harried clerks.

If you want to go shopping, walk, hail a cab, or take a bus from the ship to town and go shopping. Your time will be your own and you can muse over the relative merits of those two gorgeous straw baskets for hours if you like.

If you're a history buff, you might do well to bone up on the sights you'll be visiting, then go on your own walking or driving tour to those sights. Most shore excursions are not history oriented. A shore excursion is a must in Cancún, but be prepared for a two- to three-hour bus trip in each direction (it's well worth it, however, for a look at one of the architectural wonders of the Western world).

Garden and flower enthusiasts often really enjoy Caribbean island tours, for instance, as they generally include a look at a botanical garden and a description of odd tropical vegetation.

Look over the ship's description of shore excursions carefully, however, and ask for some very specific information on just what you will see and do.

A shore excursion we took on one Caribbean island drove endlessly around in a barely air-conditioned bus, visited a tiny, smelly, and downright depressing zoo, then stopped at a hotel for drinks. A final stop at an island church would have been the ultimate boring blow had not a lady at the back of the church been performing a pagan healing rite on a parishioner, offering us a look at the cultural elements that have been successfully assimilated on the island. That hot and dusty bus ride cost about $20 each, and was a most miserable way to blow $40.

Don't be afraid to talk with other passengers who might have visited the port before to find out whether a shore excursion is worth the money. In most small Caribbean islands you'll do just as well or better by rounding up a couple of other adventuresome types and dividing the cost of a taxi or a car. Seek out a driver with air conditioning and make sure he promises to turn it on—fuel charges are high in the Caribbean and drivers will leave the cool off if you don't make a point of it.

Don't be afraid to bargain about the price of a taxi for the day or half day, but make sure that the final amount you negotiate is as clear in the driver's mind as it is in yours. If there's a bit of a language barrier, write the numbers down on a piece of paper. Money numbers are an international language! And pay at the end of the agreed-upon time, never at the beginning.

Shore excursions are usually $20 to $35 a person, but can be $10 less or umpteen dollars more if the tour takes you a very long distance from the ship.

Don't think you are leaving civilization behind because you are visiting Mexico or the Caribbean. Rental cars are ever with us and available in practically any port. In most, your Stateside driving license will get you on the road in the flash of a credit card or cash.

It may also be wise to make rental-car reservations through a travel agent or an international company before you leave on your trip. That way you can be sure a car, and the kind of car you want, will be there when you arrive. You can also pay for the car in advance. That little bit of planning cuts down wasted time too.

Rental-car rates are generally higher in the islands than Stateside, and cars are often not the clean and serviceable autos you've come to expect here. You aren't likely to have any problems, but allow yourself plenty of time to get back to the ship just in case something breaks or goes flat. And write down the telephone number of the rental-car office.

Some travelers have been known to take bicycles with them on their journeys, wheel them off the ship onto the dock, and just ride off on their own excursions. We've never tried it, but it sounds interesting.

Among the better bargains in shore excursions, especially for first-time cruisers, are the dive-in expeditions now offered by nearly every Caribbean cruise line. These provide you with snorkel and flippers and sometimes even a commemorative T-shirt that will be instant status back in the old neighborhood. On board the day before you reach port, diving instructors who are certified scuba-divers will brief you in the best way to avoid snorkeling up half the ocean and show you how to keep your diving mask unsteamed while breathing heavily at the sight of a bikini atoll.

Once the ship has docked in port, you meet your diving cohorts and instructors for a minibus ride to the best diving areas. After hours of diving and pointing and playing with starfish, you return exhausted to the ship where you try unsuccessfully to describe the wonders you've seen in that glittering and indescribable underwater world.

Excursions like that cost about $20 to $25 on most ships, and are worth the money. If you're an experienced diver and/or know your way around an island, you can often find your own good reef, and on many islands there are fine places to dive not far from the ship. Just don't go diving alone under any circumstances. *Ever.*

9. FUN AND GAMES AND OTHER EXPENSES

While none of your food or entertainment on board will cost you a cent, you should budget some money for other small expenses.

You'll probably want to play Bingo, for which you pay about $1 a card. Bets on the ship's horse races are usually at least $1 each. On some ships there's betting on the distance the ship will travel that day—it's called "the pool"—and of course, betting in the casino.

Photographs you buy from on-board photographers will cost $4 to $5 each. You'll probably be tempted to buy at least a few of the many that will be taken of you just to be sure you have some record of this vacation event.

Shopping on board and in port will require some dollars, as will taxis or buses you take to and from the docks at some ports.

Drinks, wine, and champagne are generally cheaper aboard cruise ships than they are ashore, but will still cost something. Mixed drinks are usually less than $2, although some fancy concoctions may be $3 or so, often including the fancy glass in which they are served. Bottles of wine can range from a reasonable $8 to $10 to the heights of fancy, as can champagne.

You pay for, and tip for, drinks when they are served, unless you're traveling on one of the ships that permits you to settle your account at the end of the voyage.

Credit cards? Yes, in most ships' gift shops; maybe in the bar, maybe not. Yes, on shore in almost all shops. Check with the line for its regulations on the use of credit cards aboard and in payment for tickets.

If you're planning to call home while you're on board or in port, budget some money for the calls. They are quite expensive, so if you can avoid them, do. If it's absolutely necessary, figure at least $15 to $20 a minute.

CHAPTER III

IS THAT YOUR SHIP COMING IN?: SELECTING YOUR CRUISE

▫ ▫ ▫

1. PRICE
2. ENTERTAINMENT
3. CREW NATIONALITY
4. PORTS
5. FELLOW PASSENGERS AND OTHER SPECIAL PEOPLE
6. LONG VS. SHORT CRUISES

That "cruise revolution" the cruise industry touts is occurring for the same reason there are horse races: a difference of opinion.

It won't take you long to discover that a discussion of the perfect cruise ship is a little like talking politics or religion. People may not agree, but they will certainly have something to say on the subject.

Naturally such a wide range of opinions on what makes a cruise perfect has led to a proliferation of cruise-ship marketing approaches. Those variations in approach determine a ship's personality, and that personality determines what your fellow passengers will be like and what ambience you will find on board.

No matter what kind of personality *you* have, there is a ship that will offer you food, activities, ports, accommodations, and service that will bring you joy and joyous memories. Some will do that better than others, but all will accomplish the goal to some degree. So now's the time for a little personal assessment of your own personality and the personalities of those traveling with you.

Ships aren't anthropomorphized with that "her" label for no reason: they really do have personalities. To be perhaps a bit more accurate about that, it's really the crew, the officers, and the philosophy of the ship's owners that impart "personality" to the vessel. Food, entertainment, crew nationality, crew-to-passenger ratio, cruise length, and even historical factors all play a part in the creation of a ship's personality too.

Basically those personalities break down to informal or formal atmosphere on board. That formality, or lack of it, is reflected in luxuriousness of accommodations, cruise price, on-board entertainment, and often in crew-to-passenger ratio.

Let's take a look at some of the things that determine a cruise ship's personality.

1. PRICE

It probably will come as no surprise to you that price is an important determinant of a cruise ship's personality. On ships too, price is a very good guideline to the kind of atmosphere you'll find on board. Luxury ships that charge high prices are quite like their counterparts in the hotel business. Those who can afford them are often older, more sophisticated travelers in search of a quiet, refined atmosphere with plenty of good food and good service. So you can see that price helps determine the kinds of passengers who will be sharing your cruise.

That brings us to crew-to-passenger ratio, another indicator of personality. All ships these days tend to offer quite a lot of service and have the staff to maintain it. Those with a crewman for every two passengers or fewer are likely to offer you more, and more thorough, service than those with a lower crew-to-passenger ratio. That ratio is closely related to the price you pay for the cruise as well.

Price also determines the luxuriousness of your accommodations aboard. Luxury cruise ships with the highest per diem rates offer you very spiffy quarters that are not only attractively decorated but are also clean, neat, well cared for, and large.

2. ENTERTAINMENT

Surprisingly enough, the kind of entertainment offered on board is often a good indicator of a ship's "personality."

Some ships offer lots of crazy, ringy-dingy, ice-breaker party games on board, so naturally the atmosphere on those vessels is relaxed, casual, informal, chummy. Low- and mid-priced vessels are generally characterized by this emphasis on on-board activities.

On the other end of the spectrum are higher priced vessels that stick to educational lectures, fine musical entertainment, and quieter pursuits that tend to lure more sophisticated, upscale travelers who expect a certain degree of decorum from crew and other passengers. That generally sets the stage for a more formal atmosphere aboard.

In the middle are those lines, usually the mid-priced ships, that juggle a combination of the two, offering both quiet pursuits and lively ones in an atmosphere that's formal on special evenings, unstructured and informal all the rest of the time.

3. CREW NATIONALITY

Relax, we're not going to get into any ethnic slurs here. But it is true that certain nationalities create certain atmospheres. And nowhere will you be more aware of that than on a ship.

Italians, for instance, are exuberant, volatile folks who would jump ship if there weren't good food aboard. When the dining room staff or a majority of the crew is Italian, you can be sure the food will be wonderful. You can also be sure that your waiter will be as solicitous as Mom, admonishing you to eat your pasta or you won't grow up to be big and strong. (These fellows seem to get as much pleasure out of your meals as you do!) Italians control the dining room or the ship on Sitmar Cruises, Costa Cruises, and Carnival Cruise Lines, among others.

Greeks are much like Italians, although one suspects they will not be thrilled with that assessment. They are most hospitable, full of flashing good humor, and quite attentive to your every wish. You'll find Greeks aboard Epirotiki Lines, Royal Cruise Line, Sun Line Cruises, and Chandris Fantasy Cruises, among others.

We are convinced that Scandinavians run the cleanest, most organized ships afloat. Dust is the enemy aboard Scandinavian-operated ships, so you'll never see any. Norwegians, who run many of the ships operating in North American waters, have a droll sense of humor too. It creeps up on you when you're not expecting it. Norwegians *adore* a good joke, so have a few ready. Scandinavian officers run the show aboard Norwegian Cruise Line, Royal Caribbean Cruise Line, and Royal Viking Line.

Indonesians are much loved by many cruise enthusiasts for their polite and courteous service. Many of them work as cabin stewards on board quite a number of ships, including Holland America Line/Westours.

Dutch officers aboard the Holland America Line/Westours ships run very handsome, clean, and efficient ships.

British personnel are typically British, either quite formal or just the opposite. Of the Cunard vessels, the *QE2* is often said to have a formal stiff-upper-lip crew while the smaller ships, the *Cunard Princess* and *Cunard Countess,* are considered more casual operations, much more informal. Of P&O/Princess Cruises' three seven-day cruisers the *Pacific Princess* and *Island Princess* are somewhat more staid than the *Sun Princess.*

On many Caribbean ships much of the staff hails from one of the many islands you'll be visiting. You can learn much from them about the history of their islands, so don't be afraid to ask what life is like in Trinidad or Jamaica.

Americans are often part of the ship's crew, most frequently performing host duties assigned to employees known as the cruise staff. That often includes the fitness director, the children's program staffers, cruise director, and on-board entertainment staff. The theory is that they understand Americans well, if that's possible, and are better prepared to deal closely with them as this part of the staff must. You'll also find American crews on board the small coastal cruisers that operate in the South and Northeast—American and Clipper Cruise Lines, for instance—and on the *Delta Queen* and *Mississippi Queen* that ply the Mississippi River. Americans, many of them from Hawaii, staff American Hawaii Cruises' *Independence* and *Constitution* too.

4. PORTS

Some cruise lines want to emphasize your on-board experience. These offer you little time in port in comparison to the amount of time you spend on board. Carnival Cruise Lines, for instance, is dedicated to this precept of maximizing the on-board experience and minimizing time in port.

Other lines figure you want to see ports, so they take you to three or more on a week's voyage, offering you a day or so in each. One cruise-line president makes frequent speeches in which he maintains that ports are what sell cruises. Consistent with that philosophy, his Royal Cruise Line offers you a choice of many, many exotic stops. Others, Sun Line Cruises and Epirotiki Lines, for example, on their Caribbean and South American cruises offer you a new port each day of your cruise with only a few days spent solely at sea.

In general, ships that offer quite a number of ports tend also to offer longer and higher-priced cruises that appeal to older, well-heeled travelers.

If you love beaches, Norwegian Cruise Line started quite a trend when it bought a Bahamian Out-Island for its very own and began spending one cruise day anchored off that island. Now Admiral Cruise Line, operators of the *Emerald Seas,* has bought an adjacent island and Royal Caribbean Cruise Line has created a resort area in Haiti.

If shopping is your first and foremost interest, you'll want to sail on a ship bound for Mexico, the Bahamas, or the Virgin Islands, each of which offers you duty-free treasures, lovely straw goods, very good liquor bargains, or in the case of Mexico, some indigenous craftwork and silver at very good prices.

5. FELLOW PASSENGERS AND OTHER SPECIAL PEOPLE

It's a maxim in the cruise industry that the longer the cruise, the older the passengers. That figures. Younger passengers, however much they may dream of long journeys, usually have neither the time nor the money to spare. Retired couples, on the other hand, often have both, so they can sail off on a two- or three-week journey or longer with nary a second thought. And why not? They've certainly earned it.

That means that if you're looking for a youthful crowd you'll want to search for your perfect ship among the three- or four-day voyagers or the week-long cruises.

On Inland Waterway, U.S. Coastline, and Alaska cruises, you also will find an older clientele and/or people interested in natural beauty, history, and fascinating ports like Annapolis, Boston, Québec City, and Newport.

It's an old and overused joke in the cruise industry that the average age aboard used to be "deceased." We say "used to be" because the times they are a-changing. These days 60% of the world's cruise passengers are younger than 55 and 30% are younger than 35. So there! Whatever ship you take will probably have a wide variety of ages on board among both passengers and crew.

If you're looking for a gambling, drinking, and fun-loving crowd, you'll be happiest on one of the partying three- or four-day cruise ships or a seven-day sailer. On those you'll be caught up in the fun of Bingo and horse races, sports competitions and trivia contests, dance lessons and hula instructions, steel bands and rum punch.

Water babies should look for ships that visit several beach destinations, places like Jamaica, Grand Cayman, Cozumél. Most of the seven-day ships offer supervised diving programs that even the rankest underwater amateur can participate in and enjoy.

Ah, yes, what have we for lovers? An issue of *Cruise* magazine, a bimonthly publication for cruise enthusiasts, carried some amusing letters from lovers protesting the absence of love on all these "love" boats. How, readers asked, can you carry on a romance in twin beds, or worse, upper and lower berths? Inconveniently, that's how.

There is, however, some good news. Cruise lines in search of younger faces have realized the appeal of king-size, queen-size, and double beds, and are acting accordingly. New ships, ships being renovated, and even some of the older craft are outfitting at least some cabins with double beds or twin beds that can be pushed together to create king-size sleepers.

Regrettably for the future of love afloat, there are still not many of those cuddle quarters available. If you are thinking of a honeymoon or anniversary cruise, or think the joy of a cruise is related to your sleeping facilities, you should read the cruise line brochures carefully, speak to a travel agent, and book early.

Sad to say, you can no longer be married on board a ship, but some lines will arrange for you and the bridal party to exchange *dockside* vows, then sail away into the sunset—all of you together, if you like! At least one line, Norwegian Caribbean Lines, even has a special honeymooners program, and most lines offer you some special recognition and souvenirs if you're on your honeymoon. Tell the line or your agent about your wedding trip plans.

If just the opposite is what you have in mind—single blessedness—fear not, you're in the right place. In fact there may not be a better place to meet likely eligibles than on a cruise ship. Small ships carrying lots of passengers throw you into close proximity with hundreds of potential friends, and every ship we've ever sailed has had at least one get-together for single passengers early on in the cruise.

Norwegian Cruise Line and Carnival Cruise Lines ships are good singles hunting grounds, as are Cunard's *Countess* and *Princess,* Princess's *Sun Princess,* and three- and four-night party cruises aboard Admiral Cruise Line's *Emerald Seas* on the East Coast and *Azure Seas* on the West Coast, and Dolphin Cruise Line's *Dolphin* from Miami. For huntresses, there are some marvelously goodlooking crewmen aboard all the ships—just pick your nationality and go for it!

If you have a handicap that makes it difficult for you to move about, you will need to check ship brochures carefully. You'd be well advised to seek the help of a travel agent and to check with the line before you buy your tickets. Newer ships tend to have the wide hallways necessary to accommodate wheelchairs, and none of the high steps and barriers that make life so difficult for people with mobility problems. Older ships tend to be less accessible. If you travel by wheelchair, most lines require you to be accompanied because there is simply not enough staff to help you get from place to place. Some lines also are quite definite about the measurements of the wheelchair too.

Ask a travel agent or the line if the ship docks in port or anchors out and takes passengers to shore by tender. Travel by tender (that's a small boat) is difficult if not impossible for handicapped travelers. Check, too, on the presence or absence of elevators, and find out which of the ship's facilities may be denied you if you cannot walk to them.

Even geography will affect the kinds of passengers you find on board. Westerners are different from easterners, there's no doubt about it. On ships based in California most of your fellow cruisers will be from the western states, and will appreciate western humor, music, and Las Vegas-y entertainment. On the East Coast passengers seem to share an interest in beautiful beaches, sports, and fitness activities, along with the usual drinking, gambling, and general partying.

Kids? Kids on a cruise? Did we say bring the *kids*? Certainly we said bring the kids. Get them across the gangplank, enter them in the youth program, and don't plan to run across them for the rest of the voyage.

Once again, the changing age patterns of the traveling public have led to the emergence of cruise ships that have extensive programs for youngsters. Sitmar, Costa, Cunard's *QE2,* and Holland America all welcome the young ones, and have full schedules of activities for them, often in port as well as on the ship. Youngsters of all ages become quite popular people on board a cruise ship, both with the crew and with other passengers. They get into everything, know every inch of the ship better, it seems, than some of the crew, and they know every shred of gossip practically as soon as it's born. And they have a wonderful time too, making new friends of all ages.

6. LONG VS. SHORT CRUISES

Naturally, the first two things you'll have to consider when you begin planning a cruise are time and money.

If you don't have much of either, you might want to get your feet wet, so to speak, with a three- or four-night cruise. Most of those will take you to the Bahamas or Mexico. There are even a few one- and two-night cruises—SeaEscape, for instance—sailing from Miami, Tampa, or Cape Canaveral on one-day journeys to Freeport and back, or to nowhere at all. Some cruise lines, stuck with a day before a major cruise begins or after one ends, also will feature a day-or-two voyage to nowhere, cruising aimlessly around out of sight of land but still offering you all the sun and fun amenities of life on a cruise ship.

If three or four days sounds altogether too short to you, try a seven-night cruise. You'll have a wide range of choices from the huge *Norway* to the small *New Shoreham* or *Newport Clipper,* among others. In five nights at sea you can become a transatlantic traveler, sailing on the *QE2* from New York to England or France. On a seven-day cruise you can visit sunny Caribbean islands, Mexico, Canada, the Yucatán Peninsula, Alaska, or explore the Hawaiian Islands.

On most seven-day cruises you'll have the fun and relaxation of two or three days at sea and two or three days in port, sometimes at night, sometimes by day, sometimes both. That way you get all the experiences rolled up in one week's journey.

If you have ten days or two weeks available, you might consider cruises from San Francisco or Los Angeles to Alaska or Mexico, from New York to the Northeast and Canada, from Miami to South America or deep into the Caribbean.

In two weeks you can also sail from Florida or California on a thrilling journey through the Panama Canal or to South America up the remote Orinoco or Amazon Rivers. You can paddlewheel your way up the Mississippi River all the way from New Orleans to Minnesota, or sail down the Intracoastal Waterway from the Northeast to Florida. In ten days or more you can also sail on a transatlantic trip from Florida to Europe.

Beyond two weeks the world is yours. In three weeks you can go deep into South America, sail to Europe from California or Florida. Longer than that and you can go on an around-the-world voyage, visit the Arctic Circle and the fjords of Scandinavia, cruise to fabled ports in India, the Far East, even Russia, or sail lazily about the South Pacific visiting dream-finder ports like Tahiti and Bora Bora.

CHAPTER IV

YOUR HOME IS YOUR CABIN: CHOOSING QUARTERS

□ □ □

1. HOW IT WILL LOOK
2. CABIN LOCATION
3. SHARING A CABIN

Selecting a cabin is important, as you can see by a quick check of the title of this chapter. That is why we're discussing the ins and outs of cabin selection before presenting detailed descriptions of those dream cruise ships. Just hang in through this material, for we think it will make the next chapter more useful and meaningful to you.

There are two schools of thought about cabins. One maintains that the size of the cabin is of little or no importance because you'll be spending almost all your time in the ship's bars and lounges, dining room and nightclubs, decks and swimming pool, saunas and gymnasium. Ships that feature dawn-to-dawn activity encourage you to get out of your cabin shell and come join the fun. Some not only encourage you verbally, but their encouragement takes the form of cabins that are small enough and/or so lacking in lounging spaces you wouldn't want to spend much time in there anyway!

Another school of thought maintains that your cabin will be your home away from home and ought to offer you the option of spending as much or as little time in it as you like.

Your personality and the personality of those with whom you are traveling ought to be taken into consideration when you are selecting a cabin. If you are a reader or a crossword-puzzle fanatic, for instance, your idea of a paradisical cruise may be a thick novel or the London *Times* puzzler—and the time to pursue that amusement. If that's the case, you'll probably be happier with a cabin that has a chair or two or a bed that can be converted by day into a sitting area.

A small cabin is less important on a week-long voyage where you will be too busy to spend much time in it.

To a great extent the kind of cabin you book will depend on how much money you have to spend and how soon you decide to spend it. If you book well in advance, say, two or three months ahead of your departure date, you can usually be sure of getting exactly the kind of cabin you want.

Cruise lines generally will not guarantee you any particular cabin, but they will certainly guarantee you the price category you request, and will do the best they can to give you whatever cabin will make you happy.

Here's the good news in cabin selection: no matter how much or how little you spend for your accommodations, you will be treated to the same service, the same entertainment, the same facilities, and on all ships except the *QE2*, the same food as those paying a little or a lot more for their stateroom.

1. HOW IT WILL LOOK

So what will it look like, this place in which you are going to hang your hat and quite a lot of other things?

CABIN SPACE: Well, first of all, it will be *small*, at least in comparison to rooms in which you probably are accustomed to spending your time. Cabins simply are not hotel rooms, unless you buy a large, high-priced suite. Strangely enough, the newer the ship, generally the smaller the cabin. Many new ships have been built to maximize profits and glamorize public space. Something had to give of course, and that is usually cabin space.

On many of the most popular new ships your cabin will be long and narrow, about half the size of a normal hotel/motel room. It will have a vanity/desk/dresser with a chair, closet space that is perhaps curtained off from the rest of the room, some drawer space tucked away somewhere, and usually a nightstand near the beds.

Much as we all worship modernity, old is really beautiful on cruise ships. Not only will you find much larger cabins for the price on older ships, but you'll also find lots of interesting little touches axed by the plastic age: things like shiny wood paneling and glittering brass edgings; little drop-down trays built into the wall over your bed with a recessed section that holds a glass firm in wavy weather; railed space on the dressers so your bottles don't spill; built-in reading lamps over the bed.

Suites are, of course, the most luxurious accommodations aboard, and they are always lovely. In looking over dozens of ships we have yet to find a shabby suite. Most of them offer you lots of space for the money, with a separate sitting area outfitted with full couch or loveseat, a chair or two, a low coffee table. In a separate room, either curtained or walled off, are double, king-size, or twin beds.

Décor ranges from, say, deep hunter-green velvet and gorgeous mahogany paneling on Sitmar Cruises' *Fairwind* to soft pastel leathers on Royal Caribbean Cruise Line's *Sovereign of the Seas*. In between are contemporary and old-world looks, fancy and simple furnishings, but always lots and lots of space. If you can afford it, suite accommodations are sweet indeed.

New ships feature cabins so alike in size it seems to us ridiculous to pay for a higher-priced cabin. All you're buying is a cabin on a deck closer to the public rooms. If you'd like to save some money on one of these ships, book the least expensive inside or outside cabins—but book them early because they go fast.

To figure out how much space you are likely to have in your cabin, look at the deck plan, find the cabin category you're interested in, and examine those cabins closely. If you assume that the beds are about two feet wide by six feet long, then you'll be able to figure out how much empty space, closet space, etc., there is in the room.

On some ships you really won't notice much of a difference between your cabin and a higher-priced one. You can tell which ships these are when you see the deck plans. Deck plans are to scale, so if you can't see much or any difference in size among the cabins, it's safe to assume that there is none or so little as not to make any difference.

In general we'd say that if you're going on a long cruise of ten days or more, you probably should try to eke out a few dollars more for larger accommodations. On long voyages you'll probably want to spend more time in your room. On a short cruise you'll be home before you've tried out all the activities the ship has to offer.

BATHROOMS: These days nearly every ship afloat has a private bathroom for every cabin. If there are a few cabins available without private bath, they are noted in the ship's brochure and there will be shared facilities nearby. If that arrangement is acceptable to you, you can save quite a lot of money on accommodations without baths. Once again, very, very few ships have cabins without baths.

Bathrooms on most ships are just big enough for one, but don't drop anything—most of the time they're not large enough to bend over in without bumping into something.

Generally, more expensive cabins will have a bathtub as well as a shower. If you think you cannot get along without your bubble bath, be sure to look over the ship's brochure carefully to see exactly what you're buying. Showers are tiny, and on some ships feature hand-held shower heads that can be snapped into the wall so you don't have to hold them. These may sound strange to you, but they're a godsend if you want to shower without getting your hair wet. On a few of the very smallest coastal sailing ships the shower is not enclosed and sprays all over everything—not ideal, but you do eventually learn to cope.

You will see some very unusual plumbing aboard some ships, particularly those built a decade or three ago. We've seen ice-water spigots in the bathroom, skinny foot-long spigots, spindly legged sinks, and some real antiquarian hardware. It all worked, however, and that's what really matters. On some ships you may find a bidet in the bathroom. No, it isn't a footbath.

BEDS: That brings us to beds. On cruise ships these come in all shapes and forms. In the wake of "Love Boat" many more ships are now beginning to include some double beds in their cabin rosters. These are still comparatively rare, however, so if you want cuddle quarters you should book them well in advance of your sailing date.

Most middle-priced cabins have twin beds. On some newer ships, like Carnival Cruise Lines' *Holiday,* for instance, they can be pushed together to form a king-size bed, but on many ships that's not possible.

Cheaper accommodations have upper and lower berths. A berth is a mattress tucked into a wooden frame. Pullman berths usually refer to beds of this kind that flip up during the day, more or less the way a Murphy bed does, and tuck away against the wall out of sight. Your cabin steward will see to it that the bed is flipped up in the morning and flipped down at night. You climb up to the bed on a ladder. Youngsters adore these aeries, but adults are a bit less keen on them.

On some ships you'll find a high-backed couch or two in your cabin. At night the cabin steward pulls down the back and the whole business becomes a bed. These are strictly a ship invention, quite different from convertible couches.

On some ships the bed flips up from the floor to tuck away against the wall with one edge designed to hold your champagne bucket in daylight hours!

Beds are most often parallel to each other, but sometimes are placed at right angles, in an L shape. That latter configuration gives you more floor space and makes your quarters look larger. It's preferable if you can get it.

ELECTRICAL OUTLETS: On most ships you won't blow fuses all the way

128 □ **DOLLARWISE GUIDE TO CRUISES**

Song of America

Upper Deck

Sun and Compass Decks

Bridge Deck

Promenade Deck

CHOOSING A CABIN □ 129

Cabaret Deck   Main Deck   "A" Deck   "B" Deck

down the hall if you plug in your hairdryer, but on older ships that can happen. In deference to the widespread use of hairdryers, however, all ships have made some kind of arrangements for their use. Exactly what that arrangement is will usually be detailed in the ship's brochure. If it isn't, call or write the line and ask, or ask your travel agent. Some ships have vanity rooms in fairly convenient locations and require you to go to one of these to use your hairdryer. It's not convenient, but once again you do eventually adjust.

Outlets for electric razors seem to be available on every ship, but if the line's brochures don't answer your questions, call or write and ask.

Most ships frown on the use of travel irons in your room, but some provide small rooms set up with irons and ironing board. You can have the pressing, as well as laundry and sometimes dry cleaning, done for you on most ships too.

You may also find some ships with European outlets that require converter plugs. These are available in some drugstores and many travel shops. Little gizmos that step down the voltage also are available.

ATYPICAL STATISTICS: To give you an idea what a massive place a cruise ship can be, we thought you might be interested in taking a look at some of the things in the linen and china closets aboard the *Norway,* the largest ship afloat:

Pillows	3,600
Curtain fabric	4.38 miles
Furniture fabric	3.75 miles
Bath towels	12,000
Sheets	21,000
Napkins	18,000
Tablecloths	3,160
Glassware	32,880 pieces
Silverware	52,000 pieces
China	92,500 pieces
Art objects	1,800 pieces

2. CABIN LOCATION

As long as you're looking at those deck plans, take a look at the deck above and below you.

If you're a nightowl you may not care that your room is located near the disco which howls to the wee hours. If you rise with the robins, however, you'll go nuts in that room.

Rooms low in the ship are best for those who fear they may suffer from motion sickness. Cabins near the middle of the ship also offer a smoother ride. On most cruises you'll hardly notice the roll of the ship, but transatlantic crossings, particularly in spring or fall, can be rough. (See Chapter XII on mal de mer.)

If you have any kind of handicap that makes walking difficult, book a cabin near the elevators. However, cabins beside or behind elevators can be good price and size bargains but may also be noisy.

On some ships cabins near the ship's engines or anchors can be noisy, and cabins near the galley likewise.

Generally, the higher the deck on which your chosen cabin is located, the higher the price. That's thought to be a leftover of old transoceanic days when higher cabins were sunnier, farther away from engine noise, and the coolest or warmest aboard, depending on where you were. Today all those conditions are controlled in other ways (air conditioning, soundproofing, etc.) but the price differences remain. If you like the status of a good address, book a cabin high up on the ship. Otherwise don't bother.

Families or friends traveling together can often book connecting cabins, but you should know that the door between connecting rooms lets you *both* hear what's being said next door. Give up catty remarks and/or avoid connecting cabins.

You'll often find that cabins in the bow or stern of the ship are less expensive than those in the center. That's because the ship narrows at those points, curving inward. Cabins in those areas curve right along with it so they're often, but not always, a few feet smaller and crescent-shaped.

On some ships this kind of "smaller" means very small indeed (*Sunward II,* for example) while on others (the *Vistafjord,* for instance) the loss of space is barely noticeable, thanks to clever interior design that turns lemon into lemonade. You can often save quite a bit of money on one of these cabins, but you'll need the help of a travel agent or someone else who has seen the ship and knows if a miracle has or has not been wrought.

Obviously, if you get the least feeling of motion amidships, you get more in the bow or stern, but once again let us stress that the kind of rough seas that cause most people's motion sickness are really quite rare in today's cruise world.

INSIDE VS. OUTSIDE: Old hands at cruising may skip this sentence, but if you're new to cruises you'll want to know that outside cabins are those located on the outer edges of the ship, and inside quarters are those that run down the middle of the ship, tucked in between the outside rooms.

Which is better is a source of continuing debate that boils down to your need for a view of the outside world versus your desire to save money.

Inside cabins are darker and usually, although not always, smaller than outside quarters. If you don't care about light or space, and/or don't plan to spend much time in your cabin, go ahead and book the inside room. You may save yourself quite a lot of money. Inside cabins are great for late sleepers too—absolutely no fear that the sun will wake you.

If, on the other hand, you worry about claustrophobia, stick to outside cabins where a full-fledged window or a small porthole will let in the light and let you see what the weather is like today. Generally, the more expensive the cabin, the bigger the window and/or the more of them you have in your room.

Ships are air-conditioned these days and portholes are almost always sealed shut, so don't expect to enjoy the sea air through them. Out on deck you'll find all the sea air you can breathe.

Many ships now use contemporary lighting so cleverly that inside cabins are so bright and cheery you never miss the window. Cunard Line's *Vistafjord,* admittedly a luxury ship, has many inside cabins every bit as attractive as outside quarters.

There is one drawback to outside cabins. If the outside cabin you are considering is located in the middle of a deck (as opposed to directly on the side of the ship), other passengers strolling by can see into it. If that bothers you, either look for a cabin that's not located next to a promenade or try inside quarters.

If you're dedicated to outside cabins, you're in for a treat on the P&O/ Princess Cruises' *Royal Princess*—every cabin on board is an outside cabin!

3. SHARING A CABIN

If you don't mind sharing a cabin with one or several other travelers, you can save money. Most cruise lines will assign you a roommate of the same sex (they haven't gone coed yet), which means that you pay the normal per-person rate in that cabin price category instead of the 50% to 100% surcharge levied on single travelers occupying a two-person cabin alone.

Some lines will even assign you, or you and a friend, to a cabin for four. That way each person pays a much lower rate than if you shared a cabin. If you're lucky the line won't find two others to share it and you'll end up paying the lower rate but not sharing after all.

Ships are very competitive these days, so if they at first refuse to book you into a shared cabin until they can guarantee a roommate, persevere. Try calling closer to the sailing date. By that time your half price may look better than none.

Just as in any roommate situation, however, the shared-cabin experience can be wonderful or wearying. There are no guarantees that you and your cabinmate(s) will be compatible. At least in the beginning of your newfound friendship, however, you will have someone to talk to until you meet other new friends.

If you do share a cabin with one or more strangers, it would be wise to put your valuables in the ship's safekeeping. See the purser for information on the availability of safe-deposit boxes or other storage facilities on board.

Some ships—but not many—have cabins designed especially for single travelers. They have one bed and are, naturally, smaller than double cabins but are quite adequate for a single traveler. You'll find single cabins on Holland America Line/Westours, among others.

Chapter V

CHOOSING A SHIP: CRUISES FROM A TO Z

□ □ □

From the Admiral Cruise Line to World Explorer Cruises

Huge ships and tiny ships, tall ships and small ships, aging ladies of the sea or young whippersnappers, elite fleets and fun ships, happy ships and world-class cruisers, river trippers, island hoppers, and floating fantasylands—just as there is said to be a match for every lonely heart, there is a ship for every dreamer.

You can sail with potentates or plumbers, retirees or those who don't retire until dawn. You can travel on a budget or break the bank. You can play at sea for days on end or set foot ashore every day of your cruise.

Somewhere, right this very minute, a cruise ship's foghorn is bellowing across the water, playing your tune.

Come with us now to see what's at sea.

1. ADMIRAL CRUISE LINE

Contact: Admiral Cruise Line, 1220 Biscayne Blvd., Miami, FL 33101 (tel. 305/374-1611, or toll free 800/327-0271, 800/432-9552 in Florida); or 140 W. 6th St., San Pedro, CA 90731 (tel. 213/548-8411, or toll free 800/421-5866, 800/262-1128 in California).

Cruising Grounds: Bahamas, Mexican Riviera, Alaska.

Itineraries: *Azure Seas*—Los Angeles – San Diego – Catalina Island – Enseñada – Los Angeles *or* Los Angeles – Catalina Island – Enseñada – Los Angeles, year round.

Emerald Seas—Miami – Nassau – Bahamian Private Island – Freeport – Miami *or* Miami – Nassau – Bahamian Private Island – Miami, year round.

Stardancer—Los Angeles – Puerto Vallarta – Mazatlán – Cabo San Lucas – Los Angeles *or* Vancouver – Juneau – Skagway/Haines – Ketchikan – Vancouver.

Future Seas—a 10-day Caribbean itinerary to be announced in 1989–1990.

Admiral has been sailing its *Emerald Seas* between Miami and the Bahamas for so long that the Atlantic would look empty without her. On this run since 1971 when the former Eastern/Western Cruise Lines bought the ship from Chandris, the *Emerald Seas* offers three- and four-night cruises to Nassau and Freeport, and the line's new pride its deserted Bahamian Out Island.

As one of the oldest lines in the country, Admiral can trace its history back to 1868 when the company was incorporated in Massachusetts and had ships plying the islands off the New England coast. During World War II most of the company's ships had negative encounters with German subs. Two, however, the *Evangeline* and the *Yarmouth*, managed to escape the German navy and returned to Boston where they sailed for some years between New York, Bridgeport, and Canada.

In 1954 F. Leslie Fraser, a Jamaican living in Miami, purchased the two cruisers and brought them to Miami where they were docked right downtown in the middle of what is now Bayfront Park. (In those days three-night cruises cost a lordly $39 to $54!)

By the 1960s Fraser had bought another ship, the *Arosa Star,* renamed it the *Bahama Star,* and was doing a booming business on three- and four-night cruises to Nassau. Meanwhile the line's two original ships cruised to the Caribbean and Central and South America on longer voyages. This line also owned the *Ariadne* at one time, but eventually sold those ships, ending up with their present vessel, the *Emerald Seas.* In December of 1982 she began sailing to the Bahamas.

Once known as the *President Roosevelt,* the *Emerald Seas* was built in 1944 with an eye to sailing her around the world, and she served the country in World War II as a troopship. Broad abeam and deep of draft, she can provide a smooth ride in the worst weather.

Recently the line added a new twist—its own Out Island in the Bahamas. Called Little Stirrup Cay, this island in the Berry Island chain is for many passengers the highlight of the trip. Why? Because there's absolutely nothing to do, thus relieving you from any duty to get out there and do something. In fact, a tiny, long-abandoned stone cottage, thought to have been built by early settlers, is the only point of interest. Except, of course, crystalline waters, sands warm as Hades, coral reefs populated by the flashiest floor show afloat, and sun, sun, more sun. . . .

Little Stirrup Cay's absence of sights means you can, without guilt, obtain a frothy rum punch from the thatched gazebo, stretch out on silver sands, and tan, while you catch up on the naps you missed after two busy days aboard the ship and in Nassau.

Explorers should take a look at the ruins then head off for the far end of the island. There some thoughtful soul has strung up a couple of hammocks where you can meditate while swaying gently in the breeze.

Meanwhile on the West Coast, the line's *Azure Seas* has for several years been operating similar three- and four-day sailings from Los Angeles to Enseñada. Like the *Emerald Seas'* cruises, these voyages are nonstop parties that just happen to be floating. Nightclub entertainment, a big and busy casino, lounges, a disco, a theater, library, card room—see what we mean?

Recently the *Azure Seas* made a big splash when it became the first cruise ship to call regularly at posh Catalina Island, playground of film stars and yachtsmen.

On three-night cruises the ship leaves Friday evening and spends the next day in Catalina, then sails on to Enseñada, where most passengers drink tequila and go on buying sprees, then heads for home in the wee hours of Sunday morning (late Saturday night), spending Sunday at sea and arriving back in port early enough on Monday morning so you can get right off and almost make it to your office on time.

That same day it leaves about sunset, spends Tuesday in San Diego and Catalina, Wednesday in Enseñada, and Thursday at sea, returning on Friday morning.

Now the line has made yet another major step forward with the announcement of its plans to build a 2,000-passenger ship currently being called *Future Seas*. Measuring in at 44,300 tons, the "cruise ship of the future," as Admiral likes to call its new baby, is being built in France and is expected to begin sailing in April 1990.

Activities

Entertainment is nearly nonstop aboard these ships, which feature a lively show each evening, two seatings at dinner, a very busy casino, and the usual array of shipboard activities from gong show to trivia contest. Activities at sea and in port run from Bingo to skeet shooting and dance lessons.

In the shops on board the *Emerald Seas* you'll find some bargains on duty-free liquor and perfumes in case you forgot something on shore in Nassau.

Life aboard ship is very casual, and because the cruises are short, you don't have to pack for formal evenings. As a matter of fact, sportswear covers just about everything except the captain's cocktail party, when a suit for the gentlemen and dress for the ladies is the furthest you need to go in the direction of formality. If you like dressing up, of course, you can do that to your heart's content in port or at dinner on the ship.

EMERALD SEAS: This is a recently redecorated craft featuring spacious and well-maintained cabins. If you can afford the fare for a suite on this short voyage, you'll be rewarded with a huge room with beautiful floor-to-ceiling glass windows, a seating area, twin beds, even closed-circuit television for watching on-board entertainment in the comfort of your own quarters. All 227 outside and 164 inside cabins have private baths.

Recently painted stem to stern in a pale-green hue and renovated to the tune of $2 million, the ship now has a contemporary look.

Food aboard is plentiful: breakfast buffet style on deck or in the dining room, mid-morning bouillon, lunch, afternoon tea, dinner, midnight buffet every day, and snacks in machines in the hallways.

If you're sailing on a budget and/or are new to the whole business of cruises, the *Emerald Seas* may be just the introduction to the high seas you've been seeking. At 24,458 tons, she's quite a big ship, carrying 960 passengers and 400 crew, any one of which may be just the person you've been wanting to meet.

Public Rooms

Public rooms aboard got most of the attention in the recent renovations so you'll find a nice contemporary look throughout the ship. The Aquarius Club is particularly attractive, with a dance floor flanked by comfortable conversation areas where passengers often gather for before-dinner cocktails.

Four dance bands should be enough to provide the kind of music you'd like to hear, or you can buzz down to the theater and watch a movie. There's an amateur talent night and professional entertainment on nights the ship is at sea.

There's a similar contemporary look about the disco that spreads across the aft end of the ship on the Sun Deck. Just outside here you'll find a cute little French café that's a favorite gathering spot for swimmers in the pool just beyond.

The *Emerald Seas* sails on Friday evening, drops anchor in Nassau early on Saturday morning, and stays there until the wee hours of Sunday morning when she sails on to the Out Island, returning to Miami on Monday morning. Her four-night sojourns begin on Monday, end on Friday, and add a stop in Freeport. They naturally attract an older crowd more able to schedule free time on working days.

As one first-time sailor told us: "I didn't know whether I'd like a cruise or not but I had the best time of my life! I'm going to start saving this week to go on another one." Enough said.

Cabins

You won't find this a fancy ship, but it is quite spacious. That's particularly true of the cabins, which are among the largest of any cruise ship afloat—and one of the prides of the line. To give you an idea what that means, lanai suites are about 11 by 20 feet, mid-priced double cabins are 16 by 13 feet or 20 by 9 feet, and less expensive quarters measure about 12 by 16 feet, some smaller.

Suites are good buys for the money, but then you have to have the money. A three-night cruise in one of these will cost $755 to $945, and four nights is $875 to $1,065 per person in winter season (March through April). They're very comfortable, however, with as much space as some hotel rooms.

Prices aboard are highest in the winter months (March through mid-April) and in summer (from June through August). Off-season aboard is January to March, April to June, and September to mid-December.

You'll find rooms with queen-size beds aboard too, although those tend to be in the highest price categories.

Budgetwise cruisers will do well on the Emerald, Ruby, and Topaz Decks, where an outside cabin with upper and lower berths costs $515 to $565 per person for a three-night cruise in peak season. Cabins E77 and E76, which are smaller rooms wedged in among the suites, might be good choices in this bracket. Rock-bottom budgets can find quarters here for $425 a person for a three-night cruise in peak season, $395 per person in summer.

Third and fourth occupants of a cabin pay $190 or $250. Singles are charged 1½ fares for a cabin with upper and lower berths, two full fares for a cabin with two lower beds.

As you can see—and as the line is quick to point out—daily rates per person really compare quite favorably with any shoreside vacation you can dream up, short of camping in the Everglades. For a three-day cruise in high season you pay prices that begin at $141 a day. That figure's even lower in the off-season.

AZURE SEAS: This cruise ship operates on similar three- and four-night cruises. On these you visit Catalina Island and Ensenada in Baja California on the three-day cruise. On four-night sailings the ship stops in at San Diego too.

Like the *Emerald Seas,* the *Azure Seas* is a party ship, designed to provide you with three days of fun, frolic, and food. Built in 1955 as the *Southern Cross,* this 21,486-ton vessel (later known also as the *Calypso*) carries 734 passengers so there's plenty of opportunity to meet, fun, and frolic. An interesting historical note: She was the first ship afloat to be christened by a reigning monarch, Queen Elizabeth II. Refurbished in 1976 and again in 1983, the ship is clean and contemporary looking, with lots and lots of deck space for sunning.

While it's no luxury ship, it's popular with first-time cruisers, who have a rip-roaring weekend while they're discovering what cruises are all about.

Public Rooms

If you like to play the slot machines, you can pull until your biceps fail at the bank of 190 one-armed bandits in the ship's casino. All the other casino games are available too.

Three nightclubs ought to provide plenty of places to play, and there's always the disco for late-night howling. It's way down on its own deck so the partying goes on well into the a.m. here.

You can tone up in an exercise room, then recuperate in the whirlpool and a small spa. You can round up a fourth for bridge or go see a movie in the ship's balconied Rialto Theater.

Most of the action occurs on the Promenade Deck, site of the ship's show lounge, the Rendezvous Lounge, where a Broadway revue provides evening entertainment. Not far away, the Mayfair Lounge offers a piano bar and soft lighting. Nearby are gift shops and the theater, and back aft is the smaller Café Miramar, a self-service dining room. The St. Tropez Bar is a popular gathering spot too. It's decked out in contemporary furnishings with a bright awning overhead.

Weekend cruisers can come aboard the ship at 5 p.m., although it doesn't sail until 7:45 p.m., and enjoy a buffet dinner at an open sitting. Bars are open too, although you'll have to wait until the ship's at sea to have a go at the casino.

In the ship's 1983 renovation the Caravelle Dining Room and the Miramar Lounge, the ship's nightclub, were revamped with colored lights that bounce off the ceiling of the room. Mexican tiles at the entrance and new carpets give the room a distinctly western look, abetted by wall graphics of California scenes, Mexican villages, tropical flowers and birds.

Cabins

Recently the line also refurbished the cabins on board the *Azure Seas* so these days they're looking prettier than ever, all outfitted in contemporary earth tones. On large old ships like this one you can expect ample quarters too.

Cabins begin one deck down, on Atlantis Deck, and continue on Barbizon Deck, Caravelle Deck, Dolphin Deck, and Emerald Deck. All the cabins on board have two lower beds or a double bed, plus plenty of closet and dresser space. Some have a pullman upper berth or two so you can take the kids along if you like. All cabins are carpeted, and they all have private bathrooms with shower, telephone, and piped-in music on two channels. Bright tropical colors and lots of blue are featured in the decorating schemes.

If you elect an outside cabin, you'll find big rectangular portholes offering a nice view of the passing scene.

Prices are divided into nine categories, with Category 1 cabins the costliest, Category 9 cabins the least expensive. There are also two seasons aboard. Off-season is January through May and October through mid-December. Peak season begins in June and lasts through September, including some Christmas holiday sailings.

Let's look at prices for a three-night cruise to Ensenãda from Los Angeles in peak season. You'll pay $20 to $25 less in off-season, and four-day cruises cost about $55 to $70 more than three-night cruises.

The top cabin aboard is the owner's suite on Atlantis Deck. It has a queen-size bed, and a convertible sofa in the separate sitting area, and costs $945 per person for a three-night cruise in peak season.

Outside cabins in Categories 1 to 4 have two lower beds or a double bed, and range in price from $815 to $855 per person. Inside cabins begin in Category 4 and go through Category 9. These quarters feature two lower beds or a double bed, and cost $515 to $765 per person for a three-night cruise in peak season.

Third and fourth persons sharing a stateroom pay $190 each for the three-day cruise, $250 for four nights. Those cabins for three or four are limited though, so it would be wise to book early.

A port tax of $30 is levied on everyone.

STARDANCER: Something new in Alaska cruises hit the marketplace in the summer of 1984 when Sundance Cruises began offering three-, four-, and seven-night voyages from Vancouver to Juneau, Skagway or Haines, Tracy Arm, Ketchikan, and Misty Fjords.

Organized by Stanley MacDonald, who was influential in the creation and marketing of Princess Cruises, and by Scandinavia's Silja ferry line, the *Stardancer* offers you the opportunity to take your car with you, disembark in Skagway to tour the Yukon or Alaska, and then rejoin the cruise. That same kind of car-tour-cruise is available in winter on the cruise line's trips to Mexico.

Sundance Cruises boasted another first for the cruise industry—a father-daughter team at the helm. MacDonald's daughter, Laurie, is responsible for the smashing good looks of this ship, right down to a ship's figurehead that lords it over Stanley's Pub—take a close look and you'll discover it's a clever carving of her father's face.

MacDonald and MacDonald had a rather hard time getting this cruise line afloat. Sundance Cruises' first ship, the *Sundancer*, sank in Alaskan waters after striking a dock. A Canadian pilot, brought on board to guide the ship through the water, was held responsible for the mishap that totaled the ship.

Not ones to give up easily, the MacDonalds bought a similar ship, the *Stardancer*, and set off to have another go at the interesting itineraries Sundance Cruises had carved out with the *Sundancer*.

In 1986 the line joined forces with Admiral Cruise Line and is now part of that fleet.

In winter months, from January to about May, the ship follows a similar schedule, but in Mexico, departing from Los Angeles Friday evening, cruising Baja and the coastline on Saturday and Sunday, with one-day stops in Puerto Vallarta and Mazatlán. You can take your car off at either of those stops for a tour through Mexico, rejoining the ship later. Or you can just stay on board and sail on as you would on any cruise ship, spending a day in Cabo San Lucas, a day at sea, and returning Friday morning to Los Angeles.

For the line, it's a good deal too—it's carrying two decks of fare-paying "passengers" who don't require any service at all.

Departing Vancouver on Friday, *Stardancer* sails north, spending the following day at sea and reaching the Alaskan capital city of Juneau on Sunday afternoon. After a visit to the famous Red Dog Saloon and Mendenhall Glacier, you sail on to Skagway, the gateway to the Klondike, and on to Haines.

There you can leave the ship and tour the Yukon or the interior of Alaska for a few days or a few weeks. Then just return to one of the two villages, reboard the ship, and return to Vancouver via Tracy Arm, Ketchikan, and Misty Fjords.

"This is a chance for the rank-and-file person, the ordinary, everyday person who doesn't have an awful lot of money but really wants to see this area," a line executive told us. "The idea is to put your automobile or camper on and then forget about it and have a posh cruise with saunas, barbershop, gym, full entertainment, and gourmet dining. It's just like a regular cruise and you have the added attraction of taking a car north or southbound." He adds that the line aims its lures at passengers of varying ages and incomes (particularly incomes) with some very budget-wise fares.

Like what? Like a maximum of $2,695 per person for a week-long Alaska cruise—and that's in the owner's suite! The minimum fare for a week-long Alaska cruise is $1,295.

If the idea of cars on a ship conjures up visions of, er, rusticity, to put the best possible face on it, dispense with that vision! This ship is like no ferry afloat, and indeed is lovely enough to put a few huge cruise ships to shame. It is, in a word, gorgeous.

Activities / Public Rooms

Showiest single feature is a three-story atrium that soars to a black glass ceiling inset with tiny blue lights that form constellations in keeping with the ship's euphonic *Stardancer* name. Lights flow down one wall like an electric waterfall while other walls are adorned with striking fiber hangings, and soft sculptures.

There's a full-time fitness instructor on board to man the saunas, spas, and elaborate bodybuilding equipment. In the togged-out spa, there are even exercise bicycles that tell you how many calories you've worked off and measure your pulse beat. Those who overdo can ease tired muscles in the gym's raised whirlpool, where they can settle in to watch passing passengers through a bank of windows.

Two more whirlpools up on the teak-floored Sun Deck let you combine tanning with whirling waters. Way up on the top deck near the funnels there's a turf-topped jogging track that comes complete with Parcours stations.

Stardancer's swimming pool is quite a fancy item. First, it's unusually large for a cruise ship, large enough to cordon one section off for the youngsters and for timid swimmers. Next, it's backed by an attractive light-blue mural of stylized waves. But best of all, it features a sliding glass roof and side sheets of glass that enclose it so the air inside can be heated or air-conditioned through vents. That means you can swim in heated comfort in Alaska, and be cooled by air conditioners no matter how hot the day in Mexico. Now that's the way to rough it!

Evenings, there's always plenty of activity in the serene Sundown Lounge, a dancing spot with the ship's trademark gray carpets, here streaked with pink. Tasteful, muted gray furnishings with tiny blocks of color swirl around a room with a circular feeling to it: there's a circular dance floor, semicircular bar, and wavy free-form bar decked out in blue leather.

For dramatic views of the ship's wake streaming out behind, pull up a seat at the Star Bar, which juts 30 feet out over the aft end of the ship. To see what's coming up, head for the opposite end of the Sundown Room where the Constellation Bar awaits.

You'll find the financial action aboard in Cassiday's Casino, a long open room with slot machines, roulette wheel, and blackjack tables overlooking the sea.

Into-the-wee-hours types head for the Stardance Disco, a fascinating spot you enter through a *Star Wars* tunnel of tiny lights and mirrors. All decked out in light purples, the room sports hi-tech touches with exposed pipes painted deep purple. Brushed-steel pipes add to the modernity, as do red dividers and slick lighting effects.

A favorite gathering spot on the ship is Stanley's Pub, where deep-blue leather bucket chairs beg you to settle in and contemplate—or join in the spontaneous sing-alongs that so often occur here. Special coffees are served in the pub, which also boasts a grand piano, lots of windows, mahogany wainscoting, a semicircular bar trimmed in brass, and glowing wall lamps—quite a pubby-looking pub indeed.

Just a few steps away, the ship's library features small love seats, more wainscoting, and big glassed-in wood bookcases.

For shoppers there's a big boutique stocked with ladies' fashions, perfumes, souvenirs of all variety, scrimshaw, and Mexican pottery bargains.

For the youngsters, there's a cute two-level Kid's Club great for climbing and crawling around.

Cabaret entertainment featuring Broadway revues and variety acts takes place in the Starlight Club, a big, cozy room outfitted in burgundy velvet. Brass gleams, lights glow on double-decker brass- and copper-trimmed tables, and huge expanses of windows welcome light or night. Erté posters adorn the walls and there's a big stage, easily seen from every seat in the house.

You'll dine in Windows of the World Dining Room where there are tables for two, four, six, or eight. Overhead, bubbly circular chandeliers add a contemporary touch to an inviting color scheme that plays with delicate shades of forest green and pinks. Chairs are gold, not brass trimmed, and like everything else on this ship the public rooms have nary a touch of plastic or vinyl.

For statistics fans, the ship was built in 1982 and refurbished in 1987. It measures in at 27,000 tons and can carry 960 passengers. Her officers are Scandinavian, her crew international, representing 38 nations, with many Americans among them, particularly in hosting positions.

Cabins

Cabins have several selling points, the strongest, for some travelers, being beds that can be converted from twins to double beds with the removal of a central console and the flick of a lock to join them together. With prices aboard low enough to lure younger travelers, that togetherness has become an increasingly important selling point for many cruise lines. You'll find those switchable sleepers on Decks 7, 8, and 9.

You'll also find all cabins equipped with color television, offering several channels in port or near land, closed-circuit broadcasts at sea, meaning you can watch some good films right in your room. Cabins also sport radios and telephones that connect you to other passengers and the cruise staff.

Cabins are decorated in reds, blues, or greens, and nearly all measure in at 9 by 16 feet; those in Category B are about five feet longer, with a small sitting area. Category A covers two fancy suites while Category C through I cabins are identical in size although, oddly, inside cabins *look* larger than outside ones.

Those who like their nights quiet will be pleased to know that on this ship all the public rooms—nightclub, disco, and the like—are located from midships aft, while cabins occupy the space from midships forward, thus guaranteeing there'll be no disco stompin' over any cabin.

In a welcome, if unusual, hark back to the ship's Scandinavian origins, showers can be hand-held so you don't get your hair wet, and bathroom floor tiles are heated from beneath! The bathrooms are quite contemporary too, with plenty of storage room.

Fares aboard are divided into six categories: one for the two suites, one for the special large cabins, two for other outside cabins, and two for inside staterooms. For Alaska sailings there are peak and "value" seasons, and for Mexico sailings there are peak, "value," and economy seasons.

To simplify matters we'll look at peak rates for an Alaska cruise, the ship's most popular voyages, running from June through mid-August.

On this ship you may take three-, four-, or seven-night voyages. A wide variety of hotel and air-fare options are offered if you're opting for the three- or four-nighters. If you're planning to take your car but want to take the full seven-night trip, just let the line know you'll be getting off and returning on another cruise. You pay the straight cruise fare—no surcharge for splitting your cruise.

So here we go with fares for a seven-night Alaska cruise in peak season:

Those two quite handsome suites are $2,695 per person for a seven-night voyage, while the slightly larger cabins, dubbed Category A, are $2,335.

Category B cabins, which are outside quarters with twin beds that can be converted into doubles, will be $1,855 per person for the cruise. Category C, outside cabins with lower beds that don't slide together, are $1,735 per person.

Category D and E cabins are inside quarters. Category D's beds are convertible to doubles, and the fare in this category is $1,495. Categories E and F are for twin sleepers that stay that way, and the fare is $1,295 to $1,375. Those less expensive fares also mean the cabins are a bit lower down in the ship.

Off-season rates drop $80 to $120.

A little arithmetic exercise will show you that you're paying daily rates in the $185- to $375-per-person range for a week's cruise in peak season.

If you're taking your car or camper, you'll be charged according to its height and length. Vehicles measuring in at 19 feet long and 6 feet high or less cost $50 round trip, depending on season; larger cruisers cost $70; less off-season.

FUTURE SEAS: Although the ship was barely a gleam in some accountant's eye when this book went into print, it's already getting plenty of print for what the line promises will be futuristic design.

One special feature of the new craft will be a bilevel, 1,000-seat dining room with a panoramic view. Add to that a two-level disco and a two-level casino.

Toss in two outdoor pools, five whirlpool spas, a health club, jogging track, bilevel show lounge, shopping mall, indoor/outdoor café, seven bars and lounges, luxury staterooms with verandas, a children's playroom, video game room, television in all cabins, a library, pub, teenage club, and 30,000 square feet of open sundeck. Whew!

2. AMERICAN CANADIAN CARIBBEAN LINE

Contact: American Canadian Caribbean Line, P.O. Box 368, Warren, RI 02885 (tel. 401/247-0955 collect, or toll free 800/556-7450).

Cruising Grounds: The Bahamas, the Caribbean, U.S. East Coast, Canada.

Itineraries: *New Shoreham II—*

IN SUMMER: Warren, R.I. – Block Island – Martha's Vineyard – Newport – Warren *or* Warren – New York – Troy – Oswego – Saguenay River – Prescott – Montréal – Québec City – Tadoussac – Montréal.

IN WINTER: St. Thomas – St. John – St. Croix – Tortola – Salt Island – Cooper Island – Virgin Gorda – Anegada – Jost Van Dyke – Peter Island – St. Thomas *or* St. Maarten – Anguilla – Grand Case – Saba – St. Kitts – Antigua – Barbuda – St. Barthélemy – St. Maarten.

Caribbean Prince—

IN SUMMER: Warren, R.I. – New York – Troy – Oswego – Saguenay River – Prescott – Montréal – Québec City – Tadoussac – Montréal; and return same route.

IN WINTER: Antigua – Guadeloupe – Dominica – Martinique – St. Lucia – St. Vincent – Grenadines – Grenada, or reverse; *or* Cozumél – Tulúm – Placentia – Barrier Reef Islands – Belize, and reverse.

Mini cruise ships are a specialty of Luther Blount, president of American Canadian Caribbean Line and one of the pioneers of the mini-cruiser concept. Just 70 or 80 cruise fans sail aboard either of this line's two small ships, the *New Shoreham II* and the five-year-old *Caribbean Prince.*

If you're looking for unusual destinations not too far from home, this cruise line may be the place to begin your search. For instance, the line's 72-passenger *New Shoreham II* spends the winter in the Caribbean, where its shallow six-foot draft allows it to stop in lovely beach-lined destinations visited by few, if any, other cruise lines.

Meanwhile the *Caribbean Prince* also plies seductive Caribbean and gulf waters on stop-every-night voyages, exploring these islands' enchanting villages far more extensively than any other cruise line.

New Shoreham II has been around for many years, sailing the crystalline waters of the Caribbean or the Bahamas in winter, calling on a number of intriguing island villages.

Both ships return to Florida in April and May to sail on what cruise lines call a "positioning cruise" from West Palm Beach to Warren, R.I., their ships' home base.

Those cruises run from the end of November through April.

From there they sail up the Saguenay River and back on 12-day cruises via Narragansett Bay and Long Island Sound to Waterford, N.Y., through the Erie Canal to the tip of Lake Ontario, past the Thousand Islands and on to Prescott, Ontario, Montréal, and Québec City. You return by bus from Montréal, or take the bus to Montréal and join the cruise there, reversing the route back to Warren. It's a six-hour trip on the air-conditioned bus from Warren to Montréal.

Fall-foliage cruises begin when trees along the waterways are shining like jewels. These are particularly spectacular sailings on this line. On many summer weekends the ships feature cruises from Warren to Newport, Martha's Vineyard, and Block Island.

At the beginning of its winter cruise schedule, in December, January, and February, the *New Shoreham II* sails on 12-day trips calling at some quite remote beaches on such rarely visited islands as Domenica, St. Vincent, St. Lucia, and the Grenadines.

American Canadian Caribbean Line's newest addition, the *Caribbean Prince*, usually spends the winter roaming the British and Dutch Windward and Leeward Islands—and life could certainly be worse than that. Stops at rarely visited sunny islets, difficult or impossible to reach except by ship, make these cruises quite a memorable experience—and make for some great one-upmanship on those we've-been-everywhere braggarts.

Most of the *Caribbean Prince*'s cruises are 12-day sailings that stop in at quite intriguing stops where you swim in underwater caves or gaze at those amazingly clear, striated waters of the Caribbean from the top of a volcanic peak. Beach lovers get a chance to sun on both white sand beaches and surprisingly soft black sand beaches as well.

The *Caribbean Prince*'s Leeward Island cruises, quite fittingly, called "Smooth Water Cruises," have the distinction of calling at both Philipsburg, the Dutch capital of St. Maarten, and Grand Case, the capital of the French side of the island. No other cruise ship makes both stops.

In 1989 the line was planning a new series of destinations, focusing on several of Mexico's popular beach resorts, then moving on to tour the tiny Barrier Reef Islands surrounding Belize, one of the world's top diving and snorkeling destinations.

Cruises among this beauteous set of islands begin in December and continue through April, when the ship travels to West Palm Beach to begin its journey up the Intracoastal Waterway to its home base in Warren, R.I. From there it joins the *New Shoreham II* on summer cruises through New England waters and up the Saguenay River to Montréal.

As winter moves into northern climes, the ships reverse their bows and head south to Florida's Intracoastal Waterway, then on to the toasty waters of the Caribbean.

CARIBBEAN PRINCE / NEW SHOREHAM II: Because these ships are so similar in size, shape, and price, we'll describe them together.

Activities / Public Rooms

Summer or winter, life aboard is casual with the scenery and ports providing entertainment. You don't need an extensive wardrobe. You won't have all that much room to store it anyway, so stick to basic sportswear.

Each ship is about 150 feet long (*Caribbean Prince* is 10 feet longer) and 35 feet wide. Because they draw only about five feet of water, the ships can sail in shallow waters inaccessible to larger craft.

A special feature of both is a bow ramp that lets you walk right off the ship down a ramp and onto the beach. How's that for service? And you can clamber around off the back of the ship and drop right into the sea from a swimming platform at the stern. Dream on *that* some sleety Sunday when you're cooped up and freezing!

Dinners are served family style in the ship's small dining room. Big bowls and platters of, say, fresh lobster or papaya or mangoes right off the trees, are passed down around the tables until everyone's stuffed.

Cabins

Caribbean Prince offers you quarters in 32 staterooms with big picture windows or in six other cabins below the deck. Staterooms look a little like the compact quarters you see on a yacht, and are decorated in handsome colors echoed in fiberglass paneling trimmed in teak.

Above-deck cabins come with twin beds that can be made into a double, although that doubling up means someone has to sleep on the inside and crawl over the other. Or a double can have a small table and two chairs, with a bed for a third person included. All rooms have private bathrooms and are carpeted.

Cabin size ranges from 7 by 11 feet to 9 by 11 feet.

After dinner everyone moves into the lounge where talk, games, and cards are the order of the day. This is a BYOB ("bring your own bottle") ship; it doesn't serve liquor but does provide the setups. You can go ashore and explore too, of course.

Caribbean Prince has only three categories of cabins and all but six are outside quarters with windows. Prices for a 12-day voyage are $50 to $100 lower than those aboard the *New Shoreham II*. On summer voyages prices are $25 to $125 higher.

At Caribbean departure points the line also provides taxi chits to get you from the airport to the ship and back. Because the ship is in port for two days between departures, you can arrive a day early and move right into your cabin. The fee for those boat-as-motel days is $75 for a couple, $50 single (no such deals on the northern cruises).

New Shoreham II has five cabin classifications. Most of the accommodations on this ship are outside rooms, some with full windows, some with a porthole too high up to serve as a window. Most also can accommodate three travelers. And most, but not all, cabins have private baths. One, cabin "A," which is not available on northern cruises, does not have a private bathroom but has a bath across the hall.

Starting at the top, the two best staterooms on this ship, Cabins 91 and 92, feature twin beds, an easy chair, picture windows on two walls, and private bathroom. Located aft on the Sun Deck, these are roomy accommodations and cost $1,735 per person for a 12-day voyage in the Caribbean.

Just a little smaller are two cabins with single berths and a picture window: Cabins 81 and 82 are $1,605 per person for the trip.

The next price category down has two lower berths, a picture window, and a private bath; it can accommodate a third passenger. The rate is $1,535 per person.

Cabins 14 to 19 and 22 to 28 have two lower single beds and a porthole. Although smaller in size, these can also accommodate a third passenger (but it will be *very* cozy). The price for these is $1,095 per person.

The lowest-priced cabins on board, Cabins 31 to 34, have upper and lower berths, a porthole, and private bath. One of these cabins will cost $999 per person for a 12-night Caribbean trip.

When the ship travels to northern waters, most of its cruises are 12-day sojourns. The top price for these is $1,935 per person, ranging down to $999 for the smallest quarters on board.

Trips between Florida and Rhode Island last 15 days and are about $100 more, depending on the size of the cabin.

Summer weekend cruises, 3 nights and 2½ days, are $355 per person for the top-price quarters, $260 to $340 for less expensive cabins.

On those long summer cruises, rates include the bus trip to or from Montréal.

If a third person shares your cabin, each person gets a 10% reduction on the price of the cabin.

Singles pay 175% of the per-person fare in the lowest-priced accommodations, 200% for other quarters.

On the *New Shoreham II* a taxi chit for the ride from the airport to the ship is included in the price of Caribbean cruises.

On the Saguenay River trips there's a $50 port charge per person, $40 per person on Caribbean cruises.

One further note: You make your own beds.

3. AMERICAN CRUISE LINES

Contact: American Cruise Lines, Inc., One Marine Park, Haddam, CT 06438 (tel. 203/345-8501, or toll free 800/243-6755).
Cruising Grounds: U.S. East Coast, Mississippi River, New England.

Itineraries: *New Orleans—*
IN SUMMER: Jacksonville – St. Simons Island – Hilton Head Island – Charleston – Savannah – Amelia Island – Jacksonville.
IN WINTER: Fort Myers – Lake Okeechobee – Fort Myers.
IN SPRING AND FALL: New Orleans – Baton Rouge – Natchez – Vicksburg – Memphis, or reverse; *or* New Orleans – Natchez – Vicksburg – Baton Rouge – New Orleans.

Savannah—
IN SPRING: Baltimore – Yorktown – Williamsburg – Norfolk – Cambridge – Oxford – St. Michaels – Baltimore.
IN SUMMER AND FALL: Block Island – Nantucket – Martha's Vineyard – New Bedford/Plymouth – Newport – New London/Mystic – Haddam *or* Haddam – Port Jefferson – West Point – Kingston – New York – Greenport – Haddam.
IN WINTER: Jacksonville – St. Simons Island – Amelia Island – St. Augustine – Halifax River – Cape Canaveral – Fort Pierce – Fort Lauderdale (land tour to Florida Keys) *or* Jacksonville – St. Johns River – Jacksonville.

Charleston—
IN SUMMER AND FALL: Boston – Boothbay Harbor – Bar Harbor –

Rockland – Bath – Portsmouth – Boston *or* Haddam – Port Jefferson – West Point – Kingston – New York – Greenport – Haddam.

IN WINTER AND SPRING: Jacksonville – St. Simons Island – Amelia Island – St. Augustine – Halifax River – Cape Canaveral – Fort Pierce – Fort Lauderdale (land tour to Florida Keys) *or* Jacksonville – St. Simons Island – Hilton Head Island – Charleston – Savannah – Amelia Island – Jacksonville *or* Baltimore – Yorktown – Williamsburg – Norfolk – Cambridge – Oxford – St. Michaels – Baltimore.

Not all ships are huge floating hotels filled with a thousand or so fun-seekers. Some are small, cozy craft dedicated to simple, casual trips to interesting ports.

American Cruise Lines offers just such cruises. Now operator of three small ships, all of which were built and are operated by the company, American Cruise Lines is headquartered at 1 Marine Park in Haddam, Conn. Owned by a gentleman named Charles Robertson, the line specializes in sailing trips in and around New England, although it now branches out to the Chesapeake Bay and recently began sailing the Mississippi River. In winter one of the ships sails south to cruise the inland waterways of Florida too.

All the ships are small, and we do mean *small*. The first ship in the fleet was the *American Eagle,* which carried 49 passengers. In 1984 the brand-new 132-passenger *Savannah* joined the family, followed by the *New Orleans* and the *Charleston.*

You won't find any spangled dancing girls or poolside pillow fights aboard these ships. These cruisers are specifically designed for inland, coastal cruising on intriguing waterways inaccessible to larger ships.

Passengers aboard are in search of "a different type of experience than those who want to go gambling or to a disco," says a company official. Your fellow passengers will tend to be well-traveled people who have sailed on larger ships and are now in search of a small-ship experience.

Itineraries of the ships are carefully planned to provide you with just the right amount of time needed to see the most interesting features in the area. In some spots the line may stay a day or two; in others, just long enough for a brief shore excursion.

On these intriguing itineraries, the ships are always in sight of land, so you can expect to dock each night and spend your days gazing at the lovely scenery along the shores. In fact these cruises are about as close as you can come to the European waterway cruising experience—kind of an American Rhine River cruise.

On the *Charleston,* the *New Orleans,* and the *Savannah,* you sail the Maine coastline, visit Chesapeake Bay, chug along the rarely visited waters of Florida's giant Lake Okeechobee and the Florida Keys, or drop in on southern plantations. Because the ships are small, they can call at harbors the big-bruiser cruisers cannot negotiate.

This year the *Charleston* will sail Florida's waterways, visiting Lake Okeechobee and operating land trips from Fort Lauderdale to the Florida Keys. She will also sail from Jacksonville to ports along the coast of Georgia and the Carolinas before heading north to the coast of Maine for the summer. In fall she returns to Florida via Chesapeake Bay and Williamsburg, and remains in Jacksonville for a winter-long series of two-day cruises on the rarely explored—and north-flowing!—St. Johns River.

Meanwhile the line's *Savannah* follows a similar course but substitutes visits to the islands of New England for the *Charleston*'s Maine coast stops while the *New Orleans,* true to her name, spends most of the year on the Mississippi, tracing the routes—and roots—of Mark Twain before returning to warm Florida waters each winter.

Don't hold us to these itineraries, however. Because the ships are quite similar they sometimes exchange the line's 13 basic itineraries.

Activities

On board these ships you'll make your own fun—quiet talks with new friends, card games, a good book, a movie, perhaps nothing more rousing than a long, long look at glittering lights twinkling along the coastline.

Most of your days will be spent ashore, visiting the historic plantations of the Old South or the intriguing bays and coastline of New England. On fall-foliage cruises, nature provides a flaming show more spectacular than any Broadway revue.

Friendly and efficient pursers and hostesses are on hand to serve you, but don't look for a disco or casino aboard.

At night the ships pull up to a dock so you can go ashore and explore, then return to your floating hotel.

CHARLESTON/SAVANNAH: These two of the line's three ships are very similar in facilities, cruises, and prices. Let's take a look at what they have to offer.

Public Rooms

On ships as small as these, spending an evening in the public rooms is like going over to a friend's house for coffee. Indeed you will be traveling with no more than 131 other passengers. Both the *Savannah* and the *Charleston* are 213 feet long and have only outside staterooms. These are quite spacious accommodations too, averaging 11 by 17 feet—bigger than some ocean cruisers' staterooms.

You'll find your entertainment in four lounges on board, each with big picture windows, and there are also three sundecks for tanning or watching the shoreline slip by. No gambling aboard these craft, however.

In the ship's dining room, everyone dines at the same time, and since tips are pooled, you're free to select any table, and consequently any dining companions you like. Fare ranges from lots of ham and eggs for breakfast to soup and sandwiches or salads for lunch, American favorites at dinner. If you're touring Maine, you'll find fresh Maine lobster on the menu, and in the Chesapeake some of those famous Baltimore crabs are likely to turn up on your plate. There are, of course, always American beef and poultry selections.

Because the ship is so frequently in port, you can go ashore for entertainment. If you stay on board, however, there are movies and a player piano for amusement. Guest lecturers and musical entertainers come on board occasionally too. And you won't have to BYOB on these ships anymore—although you can, if you like—they're now serving alcoholic beverages aboard.

Cabins

On this ship you are guaranteed an outside cabin for a very simple reason: all the cabins are outside quarters! While they're not elaborately furnished —just twin beds, a small vanity with a built-in sink, a nightstand with several drawers, and a bathroom with shower—they're pleasant, attractive, and lean.

Some cabins aboard are entered from the outside decks, some from central corridors on the ship. All are located above the main deck so you have a nice view from the windows in your room as well as from the public rooms. All also have picture windows that open if you want the breezes to cool you, although there's air conditioning aboard. Some cabins have queen-size beds, and all have private showers and toilet facilities.

The *Savannah* has some handsome American artwork aboard too, much of it in cabins.

Cabin prices are divided into three categories: AA, A, and B, in descending order. Let's look at the price of a week-long cruise aboard any of the three ships.

Most AA cabins are on the two top decks. The price for a week-long cruise in one of these is $1,750 per person. Figure about $750 more per person for a 10-day cruise, and double the cost for a 14-day journey.

Category A cabins vary little except in price. For these cabins you pay $1,610 for a seven-day cruise.

Category B cabins are on the boat deck, plus a few on the main deck, and the price for these smaller quarters is $1,400 per person for a week's cruise.

Single fares are $2,100 for a seven-day cruise, $3,000 for ten days.

Two-week cruises are double the price of one-week voyages.

Per diem rates then work out to $200 to $250 per person for a seven-day cruise.

NEW ORLEANS: While the line's other two ships, the *Savannah* and the *Charleston,* are typical cruise ships, the *New Orleans* is a typical river cruiser—of 100 years ago! Built to look just like the Mississippi riverboats Yancey Derringer and his riverboat gambler cronies would have sailed, the *New Orleans* is a study in the white columns and the broad-abeam construction that characterized those picturesque river craft.

Beyond columned decks lined with zippy red trim, this chic sailor is quite a "today" craft. Inside this sleek new ship you'll find contemporary colors—peaches, pastels, soft earthy shades—and all the latest conveniences in cabins that the line claims are the largest in the cruise industry.

Built at a shipyard in Salisbury, Md., the *New Orleans* is, of course, doing what comes naturally to her kind: sailing the Mississippi River. A wide variety of cruises is available, ranging from a two-day cruise to a seven- or ten-day cruise.

Activities

There's something about the Mississippi that just brings out the sing-along in folks, so you'll find plenty of that going on aboard the *New Orleans*. Naturally, with a name like that the ship features plenty of the music made famous in its namesake city—jazz, of course.

Historians and lecturers also make an appearance to discuss what you're seeing along the river and hark back to days of Mark Twain and his amusing and amazing friends, both real and literary. Movies are also shown on board and there's a very good library of river-related books, perfect for reading in the ship's Mark Twain Reading Room.

Naturally, on a ship this small—just 126 passengers—everyone dines at once. That dining, which features much the same kind of all-American cuisine available on the line's other ships, takes place in a handsome, airy dining room decked out in rattan furnishings and pretty peach lines.

Evenings, you can select from among four lounges: the Sky Lounge up on the top deck near where you'll spend your days in the sunshine, the Riverboat Lounge, the Mississippi Lounge, and a fourth lounge on a deck quite appropriately called Lounge Deck.

Cabins

It's hard to refute the line's claim that these are the largest staterooms afloat. They are, after all, 250 square feet in area and there's no question that that's big.

All of them also have an outside veranda as well as an inside entrance so you can stand out on your private patio and watch Ole Man River roll by. All cabins have a big picture window, plus several chairs, twin beds, and private baths.

If you select the top-of-the-line cabin, you'll pay $1,750 for a seven-day cruise. Go it one better—a suite—and you pay $2,450. Per-person rates for other category cabins on a seven-day cruise are just the same as on the line's other ships: $1,610 for a Category A cabin, $1,400 for a Category B. Singles pay $2,100 for a seven-day cruise and triple rates are $1,400 per person.

4. AMERICAN HAWAII CRUISES

Contact: American Hawaii Cruises, 550 Kearny St., San Francisco, CA 94108 (tel. 415/392-9400, or toll free 800/227-3666).
Cruising Grounds: Hawaiian Islands.

Itineraries: *Constitution*—Honolulu – Maui – Hilo – Kona – Kauai – Honolulu.

Independence—Honolulu – Kauai – Kona – Hilo – Maui – Honolulu.

Aloha, mai e'ai, e alu, and especially *le'ale'a!* That's what American Hawaii Cruises, owners of two historic U.S. vessels, wishes you. And come to think of it, they provide it for you too.

From sunup to sunset, Hawaii is in evidence aboard this line's *Constitution* and *Independence,* so when your island cruise ends you'll be able to say all those words and know what they mean "Greetings, come and dine, relax, and have fun!" The *Constitution* and *Independence* provide all that and more for you, and toss in visits to those palm-fringed Hawaiian Islands, home of hula hands and silver sands.

Created in 1978, American Hawaii is a comparatively new line operating two elegant craft built in an American shipyard. They have the distinction of being the only craft operating as American-flag vessels. One of them, the *Constitution,* was thought lovely enough, in fact, to carry Grace Kelly and her wedding party across the sea to Monaco for her marriage to a prince.

American Hawaii bought the *Independence* from a Hong Kong shipping company and began operating her in Hawaii on seven-day inter-island cruises. Success on that front led the company to purchase the *Constitution,* sister ship to the *Independence,* and in 1982 this ship also became an American flag carrier.

Now both ships are sailing the Hawaiian Islands, with occasional Pacific Ocean cruises from California. Built in 1951 to carry 1,000 passengers on long Mediterranean cruises, the ships' passenger load has been lowered to 800, so cabins and public areas are spacious. The *Constitution* was refurbished in 1987, as was the *Independence* in 1988.

Glenn Ford, Anthony Quinn, Alan Ladd, Peter Ustinov, and Ronald Reagan have sailed aboard the *Constitution.* And if she looks strangely familiar to you, it may be because she's also a film star: Cary Grant and Deborah Kerr filmed *An Affair to Remember* aboard this ship. She was also the star of a "Real People" television segment.

If you like numbers, you'll find the statistics the same on both ships: both are 30,090 tons, 682 feet long, and 89 feet wide.

Recently the line introduced a new land-and-sea package perfect for those who can't make up their minds. If you're one of those, you can book a deal that offers you a three-day cruise from Honolulu to Hilo or Hilo to Honolulu followed by a four-day stay at the Kona Surf on the "Big Island" of Hawaii, the Turtle Bay Hilton on the windward coast of Oahu, or the Prince Kuhio in Honolulu. Fares, including land transfers to the ship, a rental car on Hawaii or Oahu, the hotel stay, the cruise, and an inter-island flight to get you to or from the ship, begin at $699 for a three-day cruise, $799 for a four-day voyage.

American Hawaii also has an "A-Low-Ha" standby program that lets you put your name on a waiting list and cruise when the line has the space to accommodate you. That means, of course, that you need to have a flexible travel schedule since you may or may not get the cruise dates you seek. Fares for the standby program are $1,150 per person for inside cabins, $1,395 for outside quarters.

Thanks to the ships' U.S. flag and an act of Congress, American companies can now deduct the cost of conventions aboard ship from their taxes. American Hawaii thought that was very good news and has aimed some of its marketing programs at conventioneers, so you may find yourself at a meeting aboard one of the ships.

Both sail on Saturday from Honolulu, calling at Nawiliwili in Kauai, at Hilo and Kona on the "Big Island" of Hawaii, and at Kahului in Maui. The *Constitution* overnights at Kauai while the *Independence* overnights at Maui.

Activities

On Hawaiian island cruises, Hawaii and things Hawaiian are the theme. An award-winning Polynesian revue sizzles with grass skirts and swaying hips. Big pineapples and luscious island flavors turn up at meals. Those Hawaiian shirts and muu-muus are everywhere you look, adorned with leis and boutonnieres.

Both ships also feature cabaret entertainment. On these two Hawaii-bound ships, featured performers are Hawaiian celebrities.

On shore, tours emphasize sporting pursuits, things like golf, windsurfing, waterskiing, and scuba-diving, as well as the usual visits to famous resort beaches and into the showy waterfalls and misty mountains of these islands.

A couple of unusual shore excursions for the adventurer: imagine yourself "Captain Cook for a Day" on a kayak trip into the heart of Huleia National Wildlife Refuge, where Cook once came ashore; pedal your way around on a tour of the north shore of Kauai; or chug over the wettest spot on earth on a helicopter trip above 5,000-foot-high Waialeale Crater. Other options: parasailing, a trek by horseback down the 10,000-foot summit of Mount Haleakala on Sliding Sands Trail, and rafting trips around Kauai's Na Pali coast.

On board, you can learn how to hula or create a flower lei or play the ukulele. You can try making a hat out of palm fronds, play cards, Bingo, or shuffleboard —perhaps spot a whale.

Or shed a few poi pounds at exercise and dancercize classes.

Movies? Of course. Food? Endless.

CONSTITUTION/INDEPENDENCE:
These sea ladies are not only sister ships, they're twins. So alike are they in spirit and in statistics that we can explore both at once.

Public Rooms

You'll never lack for a place to play aboard the *Independence* or the *Constitution*. Every deck has a handsome lounge, each different, each offering entertainment, be it quiet pursuits or lively ones.

Up on the Sun Deck is one very popular place, the swimming pool, and nearby the inevitable snackbar and libations arena. On the *Independence* it's the Barefoot Bar; on the *Constitution*, the Beachcomber Bar.

One deck down is the ship's main showroom, the big Pacific Showplace on the *Independence*, the Tropicana Showplace on the *Constitution*. Both have a lovely curving glassed-in section called the Commodore's/Tradewinds Terrace.

Amidships on this Promenade Deck is the *Independence/Constitution*

Lounge, where great curving banquettes divide the room into cozy sipping spots.

On the *Constitution* a small room has been set aside to honor Princess Grace. Understandably, it's called the Princess Grace Room. There are lounges called Latitude 20 Degrees on the *Independence* and Lahaina Landing on the *Constitution*.

Children are much loved by this cruise line, which provides children's playrooms on both ships and a youth recreation center on the *Independence*. In school holiday seasons youngsters have a full range of activities every bit as ambitious as those offered adults. Recreation directors oversee the activities both aboard and ashore, planning disco nights and beach parties, pizza events and even appearances by youthful stars like Todd Bridges of "Different Strokes" and Kim Fields and Mindy Cohn of "Facts of Life." Video games too, of course.

You'll be dining in the pretty Palms Dining Room on board the *Independence* and in the Hibiscus Dining Room on the *Constitution*. Favorite American steak and seafood selections are supplemented with exotic island creations: things like lomi-lomi salmon, cream of coconut aloha, crabflake cocktails, mahimahi, ono, ulua, or opakapaka. What's that? Try it and find out!

Both ships have theaters too.

Cabins

American Hawaii Cruises does the best job of any cruise line afloat in describing its cabins. Not only does their brochure allot two full pages to detailed descriptions of each category of cabin, but it also includes photographs and small sketches of each kind of cabin so you'll have a clear idea what you're buying. Sketches indicate every stick of furniture in the room, from beds and chairs to closet, sofa, dresser, shower, sink, table, toilet, window, and Pullman quarters.

A high percentage of cabins are outside quarters, so if you like the idea of a room with a view, you have a very good chance of fulfilling your desires. All rooms are air-conditioned, certainly a necessity over this way, and all have televisions, most adapted for closed-circuit broadcasts of films and activities on board.

On board both ships you'll find some very attractive quarters ranging from suites to simpler quarters. Some have king-size beds and some have nifty beds that flip back to become a couch. As is usual with older ships, spacious quarters prevail but rooms come in all sizes and quite a variety of shapes.

Prices are the same on both vessels, divided into cabin Categories A (the highest price) through J (the lowest). There are no seasons to be dealt with in these balmy all-year-round tropics.

To get an idea of what a Hawaiian Island cruise on the *Constitution* or the *Independence* will cost, here's a look at prices for a week-long island cruise. If you want the very best, book a suite, a very roomy stateroom indeed, with a separate sitting room you can close off from the bedroom. Two lower beds can be pushed together to create a king-size sleeper. For one of these you pay $2,395 to $3,295 per person for a week's cruise.

Three categories of outside rooms, Categories B, C, and D, all feature two lower beds or a double bed, and begin at a high of $2,095 per person, dropping $100 in each category to a low of $1,895 per person for the seven-day cruises.

Three categories of inside rooms have twin beds or a double bed, and the prices for these (Categories E, F, and G) cabins are $1,595 to $1,795 per person, for the island voyage.

On the *Constitution* some cabins in Categories E, F, and G have king-size beds. Prices are the same, however.

Note to bargain seekers: The line has a few outside staterooms with upper and lower berths. It calls them economy cabins and offers them for $1,595.

There are also a comparatively large number of inside cabins, also with upper and lower berths, designed for the budgetwise at $995 to $1,395 per person for a week-long cruise.

Third and fourth adults sharing a cabin pay $495 to $595; children under 17 pay $295.

Single travelers pay a surcharge of 50% to 100% more for single occupancy.

Per diem rates range from a low of $142 to a high, excluding suites, of $299 per person for a seven-day cruise. All prices are a bit higher in December. Port and service charges are $31 per person.

Air/sea packages offering round-trip air fare from a number of mainland cities let you fly to join the cruise for less than $450 per person, round trip.

5. BERMUDA STAR LINE

Contact: Bermuda Star Line, 1086 Teaneck Rd., Teaneck, NJ 07666 (tel. toll free 800/237-5361).

Cruising Grounds: Mexico, U.S. East Coast, Canada, Bermuda, New Orleans.

Itineraries: *Bermuda Queen*—
IN SUMMER: New York – Bermuda – New York.
IN WINTER: New Orleans – Key West – Playa del Carmen – Cozumél – New Orleans.

Bermuda Star—
IN SUMMER: New York – Newport – Sydney – Bonaventure Island – Perce – Gaspé – Saguenay Fjord – Québec City – Montréal *or* Montréal – Québec City – Perce – Gaspé – Halifax – Martha's Vineyard – Fall River – New York or Philadelphia.
IN WINTER: San Diego – Cabo San Lucas – Puerto Vallarta – Mazatlán – San Diego.

Veracruz—Tampa – Playa del Carmen – Cozumél – Tampa, year round.

Until 1984 Bahama Cruise Line, now called the Bermuda Star Line, operated one ship, the *Veracruz*, moving her in winter to Florida's west coast and in summer to New York. In 1984 the fleet doubled with the addition of Holland America's *Veendam*, now known as the *Bermuda Star*. Then in 1987 the line expanded again by reuniting the *Bermuda Star* with her original sister ship built by Moore-McCormack Lines and first known as the *Brazil*. Sold later to Holland America Line, which renamed the ship the *Volendam*, and then later to another company which renamed it the *Liberté* for Tahiti sailings, the *Bermuda Queen* sailed briefly as the *Canada Star* before getting her present tag in 1988 when she began sailing the line's Bermuda cruises.

Bermuda Star Line's *Veracruz* no longer follows the seasons but instead stays year round in Florida, where she sails from Tampa to Mexico's Sun Coast cities on five-day sojourns and spends the remaining two days sailing in Gulf of Mexico waters on short cruises to nowhere.

A branch of a New York transportation company called Common Brothers, the Bermuda Star Line sails its *Bermuda Star* on week-long voyages from New York up the St. Lawrence to Montréal. You can embark in New York or in Montréal and get to one of those cities on Amtrak's *Adirondack* day train or *Montrealer* night train. Several fall cruises visit Bermuda, Cape Cod, Martha's Vineyard, and Nantucket.

The latest addition to this line is the *Bermuda Queen*, which in summer sails between New York and Bermuda, a familiar itinerary for this craft. It also sails to Playa del Carmen, Cozumél, and Key West, but from New Orleans, one of the few ships to call that lacy old city home.

The *Bermuda Queen*'s unusual summer itinerary features trips from New York to two ports in Bermuda—St. George and Hamilton—so you can get a look at the colonial charm of St. George and still not miss the cosmopolitan glitz of Hamilton. These cruises arrive in St. George's in the morning and spend the night and next day there, leaving at 6 a.m. for the two-hour sail to Hamilton, where the ship remains until 11 a.m., spending a day at sea on either end of the cruise.

All these ships are venerable old ladies offering all the basic amenities, more of them on the *Bermuda Star* and *Bermuda Queen* than on the smaller *Veracruz*. Cabins and public rooms sometimes show their age on these ships.

One cannot fault the crews, however. They work hard to keep you happy and provide you with plenty of pampering.

Activities

As with many Caribbean sailers, activities on board begin early and end late, if at all, on the *Veracruz*. Each evening there's entertainment in the ship's lounge and dancing in several sections of the ship, not the least of which is the Disco just off the Lido Bar.

Life is very casual aboard this ship. You can dress to the nines on one or two evenings if you like, but you won't feel uncomfortable in jacket and tie even on formal evenings.

You won't find a full-fledged midnight buffet on board the *Veracruz*, but you can get pizza at the witching hour and stave off night starvation with some hot snacks. A coffeeshop is open until 2 a.m. too.

Casino fans will find a small game room with slots, roulette, and four black-jack tables.

If you think you have talent, you can find out whether others agree at a talent show. There's also a costume party.

A popular family ship, the *Veracruz* has special rates for children.

At 23,500 tons, the *Bermuda Star* and *Bermuda Queen* are much larger ships but carry about the same number of passengers. They have had quite respectable careers, often sailing the Caribbean. While the ships retain that play-as-you-go atmosphere that's so popular in the Caribbean, they're a bit more formal than their sister ship, the *Veracruz*. Cabins are large on board the *Bermuda Star* and *Bermuda Queen*, which were originally built as transoceanic cruisers, and many of them are outside quarters. Attention nightowls: yes, there is a full-fledged midnight buffet on these ships.

VERACRUZ: Built in 1957 by a German shipbuilder, the *Veracruz* was constructed for transatlantic service and was once known as the *Freeport II*. Refurbished in recent years, she measures in at 10,595 tons and 487 feet long, and carries about 700 passengers.

Public Rooms

The first thing you'll see aboard is Bimini Deck. It's also the place you'll visit most often during your voyage—most of the ship's playing places are on this deck. For openers there's the big Dolphin Lounge, with bars at both ends and a dance floor in the middle. This is the place to see the evening's entertainment, which ranges from singers to dancers to comedians. Two bands perform here each night as well.

On the other end of this deck is the bright Casino Lounge, where piano-bar fans will find some of their kind of music. Big curtained windows here make this a cheerful room in which to while away the day. There's a small dance floor tucked away in this room too. On really romantic evenings you can move out to the nearby observation area and dance there in the moonlight.

You'll find a pretty main staircase on board, with bright mirrors and glowing chandeliers.

Between the two major rooms on this deck is a shopping arcade where you can pick up the gift you forgot in port. Beauty salon, barbershop, and information offices are here too.

One deck up and aft is the disco, tucked in beside the circular Lido Bar.

Still one more deck up is the sunning space including a glassed-in solarium and another observation area.

Swimmers will find the ship's small round pool down on Calypso Deck. While the main part of the pool is rectangular, two eyebrow arches on either side offer shallow splashing water perfect for children and nonswimmers. Nearby is the New Orleans Terrace, home of a snackbar and purveyor of hamburgers and hot dogs.

Amidships on Delta Deck is the Bahamas Dining Room, a U-shaped room with two wings down the sides of the ship. And down in the depths of the vessel you'll find the Cinema Theater.

A simple ship, the *Veracruz* is not a luxury liner and doesn't pretend to be, so don't expect glitter.

Cabins

On board you'll find 367 cabins designed to serve as sitting rooms by day and bedrooms by night. They're equipped with a sofa bed and a recessed bed, or sometimes with a double sofa bed or two lower beds. All have private bathrooms with a shower and sink. You can use your electrical appliances here too. Some, of course, have upper berths accommodating a third or fourth person.

Once again, don't expect spacious luxury. Cabins are small, with basic accoutrements like carpeting and private bathrooms but nothing fancy.

Cabin prices run from Category 1 (the highest prices) through Category 10 (the lowest). Peak season runs from January through September, but prices are about $100 higher on Christmas and New Year's sailings.

Let's look at some of the prices for a five-day Caribbean cruise in peak season (January to September). You will pay $349 to $399 per person for all inside cabins, and $419 to $449 for all outside quarters. Some two-room suites are available.

Third and fourth persons sharing a cabin are $200 for each adult, $100 for each child under 11. Four berths are found in inside cabins only.

Some outside staterooms have double beds.

Budget an additional $23 per person for port charges.

Single travelers pay an additional 50% in any category of cabin.

As you can see, per diem costs range from a very low $70 per person to a high of $92, less in fall, making this ship one of the best budget buys afloat.

Some discounts are often available for senior citizens on certain sailings, and for payment 90 days or so in advance. On New England cruises you also get a discount if you take the two-week cruise.

Air/sea add-on rates—or freebies—are available too.

BERMUDA QUEEN / BERMUDA STAR: Built in 1958, the former *Brazil* and *Argentina* both measure 23,500 tons and carry about 700 passengers and a crew of 300. Their officers are European and the crew is a mix of nationalities.

Public Rooms

Most of your playtime will find you on Promenade Deck, where the public rooms are located. There are several shops and a newsstand on board so you can buy and read whenever you like.

Tan fans will find quite a number of open spots in which to seek the sun, but the biggest and best is on the Promenade Deck where you'll find the ship's swimming pool. A canopied area accommodates those who want the air but not the sun, and of course there's the usual snackbar and lounge right nearby.

At night that lounge turns on to the music of a dance band, and this attractive bright room is usually packed with dancers.

On the Promenade Deck you'll also find another big lounge and polygonal dance floor surrounded by long banquettes that snake about the room creating several intimate corners. Just off the open promenade at the bow is the ship's casino, which features the usual slots and blackjack tables. It's located not far from yet another lounge and dancing spot, and a card room and library are nearby.

Look up on the Observation Deck or Sun Deck for a quiet spot with lots of windows and a semicircular seating area that's a pleasant place for a chat with friends.

The ships' long rectangular dining rooms are on the main deck, and down a deck is the theater. Up a deck is a health center.

Cabins

Cabins aboard these 30+-year-old ships are quite comfortable, many of them large as befits a transatlantic cruiser. They are decked out in attractive contemporary fabrics.

The top cabins are deluxe outside double rooms with two beds, full vanity, large wardrobes, comfortable sitting area with a couple of chairs and a table, and a full bathroom with both bathtub and shower.

Dropping a category, you'll find outside double rooms with twin lower beds and similar accoutrements, but in these the sitting area is smaller. Some have double beds.

Inside double rooms are smaller but still have adequate space, with twin beds, a vanity, plenty of wardrobe space.

The lowest-priced accommodations have one lower bed, or lower and upper berths, but still have a vanity, closets, and bathroom.

The following prices are for a week-long cruise on board the *Bermuda Star* in peak summer season, from mid-July through mid-August. (You will pay $20 less in late summer through September.) Cabin price categories are numbered from 1 through 10: Category 10 is the lowest-priced, Category 1, the highest priced.

The most expensive quarters aboard feature two lower beds and a sitting area, and cost $1,395 per person in peak season.

Larger cabins, in Categories 2, 3, and 4, most of them outside cabins, are $1,300 to $1,370 per person for a week's summer trip.

Three cheaper categories of outside cabins also feature two lower beds and are $1,195 to $1,255 per person for a week's voyage.

Cabins in Categories 8 and 9 are inside quarters with two lower beds and are $1,045 to $1,095 per person for the week's voyage in high summer season.

The least expensive cabins on board feature upper and lower berths and may be inside or outside cabins. These quarters are $995 per person in peak summer season.

Singles pay $1,395 for inside or outside single rooms on the upper and main decks.

Children under 8 are free on many summer sailings.
A tip for super-budget travelers: Inside cabins dubbed "young people's cabins" are located deep in the ship on Hollywood Deck, have no elevator, television, or phone, but are just $795 per person for a week-long cruise to Bermuda.

6. CARNIVAL CRUISE LINES

Contact: Carnival Cruise Lines, 5225 NW 87th Ave., Miami, FL 33166 (tel. 305/576-9260, 305/327-2058 for bookings within 30 days of sailing; or toll free 800/327-9051, 800/432-5424 in Florida).

Cruising Grounds: Mexico (from both Florida and California), Bahamas, Caribbean.

Itineraries: *Carnivale*—Miami – Nassau – Miami *or* Miami – Freeport – Nassau – Miami, year round.

Celebration—Miami – San Juan – St. Thomas – St. Maarten – Miami, year round.

Festivale—San Juan – St. Thomas – St. Maarten – Barbados – Martinique – San Juan, year round.

Holiday—Miami – Cozumél – Playa del Carmen – Grand Cayman – Ocho Ríos – Miami, year round.

Jubilee—Miami – Nassau – San Juan – St. Thomas – Miami, year round.

Mardi Gras—Fort Lauderdale – Nassau – Fort Lauderdale *or* Fort Lauderdale – Freeport – Nassau – Fort Lauderdale, year round.

Tropicale—Los Angeles – Puerto Vallarta – Mazatlán – cruising by Cabo San Lucas – Los Angeles, year round.

You can call Carnival Cruise Lines many things but you cannot call it subdued. Glitz and glitter, socko-on-socko color and more changes of pace and face than "The Price Is Right." Those are the things Carnival's endless-party ships are made of and that's exactly how they want it.

Indeed, Carnival Cruise Lines blithely bills itself as the fun ships, folks. Nonstop activity is the watchword here, so if you're looking for action days—and nights—you'll want to see what's going on at Carnival.

Carnival's execs know exactly what market they're aiming at and they know just how to satisfy it: fun, fun, fun, and sun, sun, sun. Carnival cruisers want to get away for a week or so, see a few ports, and play to the max.

Few lines are growing as fast as Carnival Cruise Lines, which put one new ship, the *Holiday,* in service in 1985; then the *Jubilee* arrived in the summer of 1986, and the *Celebration* in 1987. And there are three more to come!

In the fall of 1989 Carnival will be welcoming the *Fantasy* to the fold. It will be the first of three new Carnival super-liners, each measuring in at 70,000 tons and carrying 2,050 passengers (more if the line lures enough passengers to fill cabins with three or four travelers). One year later, Carnival's talented hoopla experts will focus on the *Ecstasy,* and in the fall of 1991 they'll be showing the world a *Sensation.*

Much of the success of Carnival's fleet must go to its sometimes-controversial, always-a-good-quote marketing executive, Bob Dickinson and to

Carnival's energetic marketing staff, which pursues potential passengers with enthusiasm and affordable prices.

So intent is Carnival on marketing "fun" that it has made that somewhat nebulous concept part of its theme: the line's vessels call themselves "the Fun Ships," which says much to many. It should say something to you about the whoop-de-do atmosphere you'll find aboard the line's seven (soon to be ten) craft: the *Carnivale, Celebration, Festivale, Mardi Gras, Tropicale, Holiday,* and *Jubilee.*

So successfully have they pursued this sun-and-fun market, in fact, that the company now boasts occupancy rates above 100%! (If you're wondering how they manage that, it has to do with the presence of third and fourth passengers in a cabin.) Not bad for a company that once thought its ship would never come in. When Carnival first appeared back in 1972 with one ship, the aging *Empress of Canada,* things did not go well at all. As a matter of fact, they did not *go* at all: the ship ran aground. Nothing improved much for Carnival's first ship, by now called the *Mardi Gras,* until 1975 when the line's ship came in to the tune of 100%-plus occupancy.

So shoestring was the company when it first began operating that it didn't want to spend the money to do a whole new paint job on the ship's stack, so it just altered the Canadian Pacific Line logo enough to make it look different. You can still see the resemblance in the line's red, white, and blue funnels.

From there the wave of success rose higher as the company bought the *Empress of Britain* to turn it into the *Carnivale,* then used profits to buy the *Transvaal,* renamed it the *Festivale,* and treated it to a $20-million facelift. In 1982 the line floated the brand-new *Tropicale,* now sailing from California.

In recent years Carnival has been a strong and vocal supporter of the free air fare concept. That means that if you decide on a Carnival ship, even one on an opposite coast, you pay nothing (or almost nothing) to fly to that other coast to board the ship. Nothing's for nothing, they say, but these offers, which are also made by other middle-market cruise lines, come close.

Carnival's ships seem to us best suited to young and/or first-time cruisers willing to forgo elegance for a relaxed fun-jammed, action-packed week filled with plenty of piña coladas and late nights. Still, Carnival cruises attract plenty of the not-so-youthful as well. In fact one of the scheduled parties aboard is a grandparent's bragging event, so you'll find all ages aboard.

You'll also find honeymooners and singles, swingers and quiet types, midwesterners and Yankees—everyone in search of a week of fun and frolic on the high seas. Unlike many cruise ships that sell the fascination of their ports of call, the emphasis on board these ships is on the shipboard experience.

It seems fair to say that they do all they can to keep you at play aboard the ship, with about 80% of the cruise spent on board and 20% in port. So nonstop is activity aboard, in fact, that your shipboard experience sometimes seems to mimic what the ships' names suggest: a lively, party-up Mardi Gras, carnival, holiday, jubilee, festival, and celebration.

Italian officers and many Italians in the crew ensure that there will be good food and plenty of pasta aboard.

All the line's ships feature Carnival's distinctive red, white, and blue smokestack, and all are painted a snappy white to go with it.

Carnival's schedules have changed a bit in recent years as the company has brought new ships into its main Miami marketplace. When the *Holiday* arrived, Carnival moved the *Mardi Gras* to Fort Lauderdale where it began sailing on three- and four-day cruises to Nassau and Freeport.

When the *Jubilee* was about to arrive, the line moved one of its other older ships, the *Festivale,* to San Juan where it began sailing on seven-day cruises to islands Carnival had never visited before—Barbados, Martinique, and the like. Then it assigned the *Jubilee* to another new destination for Carnival: Mexico's Yucatán Peninsula, stopping at Grand Cayman and Ocho Ríos.

Carnival also get the credit for making that French/Dutch island of St. Maarten a really popular cruise port. Carnival was the first Miami ship to call there every week.

The *Jubilee* and the *Celebration* are 48,000-ton ships, the largest ever built specifically for cruising. Both are seven-day ships.

If Carnival completes its plans, by 1995 the line will have ten ships, something like 10,000 beds in its fleet, and will be carrying more than a million passengers a year.

Activities

So what is all this activity we're talking about? Well, for openers there are movies going in the ships' theaters all day and most of the night, nonstop.

There's always a party somewhere on board, be it grandparents bragging, beer drinking, pillow fighting, plank toppling, men's pretty legs, or champagne celebrations for honeymooning couples.

Following through on their "Fun Ship" theme, the line figures fun has no age limit and so plans something for absolutely everyone, from the youngsters to the oldsters and back again. As line executives like to say, at any given moment "the ship really cooks." There are bands playing outside, the casino is going, continuous movies, activities in- and outdoors, a disco rolling.

Even on its three- and four-day schedules Carnival keeps the Nassau visit to one day and then spends all day at sea to, as Carnival executives put it, "showcase" their product.

At dinner every night there's a theme evening, something like French night, for instance. And here's an interesting touch: if you have a certain age preference in dinner companions you can request that when you book your cabin.

Cruise staffers must be entertainers as well, so some nights you'll see them performing magic tricks, singing, and dancing.

Entertainment is slightly different on the *Tropicale*, where the western audiences are accustomed to glitzy Las Vegas shows and mariachi bands. You'll find both on board that ship, and sometimes even a steel band, which proved so popular in test runs that it just stayed. Definitely there will be a calypso band on Caribbean voyages.

CARNIVALE: Launched in 1957 as the *Empress of Britain,* this 27,250-ton "Fun Ship" carries 950 fun-seekers to such fun spots as Nassau and Freeport. Renovated in 1976 and refurbished in 1984, the ship retains many '50s touches, and in cabins some dated, if unabashedly tropical, color schemes.

Wood, wood, and more wood is a watchword of this ship. Fabulous lightwood paneling lines the hallways, and corners are often trimmed in contrasting dark woods. You'll see polished wood handrails and handsome wood head and foot boards everywhere you look.

In some of the hallways aboard you'll find taps for ice water, and in a couple of corners you can spot little lighted alcoves labeled "cigarette ends." Antique buffs will love exploring this ship.

Public Rooms

Carnivale's International Dining Room is down on the main deck, a dark spot lined with beautiful woods and wood columns. A burgundy color scheme here is sparked by white linens.

Dance buffs should head straight for the circular Fly Aweigh Disco, where the floor lights up, old windows feature etched glass, old fittings hark back to days gone by, and there's even a jukebox. Woodworking fans ought to love the burl door too.

Mardi Gras Nightclub is also a circular spot, but this lounge is done up in blues with chairs that give a giant "poof" when you settle into them. The stage is trimmed in shiny stars and there's live entertainment in this room, which also features a circular parquet floor.

On the same Promenade Deck you'll find the cinema not far from the children's playroom, and the ship's gift shop and boutique.

Between the Mardi Gras Nightclub and the disco (of all places!) is a small library.

As you might have guessed by now we're very partial to those long enclosed promenades, one of which you'll find here. You shouldn't have any trouble finding your way around the walkways either—big marquee signs identify public rooms like the casino, which by the way features a bank of impressive brass doors.

Art deco turns up on the doors to the refurbished cinema.

The largest lounge aboard is the Showplace, which seats 550 and is done up in plastic chairs in shades of burgundy and tan and features lots of windows.

Swimming pools? Good grief, yes. Up top on the Lido Deck the Lido Beach Club features no fewer than three pools and a wader, and way down on Riviera Deck there's yet another pool, the Coral Pool, near the ship's gym and sauna.

Cabins

If you like an early-morning dip in private, some of the ship's lowest-priced rooms—$325 to $425 per person for a three-day winter cruise—are not too far from the indoor pool.

There are 12 rate categories aboard, with the most expensive cabins in Category 12, the least expensive in Category 1. Cruises also are divided into "season" prices and "base" prices. Base prices are in effect in the slow tourist season in these waters and season prices are in effect in the most popular winter months and June through August. Exact season dates had not been set when this book went to press, but figure January to April as top-price months along with those summer months already mentioned, and everything else at base prices.

The following are the *Carnivale*'s prices for a three-day cruise in peak summer season, from June through August.

Top dollar for a three-day cruise at that time will buy a veranda suite, a very spacious suite with a big separate sitting room and a twin-bedded room with lots of closet and drawer space. Despite the veranda tag, these do not have an open balcony. They do, however, have big french doors that close one room off from the other, thus giving two couples or a family more privacy than is available on any other ship we know. That could make this a bargain for you if you're traveling with others. The price for this suite on a three-day cruise is $885 per person.

Because rooms differ so widely aboard the ship it's really quite impossible to begin describing them. Suffice it to say that the more you pay, the more space you buy—and on this ship more is plenty! Cabins are quite spacious, even in the lowest categories, and not uncomfortably crowded even at the minimum rate. That's one of the reasons some people are so partial to older ships like this one.

Outside cabins from Category 11 down through Category 6 will cost from $835 per person for a three-day trip to $695 per person, not a large gap. Cabin E73 seems a good example of Category 10, and a particularly good example of a room with lovely wood headboards. You'll also find a matching dresser and triple mirror, plus a full-length mirror. There's a separate sitting room and twin beds in this outside deluxe double.

Nearby E69 is a veranda suite with aging furnishings, a sitting room, and more of that same beautiful wood. Tub and toilet are each in separate rooms here, as they are in many cabins throughout the ship.

Category 6 cabins (inside) and Category 8 (outside) feature twin beds. One of those folds up to become a couch and one upper pulls down. A shower shoots right into the floor, testimony to the aging plumbing aboard. Of these cabins, 41 is nice. The cost of a Category 6 inside cabin is $695, and for a Category 8, $735 per person for the three-day voyage.

Category 5 inside cabins with twin or double bed are $655, and again are pretty spacious quarters.

Categories 4, 3, 2, and 1 include both outside cabins with upper and lower berths, and inside cabins with upper and lower berths, a double bed, or twins. Those with double or twin beds cost the most: $635 per person for three days. Those with upper and lower berths, or inside rooms with double beds, range from $375 to $495 per person for three days.

Third and fourth persons sharing a cabin pay $190 for adults, $95 for children, on a three-day trip.

Single occupancy of a cabin costs an additional 50% in Categories 1 to 3, and twice the price in other categories.

If you're willing to share a cabin with three other people, you pay $190 for a three-day cruise.

Port charges are $24 for adults for the three-day cruise, $26 for the four-day trip.

Per diem rates on the ship work out at a low of about $125 per person in summer and a high of $275, excluding suites. Rates are about $120 higher in winter.

FESTIVALE: Carnival has adapted some aging craft to its purposes, which means that you can expect some unusually large cabins aboard. Not that they're all huge, by any means, just that you'll find more large cabins than you might find on some other newer ships never built to pamper the demanding transoceanic traveler.

On the other hand you'll have to accept a few of the less desirable elements imposed by this antiquity. For instance, you'll have to get used to visible sinks right in your room rather than tucked away in separate bathrooms, aging electrical and plumbing systems, and dining rooms well below decks with no windows.

Public Rooms

Festivale's very best feature, to our mind, is a long, long deck, glassed floor to ceiling, where you can sit in windless, rainless comfort and watch the world go by—shades of "Bring me my tea, Jeeves."

The Tradewinds Club is a very Sidney Greenstreet spot in which to perfect your Bogart imitation, and the Copacabana Lounge, after a recent renovation, sports a custom-made carpet in a parrot motif of reds, blues, and blacks with matching banquette seating in ruby-red with black stripes and iridescent lavender chairs. Now there's a daring decorator for you!

In the Continental Restaurant you'll now see a vivid color scheme that unabashedly mixes rose, salmon, black, gray, and turquoise. After dinner—which often ends with showy presentations of flaming desserts and drinks delivered on trays balanced on the waiters' heads—head for the Gaslight for an *après* specialty coffee and pastry in what is now a coffee bar, a feature that's being incorporated into some of the line's older ships after it proved a hit on its newest craft.

The Carnivale Lounge, with its deep-burgundy accents and low contemporary chairs, art deco wood design, and tinted mirror, is the best place on the ship —nobody said we have to be objective here. The Gaslight Café is a good match for its name, with two big lanterns and a copper ceiling that give you the feeling of that era.

An entrance/reception area aboard is quite contemporary with red furnishings and attractive murals.

Backlit figures etched on glass in various colors are a don't-miss in the round Le Cabaret Room, where evening entertainment is presented. Lighted floors in the Fanta Z disco produce a light show timed to the music, and you can watch yourself at play in the mirrored ceiling. Finally, the shiny steel art deco stairways aboard ought to be designated a national treasure.

Those who visualize heaven as a place in which you drape yourself over a lounge chair beside the pool can practice up here. There are three pools aboard, two outside, one in, and one with a slide that slips you into the wet stuff, screeching with the joy of it all.

Seek out the Lido Lounge, near the indoor pool, for a look at some interesting brass ship-steering equipment, not to mention snacks.

While her antiquity is fascinating to those of us who did not live in that era, some older, more affluent travelers may not be as enchanted by this lovely old lady. Oddly enough, the *Festivale*'s antiquity appeals mightily to young travelers. One barely bearded fellow raved on and on to us about his adoration of this ship, whose best point, he said, was "its ambience, its amazing old-world travel feeling." Indeed.

Cabins

Some cabins on the *Festivale* feature double beds and even king-size sleepers, which on cruise ships is a very rare feature indeed. Upper and lower bunks are quite common aboard this craft, which makes up for its small and often dated bathroom facilities with plenty of closet space.

Let's look at some of the accommodations and the prices you'll pay for a week's cruise aboard this venerable lady in peak winter season (figure $50 to $100 less in the off-season).

The price categories are once again divided into 12 options, with Category 12 the highest-priced accommodations. There are two seasons aboard, base and (high) season. Base includes April, May, and September to December; the season is mid-January through most of April and June through August.

Those Category 12 cabins are veranda suites, very large accommodations, which sport a divider between beds and the sitting area. They're quite spacious and some even have private outdoor verandas! For one of these cabins you pay $2,095 per person for a week's cruise in peak season.

Accommodations known as demi-suites are every bit as nice as the suites. V34, for instance, has wood bedsteads and is very spacious. For that you pay $1,895 per person for the week-long trip.

Outside cabins in Categories 10 and 9 are very large outside cabins, some with queen-size beds, some with twins. One of these rooms, in either configuration, will cost $1,795 or $1,565 per person for a week's voyage in peak season.

Cabin U3 is a Category 8 cabin with a queen-size bed and an unusual arcing wall. It's small but nice for honeymooners and others who value togetherness. It's also a bit cheaper because it's smaller: $1,495 per person for that week's journey in peak season.

Cabin E147 is a basic Category 7 cabin, large with twin beds, and costs $1,445 per person for a week.

Cabin U137, a Category 6 cabin, is one of the mid-priced accommodations aboard, and has a sink in the bedroom, a queen-size bed, and a somewhat barren look to it with minimal décor elements. That one goes for $1,385 per person on the week's trip. Others in this category also have queen-size beds, but generally someone will be sleeping next to the wall.

Inside cabins with twin or queen-size beds in Categories 5 and 4 are $1,335 or $1,275 per person. An inside Category 3 cabin with upper and lower berths is $1,195 per person for the trip.

A Category 2 cabin, Cabin U143, just a few steps away, has upper and lower berths in an inside cabin and is one of just a few low-priced cabins on that deck. By low we mean $1,145 per person for a week's cruise in high season.

Lowest-price accommodation on board is an inside cabin with upper and lower berths, small but not tiny. One of those cabins is $1,075 per person for the peak-season voyage.

As you can see, per diem rates range from a low of $155 to a high of $255 per person for a week's cruise in high season, excluding suites.

Third and fourth persons sharing a room pay $395; children under 16, $195.

Port charges are $35 per person.

Single-occupancy rates are 150% of the fare in the three lowest-priced categories, 200% for higher-priced categories. Single cabins are available.

If you go for the sharing plan, four to a cabin, assigned by the line, you pay $575 per person for a week's cruise in high season—not bad at all.

CELEBRATION / JUBILEE / HOLIDAY:

As alike as three floating theme parties can be, these 1980s Carnival babies sailed into the cruise world with colors flying, quite literally. If there is any shade of the rainbow that doesn't appear on one of these ships, it must be the color Clear.

On the 45,000-ton *Holiday,* for instance, Carnival went all-out with kicky touches that range from hand-carved totem poles in one of the ship's cocktail lounges to a bright-red antique bus that's the focal point of the '40s Bus Stop Café. There are 1940 newspapers laminated atop café tables, a floor of stone and glass in the disco, and $1 million in artwork scattered about the 1,452-passenger ship.

On the *Jubilee* the Speakeasy Lounge is black and white and red, red, and red all over, right up to the arcing "piano" bar that is play-ful only in imagination. Those who tire of that scenery and can still negotiate a curving iron staircase can wind themselves right up to the casino one deck above them. Add to that the green lighted ceiling and the hot-pink floor of the Oz Discothèque . . . well, surely, or should we say colorfully, you get the picture.

As for the *Celebration,* which made its first appearance in 1987 . . . well! A Miami newspaper's architecture critic succinctly described that 1,486-passenger ship as "Mardi Gras meets *Animal House* in Las Vegas-by-the-Sea."

Carnival, which does not shrink from showmanship, is quite happy to have it that way, thank you. So happy, in fact, that they plunked millions into original artwork, much of it shiny, metallic surfaces in Day Glo–colorful hues. On the *Celebration,* a $500,000 kinetic creation graces the main lobby and a dozen neon starry constellations zap the eye at staircase landings.

Carnival's interior designer, Joe Farcus, who is responsible for the glitz and glitter of these three ships, says he got what he wanted: "I wanted passengers still to be noticing new things after a week on board."

There is little doubt that week-long cruise passengers, awestruck—or perhaps sunstruck—by hot colors, neon floors that flash and twinkle, ceilings that swoop and swirl, and clouds that glow beneath cocktail tables, are likely to be noticing new things even as they *disembark.*

Public Rooms

To give you an idea what we mean, start up on the Sun and Veranda Decks, where you'll find separate health-club facilities for men and women, saunas for each, all the latest in workout equipment, and plenty of sunning room to boot.

Each of the ships has a casual dining spot on the Lido Deck and on each the theme is nautical, from spinning directional radar arms and whirling scanners to funnels and even a closed-circuit television showing a long-running favorite: the view from the bridge.

In the *Celebration*'s Rainbow Casino, far more colors than any rainbow ever boasted streak down walls and race around the ceiling on neon tracks. So bright is it in this gambling den that, as one passenger put it, "You can wear sunglasses and still see the numbers."

Yes, indeed you can, for on this ship, when it is dark, it's very dark, and when it is not, it's shattering. Take, for instance, the liner's Red Hot Piano Bar, which tinkles by night with piano music. By day it's a wall-to-wall blitz of red-satin red guaranteed to knock your socks off, whether or not you're wearing any.

On all three ships there is at least one room that goes to the opposite extreme. On the *Celebration* it's the Admiral's Club, where soft, subtle colors are enhanced by an impressive collection of early steamship models tastefully encased in Lucite. A royal-blue rug woven with tiny red cruise ships glows in the light of a massive stained-glass chandelier depicting the *Queen Mary* and the *Normandie* steaming past each other. On the *Holiday* it's the Carnegie Library, an escapist's haven of soft light and chairs to match; on the *Jubilee* it's Churchill's, where a set of shining armor and a faux fireplace define the atmosphere.

Carnival is very proud of its showy showgirl revues and sees to it that they have a showroom to match. On the *Celebration* it's the multilevel Astoria Lounge, where marble and stainless steel are combined with hot, zappy colors and elaborate indirect lighting.

Farcus said he set out to use color and materials in a nontraditional way, and he certainly could be said to have accomplished his goal. In the *Celebration*'s Islands in the Sky lounge, fluffy white nimbi are outlined in lights beneath the convertible stage/dance floor on lighted-from-beneath cocktail tables and in colorful neon over the rear bar.

On these ships shiny metal surfaces flash, and neon and plastic are used in innovative and unusual ways. There is no single theme aboard any of the ships—far from it. Each room seems an entity unto itself with no colors or themes flowing into any other area.

Aboard the *Celebration* the Galaxy-Z Disco comes complete with underlighted black glass floors, circular ceiling bubbles with imbedded lighting, and flashing strobes mounted on anything that doesn't move. On the *Jubilee* the Park Lane Promenade focuses on a pink-pillared Victorian gazebo with turquoise railings and tiny Tivoli lights; on the *Holiday* Rick's Café Americana is a study in floating Casablanca atmosphere; and the *Celebration*'s Endless Summer lounge is trimmed ceiling to floor with peach and salmon dinghy hulls.

On these ships the staid Promenade Deck of yore retains its purpose as the place to see and be seen, but has abandoned staid with a vengeance. Instead, watchers and watchees ramble on the Promenade's Bourbon Street, Broadway, or Park Lane. Those fanciful "streets" (one even has shining steel trolley tracks) link the ships' showrooms, where flashy showgirls show quite a lot, to another large and showy lounge designed for dancing and conversation.

On the *Holiday* that quieter haven is called the Blue Lagoon Lounge, and it's painted in wavy shades of green and blue that give you the eerie feeling you're floating while floating! At night this room becomes the showroom for individual performers, singers mostly, and is a favorite dancing spot too. In between the big lounges are smaller lounges, a disco, and this departure: a cappuccino/espresso/truffles/ice cream bar outfitted, on the *Celebration* in handsome gray leather.

The *Holiday*'s enclosed promenade runs all the way down one side of the ship. Called Broadway, it's a brick boulevard with teak sidewalks. In the center you'll find a vintage bus, cozily parked in the middle of the Bus Stop Café. In the bus you'll spot '40s characters, dressed in clothes of the era, patiently awaiting arrival at their "stop."

Those who can add up to 21 faster than a speeding computer head straight for the ship's casino. On the *Holiday* that's to be found behind etched-glass doors in an atmosphere designed to evoke the concentration-and-desperation quiet of a private gambling club. If, heaven forbid, you don't do well, just sidle over to the red spiral staircase, slink down it, and you'll find yourself immersed in piña coladas and sympathy at Rick's Café, a lounge that appears by different names on each of the ships and is connected to the casino by a showy set of steppers.

Like its twin sisters, *Celebration* has two dining rooms, Vista and Horizon, both with raised center sections that serve to hide the waiters' stations from view and give diners in the center of the room a view through wide windows that line both sides of the rooms.

Décor is similar: Vista offers a salmon and sea green color scheme with banquettes backed by bevelled glass; Horizon features backlit glass trim designed to create a softly romantic mood. On the *Holiday* rosewood veneer trims one dining room, a burgundy color scheme dominates suede wall coverings, and a custom carpet adorned with a sea god and goddess is in the other.

"I'll meet you at Times Square" is a favorite joke on board the *Holiday,* where Times Square is a gathering place just off Broadway and it's also where you'll find an intriguing acrylic sculpture you walk right into—it's wrapped around the elevator doors.

Each of the ships has a Galleria Shopping Mall and a boutique that sells every manner of souvenir with Carnival's logo emblazoned on it.

Other facilities aboard all three ships include barber and beauty shops, two small boutiques, a sauna, shuffleboard, several outdoor swimming pools—four on the *Celebration*—an electronic game room, a health spa with whirlpools, a gym, and a massage room.

There's a video game room and children's playroom on board too.

Cabins

Cabins on all the ships are as alike as a mouthful of perfect teeth. They are simply furnished and large enough to contain twin beds and pull-down upper berths, a chair, dressing table, and both closed and open closet space. A few cabins at the bow and stern of the ship are horizontally placed and so seem larger. Suites sport whirlpool baths on the *Celebration* and have beds—honeymooners' alert—that can be moved together to create a king-size sleeper, a feature of both other ships too.

Cabins, with the exception of suites, of course, are quite uniform in size, reasonably spacious, and inside cabins are actually a foot or two larger than outside quarters. All have closed-circuit color televisions with continuous movies shown until 3 a.m. daily, plus stereos and televisions. All, of course, have medium-sized bathrooms with hand-held showers and quite contemporary fixtures. And all (except cabins with upper and lower beds) have twin beds that can be pushed together to become king-size sleepers.

Rates on these ships are divided into ten cabin categories and two seasons. Season prices are the highest and are in effect from about mid-December to mid-April and from mid-June through August. Base-season prices, which are in effect from mid-April to June and September through mid-December, are $50 to $100 a person cheaper.

Top-of-the-line quarters aboard are on the top deck and feature a separate sitting room and private veranda. Rates for a week-long cruise in one of these Category 12 staterooms is $2,095 per person.

Moving down the line to cabins in Categories 8 and 9, you will discover that rates for those outside cabins on the Empress and upper deck are $1,495 per person in peak season. Categories 6, 5, and 4, which cover both inside and outside cabins that are quite similar, have quite similar price tags as well: $1,275 to $1,385 per person for a week's cruise.

The lowest-priced cabins on board are those in Categories 3, 2, and 1, all of them with upper and lower berths. Some are outside, some inside quarters, and the fare ranges from $1,075 to $1,195 per person.

Add to those fees port charges of $24 each.

Third and fourth persons sharing a stateroom with passengers paying the full fare are charged just $395 for adults, $195 for children under 16. Single travelers pay a 50% surcharge for single use of a double cabin in Categories 1 through 3 and singles pay double fare for cabins in Categories 4 to 12.

Those with a nose for inaccuracies will please sit back down now: yes, we did say there are ten categories of cabins and then we referred to suites in Category 12. Don't ask us why, but there aren't any Category 10 or 11 cabins!

Doing the usual divide-by-seven process, you discover that peak per diem rates on these ships range from a low of about $155 per person a day for a cabin with upper and lower berths—of which there are very few, incidentally—to a high of $299 a day per person for a suite (there are just ten of those).

MARDI GRAS: First of Carnival's ships, the *Mardi Gras* is thought by many to be an oldy but goody. She's an incredible study in Le Style Grande, probably the most evocative-of-days-of-yore ship of any craft afloat. It takes no imagination at all to picture the fabulously wealthy trailing merrily down these wide, wide hallways or drifting about in cabins practically large enough to get lost in!

This ship is a woodworker's dream—and, in fact, pretty dreamy for anyone with an interest in antiques and the woods of which they were made. You'll see endless miles of wood aboard this ship, streaking down long wide hallways in massive stretches of paneling, and in almost all the cabins.

If you look very closely in the higher-priced cabins you'll find a tiny plaque telling you what kind of wood you're looking at—each room is different. We spotted one done in something called "grey harewood dyed," another in figured silver birch, another in "one-quarter figured mottled white ash"! None of those slick but plastic new ships can match that.

A twin to the *Carnivale* in most aspects, the *Mardi Gras* features the same beautiful woodsiness with lots of brass accents. Once known as the *Empress of Canada,* she was built in 1961 and refurbished in 1973 and again in 1985. Today her public rooms look surprisingly contemporary, although cabins hark right back to the '50s in both colors and furnishings.

At 27,250 tons, she carries 1,100 passengers and shows her age in many places, almost always charmingly. She's kept neat and clean too, which makes those few antiquities bearable.

Public Rooms

Gamesters can while away the wee hours at the glassed-in Bourbon Street Arcade while dance fans can trip the light fantastic until the wee hours at nightclubs and discos. Three bands—steel, orchestra, and "loverly"—attend to your musical needs.

In summer and for holidays there are special programs for children, and at any time of year there's plenty to keep both adults and children occupied. There are, for instance, three swimming pools aboard, two outside and one inside. One pool aboard is especially earmarked for the youngsters, who also have a playroom near the sports deck and near that youngster's-only pool.

There's a fully equipped gymnasium on the Sun Deck, a sauna near the indoor pool, and a cinema (with a balcony) on the main deck, where movies are shown continuously.

Another of Carnival's enclosed promenades turns up on the Empress Deck, where the Point After Club is a lively meeting spot. On that same deck you'll find the grand ballroom and some shops.

Mardi Gras's dining room is small and inside, but comparatively bright and cheerful. Mirrors help make it look larger than it really is, and contemporary furnishings and a red décor brighten it still more.

In the Grand Ballroom you'll find brass-trimmed glass doors with a double-winged staircase leading to a balcony that rims the room. Quite an impressive spot, it features circular banquettes in deep burgundy and blue. Way up in the ceiling tiny lights glitter.

More of that glowing burgundy shade turns up in the nearby Carousel Lounge, which features windows down both sides. A black-lacquered piano bar captures center stage in this attractive room.

Disco fans can dance up a storm in the Point After Club where a mirrored ceiling and matching columns glitter. There's a wall of windows here, so as you're dancing you can look out over a swimming pool. A massive woodcarving is a focal point on one wall of this red-and-black room.

A small nook called the Tropicale Bar opens to the deck through a glass wall for on-deck dancing. Pretty carved-wood furniture gives the room a European bistro look. Look for it up on the Promenade Deck.

Up there, too, you'll find a long, enclosed promenade known as El Patio Grande. Nobody seems to have known quite what to do with this section of the ship, so it now sports a gaggle of ice-cream-parlor chairs and tables in bright yellow, plus a couple of one-armed bandits. El Patio Grande encircles the ship's Showboat Club Casino, a huge casino with one of those big roulette wheels, craps tables, table roulette, blackjack, and slots.

Cabins

As with many old ships, the *Mardi Gras* has quite a number of cabins that are larger than some you'll find on newer ships. All of them have private facilities and the 24-hour room service offered on all Carnival ships. Many, many cabins have sink and shower in one small room and toilet in the other. Many bathrooms are tiny creatures, barely big enough to turn around in and certainly not ideal for the hefty.

If you're partial to king-size beds, you'll find some of those on Riviera Deck. They're inside cabins in Category 6, which is about mid-price for this ship. Be prepared to find that there's not a great deal of room left over, however. Some cabins also have double beds, the less expensive being inside cabins on upper, main, and Empress decks.

Again there are 12 price categories (the highest-priced is 12; the lowest is Category 1). And again there are two seasons: high season (mid-January through April and June through August) and low or base season (mid-April through May and September through mid-December). You'll pay $20 to $40 less if you're not sailing in peak winter or summer seasons.

Suites much like those on the *Carnivale* are $885 per person, and a demi-suite is $835 per person, for a three-day trip in high season. The best thing about these suites is this: if you're traveling with a family or another couple, you can have absolute privacy by closing the paned-glass doors between the two separate rooms. You'll save lots of money on those third and fourth fares too.

Categories 10, 9, 8, and 7 are all outside cabins with double or twin beds, and they are big, big, and bigger. Look at the line's brochure and you'll be able to spot the largest ones. All look much the same, outfitted (in 1985) in burgundy bedspreads. Prices in these cabins range from a high of $795 to a low of $665 per person. Cabin E28, a Category 9 cabin, is very large, large enough to accommodate two cots at night (the steward will remove them in the morning). This room is paneled in figured mottled white ash and it will cost $775 per person for a three-day journey in high season.

In Category 6, Cabin E30 is a good example of an inside cabin in this price bracket. It's small, but not uncomfortably so, and features a double bed, with a sink in the room rather than in the bathroom. There's a bathroom too, of course.

Categories 4 and 5 are inside cabins with double or twin beds. One of these costs $585 or $605 per person.

Categories 3, 2, and 1 include both inside and outside cabins, but all have lower and upper beds. Category 1 cabins have a sink in the room, but there's still plenty of space. Bathrooms are small, however.

Some of these lower-priced cabins are in a section of the ship that has wall coverings or plastic panels on the wall, so you won't see the woodwork here that you see in higher-priced cabins. Upper berths flip back against the wall during the day so there's a bit more space then. Even these quarters usually are reasonably spacious for the price. The price in these three lower categories ranges from a high of $505 to a low of $375 per person.

Third- and fourth-person fares and single-occupancy rates are the same as on the *Carnivale*. Per diem rates are the same as well.

TROPICALE: In 1984 the *Tropicale* spent its first full year as a California-Mexico cruiser, abandoning the Alaska sailings it had done under charter to another company.

Line officials are dedicated to a philosophy they call "keep it simple," with few or no itinerary changes for each ship and a steady pattern of cruising all year long to and from the same destinations. Nevertheless, Carnival was premiering summer cruises to Mexico, something rarely done in the past and never done previously by Carnival.

Entertainment on this ship is slightly different, flashier, more Las Vegas in style, tailored to the western audience, which has come to expect that kind of evening showbiz. Here, too, you'll see a salute to Mexico with a mariachi band on board, often in addition to the steel band that met with success on some trial runs.

Public Rooms

Public rooms on the *Tropicale* are very contemporary. In the Palm Restaurant you'll find sweeping circular lines, rattan furnishings decked out in burgundy and gray, recessed ceiling lights. In the Islands in the Sun Lounge, trendy Lucite discs trim the ceiling line and couches encircle a grand piano that forms one of the focal points of the room.

In the Tropicana Lounge, deep blues and a jewel-toned aquamarine are so blue you sometimes feel as if you're snorkeling your way through your margarita.

Slick brown plastics are a highlight of the Boiler Room Bar and Grill, where hi-tech touches carry out that mechanical theme.

Exta Z, the ship's disco, has lights that keep time to the music so the beat's overhead, underfoot, and in your personal rhythm section. A great favorite with the younger set—and those who still consider themselves so.

Tropicale seems a well-thought-out ship, with a game room, library, card room, casino, two lounges, and a swimming pool all located on Promenade Deck. Part of that deck features an enclosed promenade and part of it is open.

One deck higher on the ship, Lido Deck features another pool and that casual Boiler Room snackbar. Atop that, the Veranda and Sports Decks feature a gymnasium with all the required shiny equipment plus ladies' and men's health clubs, two saunas, and lots of deck room for sunning. On the Sports Deck you can practice your golf drive across the biggest water hazard of them all, or try trap shooting, table tennis, and shuffleboard.

For the youngsters there's a children's playroom tucked away on the Empress Deck right near a wading pool for the pint-size water baby.

Shops? Of course, including a beauty salon and barbershop.

Cabins

Because this ship was built for the line and not reconstructed from an older ship, every cabin on board—except suites, of course—is similar in size and shape, planned rather than carved from available space.

In outside cabins the portholes are often long windows rather than the brass-trimmed circles of days past. And almost all rooms on board have twin beds that convert to king-size beds by the simple expedient of pushing them together.

Outside cabins on the *Tropicale* are very large, and suites are really something. Cabins have closed-circuit televisions too, mounted high up in the corners of the room, so you can watch a film right in your room. There's a complete television production studio aboard too.

Price ranges are the same as those aboard the other seven-day ships—in fact they're identical, except that the two upper-level categories, 10 and 11, are missing on this craft. Veranda suites in peak season are $2,095 per person, but there are no demi-suites or extra-extra-large outside cabins.

Outside cabins begin in Category 9 and range down through Categories 8, 7, and 6. Prices go from $1,495 per person in Category 9 to $1,585 per person in Category 6, and there's little difference except overall size of the cabins.

Inside cabins begin in Category 6, but these also have twins that can be pushed together to become king-size beds.

The five lowest categories aboard begin at Category 5 and go down through Category 1, just as they do on the other ships. Prices for those categories range from a high of $1,335 to a low of $1,075 per person. In Categories 3, 2, and 1 the beds are upper and lower berths, and the top price in those categories is $1,195 per person for the week's cruise in peak season.

Single rates and charges for a third or fourth person sharing a cabin are the same as on the other ships. Children's fares are also the same.

7. CHANDRIS FANTASY CRUISES

Contact: Chandris Fantasy Cruises, 900 Third Ave., New York, NY 10022 (tel. 212/750-0044 in New York; 305/576-9900 in Florida; or toll free 800/621-3446 or 800/423-2100).

Cruising Grounds: Bahamas, Mexico, Caribbean, Panama Canal, Bermuda, South America, Mediterranean.

Itineraries: *Amerikanis*—

IN WINTER: San Juan – St. Thomas – Guadeloupe – Barbados – St. Lucia – Antigua – St. Maarten – San Juan.

IN SUMMER: New York – Bermuda – New York.

Britanis—

IN WINTER AND SPRING: Montego Bay – Aruba – San Blas Islands – Cartagena – Panama Canal – Montego Bay.

IN SUMMER AND FALL: Miami – Key West – Cozumél – Playa del Carmen – Miami *or* Miami – Nassau – Miami.

IN FALL: 47-day cruise around South America.

Galileo—

IN WINTER: Miami – Nassau – Miami *or* Miami – Key West – Playa del Carmen – Cozumél – Miami.

IN SUMMER: New York – Bermuda – New York; cruises to nowhere.

The Victoria – San Juan – St. Thomas – Martinique – Grenada – Caracas – Curaçao – San Juan, year round.

The Azur—

IN SUMMER: Mediterranean cruises from Venice to ports in Greece, Egypt, Israel, Yugoslavia, Turkey, and the Black Sea.

IN WINTER: Barbados – Martinique – St. Kitts – San Juan – St. Thomas – Dominica – Bequia – Barbados.

Romanza—Mediterranean cruises in summer only from Venice to ports in Greece, Yugoslavia, and Turkey.

Chandris is a Greek line perhaps better known in Europe than it is on this side of the Atlantic. It's particularly difficult to keep up with what Chandris is doing because they move their vessels around often and lease or sell them frequently. That makes it hard to say just what Chandris will own, operate, or otherwise have an interest in when you read this.

Don't get the idea that what you are about to peruse is written in stone. Chandris is changeable. It's a good idea to check with Chandris to see where they're going, if you have some specific ports in mind. Let's take a look at the line just so you'll have some idea what to expect generally, if not specifically.

Chandris was first organized, so the story goes, way back in 1915 by a gentleman named John D. Chandris, who sailed into the passenger cruise business in 1922. Born in the eastern Mediterranean area that has been home to such shipping magnates as Onassis and Niarchos, Chandris also made a foray into the hotel business in the Greek islands and on the mainland.

Meanwhile Chandris Fantasy Cruises bought, sold, and operated a raft of ships, including the *Ariadne, Monterey, Lurline, America, President Hoover, Aurelia,* and the *Dunottar Castle,* which were later to be renamed the *Amerikanis, Ariane, Britanis, Ellinis, Italis, Regina Prima, Romanza,* and *The Victoria,* with a few names in between.

At this moment the five Chandris vessels sailing in North American waters are the *Britanis, Amerikanis, Galileo, The Azur,* and *The Victoria.*

To give you an idea how things change while staying the same, the *Britanis* once plied the routes *The Victoria* sails.

In Europe, Chandris's *Romanza* sails the Mediterranean, concentrating on the Greek islands.

AMERIKANIS/BRITANIS: Like other Chandris vessels, these venerable craft show their age but get you there—or nowhere—with all the sizzle and pizzazz they can cook up to get things stirring.

Built in 1932, the *Britanis* is a 26,000-ton ship with 465 cabins that house twice that number of passengers, more if the usual number of four-friends-sharing-a-cabin budgeteers are on board.

Her sister ship, the *Amerikanis,* is a bit smaller—20,000 tons, carrying 610 passengers—and about 20 years younger. It was built in 1951 and was once known as the *Kenya Castle.*

Public Rooms

Either ship's days as a castle are over. These are no luxury ships, but then they don't pretend to be. They are, however, about as perfect as you can get for a first-time sailing trip, particularly if you work all week and can't get much more than a day or two off to go sailing. When we sailed on a weekend cruise aboard one of these ships, a dozen people told us they were on their first cruise and having the time of their lives!

Food aboard these vessels gets special kudos from many who sail on them. Greeks worship good food with almost as much adulation as do Italians, so it's easy to understand why they cook well, if not showily, aboard.

On either ship, you dine in one of two dining rooms, one smaller and more intimate than the other (the Coral Dining Room on the *Amerikanis,* the Silverleaf on the *Britanis* are the smaller spots). Both are on a lower deck so they aren't as glossy and showy as those you find aboard newer ships.

Activities

On the *Britanis* you'll find a nice card room near the casino, and on the opposite side of the ship the Gallery Bar is an attractive hideaway for a quiet after-dinner drink. If you smoke and are tired of hearing snide remarks from those who don't, you can join other protesters at the Smoke Bar, which features a special smoking room at one end. Nonsmokers have their special section too.

Of course there's a swimming pool on both ships, a particularly interesting double one on the *Amerikanis.* On the *Britanis* you can have your cocktail with a splash—the Marine Bar's within sight of the ship's swimming pool.

You can work off your pasta calories at dancercize classes, visit the sauna, try skeet shooting or table tennis, go to the movies. Or learn to love them and spend your time doing nothing at all—in the sunshine.

Every night there's a different show in the nightclub, ranging from high-kicking showgirls in sparkles to dance bands and singers. A casino provides gamesters with craps tables, slots, blackjack, and roulette to while away the evening.

Cabins

On the *Britanis* many cabins are inside quarters with one or two extra berths, and some can even accommodate six!

One large cabin we saw had an upper and lower berth, a chair that converted into a bed, and a couch that flipped over to become a sleeping spot. It also featured two very large closets and a third all fitted out with a bevy of drawers designed to accommodate the trunkloads of clothes travelers once packed on long transoceanic voyages.

The cabin price categories range from B to M, with B the lowest and M the highest prices aboard. Peak winter season aboard is the last week in December, and February through April. In the off-season you pay about $20 to $50 less per person for a two-night cruise. Five-night sojourns in peak season are $445 to $945 per person.

In summer, peak season is June through August, and off-season is from May to June and August to mid-December.

Let's look at some of the prices for a cabin on a two-night cruise in peak summer season. Decks on board are named after popular Caribbean ports—Aruba, Barbados, Caracas—and the highest prices are to be found on the main and upper decks where large suites and junior suites with two lower beds and a sitting room are $315 to $370 a person for the two-night cruise to Nassau. Categories J and K are outside cabins with two lower beds, somewhat larger and more elaborate than other outside quarters on board. For one of these cabins you'll pay $295 to $315 per person for a two-night trip.

Two categories of large inside cabins, Categories H and I, also feature two lower beds and are $260 to $270 per person for a two-night cruise.

Outside cabins with a double bed are $270 per person and similar inside quarters with double beds begin at $245 per person for a two-night cruise. If you don't mind sleeping in upper and lower berths, outside cabins with those accommodations are $235 per person for a two-night cruise in peak season. Similar inside cabins in Category C are $220.

Category B cabins are smaller, inside, and have lower and upper berths. One of those is $209 per person for a two-night cruise.

To partake of the rockiest of rock-bottom rates aboard you will have to give up a private bath, although there'll be a bathroom and shower nearby and a sink in your room. For one of those outside or inside cabins with two lower beds and lower and upper berths, the cost is just $189 per person for a two-night cruise.

Single rates are 150% of the fare.

Budget $17 for each adult for port taxes, $11 for each child under 16. On a five-night cruise those charges are $24 for each adult and child.

Third and fourth adults sharing a cabin pay $99 for a two-night cruise, and children under 16 are $80 each (under 3, they cruise free).

The *Amerikanis* sails on one-, two-, three-, and five-night cruises in summer, enabling even the rock-bottomest of budgets to get in on the fun.

Those short cruises go nowhere at all from New York for one night, just sailing around out there in the blue, armed with strawberry daiquiris and a foot-long activities roster.

Days, you can dally at convivial lounges or take dance lessons, and nights you can combine those pursuits at a jumpin' disco. At the ship's casino you may win the price of your cruise, but if not, you can drown your sorrows in the Aquamarine or Rendezvous Bar.

Cruise prices run $119 to $199 for a one-day cruise, $595 to $1,095 for six-night voyages to Bermuda's historic St. George's. Singles pay a 50% surcharge on prices, and port charges are $10 to $48, depending on the length of the cruise. A third or fourth person sharing a cabin pays $70 for a one-night cruise to $420 for six nights at sea.

GALILEO/THE VICTORIA: Chandris's *The Victoria*, once known as the *Dunottar Castle*, measures 19,000 tons and is fitted out to carry 560 passengers. Her size helps her work her way into small ports, so the ship often pursues some interesting itineraries.

All begin in San Juan, where you have dinner on board and sail at about midnight. By the next morning you're in St. Thomas for the day. That's followed by a day in Martinique, a day in Grenada, a stop at La Guaira (the port for Caracas), then on to Curaçao. After one day at sea you arrive back in San Juan early Monday morning. On some sailings the ship substitutes Barbados for Curaçao.

The *Galileo*, built in 1963, is the largest of the line's ships and carries 1,100 passengers off to Mexico's Yucatán Peninsula in winter and to Bermuda in summer, although Chandris often moves this ship around to new itineraries.

Public Rooms

Built in 1939 and refurbished in 1987, *The Victoria* offers a gym and sauna, plus a playroom for children. Her cinema is a two-story spot with a balcony.

Swimmers will find two swimming pools aboard. Oddly enough, they're back to back on the Lido Deck, with a cute little arching bridge crossing between the two. To reach this pool deck from the upper deck you can make quite a grand entrance on a swirling staircase. There's not a great deal of sun space aboard.

If you like to read or join some new friends for bridge games, there's a large library and card room just off an enclosed promenade area known as the Winter Garden.

Nights begin with dinner in the Roman Dining Room. Later the ship comes alive with some rousing Vegas-y entertainment. The click of the little white ball spins into the wee hours in the casino, and a nice hideaway spot is the small Galleon bar on the Rendezvous Deck.

On the *Galileo* there is more playing space but pretty much the same round of activities. This ship is a good one for the youngsters — it has its own swimming pool just for them, not to mention a playroom off-limits to adults.

Adults won't lack for places to play, however. You'll find a casino on board and all the usual gambling games, plus a big showroom where some flashy song-and-dance entertainment takes place each night.

Out on deck, well, on two different decks, there are two swimming pools and plenty of adjacent sunning space.

For escapism there's a piano bar, a game room and a nice, secluded card room.

Cabins

One of the line's more contemporary ships following a renovation in 1987, *The Victoria* has a very large number of outside cabins, so you have a good chance of seeing the Caribbean from your cabin window. That's especially nice when you're sailing, as *The Victoria* does, among many small islands.

Rates aboard *The Victoria* are divided into seven categories, plus one additional one for single travelers. They are also expressed by zone, that is Zone 1, Zone 2, or Zone 3, which refers to the line's fly/cruise packages. Cities farther away from San Juan — places like Birmingham, Milwaukee, Minneapolis — are Zone 3 and have somewhat higher fares, while those near and/or easily accessible — like New York, Orlando, Syracuse, Tampa, Providence — are Zone 1, the cheapest fares. Air fare costs determine those fares, of course.

Rates aboard *The Victoria* for a seven-night cruise range from $849 to $1,649 per person.

Let's look at some of the prices applicable to those traveling to San Juan from the East Coast.

There are six suites aboard the ship, each named after a Bahamian island — Bimini, Eleuthera, Antigua, Inagua, Andros, and Abaco. Those are the highest-priced accommodations aboard, at $1,349 for a week's cruise.

Outside cabins with two beds or a double bed start at the same price and descend in cost to $1,099. Cheapest of those would be a cabin on Coral Deck, about 9 by 15 feet.

Inside cabins with twin beds or a double bed are $949 to $1,049, and the cheapest accommodations aboard are two-berth inside cabins for $849. As we mentioned, those prices are slightly higher if you live in the Midwest or West.

Some cabins can accommodate three or four, with the third in an upper berth, the fourth in a portable bed. Third and fourth passengers sharing space pay $699.

Children under 12 pay $499, and singles can choose from eight cabins designed just for them, priced at $1,099.

That means per diem rates are comparatively low, beginning at $100 per person and rising to a high of $192 a day for a seven-day cruise.

Many cabins aboard the *Galileo* are inside quarters in a wide variety of configurations, all snuggled in around each other so there are plenty of low price options. You'll even find inside *suites,* quite a rarity on ships these days.

On the *Galileo* prices for inside cabins on a five-night trip range from $445 to $565, with those inside suites priced at $845 per person for the five-night trip.

Outside cabins with upper and lower berths are $515; those with a double bed, $605 to $665. Outside suites with a sitting area are $945.

Daily rates aboard the ship work out to a quite-low peak-season per diem of $89 to a high of $189 a day for a suite.

THE AZUR/ROMANZA: With the addition of *The Azur,* a ship formerly operated by France's Paquet Line, Chandris Fantasy Cruises now counts six passenger ships as part of its fleet. Built in France in 1971 and acquired by Chandris in 1987, *The Azur* was treated to a major facelift before her debut in the Caribbean in 1987.

Measuring in at just 15,000 tons and carrying 678 passengers, *The Azur* is small enough to work her way into unusual ports like Bequia, Dominica, and St. Kitts, and also visits the Caribbean biggies, places like Barbados, St. Thomas, San Juan, and Martinique.

In summer the ship heads east to the Mediterranean where she sails from Venice on 10- and 11-day cruises similar to those of her sister ship, the *Romanza.*

Chandris was busy in 1987: in that year the line also refurbished the *Romanza,* which was built in 1936 and purchased by Chandris in 1970. The *Romanza* measures in at 11,000 tons and carries 590 passengers.

Public Rooms

For many in these days of workout mania, the single most endearing feature of *The Azur* is a duplex sports deck complete with gym, sundeck, and volleyball/squash courts. There are also two outdoor swimming pools on board and the usual array of public rooms, ranging from romantic corners to sizzling discos, a lively casino, and a two-level cinema.

On several Caribbean islands *The Azur* has organized what they call Chandris Fantasea Sports Centers, offering a program of on-island sports facilities.

Catering to the many European families who come aboard each summer, the *Romanza* entertains the youngsters in a special playroom just for them.

Cabins

The Azur offers 344 cabins, 156 of them outside quarters. Attention, lovers: some cabins have double beds at prices from $1,100 to $1,150 on a seven-night Caribbean cruise. Other cabin prices for a week's sail in the Caribbean range from $650 to $1,150 per person double, bringing per diem rates to $92 to $164.

Prices on the *Romanza,* which has 293 cabins on its five decks, begin at $725 per person on seven-night trips and at $932 per person for nine-night cruises from Venice.

8. CLIPPER CRUISE LINE

Contact: Clipper Cruise Line, 7711 Bonhomme Ave., St. Louis, MO 63105 (tel. 314/727-2929, or toll free 800/325-0010).

Cruising Grounds: U.S. East Coast and Northeast, Caribbean.

Itineraries: *Nantucket Clipper / Newport Clipper / Yorktown Clipper*—

IN SUMMER: Boston – Nantucket – New Bedford – Newport – Martha's Vineyard – Bath – Camden – Bar Harbor – Boothbay – Portsmouth – Provincetown – Boston.

IN SPRING AND FALL: Baltimore – Yorktown – St. Mary's City – St. Michaels – Annapolis – Washington *or* Savannah – St. Simon's – Beaufort – Charleston – Hilton Head – Savannah.

IN WINTER: St. Thomas – Tortola – Virgin Gorda – St. Croix – St. John – Peter Island – St. Thomas *or* Antigua – Montserrat – St. Kitts – St. Christopher – St. Eustatius – St. Barthélemy – Anguilla – St. Martin.

In 1983 with considerable fanfare a new cruise line was born in, of all places, St. Louis! The three Clipper Cruise Line ships are the *Newport Clipper*, the *Nantucket Clipper*, and the *Yorktown Clipper*, sparkling vessels outfitted in contemporary fabrics and lovely bleached maple trim.

Aboard you'll find a clubby atmosphere enjoyed by those in search of visits to interesting ports—particularly historic American ones.

Built in St. Louis, the ships have an all-American look too, from the freshfaced young midwesterners who man them with a smile to the delicate pastel décor, wide open spaces of public rooms, and sleek contemporary furnishings.

This spiffy new line is a departure from the norm in cruise lines in many ways, not the least of which is the size of its ships. Only 207 feet long and carrying just 100 passengers, the *Nantucket Clipper, Newport Clipper*, and *Yorktown Clipper* are something between private yachts and full-fledged cruise ships. In fact they once called these ships, which are small enough to negotiate inland waterways between New England and Florida, "ultra-yachts."

"One of the worst mistakes we ever made was to call this Clipper *Cruise* Line," a line executive told us. "While the *Newport Clipper* was still being built [in 1983], we found ourselves saying 'No' to 'Does it have a casino?' and 'Does it have elevators?' We should have called ourselves Clipper Yacht Line."

Two more facts: you'll find stewardesses, rather than stewards, taking care of your cabin and serving meals and drinks; and there are no special facilities for children.

NANTUCKET CLIPPER / NEWPORT CLIPPER / YORKTOWN CLIPPER:

The three *Clippers* travel a sedate ten miles an hour, and because they have flat hulls and a mere eight-foot draft, can sail into shallow waters denied larger craft. That's why you'll find these ships visiting such exotic ports as Tortola and Peter Island. Intriguing ports are indeed what lure most passengers aboard.

The itineraries of these handsome new craft vary widely. In spring and fall when the ships are moving from their winter sailing grounds in the Virgin Islands north to New England or vice versa, they feature positioning cruises that call on cities of the Deep South—Savannah, St. Simon's Island, Charleston, antique St. Augustine, Titusville, Palm Beach, and Fort Lauderdale.

In winter you can find them sailing the serene waters of the Virgin Islands and in spring they return on a similar route, stopping both in spring and fall at a number of Chesapeake Bay ports as well.

If you've plenty of time and wanderlust, you can combine several of those positioning voyages into a 14- or 28-day sojourn that will take you all the way up or down the eastern seaboard.

In summer the ships can be found touring some of the nation's historic spots: Williamsburg, Yorktown, Baltimore, Annapolis, Boston, Nantucket, Newport, New Bedford, Martha's Vineyard.

Because the ships have such a variety of itineraries, one of their selling points is that repeat passengers can sail different itineraries four times a year if they've a mind to do so—and at about $255 a day per person.

Activities

Not even the line denies that these yacht-cruisers are designed in every way —including cost and ambience—for a certain kind of person. If you want lots of nightlife, plenty of rip-roaring on-board activities, bars, games, and organized events, the *Clippers* are not for you.

If, on the other hand, you like to keep reasonably early hours and to fill your days and nights with some fascinating sightseeing, quiet walks and talks, you ought to adore these sparkling new seafarers.

Most of your fellow passengers will be retired, affluent folks who are also sophisticated travelers to whom the intimacy and interesting itinerary of these small crafts are particularly appealing. Those we've talked to who have sailed these ships seemed quite enthusiastic about the young crews, despite some inconveniences attributable to inexperience.

These are not ships for the handicapped as there are no elevators and the stairs are steep. There are also no doctors aboard, although daily port stops mitigate this lack.

Entertainers and lecturers are brought aboard at some ports, and video movies are shown on two televisions aboard. You can also tune in the morning and evening news on these televisions.

Public Rooms

Throughout these vessels you'll see beautiful blond bleached-maple trim and light contemporary earth tones. Big, big windows everywhere make the ships as open in feeling as any craft we've ever seen.

On each ship, the main gathering spot is a forward lounge that's decked out in pale pastel shades of aqua and peach. It has a small bar, some comfortable low chairs and couches, and a bookcase in the corner that serves as library.

Sports fans jog around the deck (18 times around is a mile—that's how small we're talking about here!) or work out on the Sun Deck, but there's no pool.

Life aboard is casual, with one seating at dinner and no formal nights. They do draw the line at jeans for dinner, although your Calvins will do just fine for the occasional barbecues on deck or ashore on some of the more remote Caribbean islands visited in winter.

Decked out in green and white, each ship's dining room is small and intimate, with tall windows, tables for four and six, chic hunter-green china. With the small number of passengers there's just one seating for dinner and assigned seating only for that meal. Breakfast is at 8 a.m., lunch at 12:30 p.m., and dinner at 7:30 p.m.

Beige carpets run throughout these yacht-like ships, which have some cabins that can be converted to accommodate three. Radios in each cabin bring prerecorded music, including a jazz channel, to your room.

Lots of handsome little touches make these small cruise ships a very special place. Baskets of African violets adorn the pretty pastel lounge, and contemporary artwork is subtle and serene.

Cabins

Every cabin on both ships is an outside cabin, many opening onto an outside deck (not ideal on rainy days). Each has its own small bath and is decorated in those same light beiges and delicate earthy tones. Big windows let in lots of light and three closets offer ample space for even the most extensive wardrobes. Cabins on the forward end are quietest, and a real blessing during early-morning departures.

In the cabins you'll find a very light and airy look created by tailored cream-colored bedspreads in a heavy cottony fabric sparked with soothing earth tones. More of that handsome bleached maple appears in the dressers, wardrobes, and trim around the beds. Beds are only about six feet long, so really tall folks will have to scrunch up a bit. You can tuck your luggage in beneath the wood-trimmed beds. Pleated fabric blinds on the windows are an interesting touch.

Cabins are divided into five price categories, one of those for single staterooms. The highest price category is Category 4, with prices descending from there. To give you an idea what you'll pay, let's look at the rates for a seven-day cruise.

The prettiest cabin aboard—and the most expensive—is L24, which features huge windows, a desk (that's a feature in all rooms), dresser, and triple mirror, plus a full-length mirror. It can accommodate three, with the third occupying a pull-down bunk. For one of these outside double staterooms measuring 138 square feet the cost is $2,195 per person for a seven-day trip.

Slightly smaller outside double rooms with two lower beds are located on the bow end of the main deck and the aft end of the lounge deck. For one of these you'll pay $1,995 for a week's cruise.

Category 2 quarters are a bit smaller yet, about 121 square feet, and cost $1,795 per person for a week-long trip.

The lowest-priced category on board, Category 1, features cabins the same size as Category 2 cabins, but located toward the bow where the ship begins to curve inward so they seem a bit smaller. One of those is $1,595 per person for a week's cruise.

Single travelers will be happy to hear that there are single rooms aboard, but you pay a premium for them: $2,375 for a seven-day cruise. A third person sharing a stateroom pays $800.

Port charges are $35 per person in the Virgin Islands, $21 Stateside also.

9. COMMODORE CRUISE LINE

Contact: Commodore Cruise Line, 1007 North American Way, Miami, FL 33132 (tel. 305/358-2622, or toll free 800/327-5617, 800/432-6793 in Florida).

Cruising Grounds: Caribbean.

Itineraries: *Caribe I* – Miami – Puerto Plata – San Juan – St. John – St. Thomas – Miami, year round.

Commodore likes to call its vessel the "Happy Ship" and why not? Aboard the *Caribe I* you'll be visiting some of the Caribbean's best-loved ports and traveling on a line that's been around long enough to know how to create "happy."

The line aims to please a lively young crowd looking for a few days of fun and sun at reasonable prices, and it does that very successfully.

Based in Miami, Commodore's rainbow-striped funnels have been seen here since 1966 when a Miami Beach hotel developer named Sanford Chobol saw the wave of the future and surfed it. He bought a ship, named it the *Bohème,* and began sailing it on cruises from Miami to the Caribbean. Now owned by a Swedish company, the line operates only the *Caribe I* (once known as the *Olympia),* registered in Panama.

The *Caribe I* measures in at 23,000 tons and carries 875 passengers, with space for 300 more in extra bunks.

We'd say the line's best selling point is its reasonable price, which, at last check, for a week-long cruise ranged from $895 per person for inside staterooms with upper and lower berths to $1,395 for deluxe suites with two lower or one double bed and honeymoon staterooms with double bed and sitting area. Prices include air fare from 100 cities.

Special prices for third and fourth passengers sharing a room make these ships particularly attractive to families. You'll see many aboard.

Commodore has a reputation for good food, and is proud to say that it produces all its own goodies rather than offering the cooking duties to a concession operator as many ships do.

The *Caribe I,* departs on Saturday from Miami for week-long Caribbean cruises to Puerto Plata in the Dominican Republic, San Juan, tiny St. John, and St. Thomas. Recently the line introduced a new series of occasional cruises to the western Caribbean ports of Ocho Ríos, Grand Cayman, Cozumél, and Playa del Carmen.

Like many other lines, Commodore has instituted an on-board credit system that allows you to settle your bills for drinks, gifts, shore excursions, and the like at the end of the cruise.

CARIBE I: The *Caribe I* can trace her ancestry back to 1953 when she was known as the *Olympia,* and measures in at 23,000 tons and carries 900 passengers. You'll see fabulously beautiful signs of her age aboard in acres of handsome polished woods and curving art deco lines that can rival anything Radio City Music Hall has to offer!

Wood is everywhere, absolutely everywhere. There are wooden columns here, wood trim there, marquetry on the walls of the dining room, even an inlaid wood wall clock. As you enter the ship, a brass information desk glitters and huge brass-and-glass doors feature a deco design. Passageways are lined in wood and there are gleaming brass touches everywhere you look.

Refurbished in 1984, this handsome aging lady needed her recent facelift in some areas, but they'd better not ever touch all those woods and deco furbelows. Antiquarians, arise.

Activities

Commodore wants to create happiness aboard its single ship. One of the ways it does that is with some interesting theme cruises. For example, in the fall there's an Oktoberfest complete with oom-pah-pah band, German beer, and fat pretzels. In the traditionally slow months the line also revs up business with a popular country-and-western cruise with all the requisite nyah-nyah-nyah wailing songs and lots of clogging and cowboy boots.

In spring the line, which was once registered in West Germany, takes its cue from what goes on in Europe each spring—wine. Commodore sponsors a Mayfest featuring European wine and cheese tasting and plenty of alpine music. On national holidays like the Fourth of July, New Years' Eve, Valentine's Day, and Easter, there are appropriately themed festivites.

Even if you don't make a theme cruise, you'll find plenty of fun aboard— casinos, giftshops, snappy productions in a double-deck theater, intimate entertainment in a piano bar, steel band entertainment from the very first second aboard.

Public Rooms

Our favorite spot on the *Caribe I* is the library, which surely ranks as one of the most plushly comfy reading rooms afloat. You sink right into the overstuffed flower-print chairs scattered about this rose-and-gray, wood-paneled room. If you can stay awake, you'll think you've dropped back an eon or two into the days of quill pens and old English manse libraries where Heathcliff brooded—a dreamy spot indeed.

If you're not of a reading-meditating-napping turn of mind, head for the Grand Lounge, where chrome glitters amid beige and pink furnishings. Tall windows give this faintly circular room an airy look similar to what you'll find in the Caribbean Dining Room, where gray, peach, and rust create a contemporary look in this high-ceilinged room, which already features beautiful marble tiles and pretty tinted mirrors etched with mermaids.

There's a full casino aboard with all the requisite blackjack, roulette, and other gambling games, plus a striking black-and-red carpet adorned with hearts, clubs, spades, and diamonds.

A small showroom up high on the ship has tiny unusual hexagonal marble tables on tall spindly brass legs and chrome chairs upholstered in a pink that matches the drapes on a bank of windows down both sides. Burgundy and gray complete a very slick color scheme here.

In the Out Island Disco you can dance until you drop, but head for the Out Island Club, also up there on the Sun Deck, for a quiet drink.

Two small shops can help inveterate shoppers pass some time, and there's plenty of deck space for strolling and sunning.

A multi-million-dollar nightclub and disco were recently added to the ship's Sun Deck. Called the Mermaid, the lounge features a dance floor under a sliding-glass roof, blond woods upholstered in navy blue, and lots of brass and etched glass. Nearby, but thankfully insulated from the disco sounds, is the Commodore Lounge, a nice place for a tête-à-tête. Another addition, the Tradewinds Lounge is a cozy piano bar outfitted in deep reds and dark woods.

Cabins

Cabins on board this ship are roomy. Many of them feature pretty wood paneling, and all have some wood trim. Outside staterooms have about 200 square feet of space; inside cabins, about 142 square feet. All have wall-to-wall carpeting, radios with music channels, telephones, old but serviceable private bathrooms, and plenty of storage space.

Peak prices aboard are in effect from February to the beginning of April, from late June to mid-August, and in December. During that season prices range from $895 to $1,445 per person double. In other months prices also begin at $895 but are about $50 cheaper in each category.

Deluxe and honeymoon suites feature two lower beds or a double bed, a separate sitting area, big closets, a mini-bar, video cassette recorder, refrigerators, and a comfortable couch. In peak season they top the price list at $1,445 for a week-long cruise.

Moving down a category, outside staterooms are large enough for a family, with two lower beds and an adjoining stateroom with one lower bed that becomes a sofa. Some rooms in this category have three or four lower beds and are $1,345 per person.

Other outside rooms range in price from $1,195 to $1,245 per person for a seven-night cruise, while inside staterooms with two lower beds range in price from $995 to $1,095.

Single travelers pay 150% of any fare to secure a cabin, or can accept one of the ship's few single cabins which cost $1,045 or $1,095 for the trip. A Commodore Roommate Program, which selects an appropriate traveling companion with whom you share a cabin, is also available. That's a money-saver for singles.

Best buys on board are inside or outside staterooms with upper and lower beds, for which the fare is $895 in any season.

A third traveler sharing a cabin pays $495, while a fourth pays $449 for the trip. Some cabins accommodating five are also available. Children from age 2 through 17 can share their parents' stateroom for $249 each, and infants under 2 are charged $65.

Prices include air fare from more than 100 U.S. cities. Those who get to Miami on their own can take $300 off the prices quoted. Add $35 per person for port taxes.

Per diem rates begin at $128, rising to about $206 for the highest-priced accommodations aboard.

10. COSTA CRUISES

Contact: Costa Cruises, One Biscayne Tower, Miami, FL 33131 (tel. 305/358-7325, or toll free 800/462-6782).

Cruising Grounds: Panama Canal, Alaska, Caribbean, Bahamas, world cruises, South America.

Itineraries: *CarlaCosta* – San Juan – Curaçao – Caracas – Grenada – Martinique – St. Thomas – San Juan, year round.

CostaRiviera — Fort Lauderdale – St. Thomas – St. Croix – Nassau – Fort Lauderdale, year round.

Daphne —
IN WINTER: San Juan – St. Maarten – Martinique – Barbados – St. Lucia – Antigua – St. Thomas – San Juan.

IN SUMMER: Vancouver – Ketchikan – Endicott Arm Fjord – Juneau – Skagway – Davidson and Rainbow Glacier – Wrangell – Vancouver.

Costa's yellow smokestack with a big blue "C" in the center is a familiar sight in the Caribbean, and has recently become a familiar sight in Alaskan waters as well. It has long been a common sight in the Mediterranean, birthplace of this large fleet.

Among the world's largest passenger lines, Costa recently signed up a sixth craft, the former *Marconi*, renamed the *CostaRiviera*.

A family-owned company, Costa can trace its history as far back as 1860 when two Costa brothers began an import business in the Mediterranean. That business eventually extended to passenger ships and soon there was a fleet of Costa ships. That large fleet, some of which bear the names of Costa grandchildren, is now spread around the globe.

There are still plenty of ships remaining, so many, in fact, that the line's officials remember them as two Cs, two Ds, and two Es. Here's what that means:

Those two Cs are the *Costa Riviera*, which sails in the Caribbean, and the *CarlaCosta*, which sails from San Juan to Curaçao, Caracas, and St. Thomas.

The two Ds are the *Danae*, which sails in Mediterranean waters in the summer and on world cruises in the winter, and the *Daphne*, a winter Caribbean sailor that sails to Alaska in summer. Both are luxury cruisers carrying only 400 passengers on longer-than-average cruises.

Daphne, twin to the *Danae,* and at 17,000 tons one of the line's smaller ships, often sails on Caribbean cruises from Florida in winter. Both the Ds are luxury vessels but the *Daphne* is the one you'll see most often in North American waters. In summer the ship heads for Alaska where it sails on weekly voyages from Vancouver to Skagway, Ketchikan, Endicott Arm, and Davidson and Rainbow Glaciers. Prelude and prologue voyages take her through the Panama Canal.

Costa's two Es are the *EnricoCosta* and the *EugenioCosta.* The *EnricoCosta* sails from Genoa through the Mediterranean, and the newly refurbished *EugenioCosta,* flagship of the line, sails in South American waters in winter, in the Mediterranean in the summer.

A special note for budgetwise sun lovers: Two of Costa's ships, the *CarlaCosta* and the *Daphne,* are so sure of their sunshine they offer a warm-weather guarantee. On any day the temperature dips below 70° you get a coupon worth one free day on your next Costa cruise!

Activities

On many of its ships the crews *parla l'italiano, grazzie,* and cook *italiano* too. That *cucina italiano* is one of the line's strongest selling points, backed by some good international cabaret entertainment and a wide variety of destinations encircling the globe.

Here's a shopping tip for Costa sailors: look for goodies emblazoned with this line's logo. It's one of the spiffiest logos afloat, and Costa is so proud of it that they devote an entire shop on some ships to the sale of their logo-ed T-shirts and ashtrays, duffle bags and pencils.

Like other Caribbean vessels the Costa ships offer a full round of entertainment. On the *Daphne,* a more luxurious ship, that entertainment is apt to be just as steady but a bit more refined.

Among the activities that will fill your days are skeet shooting, shuffleboard, movies, and of course those daily port stops.

At night, consumption of some sensational dinners occupies a couple of hours, made even more entertaining by special theme evenings. Every night at midnight there's a bountiful buffet, and one night you'll be treated to an on-deck barbecue. Another evening a sumptuous spread is presented right in the polished galley so you can see what goes on behind the scenes.

In the evenings, glittery showgirls dazzle you with song and dance. International performers sing, dance, and laugh it up for your entertainment, aided and abetted by a riotous Roman bacchanal, a captain's dinner, and a farewell dinner. Every night there's a show on deck too.

CARLACOSTA:
Be at the docks in San Juan on a Saturday, summer or winter, and you'll see the *CarlaCosta* readying for her midnight departure to such alluring ports as Curaçao, Venezuela, Grenada, Martinique, and St. Thomas. What this ship lacks in glamour she makes up for with a bubbly Italian crew and good food and wine. Like the cheerful crew, life aboard is informal, with two formal nights scheduled to let you play at dress-up.

Public Rooms

You'll find plenty of public places to while away the hours. Certainly there's plenty to do aboard, and plenty of public rooms in which to do it. Most of those are on the ship's Lido Deck, where a huge circular Observation Lounge features an orchestra for entertainment and a sensational view of emerald isles on the horizon.

At the bow of the ship is the swimming pool, and in between, a balconied theater, a gift shop, several bars, and the Grand Salon, where there's always something happening.

Below on Continental Deck is the ship's dining room, where you'll always have a selection of wonderful pastas plus the usual fancy continental cooking, ranging from succulent beef and veal choices to luscious, frilly, sinful desserts.

There's a casino aboard too, for those who like to while away the hours with Lady Luck as a companion.

Cabins

All the ship's cabins have private bathrooms and are divided about equally between inside and outside cabins. Those quarters are large, as they are in most older ships, and following a recent renovation are pretty—contemporary spots to shut your eyes.

Cabin prices run from Category 1 (the least expensive quarters) through Category 15 (the costliest spaces). The *CarlaCosta* also has a "value season" and peak-season price. Figure value season as January, late April to mid-June, and August through mid-December. Peak season includes the last week in December, February through mid-April, and late June through mid-August.

Let's look at the price of cabins for a one-week cruise from San Juan in peak season (about $100 less in value season). Free or low-cost air add-on rates are available.

The most luxurious cabins are on the Promenade Deck, where quite large suite accommodations bear such names as Portofino, Acapulco, Puerto Vallarta, Balboa, Tahitian, Cabo San Lucas, Monterey. These feature two lower beds, a sitting room, and a sofa bed, and are of course quite spacious. For these you will pay $1,960 per person for a week's cruise.

If you want to go in style but just a little less in cost, you might consider a Category 12, 13, or 14 cabin on the Promenade Deck. In price Category 12, outside cabins with two lower beds or a large double bed plus bath/shower combination are $1,780, and some of those are extra-large accommodations. In Category 13 you are buying a deluxe outside cabin with two lower beds and a sofa bed for $1,820 per person for more elaborate accommodations. Measurements on one Category 12 outside room are 12½ by 24 feet, and that's very large by any standards.

Three categories of smaller outside cabins (Categories 8, 9, and 10), with two beds, and additional berths if you want to include a third or fourth person, are $1,560 to $1,670 per person for a week's cruise.

Four categories of inside cabins (Categories 4, 5, 6, and 7) include two lower beds and are $1,390 to $1,560 per person. Mid-priced inside cabins, those in Category 7, for instance, are $1,560 per person and can measure as large as 14 by 23 feet, quite substantial. Two of those are even located up on the Boat Deck where there are only a dozen or so other cabins, all of them outside sleepers with a $1,780-per-person price tag in peak season—but they're above the disco. Down on the main deck a cabin in that price category that seems especially spacious is 401, which has two additional berths as well.

Category 3 is a value-wise selection. In this category are outside cabins, but they have a lower bed and an upper berth. For one of these you'll pay $1,325 for a week's cruise.

The lowest prices on the ship are on Pacific Deck, way down in the ship where the cabins are inside cabins and some are very small indeed. However, the price is just $1,095 to $1,225 per person for a week's cruise. Some of these lowest-priced accommodations have lower bed and upper berth; others have two lower beds, and sometimes upper berths as well.

The third- and fourth-person rate is $495 for adults, $275 for children under 13 sharing a cabin with adults.

Per diem prices on this craft range from a low of $156 to a mid-price of $194 to $260, and deluxe suites at $254 to $316 per person daily. Budget $35 per person for port charges.

Singles pay $1,395 in peak season for a cabin.

The *CarlaCosta* sails from San Juan to Curaçao, Caracas, Grenada, Martinique, and St. Thomas on one-week cruises beginning each Saturday. And don't forget that you can combine the voyage with a week on the *Daphne* if you have two weeks to spare.

COSTARIVIERA: In late 1985 singer Connie Stevens wielded a recalcitrant champagne bottle at the bow of Costa's newest ship, the *CostaRiviera*. When she did finally manage to crack that stubborn bottle of bubbly, it was a splashy moment for Costa Cruises in more ways than one. Not only was this the newest addition to the line in many years, but this handsome ship is also the first Costa ship in many years to sail year round on week-long cruises from Florida.

Formerly the *Marconi*, this 1,000-passenger ship spent many months in a shipyard getting a deck-to-dining-room facelift that has turned it into quite a showy place indeed.

Costa likes to call its new 35,000-ton baby "a taste of the jet-set life of the European Riviera at an affordable price." To promote that cosmopolitanism, the line has gone all-out on the *CostaRiviera* to emphasize its Italian connections.

For openers, Italian cuisine is a mainstay of the menu—there's even a pizza parlor right on board.

Italian design ranks right up there among the most avant-garde styles in the world, so on board you'll find designer boutiques stuffed with the chic creations of Gucci, Fila, and Ferre. Ship shops also feature Florentine leathers, Venetian glass, and an exquisite array of Italian art and craft work.

There's more: decks are named after famous Italian playgrounds—Amalfi, Riviera, Portofino, Capri, Sorrento, Venice.

And this finale: there's even a flashy red Italian sports car on display at the entrance to the ship's Riviera Lounge!

Public Rooms

Costa Cruises is particularly proud of the line's chic Italian boutiques, which Costa claims are the first designer-operated boutiques aboard any cruise ship. Clustered amidships in the Galleria Via Veneto, the shops feature Gucci's famous leather products as well as Fila and Ferre haute-couture collections, even Biagiotti sunglasses at 50% below U.S. prices. In a shop called Profumissimo, Italian designer Gianfranco Ferre's new perfume, Ferre, made its worldwide debut, but many another designer perfume, from Arden to Valentino, is there for the sniffing.

Those shops and most of the rest of the action aboard can be found on Riviera Deck. Here you will find *CostaRiviera's* tiered 600-seat La Scala Show Room, all decked out in zappy shades of orange and aquamarine. Swivel chairs offer comfortable seats and a good view of the lively entertainment that takes place each evening on board.

Not far away memorabilia of the international race-car circuit trims the big Grand Prix Bar. A favorite before- and after-dinner gathering spot, this big open lounge decorated in smashing shades of raspberry features a piano bar.

At the aft end of the ship, everything seems to go around in circles as you ease into the curvilinear lines of the Riviera Lounge. Behind the stage where a band plays for dancing, you'll spot brushed-steel "stalactite" sculptures, one of many sculptural features on board this ship. Late at night this room becomes the ship's disco.

Yet another *CostaRiviera* watering hole, the Rendezvous, gets our vote for the coziest spot on board. Sneak in here for a Campari before or a cappuccino after. You can settle into the intimacy of a small cozy interior bar or wander into a second bar at the edge of the ship and pull up a chair in a garden of bromeliads lined with big windows.

Up on Lido Deck, hot "Italian" colors—bright yellow, green, and red—rim the ship's swimming pool while cabin and restaurant décor focuses on soft pinks and aquas.

If you like informality at breakfast and lunch, head for La Dolce Vita Buffet, a flagstone-floored poolside café, where you can wear a bikini to the buffet line.

More formal dining takes place in the ship's Portofino Dining Room, a bright and pleasant spot lined with windows down both sides and attractively outfitted in blending shades of blue, deep red, and green. The *CostaRiviera's* dining room is different on two counts: it's one of the few cruise ships that combines dining and dancing—an ensemble plays for dancing during dinner—and it has quite a large number of tables for two as well as the usual tables for four, five, six, and more.

Naturally enough, the specialties of the house are Italian treats, but French, American, Caribbean, and continental preparations are also on the list. The notable culinary creations include orecchiette all pugliese (fresh pasta shells with a broccoli and parmesan sauce), beef tenderloin Benedict, and roast pheasant with a grape sauce.

When all you want is pizza and beer, fear not. Just stroll on over to the pizzeria and sink into the eye-popping décor of aquamarine and orange. Then order up an on-draft imported beer, pick out a pizza, and, *voilà!* hog heaven for pie fans. It's open when the dining room isn't, so you can pop in for a pie to tide you over till dinner.

Later, ease on over to the ice cream parlor, here called a *gelateria*, to snack on luscious Italian ices.

Activities

Costa likes to say that you face the day "con brio," by which they mean "with plenty to do." You can begin with an aerobics class, move on to golf practice tees and a putting green, have a go at basketball, skeet shooting, and films in a balconied theater, and wind up somewhat more sedately at a sing-along in the Grand Prix Bar.

They even entertain you while you're doing something entertaining—performers who appear in on-board shows each evening turn up on deck by day, wandering through the ship juggling, performing magic tricks, flipping a sassy can-can skirt, doing whatever they do best just to get you laughing.

When it's time to dispense with a couple of calories, you'll find a whole deck just waiting for workouts. Called, fittingly enough, the Sports Deck, this top-of-the-ship locale is togged out with a shiny gym equipped with all those torture machines we've all grown to know and love. There's a teak jogging track up there, a sauna to sweat it out in, a massage room, basketball hoop, facial rooms, showers, and even three outdoor Jacuzzis.

Attention bridge—and other game—players. Although game rooms seem to be little more than an afterthought on some ships, on this craft the game room is a cushy place with sink-in-able beige chairs and lots of light streaming through a glass wall.

For games more serious than Scrabble, head for the ship's huge Monte Carlo casino, which is in fact one of the most notable features of this ship. Far from being consigned to some spare room aboard, as casinos are on many ships, this casino stretches right across the ship from one side to the other. In it you'll find not only two roulette wheels, four blackjack tables, a craps table, and 110 slot machines, but even this departure—a baccarat table. For newcomers to gambling, the ship offers a slick little booklet that tells you just how to play—sorry, no instructions on how to win. Friendly croupiers will be happy to help you get rolling too.

Young sailors get special attention on board and have two rooms just for their pleasure. Sorry, but parents can get in here only if invited by and accompanied by a child. Young children play in the Pinocchio Room and teenagers gather in the Teen Club. All young passengers are registered by age when they come aboard and treated to a tour of the ship. Each day they get their own daily schedule of activities that keeps them going from 9 a.m. to 11 p.m.

Meanwhile, grateful parents have their own ways to play. Evening entertainment includes the usual captain's dinner at the beginning of the cruise and a farewell party at the end. In between there's a Festa Italiana Night, a Carnival Night paying tribute to Caribbean pirate days, a Western Night, and a Roman Bacchanal that replaces the masquerade evening.

If you'd like to learn how to whip up some of those Italian goodies in your own kitchen, just mosey on down to the chef's weekly cooking lesson where you can learn the tricks he uses to feed 1,000 passengers three meals a day.

Then hie on over to the *CostaRiviera's* wine-tasting party to learn a little about what Italian wines to order with dinner and to serve with what you now know how to cook.

Cabins

On this quite large ship you'll find 492 cabins in a variety of sizes and shapes. More than half of them—296—are outside staterooms, and 52 cabins feature queen-size beds. Three inside cabins have just one bed for single travelers and 35 cabins aboard have upper and lower beds; all the rest are twin lower berths.

Cabins come in all sizes and shapes, and many open off small corridors that nip off from the wide main hallways. Fanciest accommodations are high up on the ship's Amalfi Deck, where you'll find nearly all those rooms with queen-size beds we mentioned earlier.

Because they come in so many sizes and shapes, cabins aboard are divided into no fewer than 14 price categories. To complicate matters further there are two seasons to consider: peak, from mid-December to April plus July and August; and value, which covers all the other months.

To give you an idea what you'll pay aboard, here's a look from the top down, which on this ship begins with Category 14 cabins, the most expensive. We'll just run down peak-season prices; value season prices are $30 to $50 lower.

In one of those big outside cabins featuring a queen-size bed you pay $1,670 per person for a week-long peak-season cruise. If you want an outside cabin of similar size but with two lower beds, the fare is also $1,670.

Next come four categories of outside cabins with two lower beds. They differ some, but not a great deal, in size and the fare is $1,460 to $1,600 per person in peak season.

Inside cabins with double bed are $1,460, and there are some quite roomy inside cabins with two lower beds for the same price.

The next four categories (Categories 7, 6, 5, and 4) range down in price from $1,430 for larger Category 7 cabins to $1,260 for smaller rooms.

Outside staterooms with one lower bed and one upper berth ring in at

$1,190 per person for a week-long cruise, while an inside cabin with the same set-up is $995 to $1,090.

Single travelers are assigned to rooms with upper and lower berths—Categories 1, 2, and 3—and pay about a 30% surcharge for single occupancy, lower than on most lines.

Third and fourth passengers sharing a cabin pay a flat rate of $495 for adults, $295 for children under 12, regardless of the category of cabin selected. Everybody pays an additional $33 per person in port charges.

Divide by seven and you get per diem rates that range from a low of about $155 per person to a high of $239 a day for the ship's spiffiest quarters. You can figure about $170 to $190 a day per person for inside cabins, $200 to $220 a day per person for outside cabins.

Fares include air fare from more than 125 cities, but if you're driving into Fort Lauderdale to board the ship, you get a $200-per-person break on the price. Costa also has arranged a number of money-saving post-cruise visits to Fort Lauderdale or Orlando, including a rental car.

DAPHNE: Big staterooms are the pride of this cruise ship, which boasts that even the smallest quarters measure in at 260 square feet. And some of the spiffiest —and most expensive—even have private balconies!

In winter, from about October to April, this sparkling-white craft is in San Juan each Saturday preparing for her midnight sailing to St. Maarten, Martinique, Barbados, St. Lucia, Antigua, and St. Thomas. And these appealing stops can be combined with a week's cruise on the *CarlaCosta* to make a fascinating two-week sojourn.

In summer the ship heads for Alaskan waters, where she sails merrily through the glaciers on glittering seven-day Alaskan sailings. To get into position for those sojourns, in spring and fall the ship features a Panama Canal odyssey visiting ports of call between San Juan and Los Angeles. Some of the stops on that voyage: St. Thomas, Caracas, Cartagena, Acapulco, and Mazatlán.

Once in Alaska the *Daphne* sails from Vancouver every Friday from mid-May through mid-September on cruises through the Inside Passage to Wrangell, Endicott Arm, Juneau, Skagway, Davidson and Rainbow Glaciers, and Ketchikan.

Built in 1956, rebuilt and relaunched in 1976, and refurbished in 1986, the *Daphne* is 432 feet long with five passenger decks. Life aboard is casual, but on two nights you can break out the wing collars and long gowns.

Public Rooms

The *Daphne,* at 17,000 tons, is one of the line's smaller ships and Costa likes to call her a "seagoing yacht." While that phrase has a touch of Madison Avenue to it, it is true that all cabins have two lower beds and bathtubs as well as showers, and that the ship is small enough that it could (although it does not) accommodate all 425 passengers at one sitting in the bright glass-walled Trevi Dining Room.

It's also true that some vessels of comparable size carry nearly twice as many passengers. On this ship you will find one of the highest ratios of space to passengers of any cruise ship. You are practically guaranteed an outside cabin too, since about 90% of the ship's quarters—190 cabins—are outside doubles.

Decks aboard this ship echo Italia—Portofino, Capri, Sorrento, Venice, and Riviera, the place to look for almost all the ship's public rooms. Here you will find the Trevi Dining Room, a casino, a shopping arcade, card room, library, and the big main lounge where the nightly action takes place.

Fitness buffs will find a gymnasium aboard, and up top on the Amalfi Deck there's space set aside as a sports deck. Something for everybody: gamblers will find a casino aboard.

A discothèque is up on the Lido Deck, where you'll also find the swimming pool, pizzeria, and gelateria.

Cabins

Cabins aboard are quite spacious, and with only 400 other passengers you'll find plenty of open public spaces aboard too. A low passenger count means you'll get some very good service as well, a pride of this ship.

Let's look at some of the prices you'll pay for a week-long voyage in Alaska's peak season from the end of June to September. (Value season runs roughly from May through mid-June and September. At that time you pay $100 less than peak rate.)

To show you what we mean by luxury ships, for openers there are four categories of deluxe suites on board this vessel. All of them have separate living room, refrigerator-bar, television, attractive contemporary décor, plenty of space, and a lofty view. Deluxe suites even have a private balcony for some very private stargazing! Quarters like these range in price from $2,800 down to $2,195 per person for a week-long peak-season Alaska cruise.

Outside doubles in the next six categories (Categories 8, 7, 6, 5, 4, and 3) all have two lower beds. For one of these you pay rates ranging from $2,025 per person for a week's cruise to a low of $1,625 per person on the Alaska voyage.

Finally, the least expensive quarters on board are inside cabins with two lower beds. The price for one of these Category 1 or 2 cabins is $1,395 or $1,505 per person.

Third and fourth adults sharing a cabin are $1,195; children under 13 are charged $745. Port charges are $48 per person on the Alaska cruise, and single occupants of a double cabin pay 150% of the applicable rate.

Per diem rates for this ship on its peak-season seven-day Alaska cruises run from a low of $199 to about $232 to $289 in the mid-price range, and a high of $314 to $400 per person.

11. CROWN CRUISE LINE

Contact: Crown Cruise Line, 2790 N. Federal Hwy. (P.O. Box 10265), Boca Raton, FL 33431 (tel. 305/845-7447, or toll free 800/841-7447).

Cruising Grounds: One-day cruises to nowhere, occasional sailings to the Bahamas. Cruises to begin in 1990.

Itineraries: *Viking Princess*—Palm Beach – Freeport – Palm Beach, with occasional cruises to nowhere; Caribbean cruises to be added in 1990.

Crown Cruise Line is a comparative newcomer to south Florida, where it began operating after spending many years sailing its single ship in the waters off California's San Diego.

VIKING PRINCESS: Crown Line's *Viking Princess* moved to Palm Beach in 1985 to become the first—and at the moment, the only—cruise line based in that small port.

Crown's move must have proven successful for the company: in 1988 Crown's Scandinavian owners, the Grundstad Shipping Group, signed a $60-million construction contract with a Valencia, Spain, company for a 530-passenger ship. That new ship is being billed as an "upscale" ship, which means it will be offering more service and showier amenities in an attempt to appeal to an audience that is not looking for bargain-basement cruise prices. It will be sailing on two- and five-day cruises from Palm Beach, to the Bahamas on the shorter cruises, and to some unannounced, but necessarily nearby, points in the Caribbean on its five-day sojourns.

In the meantime you can have a rollicking day at sea on this 700-passenger, yacht-like ship, setting out to sea at 9:30 a.m. and returning at midnight. Along the way you'll do what you do on any one-day cruise: get lots of sun, sing along with a calypso band, dance, dine, gamble, and be entertained by a pleasant crew. After a few hours in Freeport, where an intriguing array of international shops offers a pleasant diversion, you reboard and head back to Palm Beach with dinner, dancing to the music of a trio, a couple of yuks with a comedian, a cabaret show and dance revue, and perhaps a couple of rounds of blackjack before setting foot once again on Palm Beach soil.

If you think you'd like a place to change and take a nap during the cruise, you can book a cabin, although many of the Sunday sailors who take this cruise don't bother.

You'll find all the usual amenities aboard: a swimming pool, lots of sunning space, deck games, organized activities, and a constant barrage of snacking opportunities.

Fares are $79 per person Monday through Thursday and $89 for a Saturday trip to Freeport; and there's a $12 port tax added to the tab in each case. Cabins are $25 to $100 additional for the day, depending on their size and location. Children's fares for that day-long trip are $29 for children 2 to 7, $39 for youngsters 7 to 11, and $49 for those 11 to 17.

On Friday evening and Sunday morning the ship sails on special cruises to nowhere. On Friday evening that cruise departs at 7 p.m. and returns at 2 a.m., while the Sunday trip, billed as a brunch cruise, leaves at 11 a.m. and returns at 7 p.m., making it a good way for children to get a taste of this cruising business. Fare for either cruise is $59 for adults, $29 for children 2 to 7, and $39 for children 7 to 17. Budget an additional $4 each for port taxes.

Occasionally the line also sails on one-day cruises to nowhere along this very scenic coastline. On those trips prices are $10 cheaper—$69 for adults, and correspondingly less for the youngsters.

12. CUNARD LINE

Contact: Cunard Line, 555 Fifth Ave., New York, NY 10017 (tel. 212/880-7500 or 661-7777 for general inquiries, or toll free 800/221-4770).

Cruising Grounds: *QE2*—transatlantic New York-Southampton, Caribbean, Bermuda, and an around-the-world cruise; other ships—Alaska, Mexican Riviera, Caribbean.

Itineraries: *Cunard Countess*—San Juan – Caracas – Grenada – Barbados – Martinique – St. Thomas – San Juan *or* San Juan – Tortola – St. Maarten – Guadeloupe – St. Lucia – Antigua – St. Thomas – San Juan, year round.

Cunard Princess—

IN SUMMER: Vancouver – Ketchikan – Tracy Arm – Juneau – Skagway – Yakutat Bay – Hubbard Glacier – Columbia Glacier – College Fjord – Whittier; and return same route.

IN WINTER: Fort Lauderdale – Playa del Carmen/Cozumél – Grand Cayman – Montego Bay – Panama Canal – Balboa – Costa Rica – Acapulco; and return same route.

Queen Elizabeth 2—

IN SUMMER AND FALL: New York – Southampton, England, *or* occasional

Bermuda and Caribbean cruises and cruises to Spain, Madeira, Tenerife, Lisbon, and Gibraltar.
IN WINTER: A 60-day cruise around South America in 1989.

Vistafjord —
IN WINTER: Cruises of varying lengths from Fort Lauderdale to various Caribbean ports including Barbados, Martinique, Antigua, St. Kitts, Nevis, St. Croix, St. Lucia, Santo Domingo, Guadeloupe, Nassau, St. Barthélemy, St. Vincent, St. Maarten, St. Lucia, Tortola, St. Thomas, San Juan, Aruba, Cozumél, Montego Bay, and Grenada.
IN SUMMER: Mediterranean and Scandinavian cruises.

Sagafjord —
IN WINTER AND SPRING: Cruises of varying lengths from Fort Lauderdale to various Caribbean ports including Barbados, Martinique, Antigua, St. Kitts, Nevis, St. Croix, St. Lucia, Santo Domingo, Guadeloupe, Nassau, St. Barthélemy, St. Vincent, St. Maarten, St. Lucia, Tortola, St. Thomas, San Juan, Aruba, Cozumél, Montego Bay, and Grenada.
IN SUMMER AND FALL: Vancouver – Ketchikan – Juneau – Skagway – Sitka – Valdez – Seward – Anchorage and return same route *or* Fort Lauderdale – New York – Newport – Nova Scotia – Québec – Montréal *or* Montréal – Charlottetown – Halifax – St. John – Boston – New York – Fort Lauderdale *or* Fort Lauderdale – Cozumél – Grand Cayman – Cartagena – Costa Rica – Acapulco *or* San Diego – Hilo – Hawaii – Lahaina – Maui – Nawiliwili – Kauai – Honolulu; and return same route.

Sea Goddess I —
IN WINTER AND SPRING: St. Thomas – Jost Van Dyke – St. Maarten – Peter Island – Iles des Saintes – St. Lucia – Grenadines – Barbados *or* Barbados – Palm Island – Mustique – Antigua – Virgin Gorda – St. Barthélemy – St. John – St. Thomas.
IN SUMMER AND FALL: Madeira – Morocco – Spain, and other Mediterranean and Greek island cruises.

Sea Goddess II —
IN WINTER AND SPRING: Singapore – Jakarta – Bali – Malacca – Kuala Lumpur – Penang – Singapore, and other varying Southeast Asia ports.
IN SUMMER AND FALL: Monte Carlo – St. Tropez – Portofino – Capri – Taormina – Corfu – Dubrovnik – Venice, and other varying Mediterranean ports.

To say Cunard is to say *Queen Elizabeth 2,* flagship of this venerable old British line. No other ship is as famous as this queen of the seas whose namesake predecessor set the standards for transatlantic sailings and for cruises of all kinds.

You can see the massive 67,140-ton *QE2* in Florida's Port Everglades several times each winter season, and in summer you can spot her tooting in and out of New York Harbor.

If you're very, very lucky—and quite well-heeled to boot—you can sail with 1,800 or so other infatuees on the *Queen's* dream-machine, around-the-world-in-90-days sojourn. For a lot less money you can join one of the shorter Caribbean cruises in early winter or her regular series of five-day New York-Southampton voyages each summer.

If you're treating yourself to the best of everything, you can even combine the elegance of the *Queen* with the very New World pizzazz of that needle-nosed, sound-barrier-blasting Concorde airplane on a special fly-cruise program.

So huge is the reputation of the *Queen* that even seasoned sailors sometimes forget that there are now six other ships in this fancy fleet.

In recent years Cunard, which is part of Britain's Trafalgar House mega-conglomerate, added two ships formerly owned by Norwegian American Lines, the plush *Sagafjord* and *Vistafjord*.

Both those sleek cruisers have been highly rated, and no wonder—where else can you find ships that offer such impeccable elegance and service: terrycloth bathrobes and Lancôme soap, even personalized stock quotes and a Chinese laundry man?

And talk about dream cruises—in 1986 the *Sagafjord* sailed from Port Everglades on a 102-day trip around Australia, India, and the Orient, and in 1988 the ship was off on a 108-day excursion around the world.

If you don't have 102 days to spare, try the elegant, 25,000-ton *Vistafjord*, which sails from Port Everglades on a series of 14-day voyages to a variety of Caribbean islands and South America.

Even more recently Cunard became the operator of two small and plush ships—with matching price tags—*Sea Goddess I* and *Sea Goddess II*.

In this book you'll be introduced to some budget bargains, some mid-priced ships, and some luxury liners, so now you're ready to meet, in your dreams at least, a seaborne status symbol.

We're talking here about *Sea Goddess I* and *Sea Goddess II*, classy craft that unabashedly cater to zillionaires or to those willing to hock the family jewels for a chance to live like that way for a week.

Even to unflappable cruise-marketing executives, Sea Goddess Cruises was a startling shot at one-upsmanship. Founded in 1983, the company was created by a Norwegian shipping company A/S Norske. Not content to run just another cruise ship, that company introduced the crème de la crème of big, ocean-going yachts and began marketing it to those whose annual income is in the $200,000 bracket. Higher than that is also acceptable, of course.

Shortly after it introduced the world to $4,000+-a-week price tags on the *Sea Goddess I*, this line doubled the pleasure with the *Sea Goddess II*, a twin sister every bit as decadently desirable and subtly sensuous.

On both those ships, all rooms are suites, although some are sweeter and higher priced than others. Tabs now easily reach $5,000 a week and for the most elaborate accommodations can top $8,000 a person for a seven-day cruise.

In recent years the line was acquired by Cunard which, with the addition of these two very exclusive ships, now has a seven-ship fleet that includes the majority of the world's poshest and priciest cruise ships.

Whichever Cunard ship you sail on, you'll become part of a fascinating history that stretches back nearly a century and a half to a far-sighted Nova Scotia merchant named Samuel Cunard. Back in 1839 Cunard dreamed up a plan to operate a mail service on the North Atlantic between England and North America. First he talked the British bureaucracy into a mail contract, then he launched a 1,150-ton paddlestreamer called the *Britannia*, which sailed to Boston from England in the summer of 1840. Fourteen days later the *Britannia* reached American shores, where Cunard was presented with a huge silver cup to commemorate the historic moment. You can still see that cup at the Columbia Dining Room of the *QE2*.

Eight years later Cunard began carrying mail to New York and in 1856 he launched a ship called the *Persia*. That craft was quite a vessel for its day: with paddles 40 feet in diameter, it was twice as long as the *Britannia* and had a speed of 14 knots.

Soon the race was on. Speed became the issue and was to remain a competitive necessity through many a decade. So important was transatlantic speed, in fact, that an award called the Blue Riband was given to the fastest ship on the Atlantic. Cunard disdained participation in that race, but one of the Cunard ships always won it anyway!

It wasn't long before Cunard built two new ships that were to become the yardstick by which ships were to be judged for many a decade to come: the *Queen Elizabeth* and the *Queen Mary*. Built for speed, the two ships could travel at 28.5 knots. The *Queen Mary* was launched first in 1937, followed a year later by her sister ship, the *Queen Elizabeth*. By the time the *Queen Elizabeth* rolled off the launching pad, however, the world was at war, so she spent her early history racing across the North Atlantic ferrying troops between England and the U.S.

Tales of the ships' near-misses are legion, but both made it safely through that bitter conflict to receive the praise of a grateful Prime Minister Winston Churchill, who pointed out, quite accurately, that "the world owes them a debt it will not be able to measure."

After the war the two royal sailors began boarding royalty and servants, famous and infamous, and anyone with masses of money, for the transoceanic passage. What an elegant scene it must have been: afternoon tea on delicate china, violinists playing softly in the background, long lazy days in the sea air, long elegant nights amid fluttering fans and exotic perfumes.

Sadly, it ended in the late 1960s when the *Queen Mary* sailed on her final voyage across the sea to a new life in California, where she remains today, a tourist attraction and hotel.

Her sister ship came to an even more bitter end. She was sailed to Hong Kong to become a floating university, but sank in the harbor there, consumed by fire.

Cunard met the challenge, however. In 1967 the line launched the brand-new *QE2*, sent down the rails after a champagne christening by Queen Elizabeth II, granddaughter of the lady who christened the first *Queen*.

You'll now find the *QE2* still making those transatlantic voyages in summer. Just as Cunard was the first, it is now the last remaining line to run a regularly scheduled service from New York to England. In winter the *Queen* heads south to Port Everglades for several Caribbean voyages, and to begin her around-the-world trip, usually in early January.

Meanwhile the *Cunard Countess* is a familiar sight in Puerto Rico where she sails year round from San Juan to a variety of interesting Caribbean islands. The *Cunard Princess* spends the summer in Alaska, the winter on Mexican Riviera cruises.

Sagafjord in 1988 sailed on an around-the-world cruise, then ended the winter season with a couple of Caribbean voyages from Fort Lauderdale.

Meanwhile, the *Vistafjord* also plied the Caribbean on voyages of varying length and to a wide variety of ports including Barbados, Martinique, Antigua, St. Kitts, Nevis, St. Croix, St. Lucia, Santo Domingo, Guadeloupe, Nassau, St. Barthélemy, St. Vincent, St. Maarten, St. Lucia, Tortola, St. Thomas, San Juan, Aruba, Cozumél, Montego Bay, and Grenada.

QUEEN ELIZABETH 2: There is no more famous ship afloat than this great beauty, which since her construction in 1967 has gone around the world and gone to war. Flagship of Cunard Lines and indeed the flagship of jolly old England herself, the *Queen* is the reigning queen of the seas, no doubt about it.

It makes no matter that the *Norway* is larger, that others are newer, fancier, or more dramatically appointed. This handsome navy-blue vessel with the distinctive red-and-black Cunard funnel carries with her a history and mystique that cannot be touched by any other craft afloat.

She is magnificent, no question about it, and the sight of her sailing majestically off into the sunset is heart-stopping. There's never been one like her, and it's likely there will never be another.

Aboard the *QE2* the British caste system is firmly in place. You travel first class or transatlantic class, just as passengers did a generation or two ago. Those who pay the most dine in the choicest of the four dining rooms on board, and are treated to cocktails and afternoon tea in a private sitting room, invited to a private party with the captain.

Frankly, we don't think you'll notice these small discriminations. If you're very observant you're even likely to see some of those first-class travelers joining the lesser-class fun!

All the restaurants on board are pretty places, and there are plenty of lounges just as beautiful, if not even lovelier, than that first-class haven. So, fear not, you'll never even notice that some people are getting something you're not. And if you do, just contemplate what they're paying for it!

One cannot help but be amazed at the sheer size of everything about this ship. On a recent visit we were overwhelmed to discover the size, of all things, of the ship's hospital! When you stop to think about it, extensive medical facilities are, of course, to be expected on a ship whose long cruises naturally attract older travelers who have had the time to acquire the money and now have the time to stay floating for two or three months. Still, who'd expect to see 15 hospital rooms, plus examining rooms for the crew, a dentist's office, a pharmacy, and finally, a complete operating room!

There are many more examples of the *Queen*'s huge size: she measures 67,140 tons, is 963 feet long and 105 feet wide, and carries a crew of 1,000 to serve 1,815 passengers! She can trot along faster than any ship afloat, steaming through the seas at 32.5 knots. More? Of course. She is 13 stories tall, has 22 elevators, and a wine cellar with more than 20,000 bottles requiring, in fact, 50 workers to dispense and keep track of the ship's beverages.

For those who cannot resist awesome numbers, here's a few more: the ship has 239 waiters, eight carpenters, two nannies, and four printers on board; she dispenses 150 pounds of caviar on a five-day transatlantic crossing; and—get this one!—stocks enough ice cream on even the shortest voyages to make 24,000 single-dip cones.

The ship has traveled more than 2,000,000 miles since its maiden voyage in 1969 and served as a troopship during England's dispute with Argentina over the Falkland Islands.

In 1986 the *QE2* did what many ladies her age do with resounding success: she had a facelift—then reappeared in her glamorous new form to begin another transatlantic season.

Activities

Not even the most blasé soul could fail to be impressed by the sheer numbers of things to see and do on this ship, not to mention the sheer beauty of her deep-blue hull steaming through the seas like a great whale. In fact, the line claims that it would take one person four months to participate in all the activities offered on board this activity-packed ship.

Down by the inside pool is a branch of the posh Golden Door Spa, which will coddle you and whip you into shape, not necessarily in that order. Use of the recently expanded Golden Door Spa at Sea is included in the cost of your voyage, so you can justify your cruise by figuring you saved the $2,500-a-week that a trip to the land-lubbing Golden Door would cost! That spa includes an exercise area, sauna, massage center, 16 daily exercise classes, a hydrocalisthenics pool, whirlpool baths, yoga, aerobics, and ballet, plus a bar and solarium.

A new addition to the ship is a personal computer learning program at sea, equipped with 16 IBM personal computers, videotape machines, and a library of educational films. Every day there's a seminar showing you how to use the computers, and the center is open 24 hours a day so you can play between sessions.

Another new addition to the ship is a glass "Magrodome," a sliding roof that can be rolled out to cover one of the swimming pools if rain dares fall on the sunseekers below. At night the area becomes an indoor-outdoor disco.

Film fans will find a big balconied theater aboard where top films are shown. Of course there are church services, and there's even a small paneled synagogue tucked away on the ship.

Cunard is proud of its Life Enrichment Program, which in 1984 invited more than 300 stars and experts on board to discuss everything from financial success to psychological well-being. Among those who were featured in the program were Helen Gurley Brown, Vidal Sassoon, and Dr. Christiaan Barnard.

The entertainment on board is fabulous. Top-name entertainers appear: Rita Moreno, Ben Vereen, George Burns, and the orchestra that plays at Buckingham Palace soirées. On her world cruise one year, the *QE2* featured Patti Lupone, star of *Evita,* plus a magician, a French singing star, Latin American dance champions, two comedians, a guitarist, the *QE2* dancers, a variety act, and a classical artist. That's not even to mention lecturers, who have included Maxene Andrews of the Andrews Sisters, a photographer, a television actor, a financial lecturer, a computer expert, and a psychotherapist.

Recent renovations have expanded the Club Lido into an entertainment complex, complete with a sound-and-light show and decorated in red and black with gray touches.

Bridge players will disappear for the whole cruise, under the tutelage of world-famous experts. Crafts enthusiasts can learn everything from macramé to woodwork, and photographers can shoot 'em up at photography classes. Joggers have a track to trot on, and get this—a mere four times around is a mile!

Dining Rooms

Dining is more than an event aboard the *QE2;* it's a status game as well. Where you dine on this ship determines who you are.

The Queen's Grill seats the 188 top-paying passengers aboard. The Princess Grill serves 102 of the next fiscal group down the line, followed by the Columbia Restaurant, which provides for 616 diners. The Mauretania Restaurant serves the 767 Transatlantic Class passengers.

If you book one of the ship's five lowest-priced cabins you'll join those 767 other diners in the Mauretania Restaurant, a sophisticated spot decked out in soft mauve and burgundy colors.

Tall windows run down both sides of the rooms, and tables for two, four, and six are available, along with some banquette seating. Large paintings of famous sailing ships adorn the walls.

On the menu is an impressive list of juices, first courses, soups, fish, entrees, grills, cold meats, vegetables, salads, desserts, fruit, and cheese. Dining is more informal here than in the other dining rooms on board, but that certainly doesn't mean you wear your cutoffs and sandals. American entrees predominate too.

The Queen's Grill is a study in mahogany elegance, where chandeliers glitter in a raised ceiling. Chrome-framed Erté posters add a contemporary touch to this English library-like room, and a centerpiece made of huge seashells is a showstopper.

In this formal spot you can order anything you can dream up and it will magically appear. We're not guaranteeing ostrich eggs, you understand, but there are all manner of strange delicacies that can be produced with the wave of a whisk.

Outside the Queen's Grill is a sitting room with marble tables on which afternoon tea and before-dinner cocktails are served.

Next down in the pecking order is the Princess Grill, which has seats for 102 diners. A subtly subdued room, the Princess Grill is our favorite, an intimate spot offering fine food in beautiful surroundings enhanced by a view of the ocean through broad windows.

Those who have paid for the privilege of dining in the ship's Columbia Restaurant will find this always-bright-and-shiny spot looking even better now after a recent renovation.

Sunlight streams through tall windows down both sides of the room. Tables for two, four, six, and eight are available, and there's a pretty wing off to one side for some very private dining. If you select a cabin in Category E, F, G, H, I, or J (toward the lower end of the price list) you'll dine in this serene, and somewhat more casual, setting. There's kosher dining too.

On this ship, as on all cruise ships, all your five or six meals a day are included in the price of your passage. However, on the *QE2* you can sometimes dine in the Queen's Grill, if you like, by paying a hefty cover charge.

You may think we're going on and on about restaurants here, but remember that where you dine determines your status aboard the *Queen*. So far does the dining connection go, in fact, that some Cunard brochures once referred to cabins not by category or type but as "Columbia cabins" or "Queen's Grill cabins."

Worry not, however. Any of these restaurants is as lovely as anything the average hometown can boast, and the food varies some but not greatly. Service is good anywhere.

Other Public Rooms

Without a doubt the best shopping area afloat is here on the *QE2*. Located on a mezzanine overlooking an equally dramatic public room, the glittering Shopping Promenade fills an entire floor. Even the most antishopping soul will be lured by the sheer beauty of the displays in windows here—Cartier, Dior, Dunhill, H. Stern, Gucci, Adidas, leather wallets with an embossed *QE2* label, lambswool sweaters, Royal Doulton china, formal wear, golf shirts, you name it. You could come on board without luggage and have no trouble outfitting yourself here. Even Harrod's is on board the *QE2*!

At one end of the shopping arcade you can make a grand entrance down an arching steel staircase to the dance floor in the very contemporary room below. Decorated in dramatic hues, this multilevel Grande Lounge is furnished in slick contemporary style with several three-quarter-circle banquettes, a raised stage, and raised wings on either side of a big, big dance floor. Way at the back is our favorite seat, a big semicircular banquette where you can watch everything at once.

Want to send someone flowers? Drop by the complete flower shop on board.

Want to retreat to a small drawing room with a large something-cool? Try the Yacht Club Bar, where a dramatic décor of wood and navy blue, and a showy piano bar combine to make this spot one of the best rooms aboard.

Another top lounge on board is the Midships Bar, a satisfyingly dark spot decked out in velvet so deep green that drinking there is like sipping in a tree house. Tinted-glass doors keep it coolly verdant at any hour, and brass accents glow with constant polishing.

Another huge public area on the quarterdeck is called the Queen's Room, and features a soothing décor that's very contemporary. Chairs swivel so you can keep an eye on what's going on anywhere in the room. A beautiful lighted ceiling reigns over a big dance floor with a raised bandstand.

If your idea of paradise is hours and hours of uninterrupted reading, you'll love the library here. While its big windows offer some minor distractions, its incredible array of book titles balances those negatives nicely. This is a full-fledged library, with comfortable couches to sit in, a writing area, and walls and walls and walls of books. What's more, there's even a librarian who really looks the way you'd think a librarian should look, and she keeps things in apple-pie order, all carefully placed by subject. Books with large print are available, as are books in German, Japanese, French, probably Swahili. Beautiful paneled walls make the room a pleasure to look at whether or not you're checking out a book, and the beamed ceiling just adds to the joy of it all.

For gaming amusement there's a handsome room with chess, backgammon, and of course, card tables available. If you like games with financial rewards, there's a full casino on board as well.

For youngsters there's a big playroom with a staff dedicated to childhood amusements. Kids even have their own cartoon cinema. Teens have a hideaway too.

There's a gym, saunas, two indoor and two outdoor pools, casino, cardroom with rosewood tables, bank, on-board newspaper, paddle tennis court. There's a kennel in which to park your toy poodle, even an 80-car garage to park your Toyota!

Cabins

As for cabins, well, they come in all sizes, shapes, and prices. All have private facilities and direct-dial telephones that will connect you to anyone in the world. Some even have their own private veranda.

If your ship has really come in, you can book one of the *Queen*'s balconied suites on an around-the-world cruise for a mere $366,930. Prices *start* at $20,435 per person.

Don't panic. Cunard sells the Big Trip, but is smart enough also to sell it in small segments, 10 days to here, 30 to there, 5 to there, all the way around.

Cunard is also smart enough to sell quite a number of other cruises ranging from five-day transatlantic voyages back and forth between New York and England, and delightful Caribbean junkets in the winter sunshine.

You need not be 103 and a zillionaire to sail on the most famous ship afloat. But you can live like one: in 1988 if you sailed one way on the *QE2* New York—England voyages, you could buy a ticket back on the supersonic Concorde for just $925! You can in fact go from New York to London on the *QE2* for as little as $1,275.

So for purposes of dreaming and scheming, let's look at the price of a five-day transatlantic trip from New York to England on the *Queen*. Besides the 19 categories of cabins available, the *QE2* also has four fare seasons, known as super-thrift, thrift, intermediate, and high. Super-thrift is in effect on only two sailings in May and December, thrift on two in June and December, and intermediate from June through the first week of October. High season applies to New York-England sailings in late July and early August.

Let's look at the prices of cabins in the intermediate season, which covers most of the ship's voyages.

Top cabin in both location and price is the Queen Mary or Queen Elizabeth Suite. These are split-level apartments no less, in which you will luxuriate in huge quarters decorated in soothing colors. For one of these suites (and most definitely an invitation to cocktails with the captain) you will pay—are you sitting down?—$25,470 for the suite, which you can share with three others at no extra charge. Dropping down a tiny peg, the Queen Anne and Trafalgar Suites are $22,680.

Moving right along now, we get into figures we can at least absorb, if not afford. Top-of-the-line outside cabins with private verandas onto which you can sweep majestically range in price from $5,220 to $7,195 per person for the five-day trip. The next three categories of deluxe outside cabins with two beds are $4,190 to $4,880 per person for the voyage. In all these aforementioned accommodations you dine in the plush Queen's Grill, and are of course recipient of the best of everything.

The next category down, Category D, is deluxe outside cabins with two beds and dinner in the very pretty Princess Grill. For one of these you pay $3,795 per person for the five-day crossing.

In the next four categories in descending price order you dine in the Columbia Restaurant and sleep in outside quarters with two beds. For those accommodations you pay $2,995 to $3,390 per person for a five-day transatlantic cruise.

Now we come to the passengers traveling in a class known as Transatlantic Class, as opposed to all you've read about so far, which is considered First Class.

Transatlantic travelers have a choice of three categories of outside cabins, Categories I and J, either of which has two twin beds, and Category K, also an outside cabin but this time with lower and upper berths, for $1,995 to $2,395 per person for the five-day transatlantic crossing in intermediate season.

The lowest-price categories on board are Categories L and M, inside cabins with two beds or with lower and upper berth for $1,650 to $1,895.

Cabins for single travelers are available on board in both First and Transatlantic Class. For one of those in the intermediate season you will pay a high of $5,410 for a deluxe outside cabin and dinner in the Queen's Grill. An inside cabin is $2,110 to $3,285 and other outside cabins are $2,880 to $4,960 for the five-day intermediate-season crossing.

Third and fourth persons sharing a room pay half fare.

As long as you've gone this far, budget another $85 per person for port taxes.

There is this saving (or is that *coup de*) grace, however: your cruise fare includes a free economy-class British Airways ticket, and if you want to spring for an additional $925 you can be the first on your block to fly BA's downright wonderful supersonic transport aircraft, the Concorde.

If you can sail in that super-thrift season, rates are substantially cheaper, beginning at $1,250 per person for an inside cabin and rising to $5,505 per person for luxury outside veranda suites. The middle bracket in that season is $2,295 to $2,595 per person.

Per diem rates on those five-day voyages across the Atlantic in intermediate season work out to a low of $350 per person, rising in the middle ranges to $600 to $700, and in the highest-priced cabins, excluding suites, to $976 per person.

CUNARD COUNTESS: Some dreary day in February when the snow has lumped into great gray piles of mush and your feet are freezing, into your ungovernable imagination will come a picture of palm trees and balmy breezes. That's as good a time as any to consider the *Countess*. Heading right into the trade winds is where you'll find this Cunard ship, which sails from San Juan all year round on cruises to fabled Caribbean isles.

Built in Italy and launched in 1976, this 17,500-ton ship carries 800 passengers to Caracas, Grenada, Barbados, Martinique, and St. Thomas. An alternate itinerary takes her on what the line calls its "Seven Plus" cruise to St. Maarten, Guadeloupe, St. Lucia, Antigua, St. Thomas, and Tortola.

If you're looking for a two-week vacation, you can do those cruises back to back or get off in Barbados or St. Lucia and spend a week ashore at Cunard's Paradise Beach Hotel and Club in Barbados or La Toc Suites in St. Lucia.

Public Rooms

In 1984 Cunard embarked on a $7.5-million refurbishing project, which added an indoor-outdoor center the ship likes to call its "theater-in-the-round." Translate that to mean you can sit inside or out to view the ship's cabaret entertainment. There's dancing under the stars too, and a late-night disco featuring the latest in electronic sounds, lights, and special effects.

You can trust Cunard to do whatever it does right. For openers, all the ship's decks were replaced with teak. See what we mean?

Fitness fanatics can play in a new area called the fitness deck, where you'll find an outdoor pool, sauna, air-conditioned gym and exercise room, even a whirlpool bath. Built in several tiers, the pool is lined in mosaic tiles.

On those teak decks you can play volleyball, table tennis, and drive golf balls.

Cunard Countess's theme has a celestial focus: you'll find a Splashdown Bar, a Gemini Dining Room, a Nova Suite, the Galaxy Lounge, and Club Aquarius, even a Starlight Lounge.

As part of the renovation the ship's Splashdown Lido Bar and Satellite Outdoor Café were redesigned. Cedar blocks line the ceiling and whirring paddle fans cool the air. Decked out in yellow, blue, and white, this section of the ship is a gathering spot for sun worshippers.

In the forward lounge you can watch through tall windows as the ship plows through glittering Caribbean waters. You can play casino games or have a quiet talk in the piano bar. Some interesting glass cocktail tables convert to chess and backgammon game boards.

If you have youngsters hooked on electronic games (and enough quarters to support their habit), send them off to the Milky Way Arcade video arcade where Pac Man and Ms Pac chase those ghosties.

Meanwhile, you can escape to the newly remodeled theater where tiered seating offers a more comfortable seat for the ship's shows and movies.

In the Meridian restaurant you'll now dine amid a pretty brown, pink, and salmon décor with soft romantic lighting.

Activities

You can get in shape in the ship's gym, swim in the pool, try life in a hot tub. All day long there's a round of activity aboard, ranging from dancing classes to lectures, movies, paddle tennis, volleyball, skeet shooting, and a golf driving range.

Nights, there's a cabaret show in the ship's nightclub and festivities in the theater-in-the-round. Or dance under the stars in the ship's instant disco, alive with flickering lights, special effects, and plenty of rhythm.

Cabins

The cabins aboard this ship have been redecorated too. They're fitted out in soft pastel colors, and all cabins have private bathrooms.

The *Countess* offers both one- and two-week fares, and divides its year up into three seasons. The cheapest of these runs from July through mid-December. Slightly higher rates—about $50 more per person—apply in May, June, and September. High season is from Christmas through March, late June through August, and October through mid-December. At that time you'll pay $150 more per person above the low-season rates.

There are eight cabin categories aboard. Category A and B cabins, which are outside double cabins with bathtub and shower, and a sitting area in some, cost $1,960 to $2,415 per person for a week's cruise in the peak seasons.

Category C and D cabins are outside doubles with shower, and cost $1,675 to $1,735 per person in peak winter season for a seven-night cruise.

Inside double cabins with a shower fall in Categories E, F, G, and H, and cost $1,545 to $1,620 per person, depending on size and location of the cabin.

Finally, double cabins with upper and lower berths and shower are $1,385 per person for the week-long cruise.

A third person sharing an outside cabin pays $850 to $900, depending on season.

Better still, the price per person goes down rapidly if you're booking four or five people into two rooms.

If you're making your first foray into the lower Caribbean, this ship provides a comparatively economical way to do it. Per diem rates range from a low of $198 for a week's cruise to a high of $345.

CUNARD PRINCESS: The *Cunard Princess* is now the line's Panama Canal and Alaska sailer. Launched in 1977, the ship measures in at 17,500 tons and carries 800 passengers on 7-, 10-, and 11-day sojourns to some interesting Caribbean isles, the fascinating antiquities of the Yucatán Peninsula, through the Panama Canal, Costa Rica, and finally to Acapulco. Some cruises depart from Galveston, following a similar route, while a few others travel from Fort Lauderdale to San Juan and back through some of the most rarely visited Caribbean islands.

In June the ship points her bow north and heads for the icebergs of Alaska. In those waters she sails on one-week cruises through mid-September. On those voyages you embark in Vancouver, British Columbia, get off the ship in Alaska, and then fly home from there. The *Princess* sails back from Anchorage, of course, so you can turn the sojourn into a two-week trip if you like. There's quite a price break if you do.

You can even decide to tour Alaska, visit Mount McKinley, Nome, Fairbanks, Denali National Park, and then rejoin the ship two weeks later for its return voyage. Cunard makes that easy for you by providing a variety of land-tour programs outlined in the company's Alaska brochure, and of course, by giving you a break on the price.

Cunard likes to say that you see more of these waters on the *Princess* than on any other Alaska cruise ship because you spend a full seven days getting to Anchorage. Other ships, they point out, sail for three days or so and then turn around. They do have a point there.

Another high point of the ship's Alaskan journey is its passage up Tracy Arm Fjord, a waterway few cruise ships visit.

As for the ship itself, it can be called a princess with impunity—it was launched by the late Princess Grace of Monaco in New York Harbor in 1977.

Public Rooms

The *Cunard Princess* is a twin sister to the *Cunard Countess,* so you'll find similar public rooms, some of them even bearing the same name.

Exploring your way down from the funnel, amidships is the *Princess*'s oval swimming pool, surrounded by open deck and protected from the breeze by long windows down both sides. A pool bar nearby dispenses food and drink to tan seekers.

On Alaska voyages the Observation Deck gets crowded, for this is a prime vantage point from which to view passing glaciers.

Nights, you'll play in the Topsail Lounge, which is enclosed with windows and features a piano bar for quiet entertainment. The ship's casino, with blackjack tables and slot machines, is up here too.

At the stern you can thump away on the paddle tennis courts, visit the Outrigger Café for an alfresco lunch or breakfast, or curl up in a cozy corner of the library/writing room.

You'll dine in the Meridian Dining Room, a handsome glassed-in area with banquettes as well as chairs.

Largest lounge aboard is the Showboat Lounge, where the evening's cabaret entertainment takes place along with musical entertainment and specialty acts. A focal point here is a shining black marble dance floor. Oval windows are an unusual feature.

If you're sailing in Alaska, you can amble into the Eight Bells Club for hot spiced wine at 10 a.m. and stop by again in the afternoon to hear the naturalist's talk on whales. Later, there's easy listening music in this lounge.

Cabins

Like the *Countess,* cabins aboard the *Princess* are not as elaborate as you'll find on some of the other ships in the Cunard family. They're convenient though, in that beds become couches when you're not sleeping in them so you can have a sitting room without paying for a suite. All are carpeted, and have a radio, telephone, and bathroom.

Let's take a look at the prices aboard for a seven-day, peak-season Alaska cruise from mid-June to September, one of the ship's most popular sailings.

Top cabins aboard are Categories A and B, deluxe outside rooms, some with a sitting area, all with twin beds and a refrigerator/bar unit. Fares are $2,705 per person for the deluxe suites, $2,215 per person for the Category B cabins.

Outside double rooms in Categories C and D range from $2,035 to $2,100 per person for a seven-day cruise. Rooms in this category have two lower twin beds and some have an upper berth in case you're bringing a third person along with you.

Inside double rooms, some with an upper berth in addition to the two twin lower beds, range from $1,665 to $1,910 per person.

Finally, double rooms with upper berth of twin beds in Category H are located where the ship's structure begins to curve, thus reducing space a bit. Fares in those cabins are $1,540 per person.

Single travelers pay $3,050 for an outside single room on that cruise, $2,495 for inside quarters. A third person sharing a room pays $925.

Per diem rates for that cruise range from a low of $220 to a high (for a suite) of $386. In between, most travelers will pay a daily rate of about $240 to $300 per person on the seven-day cruise.

Cunard, like most lines these days, offers free air fare to or from the cruise to many cities in the U.S., with $50 to $200 add-ons for some cities. You'll also need to add $85 in port taxes.

SAGAFJORD: Numbered by her fans—and probably even her competitors—as among the top ships in the world, the *Sagafjord* is a classy operation, no doubt about it. Step aboard and you'll soon see why she's so beloved by her often-repeat customers. Copper and enamel sculptures grace the Veranda Deck, where elaborate woodcarvings are a feature of the Garden Bar, decked out in deep blue with tiled tables and big beautiful windows. A trio keeps 'em dancing on the circular dance floor by night, and presents concerts for afternoon tea.

Sweep up the swirling staircase from Veranda Deck and don't miss the absolutely sensational dark-wood paneling you'll see throughout the ship.

Public Rooms

Speaking of that dining room, aboard the *Sagafjord* there's only one sitting. You dine anytime you please (at tables for two, four, six, or eight) between 8 and 10 p.m. Whatever time you arrive, you will be enchanted by an open airy room done in a contemporary beige shade with just a hint of pink to it. Long windows, lighted pillars, and a raised ceiling almost two stories high add drama to dinner.

A shop aboard the *Sagafjord* is especially nice, with a very wide-open and airy feeling, quite a contrast to some ship's shops, which are so tiny and crammed you sometimes feel a little like a mole.

There's a spa program aboard if you'd like to limber up and slim down. It's got an indoor pool and a complete spa operation with fancy weight-lifting and workout equipment, bicycles, massage rooms, even a hot tub.

The tiny Lido café is a comfortable place to settle into the air conditioning while not sacrificing the feeling of being outside. Besides, the pool is just beyond the glass doors that sets off this café. Out on deck, plastic pipe furniture cushioned in orange and browns is pulled up under patio umbrellas.

A new nightclub, the Garden Lounge, was carved out of some extra space recently. You can also dance the night away in the ballroom, decked out in an attractive sprigged orange-and-red pattern on a beige background. Big curving banquettes are a special feature of this room, which has long narrow windows and a raised bandstand, plus a big, big dance floor.

You'll also find a launderette aboard with washing machines for do-it-yourselfers, as well as the usual ship's laundry services.

Cabins

Cabins are very spacious aboard the *Sagafjord,* as they really ought to be at these prices. Top of the line, no. 129, an outside double, features a suede couch and chair in a delicate pink-beige color with chocolate and rust accents. A divider sets off a sitting room from the sleeping area, which features twin beds with velvety velour spreads in a similarly delicate pink-beige.

There's a full-length mirror over a long dresser and a refrigerator built into a bar. A large table with drawers provides a nightstand between the two beds, and three very large floor-to-ceiling wood closets equipped with shoe racks offer plenty of space for everything you'd need on a cruise. Baths have tiled floors and many have tubs as well as showers.

On the Sun Deck, Cabin 105 is one of several new suites just carved out aboard the *Sagafjord*. It's decorated in rust and blues, and has a couch, two chairs, one flanked by an end table, and—get this—a private terrace with patio chairs and a table. Closets on this ship are rigged out with sliding wire baskets that help compartmentalize your belongings, and rooms have full-length mirrors.

Cabin 102 is a terrific corner suite with completely separate sitting room and two big picture windows. Decorated in rust and beige, it features walk-in closets and a very large bath, plus three more closets. This is a very, very special cabin.

Cabin 343 is an example of an outside double with twin beds and an emerald-green décor. Very trim-heavy woven bedspreads are the focal point of this room, which offers plenty of space between the beds and two portholes for light. There's a dresser with a mirror, a full-length mirror, and four closets, plus a bath with tub too.

Even smaller quarters are far from small. Cabin 305, for instance, is much smaller than some but is by no means tiny. You enter this one down a hallway, one wall of which has a small closet draped off with a floral curtain in place of a door. There's a tub and shower in the bath, and three full-length closets with doors. One bed turns into a couch during daylight hours, and there's a chair, table, two small dresser-like storage pieces (one with a mirror), and a full-length mirror.

Newly redecorated cabins are done in contemporary pastel shades—dusty roses, light blues, grays. Cabin 233 is a good example of the gray theme, and features gray and blue stripes in the carpeting, a similar color combination on the heavy checked spreads. This small corner room also sports lots of closet space and a bath with shower only.

Cabin 227 is a monster accommodation, "as big as my first apartment," laughed one awestruck peeker. This suite features beige carpets, twin beds, armchairs, dressers, and closets in one room, separated by sliding doors from an adjoining sitting room with more chairs, lots more closets... well, you get the picture. If you can afford this one, don't let it get away.

If you're looking for a double bed, you'll find one in Cabin 438, among others.

Because itineraries and prices vary so widely it's difficult to select a representative price, but let's look at the price for a ten-day Alaska cruise from Anchorage to Vancouver.

Top rate for a suite on that voyage is $5,690 to $8,910 per person, followed by outside doubles for $2,480 to $5,260 per person.

Inside doubles, which are naturally smaller than the more expensive cabins, are $2,340 to $2,630 per person for the ten-day journey.

Singles have a number of options on board, with prices ranging from a high of $5,550 to a low of $3,210 for an inside single cabin for ten days.

A third person sharing the cabin pays $1,310 for the ten-day trip.

Per diem rates then range from a low of $234 to a high, excluding suites, of $526 per person for a ten-day Alaskan cruise. Rates include transfers to the ship and back to the airport. A train trip from Anchorage to the coast is also included in the price.

VISTAFJORD: Like the *Sagafjord,* this is one of the most beautiful vessels afloat. From your first glimpse of her trim gray-and-white hull topped by the bright-red Cunard funnel, you'll know you're seeing a very special cruise ship.

Launched in 1973, the *Vistafjord* is as close as most of us can come to a floating palace: for openers, a bottle of champagne, set in a bucket of ice, awaits you in your cabin on departure day.

Beyond that, a magnificent arching staircase twists majestically through the middle of the ship, each of its steps lighted from beneath and on the sides by small white lights.

The cabins are a study in gray, peach, salmon, and meltingly lovely pastels. Brass sparkles, glass shines, everything is as perfect as a spiffy Norwegian crew can keep it—and that is spiffy indeed!

Public Rooms

The Lido Café is a handsome enclosed garden room where you can watch the swimmers outside in air-conditioned comfort. Contemporary chrome-and-reed chairs are cushioned in eye-stopping lime greens in this café overlooking the pool.

More of those arching staircases turn up on this deck, winding their way to the Club Viking, a galleried nightspot that surely must be the most dramatic nightclub afloat. Behind a wall of tinted glass here you'll see a two-story room flashing with chrome and mirrors. Decked out with high-backed gray swivel chairs, the room centers around a lacquered gray piano and white marble dance floor.

Wide glass doors at the head of the dance floor open onto a small balcony to let ocean breezes cool fevered brows. To take advantage of those tropical evenings, seek a seat on one of the two glassed-in but unroofed outside wings to this room, where you can cuddle into beige-cushioned chairs and sip something cool as the ship steams through a starry night.

Sun buffs will find plenty of deck space and pools aboard, and movie fans can see current favorites in a comfortably cushioned theater.

For more contemplative moments, head for the Norse Lounge where a deep-green décor plays counterpoint to brass-trimmed tables and watercolors adorn the walls. Nearby is a game room, and just beyond that you'll find another lounge and dance center, the Garden Room. Green predominates, from the masses of plants that encircle the white marble dance floor to the upholstery, to the accent colors on the tiled tabletops. Lamps trimmed in brass add a metallic glint to this sweeping circular room enclosed in windows.

Those streamlined lines you find everywhere on the ship extend even to the craft's boutique, where shining treasures are displayed in a glittering glass counter that swoops across the entrance.

Deep down in the ship you'll find a goodlooking indoor swimming pool backed in vivid navy tiles sparked with fiery touches of orange and lined with orange circles. In the nearby spa you can get a facial, have your eyebrows shaped, get a massage, or have some infrared heat treatments.

Everywhere you look on this ship is beautiful woodwork and lighting, cleverly designed to give the ship an airy, wide-open look. Which, come to think of it, this ship would have even *without* that subtle lighting.

Beige and mauve play counterpoint in the dining room, where you'll dine on a wide range of continental delicacies and get an opportunity to try some Scandinavian specialties too.

Much of the action aboard occurs in the big orange-and-gold ballroom in which a massive vase of silk flowers provides a focal point.

Cabins

Kept spic and span by a bevy of cheerful stewardesses, this ship has some of the loveliest accommodations we've ever seen in a hotel, let alone on the high seas. Naturally, cabins get bigger, better, and infinitely more elaborate as you rise in price category, but we've never seen an unattractive one aboard.

On this ship you'll find real wood beds with wood headboards and footboards, and wood circling all around. In the tall closets are lights that switch on automatically when you open the wood-paneled doors. In there, too, you'll find a metal bar over which to hook your shoes, hooks for hangings things, and shelves that swing up and lock out of the way or swing down for extra storage. In some of the more elaborate cabins you'll even find walk-in closets, and in many you'll find closets big enough to stroll in, plus beautiful dark-wood nightstands and dressers, all with a key-locked drawer too.

All cabins have full-length mirrors, and many have both tub and shower. In the bathroom a three-sided mirror stretches across the wall above a thoroughly modern sink outfitted with lots of storage space for shaving and makeup needs. Cabin 242 is a good example of this kind of cabin. It's decorated in soothing grays and dusty-rose shades, and features a big window, piped-in music, and an interesting chalk drawing on one wall.

The most beautiful rooms aboard are those that have obviously been recently redecorated. In those, pink and gray are the dominant colors, with drapes that blend those shades with a pale mauve hue. Older quarters are outfitted in those colors commonly thought of as tropical: orange, royal blue, gold, green. Cabin 240 is one of those gray and salmon creations with a couch that converts to a bed, set at a 90° angle to a twin bed.

Among the smallest cabins we saw aboard was Cabin 333, done in gold and blues. Nearby, Cabin 343 is another small nest with one lower bed done up as a couch in royal blue and an upper berth that pulls down. Here you'll find the same dresser and closets as are found elsewhere on the ship, plus a tub and shower in a spacious bathroom. Similar cabins: 345 and 353.

Even inside cabins are lovely on this ship; in fact some of them could challenge the outside quarters any day. Cabin 653 is an attractive inside accommodation decorated in gold. Drapes run clear across a wall behind the bed and are backlit so cleverly you're not sure there isn't a porthole behind them.

Many cabins aboard make the best possible use of whatever space could be found. Cabin 679, for instance, is an unusual shape with a couch angled to a twin bed, the whole a study in royal blue and white. Life jackets are stowed away in a nightstand. Behind the couch in this cabin, as in many similar accommodations, the curve of the ship has been traced with a shelf so you have lots of room to store the treasures you pick up along the way—then just close the drape and all the jumble disappears! Two similar examples: Cabin 690, which is a very private place off by itself, and Cabin 684, an unusual room decorated in contemporary off-white checks.

Many rooms aboard, like Cabins 676 and 678, are tucked away at the end of a small private foyer. These two are long rooms with berths that convert to a couch set at right angles to a twin bed. These two, and others like them, seem perfect for two couples or a family traveling together.

One cabin we thought especially nice for a single traveler was 576, which featured that contemporary gray and pale-pink color scheme again, with one bed tucked away so invisibly it served as a counter for the champagne and ice bucket. If you frequent the beauty salon you should like this one: it's just steps away.

If you have plenty of mad money to spend on your cruise, consider one of the suites. The Mediterranean Suite is dove gray from stem to stern, with two chairs in chrome and gray velour, a couch that becomes a bed, a dresser, lighted mirror, big closet, nightstand by one bed, two huge windows, and a lot of space. A nearby suite, the Baltic, is similarly gorgeous. If you like pink, the Atlantic Suite is outfitted in pale hues of that color with darker pink accents.

A little lower in price, but not much, Cabin 108 features a built-in refrigerator, and like other suites, can be connected to create two massive living/sleeping areas. Numbers 103 and 104 nearby are other top-of-the-line accommodations.

Our special favorite aboard is Cabin 174, a super-long suite trimmed in gray with three windows, a full couch, two beds, a chair, coffee table, full-length mirror on a deep-green wall, and a refrigerator built into a cabinet. The best feature of this one is its sitting area, which, because the room is long, is quite separate from the sleeping area. If we can't have this one, however, we'll settle quite happily for its only neighbor, 176, which comes complete with huge walk-in closet and pink décor. It's quite similar in design to 174.

One final mention for really comfortable sailing: Cabin 175 features a built-in wall unit in lovely blond wood and glass, salmon and gray color scheme, two beds that can be joined to create a king-size sleeper, two chairs, and a curving love seat.

Once again cabin prices vary widely because the ship sails on so many different itineraries. It is only to be expected that you'll pay top dollar for the elegance you get aboard this ship. On 14-day cruises in Scandinavia, for instance, per-person rates begin at $2,880 and rise to $11,530 for very elaborate suites.

Double cabins for a 14-day Baltic Sea adventure range in price from $2,880 to $6,150 per person, with suites topping out the price categories at $7,680 to $11,530.

Cabins for single travelers range in price from $4,420 to $6,150 per person for a 14-day Scandinavian trip.

Third and fourth travelers sharing a stateroom pay $1,440 for the voyage. Port charges are $125.

SEA GODDESS I / SEA GODDESS II: So what do you buy for your buck in the lofty realms of $5,100 a week? Well, for openers, as you sit at the outdoor café, a waterfall splashes and tinkles behind you, pouring ceaselessly down a section of the ship's sleek smokestack.

When you anchor in some crystalline Caribbean waters or off a glittering Greek isle, a platform at the stern of the ship is lowered and you step right off into the sea for some snorkeling, or onto a windsurfing board or small sailboat.

Swimming in the ship's pool sounds a real yawner? Then try the whirlpool right there beside the pool. Or escape from the sun to the ship's secluded Greenhouse, where you relax on comfortable couches amid a profusion of exotic blooming plants.

You just want to relax in your stateroom? Of course. Would you like us to turn on the stereo or the video cassette player, fix you a drink from your stocked in-cabin bar, or turn on the television? Perhaps a little snack from your refrigerator, carefully packed with assorted cheeses and garnis?

And what does your room look like? Well, there are no mere cabins aboard. Every one of the 60 staterooms is a suite: each has a separate living room and big wide windows overlooking the sea. Each cabin aboard is the same size, about 50% larger than the usual cruise-ship cabins. You can take your choice, however, of twin or queen-size beds. Archways and built-in cabinetry are of white oak, and the furniture is outfitted in soft contemporary colors. Plus floor-to-ceiling mirrors, a coffee table large enough for dining, deep carpets, thick walls.

Small though they are, *Sea Goddess I* and *II* are quite a bit larger than other luxury yacht-ships of this kind (about four times as large in fact): 4,000 tons, 340 feet long, and designed for 120 passengers.

In their bright dining rooms lined with moldings and mirrors, you dine when, and with whom, you please, not at some preordained hour.

After dinner perhaps you'll choose a game in the small casino, or some quiet music at the piano bar, some witty conversation with fellow passengers. Or nip into the circular Main Salon where the best of shoreside entertainers has been brought on board for your evening amusement.

You're looking forward to Bingo, grandmothers' bragging contests, arts and crafts? Then you are very likely not *Sea Goddess* material!

If you select this very posh way to sail the seas, you'll find yourself spending a summer week gliding to the very best and most exclusive ports of the Mediterranean from, say, Monaco to Ibiza, Mallorca, and St. Tropez, and wintering, as does anyone of any importance, in St. Croix and cruising from there to the best addresses of the Caribbean—Casa de Campo or Princess Margaret's Mustique hideaway.

And how much does this all cost? Well, if you have to ask . . . But since you did, a week in the Caribbean is $5,100 to $8,900 per person, double occupancy.

13. DELTA QUEEN STEAMBOAT CO.

Contact: Delta Queen Steamboat Co., 30 Robin St. Wharf, New Orleans, LA 70130 (tel. 504/586-0631, or toll free 800/543-1949).

Cruising Grounds: Mississippi, Tennessee, Cumberland, and Ohio Rivers.

Itineraries: *Delta Queen*—
IN SUMMER: New Orleans – Tennessee and Cumberland Rivers – St. Louis – St. Paul – Nashville – Cincinnati – Pittsburgh and return.
IN WINTER: New Orleans – Houmas House – Baton Rouge – Vicksburg – Natchez – St. Francisville – New Orleans.

Mississippi Queen—
IN SUMMER: New Orleans – Memphis – St. Louis – St. Paul – Chattanooga and return.
IN WINTER: New Orleans – Houmas House – Baton Rouge – Vicksburg – Natchez – St. Francisville – New Orleans.

There survives in the South a sweet, slow way of life that is both scorned and coveted by those who pursue—or is it endure?—the rapid and demanding pace of the megalopolis.

When you board one of the furbelowed steamboats operated by the Delta Queen Steamboat Co., you drop instantly out of frenzy and into the world of yesteryear where Scarlett dallied and Rhett romped.

In long, lazy days chugging up the Mississippi past sprawling columned plantations and rainbow gardens, slowly, slowly, you sink back into the glamorous world of the riverboat, a world of glittering chandeliers, shining brass, oak beams, and satin drapes.

A day or so into a trip aboard one of these craft and the sudden appearance of a white-suited riverboat gambler wouldn't even rate a second glance.

Romantic as the days of flirting fans and hooped gowns, Delta's two steamers are wonderful anachronisms authentic enough to please "Maverick" fans yet modern enough to satisfy "Love Boat" enthusiasts. These two steamboats can trace their history back to 1890 when a riverboat captain named Gordon Greene began operating packet steamers on the Ohio and Mississippi Rivers.

Riverboats remained in the Greene family until 1973, when the *Delta Queen* became part of Overseas National Airways. That company began construction of a second vessel, the *Mississippi Queen*. For a few years in the late 1970s the two ships were owned by the Coca-Cola Bottling Co. of New York. In 1986 the Delta Queen Steamboat Co. became a privately owned company operating the only two remaining overnight passenger steamboats in this nation.

There's something magical about sailing on one of the very few remaining American flag vessels, something that can be equalled nowhere in the world. It can be an especially inspiring voyage if you take the time to read a little of the history and folklore of this river that has over the centuries played such a vital part in the history of this nation.

Arise early some morning when golden rays of sunlight peek through pines along the shore as you steam through deep dark waters. Suddenly you will know why a fellow named Mark Twain never lost his fascination with this mighty waterway and the craft that ply it.

Plunk yourself down in a deck chair and lose yourself in the churning white wake foaming out behind the spinning paddlewheel. Sink into the emerald shade of giant live oak trees spreading their ivy-covered branches over sweeping, columned verandas of massive antebellum mansions. All around you is the haunting melody of the nation's most elegant and most tragic historical moments: the grim, silent battlefields of Vicksburg, the sugary sweetness of Natchez, whose stately homes were spared the ravages of the nation's most bitter conflict.

Unfetter your imagination aboard either of these two elegant ladies of the river and you'll become part of the best of the Old South for a few leisurely days up the lazy river from New Orleans, or down it from St. Louis, Cincinnati, or Pittsburgh on cruises that vary in length from 2 to 12 nights.

There are some exciting special cruises aboard both the boats. In June they duo race each other up the river from New Orleans to St. Louis—although at speeds that don't exceed a stately 12 mph . . . you certainly won't get any stock-car sensations!

In February the vessels, which spend much of their time in the New Orleans section of the river to catch the best weather, celebrate Fat Tuesday with a couple of Mardi Gras celebrations, followed by trips that will appeal to the gardeners and antiquarians among us: Victorian Lifestyle cruises that take place during the South's annual Spring Pilgrimages when riverside cities open their homes, their hearts, and their eye-popping gardens in a celebration of the South's dramatic history.

In fall, when nature turns the river's northern reaches into a flaming carnival of autumn color, the boats cruise the Ohio and Upper Mississippi Rivers. Finally, at year's end, special "Old-Fashioned Holiday Vacation" cruises depart from New Orleans for visits to plantations dressed in their holiday best.

Activities

On board either of these two boats you not only see history along the shoreline, you become part of it in a way that is at once antique and modern. Fly a kite over the paddlewheel, whizz a mean shuffleboard disc, dip in the Jacuzzi, work out in the gym, relax in a sauna.

On your way to dinner, sweep down the glamorous Grand Staircase for your own grand entrance. The *Delta Queen* gets our vote for the most beautiful staircase afloat.

Aboard either of these two vessels you'll savor American flavors, things like Louisiana oysters, Arkansas catfish, Créole flavors, crunchy pecan pie.

After dinner, get in on the fun as riverboat becomes showboat, celebrating American-Old South style with Mardi Gras parties, Dixieland bands, bluegrass banjos, a steamboat cabaret, ragtime, sing-alongs, dance music. You can even learn to play a real oldtime "Steam Pianna," otherwise known as a calliope, one of the rarest instruments around. Steam pressure produces the tunes on calliopes, which were invented by a fellow who figured they could replace church bells. His idea never quite caught on, and when you hear one of these wheezing, tooting whistlers, once called a cross between an organ and a fire engine, you'll get an idea why not!

It isn't all history aboard this line. In 1983 the line's *Mississippi Queen* was featured on NBC's "Today Show," which came aboard to film the vessel's computer-learning seminars. Talk about leaping time zones!

Life is casual and for the most part informal on these riverboats, although at dinner gentlemen will feel better in jackets and ties, ladies in the feminine equivalent.

DELTA QUEEN: In the glow of stained-glass windows and under the glitter of crystal chandeliers, you'll find it hard to believe this steamer hasn't been cruising these waters for generations. Truth is, she's been around only since the 1920s when she was built on the River Clyde in Scotland—Glasgow to be exact. Well, not built exactly but composed of a bunch of prefabricated pieces that were shipped to California where all the puzzle parts were put back together for cruises between Sacramento, Stockton, and San Francisco.

Used to ferry troops during World War II, the ship was purchased by the Greenes in 1946 and moved to the Mississippi River. That may sound simple, but it was quite a project: the boat was towed for 5,000 miles down the Pacific coast, through the Panama Canal to New Orleans. After refitting in Pittsburgh, she began in 1948 to sail on cruises between Cincinnati and Cairo, Illinois. So authentic is the *Delta Queen* that she's entered in the National Register of Historic Places.

These days you can find the *Delta Queen* sailing all year round on cruises on the lower Mississippi, the Upper Mississippi, the Ohio, and Cumberland Rivers, with stops at places like Houmas House, a classic southern mansion; St. Francisville, site of Rosedown Plantation; magnolia-trimmed Natchez; and the ramparts of Vicksburg. Other cruises stop in at Baton Rouge or journey to Memphis, Cairo, St. Louis, or Nashville.

For those who like to see a lady's figures, the *Delta Queen* is 285 feet long and has a 7½-foot draft. She weighs 1,650 tons and her paddlewheel is 18 feet wide and 20 feet in diameter. When she's pouring it on, she can go as fast as 12 mph but most of the time she sails along at a sedate 7 mph. She carries 176 passengers in 88 cabins, and has a crew of 75 to serve them.

Public Rooms

Public rooms aboard are a study in teardrop chandeliers, intricate wrought-iron staircases, stained glass, polished woods, and heavy ornate moldings everywhere.

From the top down, you'll find the Sun Deck, which, interestingly, houses all together four top-priced cabins, some mid-priced quarters, as well as several F-category, much more moderately priced rooms. Next comes the Texas Deck, where you'll find most of the riverboat's staterooms and the Texas Lounge, where the ship's entertainment takes place.

One deck lower, Cabin Deck, are two more lounges aptly named the Forward Cabin Lounge and the After Cabin Lounge so you can't get lost no matter how many Planter's Punches you've had! On this deck are the purser's office, gift shop, and several new staterooms. Follow the heady perfumes of good cooking and you'll find the Orleans Dining Room on the Lower Deck. Tables for four predominate here, although two can sometimes find a private spot.

All in all, we think that the *Delta Queen* is not as elaborate, nor as slickly turned out, as her *Mississippi Queen* sister, but that absence of modernity is the very thing that makes her every bit as charming as the *Mississippi Queen*.

Cabins

Quarters aboard range from two big snappy staterooms with king-size beds to an economical—and small—upper/lower bunk-bedded cabin. All of them are outside cabins and have beautiful moldings, oval mirrors, brass fittings, and wooden shutters, which reinforce the historic feeling aboard.

If you elect the best Sun Deck cabins, AA339 and AA340, you'll certainly be in good company—former President Jimmy Carter and his family once occupied those two. To sleep where a president slept, in a double brass-bedded room with a sofa bed, shutters on the windows, wall-to-wall carpeting, polished wood dresser, and bath, will cost you from $728 per person for a two-night cruise to $2,674 for a seven-night journey.

In 1984 the line added 22 new top-of-the-line cabins on Cabin Deck. Quite spacious accommodations, they sport large picture windows inset with stained glass. Sunlight streaming in through big windows shines on reproductions of Chippendale armchairs, Goddard chests, and antique desks. Add to that brass beds and limited-edition prints of the world's great steamboats. Fares for a seven-night cruise in one of these spiffy sleepers are $2,303 or $2,674.

Price categories aboard begin at the top with AA and work down to the low Category F rates, so you have seven price options. You also can sample the ship on a two-night cruise (although there aren't many of those) or try a four-night Kentucky Derby journey, or longer voyages lasting 5, 7, 9, 11, or 12 nights (although there are only a few of the latter lengths).

Way down the price range in those super-budget quarters you'll pay $282 per person for a two-night cruise, rising to $1,692 per person for 12 nights on the river. For a seven-night cruise, the most common offered by the company, one of the eight cabins in this bottom range will cost $1,036 per person.

A cabin in the middle price range (Categories C, D, and E) costs $1,519 to $2,002 per person for a seven-night trip. Five nights aboard in that category of stateroom will cost $1,065 to $1,405.

Most cabins have washbasins in the room (they're not in the bathroom, which in some of the lower-priced cabins is just as well since some of those bathrooms are quite tiny indeed). For Categories E and F cabins have upper and lower berths, although a few with extra-wide sleepers are available.

Cabins aboard this craft can't accommodate a third person, but you can find the space for three on the *Mississippi Queen,* which sails a very similar itinerary.

If you want cabin sizes, figure a very compact 44 square feet or so for the smallest quarters, 68 square feet for mid-priced quarters, and 135 to 156 square feet for the very top bracket.

Single travelers pay 175% of the regular per-person fare if they want exclusive occupancy of a room. The line will try to match you up with another passenger traveling alone if you'd like to share a room.

MISSISSIPPI QUEEN: What a beauty we have here! Launched in 1976 at the height of the Bicentennial celebration, the *Mississippi Queen* is about twice the tonnage of her fellow sailer, the *Delta Queen.* She measures in at 3,364 tons, and carries 400 passengers in her 200 cabins.

New deluxe suites were recently added to the top of the vessel by cranes that lifted the new quarters into place on the Promenade Deck. Furnished to a contemporary faretheewell, two of the new suites offer the lucky the same view as the ship's pilot, six flights up, through huge windows that let you look upriver and off to the sides. In that same year all the public rooms, which were lovely to start with, were redone over again.

Unlike the *Delta Queen,* this $27-million craft sports an all-steel hull and superstructure, and about all the modern conveniences the modern mind can conjure up: a movie theater, a swimming pool, a sauna and gym, a Jacuzzi, beauty salon, elevators. And all that's tied together with brass, mirrors, chrome, steel and brass, parquet dance floors, beautiful contemporary colors.

Exterior design was by James Gardner, a London designer who helped create Cunard's *Queen Elizabeth,* and the ship was built in Jeffersonville, Indiana, at the Jeffboat Shipyard that has created more than 4,800 steamboats over the years.

Public Rooms

Most of the action aboard takes place on the Observation Deck, five decks above the waterline. It's a lovely aerie from which to get a gull's-eye view of the river below. Here, perched over that churning paddlewheel is the Paddlewheel Lounge, a dramatic two-story room with a shining tile floor. Tall windows soar two stories up to give you a magnificent view of the shoreline sliding by outside. Contemporary chrome chairs are upholstered in cherry red, and from a seat on the second-level balcony you can look down on all the world, for a while at least.

Farther forward is the ship's dining "saloon," as they call it. Decked out in linens and flowers, this handsome room has windows all down the sides so there's a good view from all tables as you dine on crayfish bisque, chicken breast

Lafayette with sautéed almonds, or a brace of roast quail with wild rice. Traditional southern riverboat culinary treats—things like shrimp rémoulade—are specially marked on the menu where they're called La Bouche Créole, with a tip of the hat to that Louisiana cuisine which grew from classical French cooking.

If you're looking for an intimate hideaway bar, try the Center Bar, located fittingly enough right in the center of Observation Deck, just short of the Grand Saloon, where you can get comfortable in a plush couch or circular armchair. Nearby, the Starboard Gallery has tall windows—and more of those fancy ceilings—through which you can watch the lights glittering in plantation windows.

One deck higher, the Calliope Bar is a pleasant aerie. Not far away you'll find a full-fledged gym, with massage facilities too. A Jacuzzi on board makes for a nice afternoon dip in summer when temperatures rise.

Way down on the Lower Deck you can take in a movie in the ship's theater, and back up on the Cabin Deck, the Forward Lounge is a good place for the faster of two cohabitating travelers to await the slower. If you'd like to curl up with a good book, you'll find a cheerfully decorated library on board too.

Cabins

All the cabins on the vessel are located on four decks separate from all those public rooms. That means you'll spend your sleeping hours on the Promenade Deck, Texas Deck, Cabin Deck, or Main Deck (the one closest to the water).

If you can afford the tariff, the top-priced rooms here are worth the money, if for no other reason than that they have lovely private verandas. There are 14 of these top-of-the-top quarters available, and each boasts silk draperies, custom-made carpets, handcrafted crewel bedspreads, and brass beds. Fares in these range from $3,045 to $3,339 per person for a week-long cruise.

Quite a number of other cabins also feature private verandas—80 in fact. Those range in price from $2,191 to $2,674 per person for a seven-night cruise. In these you'll find a dressing area with vanity and closets; in some, a sofa bed. All have showers but some also offer a tub.

From there down in price we'd suggest that you spend your looking time up on deck. Although cabins in Categories C and E are outside accommodations and do have large windows, they're not always in convenient places for comfortable observation. Inside cabins, of course, don't have windows.

You'll find twin beds pushed together to create a king-size sleeper in the upper price categories, twin beds or double with an upper pullman berth in less expensive veranda quarters and outside cabins without verandas.

Families will do well with adjacent Category B and F rooms, and some in the lower-priced Category F rooms that share a common entry hall.

If you want to sail on this ship on a budget, Categories E and F cabins are the most economical. Some have twin beds, some upper pullman berth and lower twin bed. For one of those you will pay $1,036 to $1,708 per person for a seven-night cruise.

The *Mississippi Queen* sails a variety of 2- to 11-night cruises to the same destinations as her smaller sister. If this year's cruises match those of other years, as is likely, the ships will be sailing round trip from New Orleans most of the year. There are some special cruises to St. Louis, St. Paul, Memphis, and Chattanooga.

14. DISCOVERY CRUISES

Contact: Discovery Cruises, 8751 W. Broward Blvd., Plantation, FL 33324 (tel. 305/476-9999).

Cruising Grounds: Bahamas and cruises to nowhere.

Itineraries: *Discovery I*—Fort Lauderdale – Freeport – Fort Lauderdale *or* Fort Lauderdale – nowhere – Fort Lauderdale.

This line's *Discovery I* is the newest one-day sailing ship to turn up at Fort Lauderdale's busy Port Everglades. After a rather rocky start, the line seems to be firmly on course and has been operating its one-day cruises to Freeport and its single-day sailings to nowhere at all for about a year.

DISCOVERY I: Formerly a ship owned and operated by SeaEscape, the *Discovery I* craft was once known as the *Scandinavian Seas*. It was quite a luxurious ship when it first began sailing on trips between New York and Florida with a stop in the Bahamas; then it fell on some hard times and was rescued by a group of female entrepreneurs who dubbed it the *Venus Venturer*. Bought later by a Bahamas-based company, the ship got a new name and a new sailing ground in 1987 when it began operating from Fort Lauderdale.

Now it sails to Freeport every Sunday, Monday, Wednesday, and Friday, departing at 8 a.m. and returning at 10:45 p.m. Along the way you are entertained by the inevitable but pleasant syncopation of a calypso band while you swim in the ship's pool or laze around in one of three whirlpools on board. Frosty daiquiris and plenty of breakfast, lunch, and snack breaks keep you busy on the way to Freeport which looms up on the horizon about 1:30 p.m. You have about three hours to roam the shops and pubs of that Bahamian island before reboarding for the trip back.

Dinner is served on the return voyage, and there's a cabaret show, music for dancing, and of course, plenty of one-armed bandits and other forms of take-a-chance games for those determined to pay for their cruise with one roll of the dice. *Discovery I* pulls back into port in Port Everglades about 11 p.m.

On other days of the week the ship sails on one-day cruises to nowhere, departing at 10 a.m. and returning at 4:30 p.m. in time for the ship to set sail once again on evening voyages that depart at 6:45 p.m., returning at midnight.

Adult fares on the trips to Freeport are $79, including port taxes, all meals, and entertainment. Children from 1 to 12 years old pay $39; those 12 to 17 pay $59.

On the shorter cruises to nowhere the adult fare is $49; children's tab is $29 for those 2 to 12, $45 for older youngsters.

On this ship, too, you can also rent a cabin for the voyage. Lots of folks find it convenient to do that, so they have a place to change or take a nap. You pay an additional $30 to $60 for a cabin on the cruises to nowhere, $55 to $100 for a stateroom on the trips to Freeport.

15. DOLPHIN CRUISE LINE

Contact: Dolphin Cruise Line, 1007 North American Way, Miami, FL 33132 (tel. 305/358-2111, or toll free 800/521-4299).
Cruising Grounds: Bahamas.

Itinerary: *Dolphin*—Miami – Nassau – Bahamian Out Island – Miami *or* Miami – Freeport – Nassau – Bahamian Out Island – Miami.

Dolphin Cruise Line is a comparative newcomer to the Miami short-cruise scene. For years this line's only ship, the *Dolphin*, was marketed by Paquet Cruises, although it was actually owned by a Greek shipping company. In 1984 the *Dolphin* was sold to a fledgling company that dubbed itself Dolphin Cruise Line and set out to see what a success they could make in the three- and four-day cruise market.

DOLPHIN CRUISE LINE □ 209

Things seem to be going along quite well for this line. Its sole ship has undergone several renovations, proving the line's owners are trying to keep their craft fresh and clean, not just sailing it off on another ho-hum season.

After its 1987 renovation, the ship looked quite bright and sparkling, and is kept that way year round—more than can be said of some ships this age.

Built in 1956, the *Dolphin* was once known as the *Ithaca*. Quite a diminutive ship, it measures in at just 12,500 tons and carries 565 passengers. Rebuilt in 1973 and refurbished in 1986, the ship takes its 565 sunseekers on three- and four-day cruises from Miami to Nassau and Freeport all year round.

When Paquet was still marketing the ship, it added something new to the itinerary: a stop at a small island just off Nassau. Originally named Salt Cay, this small Bahamian Out Island has been dubbed Blue Lagoon Island by the *Dolphin*'s crew (on another day of the week it also welcomes passengers from a competing cruise line). Whatever they call it, this small Bahamian outpost is a spot much loved by weekend-cruise habitués who wallow in its soft sands, awesomely clear waters, and Robinson Crusoe atmosphere.

DOLPHIN: In the pre-plastic era shipbuilders created with wood. You'll see what we mean aboard the *Dolphin*, which has acres of shining dark-wood decks, wood trim around the cabin doors, wooden wardrobes, lovely paneling, small round wood cocktail tables in one of its lounges, even some pine dressers and nightstands. Greek officers add a pleasantly Mediterranean touch to the ship.

On the *Dolphin* you'll find a typical short-cruise party ship that concentrates on three days of fun and frolic. These days this small party ship is lovelier than ever, with a new look from stem to stern. Redecorated in 1987, it now looks as shiny as a new penny, with delightfully plush fabric wall coverings in passageways and cabins, contemporary and colorful décor everywhere.

Lording it over the main entrance of the ship is a shining brass-and-steel sculpture of leaping dolphins at play in a sea of silver waves.

Activities

Although small, the *Dolphin* offers all the activities that characterize these short Caribbean voyages: plenty of sunshine, gambling in the casino, swimming in the pool, entertainment night and day.

Because so many single people like to take these cruises, the voyage begins with a party for the unattached.

In the mornings there are dance and exercise classes, and in the afternoon you can practice your putting on a golf green. Daily quizzes test your trivia knowledge and fashion shows give you a look at what the shops have to offer.

There are movies in one of the lounges and a tour of the bridge. Not to mention pillow fights, Goombay music, and beer-drinking competitions.

One evening you'll be invited to meet the captain, and on the final evening of the cruise he'll preside over a farewell dinner. Most nights there are variety shows in the Rendezvous Lounge, movies, and dance contests. Before and after those evening shows, the Café Miramar is the gathering spot. Much later, the ciné-disco is the spot aboard.

Public Rooms

There's a particularly handsome swimming pool on board surrounded by the most spectacular wood decking you'll ever see. It may be mahogany, but none of the crew was a woodworking expert so we never did determine that for sure. Whatever it is, it sweeps across all the decks, and provides a raised sitting area around the edge of the small pool.

If you're taking the youngsters along, you can deposit them in a small circular pool just three feet deep while you splash in the deeper water of an adjoining pool that's lit for nighttime use. A poolside bar? Of course.

One more toy for the youngsters (and perhaps the not-so-youngsters) is up on the Promenade Deck too: an electronic game room lined with 13 of those whirring machines.

Breakfast and luncheon buffets are available in Café Miramar so you don't have to miss a minute of sunshine. A big circular bar is the focal point of this room, which features an attractive contemporary décor of Breuer chairs and spacious banquettes, lots of mirrors, a handsome wood dance floor, and a huge wood wall hanging that sparks the room's colorful décor. Lots of big windows let in the sunshine in daylight hours and a view of the stars at night, when this becomes a dancing spot.

You'll be dining in the Barbizon Restaurant, an attractive but small dining room serving excellent food up to and including some sinful French pastries. Low ceilings and new earth-tone décor make this room a rather dark, if intimate, spot, but the top-notch food aboard easily makes up for any missing décor pizzazz.

From there, gamblers can head up to the Promenade Deck to the Monte Carlo Casino, where there's even a coin-operated roulette wheel. You pick the odds and the wheel automatically revolves, paying you off if you win. What next?

Those in search of the evening's entertainment will head for the pretty Rendezvous Lounge. Velvet banquettes and chairs in handsome pastels encircle a central dance floor where the ship's nightly entertainment takes place. That show, by the way, might be a magician, a singer, or a comedian, or any combination of the above.

For a nightcap, try the Club Royal, a small, cozy spot where the bartender will whip up a very satisfactory piña colada. Dancers will beat an immediate retreat way down to Dixie Deck, where the disco is tucked away in a spot that doesn't keep anyone awake. You can party there until you drop—they'll go on just as long as you do.

A small shop aboard provides for basic needs.

Take the elevator on this ship only if you're an antiquarian or courageous or both. A real antique it is, with double doors and unpredictable behavior.

Cabins

When you do finally drop—after, we hope, the midnight buffet of fruit, cheeses, pâtés, and a thousand or so other goodies—you'll do so in one of 284 cabins found on five of the ship's seven decks.

All the *Dolphin*'s cabins were refurbished recently so you'll find plush new carpets in contemporary colors and matching bedspreads. Coordinated drapes reverse the color scheme, and all the walls have been covered in earthy-colored fabrics.

The *Dolphin* recognizes two seasons it calls "value" season and "on" season. Value season includes January, late April through May, and mid-September through about mid-December. That leaves February through most of April and June through August as "on" season, when prices in each rate category are $20 to $30 higher. As for the difference in price between a three-day and four-day cruise: you pay $120 to $140 more per person for a four-day cruise in either season.

The top-of-the-line stateroom aboard is Cabin 511, a suite with a separate entrance to its next-door sitting area. And very pretty it is too, decorated in contemporary colors and plush carpet. A handy built-in wall unit also houses dozens of glasses, each carefully set into a built-in holder to keep them steady.

Other top-price cabins are as usual located on the top decks of the ship. Aboard the *Dolphin* you pay the highest rate for a cabin on the Boat Deck, where outside rooms are extra-large with two lower beds and a full bath, including a hand-held shower, and more wardrobe space than you'll find elsewhere on the ship. All decked out in the line's new pastel drapes and bedspreads, these are large and pretty quarters. For one of these cabins you pay $755 per person if you select a room with twin beds on a three-day high-season cruise.

The next four grades of outside cabins (Categories 2 through 5) will cost you $685 to $735 per person for a three-night cruise in peak season, $805 to $855 per person for a four-night trip. The higher-priced cabins are on Atlantis and Boat Decks, with lower prices in this category found lower in the ship on Barbizon and Caravelle Decks.

Quite a number of cabins, both inside and outside, have double beds. One particularly pretty one is Cabin 400, which follows the curve of the ship and thus has a most unusual shape. It also has its own porthole, but only a view of the deck beyond. A nice sketch of an old sailing ship hangs on one wall and there's a cozy feeling to the room that's appealing. It's $695 per person for a three-night cruise in peak season. Cabin 403 is also a pretty double-bedded room. Some inside rooms with double beds, however, are set up so someone has to sleep next to the wall and clamber out over the other sleeper.

The least expensive cabins on board are inside quarters with lower and upper berth. Some of those are almost as large as some of the more expensive accommodations—Cabin 4111 for instance. That one is right near the center of activity aboard, Purser's Square, and quite close to many cabins costing almost twice as much. For one of these dollarwise choices you pay $495 per person for a three-night cruise in peak season.

Three or four adults sharing a room will do so only with good friends. While multiperson cabins are a good buy aboard and are larger than are found on some newer vessels, they're pretty close quarters for four. Nevertheless if you're willing to share your space, you'll save quite a bundle. Third and fourth adults pay just $395 ($445 for a four-night trip).

Fares include air transportation from 98 cities with a small additional charge for those who do not fly from one of those 98 cities. Port charges are $28 for adults, $21 for children.

Theme cruises are popular on this ship and include mystery weekends, Big Band sailings, and tributes to the '50s, plus the usual holiday sailings which on this ship are often extended to seven-day cruises that add Playa del Carmen and Cozumél to the usual itinerary.

Some of the more accommodating rooms we saw aboard include Cabin 421, with a fetching little shell-shaped lamp and lovely pastel décor and big porthole; Cabin 403, a nice double; Cabin 411, an inside cabin with more of that pale décor, two lower beds, and a spacious feeling despite its small size; and Cabins 501 and 502.

Radios and telephones are in all rooms. *Bonne nuit!*

16. EPIROTIKI LINES

Contact: Epirotiki Lines, 551 Fifth Ave., New York, NY 10017 (tel. 212/599-1750, or toll free 800/221-2470).

Cruising Grounds: Caribbean, Amazon River, Mediterranean, South America, Greek islands.

Itineraries: *World Renaissance*—
IN WINTER: Manaus – Boca do Valerio – Santarém – Alter do Chao –

Brèves – Devil's Island – Tobago – Trinidad – Grenada – Bequia – Guadeloupe; and return same route.

IN SUMMER: Transatlantic cruise from Guadeloupe followed by seven-day Mediterranean cruises.

Pegasus—
IN WINTER: Rio de Janeiro – Santos – Punta del Este – Mar del Plata – Buenos Aires – Montevideo – San Francisco do Sul – Rio de Janeiro.
IN SUMMER: Greek island cruises.

It's likely to come as a surprise to even the most seasoned cruise fans that Greece's Epirotiki Lines is the largest cruise line in the *world,* its fleet numbering no fewer than 11 ships. Despite the size of its fleet, Epirotiki remains little known on this side of the Atlantic where only three ships have ever appeared and those only within the last few years.

If you've sailed through the glory that is the Greek islands, however, you've probably done so on one of Epirotiki's cruisers. Eight of the company's ships ply the Mediterranean on everything from little-known one-day outings that are one of the great bargain secrets of the Mediterranean, to two-, three-, four-, and seven-day voyages to the bazaars of Istanbul and the pyramids of Egypt.

Even line officials sometimes falter, understandably, when asked to name all 11 ships. Here's a look at what they are and where they operate.

Atlas, the line's 16,000-ton flagship, takes about 600 passengers through the Mediterranean, sailing from Piraeus to the Greek islands, Egypt, Israel, and Turkey.

On the other end of the size compendium, Epirotiki's *Argonaut* is really just an overgrown yacht, measuring in at 4,500 tons and sporting only 88 cabins. You'll find this ship on year-round Europe and South America charter to a New York wholesale tour operator called Raymond & Whitcomb.

Pegasus in 1986 made its American debut when it sailed up from a winter in the Galápagos to Alaska, where it spent the summer visiting that state's dramatic ports from a base in Vancouver.

Oceanos sails the Greek islands on three- and four-day cruises from Piraeus, with shore excursions to Turkey.

Jupiter measures in at 9,000 tons, carries about 400 passengers, and sails the Greek islands, Black Sea, Istanbul, and sometimes embarks on voyages from Venice to Nice on cruises marketed in the U.S. with air fare from New York included in the price.

One Epirotiki ship, the *Hermes,* sails on one-day cruises. These are those bargain voyages we mentioned earlier. These deal-cruises pick you up by bus at Athens hotels, transport you to a nearby port, then sail you away to three Greek islands for a day-long excursion that includes 60- to 90-minute visits to the beaches and quite spectacular antiquities on the islands of Aegina, Poros, and Hydra. The price in 1988 was just $25, including lunch and a ride back to Athens!

Epirotiki's *Neptune* recently began making seven-day voyages from Athens to Barcelona with stops in Lisbon, Ibiza, Palma, Gibraltar, and Tangier.

Orpheus, a 6,000-ton ship with 152 cabins, is often chartered to England's Swan Hellenic Line, which uses it on a wide variety of Mediterranean cruises.

Meanwhile, those craft of most interest to passengers in search of a ship sailing from North or South American ports are the *Pegasus,* which in 1986 scheduled its first series of seven-day cruises to Alaska from Vancouver; the *World Renaissance,* which spends its winters in the sunny waters of the Caribbean and exploring the Amazon River; and the *Jason,* a small ship that for several years wintered in the Caribbean and South America.

Epirotiki moves its ships quite frequently, and just as frequently swaps itineraries, but any travel agent can tell you where Epirotiki is sailing and when.

It's Europe's good fortune, and our loss, that so few Epirotiki ships can be found over this way, for a voyage on this line can be quite a marvelous experience, complete with some of the most efficient and charming service you'll find on any ship afloat.

That is perhaps no coincidence: after all, the Greeks devised that word "hospitality" and on board Epirotiki ships, staffers from steward to captain seem to take their hospitality responsibilities quite to heart.

Certainly this line has had plenty of time to learn how to do what they do well—it's been around for 130 years, owned and operated all that time by the Greek Potamianos family. Heading the family business these days are brothers George and Andreas Potamianos, either or both of whom can often be seen checking things out aboard the ships of their fleet.

Epirotiki got its name from the Greek town of Epirus, the launching port of Tassos Potamianos, grandson of the line's founder and creator of Epirotiki's logo, a gold Byzantine cross on a royal-blue background. Epirotiki began, as did all lines as old as this one, as a cargo carrier, but entered the passenger cruise business in the early 1950s, expanding rapidly until today there are few spots on the globe not visited by this line.

Epirotiki has, in fact, often been credited with touching off the expansion of cruises in the Aegean and Mediterranean when it joined with the Greek National Tourist Organization to introduce cruises to European vacationers. It also became a pioneer in the European car-ferry business when it launched a ferry between Italy and Greece in 1959.

Greeks revere history, as well they should with such a fascinating national history to revere. On this line, that history plays an important part in ship décor. For openers, you'll notice that most of the ships have names that recall Greek myths or history. On board nearly all the ships, décor provides a short course in mythology. You'll see trident carpets aboard the *Neptune* and a massive tapestry of Jason on a bull-snaring expedition aboard the *Jason*. Throughout many of the ships you'll spot murals, tapestries, mosaics, and sculptures that outline the antics of Greek mythological figures.

Epirotiki's most frequented ports of call remain the Aegean Sea, Israel, Turkey, and Egypt. In recent years, however, the line has added transatlantic cruises, visits to some intriguing Caribbean islands, to South America's Amazon River and the Galápagos Islands, to the Black and Baltic Seas, and even to Alaska.

Epirotiki also has the advantage of operating comparatively small ships, so you'll find service extra-specially rapid and personal. To give you an idea what we mean: your cabin will be cleaned practically the second you leave it and all your clutter will end up quite tidily organized; and Nicholas, an exemplary lounge waiter was so observant that from our second day on board he could tell either of us where the other was last seen!

Greek maritime unions initiated the custom of anonymous tipping aboard Greek ships, and Epirotiki sticks to that to the letter. When the final day arrives, you put your tip in an envelope and drop it in a box at the reception hall. Later all tips are tallied and divided equally among the staff. Somehow that seems eminently fair, and certainly it removes that uncomfortable waffling over how much and to whom.

Because Epirotiki's ships are small, they're quite delightfully intimate and informal. No fancy invitation to the ship's bridge here—you just walk on up there for a look around, and as likely as not, you'll find a quite charming captain on hand to show you what he does for a living.

Activities

That ship "personality" we're always talking about might, on this line, more accurately be called a *split* personality. Epirotiki's European cruises lure a wide variety of passengers who hail from all parts of the world, although many, if not most, are Europeans. Because the line's Mediterranean cruises come in a wide range of prices from $25 to $5,000, passengers on those ships fall in all age, financial, and educational categories.

Epirotiki ships sailing in this hemisphere, however, feature longer, more luxurious cruises designed to appeal to well-traveled passengers in search of off-the-beaten-sea cruises. For that reason you'll often find older, wealthier travelers cozily ensconced in the deck chairs aboard the *World Renaissance* and *Pegasus*. And for that reason you'll also find entertainment aboard carefully geared to be as educational as it is diverting, with lecturers and opera singers joining leggy, spangled dancers and puppeteers on the daily entertainment sheet.

Perhaps because Epirotiki's roots are European, there's quite an emphasis on showy evening entertainment aboard all the ships, so nary a night goes by without a full show. On a recent voyage aboard the *World Renaissance,* every evening featured performances by showily costumed dancers, a magician, a comic, two singers, and a troupe of delightful marionettes. In ten nights aboard they never repeated any performance.

While dining perhaps does not quite qualify as an "activity" in shoreside life, on ships it ranks right up there with Bingo as one of the highlights of the day. That's certainly true on Epirotiki ships, where the menu is a happy compilation of nationalistic touches and dining is a rather formal event much of the time. In fact, on an 11-day cruise four evenings are officially dubbed formal evenings, so there's plenty of opportunity to wear the long dresses and tuxedoes if you like.

On this ship as on many others today, however, most passengers turned up even on formal nights in nothing more formal than you'd wear to a restaurant. Very few tuxedoes were in evidence, although plenty of long dresses were sweeping around the decks.

Thanks to the line's Greek origins, you can rest assured you will never go hungry on an Epirotiki ship. Those of us who can never have enough Greek salads can feta themselves into oblivion—they'll bring you one of those olive-laden creations every night at dinner if you like, will serve you one at lunch, and will certainly do their darndest to rustle you up one for *breakfast* if you've a yen.

Pastas are marvelous and appear on the menu most every evening. If you like one dish in particular (hint—the fettuccine Alfredo is to die for), just give them a little advance notice and there it will be on your table that evening. Greek retsina wines make an interesting taste test for the uninitiated and go well with moussaka, avgolemono soup, and the myriad Greek treats that turn up at lunch and for the Greek Night dinner. If Greek's not your dish, rest easy—there are plenty of American and continental favorites available. It's also worth staying up for the midnight buffet when they're serving pizza—terrific.

As for other activities, you'll find the usual dance lessons including Greek dance steps taught by a quite breathtakingly handsome Greek song-and-dance man, plus Bingo, trivia games, bridge, Scrabble, a daily quiz that challenges the memory. Epirotiki ships fit many ports into their itinerary so there are perhaps fewer on-board activities than on lines that want to keep their passengers on board more than they're on shore.

Highlights of Epirotiki's *World Renaissance* and *Pegasus* cruises are lecturers of impressive credentials who are on board to help you understand what you're seeing. On *World Renaissance* cruises, for instance, lecturers included a university Amazon authority, a writer who'd spent many months researching the convict life on Devil's Island, and an astronomer who dutifully rose at 5:30 a.m. to help stargazers peer into the cosmos. A group of opera singers also performed several times during the voyage.

So let's move right along now for a closer look at the Epirotiki ships that sail in this hemisphere—the *World Renaissance* and the *Pegasus*.

WORLD RENAISSANCE: Among the most interesting cruises on this line are the *World Renaissance*'s trips down the jungle-lined Amazon River and through some rarely visited Caribbean islands. Not only are the ports fascinating spots, but the crew has come up with quite an innovative ship-to-shore program. Here's what's happening.

Capt. Yiannis Papadopoulos and his crew, discovering a need for basic food, clothes, and medicines among the people who live in the remote jungles along the riverbanks, began collecting from the crew an assortment of shirts and shoes to give to the people ashore. On a ship this small, passengers know everything that's going on aboard so it wasn't long before they too began contributing clothes and money.

Now, on each voyage the crew seeks donations and uses them to buy food, medicine, toys, and clothes. When they've got all that lot together, they parcel it out into small plastic bags. Then as the ship cruises down a compact section of the river called The Narrows, passengers and crew gather on the bridge to toss the dozens of plastic bags down to waiting families who paddle out in dugout canoes to grab the goodies. There's lots of waving and smiling at this grab-bag event that has become one of the highlights of the cruise.

Public Rooms

Built in 1966 as the *Renaissance,* flagship of Paquet Line, the *World Renaissance* is, at 12,500 tons, among the biggest Epirotiki ships, although it's certainly not a large ship. Built to carry just 470 passengers, it is small enough to be cozy, large enough to give you plenty of space to roam.

Refurbished in 1985, the ship is now all decked out in tranquil, contemporary pastels that range from creamy cushioned chairs in the main El Greco Grand Salon to pale-aquamarine furnishings in the Pelagos Dining Room.

Up on the top deck there's a gym and sauna where an aerobics class huffs and puffs every day. Down on Hera Deck you'll find the first of the ship's two swimming pools, backed, of course, by the Helios pool bar.

The central strolling spot aboard is Apollo Deck, which houses the ship's beauty/barbershop and its very small boutique well stocked with Gucci bags and every known brand of perfume. After dinner each evening, the determined gamblers aboard trickle into the casino where they can play at two blackjack tables or a couple of banks of slot machines.

Most of the crowd ambles up from the dining room and heads straight for the El Greco Grand Salon where dance music plays until the show goes into action. This wide bilevel salon rimmed by big windows is the central meeting spot aboard and the site of most daily activities, the staff's port preview talks, and even the daily buffet lunch.

One deck down on Venus Deck is the ship's disco, the Taverna Bar, which although it's called a disco is more cozy pub than disco. In the wee hours after the evening show the disco becomes the gathering spot for the ship's officers and for everyone young enough in age or spirit to while away the wee hours among the plants and rattan furnishings here.

Just down the hall is the ship's movie theater where on South American voyages films are chosen to increase your knowledge of the ports you're seeing—one is a fictionalized tale based on the life of rubber plantation barons who built Manaus and several other cities along the Amazon. Lecturers often give their presentations here too.

The crew on board the *World Renaissance,* as on other Epirotiki Lines ships, is Greek, Greek, and Greek, which you may translate as marvelously responsive, quick, efficient, observant, concerned, all-round wonderful, and possessed of at least one relative in the U.S. The only exception to that Greek orientation, which stretches from a suave Capt. Yiannis Papadopoulos through a bevy of model-handsome officers, is the cruise director's staff. There you'll find every nationality from Italian to Norwegian, Dutch, and English.

Cabins

Cabins are rather uniform in size aboard the ship, although they differ in configuration. They're quite contemporary in décor, with amusing prints on the wall and serene earth tones covering walls and beds.

You'll find plenty of closet space, one for gentlemen, one longer closet for ladies' long gowns, and a third storage area at the front of each cabin that's just right for the handmade bows and arrows many passengers buy from jungle salesmen.

An interesting touch—bedside tables provide drawer space, each top drawer covered with a hinged surface that swings up to reveal partitioned storage bins and a makeup mirror. When you put it down again, it becomes a tabletop for room service, which, by the way, is available day and night for all meals.

There is just one official suite aboard, VSS 67, which is actually two connecting rooms ideal for families or friends who want to roam in and out of each other's rooms.

On that same Venus Deck you'll find six rooms with double beds, quite roomy, airy quarters decked out in cream bedspreads and shiny contemporary décor.

Elsewhere on board the cabins are rather uniform in size, many of them L-shaped with one bed stretched out under a porthole, the other at right angles to it along a wall. Each has its own reading light, and rooms also have telephones and three-station radios.

Bathrooms are comparatively modern and everything works, particularly toilets that flush with a resounding roar. There's plenty of space under the sink and in the lighted medicine cabinet, and always enough towels around to dry an army.

Electric current is compatible with your U.S. appliances (110 volts A.C.), and there's reasonably priced laundry service on board but no dry-cleaning facilities.

Price categories number ten on board this ship, seven of them for outside cabins, three for inside quarters. They are not broken down into the usual A, B, C ranges, but instead bear SS (for special suite), S or SU (for special staterooms), T, A, B, and C for other outside rooms, and D through F for inside accommodations.

Fares include air fare on a chartered aircraft that takes you straight from Miami to your starting point in either Manaus or Guadeloupe. A chartered aircraft also brings you back from either point, which means you can buy anything you like—up to and including the four-foot-high vases you'll find at downright irresistible prices in Belem's Paratur craft shop—and have it taken right to the plane and shipped on to Miami, no pain.

Because the ship's drydock session in 1988 interrupted its usual schedule of winter South American sailings, no current prices for this Brazilian adventure were available at press time. To give you an idea what prices are aboard this sleek ship, however, here's a look at the fares on a 14-day Greek island cruise in peak season from September through October. Sailings in summer months are about $300 cheaper.

That special suite, really two rooms, is $3,805 per person for the cruise.

Next category down in price are special staterooms, all of them large with twin or double beds, lots of floor and storage space, a comfortable chair or two, and tubs as well as showers. Double-bedded cabins actually have queen-size beds, and the price for these staterooms is $2,925 to $3,340.

Categories T, A, and B each offer basic outside staterooms with twin lower beds, priced in descending order at $2,675 to $2,550, while Category C features outside cabins with one lower bed and one upper berth for $2,295.

Most inside cabins are down on Nereus Deck, where there are no portholes although a few are scattered about on the center of other decks. If you're opting for inside quarters, you'll find that those on the upper decks are nearly the same size as outside quarters. Inside cabins on Apollo Deck—or outside cabins, for that matter—are conveniently close to the main lounge, beauty salon, shop, and casino.

Category D cabins with twin lower beds or lower and upper beds are $2,170 to $2,295 per person.

As you can see, that works out to per diem prices that top out at about $272 per person for that top-of-the-line suite for four, down to about $155 a day per person in inside cabins with lower and upper beds. Add to that port taxes of $180.

Single travelers need to add an additional 50% to those fares for the single use of a double cabin. If you're traveling in threes or fours the rates for the extras go down 25% for the third and fourth persons, 50% for children.

PEGASUS: *Pegasus* made its North American debut in Alaskan waters in the summer of 1986 and often sails in and around South America.

Refurbished for millions of dollars in 1984, it is now the largest Epirotiki ship, measuring in at 18,000 tons and carrying 750 passengers.

Public Rooms

Eight stories tall, it has just about any amenity you can dream up. On the top deck there's a big solarium and Jacuzzi, and way down on a bottom deck there's an indoor swimming pool, another Jacuzzi, a gym, massage rooms, saunas—all part of the Olympia Fitness Center.

You'll never lack for a cool one on this ship, which has a cocktail lounge or bar just about everywhere you look, from Helios Sky Bar on the top deck to the Nymphs Night Club down a few levels on Apollo Deck—seven of 'em, in fact.

You'll find pleasant promenade areas on two decks, a big casino backed by yet another bar, even an art gallery.

Evening entertainment takes place in the Argonaut Grand Salon, a multilevel spot where there's always a good view of the stage and of the outside world through big windows.

Down on Dionysios Deck is the Dionysios Dining Room, where tables are tucked in under tall windows and quite convenient to the swimming pool and pool bar.

You'll find two theaters on board, a children's playroom, and a handsome gallery and veranda that's near enough to the dining room to make a good spot for the quick-change artists to while away some time waiting for those who take forever to get ready for dinner.

Down on Venus deck is the ship's boutique and Adonis Beauty Salon (don't you love that name?) plus a library/card room and the Lounge of the Poets.

Cabins

You'll find three two-room suites on board, one lodged high up on the ship on Jupiter Deck where all the cabins are outside quarters and two down two decks at the bow of the ship.

Because this is such a tall ship it offers quite a number of outside cabins with portholes but a fair number of money-saving inside quarters as well.

Decked out in soft contemporary colors, the ship's cabins are rather uniform in size so unless you're splurging for a top-priced cabin, you won't be buying a great deal more space no matter which category you choose.

On its South American cruises in 1988 the line was charging prices ranging from $2,060 to $3,690 for 14-day cruises. Prices in any one cabin category vary by no more than about $150 and fares include round-trip air fare from New York or Miami.

17. EXPLORATION CRUISE LINES

Contact: Exploration Cruise Lines, 1500 Metropolitan Park Building, Seattle, WA 98101 (tel. 206/625-9600 or 624-8551, or toll free 800/426-0600).

Cruising Grounds: U.S. East and West Coasts, Alaska, Pacific Northwest inland rivers, Panama Canal, Mexico, Caribbean, Tahiti.

Itineraries: *Great Rivers Explorer / Pacific Northwest Explorer*—

IN SUMMER: Ketchikan – Misty Fjords – Wrangell – Sitka – Glacier Bay – Skagway – Haines – Juneau – Tracy Arm – Petersburg – Le Conte Glacier – Ketchikan.

IN WINTER: Panama City – Pearl Islands – the Darien Jungle – Balboa – Panama Canal – San Blas Islands – Colón; and return same route.

Majestic Tahiti Explorer—Papeete – Raiatea – Bora Bora – Taha'a – Raiatea – Huahine – Moorea – Papeete, year round.

Glacier Bay Explorer—

IN SUMMER: Ketchikan – Misty Fjords – Wrangell – Sitka – Skagway – Haines – Tracy Arm – Juneau – Petersburg – Ketchikan.

IN WINTER, SPRING, AND FALL: San Francisco – Sausalito – San Joaquin River – Stockton – Sacramento River – Sacramento – Locke – San Francisco.

Colonial Explorer—

IN SUMMER: Portland (Oregon) – Bonneville Lock – McNary Lock – Lewiston – Clarkston – Richland/Pasco/Kennewick – Columbia Gorge – Astoria – Portland.

IN WINTER: St. Thomas – Jost Van Dyke – Salt Island – Tortola – Norman Island – Virgin Gorda – St. Croix – St. John – St. Thomas.

North Star—

IN SUMMER: Prince Rupert, B.C. – Misty Fjords – Ketchikan – Sitka – Glacier Bay – Skagway – Haines – Juneau – Prince of Wales Island – Prince Rupert.

IN WINTER: La Paz – Cabo San Lucas – Mazatlán – San Blas – Puerto Vallarta – Manzanillo – Zihuatanejo/Ixtapa – Acapulco.

Explorer Starship—

IN SUMMER: Prince Rupert, B.C. – Ketchikan – Juneau – Haines – Skagway – Glacier Bay – Sitka – Yakutat Bay/Hubbard Glacier – Anchorage.

IN WINTER: San Juan – St. Thomas – St. Kitts – Saba – Martinique – Grenadines – Grenada – Barbados *or* Barbados – Bequia – St. Lucia – St. Barthélemy – St. Maarten – St. Croix – Virgin Gorda – Peter Island – San Juan.

IN SPRING AND FALL: San Diego – Isla Cedros – Cabo San Lucas – Puerto Vallarta – Acapulco – Costa Rica – Panama Canal – Curaçao – Barbados.

Exploration Cruise Lines got its start a decade ago as Alaska Tour and Marketing Co., operating land tours to the dramatic Alaska, Arctic, and northwestern U.S. scenery. In 1981 the company bought its first ship, the *Pacific Northwest Explorer*, and began sailing from Seattle on cruises to the San Juan Islands and Puget Sound.

Combining a familiarity with the region and a belief in its saleability, a year later the company bought two more ships, the *Great Rivers Explorer* and *Majestic Explorer*. Family owned, Exploration Cruise Lines is operated by Robert Giersdorf, president of the line, and his son, Dave, and their families.

By 1985, Giersdorf says, he had decided that to expand the line he'd need to take his company public or look for private resources. That's when Exploration Cruise Lines teamed up with Anheuser-Busch, which bought a major interest in the line.

Things then began to pop. In December 1985 the line added an unusual ship to its fleet, the *Colonial Explorer*. Formerly the *Pilgrim Belle* operated by Coastwise Cruise Lines, the *Colonial Explorer* is a new ship designed to look like an old one. A 102-passenger craft, its resemblance to an old coastal steamer helps it blend right into its itinerary, which takes it on visits to the nation's colonial roots via Lewis and Clark's route.

In 1986 Exploration added the *North Star*, a 156-passenger craft, to the fleet. A year-old ship formerly sailing in Europe, the *North Star* now calls Alaska home in the summer but heads to the warm waters of Mexico in the winter.

About that time it contracted for construction of a new ship to be called *Explorer Starship*. This new craft is quite a departure for the line in more ways than one. *Explorer Starship*, the company decided, would aim its pretty new nose directly at those upper-crust sailors who now frequent Sea Goddess Cruises at weekly fares in the $4,000-per-person stratosphere.

"With that base, we're going to increase the development pace substantially so we can acquire and deploy vessels on a more aggressive schedule," Giersdorf promises. That means, he says, that the line, which now is operating seven vessels, expects to have added four more 200-passenger craft by 1990.

At this point Exploration Cruise Lines has what Giersdorf quite accurately calls an "extremely strong presence" in Alaska where the line got its start. Exploration now has five ships—the *Explorer Starship, Glacier Bay Explorer, North Star, Pacific Northwest Explorer,* and *Great Rivers Explorer*—operating there and in the Pacific Northwest. In the summer of 1987 the line's newest ship, the *Explorer Starship,* joined the crowd, replacing the *Majestic Alaska Explorer,* which moved to a permanent base in Tahiti to become the *Majestic Tahiti Explorer.*

Cruises on these ships are for people who want to combine a look at the stupefyingly impressive scenery of this region with the ease and comfort of ship travel. These are not large ships, so your entertainment will be almost solely scenic, although the line does have a cruise director.

A special feature of most of these ships is a plated bow piece that can be slid aside to allow stairs to be lowered so you can walk right off the ship and onto an iceberg!

Activities

As on most small ships you won't find a raft of lounges, discos, or gymnasiums, so don't expect rousing entertainment or a daily schedule of events. Cruises on these vessels feature the destination more than cruising itself, concentrating on offering passengers a close-up look at awesome scenery and some interesting shore excursions. Many of those shore excursions, by the way, are included in the price of the cruise.

On small ships like these, cruises are also more casual. Passengers spend more time together and get to know each other better than they would on a large cruise ship. To encourage friendships, the ships plan entertainment that gets passengers mingling and mixing. Activites on board are coordinated by a cruise director, and include things like talent contests, Bingo, and slide shows or movies. In some ports—Tahiti, for one—the line brings entertainers on board several different evenings. A player piano often gets the fun going, and there's a full-service bar open whenever anyone wants it to be.

There are some attractive sundecks where you can pull up a chair and gaze at snow-clad mountains rising in regal splendor along sapphire waterways.

Life aboard is very casual, so don't bother to pack a black tie. You can dress up for the Captain's Gala dinner if you like, but you won't feel the least bit out of place if you don't.

At happy hour you'll find trays of appetizers circulating, and you can get tea, coffee, or hot chocolate at any time of day or night.

PACIFIC NORTHWEST EXPLORER/GREAT RIVERS EXPLORER/ MAJESTIC TAHITI EXPLORER/NORTH STAR/GLACIER BAY EXPLORER/COLONIAL EXPLORER: So much alike are these six small sailers that we'll explore them all at one time.

Largest of the sextet is the *North Star*, which measures in at 3,095 tons, is 295 feet long, and can carry 156 passengers. All the others range in size from 125 feet to 150 feet long and carry about 60 to 120 passengers.

Pacific Northwest Explorer, Great Rivers Explorer, Glacier Bay Explorer, and *Majestic Tahiti Explorer* are as alike as peas in a pod. *Colonial Explorer,* however, was built to resemble an oldtime river steamer and is fitted out with lots of wood, brass, and etched glass. This one carries 102 passengers and can cruise at speeds up to 15 knots, a bit faster than the others.

Public Rooms

Dinner in the Explorer Dining Room is the main event of the evening, followed by some congenial gatherings in the Vista View Lounge. Both are on the main deck, and feature big windows on both sides so you need never miss any of the view passing by outside. In the lounge you'll find a small bar dispensing libations and some comfortable chairs and banquettes. A piano sets off occasional sing-along evenings, and card games are popular.

Dining is family style at long tables down which are passed the dishes *du jour*. Those will include fresh fish and fruit or the specialty of the region. Cooking is basic American, with the emphasis on foods favored by American diners.

There is no beauty salon or barbershop aboard, and no laundry facilities. Most electrical equipment can be used, but no irons or small appliances exceeding 500 watts.

Cabins

All cabins aboard are outside accommodations, brightly decorated in cheerful colors. While not elaborately appointed, they're clean and cheerful, and seem quite comfortable for the amount of time you'll be spending in them (who would want to miss this scenery?). All are carpeted and have private bathrooms, mirrors, and individual reading lights.

It seems quite amazing that with just 40 or so cabins aboard there could be four price categories, but that's the way it is. The top-of-the-line cabins are deluxe staterooms that measure 10 by 14 to 20 feet and include a small table and chairs by the window, a double bed, a sink in an alcove, and a shower in the bathroom. A closet in one corner provides for your storage needs. Biggest draw here is the view through big windows. A convertible sofa can accommodate a third person. For one of these cabins the fare on a six-night peak-season Alaska trip is $1,975 per person.

On the main deck are rooms with double or twin lower beds, a small table and chairs, and perhaps an upper berth. One of these Category AA staterooms is $1,935 per person.

In Category A staterooms often have twin beds set at right angles to each other, leaving the maximum floor space visible. A small bathroom with a shower is off one side of the room. The fare for one of these cabins is $1,795 per person for a six-night trip.

The lowest price on board the ships is a Category B or C cabin, with two lower berths, one of them extra wide. Although there's a window, it's high on the wall so it's more for light than for view. These may be small rooms, measuring 7 by 10 feet, and there are no closets—just some hanger-bars for your clothes. A six-night fare is $1,375 to $1,705.

A third occupant of a stateroom, adult or child, is charged the minimum cruise fare (the cost of a Category B cabin). Single travelers occupying a stateroom alone pay 130% of the price per person for a Category B cabin, 150% for all other categories.

EXPLORER STARSHIP: The *Explorer Starship* is quite a departure for this line. In fact, it would be quite a departure for nearly any line! Designed to be what Giersdorf calls an "ultra-deluxe" 250-passenger vessel, the ship aims at the very top of the cruise market, those who can afford to pay rates of $380 or more per person a day.

In summer this luxurious craft joins much of the rest of Exploration's fleet in Alaskan waters, and in winter it heads south to the Caribbean where it goes head to head with another very posh cruiser, *Sea Goddess I,* which sails on a similar itinerary and at similar—but slightly higher!—prices.

Each of the cabins aboard is designed to pamper passengers to the *n*-th degree with such goodies as a stocked mini-bar/refrigerator, color televisions and VCR players, a film library, a complete sound and video system, and very large staterooms. Giersdorf bills his line's offerings as "the Explorer Class Experience," which means, he says, that because the line's ships are so small they can tie up in ports "that could not be delivered to 1,200 or 1,400 passengers—special spots, beautiful Shangri-Las that are the hidden treasures of those areas we specialize in."

Like one other vessel in the line, this craft has a small tender attached to its stern to take people ashore in remote locations.

Giersdorf says frankly that the new vessel is designed to compete with the *Sea Goddess* in amenities and appointments, but charging somewhat lower fares, in the $350 to $400 a day range.

"We feel there's a market for those who want deluxe amenities on the ship but want the approach to cruising we deliver—destination intensive," Giersdorf says.

Explorer Starship concentrates on ports larger cruise ships do not or cannot reach, places like Saba, Virgin Gorda and the Baths, Nevis and St. Kitts, St. Barthélemy, Bequia, Mustique, the Tobago Cays, and Grenada, plus a few of the most popular ports like St. Thomas and St. Croix tossed in for good measure.

Public Rooms

Exploration Cruise Lines is very proud of its newest ship, and rightfully so, for it is indeed a handsome craft, filled with original artwork and outfitted in sleek, contemporary style.

Focal point of the vessel is a three-dimensional mirrored diorama that soars up all seven decks and spotlights the ship's destinations. Each deck sports a different theme complete with themed objets d'art ranging from bronzes to relief sculptures and fabric creations. Soft shades of purple, rose, and aquamarine blend softly into each other throughout the ship and are abetted by lots of mirrors and sleek pale woods.

Best hideaway on board is up on the Observation Deck, where the view from the aptly named Observation Lounge enclosed in glass seems never to end.

You can while away an evening in the small but chic casino or wander into the adjacent Explorer Lounge for dancing or one of the nightly revues. Those whose day begins at about 10 p.m. can be found in the marble-floored disco, which sports something called sequential Tivoli lighting and a fog machine, and a piano bar.

Dining occurs in the Galaxy Dining Room, a small but significant spot with a bevy of windows and tables for two, four, and six. Each evening a pianist provides music to eat lobster medallions, Alaska king crab legs, and Pacific salmon by, not even to mention the notes that accompany radicchio-with-raspberry-vinaigrette salads and chocolate chess-set desserts.

There's a cute little "Baby Starship" to whizz you off to shallow-water explorations and a Jacuzzi that's very popular in the Caribbean.

Those with a more intellectual bent can head for the library, where an array of bestsellers and videotapes are available. Fitness fans will find a health club with spa, sauna, and a daunting array of shiny workout equipment.

Cabins

Because they charge plenty for the privilege of sailing the *Starship*, the line naturally provides the poshest service and some very handsome cabins. Ranging in size from large to very large, these subtly decorated quarters are all outside cabins, thus guaranteeing you a look at the fascinating scenery of the Caribbean and Alaska.

Each has a separate sitting area and all have closed-circuit color televisions, video cassette players, a radio, telephone, stocked refrigerator, built-in hairdryer in the tile baths, and key-card door locks. Video programs relay everything from arrival and docking information to lectures and the evening entertainment for those feeling too lazy to go down to the showroom in person.

If you're prepared to travel the firstest of first class, book a veranda suite, which sports sliding glass doors leading onto private verandas. Beds here, as in other cabins, are twin-size and can be pushed together to create a queen-size sleeper. Such accommodations, which measure a ship-spacious 17 by 19 feet, are $4,795 per person for a seven-night Alaska cruise in peak season.

Next down the line are deluxe staterooms, measuring about 11 by 16 feet. Those are $3,395 per person for that seven-night Alaska cruise, while slightly smaller, but still more than adequate, quarters range in price from $2,695 to $3,195 per person for that Alaska voyage.

A number of cabins can be joined to create a two-room parlor suite.

18. HOLLAND AMERICA LINE / WESTOURS

Contact: Holland America Line / Westours, 300 Elliott Ave. West, Seattle, WA 98119 (tel. 206/281-3535 or 281-1970, or toll free 800/426-0327).

Cruising Grounds: Mexico's Yucatán Peninsula, Caribbean, Mexican Riviera, Alaska.

Itineraries: *Nieuw Amsterdam*—
IN SUMMER AND FALL: Vancouver – Ketchikan – Juneau – Glacier Bay – Sitka – Vancouver.
IN WINTER AND SPRING: Tampa – Playa del Carmen – Cozumél – Ocho Ríos – Grand Cayman – Tampa.

Noordam—
IN SUMMER AND FALL: Vancouver – Ketchikan – Juneau – Glacier Bay – Sitka – Vancouver.
IN WINTER AND SPRING: Fort Lauderdale – San Juan – Tortola – St. Thomas – Nassau – Fort Lauderdale.

Rotterdam—
IN SUMMER: Vancouver – Ketchikan – Juneau – Glacier Bay – Sitka – Vancouver.
IN WINTER: Fort Lauderdale – Curaçao – Caracas – Grenada – Martinique – St. Thomas – Nassau – Fort Lauderdale.

Atlantic— 1989 itinerary unannounced at press time.

Westerdam—Fort Lauderdale – San Juan – St. Maarten – St. Thomas – private Bahamian island – Fort Lauderdale *or* Fort Lauderdale – Ocho Ríos – Cayman Islands – Merida – Fort Lauderdale.

In 1983, this elegant old line introduced the newest star in its firmament, the *Nieuw Amsterdam*. A 32,000-ton French-built vessel, she is a smashing beauty Holland America describes as "an extraordinary marriage of art and technology." But a year or so later the *Nieuw Amsterdam*'s sparkling newness was matched by yet another new Holland America ship, the *Noordam,* a twin to the *Nieuw Amsterdam*.

Holland America is inordinately proud of its big luxurious ocean liners, so proud, in fact, that the line has trademarked the term "Ocean Liner Service." Oldtime elegance is the watchword of Holland America, and that isn't just Madison Avenue hype either. You can sample the finest example of that service in glamorous style aboard the company's oldest and most stately vessel, the *Rotterdam*.

Aboard the line's other shining ships you'll find that same touch—or touches—of class. Holland America spent thousands of dollars to equip the *Nieuw Amsterdam* and the *Noordam* with a fortune's worth of historic art treasures: museum-piece glassware and silver from the 17th and 18th centuries displayed in glass showcases. Navigation instruments from those long-gone days are proudly on display in a lounge. A massive wooden mermaid looks soulfully down from her perch and a 16-foot mosaic mural graces a balcony perch.

And to make matters even classier: there's a welcome no-tipping-required policy aboard all Holland America ships, so the crew works for your smiles instead of your little white end-of-cruise envelopes. You can, of course, cross some palms with green, but you won't have to endure any of the tacky talks on tipping that are so prevalent on many cruise lines these days.

Dutch officers keep things humming, and a smiling Indonesian crew can't seem to do enough for you. They are there to escort you to your room when you step aboard that first day, and they're there every minute thereafter to see to your every whim.

Once you're aboard you can sign for purchases, then pay your bill on your last day—no cluttering your pockets with wrinkled bills.

Holland America has quite a fascinating history, one that stretches back to 1872 when two Dutchmen began sailing the first *Rotterdam* to the U.S. from that Dutch city. In those days eight lucky passengers could travel first class, about 400 others went in steerage, and cargo was what kept it all afloat financially.

A year later the two formed the Netherlands-American Steam Navigation Co., which became known in 1896 as Holland America Line. It has kept that name all these years and bears it still, although the company is now owned by Seattle-based Westours, which first found its niche in the travel marketplace selling Alaska tours. Westours backed into the shipping business, acquiring this famous line after having chartered her ships several times for Alaska voyages.

Over the years Holland America has owned ships called the *Noordam, Maasdam, Statendam, Ryndam, Potsdam,* and more recently the *Veendam* and *Volendam*. If you've loved cruising for a long time, you will recognize some of those famous names.

HA's original *Statendam*—all 32,000 massive tons of her—had the misfortune to be launched about the time the Germans were discovering U-boats. She was sunk by one of those lethal craft before she could board her first paying passenger. A namesake ship was launched in the late 1920s, sadly at the opening of a miserable economic decade and just prior to another World War that was to force the Dutch company's operations out of the land of dikes to the Dutch-owned isle of Curaçao.

Holland America's latest *Statendam,* a 24,294-ton vessel carrying 850 passengers, was until recently sailing under Paquet Cruise colors as the *Rhapsody* and is now a Regency Line ship. Meanwhile the *Maasdam* and *Ryndam* went off to become the *Stefan Batory* of Polish Ocean Line and Epirotiki Lines' *Atlas*.

In 1983 Holland America became part of Westours and sold its *Veendam* and *Volendam* to shipping magnate C. Y. Tung, who in turn sold the *Veendam* to Bermuda Star Line. The *Volendam* became Bermuda Star's *Bermuda Queen*.

The current *Rotterdam* is the fifth ship to carry that venerable old name. Launched in 1957, this 38,000-ton cruiser, christened by Queen Juliana, has been the flagship of the fleet for nearly three decades.

Now the *Rotterdam* is based in Fort Lauderdale's Port Everglades, where she sails on Caribbean cruises from late September to April. In April she sets off to go through the Panama Canal and up to Alaska for the summer. In the fall the process reverses, giving you lots of chances to sail to many ports on segments of this ship's busy schedule.

The *Nieuw Amsterdam* winters in Tampa, sailing from that west coast Florida city to the silvery beaches and swaying palms of Jamaica, Grand Cayman, and the Yucatán Peninsula. She returns to Alaskan waters in summer.

Nieuw Amsterdam's twin sister, the *Noordam,* is now based in Fort Lauderdale where she sails on seven-day Caribbean cruises, shifting operations to Alaska in summer where she joins the *Rotterdam* and the *Nieuw Amsterdam*.

In 1988 Holland America surprised the cruise world by announcing its purchase of Home Lines, which had been in business for many years, operating in recent memory two very handsome ships, the *Homeric* and the *Atlantic*. Both are comparatively new ships: the *Atlantic* is a 33,800-ton vessel built in 1982, designed to carry about 1,000 passengers and able to clip along at 23.6 knots; and the *Homeric,* a ship built in 1986 in West Germany.

When Holland America bought the two ships, it immediately renamed the *Homeric* the *Westerdam,* in salute to a ship Holland America owned from 1946 to

1960. At press time, however, no one was saying just what would happen to the *Atlantic,* a craft we found particularly appealing with its lots-of-leather décor and sleek contemporary styling.

As for the *Westerdam* (née *Homeric*), she fits easily into the Holland America fleet and at 42,090 tons is the largest ship now sailing under Holland America colors. Built at a cost of $150 million, the ship was, and is likely to continue to be, staffed with a crew and hotel staff of Italians, and a cruise staff of Americans.

On board this expensive lady of the sea you'll find 1,104 passengers roaming about eight spacious decks while the ship clips along at a quite respectable 22.6 knots.

In line with most new cruise ships these days, the *Westerdam* has many more outside cabins than inside—specifically, 365 outside sleepers and 187 inside. Cabins are quite respectably spacious, ranging from 146 to 245 square feet, plus suites that measure in at 435 square feet. All cabins have televisions too, so you can pick up the six o'clock news near shore and watch movies when the networks fade.

Every conceivable amenity can be found on board, from children's nanny-counselors in summer season to a computer instruction center, a casino, golf practice court, gymnasium full of shiny grief-machines, a massage room, saunas, and a video game room.

There are not one, but two swimming pools aboard, one of them with the sliding "magrodome" roof that once was a trademark of Home Lines. That roof slides open on sunny days and closes to let you swim if there's rain.

NIEUW AMSTERDAM / NOORDAM:

As the new twins of the line, the *Nieuw Amsterdam* and *Noordam* replaced former ships of the same names. These two ships, built in French Chantiers de l'Atlantique shipyards, are look-alikes right down to the last inch of their 33,930 tons.

This winter you can see the *Nieuw Amsterdam* in Tampa where she'll be sailing into the sunshine of Grand Cayman, Jamaica, and the Yucatán Peninsula with a special 12-day Christmas journey to the Panama Canal with stops at several Caribbean islands.

You'll spot the *Noordam* in Fort Lauderdale, her winter home, from which she sails to Nassau, St. Thomas, and San Juan.

And they're worth seeing! With deep-blue hulls topped by a white superstructure, they slip showily through the seas carrying 1,200 passengers in considerable splendor.

Activities

You'll find all the usual exercise classes, gymnasium, crafts classes, and deck games, but life aboard these ships is not typically seven-day raucous. There's plenty to do and plenty of lovely places to do whatever you like to do, but you won't find any male nightgown competitions.

In the evenings, dinner is a production and features some wonderful Dutch and Indonesian treats as well as the more familiar continental flavors. Later, bands play, the casino clicks and whirrs, and flashy shows take place in a beautiful two-story showroom.

Public Rooms

As alike as two peas in the proverbial pod, the 33,000-ton *Noordam* and *Nieuw Amsterdam* are twins, with cabin sizes and layouts the same, deck plans the same, and public rooms the same—some even with the same name.

None of that makes them any less glamorous, however. On both you'll find dozens of museum art pieces from the 17th and 18th centuries carefully scattered about to keep you aware of the line's Dutch East India Company theme. After all, that historic old firm spurred the creation of early trading routes and encouraged seafaring adventures that were to change the world.

On board both ships you'll find more than 20 public rooms, places like the *Noordam*'s Amsterdam Dining Room, where 106 floor-to-ceiling windows overlook the shining sea below. In the Admiral's Lounge an atrium soars two stories high, and Tasman's Terrace, named for Albert Tasman, discoverer of Tasmania, is one of many cozy lounges aboard. For dancing, head for the Hornpipe Club.

For a more detailed look at these two ships, let's tour the *Nieuw Amsterdam*, keeping in mind that rooms and décor aboard are very similar, if not twin to, those on the *Noordam*.

There is no more beautiful lounge afloat than the *Nieuw Amsterdam*'s Stuyvesant Lounge with its shining dark woods and high ceilings. A massive lion-bedecked gold crest backs the raised stage where gleaming chrome trims the band's royal-blue music stands and flashy entertainers perform. Subtly tasteful woven fabric covers wood-trimmed armchairs. A shining wooden dance floor, glittering in the glow of round lights set into chrome squares, is a sight to behold. On a glass-trimmed balcony, named Minnewit Terrace in honor of that shrewd trader who spent $24 to buy Manhattan, you can peer down at the dancers swirling below.

A look at some of the room names on board will quickly clue you in to the theme aboard: Old New York a/k/a Nieuw Amsterdam. That, thank goodness, is as far as the resemblance to the *old* of Old New York goes. Everything else aboard is spanking new, with the best of the Old World represented in polished wood, shining brass, acres of teak deck, and some very courtly service.

We could go on rapturously here with description after description of handsome public rooms, but our vote for the best home-away-from-home drawing room on any ship afloat goes to the Explorers Lounge. Settle into an earth-toned, wood-trimmed couch or chair here, turn on one of the shaded brass table lamps, open a Robert Ludlum thriller, and lose yourself in scrunchy comfort. Or if you're not the reading type but do occasionally interrupt your pursuit of activity for a breather, take that breather here, where you can gaze through tall curtained windows at sapphire seas below. Afternoon tea, complete with violins, is served here too.

Fittingly, the serene Explorers Lounge merges right into the ship's Book Chest Library and an adjoining card room. A few steps away you'll find the Princess Theatre, where films are shown daily. This general area also makes a good waiting spot for those whose contribution to the shopping expeditions in nearby boutiques is to sit and wait, more or less patiently. Nothing on this deck is far from the popular Henry's Bar, where a long serving bar streaks in marine-blue splendor down one wall and comfortable chairs in the same riveting hue pull up to small square tables.

Nine decks high and 704 feet long (that's only 4.3 times around for a mile, joggers!), this glamorous ship could be overpowering, but clever designers have turned her busy Promenade Deck into a series of unusually shaped nooks and crannies.

No matter how many fun seekers there are aboard you can always find a quiet spot somewhere for an intimate tête-à-tête. If you're looking for such a spot, try one of the remoter corners of the Hudson Lounge. Or go way up to the Sun Deck where you can become part of the big circular bar in the Crow's Nest, or find a spot near the windows for a magnificent ocean view.

Exercise buffs can tone up in two outdoor pools, then snack and drink at the Lido Restaurant and Bar, just steps away. Right here's where you find the 60-foot buffet presented for breakfast, lunch, or late-night supper. Three decks up on the Navigation Deck there's another swimming pool. In salute to the nation's fascination with physical fitness, the *Nieuw Amsterdam* now features an ocean-going gym. In it you'll find Universal weight machines, a treadmill, bicycles, dumbbells, and an inclined plane. If it's any consolation, you can enjoy a lovely view out over the Navigation Deck and swimming pool as you huff and puff.

One deck up, on the Upper Promenade Deck, you'll find the balcony half of that gorgeous Stuyvesant Lounge and a gambling spot called the Wampum Casino. That name carries this theme thing to ludicrous depths, but this spot nevertheless offers attractive quarters in which to take your best shot at a lady named Luck.

During blackjack breathers you can hoist one at the glowing wood Partridge Bar, which is (get this) just off the Peartree Club. Both are named after a pear tree old Peter S. planted a couple of centuries ago. Plump with comfortable barrel chairs and ocean shades of blue and green, the Peartree grows on you. Disco fans can boogie in the Peartree, which rocks to the wee hours every night.

When the sun drops over the yardarm you will dine under the sparkle of dozens of contemporary chandeliers glowing over the massive Manhattan Dining Room, which seats more than 700 diners. Tall windows fill the room with light at lunch and give you a glimpse of the stars at dinner.

Most of the tables in this restaurant room are for six, but down the center you'll find some tables for two and four. Two wings on one end of the room are called the King's and Queen's Rooms. Wherever you sit, you'll dine on topquality cuisine, sometimes featuring some of those delectable Indonesian dishes so popular in Amsterdam, and even occasionally get to try some Dutch treats. You'll also dine on Rosenthal china with silver created in the same mold that formed the silver on the original *Nieuw Amsterdam*.

Cabins

When you're finally beginning to flag after a long luxurious day of dance lessons, bridge tournaments, deck sports—you can even practice your service on tennis practice courts—trap shooting, golf lessons, nightclub entertainment, and sightseeing, it's off to sleep in the most contemporary of cabins. For openers (literally and figuratively), you get into your cabin by inserting a little plastic card in a slot until you hear the door click open.

So many cabins are there aboard these big ships that you'll find some on nearly every deck (except Promenade). No matter what kind of sleeping arrangements you prefer, you're sure to find them here: king-size beds, queen-size beds, a room with a king-size bed and a sofa bed, a room for four with two lower beds and two pullman uppers, connecting rooms, nonconnecting rooms, rooms with bathtubs, rooms with showers, rooms with both.

Of the 600 or so rooms on board, more than 400 are outside cabins. All of them have a multichannel music system piped in, closed-circuit television, telephone, and individually controlled air conditioning. All have pretty plush carpeting on the floor, and bright contemporary colors abound. You'll find lots of green, striking red with white accents, earthy contemporary tones, delicate floral prints. Drawer space is tucked away in nightstands and beneath vanity/writing tables.

In some rooms couches flip over to become beds; in others, beds with flouncy skirts serve as pillow-backed sitting areas during the day. Outside cabins feature long rectangular windows rather than portholes, walls are covered with light paneling, and there are lots of closets. Many rooms have a couple of deep easy chairs or contemporary tub chairs for extra seating.

The least expensive rooms aboard either ship are, as usual, inside cabins. There are some on every level from the main deck down to and including C Deck. Even in these cabins you'll find two double closets, a contemporary bathroom, a lighted makeup table, and a big dresser. Of the two lower beds, one serves as a sitting area during the day.

These are the smallest rooms aboard, and the beds are often placed in an L shape to give you the most walking-around space. They're small, yes, but we've seen tinier. Cabins 705, 702, and 661 offer a little more space than others. The price for accommodations in these cabins is $1,295 to $1,395 per person for a seven-day Caribbean cruise in peak season.

Which brings us to peak versus off-season aboard, and thank goodness, it's simple. For a one-week cruise on either ship you pay $100 more for any room in peak season, which begins in late January and lasts through March.

Moving up the cabin ladder there is one more category of inside double rooms. These are a bit larger, large enough in fact for some to accommodate a queen-size bed. For these accommodations you pay $1,445 to $1,555 per person. For just $50 more you can have an outside cabin of the same size, although with twin beds (seems worth it to us, especially for Cabins 620, 621, 618 and 619).

From there on up prices range from $1,555 to $1,755 per person for a seven-night voyage in cabins called double, large double, and deluxe double, in ascending price order.

The outside doubles in the lowest of the upper price categories offer two beds and four double closets. Two particularly good buys in this category are Cabins 064 and 067, which are way up on the Navigation Deck, just down the hall from the ship's highest-priced quarters.

Large and deluxe double rooms, which range in price from $1,695 to $1,755 per person, are very pretty, quite large, and furnished with twin or queen-size beds, and the higher of those two prices includes a sweeping picture window, a separate sitting area, dual dressers, and bathtub as well as shower.

Suites? Of course, 20 of them in their own private wings on the Boat and Navigation Decks, with a king-size bed, twin dressers, a separate sitting area with couch and chairs, lots of space, and costing $2,015 per person for a week's Caribbean cruise in high season.

All prices are the same on both ships.

Third and fourth room-sharers pay $495 for seven-day cruises.

And here's a bargain break: if you don't need transportation to or from port (which usually applies to those who drive in from other parts of Florida or nearby), you get a $200 credit toward the price of your stateroom. (What they're really offering here is a $200 credit to anyone not participating in the line's air/cruise programs.)

Single sailors pay an additional 30% to inhabit a cabin alone.

If you're figuring per diem charges, in peak season you'll pay a low of about $185 per person for a week's cruise, to a middle range of $222 to $250, excluding suites, which are $289 per person daily. Budget about $45 per person for port charges.

And on both these ships the price includes air fare and a Dutch (what else?) chocolate on your pillow each night!

Holland America also has several money-saving programs—if you have the time and the money to save on them. One of those offers you a $900 saving if you book what the line calls its "7 plus 7" program by combining a seven-day cruise on the *Noordam* with a second seven-day cruise on the *Nieuw Amsterdam*. Air transportation between Fort Lauderdale and Tampa is included, as are transfers to the ships. Another program called "Dutch Incentive" offers reductions on cruises booked well in advance of sailing.

ROTTERDAM: As grande dame of the fleet, the *Rotterdam* has been riding the waves for a quarter of a century. In an age that venerates youth, the *Rotterdam* retains an aloof disdain for discussion of age and even goes so far as to celebrate her years. In 1986 the ship's glamorous world cruise saluted itself with a Silver Anniversary Cruise.

Whether or not the world was more innocent in those days (or just choosier about the people with whom it shared secrets), the *Rotterdam* seems the perfect place to glorify glamorous days when evening meant black tie and long gowns, champagne and caviar, tea dances, the Charleston, Fred Astaire, the Ziegfeld Follies, a Gershwin tune.

Cruise ships somehow seem to epitomize that bygone era when the rich were richer, or at least far more innovative in their use of wealth. And what better place to celebrate the creative use of wealth than aboard this massive ship where it requires very little effort to imagine Fred and Ginger floating down the great curving staircase that sweeps up to the balcony of the Ritz Carlton Room.

At 38,000 tons, the *Rotterdam* is 6,000 tons heavier than her sisters in the line, and carries fewer passengers—1,114—which of course means more space for everyone.

Public Rooms

Ten decks high and three-fourths as long as the Empire State Building is tall, the ship combines the extravagance that could still be afforded in the '50s with the contemporary look that was born in those days. You'll still see unmistakeable signs of the '50s on board in things like tapered chair legs, but the ship was designed with such clean, simple lines that she looks almost as modern as her newer sisters.

In the Ocean Bar, for instance, you'll find big windows sweeping to the ceiling, circular tub chairs decked out in red plaid, and a long arching bar under a shining ceiling scattered with small spotlights.

Acres of wood spread throughout the ship on swirling polished dance floors and what seems to be miles of paneling. So civilized is life on board that there's even a handsome smoking room filled with plushy velvet armchairs gathered into cozy circles. Beautiful wood paneling provides a backdrop for an intricate metal sculpture, one of many you'll spot on the ship.

On the glass-enclosed Upper Promenade Deck you'll find the ship's big 610-seat CinemaScope Theatre with its second-level balcony. Here, too, is the ship's flash-and-dazzle center, the slick Ambassador Room. A rocking spot, this room's a study in circles, from divider walls of glass circles to a circular dance floor filled with a myriad of starburst-inside-starburst, and overhead a spiffy white circular ceiling.

Gift shops, a boutique, even a drugstore are tucked away on this deck, and it's here you'll go to find something to read in the ship's library or to gamble on your luck in the casino.

One deck lower, on the Promenade Deck, you'll dance away the evenings in the big Queen's Lounge with its kidney-shaped polished-wood dance floor and elegant grand piano. Or sneak into the Ocean Bar for a quiet moment. If you play cards you'll have plenty of space to play them at the big card room set off the glass-enclosed promenade. There's a shopping center on this deck too.

Finally the Lido with its semicircular bar and big Lido Terrace café winds about the swimming pool so you need not fear starvation or thirst after a day in the sun. There's an indoor pool too.

While you're out in that sun, by the way, you might as well make the most of your time and get in a little tennis on the practice courts, take a couple of golf lessons, or try trap shooting or weightlifting. Send the kids off to the video games.

Perhaps the single best-known spots on the ship are down on B Deck—the bright and elegant La Fontaine and Odyssey Dining Rooms. Decorated in red and royal blue, this domed dining arena is lined with golden columns lit by dozens of upturned glittering lamps that bounce light off the ceiling. The dining rooms offer mirrors and murals, red-jacketed sommeliers, shining gold buttons, white gloves, and course after course of delectable treasures ranging from lobster to steaks to kiwi fruit and chocolate mousse pie. Chefs on this ship and all others in the line are members of the select Confrérie de la Chaîne des Rôtisseurs, the international group of gifted chefs and food lovers.

Dinner is even announced with elegance: not the usual loudspeaker to disturb your meditation but the soft ring of brass chimes.

Activities

Evenings find a pianist/singer in every lounge, a dancing-singing revue in the main lounge, the usual sounds in the disco, a string quartet, big-band sound, even a midnight show. Not to mention the casino.

If you like quiet spots, stop up to the small Sky Room on the Navigation Bridge Deck where you can sit out on the observation deck or terrace and, well, muse.

If you're wondering how your wardrobe is going to stand up to all this, let it be known that the *Rotterdam* gets rave reviews for its laundry and dry-cleaning service. So good and so inexpensive is it that some people say they have contemplated saving up their laundry and bringing it on board to have it done here.

Cabins

At last full days become full evenings and turn finally into exhaustion. You wend your way back to your cabin, a spot that can come in many sizes and shapes.

If you've secured one of the top cabins aboard, an outside double room in Category B, you'll be returning to a room with twin beds outfitted in a contemporary print. Off to one side of the room, built-in wood cabinets rise to the ceiling matching the tiny strip of molding that edges the ceiling. You're likely to have two portholes, covered with tied-back curtains that match your bedspread and the drape that sets the sleeping area off from the couch and chairs in your sitting room.

If you have a slightly less expensive outside cabin, called a "large outside double room" on this ship, you're still likely to find one of those massive built-in wall units in your room, complete with drop-down bar/desk. Twin beds often sport a fluffy dust ruffle, while a couple of chairs provide a seating area for cocktail time. Signs of the '50s in these rooms range from Formica-clad furnishings to Danish modern chairs and the tapering wooden chair legs that were so popular in those days.

If you've chosen an inside double room, Category D, you'll be occupying a room with twin beds and often a couple of chairs in a small seating area.

The least expensive categories are economy outside or inside rooms that are compact with upper berth and lower bed. Some have bathtubs as well as showers.

On board this ship, as on few ships, there are single rooms designed especially for the unaccompanied traveler. Granted, they're small, but then the price is in line for single travelers who often have to pay much more elsewhere.

It's quite difficult to tell you just what a cruise will cost here since there are so many possible options. For the sake of comparison let's look at the fares for a ten-day trip aboard the *Rotterdam* sailing from Fort Lauderdale to Curaçao, Caracas, Grenada, Martinique, St. Thomas, Nassau, and back to Fort Lauderdale.

On this cruise, one of those inside single rooms will cost $1,925. An outside room for a person traveling alone is $2,235.

Economy inside double rooms range from $1,595 to $2,095 per person, rising to $1,845 to $2,525 per person for similar outside quarters.

If you're really going first class, you'll pay $3,045 per person for a deluxe stateroom with separate sitting area and the best of everything.

As you can see, that works out to a minimum of about $159 per person a day, rising to $252 in larger or outside quarters, up to $305 per person daily for a ten-day cruise in a suite.

Extra passengers sharing a stateroom with two full-fare guests pay $595 for a ten-day voyage, proportionately higher on longer trips. All these rates include air fare, but there's a $200 credit for those who do not require transportation to or from the embarkation point.

ATLANTIC: Launched in 1982, this snappy craft was designed inside and out by a bevy of European architects and interior decorators. Said to have the largest outdoor deck of any cruise ship afloat, the *Atlantic* sports a weather-guaranteeing sliding glass "magrodome" roof over the pool.

This is one beautiful craft, so stunning in décor that each room you visit seems more beautiful than the last. With no fewer than 23 public rooms, the ship offers plenty of places to see and be seen, to meet and to greet, to play and to do nothing at all.

Public Rooms

For openers, it seems safe to say that there's more leather aboard this ship than on any other craft afloat. Everywhere you look are acres and acres of glove-soft leather chairs, and in at least two of the lounges even the bar is made of silky leather.

Among the cozier places on board is the Rendezvous Bar, where you can plunk down in a tan leather chair—or a matching leather bar stool—while a small combo entertains for dancing on the postage-stamp dance floor. This lounge runs right down the side of the ship, so you can watch through tall windows as the *Atlantic* pulls out of port.

On the opposite side of the ship you'll find another lounge with an odd name: The Quiet Room. What exactly makes it quiet is anyone's guess, but it certainly is attractive. Those same tan leather chairs appear here, but now in a setting replete with cream-colored drapes and matching wallpaper of tranquil waterside scenes.

Between the two is the spectacular glassed-in Observation Lounge, furnished wall to wall with black and beige leather tub chairs.

In the evenings you'll be entertained in the Atlantic Lounge, a handsome multilevel room with white translucent lights overhead, comfortable couches and chairs in beige tweedy fabric, a raised stage, and a dance floor. Tinted-mirror cocktail tables are rimmed in chrome, and a steel bar shines at the rear of the room. Banks of windows stretch down both sides of this very contemporary setting that's an all-day meeting spot as well as an evening haven.

Throughout the ship you'll see beautiful contemporary glass and metal sculptures, the most impressive of which is a giant bronze Atlas holding up the world. Look for it in the main foyer, where you can settle into a dark-brown leather chair and meditate upon the difficulties of Greek gods.

It's difficult to meditate much on board this ship, however. There's always some temptation to lure you away. Tops among those are the ship's shops, which are certainly among the most spacious and beautifully designed shops afloat. One purveys perfumes, another those delightfully humorous Italian ceramics. Both are glass enclosed. Unlike some vessels where shops are tucked away in dark corners, the *Atlantic* puts them right down the side of the ship alongside big portholes that let light stream in to bounce off shining crystal and porcelain treasures.

Even the youngsters have been considered here: there's a small electronic game room.

For adult gamesters there's a spacious two-room casino featuring slot machines in one room, blackjack tables in another.

Card and Scrabble players have a room all to themselves too, a beautiful spot decked out in green and gold with dark-wood furniture and brass-trimmed tables. This bright, airy corner with its shaded wall lamps is as quietly lovely as a library in an English manor house.

When quiet is not what you have in mind, head for the Disco Nite Club, yet another gorgeous room. This one is outfitted in deep-burgundy velvet banquettes and chairs, and lit by U-shaped graphic designs on the walls. Overhead a black ceiling is dotted with round white lights. Take all this glamour in, then step up to the S-shaped bar and run a hand over its silky surface—yes, the entire bar is glove-soft burgundy leather!

If you're looking for sports, there are plenty: in the ship's big gym you can bike on the exercycles and lift on the weight machines, then ease the pain at a massage room or in the sauna. Walk a few steps farther back on the Lido Deck and dive into the Veranda Pool, surrounded by that movable "magrodome" roof. Or walk a few steps in the other direction and splash in the Lido Pool, then sun on the open end of the Lido Deck.

If you're feeling particularly martyred after your efforts, drop by the soda fountain or try a long cool one in the cheery La Baracca snackbar or at the soda fountain in the Lido Bar.

Even the theater is something to see: its 250 seats have cocoa-brown velvet upholstery and leather arms. Small white lights on the dark-brown walls create a graphics effect. Look for it on the Pacific Deck.

Deck names aboard the *Atlantic* are twins to those on the *Westerdam*—Belvedere, Continental, Oceanic, and the easy-to-remember Restaurant Deck.

On that latter deck is the *Atlantic*'s 600-seat restaurant, decked out in deep-purple décor sparked with lavender and rose touches. A high domed ceiling in the center features indirect lighting to highlight the silver sculptures that adorn the room's silver pillars.

One final spot to explore: the Bermuda Lounge, a vast, glass-enclosed room in tropical orange, lime, and gold velvet décor that is continued in the adjoining Hamilton Bar. In that bar be sure to look up at the very unusual windmill-like copper lighting fixtures hanging over the (you guessed it) all-leather bar!

Activities

La dolce vita aboard this ship begins whenever you want it to, but always with a couple of cheerful *buon giornos* from this Italian crew.

You can start the day with breakfast in the Observation Lounge and move on later to a swim in one of the two pools. That sliding-glass roof over one splashing spot guarantees swimming in any weather.

Golfers can drive a few off the deck into the sea while games fans plot strategy in a backgammon tournament and trap-shooters down clay pigeons.

Afternoons you can nibble on some delicious Italian ice cream at the Lido soda fountain or browse in the ship's shops.

An energetic crew provides plenty of other distractions as well, ranging from afternoon tea to fashion shows, trap shooting, a white elephant sale.

Every evening there's entertainment in all the ship's major show rooms, so much of it in fact that you'll be humming a variety of Italian favorites—maybe even in Italian—by the time you get back home.

While there's plenty to do aboard, the number of ports visited on this ship's cruises means you'll find fewer on-board competitions and scheduled events, at least during daylight hours. This is a somewhat more formal ship too, one on which you can expect to put on your finery every night the ship is at sea for the whole day, about three nights in ten. As is customary aboard cruise ships, dinners are informal when the ship has been in port that day, but gentlemen are requested to wear jacket and tie every evening.

Each evening dinner is a theme event too. One night there's a Mexican dinner, on another a Bahamas celebration, on yet another a French feast. Halloween fans can think up a costume for the masquerade evening, and one evening you'll be treated to bottles of bubbly champagne.

Each evening the disco goes on to the wee hours, accompanied for many of those by the action in the casino. Night snackers will be relieved to know they can always sneak out for a 2 a.m. pizza!

Cabins

All this glamour extends to cabins too. For openers, more than 75% of the ship's 543 cabins are outside, and they're big: deluxe cabins feature 200 square feet of space with bedroom, sitting room, and full bath with tub and shower.

All cabins feature piped-in music (three channels of it), and many even have closed-circuit television.

Try as we would, we couldn't find one really undesirable cabin aboard this gleaming vessel. Every one we explored was large, comfortable, bright, and contemporary, and the suites—well, some apartments aren't as gorgeous as these suites!

To travel in one of these suites is to know you've arrived: two full couches upholstered in soft butterscotch leather and a big matching easy chair, beautiful walnut paneling, a television on a stand that opens to reveal a small refrigerator, twin beds in subtle earth colors occupying a big walled-in alcove that closes off from the rest of the room with both a door and a drape, bright mirrors, a bank of tall windows, contemporary shaded lamps, a low coffee table, and a walk-in closet practically big enough to jog in! In the bathroom are sleek bright-blue contemporary fixtures, a floral bouquet painted on the mirror . . . well, you get the picture. You can occupy one of these beautiful suites on a ten-day Caribbean cruise for $3,570 per person.

If that's strictly Dream City for your budget, don't despair. There are lovely quarters on every deck of this ship and in a comparatively wide variety of price brackets.

You'll discover shortly that reading the rate sheet for this ship is a day-long job. There are 14 categories of cabins, and prices for cruises of varying lengths from 6 to 14 days in high winter season and in seasons the ship calls economy and intermediate. No matter what category of cabin you select on this contemporary ship, you'll find lovely quarters. Even the single cabins, which on other ships are often either nonexistent or stuck in some dark corner, are lovely on the *Atlantic*.

Each cabin deck features different colors, so you'll find some cabins outfitted in apple green with cream-colored drapes that feature a palm pattern in coordinating shades of green. Outside rooms on the Oceanic Deck, 036 for example, look just like that, but also have a seating area with two comfortable armchairs, a couch, television, small cocktail table, and a big mirror that makes all this look even larger. In the big bathrooms, coordinating wallpaper carries out the color scheme amid very modern plumbing. For a room in that price category, Category 6, about midway in the list, you'll pay $1,435 per person for a seven-day April Caribbean cruise.

An outside room for a single traveler, Cabin 012 for instance, is much smaller but plenty of room for one. It has all the same amenities too: a small dresser with a slide-out board that converts it to handy desk space, another dresser in the foyer, big closets, even a green telephone. That and similar cabins are $1,350 for a seven-day Caribbean trip.

The lowest-priced double cabins on board are inside Category 13 quarters that are a bit more spartan but nothing you'll find oppressive. These cabins feature the same lovely color schemes, but in these you'll find one twin bed at a right angle to the other with the second fitted out with big blocky cushions so it doubles as a couch in daylight hours. You'll still have plenty of dresser and closet space, and a reasonably sized bathroom. For one of these you pay $1,115 per person for a seven-day cruise.

In the middle ranks are inside cabins similar to the one we just described, barely varying in size. Outside quarters are quite similar in size throughout the ship too, and even those in Category 7, a mid-priced category, include sitting areas. The cost of one of those is $1,385 per person for a seven-day cruise.

Prices go down as you go lower in the ship. Deluxe outside cabins in a top price category with two beds and sitting room on the Belvedere Deck ring in at $1,690 per person for a seven-day cruise. Prices drop $80 for similar accommodations on Oceanic Deck, and finally go as low as $1,385 for an outside room with two beds and bath on Oceanic or Pacific Deck.

Singles get what seems to us to be a bit of a price break on this ship. Single outside cabins can be found at the bow of the ship on Pacific, Oceanic, Restaurant, and Europe Decks, all priced at $1,515. That's within $100 of what a couple pays per person for an inside room of quite similar size nearby.

The rate range, then, goes from $1,115 to $1,690 per person double for a seven-day peak-season Caribbean cruise, and $1,515 single.

The daily rate per person for a winter Caribbean cruise runs $159 to $241, excluding suites.

With such a variety of cruise lengths available (4, 6, 7, 9, 10, 11, and 14 days), you ought to be able to find a cruise and a cabin that fit right into your bankbook.

WESTERDAM: One of the new additions to Holland America Line / Westours' fleet, the *Westerdam* makes quite an appearance. For openers this new ship, constructed in West Germany, features a magradome, a movable roof that rolls right out over the pool so you can keep swimming even when the weather doesn't cooperate.

Beyond that the line has gone all-out on board this ship to repeat the classiest elements of its very-classy-indeed *Atlantic,* and added to that a forest of shining brass railings, beautiful jewel-toned furnishings, and an all-round snappy style visible in every nook and cranny. There seems to be nothing missed in quality, right down to door handles in the form of shining brass crescent moons.

Public Rooms

A few cruise lines have eschewed the copycat look of pale pastels that has swept American décor, opting instead for lavish use of handsome jewel tones. This line is one of those, so its new ship sports some quite tastefully dramatic interiors that glow rather than glitter.

In the curving Vista Lounge, for instance, you can settle into sapphire-blue velvet banquettes backed by gleaming brass rails and glide through the seas, watching the world pass by outside the acres of windows that enclose this attractive curving lounge.

As it is on many ships, the Lido Lounge is a casual buffet dining spot that's a favorite with swimmers and tan fans who nip in here for quick snacks on a busy sunning day. Even inside they're not likely to miss much: large windows line both sides of this serene snack center.

Greeks are rightfully proud of their heritage, and on this ship salute it colorfully on the ship's main Belvedere Deck where gods and goddesses of legend cavort across a massive mural. Here, too, are the ship's sparkling shops, one of them devoted entirely to glittering crystal, another sporting a wide variety of I-can't-resists up to and including amazingly lifelike ceramic dogs and cats.

Red, they say, jostles even the most sluggish corpuscles so that color is the favorite hue for nearly every ship's casino. That's no less true on the *Westerdam,* where shades of red form the backdrop for the ship's small but sufficient casino equipped with roulette wheels, blackjack tables, and a respectable number of slot machines.

You'll find our favorite hideaway, the Monte Carlo Bar, right next door, a quiet haven decked out, corner to corner, in a subtle Victorian shade of rose that's perfect for the hint-of-Victoriana furnishings in this piano bar. Another quiet spot is the Americana Bar, where deep reds and slate-gray marble tables create a cozy, club-like atmosphere.

Those same soft rose hues curve right into the Coral Lounge where they're abetted by three smashing shades of purple, progressively darkening into a brilliant royal purple. In the center of this curving lounge trimmed with brass railings and rimmed in windows is a big dance floor.

Nearby, the ship's disco, called Strawberry Fields, heats up those same colors and adds a few other lively shades to create a zappy room that's also used as an activities center for the line's youth program. Several video machines here provide a diversion for both young and not-so-young.

We'd say the *Westerdam* has quite the handsomest beauty/barbershop of any ship afloat. While hairdressing may not seem to require a chic setting, it's nice to see this bright, airy spot right in the middle of the ship instead of tucked away in some dismal corner as it is on most ships.

There are enough brass railings on board this ship to line several Main Streets, and following their glittering trail will take you to the main lounge, where the ship's showy evening entertainment takes place. This one puts the lie to our claim of deep colors: it's color scheme leans to placid shades of blue and soft pinks sparked by some very unusual backlit oval walls, the lighting abetted by shining tubular crystal chandeliers and sconces.

At the bow of the ship the Galaxy Lounge and American Bar are downright gorgeous, furnished in burgundy velvet and trimmed in black. A striking wall hanging adds daring yellows, oranges, and purples to the burgundy, and provides a vivid focal point here. There's a circular central dance floor of mosaic tile with a huge chandelier overhead, and big windows to provide starlight by night, sunshine by day.

Those bent on quieter moments can head for the library, where soft shades of green encourage contemplative pursuits.

There is, of course, a flashy fitness center equipped with all the requisite torture equipment and two swimming pools: one with that moving roof and mosaic-tile deck trim, the other down two decks with plenty of sunning room. And for the truly dedicated, five laps around Lido Deck is a mile.

Evenings, you'll dine on such tempters as vichyssoise, grilled rock lobster, cherries jubilee and dramatically presented baked Alaska in the La Coupole restaurant, where a huge lighted octagonal dome rimmed in copper glows down on ivory velvet furnishings. There is a pleasant variety of seating arrangements with even a few tables for two, a rarity on cruise ships.

There is even an ice-cream parlor serving excellent Italian ices, sundaes, sodas, and ice-cream cones. And for traditionalists: bouillon is served promptly at 11 a.m. daily, tea at 4 p.m.

The *Westerdam* sports perhaps the most luxurious cinema aboard any ship: it's furnished in cream velvets backed by navy-blue carpeting on floors and walls.

Throughout the ship you'll see colorfully contemporary woven-wool wall hangings and flashy mosaic creations, good examples of the former in the dining room and of the latter out by the swimming pools.

Cabins

Throughout the ship there is an airy feeling of openness and space, a feeling that continues right into restfully decorated cabins. Unusually spacious, the *Westerdam*'s staterooms are very well designed, with storage space for shorts and snorkels, long dresses and suitcases. The ship's fanciest suites measure 435 square feet, while other less sumptuous quarters still measure in at a quite respectable 210 square feet.

Rooms have mirrors on the door, full-length closets, hanging and drawer space, and a long dressing table that serves as both vanity and desk. Those who read themselves to sleep can just reach out to a panel that controls the reading lights, room lights, radio, and television.

A sitting area large enough for a convertible couch can be found in all but the least expensive inside cabins, and some quarters also sport queen-size or double beds. You'll find soothing ivory and cream shades dominating the décor, trimmed with light woods with occasional touches of walnut. Soundproofing is quite good aboard this ship.

Baths are naturally quite modern and a bit larger than on many ships. Some have massage showerheads and bathtubs, and all are stocked with lotions and shampoos.

Rates on the *Westerdam* are divided into 14 categories and three seasons, so to give you an idea what you'll pay, we'll give you a look at some of the prices for a seven-day cruise in peak winter season when the ship sails from Fort Lauderdale's Port Everglades to San Juan, St. Thomas, and Nassau.

Suites, which are quite large and have distinctly separate sleeping and living quarters, are $2,875 per person for that peak-season Caribbean cruise.

Outside cabins are divided into nine price categories, determined largely by size and elaborateness of the accommodations, and partially by deck. Prices for those range from $1,670 to $1,860 per person. Two categories of larger outside accommodations, Categories 2 and 3, may have queen-size beds and ring in at $1,935 and $2,080 per person in peak season.

Many, if not most, outside cabins have an unusual sleeping arrangement: one twin bed and one pull-out couch bed. That provides more floor space, but won't make you happy if you don't like convertible-couch sleeping arrangements.

There are five categories of inside cabins—Categories 9 through 13—varying in price from a low of $1,390 to $1,605 per person for a seven-night Caribbean cruise in peak season. Interestingly, all inside cabins have twin beds—none of them is furnished with the twin bed/sleeper-couch combination of many of the more expensive outside cabins.

Unlike most ships which just require single travelers to pay an additional

50% or 100% for single occupancy of a cabin, the *Westerdam* has some cabins specifically designed for single sailors. These are Category 14 quarters, with one sofa bed and, naturally, a bathroom. In peak Caribbean season one of those cabins is $1,715, and all of them are outside quarters too. If those cabins are all booked, the single supplement to any of the prices listed is $695 for a week-long cruise in peak winter season.

That works out to a per diem rate ranging from a low of $199 to a high of $297, excluding suites. Port charges on a seven-day Caribbean cruise are $30 per person, and third and fourth passengers pay $450 each to share a cabin.

19. NORWEGIAN CRUISE LINE

Contact: Norwegian Cruise Line, 2 Alhambra Plaza, Coral Gables, FL 33134 (tel. 305/358-6680, or toll free 800/327-7030, 800/432-9696 in Florida).

Cruising Grounds: Bahamas, Caribbean, Mexico.

Itineraries: *Norway*—Miami – St. Maarten – St. John – St. Thomas – Great Stirrup Cay – Miami, year round.

Seaward—Miami – Great Stirrup Cay – Ocho Ríos – Grand Cayman – Cozumél – Miami, year round.

Skyward—Miami – St. Thomas – St. Kitts – Barbados – Grenada – St. Lucia – St. Maarten – St. Croix – San Juan or reverse; *or* Miami – Great Stirrup Cay – Ocho Ríos – Grand Cayman – Playa del Carmen – Cozumél– Key West – Miami, year round.

Southward—Los Angeles – Catalina Island – Enseñada – Los Angeles *or* Los Angeles – Enseñada – San Diego – Catalina – Los Angeles, year round.

Starward—San Juan – Barbados – Martinique – St. Maarten – Antigua – St. Thomas – San Juan, year round.

Sunward II—Miami – Nassau – Great Stirrup Cay – Miami *or* Miami – Nassau – Great Stirrup Cay – Freeport, year round.

As one of the largest and most successful cruise lines in the world, Norwegian Cruise Line makes it their business to know where and how people want to play. That's why you'll find this line offering cruises to the Caribbean's best-loved destinations aboard ships that feature nonstop and showy, often top-name, entertainment.

The flagship of the line is none other than the massive 69,500-ton *Norway*, the world's largest cruise ship, home to as many as 1,800 passengers. Six city blocks long, the former S.S. *France* has more than a million dollars worth of art on board, and features some of the biggest names in show biz in her huge Saga theater. If you like your entertainment intimate, you can play tête-à-tête in a dozen different lounges or "21" in a full-fledged casino.

The *Norway*'s smaller sisters are just as popular. NCL's *Skyward* sails on seven-night sojourns from Miami, while the line's smallest ship, the 14,100-ton *Sunward II*, features three- and four-night getaways to Nassau and the line's Bahamian Out Island, Great Stirrup Cay.

With the arrival in 1988 of the line's newest offspring, the 1,534-passenger *Seaward*, NCL altered the itinerary of several of its ships, sending the *Southward* off to California to compete in the three- and four-day cruise arena with voyages to Catalina Island, Enseñada, and San Diego from Los Angeles.

Longer cruises are beginning to increase in popularity and NCL is ready with its *Skyward*, which sailed for many years on seven-day cruises, then in 1988 began eight- and ten-day cruises to some of the more distant Caribbean islands.

To give repeat passengers an even greater number of port options, the line stationed its *Starward* in San Juan, where it sails on seven-day cruises to some of the Caribbean's best-loved ports.

As for its newest ship, the *Seaward,* that ship took over the *Skyward*'s western Caribbean route, plying the waters between Miami and Cancún with stops at Jamaica and Grand Cayman as well as the line's private Bahamian Out Island.

This conglomerate of cruisers got its start nearly 80 years ago when a seafaring Norwegian named Lauritz Kloster bought an 830-ton steamer to haul ice and coal between Norway and Great Britain. Ten years later that one vessel had been joined by a merchant fleet, seemingly invincible even during the tribulations of World War II.

In the mid-1960s the company, now known as Klosters Rederi A/S, began examining the opportunities for specialization and shortly established a U.S. cruise division, then called Norwegian Caribbean Lines. Over the years the leadership of this influential shipping company has passed from its founder to his son, Mogens Wiig Kloster, and in turn to his grandson, Knut Utstein Kloster, current board chairman of Klosters Rederi A/S.

In 1966 NCL brought the 11,000-ton M.S. *Sunward* to Miami, where she was the first ship to call this then-small port home. In those days the ship pulled into a berth at what is now Bayfront Park in the middle of downtown Miami!

People laughed. How could a shipping company be successful in a little port like Miami, which in those days was about as important a cruise center as Des Moines. But NCL was to prove them very, very wrong, as it turned its single one-class little ship into a fleet that today includes the largest cruise ship in the world.

With all those experiences under its waterline, the company has learned many things about its marketplace. It has used those lessons to keep its fleet filled with laughing passengers in search of fun and frolic on the high seas, some intriguing port visits, and enough rum punch to fill the Atlantic.

When it feels things are slowing up a bit, NCL may switch a few itineraries around to give its significant numbers of repeat customers someplace new to explore. Generally, however, you can depend on the ships to maintain regular schedules from Miami year in and year out, all year round. "White" ships in the fleet (the *Norway*'s blue hull has earned her a "blue" ship nickname) are switched about on different itineraries occasionally, but the vessels are so similar in ambience and size that you'll hardly notice the difference.

When NCL decided it might be time to try something really new, it just went out and bought its own island! Called Great Stirrup Cay, the island was one of hundreds of deserted Bahamian isles. It's deserted no more. These days you'll find it filled with sunning, swimming, snorkeling passengers having one whale of a time drinking in sun and rum punch on a one-day stop there.

Despite occasional surprises, the line sticks close to its successful formula which, in a nutshell, is seven-day Caribbean cruises to the best-loved ports and to a deserted sand-trimmed island. Just to keep up with the competition and to give the first-time and/or low-budget cruiser a taste of the seafaring life, the line keeps its three- and four-day sailer, the *Sunward II,* plying the party-ship waters.

To give the cruising world something to ponder, the line in 1982 became the first cruise line to advertise on network television. And what spot do you suppose it chose? A couple of minutes right in the middle of "The Love Boat," what else!

What surprises does this line have in store next? That's anybody's guess, but owner Knut Klosters has spent $1 million or more on construction of a model of a massive new cruise ship that will carry—are you ready—4,000 passengers!

On this line you pick ports more than ship (except on the *Norway*) because the ships are so similar in all things from cabin size to on-board activities. When

NCL hits on a good idea, it introduces it on every ship. Witness the ship's Olympic games, tee-up golf programs, western evenings, Fit With Fun fitness programs, jazz fests, and Dive In snorkel-scuba shore excursions available on all ships.

NCL's ships are kept very clean, and they're decorated tastefully, if not always elaborately. A $62-million refurbishing campaign recently updated décor in all the staterooms of every ship. We saw some of that renovation in its early stages and found it downright magical—from dated '50s to contemporary '80s décor in the flick of $62 million. Now the job's complete and these ships are certainly among the best-dressed ships in the Caribbean.

Cabins, with the exception of suites, are of just-average size, not what you'd call huge but big enough to share comfortably with another sailor.

NCL's *Sunward II, Southward, Starward,* and *Skyward* are not elegant or formal ships, but they're solid, well-maintained contemporary craft sailing to appealing ports. On them you will find dedicated service, some good, simple cooking, and a cosmopolitan international crew overseen by friendly Norwegian officers who speak perfect, delightfully accented English.

If you have only three or four days to spend, you can try life aboard the partying *Southward* or *Sunward II,* where spirits are free and the partying is nonstop.

If you have a week, here are some tips to help you decide.

The *Norway,* sailing to St. Thomas, St. Maarten, tiny St. John, and that private Bahamian island, is spectacular in both size and variety of entertainment possibilities.

The *Skyward* is relaxed and casual, and visits more ports than any of the other ships: sunny St. Thomas, old (and very new) San Juan, the silvery beaches of Barbados, and romantic St. Croix.

The *Starward* travels to less-frequented ports, visiting Martinique and Antigua.

Finally, the *Seaward* is for beach lovers. It offers you a look at sand-trimmed Ocho Ríos, a chance to dive in the colorful, crystal waters of Grand Cayman, and sun on the jet-set beaches of Cozumél and Playa del Carmen.

NCL stays right with the competition in offering free or very low-cost air fare from dozens of cities across the U.S. Your travel agent can help, and the line's brochures will help you figure what your cruise will cost.

Activities

NCL has found a very secure niche by appealing to people who want to visit some interesting sun destinations without spending a great deal of money. It provides informal cruises jam-packed with day-into-night activities designed to appeal to those who love a casual party. There are, of course, a couple of dress-up evenings aboard, but you'll wear your flip-flop sandals and T-shirts much more often than black ties or glass slippers.

Passengers aboard these ships don't seem to fall as neatly into categories as they do on some other ships. Most, one would guess, are middle-income, middle-age-bracket travelers, many taking their first cruise, and all of them ready, willing, and able to have a good time.

NCL provides for that with masquerade parties and Western Night barbecue-hoedowns on deck; with a hilarious ship's Olympics that involves, among other games, carrying a balloon between your knees and passing it off to another Olympic star; and with professional entertainment every single night.

Now on the *Norway,* well, that's different! On that ship you'll often find top-name entertainment as well as the line's high-kicking, spangled Sea Legs Revue, song and dance-sters that would do Broadway proud.

In recent years NCL has taken to theme cruises like, as an apt proverb puts it, a duck to water. A particularly popular theme focuses on sports stars, bringing aboard champion basketball, football, or baseball players who show and tell how they do what they do.

Golfers often resist cruises because no ship afloat has—yet!—installed an on-board golf course. NCL has thwarted those objections by plotting out elaborate events called "Tee-Up" programs which let players putt, chip, and drive aboard and ashore. There are on-board putting contests, lectures and workshops with professional golf instructors, video analysis of swings and putts—even 19th hole parties! For those who seek new golf course experiences with collector-fervor, the line will arrange reserved tee times on challenging courses on island ports its ships visit.

A similar emphasis is given to tennis and to a dive-in program that teaches you how to snorkel.

At regular intervals the line also features Fitness and Beauty Cruises, complete with lectures in sports medicine, fitness, health, skin and hair care, shoreside fun runs, and appearances by top sports stars.

Music fans can tune into country-and-western music, jazz, golden oldies, Big Band sounds.

Add to all that this new twist in theme cruises: hand-is-quicker-than sailings featuring some of the nation's top magicians.

NORWAY: To speak of this ship is somehow always to use awed, if not hushed, tones. There's no question about it: this stately grande dame can steal any show.

It's a trip just to tour this massive vessel and that's before she's even left the dock! How big is she? Well . . . once France's pride, *joie,* and national flag carrier, this 70,200-ton bruiser-cruiser is so large the *Sunward II* could fit inside just her forward engine room without touching any of the walls! To get this beauty on the road . . . er, sea . . . takes 24½ gallons of gas just to move the ship her own 1,035-foot length.

One crew member told us that when he met a friend in a corridor aboard one day, the other fellow welcomed him back from vacation. "But I wasn't on vacation at all," the crewman reported. "I just hadn't seen that guy aboard for three months!"

So huge is the *Norway* that the 800-person crew of this craft has an entire world of dining spots and lounges all to itself, while the 2,000 passengers aboard can choose from a dozen bars, two perfectly gorgeous dining rooms, a maze—and we do mean maze—of public rooms and boutiques.

This ship is so big they have international symbol signs to help you find your way around. And that's not to mention 63 ship's directories, each with a locator map of key shipboard facilities and an overview of each passenger deck.

Public Rooms

So you'll know how to read those deck signs, starting from top deck down they show a sunburst for Sun Deck, some pine trees and rippling water for Fjord Deck, a snowflake for Oslo Deck, a stylized globe for International Deck, some waves and a railing for Pool Deck, a Viking helmet for Viking Deck, a Norwegian flag for Norway Deck, lots of waves for Atlantic Deck, a palm tree for Biscayne Deck, and a jumping dolphin for Dolphin Deck. Got it?

When you find your way to the shopping center on International Deck, you'll discover not one small souvenir shop but an entire shopping center called International Promenade. Jade and Cartier gold, T-shirts and tennis shoes, aquamarines and aspirin, follies and furbelows, it's all there. You can browse in shops like Upstairs at the Downstairs, featuring everything from cameras to porcelain; Le Drugstore, for everything from basic toiletries to ashtrays; Dimensions, for swim wear and clothing; Scandavia, for those intricately knitted Norwegian sweaters, fashionable Swedish glass, or enameled jewelry from Denmark; East of Eden, for Oriental silks and jade; the Golden Touch, for 18-karat gold jewelry.

If you don't care anything about shopping, fear not. There are 40 or 50 other things for you to do. For instance, participate in the line's Fit With Fun program, that works its way through weightlifting, to brisk walks and runs, and aerobics. Try arts-and-crafts classes in flower making, ice carving, collage, or magic. Or play Bingo—sometimes the jackpot is in the thousands!

Listen to the cruise director expound on the next port. Jog around the one-eighth-mile track on Oslo Deck or on shore, using a handy Joggers Cruise News map provided by the line.

Take in a movie in the 500-seat theater or try trap shooting. Drop in on one of the multitudes of parties ranging from a Honeymooner's Champagne Party to a Grandparents' Party to an Unattached Party, or the ship's Olympic games.

You can play volleyball, nine-hole miniature golf, or golfball driving. Or take aerobic or social dancing classes, inspect the bridge, or try on-board horse racing, with bets of course.

You sedentary souls and anti-group-activity types can scrunch into an easy chair on one of the *Norway*'s huge enclosed decks and meditate on the history and glory of it all as you let the porpoises provide a floor show. Explore acres of polished wood rails and slate floors, marble-topped tables, and teak decks so long you think surely they must reach port hours before you do.

Stroll down one side of the ship and you're an entrepreneur exploring posh Fifth Avenue lined with ornate wrought-iron furniture. Walk the other side and you're a boulevardier on the Champs-Élysées. Or stop by the card room and its adjoining Henrik Ibsen Library, decked out in pale aquamarine velvet Austrian drapes set off by velvet-topped tables and find a like-minded player.

While you're having this marvelous time, rest assured that any youngsters you might have brought along will be doing even better. For the little ones there's Trolland, a playroom full of the child's equivalent of adult toys. It's open daily and when the ship's in port.

As you explore this massive vessel, whose funnel soars 17 stories high, you see a fortune's worth of artwork including beautiful tapestry weavings.

Three pools offer plenty of places to paddle, but if you're looking for the most swimming space, head for the pool near the Lido Bar—it's the largest sunning-swimming spot.

Will you starve? Not a chance! Begin with breakfast in the dining room, or on deck in the ocean breezes, or in bed. Lunch on a cold salad bar, hot dogs, and hamburgers at the Great Outdoor Restaurant, or go for the full sit-down multi-course luncheon. As the sun slides gently over the horizon, you sip your final pre-dinner (or post-sunbathing) libation in the West Indies Bar, the Windjammer Bar, the poolside Sunspots Bar, the Café de Paris, the North Cape Lounge, or the Lido Bar.

Then it's on to dinner in the dramatic formal Windward Dining Room, where tiny lights sparkle in the huge domed ceiling and subtle sconce lighting turns the room into a wonderland. Or in the Leeward Dining Room, where more than 500 diners can be accommodated in this two-story wonder that features a stunning brushed-steel circular staircase curving elegantly down from a second-level balcony to the main-floor dining area. Once upon a time this impressive dining room was for second-class travelers(!), while high rollers were assigned to the elegant Windward Dining Room with its wide and equally grand staircase.

Want something special that isn't on the menu? Seek and ye shall find it delivered.

Enough? Certainly not. After dinner it's on to the glittering sequined razzle-dazzle of the leggy Sea Legs Revue, equal to anything Vegas has to offer. Auditions for these shows' performers occur three times a year and are as competitive as anything *A Chorus Line* ever saw.

Or take in a show featuring Vic Damone, Shirley Jones, Diahann Carroll, Roger Miller, Buddy Greco, Jim Nabors, or the Smothers Brothers, among others. So top-notch is the entertainment aboard that seasoned cruise passengers book a cruise only after they've selected which performer they want to see.

There's a 15-piece band in the North Cape Lounge and piano players in the bars.

We don't think even the competition would argue with the *Norway*'s claim to some of the best entertainment afloat. The toppest in top-name stars make guest appearances aboard. If you love entertainment, you hardly need read further for you have found your dream boat.

The *Norway*'s Monte Carlo Room casino claims honors as the largest casino afloat, featuring 180 slot machines, eight blackjack tables, roulette, and craps.

Or make your way to any of a dozen lounges on board or to the A Club Called Dazzles disco where a rainbow-lit glass floor flashes, and the splashy neon trim is as contemporary as the silvery décor. While you're dancing, you can look through portholes into an illuminated swimming pool. Relax, the room's soundproof so you can sleep even if you're in a nearby cabin.

At Checkers Nightclub you'll find deep-red décor trimmed with onyx as black as night and a dance floor created with checks of black and white marble.

High ceilings, shining chandeliers, and great open spaces recall the vessel's venerable past in the ship's "living room."

From racquetball to clown-and-popcorn Carnival Night, from sequined showgirls to lazy afternoons on deck, you'll never want for something to see and do.

Cabins

Now primarily a seven-day sailer visiting St. Maarten, St. Thomas, St. John, Nassau, and the line's Bahamian Out Island, the *Norway* has recently been redecorated so she's more luxurious than ever. The cabins are all decked out in contemporary plaids in deep blues or soft earthy shades. The walls are creamy white, making the rooms seem larger.

In peak Caribbean season, which on this line runs from about February to April, cruise prices rise $50 to $75 in each of the 12 price categories. Category 1 is the highest-priced quarters and Category 12 the lowest.

So varied are cabins and prices, the mind boggles. There are fabulous suites with big separate sitting areas, billowing drapes, and touches of art deco in the décor. Those very grand suites cost $5,095 per person for a seven-night peak-season Caribbean cruise. There are slightly smaller versions of that with a king-size bed, Moorish windows, big wardrobes, and contemporary sofas for $2,950 per person—quite a drop.

As you move down to Category 3 cabins, you'll find junior suites with twin beds outfitted in the line's new-look tailored bedspreads with contemporary plaids in subtle colors. In these cabins there is often a love seat and chair in a separate sitting area, and needless to say, big windows. These quarters are $2,250 per person for a seven-night Caribbean cruise.

One category down, Category 4, in the ship's deluxe outside rooms, the cabins get a bit smaller and one bed serves as a couch during the day; some have a double bed. Outside cabins have a big window, however, and like all cabins on board, a closed-circuit television and telephone. A cabin in this price category costs $2,065 per person for a week's Caribbean cruise.

In four other categories, outside double rooms with twin or double beds or upper and lower berths, you'll pay $1,415 to $1,995 per person for a seven-night sojourn.

If you don't mind doing without a window, a superior inside room with twin beds is $1,795, the ship's mid-priced cabin. These come in a variety of shapes and on several decks, but NO83, NO79, NO80, and NO84 are among the larger cabins in this category.

Three categories of inside rooms with twin or double beds or upper and lower berths—Categories 9, 10, and 12—range in price from $1,295 to $1,625 per person for a week's peak-season trip.

You can figure that prices on board for the seven-day cruise range from a low of $185 to a high of $295 per person daily, suites higher.

A third or fourth person sharing a room pays $545. The single rate is $1,785.

SKYWARD: Perhaps the most unique element of the *Skyward* is an open-air, balconied lounge on the aft end of the ship. When this ship sails on its "Mexibbean" cruises to the Yucatán Peninsula/Cancún area, this tropical half-roofed three-story lounge is outfitted in palm branches and adorned with replicas of famous Mayan sculptures, one of which features a somewhat bemused fellow balancing a plant on his belly.

After many years as a seven-day sailing ship, *Skyward* in 1988 became the first NCL ship to sail on eight- and ten-day cruises. Quite interesting sojourns they are too, with stops in eight ports including, a visit to San Juan where you join or leave the ship for a cruise to or from Miami.

Public Rooms

Elsewhere on this 16,250-ton ship, look for a gorgeous Lucite etching of a ship under full sail and check out the brass sculpture in the Pot of Gold piano bar. In the Starlight Dining Room you'll find an impressive fiber wall hanging that plays perfect counterpoint to the soft pastel color scheme here.

For entertainment, head for the Lido Disco, which features tropical furnishings and a round steel floor. There's a flashy stage show too, and it has something going on every single night. In addition to a masquerade ball and strolling Mexican singers at dinner, there's a Mexican folkloric show to get you into that "South of the Border" mood.

Here, too, as aboard other NCL ships, one evening is devoted to a Country and Western Night. Jeans, boots, ten-gallon hats, sombreros, big belt buckles, and anything remotely western is dress of the day. Western dance lessons too. Barbecued ribs and chicken stave off midnight hunger pangs.

Dancing girls—and guys—put on a terrific show, similar to (but not as large as) the show aboard the *Norway*. It takes place in the Paradise Lounge, where you'll find an unusual color scheme that somehow successfully mixes burgundy and oranges around a parquet dance floor.

Just off that lounge is the Viking Bar, a smaller sipping spot that's a wonderfully intimate corner for private tête-à-têtes.

The Cumuku Bar up on Compass Deck is a pleasant hideaway, and in the Pot O'Gold Room down on Rainbow Deck you can pursue that glitter at the tables or machines. Or take in a movie at the ship's theater or go shopping in a row of gleaming shops and boutiques.

On every deck you'll find Fiberglas walls depicting that Mayan theme too.

Naturally you'll find a swimming pool on board—this one's figure-eight-shaped to inspire you to match it.

Cabins

Cabins on the *Skyward* are done in the company's theme colors: blue and beige checks with cream walls—very contemporary, very attractive. Most cabins are medium-sized, long and narrow with two twin beds separated by a nightstand and often backed with a porthole. There's a desk/vanity in most rooms, and of course more space in the suites.

Rates aboard are divided into 12 categories, from Category 1 (the highest prices) through Category 12 (the lowest). There are three seasons aboard this Yucatán sailer: the high season, roughly from late January to April and June to August; and the least expensive cruising season from April to mid-June and September to mid-December.

NCL has its rate categories divided up by decks, which makes prices a bit difficult to ferret out, but if you want to be on a certain deck of the ship you can see what's available on that deck quickly.

All cabins are carpeted, and have private bath, radio, and phone.

Let's look at the price of cabins for an eight-day voyage in peak season.

Top accommodations aboard are big suites on Boat Deck. These have a sitting room with a convertible sofa, lounge chairs, bedroom area with double bed, and *two* private baths. For one of these suites you pay $2,145 per person for the eight-day peak-season trip to Cancún, Cozumél, Grand Cayman Ocho Ríos, and Key West. Slightly smaller suites on this deck are $1,875 per person for the trip.

Inside rooms on this deck occupy space between the suites. For this good address the cost is $1,525 per person for a cabin with double bed and folding upper berth.

Outside rooms with double bed or two lower beds that can be pushed together to create a double are $1,225 to $1,675 per person. Inside rooms with a double bed and folding upper berth are $1,300 to $1,525 per person for an eight-day trip.

A cabin for four on the *Skyward* has upper bunks that sport a slide-and-pull mechanism that lets you lower them and use them for storage of extra luggage if all four aren't being used for sleeping. That extra storage space may not seem important, but it's surprising how much you can acquire on even a brief voyage.

Third and fourth persons sharing a cabin pay $495 for eight-day voyages in any season.

Single travelers pay $1,495 or 150% of the fare.

Port charges on board are $25 per person, adult or child.

Per diem costs range from a low of $153 to a high, excluding suites, of $209.

Very competitive air/sea programs are available from many cities in the U.S. to get you to Miami at little or no additional cost.

SUNWARD II: Once called the *Cunard Adventurer,* the *Sunward II* is the second ship of this name to sail under NCL colors. This *Sunward,* a 14,100-ton vessel carrying 718 passengers, was rebuilt and relaunched in 1977 when she was given her new name. Now she sails happily between Miami and the Bahamas, filled with sun-seeking passengers in search of a days-long "Bahamarama" beach party. They get just that at the line's Out Island, Great Stirrup Cay in the Berry Islands.

A bit smaller than some of the line's other ships, the *Sunward II* offers dining in the Sunburst Dining Room, decorated in earthy colors with chrome accents. Etched-glass dividers add sparkle to the room, which has some unusual banquette seating as well as tables.

Aboard all NCL ships you'll see some handsome Scandinavian craft work. On this ship the rya wall hangings on each landing are particularly dramatic.

Public Rooms

The Bahamarama Lounge is a goodlooking spot outfitted in burgundy upholstery and featuring a big ceramic sculpture as its focal point, lots of etched glass, and mirrored columns, plus a stainless-steel dance floor. In this room you'll watch the ship's nightly entertainment.

Another steel dance floor turns up in the Lido Café/Disco, and at horse-racing time some ornate carved wooden equines provide an interesting departure from the usual plywood nags.

Sunward's movie theater has an unusual and bright décor, and frequent top-quality films. There's also a big swimming pool and plenty of sunning space, plus sauna and massage rooms too.

There are some homey touches aboard—things like sheer white curtains trimmed in burgundy and tied back around the portholes—that make this a particularly cozy weekend home.

A large casino offers five blackjack tables and two banks of slot machines, plus the ever-present roulette wheel.

An interesting feature aboard is an artist who occupies a kind of second-story den overlooking the casino. He'll whip up a portrait of you in practically no time at all.

In the Crow's Nest nightclub you can pretend you're captain at a big ship's wheel. Outdoor types can sip at the roofed-in outdoor Buccaneer Bar, snappily trimmed out in navy and white.

Shoppers will enjoy the impressive shopping arcade studded with treasures from around the globe.

Cabins

Most of the 359 cabins aboard the *Sunward II* are average or small in size, certainly not huge, and sometimes tiny, although some of the outside staterooms are quite spacious, as are the suites of course. Cabins that are small are *definitely* small, however. Don't plan on spending a lot of time in one of those.

High season aboard this ship is roughly the same as aboard the line's other cruisers. On the *Sunward II,* however, add sailings from mid-June to mid-August to the peak season. Favorite vacation periods turn those months into an extra peak season for these short party cruises.

Let's see how much you will pay for a cabin in that peak season for a three-night cruise to Nassau and the line's private island. Four-night trips are $170 more.

Top price aboard will buy you an outside stateroom with two lower beds and sometimes an upper folding berth. Again, all cabins have private bathrooms. One of these rooms will cost $675 to $695 per person for the peak-season three-night cruise.

Three more categories of outside cabins with two lower beds or upper and lower berths are $575 to $615 per person for the peak-season cruise.

Three categories of inside cabins, ranging from Category 6 through Category 8, are $375 to $550 per person. Some of these rooms have two lower beds and some have upper and lower berths (your travel agent can help you secure the kind of cabin you want). The lowest price aboard is $375 per person for an inside room with upper and lower berths for the three-night cruise in peak season. You pay $20 to $25 less in other months.

Third and fourth adults and children pay $150 for a three-night cruise in any season or category.

Port charges on a three-night cruise are $19 per person; on a four-night trip, $21 each. Christmas and New Year's sailings are higher in price.

Per diem rates for a three-night peak-season cruise work out to a low of $125 per person and a high, excluding suites, of $205 per person.

SOUTHWARD: This 16,607-ton craft is very like her sisters, the *Starward* and *Sunward,* in size and ambience, and has an interesting new itinerary that is quite a departure for this ship which has for many years been sailing on seven-day cruises. Now, however, she's off on three-day adventures, NCL's first appearance on the nation's West Coast.

Based in Los Angeles, the *Southward* is now sailing on three-day trips that call in Ensenada and at the ritzy yachtsman's haven of Catalina Island. On four-day voyages the ship adds a stop in San Diego.

The *Southward* joined the line's fleet in 1972 and inaugurated a 14-day itinerary from the Port of Miami. In 1975 NCL bet its future on seven-day cruises and the *Southward* sailed on many of those before beginning this new itinerary from California. That itinerary will include shore excursions to Disneyland, Universal Studios, and Knott's Berry Farm.

Before it began that itinerary, the ship underwent a major renovation and now sports a spiffy new look in all public rooms and cabins.

This ship has an atmosphere very similar to that on the line's other vessels, and many of the same activities, ranging from a masquerade ball to a country-and-western evening and in-port dive-in snorkeling excursions.

Public Rooms

The big and shining El Dorado Dining Room offers a lovely view of misty green islands sliding by outside. One evening during your cruise you'll be treated to a fiery display of baked Alaska, paraded around the room in glittering splendor by waiters who sometimes balance the trays on their heads.

A recent addition aboard is a set of shining exercise equipment tucked away in a corner of the ship. You'll find everything here from an exercycle to chin-up bar, with weights you add on with the flick of a key.

The main lounge aboard is the bilevel Clipper Lounge, the center of attention each evening for showy entertainment flown in from one of the other ships or some amusing slapstick comedy provided by a hard-working staff.

A bank of slot machines is set off in a small separate room that's a favorite spot for some of the more dedicated gamblers: we watched one lady work two machines at a time every night and many afternoons every single day of the cruise! (Yes, she won—quite a lot!) Others were content to join a few blackjack players busy computing combinations of 21.

You can find the young and young-at-heart set rocking in the Crow's Nest Nightclub, a lively spot so dark we couldn't tell you *what* color it is in there. Nearby there's a small but impressive observation post where tall, tall windows offer you a look at the same view the captain's seeing.

For an even better captain's-eye view, take one of the ship's tours of the bridge.

Up on one of the wings that rise at the rear of the main lounge aboard you'll find a small library and a card room. Lovers should head for the opposite side of the ship to search out a tiny lounge that's small as a cozy living room, with comfortable couches and chairs, a piano, and usually few other people.

If you don't want to leave the sunshine on Beach Deck (which is where you'll find the larger of the two swimming pools aboard), pick up a hamburger or hot dog or danish at the casual Riviera Bar.

An energetic crew of all-American types keeps you going with all kinds of activities ranging from aerobics to arts and crafts. You can learn the merengue, that step-drag-step-drag dance so popular in the Dominican Republic, at dance lessons or try skeet shooting with one of the Norwegian officers. On shore, the cruise director can lead joggers in the best jogging directions and a couple of underwater enthusiasts will teach you how to snorkel.

Cabins

Cabins aboard are just about the same as on all the ships, although some are larger than average. An outside cabin will have twin beds, decorated in blue and cream.

There's a desk/vanity, a couple of closets quite big enough for this short journey, and plenty of drawer space to stow your belongings. Portholes are the traditional circles rather than the large windows found on some newer ships, but they're large enough to keep things bright, especially in the West Coast sun.

All quarters on board have compact private bathrooms, some with both tubs and showers, others with showers only.

On the *Southward,* prices begin with Category 1 suites and work down through Category 15 cabins, which are the lowest-priced accommodations aboard, yet are outside cabins! That's quite a departure, but there's a catch: the beds in these cabins are what the line calls "oversize" lower beds. Translate that to mean a bed that's smaller than the normal double bed yet larger than a twin. Definitely not recommended for light sleepers or chunky folks.

On this ship there are three seasons. Cabins do not differ much in size but do differ in price from deck to deck, decreasing as you go lower in the ship, farther away from the topside entertainment facilities. This means that cabins on Atlantic Deck will cost more than identical quarters on Biscayne Deck, one deck lower, which in turn cost more than the same quarters on Caribbean Deck.

Prices for a three-day cruise, departing Los Angeles on Friday and returning early Monday morning, range from $345 to $735; four-day trips are $445 to $885. Third or fourth persons sharing a cabin pay $150 for the three-day cruise, $195 for the longer voyage. Peak season in these waters, by the way, is May through September, with lower rates in effect in other months.

Single rates are $745 in the off-season, $50 more in peak season.

STARWARD: As the first ship to join the present fleet, the *Starward* bears a very close resemblance to the *Skyward*. She weighs 16,000 tons, and carries 740 passengers and about half that many crew. The *Starward* joined the fleet in 1968, two years before the *Skyward*.

This is the unusual-ports lover's ship. It visits the split-personality island of St. Maarten-St. Martin; the rarely visited port of Antigua; lovely Barbados, which many travelers number among the most beautiful of all Caribbean islands; and the French enclave of Martinique; as well as the shoppers' paradise, St. Thomas. Departing as it does from San Juan, the ship is able to cover five ports in a week.

If you're planning a trip on this one, add a couple of days before or after the cruise to wander the historic and ornately scenic streets of Old San Juan.

Public Rooms

There are two swimming pools on board, one near a pool bar on the Boat Deck, the other one deck down near the Lido Bar.

If you're looking for an intimate get-together spot, the Topsiders Lounge gets our vote. It's a lovely spot, high up on the Compass Deck.

Entertainment on board takes place in the Starlight Cabaret, a big room with tables and banquette seating in the center of the room and similar arrangements down both sides so everyone has a good view.

A few steps away is the Windows on the Sea Dining Room, where tables for four and six predominate. On this same deck, Cabaret Deck, you'll find the ship's small casino and the adjoining Reflections Lounge, an unusually shaped room that winds around a dance floor and has lots of windows through which you can spot real reflections.

There's even a two-level theater where you can catch that film you missed at home.

With a lovely name like *Starward*, it stands to reason that the ship would have more than a passing interest in those stellar glimmers. That's why you'll find on board an observation platform that's home to the *Starward*'s Star Planetarium! Now that's surely a first for a cruise ship.

Cabins

Cabins aboard are average in size, although larger outside cabins offer a bit of moving-around space. On this ship price is determined by the deck your cabin is on. As you go farther below in the ship, the price gets cheaper, although the sizes of the cabins do not vary. This means that a cabin on Atlantic Deck will cost you more than one directly beneath it on Biscayne Deck or Caribbean Deck.

Suites feature double beds and small sitting areas, but in some of the doubles the beds take up most of the room. Closet space is curtained off in some rooms, but there's enough wardrobe space to accommodate a week-long voyage.

All rooms have private bathrooms, some with tubs but most with shower only (no tub). Recently the line began renovation of this ship, so you now see pretty blue bedspreads, cream-colored walls, and coordinated draperies in *Starward* cabins.

Peak season on this ship is the same as on all the line's ships.

The fares below apply to a week's trip from San Juan to Barbados, Martinique, St. Maarten, Antigua, and St. Thomas, in peak season.

Starting at the top on Atlantic Deck, you'll pay top price aboard for a week's cruise in the comfort of a suite with a double bed, sofa, chairs, sitting area, and bathroom with both tub and shower. Suites like this are $2,145 per person, while somewhat smaller but similar accommodations (with a convertible sofa bed in the sitting area) are $1,945 per person for the week-long trip.

Outside rooms with a double bed or two lower beds that can be pushed together to become a double bed are $1,525 to $1,800. Slightly smaller outside rooms with upper and lower berths are $1,195 to $1,375 per person.

Inside cabins with a double bed and folding upper berth or upper and lower berths are $1,375 to $1,525 per person.

Third and fourth adults sharing a cabin and children pay $545.

Single occupants of a cabin for two pay 150% of the fare, although the line offers a program in which you pay just $1,645 for a week-long cruise if you accept any cabin assigned by the line.

Port charges are $35 per person, adult or child, and holiday sailings are higher. Low-season sailings are $110 cheaper in any cabin.

Per diem rates, as you can see, work out to $170 to $257 per person, excluding suites.

SEAWARD: In 1988 NCL introduced its newest liner, the *Seaward*, one of three new vessels it plans to debut in upcoming years. Built in Finland by the

Wartsila Shipyard, which has created many of the newest ships at sea, the *Seaward* measures in at 42,000 tons and carries 1,534 passengers off to the best-loved ports of the western Caribbean—Ocho Ríos, Grand Cayman Island, and Cozumél, with a rest stop at the line's private Bahamian island, Great Stirrup Cay.

Public Rooms

Focal point of the new ship is the Crystal Court, a two-story-high main entrance hall sporting a crystal-and-water sculpture with cascading fountain that splashes into a lighted marble pool. Stationed subtly around the showpiece are furnishings of mahogany and leather.

Designed to turn the inside out and vice versa, the new ship features two glassed-in staircase towers and floor-to-ceiling windows in the top-deck Palm Restaurant, where there's even more starshine glittering through a central skylight.

Observation lounges are popular at NCL, which features them in some form or other on all its ships, no less so on the *Seaward,* where you can sip something cool in a spectacular setting as you watch the seascape, unfolding before you.

On this craft, NCL chose to mimic the many blue hues of Caribbean sea and sky with contrast provided by muted shades of coral. Mirrored walls and brass accents add sparkle to the very contemporary environment the line has created aboard its newest creation.

In the first of several departures from the norm, the *Seaward* is introducing a new concept: a dining room called the Palm Restaurant in which you reserve a table and pay a moderate surcharge to dine in an intimate setting featuring an à la carte menu and white-glove service. Dining in the ship's two main dining rooms, the Seven Seas and the Four Seasons, is included in the cruise price, of course.

Those who like to do their nibbling in more casual surroundings can wander up to the indoor Big Apple Café or the alfresco East Side/West Side Patio, with perhaps a stop at the All Around the Town Bar. Sportswear and casual clothing are quite acceptable here, thus answering the prayers of those who don't want to dress to the nines for dinner every night. Both these cafés are open for all meals, and even for a midnight buffet. They're also a welcome taste for diners whose hunger pangs don't coincide with the set dining times in the main dining rooms.

Yet another departure is a wine bar called Gatsby's, which purveys vintage grape selections, caviar, and toney hors d'oeuvres, and is the penultimate spot for pre-dinner imbibing. During each voyage several wine tastings take place in this cozy spot outfitted in comfortable sofas and café tables.

For a livelier atmosphere, head out to the forward outdoor bar where Coconut Willy's whips up piña coladas and similar sins.

Finally, for the child in all of us, an ice-cream parlor with perhaps the most imaginative name of any room afloat: Lickety Splits.

Another rarity debuted by NCL on this new ship: strolling musicians in the two main dining rooms.

As is usual aboard NCL ships, the showiest of the ship's entertainment takes place in the Cabaret Lounge, which seats 740 passengers at sleek banquettes fronted by brass tables. A new show "Sea Legs Express" was introduced aboard this ship in 1988 and entertainment includes a full-scale Broadway production similar to the *Barnum* and *My Fair Lady* spectaculars that are now legendary in floating showbiz history.

At the aft end of the ship, the Stardust Lounge provides a backdrop for afternoon concerts, cocktails, and the line's popular late-night adult comedy shows.

A piano bar called Oscar's makes a good hideaway for quieter moments and sing-along sessions, while those who have dreamed of dancing beneath the stars can do so beside the top-deck swimming pools.

Those who opt for rousing entertainment can get out there and stomp at Boomer's, the ship's nightclub, while high-rollers sidle off to the Monte Carlo Casino where 155 slot machines, roulette wheels, and blackjack tables keep the night going long into morning.

Theme cruises featured by the other ships also appear aboard this new entrant to the NCL family.

Sports fans will be relieved to discover that they need not abandon their fitness programs even for an hour. There are two swimming pools and two whirlpools, one of which becomes a fountain by night. One pool measures in at 14 by 42 feet, a size NCL claims is the largest on any cruise ship, and we must admit that we're not prepared to dispute that. A "Dive-In" snorkeling center is right here at poolside, in easy proximity to instructors who will begin snorkeling lessons in the pool nearby.

A health center is equipped with all the latest in torture machines, and up on the Promenade Deck joggers can race around the entire ship, running their hearts out on a special deck surface designed to cushion impact. Another first here: the first shipboard Vita exercise course.

The Promenade Deck also is the spot for basketball, volleyball, skeet shooting, and golf driving.

For more contemplative moments there's a library and a card room.

Those of us who consider ourselves Olympic shopping champions will head straight for Everything Under the Sun, a terrific shopping arcade displaying every kind of temptation from crystal to porcelain, furs and jewels. Some of the world's top designers hang their creations in the clothing shops, and Fendi and Gucci are there to complete the look.

Cabins

In keeping with its accent on airy, inside-out design, the *Seaward* has many outside cabins. Two-thirds of the total of 767 staterooms in fact sport windows on the world. All cabins have telephones, televisions, and built-in hairdryers, plus beds that can be converted from twins to doubles in the flick of a steward. Four cabins aboard are designed for wheelchairs.

Room service is of course available, as are dry-cleaning and laundry services.

Fares range from $975 per person for inside quarters to $2,145 for elegant and handsomely appointed suites. Third or fourth passengers pay $495.

20. OCEAN CRUISE LINES

Contact: Ocean Cruise Lines, 1510 S.E. 17th St., Fort Lauderdale, FL 33136 (tel. 305/764-3500, or toll free 800/556-8850, 800/528-8500 in Florida).

Cruising Grounds: Caribbean, Orinoco River, Amazon River, Mediterranean (particularly the Italian coastline), Scandinavia, Russia, the fjords, the Baltic Sea, China, Indonesia, and Malaysia.

Itineraries: *Ocean Princess* —

IN WINTER: Aruba – Caracas – Tobago – Devil's Island – Amazon River – Manaus *or* Manaus – Amazon River – Fortaleza – Salvador – Santos – Puenta del Este – Buenos Aires – Florianopolis – Santos – Rio de Janeiro *or* Rio de Janeiro – Salvador – Fortaleza – Belem – Devil's Island – Tobago – Caracas – Aruba or reverse.

IN SUMMER: Scandinavian fjord and Russia cruises.

Ocean Islander—
   IN WINTER: Barbados – Bequia – Mustique – Palm Island – Orinoco River – Ciudad Guayana – Tobago – St. Lucia – Martinique – Barbados.
   IN SUMMER: Mediterranean cruises.

Ocean Pearl—Hong Kong – Shanghai – Qingdao – Yantai – Qinhuangdao – Beijing – Dalian – Pusan – Kobe or reverse; *or* Bangkok – Singapore – Bali – Mataha Island – Manila – Whampoa/Canton – Hong Kong or reverse; *or* Bangkok – Singapore – Malaysia – Brunei – Manila – Wampoa/Canton – Hong Kong or reverse; *or* Singapore – Jakarta – Bali – Indonesia – Kuala Lumpur – Bangkok or reverse, year round.

A new line that just got sailing in 1983, Ocean Cruise Lines is now headquartered in Fort Lauderdale but operates its ships, the *Ocean Islander* and the *Ocean Princess*, in the Caribbean and South America in winter, Europe and the Baltic in summer.

In 1987 the line teamed up with Pearl Cruises of Scandinavia, one of the pioneers in Orient and Indonesian cruises, and now operates that line's *Pearl of Scandinavia* as the *Ocean Pearl*. It is now the only ship operating year round in the Far East.

Built in 1967, the *Ocean Pearl* was once known as the *Finnstar*. Over the years it has been rebuilt twice, one in 1978 and again in 1981 when the ship was converted for deluxe cruising by a Danish shipbuilding firm. Now carrying 425 passengers and a Scandinavian and Indonesian crew, the ship underwent a multi-million-dollar refurbishment in 1988 when it became the *Ocean Pearl*. During that facelift 12 feet where added to the ship and all the interior of the craft was redone, right down to new names for the decks.

Now those lucky enough to have the time and money for a 14- to 20-day trip to exotic ports like China, Bangkok, Bali, and the like will find subtle reminders of the Orient throughout the ship, from the delicate pastels of the Orchid Room dining room to the teak and rare woods everywhere.

There's one crew member to every two passengers here, guaranteeing you drop-of-the-hat service. And there are now 12 new two-room suites aboard for those intent on going really first class. Prices range from $2,750 to $6,195, excluding suites, for the line's 14-day China Discovery cruise.

When you get a look at either of the sleek *Ocean Islander* or *Ocean Princess*, you will see what $25 million can do. You will, in fact, have trouble believing that these are older ships that have been revamped to quite glittering modernity. That's a tribute to the skills of Greek designer Michael Katsourakis, a man quite well known in marine décor circles.

Ports are a major selling point for this line, which visits a bevy of secluded Caribbean islands in winter and some quite entertaining European cruising grounds in summer.

Line officials say that although Ocean Cruise Lines' seven-day schedule, and therefore tempting prices, make the line equally appealing to first-time and seasoned cruise passengers, the majority of those aboard are likely to be travelers who have been on several cruises and are lured to this line by its unusual itineraries and small-ship ambience. Average passengers aboard, they say, are "in their 40s, high income, well-educated—we've had a dozen university alumni associations, for instance."

That's just the way the line planned it, encouraging those kinds of travelers by offering stops at small, exclusive Caribbean and European ports like tiny, idyllic Bequia, the beach-rimmed Grenadines, and the Orinoco River where the ship stops off for a look at Venezuela's towering Angel Falls.

"We don't want to compete with the big guys so we've tried to provide itineraries that are unique and in keeping with the size of the ships. Our passengers are people who don't want to be with a thousand other people," they say.

Aiming squarely at the upper end of the market, the ships appeal most to sophisticated travelers who have been around a bit and want their surroundings to be as chic as they are comfortable.

Because they are small, both ships, but particularly the *Ocean Islander*, are really more like very large yachts than the traditional pack-'em-in cruise ships. Crewmen are downright delightful fellows who go the extra mile to please passengers, who often become friends as well as customers.

Informality is a trademark of this line. You can, for instance, stroll up for a look at the bridge just about any time you like and you'll be welcome to take a look at what keeps things running. That doesn't mean, however, that there are no formal nights; it does mean you won't feel out of place if you don't wear a tux or long dress on the two nights that are officially deemed **formal**.

To avoid competing with the raft of ships that now depart from Florida, the line stations its two craft in Caribbean ports each winter. Which means you can get the mood going—or keep it going—with a few days' pre- or post-cruise stay in Rio de Janeiro, Barbados, or Aruba.

OCEAN ISLANDER:
Talk about tiny, now this is tiny! *Ocean Islander*, which measures in at just 5,000 tons, can practically guarantee you will never stand in a line, never wait for anything, and certainly never trip over 500 sunseekers scattered about the pool. They can make that latter guarantee with confidence since there are just 127 cabins aboard this small sailer, ensuring that there are never likely to be more than 250 or so aboard.

Originally called the *San Georgio*, the *Ocean Islander* was operated by Italy's Adriatica Lines as a freighter and passenger ship for years. Later it became the *City of Andros* sailing under the colors of Greece's Cyclamic Cruises. Now more than 30 years old, this ship certainly does not look its age, thanks to the $15-million renovation that occurred aboard.

Laid out a bit differently than its larger sister ship, the *Islander* has all its public rooms and dining room on two upper decks, the Sun Deck and the Promenade Deck, and its cabins on the next three decks down. What's more, it now goes one knot faster and is freer from vibrations following repairs that took it out of service for part of 1986.

Public Rooms

Every bit as glitteringly lovely as its sister sailor, the *Ocean Islander* is also similar to its sister ship in color and interior design.

Starting from the top, the Lido Deck is the spot for fitness fans who can work out on the equipment at the Fitness Center then whiz down one floor to the Promenade Deck to cool off in the pool.

On the *Ocean Islander* all the action's on the **Promenade Deck,** site of all the ship's public rooms. At the bow is the ship's main entertainment lounge, the Marco Polo Lounge, sporting a new hi-tech sound system. Here, tables and banquettes curve around a clover-shaped stage and part of the lounge arcs around in the opposite direction to become the Explorer Bar, a favorite before-dinner gathering spot featuring great views and a pleasant intimate atmosphere.

On this same deck is the Belvedere Restaurant, the ship's lovely main dining room, a study in peach with tables for four running down the middle and tables for eight set lengthwise to tall windows so everyone has a dinner view of sea scenes.

Buffet lunches, barbecues, and breakfast are served beside the swimming pool and near a cool pool bar.

There's a glass-enclosed card room next door to La Boutique where a glittering array of buyable baubles are displayed.

Naturally, there's a casino on board, and this one's also decked out in quite contemporary colors, up to and including those lavender-topped gaming tables.

Activities

Like the *Ocean Princess,* the *Ocean Islander* keeps its entertainment entertaining but not flashy. A multitalented staff comes up with all kinds of diversions from magic tricks to songs, hypnosis, dance, and the like, and there's always music for dancing in the Marco Polo Lounge or up top on the Sun Deck in the Peppermint Lounge and Piano Bar.

You won't find any lack of daytime diversions either. Daily Bingo matches get a lot of attention and attendance swells when the snowball Bingo event offers $1,000 or more for the winning card. Wooden horses, moved to the throw of the dice, create horserace gambling events and there are always blackjack lessons, chess, Scrabble, bridge and backgammon tournaments, trivia games, skeet shooting. Movies are shown on board each day too. On some cruises there are lecturers aboard to help you understand more about what you're seeing.

Theme evenings are a regular event too, with steel drum salutes to the Caribbean, Latin fiestas, and Carnival costume parties.

Cabins

Almost all cabins on the *Ocean Islander* are outside quarters with just a few inside cabins tucked away on three decks. What's more, almost all cabins are the same size, measuring in at about 125 square feet. Suites are bigger, naturally, but there are just six of them.

Rates vary some according to season, with the highest rates around Christmas and in February and March. You'll pay about $75 to $350 per person less in December and January. The same goes for the line's summer cruises, when the height of the season in July and August is the most expensive time of year; shoulder-season sailings in May and September-October ring in at lower fares.

To keep from driving you crazy with numbers we'll give you the highest fares, those applicable in February in the Caribbean.

All rooms have private bathrooms, each tiled and outfitted with an amenities basket. All rooms also have full-length mirrors, pullout desk tops, and 110-volt A.C. (that's standard American current), electric outlets for hairdryers and small appliances.

Quarters begin on Riviera Deck where most of the cabins are located, with a few others on the next two decks down, Pacific Deck and Caribbean Deck.

There are eight cabin price categories on board, from A, the top, to H, the least expensive.

Those Category A cabins are described as "deluxe" and indeed they are—large enough to include two beds, a large dresser between them, a convertible sofa, and a coffee table. Quite spacious, they have big windows and lots of closet space. For one of these you'll pay $2,195 for a seven-night Caribbean cruise.

Categories B, C, D, E, and F are too similar to warrant individual description, so suffice to say they each offer outside cabins with twin beds, probably outfitted in coral or light blue. You'll find a dresser between beds, plenty of closet space, and of course a window or porthole. Rates are $1,650 to $1,950.

Categories G and H are inside cabins. If it's one of these money-savers you want, you'll have to get your bid in early: there are only 16 of them on board.

Fares in these quarters range from $1,495 to $1,575 for a seven-day Caribbean cruise in peak winter season.

Those dedicated to double beds will find several cabins aboard feature that kind of sleeper, and some cabins also feature fold-away upper berths if there's a child or third person traveling with you.

Single travelers pay a 50% supplement on those rates, and a third person sharing a cabin pays 50% less on each rate.

OCEAN PRINCESS: The *Ocean Princess,* once known as the *Italia* and operated at different times by both Princess and Costa Lines, has like its sister ship been revamped by Greek designer Michael Katsourakis. Built in 1967, the *Ocean Princess* was treated to a $15-million stem-to-stern revamp in 1984. About twice the size of her smaller sister, the *Ocean Princess* measures in at 12,500 tons and carries about 500 passengers in 249 cabins.

Public Rooms

Quite a chic creation, this ship is a stem-to-stern study in modernity. In the *Princess*'s sleek Four Seasons Dining Room you'll find shining etched-glass panels playing backdrop to a peach décor highlighted by art deco touches. Tables for eight or ten are scattered down the center of this airy room while along the sides you'll find a marine rarity: cozy high-backed banquettes. Fresh flowers are here every day, often bright-red anthuriums that add a starkly elegant touch that fits right in with this bright, contemporary décor.

Not only the room is elegant, however. You'll also find quite a high-toned menu, with selections like beef Wellington, coquilles St-Jacques, pâté en croûte, duck à l'orange, and cherries Jubilee featured.

Perhaps the single most awe-inspiring feature of this ship is its treasure-laden shop. Stripped down the center of Riviera Deck's Rendez-Vous Square, the boutique is rimmed in wide windows that feature a hopelessly tempting display of topaz, emeralds, diamonds, silks, gold, and designer labels at bargain prices. There's an aquamarine-and-diamond necklace there that's . . . well, someday going to be, ahh . . . ours.

The open, airy feeling that characterizes the ship's dining rooms and shops is the single most distinguishing feature of these sleek new ships. Everywhere you look light streams through banks of windows that frame the sea beyond into hundreds of postcard-pretty vignettes.

Even the casino, which on many ships is a dark, back-roomy sort of place tucked away in a corner, on the *Ocean Princess* is all rimmed in glass and outfitted in blues and lavenders—right down to lavender-topped blackjack and roulette tables!

Most of the action aboard occurs on Riviera Deck, the ship's main public area. Here you can seek 21 in that glitzy casino or stroll to the opposite side of the ship and settle into a comfortable couch at Harry's Bar, yet another view-ful spot aboard.

So cleverly is color used throughout the ships that everywhere you look rooms ebb and flow into each other, their colors streaming from one room to the next blending and merging and changing.

Up on Riviera deck you can pull up a purple bar stool and settle in to gaze out through a bank of windows at the sea beyond. Here, too, is the Marco Polo Lounge, a multilevel entertainment area that slopes up at the entrance, then down to the stage so everyone has a good view of the entertainment. A rainbow of blues and pinks, this handsome lounge is reflected in mirrors, mirrors, and more mirrors with lots of greenery filling in the corners. Comfortable club chairs in shades of pink glow under contemporary chandeliers.

On the Lido Deck you'll find the Café de Paris, a study in bleached-wood floors and light contemporary rattan furnishings cushioned in heather blue offset by aquamarine, all very tropical and cool.

If you like informal buffet breakfasts and lunches, not even to mention midnight snacks, this is where you'll find them, served buffet style in a handsome room with some of the best views on the ship. The focus of the room is a lacquered white piano. There's a semicircular bar also decked out in that delicate heather hue, and beyond the big windows those same colors reappear in a wavy mural that forms the back wall of the swimming pool.

Even the deck chairs are color coordinated on this designer-labeled ship—they're strapped in navy blue to contrast chic-ly with blue mosaic tiles that trim the pool.

Those whose many trips to the midnight buffet must be balanced by an equal number of trips to the exercise floor will not be disappointed: the ship has a fully equipped health club.

Evening entertainment is not glitzy aboard small ships like these, but a talented staff performs everything from magic to hypnosis to song-and-dance numbers. There is, of course, dancing, which goes on until the wee hours in the ship's shiny-bright Raffles Piano Bar and Discothèque. A study in shades of coral and orange, the room goes around in circles—literally. Its windows are round portholes; the room itself is horseshoe-shaped and filled with comfortably rounded, cantilevered chairs and banquettes that follow the room's curves.

Cabins

You'll find cabins on every deck here, from sunny spots on the Lido Deck down to a large number of inside cabins on Capri Deck. No matter where you sleep, however, you'll find that your quarters are quite a respectable size, some of them actually larger than they were when the ship was built, thanks to extensive renovation.

The *Ocean Princess* sports a comparatively simple pricing system, with cabins ranging from highest-priced A category quarters to lowest fares in category J. There's a low season—usually a couple of weeks in mid-May and the first week or so of October, when prices are about $200 cheaper per person. All the rest of the year, however, prices stay at a single level for seven-day cruises, higher of course for longer Christmas and New Year's cruises or for bargain-priced transatlantic sailings.

Let's take a look, then, at prices and cabins from the top down. All cabins, by the way, are decorated in one of three color schemes—soft pinks or blues and bright oranges—carried out in bedspreads that feature wide stripes of color that merge softly into each other. Baths on board are quite modern, tiled, and come complete with towels in contemporary colors and little baskets of what hoteliers like to call "amenities" (translation: little bottles of shampoos, lotions, and the like)—a nice touch.

As usual, Category A cabins are top-of-the-line accommodations. On this ship that means outside staterooms with a convertible sofa, two beds, loads of closets, and lots of windows (four or more in some). Bathrooms include both tub and shower. There's plenty of stretching-out space in these attractive quarters found on Riviera and Promenade Decks. The fare in one of these beauties is $2,970 for a ten-day Amazon cruise.

Category B, C, D, and E cabins are outside quarters, comparatively uniform in size and scattered about on five decks from Lido right down through Belvedere Deck. Twin beds are the order of the day, although a few Category C cabins have double beds. While double beds are nice, perhaps mandatory for some, on this ship they may be tucked away in toward the bow where the ship curves. One we saw was smack up against a wall and looked less romantic, all things considered, than twin beds. Fare is $2,450 to $2,675 per person, double, for ten days.

Cabins in Categories F, G, H, and I are inside quarters, each with twin beds and shower in the bathroom. You'll be hard-pressed to tell the difference in size between the inside quarters and the outside, and indeed there may be none. We were inclined to prefer some of them to higher-price-category cabins, so if you're thinking about saving a few pence, don't be afraid of these inside rooms. Fare per person, double, is $2,030 to $2,275 for a ten-day Amazon cruise.

Lowest-priced category on board, Category J, is an inside stateroom with one lower berth and one upper one, not bad for anyone but particularly appealing, in both price and ambience, for single travelers. You'll pay $1,845 per person, double, for that category of cabin on a ten-day Amazon trip.

On this ship single travelers pay a 50% surcharge, a third person sharing a cabin pays 50% of the rate for that cabin, and children under 12 pay 10% of the fare.

Port charges are $55 to $125 on 7- to 19-day Caribbean and South American cruises.

21. PREMIER CRUISE LINES

Contact: Premier Cruise Lines, 101 George King Blvd., Port Canaveral, Cape Canaveral, FL 32920 (tel. 305/783-5061, or toll free 800/327-7113, 800/432-2545 in Florida).

Cruising Grounds: Bahamas.

Itineraries: *Starship Royale*—Port Canaveral – Nassau – Bahamian Out Island – Port Canaveral, year round.

Starship Oceanic—Port Canaveral – Nassau – Bahamian Out Island – Port Canaveral, year round.

Premier made its première in the spring of 1984 when it bought Costa's *Frederico C,* then painted, primped, and polished her up to present her to the cruise world as the *Starship Royale.*

As the latest entrant in the three- and four-day cruise marketplace, the *Starship Royale* was greeted with loud huzzahs by officials of Central Florida's Port Canaveral. They'd been trying for years to lure a cruise line to this small port hard by the Kennedy Space Center.

Rigged out in shiny red and topped by a white smokestack emblazoned with a P for Premier, the *Royale* steamed into port to begin year-round cruises to the Bahamas. Owned by Greyhound Corporation, the line is tapping what it sees as a lucrative market of 24 million Central Florida visitors who come here to visit famed Walt Disney World.

Premier has in fact worked out a package program in which you can spend three or four nights at sea with the dolphins and three or four nights on land with the Mouse.

Recently the line went and did it again. This time the purchase was Home Line's big *Oceanic,* a 39,214-ton beauty built in 1965 and among the first ships to be constructed especially for cruising, as opposed to transatlantic passenger service.

Premier's whiz kid, Bruce Nierenberg, figuring that once you've perfected a product you might as well exploit . . . ah, er, perfect . . . it, set about to turn the very big *Starship Oceanic* into the line's second three- and four-day cruiser. That's why much of what you'll see—from interchangeable panels in the dining room to slick, contemporary design and even lounge and cabaret names—are twin to the line's *Royale*.

These two cruisers even go to the same place, one departing just 30 minutes behind the other, their two red hulls creating quite a rosy picture when they pull into port in Nassau.

Many of the line's promotional activities are connected to Orlando's famed Walt Disney World, an entity we surely do not need to describe. We add, ever so humbly, that if you'd like to know everything there is to know about Disney World and EPCOT, we just happen to have written another book called *Frommer's Orlando, Disney World, and EPCOT* that has the complete scoop.

Premier has teamed up with the Mouse to offer a seven-night package that includes a three- or four-day cruise and three or four nights in a good hotel near Walt Disney World or, thanks to the line's new status as Official Disney World Cruise Line, on Disney property. As part of the deal you'll also get a three-day World Passport to the Magic Kingdom and EPCOT, tours of Spacesport USA (the Kennedy Space Center), and several other goodies on the ship for prices beginning at $450 per person for a week if you drive here, $540 if you want a rental car!

Premier is so thick with Disney creatures, in fact, that none other than Her Highness—blare of trumpets—Miss Minnie Mouse christened the line's new *Starship Oceanic*! A historic moment: the first time Minnie ever touched champagne.

Activities

Entertainment from dawn to dusk and well beyond is a mainstay of these three- and four-night cruises. Topping the list of diversions, however, is the line's new "It's Your Party, America" show, a star-spangled revue dreamed up by one of the creators of Walt Disney World shows and the Liberty Weekend celebration honoring the Statue of Liberty. Twelve singers and dancers use more than 70 costumes during the 45-minute production which focuses on cameo performances by everyone from W. C. Fields and Mae West to The Monkees and Charlie the Tuna.

When you're not watching that extravaganza, you can become a performer at aerobics classes out on deck, at the Sea Spa Health Center, which features all the latest in electronic gymnastics, or on the jogging track that encircles the Sun Deck.

If you want to see the stars *of* the sea, you can enroll in the ship's Splash Down snorkel program. They'll teach you how to snorkel in shallow water just offshore and reward you with an official Splash Down certificate.

You can nibble wine and cheese at a tasting, and find a variety of other entertainment in several lounges aboard each of the ships.

There are first-run films in the theater, big-band sounds in the lounges, movin' music in the disco. If you can stay awake until midnight, you can nibble at the special outdoor midnight buffets.

Nonstop diversions are a feature of most three- and four-day cruise ships, and these two cruisers are no exception.

There are some amusing diversions for you on shore as well. You'll be greeted by a cannon salute as you step ashore, and later a gang of marauding "pirates" will visit. You can also go on a treasure hunt to pirate Henry Morgan's cave.

STARSHIP ROYALE: Built in 1958, the *Starship Royale* is a 21,000-ton ship designed to carry 834 passengers. She's carrying those passengers to Nassau and an Out Island of the Bahama Islands on the three-day cruise, and increasing the journey by one day by spending an extra day at sea on the four-day trip.

They're going all-out to provide the best of seven-day amenities—and then some—to passengers on these shorter cruises. Bruce Nierenberg, who for years was an executive at Norwegian Caribbean Lines, says Premier wants to bring some of the elegance to the three- and four-day cruises with things like delicate little treats for tea time, "not a plastic cup and a Lorna Doone."

Themed dinners are another way they add that elegance, he says. Each evening is French or Italian or Caribbean or American Night, and everything in the dining room, right down to interchangeable paneling on the walls, reflects the theme. On French Night just remember to call your waiter François, not Frank!

Public Rooms

On board this craft you'll find lots of deck space, probably the single most important item to cruisers looking for a couple of days of Bahamian sunshine.

This close to the Kennedy Space Center it's only natural to think celestial thoughts, which accounts for the interplanetary monikers that appear on every public room.

If you're sailing with children, send them on up to the Bridge or Lounge Deck where the Big Dipper Ice Cream Parlor and Starfighter Video Arcade will keep them occupied tummy and soul.

One deck down, you can soothe away your tensions in a big oval whirlpool backed by a pool bar with a perfectly wonderful name: Mars Bar. At the bow on this deck, in the Apollo Observatory, you can get a look at the starry world that inspired the names aboard.

If you have something a bit more starstruck in mind, you might begin looking down on the Lounge Deck where the Starlight Cabaret offers an oval dance floor surrounded by a cluster of chairs and love seats. On this deck you'll also find the ship's casino, a big, wide-open spot with a bank of slots and the usual gambling games.

Major entertainment on board occurs in the ship's big Club Universe, where a rectangular stage is the focal point for a room outfitted in snappy colors. Up here too you'll find a small Satellite Café for snacks and buffets.

Not worn out yet? Okay, on the Promenade Deck you'll find the Saturn Lounge piano bar tucked away near the ship's big swimming pool. Down a deck, on the Restaurant Deck you can watch a film in the Mercury Theater, and down one more deck, on the main deck you can party at the Outer Limits disco, a slickly contemporary circular room.

You'll dine aboard in the Galaxy Dining Room, a long U-shaped room featuring many tables for four and six, a few for two.

Cabins

Cabins are about equally divided between inside and outside quarters, with 243 outside accommodations and 174 inside cabins. That's as much uniformity as you'll find, however. To take a look at the ship's deck plans is to wonder if there are any two cabins alike on this craft.

So different are they, in fact, that there are 11 rate categories, and a 12th to cover single-parent accommodations! (Here's where you'll really discover how wonderful your travel agent is.) To complicate matters further, the rate list is divided into three season departures. On-season runs roughly parallel to the prime season in Central Florida: June through mid-August, when the youngsters are out of school and visiting Disney World, and over Christmas. Off-seasons range from March to June and from late August to about December 21.

The following prices are for a three-night peak-season cruise. Figure $175 to $250 more per person for a four-night trip.

The top accommodations on this ship are outside suites on the Promenade Deck. These have two single beds and a sofa bed in a separate sitting area. They're decorated in tropical colors, and like all the cabins aboard, have a little wicker basket full of shampoo, fancy soaps, shower caps, and the like. The cost of one of these suites is $805 per person for a three-night cruise in peak season, $990 for a four-night trip.

Moving down a bit, Category B cabins are larger outside staterooms with two lower beds or a double bed. Four of these cabins (P17, P18, P19, and P20) have a queen-size bed. A Category B cabin costs $775 a person for a three-night cruise; $945 for a four-night trip in peak season.

Categories C, D, and E are standard outside cabins with two lower beds or a double bed. These accommodations range in price from $640 to $710 per person for a three-night cruise in high season.

Three categories of inside cabins with two lower beds, a double bed, or upper and lower berths are priced from $445 to $640 per person.

Among the better outside cabin buys on board, although they are narrow or oddly shaped, are Category H cabins, which have upper and lower beds. There are not many of these on board and they're scattered about on several decks. For one of these you will pay $445 per person for a three-night cruise in high season.

Single rates are $545 for an outside cabin, $445 for an inside cabin, in peak season for a three-night cruise.

Port charges are an additional $28 per person.

Third and fourth persons sharing a cabin with two passengers paying full fare are $190 per adult for a three-night cruise. For a four-night trip the fare is $295 for adults.

Premier has air / sea add-on fares from a number of cities.

STARSHIP OCEANIC: While that name sounds a bit on the hype-y side, the line swears that is really this ship's original name and the one that appears in ship's registry records. Whatever its name, this was and remains quite a showy craft, complete with two sensational swimming pools covered by what's called a "magradome" lid—it rolls back when the weather's sunny, or covers the pool so you can swim when it's raining.

Public Rooms

About twice the size of the *Royale,* the *Oceanic* these days bears quite a noticeable resemblance to its sister ship. Certainly the two travel to the same ports at the same time and feature the same activities, but they also share many outer-space names that first appeared on the *Royale*—Mars Bar, Saturn Lounge, Satellite Lounge, for openers.

Built in 1965, the ship had such large open areas that Premier was reluctant to change it too much or do anything to destroy the wide-open-spaces feeling of the ship. That's why those who have traveled on the *Oceanic* will find it different but won't have trouble finding their way around.

"We only had to contemporary-ize it," Nierenberg says. They did that by tearing out a few walls to open up several areas of the ship, then adding lots of bright colors "but basically we maintained the integrity of the ship," the line hastens to add. Showrooms and lounges are now in different places but the ship was not vastly altered to accomplish that, line officials say.

Talk about seeing stars! On this ship with its outer-space theme you'll find stars everywhere you look—stars on the doors of each cabin, stars on the carpets, stars on the floor, stars on the ceilings.

You'll find new teak planks covering the ship's ten passenger decks and a big new children's recreation center that's dream city for the small folk.

An indoor-outdoor facility, the children's center is, of course, designed to provide even more of a lure for families who want to team this cruise with a visit to Walt Disney World—a little comic relief for mom and dad, but no sacrifice for the little ones. Anyway, that center boasts its own outdoor deck, a learning center, an arts-and-crafts room, jungle gyms, and its own splash pool. Naturally there are many Disney touches in evidence here too.

For teenagers there's a teen center called Space Station where Disney films like *The Black Hole* and *Twenty Thousand Leagues Under the Sea* provide the décor theme. There's a disco built into the center too.

When the line discovered that passengers didn't want to give up even a minute of sunshine—or moonshine for that matter—they created a dining room called the Satellite Café. It's designed to handle large numbers of people quickly, yet give them something more elaborate to eat than hot dogs and hamburgers. You can also lunch outside at tables beside the swimming pool. If you're seeking solace from the sun, head for the indoor and informal Sunrise Terrace.

On this ship the pool bar's quite a fancy affair, all decked out in Casablanca style with paddle fans and sundry exotic accoutrements.

Dance fans will find a disco called the Galaxy Disco, a spaceship-y sort of place filled with galactic whirly-twirlies to get you rocking.

Hedonists will discover a gym, whirlpools, and a Jacuzzi spa on the Pool Deck, which brings us to a new renaming system aboard. Decks that used to have obscure names like Belvedere or Riviera are now plain and simple Pool Deck or Lounge Deck, named after the most notable feature on that deck.

At the bow of the ship the *Oceanic's* former first-class lounge, the Italian Hall and adjacent Mayfair Bar have been gutted, joined, and converted into a very big and glitzy room that seats 600 and is called the Broadway Show Room. Unlike the show rooms on many ships, it was designed specifically as a show room for major entertainers, so that's all that happens in this room. No Bingo games or port lectures occur here and sound, lighting, and seating is all designed to replicate Las Vegas show rooms.

The *Oceanic's* main lounge also was swept away and given a new life as a central forum, a Times Square kind of space you walk through to reach several rooms that surround it. Among those is the ship's Heroes and Legends Pub, a stained-glass-trimmed, beer-and-a-shot spot that, despite its British pubbiness, is dedicated to famous *American* heroes. On the walls here you'll find sepia prints of Babe Ruth, Lindbergh, and the like.

Other rooms located just off this central forum are the Mars Bar, a piano bar, several sitting areas, a gift shop, and the casino.

At the opposite end of the ship, the former casino and another small nightclub have become the Saturn Lounge, designed for quiet, more intimate moments.

To hear single entertainers, comedians, singers, guitarists, and the like, head for the Starlight Cabaret, a traditional shipboard main lounge decked out in mauves, blues, and chrome.

As you might have guessed by now, many different themes are visible throughout the ship—a Mediterranean, tropical ambience in the Tropicana Club; a glitzy, Broadway look in the main showroom; klieg lights, brass, and bronze in the central forum.

There's a 450-seat movie theater on board, and if numbers don't mean much to you, take it from us, that means big. It's equipped with both video beam and 16-mm projection equipment so the theater can show all kinds of unusual films.

Nierenberg calls the ship's burgundy-and-mauve dining room "really something special," and while he may not be the most unbiased source, no one would deny that this is quite a dramatic spot. For openers, it's two stories tall and now sports a spectacular chandelier towering over the center of a room liberally trimmed with brass. Large enough to seat 750 diners at a time, the room features the same switchable panels as the *Royale,* making it an easy matter to change the theme of the day, as they do, from Italian to French to Caribbean.

Cabins

Premier claims that the *Oceanic* has the largest cabins of any cruise ship in the world carrying more than 400 passengers. They also claim to have larger cabins and more space per passenger than the world's largest cruise ship, the *Norway.*

Claims aside, the *Oceanic* has always been known for its large cabins. Nothing has changed but the décor, which now comes in blue, yellow, red, or orange, your room décor matching the color scheme of the corridors on that deck and repeated in star-strewn carpets. If your room is blue, even your cabin door is blue. So if you're not color-blind, you'll have a really easy time locating your cabin—even after a long night in the disco.

Premier has kept this ship's smashingly beautiful veranda apartments and added contemporary touches like double and queen-size beds.

Prices are identical to those on the line's *Starship Royale.*

22. P&O / PRINCESS CRUISES

Contact: P&O / Princess Cruises, 2029 Century Park East, Los Angeles, CA 90067 (tel. 213 / 553-1770 or 553-7000, or toll free 800 / 821-0522).

Cruising Grounds: Panama Canal, Caribbean, Mexico, Alaska, Orient, Europe, South Pacific.

Itineraries: *Pacific Princess—*
IN FALL, WINTER, AND SPRING: San Juan – St. Maarten – Martinique – Mayreau – Barbados – Antigua – St. Thomas – Miami, or return same route.
IN SUMMER: Mediterranean cruises.

Island Princess—
IN SUMMER: Vancouver – Ketchikan – Juneau – Skagway – Glacier Bay – Columbia Glacier / College Ford – Whittier, or return same route.
IN WINTER: Miami – St. Maarten – Mayreau – Martinique – St. Thomas – San Juan, or return same route.

Sun Princess—
IN SUMMER: Vancouver – Juneau – Skagway – Glacier Bay – Ketchikan – Misty Fjords – Vancouver.
IN WINTER: Los Angeles – Cabo San Lucas – Mazatlán – Puerto Vallarta – Zihuatanejo / Ixtapa – Acapulco, or return same route.

Royal Princess—
IN SUMMER: Vancouver – Juneau – Valdez – Columbia Glacier – Seward – College Fjord – Glacier Bay – Ketchikan – Vancouver.
IN FALL, WINTER, AND SPRING: Acapulco – Panama Canal – Cartagena – Aruba – Martinique – St. Thomas – San Juan *or* San Juan – St. Thomas – St. Maarten – Martinique – Curaçao – Panama Canal – Panama City – Acapulco.

Sea Princess—
IN FALL, WINTER, AND SPRING: Singapore – Bali – Darwin – Whitsunday Islands – Brisbane – Sydney *or* Sydney – Bay of Islands – Auckland – Tonga – Fiji – Sydney or Sydney – Bay of Islands – Auckland – Fiji – Pago Pago – Bora Bora – Moorea – Papeete, or return same route; *or* Hong Kong – Canton – Manila – Borneo – Bangkok – Singapore, or return same route; *or* Hong Kong – Beijing – Dalian – Yanta – Shanghai – Pusan – Hiroshima – Kobe, or return same route.
IN SUMMER: Vancouver – Juneau – Skagway – Glacier Bay – Ketchikan – Misty Fjords – Vancouver.

Born in the early 1800s, the Peninsular and Oriental Steam Navigation Company grew and prospered over the years until today it owns and operates some of the finest ships afloat and is England's largest passenger line. In fact it was on P&O ships that a word you have heard many times was born: posh. Although posh now means something elegantly upper crust, the word has some very humble beginnings as nothing more than a four-letter designation stamped on certain steamship tickets. That POSH stamp on an Egypt to India ticket indicated the ticket was the possession of a passenger traveling Port Out, Starboard Home, the coolest, and thereby best, cabins on board.

A new arrival in this hemisphere is P&O's *Sea Princess,* formerly called the *Kungsholm,* which turned up in Fort Lauderdale's Port Everglades in the fall of 1985, sailed one season on seven-day cruises to the Caribbean, and headed for a major renovation. Now marketed by Princess Cruises, the ship was sent off to the facelift factory to be brought up to the line's rather demanding decorative standards. All is now changed throughout this 20+-year-old ship, which was transformed into a shining, bright new craft in 1987.

Much better known in North America is the P&O-owned Princess Cruises. Princess may in fact be the best-known line in the world, thanks to television, for Princess is none other than . . . blare of trumpets, the "Love Boat" line!

Now, let's get what you really want to know right up front here. No, Gopher and Captain Stubing and Julie and Doc and Isaac are not real people and they do not spend their nonfilming hours working on the *Royal Princess, Island Princess,* the *Pacific Princess,* or the *Sun Princess*. Travel agents tell us it's downright amazing how many people are *crushed* to discover that the stars of "Love Boat" do not actually work on one of the Princess ships! Which says a great deal, of course, for the talented performances staged by the "Love Boat" crew of actors in the series.

Now that we've crushed your fondest dreams, let us add that you can sometimes see the stars who play those parts on board one of the Princess ships. They go aboard occasionally for promotional filming.

Even if you don't see your favorite stars on board, you'll hardly notice the difference—and hardly care. On these ships Gopher's equivalent actually does wear those knee socks and Bermuda shorts, although he's more likely to have a British accent than an American one.

What's more, these ships are downright gorgeous. They're contemporary to a fault, as bright and airy as a garden room and as elegantly appointed as a penthouse.

You'll feel like Midas aboard one of these showboats as you journey off to ports in Alaska, the Caribbean, and Mexico.

If you're looking for Caribbean sunshine your choice will be the *Island Princess* or the *Pacific Princess*. From October through May they sail on cosmopolitan seven- and nine-day journeys from Miami or San Juan.

Meanwhile the *Sun Princess* does what her name suggests. She sails in sunny Mexican waters from October through mid-May.

In mid-May the ship leaves Mexico to join other Princess ships in Alaskan waters. There she sails on seven-night trips from Vancouver to Juneau, Skagway, Glacier Bay, Ketchikan, and Misty Fjord.

The *Pacific Princess* embarks on a variety of itineraries during the year. From January through March she cruises the Caribbean, and sometimes sails northern Europe and the Mediterranean in summer and fall.

Each of the ships breaks its steady pattern with one or more cruises of 9, 10, 11, or 14 days, and on some sailings you can combine voyages to create a two-week round-trip cruise.

So let's take a look at this famous Love Boat line and see if this is where your cruise future sails.

ROYAL PRINCESS: Princess Cruises has a marine lock on imposing staircases, but aboard the *Royal Princess* they've even managed to outdo themselves! Perhaps the most heralded staircase afloat, that arcing sweep of risers earned gallons of ink when the ship debuted in November 1984 and has seen many a grand entrance in ensuing days.

Perhaps the most notable of those dramatic entrances were made by the "crew" of television's "Love Boat"—Gopher, Doc, Vicki, and the rest—who all were aboard the inaugural cruise and filmed segments of their popular show on this sleek new craft.

That fancy glass- and brass-lined staircase that soars up through two stories of the ship and is festooned with flying bronze-and-steel seagulls is without question the single most riveting fixture of this ship—but it is certainly not the *Royal Princess's* only attraction.

A very showy ship indeed, the 1,200-passenger *Royal Princess* is a study in avant-garde ship design. For openers, every cabin has a window on the world for one very unusual reason—on this ship *all* the cabins are outside quarters, a claim no other ship in the world can make.

In fact there seem to be windows, and the gorgeous views that go with them, everywhere you look on this quite dazzling cruise craft. You can watch the view go by as you work out on the ship's elaborate exercise equipment. You can gaze at mountainous tropical islands as you sip a cool one in the cozy-elegant splendor of the Princess Court lounge. You can pull a chair up to a mosaic-tile table in the window-lined Lido Café and dine while the world slides by outside a bank of windows. For those with a touch of claustrophobia, this ship should be heaven.

Jaded would be the soul who is not impressed by the spacious openness of this new cruise ship, which measures in at 45,000 tons. At $200 million it was, at the time of its construction, the most expensive cruise ship ever built and is likely to hold that record for a few years yet. Naturally, a ship with such a regal name needed a royal christening, so the honors were done by none other than Her Royal Highness, the Princess of Wales, the glamorous bride of Britain's Prince Charles.

Public Rooms

Life aboard the *Royal Princess* is first class all the way. Outside you can romp over two acres of teak decks that sport pools, pools, and more pools. There are whirlpools and spa pools, a lap pool, a freshwater pool, a saltwater pool, heated pools, and cool pools. Most spectacular of all is a five-pool combination surrounded by live tropical plants—well, what else but a Hollywood set would you expect from a California-based ship?

While it is Hollywood-showy, the *Royal Princess* is certainly not Hollywood-garish. Soft, subtle colors abound from the beige tub chairs in the two-story Riviera Club to the blue-and-white patterns in the airy Lido Café.

Perhaps the single most glittering room aboard the *Royal Princess* is the Horizon Lounge, where you can indeed see the horizon—in every direction! Tracing a full circle, the room is edged by tall sloping windows that offer dozens of different looks at the passing scenery.

The best combination of glamour and intimacy aboard is the Riviera Bar where bright-red chairs and couches are played off against muted shades of gold. Overhead a mirrored ceiling glitters. On the opposite side of the ship the Terrace Room welcomes you to yet another inviting gathering place.

Dining takes place in the curvilinear elegance of the Continental Dining Room. A bilevel spot trimmed with arcing brass rails and lined with windows, this handsome contemporary dining room has tables for two for those who want to talk only to each other, and larger tables of four, six, and eight for those in search of dining companionship. Waiters are togged out in formal attire and are quite skilled at dramatic tableside preparations of such culinary adventures as fettuccine Alfredo, steak tartare, crêpes Suzette, and cherries Jubilee. And one night is always dedicated to that cruise-ship flaming favorite: baked Alaska.

Activities

As on all this line's ships there's never any lack of diversions.

Evenings, the ship's big circular International Lounge is the setting for elaborate entertainment. Princess has a team of professional writers, choreographers, customers, and arrangers who no sooner finish working out the 35 or more costume changes for one show than they begin working on another production.

Gamblers can try their skills, or their luck, whichever prevails, in the ship's Crown Casino, a large gaming center complete with blackjack, craps, and slot machines.

Those whose taste in card games is somewhat more esoteric can find likethinkers and head for the ship's handsome Bridge Lounge where Scrabble, Trivial Pursuit, and other board-game players congregate. On the opposite side of the ship, a small library calls to those who have been waiting all year for the chance to curl up with a good book.

Shopping doesn't usually qualify as a shipboard activity, but it does on this ship. Right next door to the casino is the ship's glittering Princess Boutique, a very spacious showy shop stocked with a wide variety of irresistibles from T-shirts that proclaim you as royalty to leather, perfumes, jewelry, sports clothes, you name it.

Film fans can be found in the Princess Theater on Riviera Deck, while shuffleboard and table tennis enthusiasts can bat a few around up on Caribe Deck where one whole end of the deck is reserved for those kinds of fun and games.

Theme dinners are a specialty of the ship, with ethnic specialties featured at Italia de Sera, La Nuit Française, and Ye Olde England nights. To go with it the ship stocks 10,000 bottles of wine.

Cabins

From the moment you open your stateroom door by slipping a plastic "key" into the coded lock, you'll know you're in a modern place indeed.

If you've got a room with twin beds and you want togetherness, *voilà*! just a couple of flips and you've got a queen-size sleeper. During the day when you'd just as soon have the space as the super-sleeper, no problem—one bed folds into a wall so you can spread out in your space. Every cabin has a dressing table with three mirrors that let you see all sides of yourself and bright lights that let you turn the truth to your advantage.

You'll find lots of wood aboard, a detail that required special fire-prevention building techniques. The drawers in the dressing tables are wood, for instance, and there are three closets large enough to accommodate even the most elaborate wardrobe. You'll even find a self-service laundry on board to keep that wardrobe as elaborate on debarkation as it was on embarkation.

Rooms also sport color televisions with an information channel to let you know what's going on aboard, plus four off-air channels, two video channels, and a live channel.

If you're a midnight snacker too lazy to hit the midnight buffet, no problem. Just stock your room's mini-refrigerator and you're ready for any snack attack.

In the bathrooms the line seems to have thought of everything: there's even a retractable clothesline. You'll also find soft lights, a big three-way mirror, tile floors, and typically American showers. All baths have both tub and shower.

If price is no problem, you can sail away amid the elegance of a suite. Some of those are furnished in leather and every one of them offers you a chance to get the absolute most from the sun on your private veranda overlooking the sea.

Quite a number of other cabins also have private verandas, and as we mentioned before, all the rooms are outside quarters so all have windows. Some, however, have the view blocked by the ship's lifeboats so you get a break on the price in those rooms. Once you get down to the lower price categories, however, you'll find very little difference in cabin size.

To give you an idea what a cruise aboard this sleek new ship will cost, here's a look at prices for a ten-night Alaska cruise aboard the *Royal Princess*.

There are 12 price categories aboard this ship, topped by Category AA, very large luxury suites with separate sitting room, floor-to-ceiling windows, and outside veranda. Next come four price categories of slightly smaller suites and rooms, all with private verandas, followed by three price categories of twin rooms, all of which have twin beds that can be converted to a queen-size sleeper. The four lowest-priced categories are all for cabins in which the view is "moderately," "partially," or "largely" restricted or obscured by safety equipment.

On that ten-night Alaskan cruise, you'll pay $7,130 per person for the best suites on board, $3,350 to $5,100 for Category A through D cabins, which the ship calls "deluxe" rooms with verandas.

Category E, F, and G cabins are twin rooms, no verandas, ranging in price from $2,700 to $3,250; while Categories I, J, and K, with restricted or nearly obscured views from cabin windows, are $2,100 to $2,650.

You can see that that works out to per diem charges that top out at $713 pe person and range down to $335 to $510 per person for top-priced cabins with sitting rooms and verandas. From there down in price, per diem rates range from $210 to $325. Yes, they're high, but this is quite a spiffy ship which figures that its first-class service and surroundings entitle it to charge premium prices.

ISLAND PRINCESS / PACIFIC PRINCESS:
As you might have noticed, we come to a bit of a departure here, describing two ships at once. That's because these two vessels are twins. What you find in one is found in the other, right down to the last lobster fork.

Both were built in West Germany, both are 550 feet long, weigh 20,000 tons, and carry 630 passengers plus 352 in the crew. Both have seven beautiful passenger decks. You may find a few color differences here and there, but the only real difference between the two is their itineraries.

Launched in 1974, the *Island Princess* carries 626 passengers off to what her name suggests—islands—all winter long, switching to Alaska in summer. Her sister ship, the *Pacific Princess,* was launched a year later.

If you watched "Love Boat" occasionally, by now you probably recognize the emerald-green and royal-blue Princess logo—a female face with streaming hair emblazoned on the ships' soaring funnel.

Once you've been aboard a craft sporting that logo on her smokestack, you'll be convinced that it really is royalty pictured up there!

Activities

Speaking of razzle-dazzle, wait until you see the entertainment here. Beautiful women and handsome men dancing and singing in full-production revues featuring some of the loveliest costumes afloat: not only glitter but beautiful feathery headdresses, period costumes, top hat and tails, professional singers, dancers, comedians, magicians, special lighting and musical scores, the lot.

If a cruise without a little casino action is unthinkable, rest easy. You can play the slot machines aboard until your biceps rebel, or try craps, roulette, or blackjack.

On board the *Princesses,* you'll never lack for things to do, from the early-morning deck walk to aerobics, dance classes, even a workout in the gym if you like. Bingo and backgammon, trap shooting or a ship tour, flambé cooking demonstrations or afternoon tea—it's all there to keep you every minute as jammed or as lazy as you like.

Public Rooms

Among the things that will convince you these are royal ladies indeed is the two-storied magnificence of the Pursers' Lobby with its glamorous staircase sweeping down from a mezzanine to a wide reception area.

Every bit as showy as any modern hotel lobby you've ever seen, this gleaming deck exhibits the loveliest architectural design afloat. Overhead, subtle lighting gleams down on bright-blue carpeting and accent lights focus on a shining contemporary sculpture. All around you, glass soars to the ceiling and transparent surfaces gleam.

In the purser's office here you'll meet smiling faces prepared to produce all the information you need to know about anything on the ship. Shoppers will quickly find this spot too—a showy glass-fronted boutique here offers treasures from around the world.

After that glamorous introduction, sweep majestically (Loretta Young–Bette Davis style fits right in here) up that grand staircase. On the mezzanine above you'll find a long, library / writing room just begging for you to curl up with a good book or to get some of those postcards written. Nearby are beauty salons and barbershops, and the ship's photo studio.

Both these decks, Fiesta and Aloha, are lined with cabins that run down both sides of the deck, with some inside quarters tucked away in the center (more on that later).

One deck up, the Riviera Deck, is where all the fun begins. Here you'll find the handsome Carousel Lounge, where things go around in circles, literally and figuratively. Comfortable couches and chairs in subtle tones fan out in a wide arc from the circular dance floor fronted by a stage. Off in a corner you can huddle with new friends in the Carousel Bar.

Amidships you'll find the showy Princess Theater, where both ships present what the line calls its Princess Discovery programs. Elsewhere these are known as port introductions, but on board this ship the cruise directors use slides and movies as well as words to tell you a little about the history and culture of each destination. The multilevel theater also doubles as a movie theater.

Flanking the theater are two wings in which you'll find on the port side the International Lounge with an arching bar, on the starboard side a matching reverse image of that lounge, this one called the Bridge Lounge. Both are wonderful places to watch passing scenery, both inside and out.

Amidships is the Pirate's Cove Bar, which by night becomes an action-packed disco.

While you're up on the Riviera Deck, walk toward the aft end of the ship and have a look at the Carib Lounge (called the Pacific Lounge on the *Pacific Princess*). Here's another sweeping staircase, this one joining this airy lounge to the smaller Terrace Room up on the Boat Deck. If you don't look beyond the soaring wall of glass here, you could swear you're in some posh penthouse lounge in Manhattan sipping a few while below the world scurries about on its mundane, trivial business.

Look around you and you'll see lovely aquamarine sectionals in channeled fabrics offset by creamy chairs, lots of shining chrome, a gleaming dance floor and stage. Slim glass panels soar two stories high to enclose both this lounge and the Terrace Room above, offering both a view out across a swimming pool and tanning deck to miles of glittering ocean beyond.

On the port side there's a lovely boutique where shoppers can lose themselves among the treasures after depositing nonshopper companions in cozy seclusion just outside the doors in the Veranda where they wait in royal splendor while gazing at nature's floor show slipping past outside the windows.

And there's a swimming pool here on the Riviera Deck, just outside the Carib / Pacific Lounge.

Up on the Sun Deck, amidships is the ship's cloverleaf (well, three-leafed clover) Crystal Pool swimming hole, a beautifully designed splasher that features a sliding cover called a Sun Dome. Naturally, sun is the name of the game on every cruise, so that dome remains open most of the time, closing only if you-know-what falls from the sky.

You'll also find another set of slot machines up here on the Sun Deck not far from a spot with the lovely name of Starlight Lounge. This is something to see: sunlight streaming through a curving wall of glass and glinting off the latest in contemporary chrome furniture in creamy earthtone colors, glass tabletops, lots of growing things, a sweeping curve of bar, and a view that goes on forever. Also, don't miss the elaborate and perfectly gorgeous buffets on deck either.

That brings us ever so neatly to dining on board. Despite its British officers and crew, the ship has Italian personnel in the kitchen and dining room. Princess Cruises has a very good reputation for providing excellent cuisine, and pasta lovers certainly will never go hungry. Nor, of course, will anyone with five meals or snacking sessions plus midnight buffets available.

You'll dine in the Coral Dining Room, a handsome spot on either ship. You'll find quite a few tables for two aboard either ship, even more tables for four, fewer for six, all with small dome-shaded table lamps. International nights are celebrated each night aboard the ship. Some nights your waiters will turn up wearing French berets and serving soupe à l'oignon and peppered entrecôte. Another night they'll be serving beef Wellington, roast beef, and Yorkshire pudding, or celebrating Italy with creamy fettuccine Alfredo.

Cabins

On these ships the staterooms are comparatively uniform in size and shape, although naturally the more you pay the more space you get.

Basically there are three configurations of cabins aboard. First of these is an outside or inside twin-bedded room with a sofa that converts to a bed by lifting off a cover and bolster, plus a recessing lower bed that folds neatly into the wall and out of sight during the day.

Next up in luxury is a "deluxe" outside twin-bedded room with two beds that convert to sofas for daytime sitting, plus a couple of chairs and a small table.

Finally, the top-of-the-line cabin is a deluxe suite with twin beds, a separate sitting area, which includes a sofa that can be converted to a bed (and curtained off for privacy), plus a table and chairs for snacktime. These are fancy quarters like the ones you see on the television show.

All cabins have private bathrooms with a shower, and the more elaborate have tubs as well. A music system piped into your room provides music if you want it, and all cabins have wall-to-wall carpeting and telephones. They're decorated in handsome colors, many of them deep greens or corals offset by subtle contemporary prints. The furniture has clean contemporary lines, often with brass trim, and every room has a dresser / vanity / desk combination with a big mirror. There's plenty of closet space too, and lots of light through big rectangular windows.

Naturally, with cruises of such different lengths the rate schedules are lengthy. Let's just look, however, at prices for a week-long cruise aboard the *Pacific Princess* to the Mexican Riviera. You will pay proportionately more for longer cruises, and also for a week-long voyage on the *Island Princess* Alaska cruises.

Rates on both ships are divided into ten price categories, ranging from those deluxe suites at the top of the price range to inside twin rooms at the bottom of the range.

On the *Pacific Princess* nine-night Caribbean cruises there are two fare seasons. You will pay less if you can plan to travel in January or late March through mid-April, slightly more in February and March or November through mid-December.

Suites come in two configurations, one with a separate sitting room and one slightly more compact with just a sitting area. Both have refrigerators. For one of these two kinds of cabins you'll pay $2,930 to $3,320 per person in the more expensive sailing season.

Singles are provided for on these ships as they are on few others. On both ships a number of cabins are designed for those traveling alone. For one of those outside rooms, which also feature in-room refrigerators, single travelers pay $2,870 to $3,020, depending on season.

The "deluxe" rooms, inside or outside, cost $2,300 to $2,640 per person in high season for a nine-night Caribbean cruise. As you can see, you can save quite a bit of money if you're willing to settle for an inside cabin. There are very few of these in this price category, by the way, so you'd do well to book as far in advance as possible if you're hoping for one of these rooms.

Most of the cabins on the ship are located on Aloha and Fiesta Decks. On these decks you will also find the more moderately priced cabins, those in price Categories F to K (A is the highest price category). Outside twin rooms will have two beds and a shower in the bathroom. They're not as large as those higher-priced staterooms you've just been reading about, but as ship's cabins go they're spacious. For the higher-priced among these cabins you will pay $2,200 in the more popular sailing months. Cheaper outside rooms can be had for $1,990 to $2,080 per person in peak times.

Dividing those numbers by nine, you get a per-day cost of about $221 to $244 per person in the minimum-price cabin, $255 to $292 in outside twin rooms in the middle-price bracket, and $355 to $377 per person for the highest-priced outside double room, excluding suites.

Prices on the seven-day Alaska sailings of the *Island Princess* range from $1,360 per person to $3,300 per person for suites.

A third person sharing a room pays 50% of the minimum cruise fare and can take advantage of the line's fly-free programs, which offer free or low-cost air fare from many cities in the U.S. and Canada. Children aged 2 to 12 pay half the adult fare (except in some of the higher-priced accommodations where they pay the full adult fare). Children under 12 months old are not permitted on the ships.

Princess also has a liberal program for exclusive (that means single) occupancy of a double stateroom. The single supplement is just 25%, way below the 50% to 75% or more charged by many other lines.

SUN PRINCESS: Launched in 1972, the *Sun Princess* was once known as the *Spirit of London*, a moniker that rather typifies her current lifestyle if you visualize today's Londoner as contemporary, casual, and just a little jazzy, as they used to say.

Less luxuriously showy than her two sisters in the line, the *Sun Princess* is also smaller, just 17,370 tons. On board are 700 passengers in search of shorter, less expensive, fun-filled cruises typical of the middle-income bracket, seven-day market. Her interesting itinerary takes her to the Mexican Riviera.

Perhaps the raciest looking of the three ships, the *Sun Princess* features streamlined long paned-glass panels that run the length of the ship, curving toward the aft end and making her look as sleek as a sportscar.

She's quite typical of many seven-day cruisers in that she carries a comparatively large number of passengers on short journeys at reasonable prices. What's more, she provides for those passengers just as sumptuously as the other ships in this line, offering them every bit as much service, food, and fun.

Public Rooms

Start your tour on the Riviera Deck, where most of the ship's public rooms are located. Here, for instance, is the Monte Carlo Room, housing the ship's slot machines. Those who like to keep their gambling to a marathon penny-a-point bridge game can do so in the card room nearby, while those who only want to read about the world's gamesters can do so in the reading room on the port side of the ship.

Before dinner, save a few minutes to stroll along the lovely open Promenade Deck, where cool evening breezes brush by as the sea, now as black as the night sky, rushes away beneath you in a cloud of white foam.

Then find your table in the ship's Continental Dining Room, plunked down right in the middle of this deck. This long room is now a study in contemporary elegance, with comfortable upholstered armchairs. Clever use of glass room dividers, each featuring a stained-glass landscape scene in glowing colors, helps keep the long room cozy and inviting.

As on the other ships of this line, the *Sun Princess* presents outstanding cuisine, delicacies like beef Wellington, succulent lobsters, rosy Alaskan salmon, followed by desserts as elaborately picturesque as they are scrumptious—and calorically disastrous.

Evenings will most likely find you headed toward the International Lounge, home for some of this line's showy entertainment. A multilevel room, the International Lounge offers good views from every direction, a good thing since you won't want to miss the elaborate production numbers created for your entertainment.

Later, stroll up to the Observation Deck where you'll find the Starlight Lounge, a handsome spot that turns into a sound-and-light show for dancers each night. Or stop by the Union Jack Bar, a casual meeting spot whose décor is as red as the cross in the flag whose name it bears. Or—perhaps and—sip an after-dinner libation at the rectangular International Bar.

By day, it must be admitted, there are some people who don't partake of all the activities the ship has to offer. Instead these sluggards head straight for the pool as soon as the sun peeps over the horizon and there's no budging them from there until they can no longer feel the heat. If you know one of those, you'll likely locate the worshipper on the Lido Deck. It won't do any good to tell them lunch is served in the dining room because tan fans just stay right out there in the rays at lunchtime, partaking of the ship's on-deck buffet. The Union Jack Bar gets plenty of attention too.

If you've lost a shopper on board, begin your search on the Aurora Deck where the ship's big Princess Boutique holds forth down one side of the ship; a Sundry Shop takes up some space across the way.

If it's a movie fan who's suddenly disappeared, you should begin searching on Baja Deck or Capri Deck, where the two-story Princess Theater can be found filling eyes and ears with top-flight movies.

Cabins

When you do finally give up and head back to your cabin, you'll find rooms a little less sumptuous than their counterparts on the line's other four ships. They're nicely if not elaborately decorated, however, and many have one or two upper pullman berths.

So here we are at prices again. In the Caribbean this ship features three price seasons: the cheapest in January and late April through the beginning of May; the next highest from February to mid-April; and the most expensive in the holiday period in the last two weeks of December. Sample prices we'll detail in the next couple of paragraphs will refer to the lowest prices available. If you want to sail in prime time, figure an additional charge ranging from about $70 to $150 per person for the lowest-priced cabins and about $132 to $180 or so per person for the top-priced accommodations.

On this ship the most luxurious quarters aboard are several suites on the Promenade Deck. Two of the six suites available here (PR6 and PR7) have quite an unusual shape, with one wall sweeping around in a curve. Inside that curve snuggles a couch, coffee table, and chairs placed to form a separate sitting area. Called deluxe suites, these rooms also have double beds, bath with tub and shower, nightstands, lots of closet space, a refrigerator, and a curtain that pulls across to separate the sleeping quarters from the suite's living room. Room numbers of these accommodations are PR1, PR2, PR6, PR7, PR24, and PR21. The price for a week's Mexican Riviera cruise in peak season one of these top-notch nests is $2,500 per person, a very nice buy if you can afford it.

Moving down a peg to a deluxe outside room with twin beds that can be converted to a double bed, a separate sitting area, and a refrigerator, you'll pay $2,250 per person for a week's Mexican cruise in peak times.

The *Sun Princess* also has some single outside rooms for those traveling alone. For one of those you'll pay $1,950.

Outside cabins with twin beds, many of which can be converted to a double bed, are available in four descending price grades, Categories D, E, F, and G.

Eight of the most expensive rooms in this middle-price category are in a nice neighborhood up on the Promenade Deck snuggled in between the ship's big suites. For one of those the price in peak season is $2,020 per person for a week's Mexican cruise.

Smaller rooms in this price bracket are located on Aurora Deck, Baja Deck, and Capri Deck, the three passenger decks deepest down in the ship. All of these rooms are outside cabins, however, which makes them quite a good buy for the money. Rates for these cabins range from $2,330 to $3,030 per person for a week in peak season.

Finally, the four least expensive fares on the ship cover one category of inside double rooms and one (Category H) of outside rooms with double bed. That latter category, for which you pay $1,540 per person for a week's cruise, is Category H, and there aren't a lot of those available. If you want a double bed, speak up early and take a deposit to your travel agent as far ahead of sailing as you can.

Inside cabins come in three price brackets, Categories I, J, and K, in descending price order. Once again, if you like a nice address, there are some Category I rooms up on the Promenade Deck near the ship's suites and deluxe rooms. The cost for one of those is $1,430 to $1,540 per person for a seven-night cruise.

Finally, for inside cabins in the two lowest-priced categories you'll pay $1,320 to $1,420. Cabin C13, despite the off-putting number, looks a good choice in this budget category.

As you will see when you look over the deck plans of these ships, the majority of cabins are in the middle price range. Dividing by seven to get per diem rates, you come up with a range of $188 to $288 per person, excluding the two upper brackets of rooms and suites.

Alaska cruises aboard this ship are also seven-night adventures, with one eight-night sailing. These are divided into two seasons, the least expensive running through early June and September, the higher prices applicable throughout the summer months. Lower prices range from a low of $1,140 to a high (for a suite) of $2,600, with the middle ranges running about $1,240 to $1,700 per person for a week's voyage.

Third-person fares, children's fares, and single supplements for single travelers seeking exclusive occupancy of a double room are the same as aboard the *Island Princess* and the *Pacific Princess*. Fly / cruise programs also are the same.

23. REGENCY CRUISES

Contact: Regency Cruises, 280 Madison Ave., New York, NY 10016 (tel. 212 / 972-4774, or toll free 800 / 457-5566, 800 / 341-5566 in New York State).

Cruising Grounds: Caribbean, Alaska, Mexico's Yucatán Peninsula.

Itineraries: *Regent Sea —*
IN WINTER AND SPRING: Tampa – Playa del Carmen – Cozumél – Montego Bay – Grand Cayman – Tampa.
IN SUMMER AND FALL: Montego Bay – Costa Rica – Panama Canal – Cartagena – Aruba – Montego Bay.

Regent Star —
IN SPRING AND SUMMER: Vancouver – Ketchikan – Juneau – Skagway – Sitka – Columbia Glacier – Anchorage, or return same route.
IN FALL AND WINTER: Montego Bay – Costa Rica – Panama Canal's Gatun Lake – Cartagena – Aruba – Montego Bay.

Regent Sun—
IN WINTER: Montego Bay – Costa Rica – Panama Canal's Gatun Lake – San Blas Islands – Cartagena – Montego Bay.
IN SUMMER: Unannounced

Regency Cruises is one of the newest kids on the marine block. Set up in 1985 by a former Paquet Cruises official, William Schanz, Regency Cruises soon announced its purchase of a 22,000-ton ship. That ship has a lineage quite well known in cruise circles: it began its career as the *Gripsholm*, operated by Swedish America Line, and was most recently known as the *Navarino* operated by Karageorgis Cruises, a Greek company.

When Regency Cruises bought the *Navarino*, it ordered extensive renovations of the craft. In November 1985 the ship, now renamed the *Regent Sea*, emerged from its million-dollar facelift to sail for its new homebase in Jamaica's Montego Bay. There it began sailing on winter Caribbean cruises that take it as far as the Panama Canal's Gatun Lake, an unusual itinerary for a ship sailing on seven-day voyages. In the spring of 1986 the ship headed north to Alaska to pursue its first summer in those waters.

Schanz is credited with teaming Paquet up with its first ship designed exclusively for cruising. That marriage turned the *Renaissance* into a Paquet ship, but it was later sold to Epirotiki Lines, which now operates it as the *World Renaissance*. Schanz is also credited with pioneering unusual theme cruises, including Paquet's Music Festival at Sea, which won enormous popularity among cruise and music fans.

Accommodating 711 passengers, the *Regent Sea* shortly acquired a sister, the *Rhapsody*, formerly the U.S. flagship of Paquet Cruises. Regency treated the *Rhapsody*, which was already quite a handsome ship, to a major renovation, and sent her into the Caribbean as the *Regent Star*.

Now both the *Regent Sea* and the *Regent Star* are familiar sights in the Caribbean, the *Sea* sailing from Montego Bay to Costa Rica, the Panama Canal's Gatun Lake, Colombia, and Aruba in summer when the *Star* is in Alaska, then returning to its winter schedule of cruises from Tampa to Playa del Carmen, Cozumél, Montego Bay, and Grand Cayman.

Meanwhile the *Regent Star* pursues its Panama Canal itinerary from Montego Bay until late spring when it heads north to Alaska for a summer among the glaciers, sailing from Vancouver to Anchorage or the reverse, with stops at Sitka, Juneau, and Ketchikan.

In 1988 the line added some new royalty to its regents: the *Regent Sun*, formerly the *Royal Odyssey*, operated by Royal Cruise Line. Another quite handsome ship, the *Royal Odyssey* was scheduled for drydock and renovations in late 1988, just prior to beginning a series of cruises from Montego Bay to the Panama Canal and back with stops in the San Blas Islands, Costa Rica, and Cartagena, Colombia.

In recent years Regency Cruises has been touting itself as the ideal cruise line for those who have already been on a cruise and are now in search of a cruise with an unusual itinerary. As you can see, Regency provides that.

REGENT SEA: Aboard the *Regent Sea* you'll still find the elegant old-world atmosphere that prevailed in days of yore when all cruise ships were transatlantic sailors.

Lovely wood paneling still glows, rooms are wide and spacious and multitudinous, and the colors are subdued and soothing. As one enthusiast put it: "You really get the feeling of being on a ship at sea instead of on a floating Howard Johnson's."

Activities

When Regency sailed into the Caribbean cruise market, it targeted affluent and experienced travelers and carried out that emphasis with lecturers, bridge tournaments, afternoon tea, events, and entertainment designed to appeal to sophisticated travelers. That emphasis continues, so the activities on board include no boffo pillow fights, but instead concentrate on lectures, films, games, or gambling in the ship's large casino.

One unusual touch aboard is a Computer Room where instructors will get you up and running.

If you interpret up and running more literally, there's a gym for pumping iron and a big deck for jogging—a mere seven times around is a mile. Scuba and snorkeling instruction, from certification to underwater safaris, is also a feature of shipboard entertainment.

Evenings, the entertainment aboard centers around bespangled dancers performing in Las Vegas—style revues, perhaps a Broadway mini-musical, magicians, singers, ventriloquists, often European performers and tunes. Folkloric dancers also make occasional appearances aboard.

To give you an idea just what sort of upscale audience we're talking about here: some of the lectures anticipated by the line run from a fashion show with color analysis to a demonstration of crêpe Suzette cookery and a pre-Colombia discussion on "Buying the Perfect Emerald." There's also an unusually high crew/passenger ratio, about 1:2, meaning there's a crewman for every two pampered passengers.

Public Rooms

A comparatively small ship with just 700 passengers, the *Regent Sea* nevertheless offers you nine lounges and three bars, a sports deck, disco, buffet, duty-free shop, boutiques, casino, the list goes on.

Starting at the top, up on Sun Deck you'll find the ship's sports deck, where just seven times around is a mile's worth of jogging. There's exercise equipment, a sauna, whirlpool, and massage rooms way down in the depths of the ship on Dorado Deck.

One deck down on the Verandah Deck is where nearly every other activity on board occurs, however. On this deck you can use a bank of computers to try to figure out how to beat the odds in the ship's big Casino Royale, just down the hall.

At the bow the Rendezvous Lounge offers smashing views of land ho—or miles of ocean ahead—while at the stern the Lido Discothèque overlooks the swimming pool. Nearby the Lido Café features casual breakfast and lunch buffet dining when you want to stay in your bikini and miss not a moment of sun.

All those ties to the very *française* Paquet line seem to have led to Regency Cruises' emphasis on *la vie* French, most notably the ship's culinary offerings prepared by a French chef. You can see what the French influence has wrought at a table in the ship's Caravelle Dining Room. This attractive window-lined room features quite a large number of tables for two or four, and another interesting departure: comfortable high-backed banquettes alongside the windows.

Later you can walk a few paces to the ship's theater to watch a film or head back upstairs for dancing and a show in the bilevel Regency Lounge.

Cabins

Cabins aboard this ship are just what you'd expect from a ship designed as a transatlantic voyager. Among the largest afloat, they measure in at 200 square feet. Deluxe quarters are even bigger, measuring 280 square feet.

Although the ship can't claim to have all outside quarters as does one brand-new ship, this one is quite a departure for its time: about 92% of its cabins are outside quarters.

All have private bathrooms, a multichannel radio, and telephones for either on-board or ship-to-shore telephone calls.

In a bit of a departure from the norm, you'll discover that your cabin attendant on this ship is a *stewardess,* a rarity on sailing ships.

About half the rooms on board have both bathtub and shower, and 50 cabins offer double beds.

To give you an idea what you'll pay aboard this craft, here's a look at what the line was charging in 1988 for a week-long Caribbean cruise that enters and then backtracks through the Panama Canal. Peak rates are in effect over the Christmas and New Year's holidays and from June through August. At other times you'll pay $70 to $100 less per person, depending on what date you're sailing.

There's one very large suite on board, the Regency Suite, a big and showy spot featuring a sitting room and bedroom with a large double bed for $2,125 in peak season.

Seven suites on board are outside staterooms with two lower beds or a large double bed. These cost $1,995 per person in high season.

From there down in price, cabins are divided into Categories 1 through 8, in descending price order. As the price goes down, so does the size of the cabin and the deck on which it's located—generally the lower the price, the lower the deck.

Cabins in Categories 1 through 4 are all outside quarters with two lower beds or a large double bed, all with bathtubs and showers. The fare for a week-long Caribbean cruise in peak season is $1,615 to $1,855 per person.

Most Category 5 cabins are on Allegro Deck, where the dining room and movie theater are located. Fares in those outside cabins, which have two lower beds or a double bed and both bathtub and shower, are $1,515 per person in peak Caribbean season. Category 6 cabins are quite similar, although located one deck lower in the ship. The fare in one of those outside cabins is $1,395 per person.

It's quite unusual to find a ship on which a less expensive cabin is an outside cabin, but you'll find that on the *Regent Sea.* Category 7A outside cabins with upper and lower beds, bathtub or shower, are $1,215 per person for a week's Caribbean cruise in peak season. The lowest price on board is $1,065.

All the fares quoted are based, as are all prices in this book, on double occupancy of a cabin. Singles traveling alone can have a Category 6 outside cabin with upper and lower beds for a lower-than-usual 30% surcharge. If you're traveling alone and want a cabin in any other price category, you pay a 50% surcharge, the same singles surcharge levied by nearly every cruise line. There's no surcharge for singles if they opt for cabins in Category 7, 7A, or 8, which are inside or outside cabins with upper and lower berths or an outside cabin with two lower berths. Fare in those quarters ranges, then, from $995 to $1,145.

For single travelers, Regency also touts a program called "Regency Roommate"—they'll team you up with another single traveler of the same sex so you can get in on the lower per-person double rates. If you sign up for the deal and they don't locate someone to share with you, you still get the price break.

Working out the daily cost of a cruise on this ship, you can see you'll be paying a per diem rate that, excluding the single fancy suite aboard, ranges from a high of about $285 a day per person to a low of about $152 a day per person.

Third and fourth adults sharing a cabin with two full-fare-paying passengers pay $795 each for a week's cruise; if that third or fourth is a child under 18, the extra fare is $695 per child in peak season. Those low third- and fourth-passenger add-ons include air fare too.

To all fares, add $72 for port charges per person, and remember that rates include free air fare from 12 U.S. cities. Comparatively low air-fare add-on prices are available from 62 other cities. If you're making your own air-fare arrangements, you can deduct $200 from the price too.

Regency Cruises also has shoreside hotel packages that may save you money if you'd like to stay over in Jamaica or Tampa before or after your cruise.

REGENT STAR: It's easy and also punningly tempting to wax, er, rhapsodic over this 24,500-ton vessel formerly known as the *Rhapsody*. Long a familiar sight in the Caribbean and Alaska, this ship has had a long and fascinating history since her construction in 1957. Many of those years were spent as one of the showpieces of Holland America Lines, which once operated her as the *Statendam* on cruises to Bermuda and the Caribbean.

Public Rooms

Perhaps the single most dazzling feature of the *Regent Star* is a series of glittering chrome lighting fixtures that plunge down alongside the main stairway from top to bottom deck. Look up or down at these as you pass by and you'll gaze upon a maze of gleaming, glowing metal and seemingly infinite white light.

Now all decorated in contemporary colors and fabrics, the ship's Promenade Deck is the heart of this craft and is the place to see everything from dancing girls in the cabaret to would-be card sharks in the casino.

Evening entertainment takes place in the Regency Lounge where diversions range from glittery revues to magicians, comedians, and singers. Windows down both sides of the room fill this lounge with light and a big raised bar set with glass sculptures offers a nice vantage point for both interior and exterior sights.

Those in search of a private moment can sneak off to the Anchor Bar where the sounds and sights are subtler.

For unfilled moments, if you have any, you'll find diversions in the card room, the library, several ship shops, and the Lido Café for snacks.

Which brings us around to food. Throw away your scales and prepare to find yourself staring down the business end of a flaming baked Alaska or putting away such offerings as Caribbean lobster Four Winds, chateaubriand bouquetière, or roast quail with juniperberry sauce and cranberry-mushroom stuffing. All of that and much more, from morning coffee to lunchtime fettuccine Alfredo, takes place in the aptly named Cordon Bleu Dining Room, a handsome spot outfitted in reed-and-chrome chairs upholstered in navy. And one evening you'll be dazzled by the Buffet Magnifique, the chef's *pièce de* no *résistance*.

Later, walk off some of those calories on the Upper Promenade Deck where you can march on an open deck at the stern or take shelter from the breezes in a short glass-enclosed promenade.

Hedonists can head for the Bridge Deck where two Jacuzzis offer warm, whirling waters, while optimists head for the casino and masochists zip way down into the depths of the ship to Domino Deck where there's an indoor swimming pool, sauna, massage rooms and gym equipped with all the requisite instruments of torture. Naturally, there's also an outdoor pool up on Promenade Deck and a movie theater down on Concerto Deck.

Activities

Activities aboard all Regency's ships are similar, with the accent on pursuits somewhat more refined than the water fights and zany competitions that are the mainstays of some other cruise lines.

Here you can improve your bridge at games with the ship's resident pro or bone up on gourmet French cooking. Poolside aerobics can start the day and a dip in the Jacuzzi can end it.

Lively entertainment each night ranges from magicians to Broadway-style revues and performances by an international dance team.

Here, too, the line has installed a computer room to give you a chance to try out those incredible machines for fun or profit.

Cabins

Outside cabins predominate aboard the *Regent Star,* with 295 cabins offering windows on the world and 180 perfect roosts for those who would rather not see the morning sun.

Soft earth tones predominate and larger quarters are enhanced by attractive wood furnishings.

In deference to lovers, the line provides some cabins with double beds.

Prices on board the *Regent Star* are slightly lower for a seven-night Panama Canal/Caribbean trip than are fares for a seven-night cruise on the *Regent Sea.*

If you opt for the top-of-the-top, you'll sail in an outside cabin with two lower beds, sitting area, and bathtub as well as shower. Rates for those top quarters are $1,915 for a seven-night trip in peak season.

Other outside cabins range in price from $1,475 to $1,785, the highest price buying you particularly large quarters on the top deck, the Sun Deck, with a great view of what's coming up ahead. Those two cabins would be particularly ideal for four traveling together since there's a sitting room between them that could be shared. And if you don't mind a view partially obscured by lifeboats, cabins on the Bridge Deck, particularly the large B1 cabin, are a good buy.

Inside cabins are in Categories 7 through 11 and vary in price from a low of $1,095 per person double occupancy for a week's cruise to $1,405. Inside cabins on the Promenade and Upper Promenade Decks are tops among the no-windows quarters.

On this ship, children under 18 pay $695 for the week-long cruise, $100 more for those older than 18. Singles can occupy a cabin alone for 130% to 150% of the fare, depending on price category of the cabin. Those who choose the three lowest categories aboard pay set rates about $200 higher than those who are sharing a cabin. Once again, the line offers a "roommate" program under which they will team up a single traveler with a roommate of the same sex to enable both to pay the lower fare for double occupancy of a room. Gamblers note: If the line fails to find you a roommate, you don't have to pay the single supplement.

Port fees are $72 per person.

Fares include air fare from 12 major cities with low add-on air fares available from 62 other cities.

REGENT SUN:
Certainly the 818-passenger *Regent Sun,* built in 1964 and rebuilt in 1982 when Royal Cruise Line bought the ship, is testimony to what $20 million can do. Yet another facelift occurred in 1988 when Regency Cruises bought the ship and renamed it the *Regent Sun.*

Spacious, handsomely decorated quarters, soft leather furniture, polished woods, plush carpets, and lots of glittery chrome and steel combine to create a dramatic contemporary décor that's as eye-satisfying as it is subtle.

So popular, in fact, was this ship when it was operating under the aegis of its former owners, that some of its passengers were booked on their 14th cruise aboard!

Public Rooms

Most of the ship's public rooms are located near the top of the vessel. Under a high domed ceiling is the ship's big entertainment center, a large lounge outfitted in dramatic plum, blue, and magenta décor. Here the ship's dancers, singers, and comedians perform for you nightly—and occasionally lure some passengers up to the stage to get in on the fun.

Not far away is another good-looking lounge, this one outfitted in pink and orange. Shining wood floors are reflected in glittering mirrors and big curving banquettes encircle the central dance floor.

One deck up via a curving outside staircase, the Promenade Deck provides a sunning space handsomely outfitted in brown and russet tones. Yet another deck up is more room for sunseekers, plus a snackbar and deck tennis courts protected from wayward breezes by glass walls.

Out on several other deck levels you'll find open sunbathing areas decked out in royal-blue cushions. Right up here, too, is an unroofed but glassed-in sundeck where you can perfect your tan without ruffling your feathers. Unusual lounge chairs and the off-the-beaten-track feeling of this spot win it special honors.

Movie buffs will love the theater aboard. It features a raised wood platform that shines like a new penny and orange theater seats tucked in between long expanses of stained glass. First-run films are shown daily.

Those of you who can count to 21 faster than a speeding croupier can tote your winnings in the ship's casino. You'll find it snuggled in between two lounge areas that rim the center of the ship. One's a colorful purple-and-aquamarine bar with a flashy white piano that's the star of this entertainment area. A low silver ceiling is studded with round orbs that shed an intimate light over this dramatic lounging area.

Pink and lavender team up with deep purple in the dining room, where a brushed-steel ceiling glitters over tables for two, four, and eight. Low ceilings give this small but handsome room an intimate feeling, and at breakfast and lunch you have a nice view of the ocean from some tables.

Shoppers should head straight to the shopping arcade, where a maze of reflective surfaces from glass to mirrors and shiny metal reflect a glittering array of treasures.

Among the favorite quiet spots on board is the Panorama Lounge, where you can sink into a black leather chair and watch the dancers swirl amid chrome and glass accoutrements. It's a lovely place to while away the day watching the sea too.

Particularly good chrome deck maps show you just where you are on board and help you figure out what's up and what's down from where you're standing. That may not sound like much, but on a ship of this size and complexity you'll be glad to see those maps.

If you like swimming but don't want any more sun, you can hike down a few decks to the ship's indoor pool. Here also are a gymnasium, professional masseur, and saunas for both men and women. Up higher on the ship, of course, is the ship's outdoor pool.

Cabins

Accommodations aboard are top-notch. For openers there are 280 outside staterooms plus 55 suites, and only 73 inside cabins. All have wall-to-wall carpeting, two channels of music if you like, a telephone for room service, attractive wood furnishings, and vanities. Most have a writing table and full-length mirrors. If you're a clothes hound, you'll find plenty of closet space, usually at least two full-length closets in each room, and modern baths with a dressing table extending across the sink in the bathroom.

Décor differs from room to room, but all cabins feature quite contemporary décors in deep jewel tones or soft pastels.

Cabins are comparatively large, with the top cabins offering 268 square feet, the mid-priced quarters offering 178 square feet, and the budget rooms measuring in at 122 square feet.

Room keys are color coordinated to deck colors, a nice touch that can help you find your way around as well.

To give you an idea what you'll pay aboard, let's take a look at the prices for a seven-day cruise.

If you're traveling really first class (and price), you could hardly do better than the Cannes Stateroom. It's a beauty, a study in beige with a semicircular look and L-shaped couches in a separate seating area. The Marbella Suite features a double bed and couch in similar décor. For accommodations in this upper price bracket, the seven-day Caribbean cruise costs $2,135 to $2,245 per person.

Cabin 5040, called a junior suite, is quite a comfortable spot, featuring a couch and two twin beds for $2,025 per person for the trip.

Rooms with numbers in the 6000s and 7000s are a bit lower in price and still quite lovely. Cabin 7019, for instance, features beige couches and a large double bed, while cabin 6005 is done in deep blues with one bed stretching along under the porthole, the other along a wall, with a bath tucked off to the side. Those rooms are all outside cabins for which you pay $1,775 to $1,845 for a seven-day Caribbean adventure.

Rooms with numbers in the 5000s are stunners. Cabin 5056 is particularly lovely, decked out in a dark dusty-rose color teamed with brown in the carpet, bedspread, and accent pillows. It's very similar to other rooms in this price bracket, but in this one the bath is off on one end of the room so the cabin looks slightly larger. It features tub and shower too, if you're given to bubble baths.

A good mid-priced choice aboard is Cabin 4037 and its counterparts, where burgundy and pink are teamed everywhere from the strip in the carpet to the tiny pink dots in the bedspread.

These kinds of outside staterooms range in price from $1,535 to $1,925 per person double for a seven-day Caribbean voyage in peak season from mid-January through March.

Inside staterooms begin at $1,235 for those high-season seven-day journeys, and rise to $1,465.

On a per diem basis, then, this ship rings in at $176 to $290, excluding suites, for a seven-day peak season Caribbean cruise.

Third persons sharing a room pay $845 for that seven-day cruise, $100 less for children under 18, and port charges are $72 per person.

If you're traveling alone and want to occupy a cabin by yourself, the single fare is a flat $1,545 for an inside cabin. As with all ships, rates are a bit higher over the Christmas holidays.

24. ROYAL CARIBBEAN CRUISE LINE

Contact: Royal Caribbean Cruise Line, 903 South America Way, Miami, FL 33132 (tel. 305/379-2601, or toll free 800/327-6700).

Cruising Grounds: Mexico's Yucatán Peninsula, Bahamas, Caribbean.

Itineraries: *Nordic Prince*—
IN SUMMER: New York – St. George and Hamilton (Bermuda) – New York.
IN WINTER: Miami – St. Thomas – Antigua – Barbados – Martinique – St. Maarten – Miami.

Song of America—Miami – Playa del Carmen – Cozumél – Grand Cayman – Ocho Ríos – Haiti – Miami, year round.

Song of Norway—San Juan – St. Maarten – Martinique – Barbados – Antigua – St. Thomas – San Juan, year round.

Sovereign of the Seas—Miami – Haiti – San Juan – St. Thomas – Miami, year round.

Sun Viking—
IN SUMMER: Miami – Playa del Carmen – Cozumél – Grand Cayman – Ocho Ríos – Haiti – Miami.
IN WINTER: Miami – Haiti – San Juan – St. Thomas – Ocho Ríos – Grand Cayman – Playa del Carmen – Cozumél – Miami.

You can tell an RCCL ship anywhere: just look for the classy glassy "Crown" lounge that forms a shining coronet high up on the funnel stack of every RCCL liner. That ten-stories-up lounge is the line's trademark.

Now, however, there is quite another trademark, and what an unmistakeable one it is. In 1988 RCCL launched the world's largest cruise ship, the 2,282-passenger *Sovereign of the Seas*!

Until then the pride of the fleet was the 1,400-passenger *Song of America*, 32,000 tons of Norwegian fun with twin swimming pools and a lounge/showroom that will knock your socks off if you're wearing any—which on these casual sun sailors is unlikely.

On the other end of the size spectrum is the smallest ship in the fleet, the *Sun Viking*, an 18,559-ton ship specializing in longer cruises to fascinating Caribbean ports. The *Sun Viking* visits such sun spots as St. Maarten, Martinique, and Barbados.

Occupying mid-size space between the *Sun Viking* and the *Song of America* are the 23,000-ton *Nordic Prince* and the 23,005-ton *Song of Norway*. Both of these ships are fine examples of an innovative idea in ship construction called "stretching."

Here's what that means. Faced with a desire to carry more passengers but possessed of ships that simply couldn't accommodate greater numbers, the line charted an unusual course. It sent the ship back to the shipyard where it was cut in half. Then an 85-foot section was added to the middle of each of the two vessels and they were put back together again. *Voila!* Two "new" ships and no stretch marks!

Thanks to those stretching changes, the *Nordic Prince* and *Song of Norway* are now 4,500 tons larger, 85 feet longer, and can accommodate about 1,000 passengers each, 300 more than pre-stretch. A similar stretching job was rumored to be imminent for the *Sun Viking* some years ago, but no talk of that lately.

Royal Caribbean Cruise Line hoisted its sail in 1970 and is today owned by three Norwegian shipping companies. One of the first lines to take a shot at year-round seven-day cruises from Miami, RCCL maintains a very steady and predictable schedule, rarely changing itineraries or voyage lengths—but always keeping its spic-and-span craft up-to-date!

Ships and cruise lines have personalities, we keep saying, and the personality you'll find here is refined and classy. No, we don't mean stuffy. What we mean is, if this were humor we were discussing, Royal Caribbean's ships would be wit, while some other ships in similar cruise-length categories would be slapstick.

This cruise line must be doing something right. It's gotten special kudos for its food from La Chaîne des Rôtisseurs, an esteemed gourmet group, and for its overall ambience from magazine readers and cruise enthusiasts around the world.

Service is very good on these ships, and you'll delight in the little extra touches: fresh fruit in a basket every night, a bucket of ice and a continental breakfast in your room until 11 a.m.

Even the youngsters are well looked after, with a carload of activities planned just for them in the usual summer holiday period. The line even provides incentive and performance rewards from T-shirts to watches and radios.

Ports are important to this line, which meets its competition by offering both the old-favorite ports and some less-visited ones. On nearly any voyage on this line's ships you will visit at least three ports and often many more than that.

Air/sea programs, to which the line has been committed for years, enable passengers from anywhere in the nation to fly to Miami and cruise on these ships at no or very low additional fees.

As for itineraries, well, there's hardly anyplace in the Caribbean you *can't* go on one of these well-organized smooth-sailing ships. You can expect to see the *Song of America* sailing seven-day cruises from Miami to Grand Cayman, Jamaica's Ocho Ríos, Playa del Carmen, and Cozumél. She makes that stop in Playa del Carmen, by the way, so history lovers can go ashore and see the ancient Mayan ruins there.

Meanwhile the *Nordic Prince* sails on cruises to the gleaming waters of the eastern Caribbean. On her ten-day sojourns the ship is a port-collector's dream. On those trips she visits St. Thomas, Antigua, Barbados, Martinique, and St. Maarten. The *Nordic Prince* also schedules interesting summer sailings from New York to Bermuda.

The *Sovereign of the Seas* sails on a predictable seven-day itinerary that takes you to Nassau for the day then on to San Juan and St. Thomas, before returning to home port in Miami.

Now stationed in San Juan, the *Song of Norway* sails on seven-day cruises deep into the southeastern Caribbean.

Finally the line's longest winter cruises occur aboard the *Nordic Prince* and the *Sun Viking*, which sail on eight- or ten-day cruises deep into both the eastern and western Caribbean.

Recently, Royal Caribbean Cruise Line spent many millions of dollars to turn a tiny Haitian enclave called Labadee into a posh private retreat for RCCL passengers. Now several of the line's ships stop there to let passengers play on white sands at the cruise-ship equivalent of a private club. When Haitian political difficulties crop up, as they have been doing often in recent memory, the line cancels that call and substitutes some other stop, even though Labadee is far removed from Port-au-Prince, the island's volatile capital city.

To give you an idea of what this new stop looks like: Labadee is 260 acres of beautiful beaches and tropical ambience on the north coast of Haiti, not far from Cap-Haïtien. Reputed to be a landfall of Christopher Columbus, the port features crystal waters, wide sweeping sands, lush rolling hills, and intriguing historical landmarks like Fort Belli, Nellie's Place, and the Bell Tower.

Activities

In daylight hours the gamblers aboard will head for the pool deck where volunteers move wooden horses toward the finish line to the roll of dice. You can bet on the winner, and you're paid off at odds just as you are at a real racetrack. And whatever you may think of Bingo, you'll soon find yourself joining all the others and hoping you've got that magic winning card!

White elephant sales of all the things you bought—or brought on board—and now want to . . . um, well, unload, are popular events, as is the ice-carving demonstration out by the pool.

Every night at dinner all the restaurant staff dresses in costume to celebrate the theme of the evening. Just before dessert, waiters and assistants suddenly disappear to reappear again a few minutes later parading about the room to musical accompaniment. After you get into the swing of things aboard, this costumed nonsense is likely to become a high spot of your evening. Costumes and entertainment range from French berets on a Gallic evening to a fire-breathing dragon on a Chinese night. Passengers get so caught up in this entertainment, they cheer for "their" waiters, and are doing standing ovations by the end of the cruise. On Caribbean Night those talented islanders on the staff carry dozens of filled liqueur glasses on a tray—on their heads—while they dance!

Each of the ships features similar entertainment. RCCL jets its professional entertainers around so all passengers can see the glittery Las Vegas–type revues, talented singers, dancers, and variety acts. Performing cruise staffers sing and dance too, so you'll see them stomping up a storm during your cruise.

If you think you're as talented as anyone, you can prove it at passenger entertainment night. It's surprising just how talented some of your fellow passengers are too!

On all ships in the line there are the usual rounds of dance classes, aerobics exercises, arts and crafts, and special events like grandparent's bragging sessions, singles parties, skeet shooting. As with all ships, there's no charge for any of these activities (except trap shooting, for which you pay a small charge to cover the cost of the clay pigeons).

Every single night there's dancing in several places aboard, and you'll often have poolside entertainment as well.

If you can stay awake late one night during the voyage, you can listen to a comedian's adult entertainment (translate "adult" to some very risqué jokes and language, scheduled for late hours to be sure the youngsters are well tucked into slumberland). If you find this sort of entertainment offensive, you need not go, of course. You'll be told what's doing long in advance.

SOVEREIGN OF THE SEAS: This gleaming bruiser-cruiser burst onto the sailing scene early in 1988 with the maximum fanfare and almost nothing that could be called minimal. A huge ship, this new Royal Caribbean baby is running neck-and-neck with Norwegian Cruise Line's *Norway*, the former *France*, for kudos as the world's largest ship.

To get that debate out of the way right off of the bat: the *Norway* is the largest ship ever built for transatlantic travel, and is 4 feet wider and 155 feet longer than the *Sovereign of the Seas*. However, the *Sovereign of the Seas* is the largest ship ever built specifically for cruising, and in gross tonnage, a measurement of enclosed area aboard, easily outmeasures the *Norway's* 66,000 tons.

Briefly put, the *Sovereign of the Seas* is a very large ship indeed.

It glitters; it gleams; it's stocked with rainbow-hued crystal, fox coats, teeny bikinis, and trolls. This sea sovereign, built in France at a cost of $185 million, is indeed something to see.

Sliding through the sea like a giant floating Hyatt Hotel, to which it has frequently been compared, the new ship sports lighted glass elevators rising between shining brass walls. It has tinkling fountains playing counterpoint to the tones of a grand piano, and there's enough brass and glass and chrome and glitz to dazzle a skyscraper architect.

There are those among us who love a number, no matter where they find it. For that crowd, here are some of the admittedly awesome numbers that make this ship such an awe-ful eye-full: the ship has 14,000 tons of steel, twice as much as the Eiffel Tower and 70 times as much as the Statue of Liberty; there are four miles of corridors, 2,000 telephones, 118 elevators, and open deck areas equivalent to 50 tennis courts or three football fields; ice machines produce 18.5 tons of ice daily, enough for 800,000 drinks; and the ship is 171 feet high, eye to eye with the Statue of Liberty, one-sixth the size of New York's World Trade Center.

Public Rooms

Dominating center stage in this floating drama is the ship's Centrum, a five-deck-high atrium that's the focal point of the vessel. People meet there and greet there, make grand entrances down the sweeping two-story staircase there, and loiter there ogling everyone else loitering there.

Bearing an unmistakeable resemblance to Hyatt's famed glass-elevatored atriums, the Centrum is the biggest, if not the first, atrium of its kind on any cruise ship, and is made even showier by the presence of a tuxedoed grand piano player plinking away, surrounded by fountains splashing into circular pools.

A ship-shopper's paradise, *Sovereign of the Seas* salutes its Norwegian connections with a shop that sells that nation's popular bulky hand-knitted sweaters and winsome hand-carved trolls. To match the ship's own glitter, one of the vessel's eight shops is aglow with a sparkling array of gems. A mannequin dressed in blue fox beckons passengers into yet another shop stocked with sequined evening wear. Austrian crystal shoots rainbow beams from the china shop's windows and sweet scents drift through the door of the perfume shop.

Décor throughout the ship is soothing, with $2.7 million in original artwork, including many Scandinavian touches, from weavings and Rya wall hangings to a sleek glass clock.

Food is typically seven-day Caribbean, leaning to simply prepared beef, poultry, and seafood selections. Breakfasts can be quite sumptuous. For those inclined toward most-important-meal-of-the-day lectures, there's everything from bagels and lox to banana pancakes on the menu. Both lunch and breakfast buffets are offered as well as dining room service. *Sovereign of the Seas* sports two handsomely decorated dining rooms with tables of varying sizes, but none for twosome tête-à-têtes.

Likewise the chances of finding a hideaway for intimate moments are slim and none. Finian's Rainbow Lounge, which does indeed sport a rainbow of pastel furnishings, is quite large, as is the ship's balconied, multi-level showroom outfitted in deep burgundy. A disco flashes with lighted glass floors and three intriguing holograms that seem to leap out of the walls, but it, too, is a large room. Even these large lounges however, are carefully designed so as not to overwhelm with color or size.

Perhaps the best quiet-talk spots on board are the circular Crown Viking Lounge, an RCCL trademark way up high encircling the funnel; the small Champagne Bar, outfitted in pale green-gray leather and dedicated to the purveyance of bubbly; and the Schooner Bar, decked out in hemp and sails.

Those who do not see their future in a glass can hie off to the bright, window-rimmed library which is far and away the best-stocked library on any seven-day cruise tripper. All the showy coffee-table volumes you always wanted to read but hesitated to shell out for are here, along with hundreds of bestsellers. This is the spot for gamesters who can sneak off to the privacy of an adjacent card room while readers sink into leather chairs and couches.

For other kinds of games, there's a large casino with everything from five-cent slot machines to roulette wheels and blackjack tables.

Entertainment focuses on sequined showgirls, singers, a 25-piece orchestra with Big Band repertoire, a trendy six-piece band, strolling musicians in the dining rooms, (and at cocktail hour, in the lounges), a steel band, harpist, pianist, and to complete the spectrum, a disc jockey in the disco.

"Fabulous Follies," featuring 16 singers and dancers performing in two different revues during each cruise, is abetted by cabaret acts ranging from magicians to jugglers and singers. There's a tea dance every afternoon, adult late-night comedy, and seven films shown daily from morning to midnight in twin cinemas.

Cabins

Sovereign of the Seas has more than its fair share of "firsts," the most intriguing of which is a $1.2-million Cruise Control video system that operates through cabin televisions.

A touch-responsive system, Cruise Control includes information on everything from how to get from your cabin to where you want to go to what library books are available, what movies are showing, what's for dinner, and what's going on where. Cruise Control can tell passengers what shore excursions are available and how much they cost, then take their order and charge tickets automatically to their account—no waiting in line. It can order from room service, display and select a wine for dinner, schedule a wake-up call, and check a running beverage tab, all at the push of a button. It's also hooked up to Cable Network News and shows late-night movies at the push of a button.

Cabins on board this craft cannot be said to be large. That, too, is a trademark of Royal Caribbean Cruise Line, where an official once blithely told us that all rooms are the same size anyway when you're asleep. While there's no faulting *that* logic, one does eventually have to wake up and look around. It is then that you will notice you are in small but very attractively decorated quarters, all done up in soothing pastels.

Each has its own hideaway refrigerator, a vanity that does double duty as a desk, and soothing but adequate lighting.

Storage space is limited but adequate for a week-long cruise, with full-length closets and plenty of drawer space. Some who have sailed on this ship complain that already-limited closet space in cabins for three and four is reduced even further by built-in televisions. Line officials say they are reworking those cabins.

Bathrooms are quite contemporary, naturally, and sport marble vanities and toilets that flush with a terrifying whoosh.

Let's take a look at the 1989 prices aboard *Sovereign of the Seas* Caribbean cruise in peak season.

Accommodations aboard this ship come in four basic configurations—suites, standard inside or outside staterooms, and larger outside staterooms.

Those labelled "deluxe staterooms" do indeed deserve the deluxe appellation. Equipped with twin beds that are pushed together to create a double sleeper, they're also decked out in plush carpeting and soft colors. Quite expansive, these rooms have a separate sitting area, quite a lot of storage space for this ship, a bath with tub and shower, even a small refrigerator. If you sail in one of these you'll find a bottle of champagne in your stateroom, too. For these kinds of suites you'll pay $2,000 to $2,495 per person in peak winter season from January to April.

From there down the price ladder you will not find a great deal of difference in cabin size or configuration. Higher-priced cabins are higher up on the ship but beyond that we can't see much difference in them. Outside cabins range in price from $1,615 to $1,850.

Inside quarters also differ little in size and come complete with all the accoutrements—television, telephone, bath with shower and closets—although for three or four sharing a cabin these lower-priced quarters are short on storage space and require you to be *very* good, elbow-bumping friends. Inside cabins range in price from $1,145 to $1,610 for a week's Caribbean cruise in the 1989 peak season.

Single travelers can pay a 50% surcharge for single occupancy of a double room, share a cabin for $1,415 to $1,530 per person, or pay a "guaranteed single occupancy fare" of $1,475 in off-season, $1,845 in peak season. If you participate in that latter program guaranteeing you the rate quoted, your stateroom will be assigned by the line at embarkation.

Third and fourth travelers, including infants and children, sharing a cabin pay $645 in any season. Port charges for each passenger are $35.

SONG OF NORWAY: With such a musical name it seems only natural that RCCL's *Song of Norway* would have a special affection for music. Indeed it does, as you'll see aboard this ship where everything in sight seems to be named after something musical. There's the King and I Dining Room, the South Pacific Lounge, the My Fair Lady Lounge . . . well, you've got the picture (or should that be tune?).

This sleek craft offers much else that is harmonious too: attractively decorated public rooms, a long hall of glittering shops, a delightful Norwegian crew.

Christened in December 1969, the ship made her maiden voyage almost a year later and sailed on week-long voyages for eight years before her return to the Wärtsilä Shipyard in Helsinki. There she was lengthened in 1978, returning to Miami in December to make what the line likes to call her "second" maiden voyage.

Public Rooms

As with all RCCL ships you'll find plenty to do aboard: casinos (except the *Sun Viking*), good looking lounges, cafés, even a late-night spot called the Lounge of the Midnight Sun that rewards your staying power with a night-owl patch if you manage to stay upright, preferably dancing, until 3 a.m.

On this ship, as on others in the line, there is some lovely artwork. Handsome circular photographs hang on many walls aboard the *Song of Norway*, and some very colorful tapestries grace the stair landings. Our special favorite small touch on this ship is an etching of a fjord, the land of this line. You'll find lots of wood in the passageways of this vessel too.

If you like activity, you'll always find something going on in the My Fair Lady Lounge, a rather contemporary spot decked out in pink and orange with lots of shiny metal surfaces.

In the King and I Dining Room you'll dine each night to a different theme with seven appetizers and five entrees offered for your chowing pleasure, not to mention all the other courses. The décor is a smashing combination of black with navy-blue chairs and some green touches here and there.

You'll find a whole acre of deck space on this sun sailer, most of that right around the outdoor pool and its sidekick pool bar. Lounge chairs around the pool are outfitted in green and blue, and on the side decks is still more sunning space, decorated in gold and brown. The teak decks aboard are beautifully maintained.

The South Pacific Lounge is a pretty place, decked out in cool greens and blues and encircled by a bright-green rail. There's a different show here each night, some provided by talented staffers, some by professional entertainers—and some by you on passenger entertainment night.

Disco fans will head straight for the Midnight Sun Lounge, where a slide show offers visual accompaniment to the music. Glass tables are cleverly lit from beneath, and there's a circular bar and dance floor rimmed by banquettes.

About 4:30 p.m., head for that circular Viking Crown Lounge way up on the funnel stack, where you'll have the loveliest of all possible views of the sun sinking slowly into the flaming sea.

There's quite a large outdoor swimming pool up on the Sun Deck, and it's accompanied by the inevitable pool bar and café where you can have breakfast or lunch if you don't want to bother dressing for the dining room.

Cabins

Pretty as are all the RCCL ships, their cabins are disappointingly small. Not uncomfortably, you understand, but far more compact than you'd expect on a ship with such elaborately decorated public rooms.

RCCL's response to this, of course, is that they want you to get out of your cabin and join the fun. And the ship does go out of its way to provide amusements that promote passenger togetherness and full use of the ship's facilities.

Cabins vary only a little in size and barely at all in shape. Most have twin beds that share a nightstand, a desk / vanity, a couple of closets, and a small bathroom. All have a three-channel radio by the bed, and reading lights that are ideally placed for some late-night reading. You'll also find full-length mirrors, wall-to-wall carpeting, and private baths. Electricity is modern too, so you can use your hairdryers and shavers in your room without blowing a fuse down the hall.

You'll be happy to discover that all the cabins—and every other room aboard the ship—display the Scandinavian spic-and-span approach to living.

If you take a look at the deck plans of the ship, you'll see cabins so uniform in size it's difficult to tell the difference between the top accommodations and the lowest-priced cabins aboard (good news for budget-watchers). You'll soon spot the largest accommodations and the smallest, and discover matching price tags.

There's only one suite aboard, so you probably won't have to worry about whether to choose that or not.

Beyond that, there are 328 outside staterooms and 183 inside rooms. If you want a double bed, you'll do well to book early as there are only about 60 of those cabins on board. If you're sailing with a family or a couple of friends, you might ask about the availability of connecting staterooms.

Price categories run from A to M (A is the most expensive) and the top three of those categories cover only a very few of the largest rooms. Off-peak rates are in effect most of the year, with peak rates beginning in mid-January and lasting through March. You'll pay $50 to $110 more per person in that prime-time period. You must also figure $100 per person more than the off-peak prices for sailings during the two-week Christmas holiday period.

In peak winter season, top dollar buys an outside deluxe stateroom on the Promenade Deck. The cost, depending on the size of the cabin, is $2,000 to $2,150 per person for a week's cruise. Cabins 840 and 838 seemed to us to be about par for this price category. The former features green and beige floral print, a very large louvered closet, and a small bathtub as well as shower; the latter is done in beige, light blue, and burgundy, with a large dressing area but limited sitting-around space.

You'd be hard-pressed to see much difference between cabins in the next four price grades, Categories D through G. They're also outside quarters with two lower beds, and are rather uniform in size. About all that seems to differ is the price, which ranges from $1,750 to $1,800 per person in the winter months. In these price categories we found Cabin 536 and the similar Cabin 534 quite nice. The latter is decorated in green and blue, with twin beds set in an L shape so you have a little more moving-around space.

The configuration of the four lowest-priced cabins aboard varies. In any one of four categories you'll find both inside and outside staterooms for the same price, and the bed setup may be one double bed plus a pullman berth or two lower beds. Naturally you can ask for what you want, and if you book early enough, you can get it. Cabins in these lower price categories range in those three winter months from $1,430 to $1,615 per person.

Third and fourth persons, including children, pay $745 for a week's cruise any time of year.

Single travelers pay 150% of the fare if they choose the cabin, $1,890 in peak season for a Caribbean voyage if the line chooses the cabin at time of embarkation. You pay nearly $400 less in the brief January value season. There is one other program for singles, a share-a-cabin deal that costs $1,525 and places you in an inside cabin down low on the ship.

Discounts of 5% to 20% are available for bookings made six months in advance of sailing date.

Port charges on Caribbean cruises are $40 per person.

Those rates work out to a per-person per-day rate ranging from $205 to a high of $308 for the top-of-the-line cabins.

SONG OF AMERICA: To us this is one of the most beautiful ships afloat. From the second you step on board this wide and glittering ship you'll know you're somewhere special.

First, the wide open spaces are really remarkable—none of those narrow, dark little corridors typical of some of the older craft; none of those dark dining rooms or cramped shops. Broad of beam and blocks long, this lovely beauty has made the most of her modernity.

Not only does the *Song of America* have one of those distinctive Viking Crown Lounges high above the sea, but on this ship it offers you a 360° look at that watery world you've come to see!

Christened in 1982 by opera star Beverly Sills—and who better to christen the *Song of America?*—this lovely lady of the sea was constructed in that same Helsinki shipyard. Registered in Norway, the ship has Norwegian officers and an international staff of 500 to care for 1,400 passengers. She measures in at 32,000 tons, is 705 feet long, and is the largest passenger cruise ship ever built in Scandinavia—although she may be upstaged any minute by one of the new ships under construction.

She's very new, so of course she's very contemporary. You'll find lovely color schemes aboard, interior design that glitters and gleams, jewel tones that glow.

Public Rooms

As one of the widest ships afloat—line officials say it's among the widest ever built—you get such a feeling of space that any claustrophobic fears lurking in your subconscious will be instantly dissipated. There is a more spacious feeling here than you'll find in many hotels!

As on the line's other ships, public rooms aboard the *Song of America* are named for famous musical shows, so you'll find an Oklahoma Lounge, a Can-Can Room, a Guys and Dolls Lounge, the Madame Butterfly Dining Room.

In that Madame Butterfly Dining Room you can down banana pancakes for breakfast and coq au vin au chambertin or Kansas prime ribs for dinner. Whatever you choose, you'll consume in an elegant dining room decked out in dusty rose offset by deep-red touches and brushed-brass accents. Tables for four and six predominate.

Off in two cozy wings of the main dining room are smaller tables, many of them along the big portholes here. Of the two wings, the Ambassador Room and the Oriental Terrace, the Ambassador seems the more darkly dramatic, decorated in royal blue with gold accents, while the Oriental Terrace is brighter with a lively gold décor accented with light blue.

As you wander along the passageways, you'll notice they're decorated in tranquil beiges with dramatic navy touches and plenty of brass accents. A special feature you'll see on this ship and no other is a Photo Gallery, hung with some eye-catching photographs of sea scenery.

If you love those machines with the single metallic arm and the three eyes that spin, head for the Casino Royale where there's a healthy bank of those bandits.

Song of America has its own cinema, and pretty it is too, all done in blue and green.

Our special favorite place aboard is the Americas Cup Bar, a dark and dramatically decorated room outfitted in bittersweet chocolate-brown leather and a small piano bar. Sailing fans will love this intimate corner: the theme of the room centers on the New York Yacht Club.

The largest lounge aboard is the splashy Can-Can Room, where lively shades of lavender and hot pink adorn a multilevel room that encircles a round dance floor. Brocaded fabrics and velvets add a lush touch to swivel chairs, and atop it all is a huge chandelier made of shining glass bubbles.

The Guys and Dolls Lounge is perhaps the loveliest room on the ship. Outfitted in beige and hot pink with big circular banquettes, chrome-trimmed smoked-glass tables, and a steel dance floor topped by two flashing mirrored orbs, this spot is disco heaven for dance fans. A massive light-and-sound room keeps things lively. Nearby here you can catch an elevator up to that lofty Viking Crown Lounge.

On the main deck, which is, to put it mildly, simply sensational, don't miss the glass sculpture with royal-blue accents. It's near Purser's Square, which is itself something to see: acres of glass and subtly muted colors that herald the kind of glitzy modernity you'll see throughout the ship.

Start at the top where you'll find not one but two big swimming pools perched up on the Sun Deck and surrounded on the next deck up by a delightful sundeck. That means, of course, that the pools are open to the sun above but carefully shielded on the sides by dozens of transparent panels.

One deck down, on the Bridge Deck you'll find the ship's snazzy gymnasium and saunas for both men and women.

Cabins

Cabins aboard the *Song of America* are almost evenly divided between inside and outside cabins, with 395 outside staterooms, 300 inside. Most cabins have two lower beds, some of which (especially in inside rooms) can be converted to double beds. Some staterooms have third and fourth berths, but those are in the minority so book early if you're planning on sharing your space with friends or family.

On this ship you'll find a three-channel radio in your room and individual controls for the air conditioning as well. Standard 110-volt A.C. electrical connections make it possible for you to use your hairdryer and other travel appliances without concern. All rooms have private bath, but only a few of the top-priced cabins have both bathtub and shower (others are showers only).

Once again, cabins (with the exceptions of suites) are not large. Many of them feature one twin bed with back cushions that turn it into a couch, plus a fold-down twin bed that flips up in daylight hours to give you extra floor space. The décor runs to bright blues and lively tropical colors.

There are two rate seasons on this craft too. Most of the year you pay peak rates, but in the months of January and April through December, rates fall. Prices are also higher during the three weeks around the Christmas holidays, roughly the last two weeks in December and the first in January. At that time of year figure to pay $100 a person above peak-season rates, which are themselves about $100 more than off-season prices.

The following are the peak-season prices on the *Song of America*.

There's one giant suite on board, Cabin 7000 on the Promenade Deck, and it's as costly as it is lovely. You pay $2,355 per person for a week-long voyage in peak season.

On the Promenade Deck you'll find the most luxurious quarters aboard. Each has twin beds topped by pretty cream-and-russet print bedspreads, a separate sitting room providing lots of space, plus a full bath and all the accoutrements for a week of plush living. A week in this lovely room will cost $2,045 per person in winter.

Down the line a bit on a partial deck between the Promenade Deck and Cabaret Deck you'll find a cluster of outside cabins that are a bit less costly. Called Categories B and C cabins, they're virtually the same size. A cabin in either of these two categories in the height of the winter season costs $1,740 to $1,835 per person for a cruise.

A large number of mid-priced outside cabins fall in rate Categories D, E, F, and I. All have two lower beds and prices range from $1,580 to $1,740 per person.

Inside staterooms are of course less expensive. The *Song of America* has five prices for inside staterooms, all with two lower beds, some that convert to double beds and some that have one or two upper berths. For one of these you'll pay $1,380, the minimum peak-season price on board, to $1,575 per person.

Third and fourth persons sharing a cabin—and that includes children—pay $645 all year long, except for peak holiday sailings.

Single supplements are 150% of the fare if you select your cabin, but you pay a guaranteed fare of $1,845 if you let the line choose your cabin and tell you where it is on the day of embarkation.

Per-person daily rates aboard range in peak season from $197 to $292. Suite prices get up into the range of $336 per person per diem.

NORDIC PRINCE: Christened in 1970 by actress Ingrid Bergman, this 23,000-ton ship made her maiden voyage in July 1971 from the Port of Miami. Stretched in 1980, she now carries 1,038 passengers and 400 crew on her Caribbean voyages. That stretch project enabled the line to increase the size of the ship's public rooms, which are now quite spacious and lovely. While the number of cabins aboard increased by about a third, the size of the new cabins is about the same as those that were already there.

Real sailors among us might be interested to know that the *Nordic Prince*, like the *Song of Norway*, *Sovereign of the Seas*, and the *Song of America*, has two gizmos called "bow thrusters" that enable the ship to maneuver by itself without tugs. To see her and her sisters leave the Miami harbor is quite a miraculous sight. They just get those bow thrusters going, roil up the water a bit, and ease on out into the channel. What won't they think of next!

Public Rooms

Way up top, you'll spot that circular Viking Crown Lounge, lording it over the ship's seven passenger decks.

Among those decks, the top fun spot in daylight hours is the Sun Deck, where everyone gathers about the big swimming pool. Like the *Song of Norway*, the *Nordic Prince* has a very large swimming pool, 598 square feet of watery fun. Only the center of the pool is deep, so even nonswimmers can enjoy just splashing about in the wide strip of shallow water around the sides. If you get hungry there's a Pool Café for snacks and a bar for a frosty daiquiri.

This deck is also home to the ship's well-equipped gymnasium. For the sore muscles you acquire in the gym, walk just a few steps away and steam in the sauna for a while. You'll also find a masseur and masseuse aboard, and they hold court up here on the Sun Deck.

Joggers will soon discover the wonders of the Promenade Deck. Those who only sit and wait for joggers to return can do so in the vicinity of a lovely lounge with an equally lovely name: Midsummer Night Lounge. This goodlooking spot gets really lively at night, when you can dance to the wee hours.

Most of the after-hours action occurs down on the Restaurant Deck, where you'll find the ship's Camelot Dining room. Here you gorge (and hate yourself for a few minutes, at least) on broiled lobsters and filet mignon, salmon and sauces, sinful chocolate creations. You'll do so in a room decked out in handsome contemporary furnishings.

After dinner, stop in at the lively set in the Carousel Lounge, a circular room with a central dance floor flanked by banquette seating. And way on the other end of this deck is the Showboat Lounge, another showy room. There's dancing here every night too.

One deck down, on the main deck, the main entrance hall of the ship is right in the middle of a long hallway called Karl Johans Gate. Along this "Main Street" of the *Nordic Prince* are the information office and cruise director's headquarters, plus a beauty salon and a bank of gift shops.

Throughout the ship the main passageways bear names: there's Helmsman Lane, Sailmakers Lane, St. Olave's Gate, Kristian IV's Gate.

Cabins

Cabins aboard this craft are quite similar to those found on other RCCL ships. In fact, the cabins in various price categories seem so similar to each other that unless you can afford a full-fledged suite you might just as well go for budget quarters. There's not a lot of difference in size, and little or no difference in décor.

The *Nordic Prince* has seven-, eight-, and ten-day sailings, and peak or off-peak rates. Peak-season rates are in effect from about January through March, off-peak rates effective in other months.

The following prices are for an eight-day cruise in peak winter season.

Suites (they're called outside deluxe rooms in the rate schedule) are gorgeous quarters, from the name on the door to the décor inside. Named after famous ships—*Golden Fleece, Cutty Sark, Great Republic, Flying Cloud*—each offers quantities of space and is decorated in striking colors: rose, burgundy, deep greens, light blues, mauve.

Suites contain beautiful wood paneling, plush carpets, big bathrooms with both tub and shower, four big closets, a television and stereo built into a wall unit, even your own refrigerator. Through portholes in the passageway here you can look right into the swimming pool. For an eight-day cruise in peak winter season one of these suites will cost $2,825 per person.

Up on this same deck, a large inside cabin is a good buy at $1,965 per person for that eight-day cruise. There are also somewhat smaller and less expensive outside quarters with two lower beds, which cost $1,815 per person for an eight-day cruise in peak winter season.

Moving down a couple of decks you find outside cabins with two lower beds (Categories C and D) for $1,715 to $1,765 per person.

Category E quarters include both inside and outside staterooms, some with two lower beds, some with a double bed. They're pretty uniform in size and cost $1,640 per person for that eight-day cruise.

The least expensive cabins on board are in Categories F, G, and H. Some of these are inside cabins, some outside; some have a double bed and pullman upper, some two lower beds. Prices in these categories are $1,380 to $1,580 per person for an eight-day cruise in peak season.

Ten-day cruises cost about $700 more per person.

The per diem rates in peak season work out to a low of $173 per person and a high of $240 per person. RCCL calls its low season "value season," which includes sailings from April through mid-December.

Third and fourth persons, including children, sharing a room pay $645 for an eight-day cruise in peak season, $795 for a ten-day voyage in any season.

Single travelers occupying a room alone pay 150% of the fare or $1,845.

SUN VIKING: This cozy ship is the line's smallest vessel and the one that makes the longest voyages. There's a solid marketing reason behind that: fewer people can afford the extra time or money, so it makes sense to use the smallest vessel for the longer excursions offered by the *Sun Viking*.

If you can stay aboard, you'll visit some fascinating sights: the beautiful beaches of Barbados, Martinique, and St. Maarten, and the treasure-laden shops of St. Thomas and San Juan.

Life aboard this cruiser is a steady round of sun and fun. There's a polite but casual air on board, and fine service tailored to passengers who are a bit more sophisticated. Thus there are fewer of the more rousing shenanigans that are such an integral part of some ships.

Ports play a very big role on *Sun Viking* cruises. It seems safe to say that most of the people aboard are here *just* because they want to visit these enchanting ports in the easiest, most satisfying way.

Public Rooms

The major passageways are named on this ship too: Court of the Antilles, Kon Tiki Passage, Prinsens Gate, Kristan Augusts Gate, and that RCCL "Main Street," Karl Johans Gate. Along "main street" are the ship's boutiques, where you can buy everything from a sailor's mug that's tilted so it won't slide off a table to fine perfumes and Lladro figurines. The shops' glass windows display all the treasures so you can window-shop here even when the shops are closed.

Up on the Restaurant Deck is the ship's H.M.S. Pinafore Dining Room, a pleasant place decked out in tropical colors. A wing of the room extends down the port side of the ship and has quite a number of tables for four along the windows.

In the evening you'll probably head first for the Annie Get Your Gun Lounge, where the ship's nightly shows take place. A big multilevel room, the lounge is also the place to go for Bingo games and dance lessons.

If you're set on a dancing evening, head for the Merry Widow Lounge, where a combo holds forth to the wee hours in a big circular room. Disco fans will head for the Lounge of the Northern Lights, where pretty lighting almost makes you think you're seeing those northern lights!

There's now a casino aboard too.

If someday you're looking for a quiet place to curl up with a book, the pastel shades of the tiny Sextant Room, up on the Promenade Deck, is one of the most tranquil hideaways on board.

On those balmy Caribbean days a big swimming pool on the Sun Deck provides a cooling-off spot. If you select a perch on the surrounding sun walk on the Compass Deck you can snag some terrific photos of the ice-carving exhibition, which, despite the sun's withering effects, takes place beside the pool. And naturally there's a pool bar, which is a good place to head after you've shed a few pounds of water in the saunas aboard.

Of course, there's one of the line trademarks: the Viking Crown Lounge. On this ship it's been newly redecorated in glittering bronze.

Cabins

As on other ships in the line, even the top-priced cabins here are not massive quarters. They really are *intent* on getting you out of your cabin and into the fun on board or in port.

You'd do well to seek a room with beds set in an L shape, for those offer more walking-around space. Otherwise, twin beds set parallel to each other have only a few feet of space between them.

Let's take a look at the price of a ten-day peak-season cruise, roughly from mid-December through March.

A top-of-the-line cabin, a Category A outside deluxe stateroom with two lower beds and small sitting room, costs $2,755 per person for the ten-day trip. Outside staterooms in Categories B, C, and D are $2,400 to $2,540 per person for the trip.

In the mid-price bracket are both inside and outside cabins in Categories E, F, and G. Some have a double bed, some twins, and some of the rooms also include pullman upper berths. The highest price in these three categories is $2,290 per person, moving down to $2,205 per person for a ten-day cruise.

The lowest rate you can pay for a ten-day cruise on the *Sun Viking* is $1,940 per person, which will get you an outside stateroom with a double bed and pullman upper, or an inside stateroom with two lower beds or a lower bed and pullman upper.

The per diem rate begins at a quite reasonable $194 per person, rising in the highest rate level to $275.

Third and fourth travelers sharing a cabin pay $795, year round.

If you don't need transportation to Miami, you pay $250 less per person.

Single cruises are charged 150% of the fare or $2,640 for ten days aboard.

25. ROYAL CRUISE LINE

Contact: Royal Cruise Line, One Maritime Plaza, Suite 660, San Francisco, CA 94111 (tel. 415 / 956-7200, or toll free 800 / 792-2992 in California).

Cruising Grounds: The Orient, Mexican Riviera, Panama Canal, Europe, Hawaii, Scandinavia, South Pacific.

Itineraries: *Golden Odyssey —*

IN WINTER: Bangkok – Singapore – Semarang – Bali – Manila – Hong Kong, or return same route *or* Hong Kong – Shanghai – Japan – Korea – China, or return same route.

IN SPRING, SUMMER, AND FALL: Mediterranean cruises.

Crown Odyssey —

IN WINTER: Los Angeles – Honolulu – Maui – Christmas Island – Bora Bora – Moorea – Papeete and return same route *or* San Juan – Santo Domingo – Ocho Ríos – Curaçao – Caracas – Grenada – Barbados – Martinique – Antigua – St. Maarten – St. Barthélemy – St. Thomas – San Juan *or* Los Angeles – Puerto Vallarta – Zihuatanejo – Acapulco – Caldera – Panama Canal – Cartagena – Aruba – St. Croix – San Juan – Miami, or return same route.

IN SPRING AND FALL: Mediterranean cruises *or* New York – Bar Harbor – Halifax – Saguenay Fjord – Québec – Montréal, or return the same route.

IN SUMMER: Scandinavian cruises.

Royal Cruise Line's president, Richard Revnes, has become something of a phenomenon on the lecture circuit, and his popularity is well deserved: he's a top salesman and a very, very good speaker selling a top-notch product.

Revnes claims that ports sell cruises, which may be why this line's two ships visit the most fabled ports of history from the Mediterranean Sea to the Scandinavian fjords. With just two ships in its retinue Royal is not one of the world's largest cruise lines, but its marketing efforts and its fascinating itineraries have made it one of the most popular.

Royal Cruise Line is a comparative newcomer to the industry. It began operating in 1972 when a Greek company was formed by P. S. Panagopoulos, who dreamed of creating a fleet of deluxe cruise ships sailing to fabled ports. He carried that dream to its logical and luxurious conclusion with two ships, the *Royal Odyssey* (now Regency's *Regent Sun*) and the *Golden Odyssey*. Two years later the U.S. branch of the company was incorporated, with main offices in San Francisco.

First to sail under the Royal flag was the *Golden Odyssey,* launched in 1974. Carrying just 460 passengers, this small, 10,500-ton ship concentrates on the Mediterranean, where you can see her in spring, summer, and fall, though some summers she visits Alaska. In winter she sails off to the Far East on cruises with evocative names like the Route of Marco Polo and Magnificent Odyssey.

Meanwhile you will soon see the much larger 40,000-ton *Crown Odyssey,* here in the U.S., but you have to look fast. She, too, spends much of her sailing year in European and Scandinavian waters, but in winter she heads for the Caribbean sun.

A brand-new ship, the *Crown Odyssey* was scheduled to make her debut in the summer of 1988. This latest Royal Cruise Line ship carries 990 passengers and clips right along at a respectable 22 knots. There will be 470 crew on board, most of them Greek.

Royal Cruise Lines also pioneered a new culinary twist: in addition to its excellent continental menu, the line now also offers entrees prepared in accordance with dietary recommendations of the American Heart Association. A brochure distributed by the line offers you pictures and descriptions of the not-at-all-spartan cuisine and details everything about it, right down to the grams of cholesterol and sodium. Called the "Dine to Your Heart's Content" program, the culinary additions are also ideal for those who want to return from a cruise wearing something tighter than a muu-muu.

You can of course join any of these cruises with the line's fly/cruise program, which offers reasonable air fares to passengers who join a cruise in Europe, the Far East, or anywhere. Royal Cruise Line says it owes much of its success to its commitment to air/sea programs.

Activities

This cruise line presents what is certainly the most innovative and intriguing entertainment idea aboard any ship afloat: dance partners. Because so many women travel alone on cruises, Royal's creative and energetic staff one day dreamed up this idea: why not give some carefully screened gentlemen passage aboard the ship in exchange for their participation in what the line likes to call its "host" program?

The function of this gentleman—who must be over 50, single, a good dancer, and a gregarious type—is to dance with unaccompanied women, be a fourth for bridge, and provide some friendly conversation. Proper introductions occur early on in the cruise when all the single femmes aboard are invited to attend a special cocktail party at which the hosts are introduced.

Begun as a project designed to last only one season, the host program was so successful it was repeated and repeated and repeated. Hosts, often recommended by travel agents, are interviewed and screened by the line. Several hosts travel on each cruise and dance each evening with 25 or 35 women. (Now there's the perfect vacation!)

Late risers will be thrilled to hear that breakfast on board is open seating, meaning you can show up anytime during the two hours or so the restaurant is serving breakfast.

Both ships maintain formality at dinner, so gentlemen will have to have a jacket, although there's nothing in the fine print about ties.

One night, the ship throws a Pastel Night party when everything's decked out in pale hues, so you might want to pack your pinks for that event. Costume-party fans, by the way, should begin dreaming up their outfit for that event (participation is strictly voluntary), although the ship's crew will be happy to help you with some props.

GOLDEN ODYSSEY: Certainly the *Golden Odyssey*, built in 1974, is testimony to what this line and $10 million can do. In 1988 this small but significant ship debuted a new look fore-to-aft that extended from new fabrics everywhere to new furniture, fixtures, colors, carpets, wall paneling, lighting, and artwork.

Now her 460 passengers sail off to some of the world's more exotic ports amid décor that flies flatly into the face of that now utterly boring scenario of colors decorators like to call Seafoam Green, Victorian Rosebud, Greige, and Petal Peach.

Instead this line chose hunter green, deep sapphire blues, and glowing cranberry hues as the mainstays of its refreshing and glittering new décor.

Public Rooms

Now you'll be greeted in the foyer by hunter-green leather Corbusier-style chairs and couches. Beside them are green Italian marble tables and under them are custom-made gray carpets bordered in cream. Adding a touch of glitter are silver wall-length mirrors and etched glass.

Elsewhere on the same deck you'll spot what looks like a couple of acres of teak, etched and inlaid with ebony and mother-of-pearl. Teak-trimmed glass showcases display far too many boutique temptations.

A favorite spot on board for many years has been the Wooden Horse Bar, which these days is sporting a new mixology center made of deep-green imported marble framed by an edging of gray leather. Beneath your feet is matching gray carpeting, and scattered elegantly about, gray leather chairs and couches, plus granite cocktail tables in black and salmon. That bar's wooden horses remain but are now abetted by a dramatic painting on the same theme, an Italian multicolored glass creation and a handmade Greek tapestry.

The *Golden Odyssey*'s main lounge, which is a gathering spot night and day, is now decked out in vibrant burgundy sparked with teal-blue and gray accents.

Down on Laguna Deck in the Lotus Restaurant you dine surrounded by jewel-like shades of blue and lotus-flower printed fabric as you gaze through big banks of windows draped in a pale powdery-blue hue.

Later, head for the action in the Calypso Lounge, which does double duty as a poolside lounge by day, a disco-by-the-water at night. There you'll dance in a color scheme of salmon and blue banquettes and couches fronted by white marble tables and bars.

Game players will find new décor in the card room and theater-goers will find a new look in their favorite retreat.

Cabins

This predilection toward glowing colors continues right on through the corridors and staterooms where slate blue carpeting plays counterpoint to silvery-gray, powder-blue, Nile-green, and light-salmon touches that make it easy to figure out where your stateroom is—as long as you're not color-blind.

The *Golden Odyssey* always had staterooms of more than ample proportions and now those quarters are handsomer than ever, all decked out in bird's-eye maple furniture with walnut trim. Every stateroom now has a pull-out, free-standing occasional table hidden away underneath the vanity—and there's a new telephone system aboard too.

A 14-day Orient cruise between Hong Kong and Beijing, China, ranges in price from $5,348 per person for a suite with bedroom and sitting area to a low of $2,448 for an inside stateroom. Medium-priced cabins for that 14-day adventure range from $3,848 for an outside cabin with portholes to $4,998 per person for a cabin higher on the ship and with full windows in place of portholes. All cabins have lower beds, although some have upper berths as well, enabling them to accommodate four travelers.

CROWN ODYSSEY:
This new entrant in the Royal Cruise Line two-ship fleet takes its décor cues from the art deco era of the 1920s and 1930s when brass, glass, marble, and wood were the order of the day.

Focal point of the new ship is the Top of the Crown Lounge, a glass-enclosed circular lounge topped by a glass dome. From this shiny aerie you can watch the world go on about whatever it is it does when it isn't sitting in splendor in the Crown Lounge.

There are seven bars and lounges aboard, four on Odyssey Deck where most of the ship's action occurs. Among those is the Odyssey Show Lounge, an eight-tiered creation with a raised orchestra platform and movable dance floor that converts to a stage for the ship's nightly cabaret entertainment.

At the rear of the main lounge is a bar with a pleasant touch: it's named Theo's Bar in honor of the *Golden Odyssey*'s longtime bartender, Theo Sourtzis, who has been stirring things up in that ship's Wooden Horse Bar for ages. This is the ship's premier hideaway, seating only 61 imbibers.

Front and center aboard is the Monte Carlo Court, where a pianist provides entertainment while all and sundry can see and be seen. Right next door is a showy circular staircase and a well-stocked shopping arcade.

Naturally, there's a casino aboard for blackjack and slot-machine enthusiasts.

Fitness fans will find two outdoor swimming pools and two outdoor whirlpools aboard, as well as a golf driving range, exercise facilities, an indoor pool with two whirlpools, a juice bar, gymnasium, sauna, and massage room. So there!

Movie buffs can view the celluloid in the two-tiered Coronet Theatre, while card and game players head for a quiet spot near the Lido Bar and Grill.

For the best view in the house, head for the Penthouse Deck's Observation Point, where you can see things even better than the captain is seeing them from his post one deck down on the bridge.

Cabins

Among the features of this new ship are expansive bay windows on all outside staterooms on Riviera Deck. So large are the windows, in fact, that by day the deck seems to be made of glass and by night it glitters with cozy light.

There's a Penthouse Deck where 16 upper-crust apartments come complete with large private decks with patio lounge chairs where you can watch the sea go by your toes, plus separate sitting rooms and marble bathrooms with whirlpool tubs!

To drive the price-conscious crazy, there are 18 categories of staterooms on seven decks. Most outside cabins have large windows, although some have portholes. All have mirrored closets, tie racks, shoe racks, and hand-varnished, solid hardwood furniture and cabinetry.

For a seven-day New England/Canadian cruise aboard the new *Crown Odyssey* you'll pay $4,078 per person for one of those penthouse apartments with private veranda.

Just a tiny step down the price ladder are Penthouse Deck apartments with bedroom, sitting room, and private deck for $3,798, and one slightly less elaborate category with, nevertheless, whirlpool bathtub, for $3,498.

Quarters called "junior" suites are slightly smaller but still have a sitting area as well as a bedroom and are $3,048 to $3,198 per person for a seven-day New England cruise.

Other outside staterooms range from $2,148 to $2,928, while inside quarters begin at $1,698, rising to $1,888 per person for a seven-night cruise.

Singles pay an additional $1,395 while third and fourth travelers sharing a cabin pay $1,100 each for that seven-day cruise.

Port charges are $59 per person.

Royal, like most cruise lines, offers a variety of discounts, including fare savings for those who book well in advance of sailing dates.

26. ROYAL VIKING LINE

Contact: Royal Viking Line, 750 Battery St., San Francisco, CA 94111 (tel. 415/398-8000, or toll free 800/422-8000).

Cruising Grounds: Panama Canal, Caribbean, South America, Mediterranean, Scandinavia, Alaska, South Pacific (itineraries vary and are complicated, so check with Royal Viking or your travel agent).

Itineraries: *Royal Viking Sky* —

IN WINTER AND SPRING: Fort Lauderdale – Playa del Carmen – Cozumél – San Blas Islands – Barbados – Martinique – St. Thomas – Fort Lauderdale *or* Fort Lauderdale – San Juan – Grenada – Trinidad – Devil's Island – Fortaleza – Salvador Bahía – Rio de Janeiro and return, with some cruises between Rio and Buenos Aires.

IN SUMMER AND FALL: Mediterranean, North Cape, and British Isles cruises.

Royal Viking Sea —

IN WINTER: South Pacific cruises.

IN SUMMER: San Francisco – Seattle – Victoria – Sitka – Skagway – Haines – Juneau – Ketchikan – Vancouver, or return same route.

IN SPRING AND FALL: China and Orient cruises.

Royal Viking Sun —

IN WINTER: Around the world cruise *or* Fort Lauderdale – Playa del Carmen – Cozumél – San Blas Islands – Barbados – Martinique – St. Thomas – Fort Lauderdale *or* similar trans–Panama Canal cruises.

IN SPRING AND SUMMER: Mediterranean and North Cape cruises.

IN FALL: New York – Cape Cod – Bar Harbor – Halifax – Québec – Montréal – Charlottetown – Sydney – Boston – Newport – New York *or* similar New England/Canada cruises.

Royal Viking likes to call its service "World Class" (as opposed to mere first class, you understand), and when you step aboard one of these floating palaces, you'll soon find yourself agreeing.

Not even Royal Viking's competition denies that these are elegant, beautifully appointed ships on which there is only one class—first class.

As history goes, Royal Viking Line is one of the newer kids on the block. Formed in 1970, Royal Viking was at first a composite of three companies—Bergen Line, Nordenfjeldske, and A. F. Klaveness—until Klaveness dropped out of the group. The line was purchased by Kloster Cruise A/S in 1984.

As you might have guessed from the names, this is a Norwegian operation, so you'll find delightful Scandinavians in charge aboard all the ships.

You'll see Royal Viking's white stack emblazoned with a soaring red sea eagle in such diverse climes as the Norwegian fjords, the Black Sea, the South Pacific, the Orient, and the Caribbean. So varied are the itineraries, in fact, that the line's brochure is thicker than most monthly magazines.

As for the ships beneath those smokestacks, well, prepare to be stunned. These are true luxury cruising ships. Contemporary and elegant, they're kept so spotless you'll be convinced an army of workers is on board picking up after each passenger. Everything from the brass trim to the glass portholes shimmers and shines, kept neat as a bandbox by smiling Norwegian stewardesses.

Royal Viking's *Royal Viking Sky* and *Royal Viking Sea* are identical, or as close to that as ships can get. Each was launched in the early 1970s, so features the latest in modern design, both in the public rooms where you can see it and below decks where you can't.

In recent years all the ships have been "stretched" with multi-million-dollar, 93-foot additions added to the midsection, enabling the vessels to carry more passengers and to expand the size of public rooms. That means you'll now find 710 passengers aboard each of the ships, which measure in now at 28,000 tons and are 674 feet long.

In 1972 the line began sailing its first ship, the *Royal Viking Star,* which remained one of the mainstays of the line for many years until recently when Royal Viking and Norwegian Cruise Line were united under one operating company. In 1988 Royal Viking turned the *Royal Viking Star* over to NCL.

Next to join the fleet was the *Royal Viking Sky,* launched in 1973, followed a few months later by the *Royal Viking Sea. Star* was expanded in 1981, *Sky* in 1982, and *Sea* in 1983.

To offer new sights and seas for its many repeat passengers, Royal Viking Lines moves its ships around frequently, rarely repeating an itinerary exactly from year to year. It would take pages and pages to detail exactly where the ships go as you will see if you look at one of their brochures, but here's a general outline of the fascinating regions each of the vessels visits.

Royal Viking Sky often begins its season in Fort Lauderdale where it sails on Caribbean and transcanal voyages or to a variety of interesting ports in South America.

Meanwhile, *Royal Viking Sea* spends much of her year in the South Pacific and the Orient, sailing over to Alaska in the summer before returning to the East.

In 1988 the line added a new ship, the *Royal Viking Sun,* which will be sailing on a fantasy around-the-world cruise, followed by Mediterranean and Scandinavian sojourns and a fall tour of New England.

In 1987 the *Royal Viking Sea* and the *Royal Viking Sky* underwent extensive refurbishment, getting new interior décor and a new health club with all the requisite shiny workout machinery.

To extend its shoreside program even further, the line in 1987 created a division called Royal Viking Tours, which organizes the company's extensive array of overland tours to areas not accessible by ship.

Activities

Naturally, on a line that features many long cruises, a very elegant atmosphere, and some prices to match, most of the passengers are likely to be more mature and sophisticated travelers who have spent years earning their right to this kind of luxury. That means that although there's no dearth of activities aboard, those you do find are quieter, more refined pursuits (definitely no suds-swilling competitions here).

Recently the line has been trying some interesting sports-oriented cruises focusing on tennis clinics presided over by top-ranked tennis players. Golfers have their day too. Royal Viking now has a Worldwide Golf Program designed with the help of golfing great, Gary Player. In Europe duffers can get out there on the most famous course of them all, Scotland's Old Course at St. Andrews, where the sport is said to have been invented. In Ireland, Hong Kong, the Virgin Islands, and New Zealand, among others, there are world-class links visits to give golfers a chance to add another famous tee to their talk. Other kinds of sports celebrities also sail on many cruises.

What Royal Viking likes to call "state-of-the-art" exercise equipment now appears on board its ships in the new Royal Viking Health Studio Clubs. Daily fitness programs are offered and instructors are on hand to help with personalized fitness programs.

One of the most popular programs aboard is one that features a guest chef and wine lecturer.

In 1987 the line also debuted a number of full-scale production shows, including one called "Salute to the Best of Hollywood" and another, "That's the Way It Was," toasting the glories of yesteryear. Elaborate sets, costumes, and choreography have garnered these shows rave reviews among passengers.

You'll now also find new exercise and sports facilities aboard the ships, including Parcours equipment that leads you through a complete 30-minute workout.

A paddle-tennis court offers you the opportunity for some exercise, and there's a ball machine for honing your tennis stroke. You can dunk a couple of basketballs on board or work out at jazzercize classes offered twice a day when the ship's at sea.

On board ships of this caliber dinner must be numbered among the day's activities, for it's a scheduled event, every bit as showy in its way as a nightclub performance. From Swedish pancakes with lingonberries or fruit-topped Belgian waffles in the morning to filet of beef tenderloin, poached ocean perch Florentine, or breast of chicken with wild rice and bing cherry sauce, you will wine and dine royally.

Royal Viking Line food has an outstanding reputation, and the surroundings in which it is served are equally outstanding. Ease into a comfortable chair by the window and gaze at the scenery passing by as you dine on Malasol caviar and beef Wellington prepared by top-ranked chefs. Royal Viking Line even likes to say you can almost chart the ship's course by what you see at dinner—exotic fruits and herbs, unusual spices.

Lavish presentations of menu selections is a pride of the line too, so you'll see delicacies presented on silver trays and served on hand-painted china and delicate Scandinavian crystal. There's only one seating on board these ships, so you can enjoy a leisurely dinner and take all the time you like.

If you don't want to miss a minute of sunshine, you can visit the showy luncheon buffet on deck where immense bouquets provide a focal point for elaborately presented lobster salad or open-face sandwiches.

If you want something special, all you have to do is ask and it will be prepared for you.

A new feature of the line is the Supper Club, an intimate 60-seat room in which you can reserve a table, then dine and dance with new friends. There's a separate menu here, and entertainment too (no extra charges, however).

Guest speakers are often on board to discuss everything from bridge to vodka, politics, history, or the cosmos. Recent speakers have included Jim Nabors, Burt Bacharach, Yakov Smirnoff, Rita Moreno, Omar Sharif, and Victor Borge. And with such exotic ports to visit, even port talks are thrillers.

You'll get a chance to learn a little more about Norwegians when the crew dons traditional handmade costumes called *bunads* and invites you to join in for a festive evening of song and dance. Other nights, dazzling stage shows entertain you with feathers and sequins, glitter and glamour. In addition to classical music or operatic theme cruises, you can now select cruises with themes ranging from Swing Era Music to Food and Wine, Theater at Sea, and Castles and Kings.

On stage, Royal Viking ships feature world-class entertainers, like Al Hirt, George Shearing, several "big-band" orchestras, Sid Caesar, and Leslie Uggams.

So, sit back and sip up. There's an icy glass of aquavit waiting for you.

ROYAL VIKING SKY/ROYAL VIKING SEA: First, let's take a look at the ships' statistics. Both *Sea* and *Sky* are 674 feet long and 83 feet wide, weigh 28,000 tons, and carry 710 passengers. As ships' ages go, these are all among the newer ships afloat, originally constructed in the early 1970s.

Best of all, each of the ships is a luxury sailer and a study in small, thoughtful touches. Along the passageways are ceramic mosaics and delightful small decorative pieces. In the spacious cabins you'll find woolly afghans draped casually over the beds, one of which often also serves as a couch during the day. Everywhere you'll see shining brass accents, glowing carpets, fresh flowers, glittering crystal, acres of open space, and extra touches that let you know in a wink that you're aboard a very special craft.

Public Rooms

Drama, tastefully executed, is in fact a byword of the décor aboard. On these ships you'll see leather and rosewood, teak and crystal, oil paintings and gold leaf. You'll find original artworks everywhere you look, and interior design so stunning you'll never quite get used to the luxury of it all.

In the airy dining room aboard the *Sky*, for instance, is a crystal fountain glittering amid the contemporary pastel décor. Glass dividers section off areas of the room, and a small dining area off to one side is a particularly intimate dining spot.

Perhaps the most dramatic room on the ship is the Discovery Room (called the Windjammer Room on the *Sea*), an oval room encircled by tall windows through which sunlight streams across a deep-green décor.

Furnishings throughout the ship are subtly contemporary. In the Prince Olav/North Cape Lounge a ship's bowsprit in gleaming gold leaf provides a striking focal point. You'll get a look at this room if you attend one of two evening shows that take place here.

Curving leather love seats are a feature here, and plush leather shows up again in the writing, card, and library rooms, which are downright gorgeous, equipped with chess boards built into tables, a huge dictionary and atlas, comfy chairs.

If you're looking for a nice before-dinner retreat, find your way to The Cove, a cozy, tiny room that has a couch, three chairs, contemporary paintings, a table for four, and plants in the windows overlooking an open promenade.

A similar getaway room is called The Snug, and is done up with cute etchings on the wall. One shows a musician haughtily intoning: "I really prefer to play here alone, then I can always play *first* violin." Talk about snug—there are just 11 seats here!

Among the larger public rooms is the Trondheim/Oslo Lounge done up on the *Sky* in a soft pastel color scheme with lots of contemporary chrome accents and big windows. Filled with fresh flowers, this large two-level room is a study in shining brass. It's here you will head to watch the ship's main evening entertainment.

In the striking Finlandia/Dolphin Bar a pianist/singer performs before lunch and dinner. Complimentary cappuccino is a lure in that latter room.

Gamesters can spend their waking hours in the handsome Casino Royale playing blackjack, roulette, and slot machines (the croupiers wear white gloves). You'll find it tucked away on the Promenade Deck. Meanwhile movie fans can head down to the Mediterranean Deck where they'll sit in the regal splendor of the domed Skylight/Saga Theater and watch a top film.

Up on Atlantic Deck you can get any question answered 24 hours a day by the cruise industry's first shipboard concierge.

One deck farther up, the Scandinavia Deck, you'll find a big heated swimming pool, one of two pools on board. Finally, up on the sports deck you can get some outdoor exercise and down on B Deck you can work out in the gym and recover in the sauna.

There are, of course, many things to do on these ships, but perhaps the most enchanting "do" of all is nothing more complicated than an exploration through the wide passageways and open promenade deck of the ship.

And don't miss sending a postcard, if for no other reason than the fun of dropping it into the cutest little red Scandinavian mailbox you've ever seen (it's outside the purser's office).

Cabins

As you would expect, your cabin will be as luxuriously handsome as everything else aboard this ship. You'll find a cozy afghan spread across a couch, a basket of fruit awaiting, two terrycloth robes, and a tiny mint on your pillow each night.

Every cabin has a private bathroom, and there are built-in bars, drawers you can lock, rosewood cabinets, a three-channel radio, telephone, color television, and modern electrical outlets.

A nice touch aboard is a small launderette where you can throw a few things in the washing machines for yourself, although those services are available from the crew too.

Because these are fairly new ships, within each category accommodations are quite uniform in size and décor. What's more, prices on all the ships are the same for each cabin price category. Itineraries on the Royal Viking line change frequently, however. For the sake of comparison with the majority of other ships, let's look at some of the cabins and the prices you'll pay for a seven-day New England cruise on one of the line's ships.

The top cabins are called Penthouse Suites, which are really quite something: twin or double bed in a separate room from the sitting area. A comfortable couch in glowing hues stands beside a built-in wall unit in which you'll find a television, refrigerator, telephone, lamp, and plenty of storage space. Plunk down in a comfortable swivel chair and look out across your private veranda to the ocean beyond. Your ship has come in, no question about it. One of these elegant staterooms costs $5,365 per person. (Don't panic—a suite is, after all, the very best you can buy.)

Moving down a bit, there are two additional categories of suites, which cost $3,734 to $4,210 per person for the cruise, depending on the elaborateness of the cabin you occupy.

Deluxe outside bedrooms are the next two price categories, Categories A and B, on Promenade and Atlantic Decks. Each offers a small sitting area with a couch, a pretty wood desk, two chairs, and a small cocktail table. For one of these handsomely decorated twin-bed quarters you pay $3,153 to $3,538 per person for the seven-day voyage.

Single travelers get special notice, with cabins in Categories CB, CC, C, and N. The top-priced of these (CC) is an outside single with a bed that becomes a couch by day. Lots of closet space and a comfortable chair make these cabins very comfortable for the single traveler. In these price categories singles pay $2,803 to $4,784 for the voyage. Category C single cabins are somewhat smaller but feature about the same furnishings.

Moving on down the price and size brackets, there are a whole raft of outside double cabins, all with two lower beds and some with upper pullman berths to accommodate a third person. Some have both bathtub and shower, but most have shower only. These are really quite adequate in size, and carefully designed to offer you the maximum amount of moving-around space. Some, however, have quite small bathrooms, which may be a tight squeeze for heftier travelers. Prices in these eight categories of outside double cabins range from $2,187 to $2,782 per person for the seven-day voyage.

Lowest-priced accommodations are inside double cabins on Pacific and Mediterranean Decks, two of the lower passenger decks aboard. These feature two lower beds and have a shower, no tub in the bathroom. For one of these bedrooms you pay $2,047 per person for the journey.

Per diem costs on these voyages range from about $292 to $505 per person, excluding suites. Air fare is included.

Single occupancy of suites, and some cabins, is double the fare, and exclusive use of standard double cabins costs 160% of the per-person rate.

A third person sharing a stateroom pays the minimum fare for that cruise. Children under 12 in a double room with an adult pay half fare while youngsters 12 and older pay full adult fare. In suites, deluxe cabins, and single rooms, children occupying regular accommodations are charged as adults.

Royal Viking also has fly/cruise fares in which you add on varying amounts for air fare from your hometown to the embarkation point.

ROYAL VIKING SUN: Royal Viking Line is not one to seek headlines with massive ships carrying umpteen passengers. For openers, their quite select clientele would not be found lining up like bourgeois lemmings, certainly not.

That's why this line's new ship is yet another comparatively small craft, carrying just 740 passengers off on dream-machine around-the-world and around-South America cruises.

Measuring in at 36,000 tons, this new $125-million vessel will be a third larger than Royal Viking's two other ships, and will have larger staterooms, more open deck space, and, the line claims, more space per passenger than any other cruise ship afloat or under construction. Another first aboard: walk-in closets, the first in the cruise industry.

That will be accompanied by a suitably high crew-to-passenger ratio, so you can expect the line's reknowned service to continue aboard this new vessel.

Public Rooms

Workout fans will find a spa and health club located high up on the ship so you can watch the sea while you work it off. Two pools can cool down the warmest workout.

RVL's showy new entertainment takes place in a big entertainment lounge that can seat all passengers at once, and the same can be said for the dining room, which has only one seating.

Up at the top of the ship is the line's now-popular 60-seat Supper Club, where you reserve a table and are served dinner by white-gloved waiters and amused by entertainers.

On this ship as on other Royal Viking ships, the menus are new daily and are never repeated, even on a 100-day cruise! Round-the-clock room service, including full dinner service in your room, is another popular feature of this and other Royal Viking ships. RVL cuisine, by the way, is described by the line as "Americanized European," with an accent on light foods now demanded by American palates.

Cabins

More than a third of the ship's 370 staterooms will feature private verandas. All cabins have walk-in closets, a bar with refrigerator, a television, and a video cassette player.

Fares will be similar to those aboard the line's other ships.

27. SEAESCAPE

Contact: SeaEscape, 1080 Port Blvd., Port of Miami, Miami, FL 33132 (tel. 305/379-0000, or toll free 800/327-7400, 800/432-0900 in Florida).
Cruising Grounds: Bahamas or cruises to nowhere.

Itineraries: *Scandinavian Saga*—St. Petersburg – nowhere – St. Petersburg, with occasional trips to Mexico's Yucatán Peninsula.

Scandinavian Sky—Port Canaveral – nowhere – Port Canaveral.

Scandinavian Star—Miami – Freeport – Miami, and Saturday day and evening mini-cruises to nowhere.

Scandinavian Sun—Fort Lauderdale – Freeport – Fort Lauderdale.

Undisputed master of the one-day breakaway cruise, SeaEscape offers the perfect solution to what to do with a beautiful day. Sail it away to the Bahamas or to nowhere at all.

While you're at it you can chow yourself into blimpdom, dance to the twangs of a steel band, rum punch yourself, sun the body beautiful, splash happily in the pool, find a quiet contemplation corner.

Novice cruisers may find this the perfect way to get an idea what this cruise business is all about while spending the least amount of time and money. On the other hand, a one-day voyage is a very minimal look at what cruise ships have to offer. Still, if you're not doing anything this Saturday (or any other day of the week), why not trip off to Miami and give this day of wine and sun-shine a try?

The Miami-based *Scandinavian Star* sails one-day sunseekers off to Freeport where they can stay for a couple of days, if they like, returning on one of the ship's other daily trips.

It has not been all beer and skittles for the folks at SeaEscape. In fact when this cruise line got started just a few years ago, the industry broke out in one long guffaw. One-day cruises? It can't be done, the three-, four-, and seven-night cruise executives snorted.

But it has been done and with comparative success; witness now *four* ships plying the Florida waters to nowhere and to Freeport.

This day-long cruise idea was born back in 1980 when an old and respected shipping company, United Steamship Company of Denmark, known as DFDS, backed the idea and launched the North American Company. It purchased the *Caribe*, then being operated by Commodore Cruise Lines, and turned it into the *Scandinavian Sun*.

In 1982 the line began operating a new 20,000-ton vessel, the *Scandinavia*, on runs from New York to Florida. To avoid the constrictions of U.S. maritime laws, the company routed the voyage through Freeport, where passengers—and their cars, if they brought them along—got off and boarded the *Scandinavian Sun* for the run to Miami.

That nice try at the big bucks of the New York-Florida market was a flop, so they abandoned the project in 1983, sending the *Scandinavia* off to Scandinavia where it shuttled cars and people on a ferry run from Oslo.

Once known as Scandinavia World Cruises, SeaEscape certainly seems to have recovered from its temporary malaise and now operates four ships, three of them sailing from Florida's east coast and one from the state's west coast.

If you're in Miami or Fort Lauderdale, you can sail away for the day aboard the *Scandinavian Star* or *Sun*. They lift anchor every morning bound for a day of fun, frolic, and all the sunshine you can tan in. Halfway through the cruise, the ship makes a stop in Freeport for a couple of hours of intensive shopping in the maze of International Bazaar duty-free shops.

If you're closer to Orlando, you can spend a day at sea aboard the line's *Scandinavian Sky*. That ship departs daily for a sailing adventure that takes you nowhere but gets you there with a lot of laughs. There's plenty of calypso music, fancy island drinks, sun, swimming, and gambling too.

For those living on or visiting Florida's west coast, SeaEscape's *Scandinavian Saga* departs from St. Petersburg each morning for day-long cruises in the Gulf of Mexico. Once again, the cruise goes nowhere, accompanied by lots of sun and fun.

On board these former ferries you will find cabins-for-a-day, outfitted more as a resting and changing spot than as a place to spend much time. So it's not a cabin you're buying here but a round of activities that begins with breakfast in the sunshine and ends with dancing under the stars.

SCANDINAVIAN SAGA / SCANDINAVIAN SKY / SCANDINAVIAN STAR / SCANDINAVIAN SUN:
A 10,000-ton ship, the *Scandinavian Star* leaves Miami each morning at 8:30 a.m., arriving at Freeport, Grand Bahama Island, about 4:30 p.m. and gets back to Miami at 11 p.m. Cruises from Fort Lauderdale aboard the *Scandinavian Sun* keep the same hours.

At Port Canaveral, port for Florida's Walt Disney World, SeaEscape's *Scandinavian Sky* lifts anchor at 10 a.m., returning 12 hours later.

The *Scandinavian Saga* departs St. Petersburg at 10 a.m. and returns at 10 p.m. after a cruise around the Gulf of Mexico.

Round-trip deck passage, including port charges, is $79 from St. Petersburg and Port Canaveral, $99 from Miami or Fort Lauderdale.

Children from 12 to 17 pay $39 from St. Petersburg and Port Canaveral, $59 for cruises from Miami or Fort Lauderdale. Younger children pay $29 from St. Petersburg and Port Canaveral, $49 from Miami or Fort Lauderdale.

If you'd like to reserve a cabin aboard, add $45 for an inside cabin, $65 for outside quarters, and $100 for a suite.

Senior citizens get a bit of a price break from SeaEscape, paying $10 less from any port, $20 less if they sail during the line's "Senior Spring Break" which is in effect from April to July.

In summer the line salutes childhood by offering free passage to children sailing from Port Canaveral and St. Petersburg. Freebies for kiddies may also be offered during some other months, usually for cruises from Port Canaveral. Check with the line to see if there's a deal on for the dates you're planning to sail.

Recently SeaEscape added a new twist in cruises: Saturday "Sampler" cruises departing from Fort Lauderdale at 10 a.m. and returning at 4 p.m., or sailing off at 6:30 p.m. and returning at 1 a.m. Fares on those cruises are $49 for the evening cruise, $44 for the daylight voyage. Children pay $49 or $39 for the mini-cruises, depending on their age.

Free bus transportation to the ships is available from many cities in Florida.

Activities

You'll find a full casino on board, a swimming pool, gift shop, cabaret, video game room, and disco. Use of all the facilities on board is free.

Activities on board these ships go nonstop from departure to return.

You can party in any of four lounges on the *Scandinavian Sun,* watch a movie, play in the disco. There are games and activities out around the big swimming pool, snacks in the snackbar, elaborate buffets.

Often the line schedules theme cruises ranging from a soap opera week, with stars of those soupy soaps on board, to a Miami Dolphin weekend featuring Dolphin football players, to Irish celebrations, and big-band days.

Music from different eras and in different styles may be featured, or a Latin Week, Country Jamboree, Jazz Notes, even a Rock and Roll Revival.

28. SITMAR CRUISES

Contact: Sitmar Cruises, 10100 Santa Monica Blvd., Los Angeles, CA 90067 (tel. 213/553-1666).

Cruising Grounds: Caribbean, Panama Canal, Mexican Riviera, Alaska.

Itineraries: *Fairsky*—

IN WINTER AND SUMMER: Fort Lauderdale – Nassau – St. Croix – St. Thomas – Jamaica – Cayman Islands – Cozumel – Fort Lauderdale *or* Fort Lauderdale – Nassau – St. Croix – Antigua – Barbados – Martinique – St. Thomas – Fort Lauderdale *or* New York – Newport – Bar Harbor – Halifax – Nova Scotia – Prince Edward Island – Bonaventure Island – Saguenay River – Quebec City – Montreal or reverse.

IN SPRING AND FALL: San Juan – Barbados – Trinidad – Devil's Island – Fortaleza – Recife – Salvador – Rio de Janeiro or reverse; *or* San Juan – St. Thomas – Martinique – Devil's Island – Amazon River – Santarem – Alter do Chao – Boca do Valerio – Manaus or reverse.

FairMajesty—

IN FALL AND WINTER: Fort Lauderdale – Nassau – St. Croix – St. Thomas – Jamaica – Cayman Islands – Cozumel – Fort Lauderdale *or* Fort Lauderdale – Nassau – St. Croix – Antigua – Barbados – Martinique – St. Thomas – Fort Lauderdale.

IN SPRING AND SUMMER: Vancouver – Ketchikan – Juneau – Skagway – Hubbard and Columbia Glaciers – Anchorage or reverse.

Fairsea—

IN WINTER AND SPRING: Tahiti – Moorea – Bora Bora – Pago Pago – Fiji –

Auckland, N.Z. – Sydney, Aust. *or* Sydney – Whitsunday – Cairns – Vanuatu – New Caledonia – Auckland *or* Tahiti – Moorea – Bora Bora – Christmas Islands – Hilo – Lahaina – Honolulu – Los Angeles or reverse.

IN SUMMER AND FALL: Los Angeles – Cabo San Lucas – Mazatlan – Puerto Vallarta – Los Angeles *or* Vancouver – Ketchikan – Juneau – Skagway – Hubbard and Columbia Glaciers – Anchorage or reverse.

Fairwind—
IN WINTER: Tahiti – Moorea – Bora Bora – Pago Pago – Fiji – Auckland, N.Z. – Sydney, Aust. or Sydney – Whitsunday – Cairns – Vanuatu – New Caledonia – Auckland *or* Tahiti – Moorea – Bora Bora – Christmas Islands – Hilo – Lahaina – Honolulu – Los Angeles or reverse; *or* Los Angeles – Cabo San Lucas – Mazatlan – Puerto Vallarta – Los Angeles.

IN SPRING AND FALL: Mediterranean and Baltic Sea cruises.

In 1984 Sitmar Cruises officials were excited as a new daddy pacing outside the delivery room. What they were palpitating over was every bit as important to them as a new baby, and in fact was a new baby—a 46,000-ton, $150-million cruise ship that rounded this line's "family" of cruise ships out to three.

Sitmar already had twins: two historic turbine steam ships, the *Fairwind* and *Fairsea,* once part of the Cunard family of elegant vessels. And now the *Fairsky* had been delivered into the world of cruising where her glitter and gleam were to lure passengers bound for the Caribbean year round.

In 1988 the line again began anticipating a new arrival: in January 1989 the *FairMajesty* is scheduled to float away from the French shipyard in which she was built and head for Caribbean sun. There she will spend the cooler months on cruises from Fort Lauderdale to the fabled islets of the eastern Caribbean, the beaches of Mexico's Yucatán Peninsula, and the islands of the western Caribbean; the warmer months she will sail the Alaska waters.

Meanwhile her twin sisters, both 25,000-ton vessels, sail on warm-weather adventures, the *Fairwind* through the Panama Canal to San Juan, the Caribbean, and the Amazon, and the *Fairsea* to Mexico the South Pacific and Alaska.

Both these ships got a sparkling $25-million facelift in 1985 and are now decked out in acres of pretty pastel colors—soft greens, creams, and blues. That renovation process extended from top to bottom, adding lots of brass and etched glass, as well as spiffing up every cabin on the ships.

Sitmar Cruises is another of those cruise lines spawned in the 1970s during the renaissance of cruising in the Western Hemisphere. Begun by former airline executives, Sitmar began operations with the purchase of two Cunard liners, the *Sylvania* and the *Carinthia,* which were built by the John Brown & Co. shipyard on the River Clyde in Scotland. Sitmar rebuilt and refurbished both vessels for cruising and renamed the *Sylvania* the *Fairwind* while the *Carinthia* became the *Fairsea.*

Then a third ship arrived, and quite a big and handsome ship it is. Measuring in at 38,000 tons, the *Fairsky* is 790 feet long and carries 1,212 passengers on 11 public decks. Like its sisters, the ship has larger-than-average cabins and a laughing, dedicated Italian crew, including some outstanding Italian cooks to maintain the line's top reputation for outstanding cuisine.

Children get special attention from this line, which has set aside special play areas for youngsters from 2 to teens, and there's an impressive round of activities for sailing youngsters.

Finally, here's one special Sitmar trademark we especially love—each ship has a pizzeria!

Activities

Sitmar is one of the few lines around that has considered—and welcomed—the possibility of sailing with children, and then taken action to arrange as much fun for them as for their weary progenitors.

On these ships youngsters will find a Soda A Go-Go game room strictly for teens (adults need not apply), with all those whirring electronics the kids love, some game tables, soft drinks, and cookouts on deck. There's even a pool nearby earmarked for the youngsters. They're very strict about keeping out adults, a rule the youngsters love and adults appreciate too.

So far do they go with this youth program (which is offered every day, not just on holidays, from 9 a.m. to midnight, in port and at sea) that the kids have their own specially printed activities schedule delivered to their cabin. On it they'll find a round of activity ranging from pizza parties to ice cream time, arts and crafts, board games, and story hours for the 2-to-12 set. There's even a nursery for the very small fry.

For those worldly teenagers there are dance contests, theatrical activities, beauty demonstrations, weight-training classes, games, and even Italian language lessons. In holiday season teens have use of the ship's discothèque from 8 p.m. to midnight, and are treated to late-night movies on some evenings, as well as wide-screen video programs.

Fear not, Sitmar hasn't overlooked grownup entertainment. A specialty of the line is theme cruises featuring big-name entertainment. There are five lounges and a raft of pubs, and entertainers have ranged from kootchy-kootchy Charo to Tony Bennett, Ben Vereen, Rita Moreno, and Florence Henderson.

You can win master points in bridge tournaments, take a shot at trap shooting off the stern of the ship, try shuffleboard or table tennis.

You can take a sedate stroll on four open decks, waltz to a dance band, or boogie up a storm in the ship's disco.

You can learn Italian, play Bingo, watch a first-run movie, work out in a gymnasium, steam in a sauna.

FAIRWIND / FAIRSEA:
Once again we are going to introduce you to two ships at once because in everything except color schemes these vessels are twins.

Italians haven't come by their reputation as food fanciers for nothing, as you'll discover aboard these vessels. Meals are eagerly awaited events that feature everything from cannelloni in lobster sauce to veal Oscar and cherries Jubilee, even "Slim and Trim" selections for weight-watchers. Sitmar is proud that all the food aboard is prepared by employees of the shipline, not by the independent caterers that cook on some ships. Finally, of course, there's that delightful brick-lined pizzeria!

Public Rooms

From the moment you step aboard and are greeted by a bevy of white-gloved, smiling crew members you know some special things will be happening. And as you explore the ship, you'll discover where some of those special things are happening—places like the splashy round Mistral Nightclub (it's called the Dolphin on the *Fairsea*), where you can watch the stars outside through tall windows as you dance the night away on a big round dance floor.

A disco is decorated in burgundy with gray accents. Seating is on circular contemporary chairs plus cozy couches, and there's a stainless-steel circular dance floor.

The Windward/Seaward Lounge, a main show room aboard, features cocktail music before dinner and nightly entertainment à la dancing girls and guys in elaborate costumes. This room itself is entertaining, outfitted on the *Fairwind* in pale pastels with comfortable U-shaped chairs and love seats. And here's a neat trick: on the *Fairsky* the stage show can also be seen on your cabin television!

For a more intimate setting, seek out the Caribbean/South Pacific Lounge, where a combo plays for quiet dancing on a steel floor and seating is on low modern chairs and love seats in teal blue. The lounge is right on deck so you can dance out into the starlight glittering down on one of the ship's three swimming pools.

On both ships you'll find some gambling action in the casino.

Shops on board are good-looking too, with floor-to-ceiling glass windows. That shopping area is called Fifth Avenue aboard the *Fairwind,* Bond Street on the *Fairsea,* which should give you an idea of the quality of the tempting merchandise. There's a shop for clothing, one for perfumes, one for china, all of them heaven for compulsive buyers. On the line's *Fairsky* the shops are on Rodeo Drive!

We're especially partial to the Mediterranean/South Seas Lounge, where piano music tinkles as you relax in deep white or teal-blue chairs. Beneath your feet on the *Fairwind* is more of that lush pastel carpeting you'll find in many places throughout the ship, and above your head a shiny black ceiling. It's a very understated and tranquil setting indeed, flanked by an equally sublime, petite cocktail lounge.

For quieter moments there's a very nice library aboard, complete with glass-enclosed bookcases, comfy armchairs, and paneled walls. There's also a card room for long-into-the-night bridge games.

One more small bar is a nice spot for post-show libations, the tiny Moby Dick Bar (called Harry's Bar on the *Fairsea),* where a few comfortable couches and chairs offer a quiet retreat.

And then there's the pizzeria. Open from 11 p.m. to 2 a.m. for adults only, this bilevel room focuses on its pizza ovens and smells wonderful all the time. Kids are welcome at certain times of day, but at night it's a strictly adult haven.

Down on D Deck you'll find the ship's balconied theater (the balcony's one deck up, of course, on the Continental Deck).

Finally, down on the Riviera Deck you'll find the ship's two dining rooms, the Ritz and the Lancaster on the *Fairwind,* the Grosvenor and the Dorchester on the *Fairsea.*

If you're one of those people who's always ready on time for dinner and your companion is just the opposite, seek out the tiny garden room for your toe-tapping wait. It's just a small spot, but the palms rustling in the background ease waiting pains.

Both ships are equipped for wheelchairs too.

Cabins

An especially nice touch occurs the minute you step aboard this ship: white-gloved attendants meet you and take you to your cabin so you're not left wandering aimlessly about. Cabin service is quite good and the accommodations are kept spic and span. A friendly steward will bring you fruit juice and small sandwiches.

Cabins are unusually large, due in part to the spaciousness you often find on older ships. You'll find full-length wardrobes in your cabin, private bathrooms in all of them, and closed-circuit television in suites and mini-suites. All cabins are carpeted and feature four channels of music on the radio. Telephones let you call new friends aboard or at home, as well as on-board services.

Cabins with two lower beds also have two upper berths that swing back into the wall during the day so you don't even know they're there.

Some outside cabins with portholes don't have much of a view but they do let in the sunlight. Sitmar is scrupulous in telling you, pre-purchase, about any obstructions to your view, so if you feel that's important, do inquire.

Electricity on the *Fairwind* is a little antiquated so you have to go to special hair-drying rooms if you want to use those powerful hair blowers. One very nice feature, to my way of thinking, is a self-service laundry with an ironing board and oldtime flat irons. You can also send your things to the on-board laundry, which has rapid service.

The *Fairwind* is kept scrupulously clean and refreshingly shining, so her few signs of age are less apparent.

In the poshest cabins there are no fewer than three stewards to see to your every need, if you can come up with that many needs. In fact, so quintessentially Italian are they aboard this craft that stewards have been known to put the arm of Herbie's jammies around Molly's nightie when they turn down the bed!

Price categories are numerous aboard Sitmar ships, ranging from the top-priced Category A to the lowest-priced Category P, a total of 15 price levels, but there are no peak and "value" seasons on these cruises anymore.

Let's take a look at some of the cabins and their costs for a ten-day Caribbean voyage.

If price is no object, the deluxe Ocean Capri Suite is a smashing sight—bath with bidet and tub, dressing area, refrigerator, built-in bar, large television, Haitian cotton bedspreads, a full couch, and two chairs, and all of it in brown, beige, and deep-green velvet. A special favorite is a suite called Ocean Antibes, a study in royal-blue carpet, burgundy velvet couches, and drapes screening off the sleeping area where a queen-size bed reposes in regal splendor. Gorgeous dark wood, mahogany, rosewood perhaps, is everywhere. For one of these really magnificent and beautifully decorated suites you'll pay $3,340 per person for a ten-day Caribbean cruise.

There are 26 mini-suites aboard, featuring twin beds with drapes that close off the sleeping area from the sitting area and its L-shaped couches and chair—very comfortable indeed. Televisions show closed-circuit movies. Mini-suites are a bit lower in price—$2,590 per person for this cruise.

Cabin 0154 is a typical example of a Category C cabin, an outside double room with two lower and two recessed upper berths, a central dresser, a big window facing an outside stairway, and a nice long mirror for before-dinner primping. The charge is $2,240 per person for a ten-day cruise.

Outside double cabins with two lower beds and two recessed upper berths range on down in price from Category D through Category G. One of those outside staterooms costs $2,015 to $2,165 per person.

Categories I and J are inside cabins with the same upper and lower bed setup, this time on Acapulco and Riviera Decks, comparatively high up on the ship. These inside accommodations are $1,845 to $1,885 per person for that ten-day Caribbean trip.

Less-expensive outside cabins in Categories K and L offer one lower bed and an upper berth. For one of these cabins the cost is $1,785 per person for double occupancy on a ten-day cruise, $2,280 single.

On the Europa Deck Cabin 189 is long and narrow, a comfortable nest for a single person and quite spacious. This is also a low-priced cabin aboard, costing $1,625 for a ten-day cruise.

Accommodations on Europa Deck are Category N inside cabins with one lower bed and one upper berth for $1,625 per person double, $2,280 if you are occupying the cabin alone.

In a lower price bracket, Cabin 176 on Ocean Deck is an inside single with an upper bunk. Although the room is quite small, it has a very good address if you'd like to buy a little status cheap. This Category P cabin is an example of the lowest-priced quarters aboard, and can be yours for a ten-day cruise for $1,545.

Third and fourth adults sharing a cabin with two full-fare adult passengers pay $945 for the ten-day cruise in peak season, while children under 12 pay $755.

The per-person, per-day rate begins at about $155, rising in upper price brackets to $224 per person daily, higher in suites.

Sitmar has some money-saving fly-free programs designed to lure you to its cruises.

FAIRSKY: Constructed at the French CNIM (Construction Navales et Industrielles de la Méditerranée) Shipyard in La Seyne-sur-Mer near Toulon, the *Fairsky* measures in at 46,000 tons, carries 1,200 passengers and cost a whopping $150 million.

Public Rooms

On board are 11 public decks with 606 passenger cabins (350 of them outside cabins, 218 inside), plus 28 mini-suites and 10 larger suites. All cabins have color television and 110-volt A.C. current. Like her sister ships, she has ceiling-recessed upper berths in many cabins, a particularly appealing feature for families.

For fitness fans the ship has a jogging track, a sports deck for paddle tennis, and a health center with exercise equipment of all kinds. Called the Spa, this health center includes a whirlpool bath, two saunas, and a massage room, all on the Sun Deck.

You'll also find a complete casino with blackjack and roulette tables and 85 slot machines.

A main showroom on board, the Fairsky Showroom, is *big:* 11,000 square feet, one of the largest afloat and able to accommodate 800 passengers at a time.

Special pains have been taken with a forward observation lounge where floor-to-ceiling windows offer a glamorous view the line calls a "captain's-eye view" of the ocean outside.

There are three swimming pools aboard, including one in the Spa, and acres of sunning space.

A favorite before-dinner retreat on the ship is the intimate Piano Lounge and adjoining Melody Bar where a pianist's quiet melodies provide background for a tête-à-tête. There's something about a lone pianist that encourages budding Carusos, so you often find a sing-along going on in here.

The *Fairsky*'s pizzeria is a welcoming place, bright and airy and just as tempting to the eye as it is to the stomach. That's why many people aboard gravitate there as they would to an outdoor café and end up sitting there for hours watching passersby or screeching over a mistake in a game of Trivial Pursuit.

If it's a cocktail lounge you're seeking, try the banquettes of the Horizon Lounge, where you can watch the scenery slipping by the tall windows that trim this room.

Many are those who escape to the intimacy of the Rainbow Bar, where more windows offer you a view both from tables scattered about the room and from the circular bar.

More lounges? Of course, six in all, including the big, bright Veranda lounge overlooking one of the ship's swimming pools and the Starlight room where curvilinear lines seem to wrap around you.

Shoppers do their exercises on Rodeo Drive where glittering boutique windows are filled with irresistibles. Sitmar is smart enough to bring some local craft work on board at each stop, so if you forgot to buy something for Aunt Jane in the last port, you get another chance when the ship lifts anchor and the shop reopens.

A tip of the toque to Sitmar's chefs, who come up with some of the most unusual and most mouthwatering pastas of any ship afloat. We defy you, absolutely defy you, to resist after you get a look at some of these creations.

You will get that look in one of two separate but equal dining rooms aboard, the Savoy and the Regency. Both boast handsome contemporary furnishings in earthy tones and have quite a number of tables for four stretched out alongside big banks of windows. Larger tables for six march down the center of the room but share the view.

A beauty and barber shop and the ship's movie theater are tucked away on lower decks where you'll also find a real convenience—a self-service laundromat.

Cabins

After you've dreamed over the suites—or perhaps gone all-out and booked one—you'll find cabins aboard quite uniform in size.

Perhaps the single best thing about them, however, is the closed-circuit television in each. On those you can while away a (heaven forbid!) rainy day or a lazy sunny one watching some of the films you've been meaning to see but haven't.

Many cabins also have two recessed upper berths as well as two lower beds, perfect for sailing families.

There are plenty of closets and drawer space, good reading lights, a telephone, and four music channels on the radio.

Décor is soft and soothing, as is the service of the stewards who will bring you breakfast in bed at any morning hour you specify and see to feeding you 24 hours a day if that's what you want.

Deluxe suites have private balconies, loads of space, and separate sitting areas. Mini-suites share the latter two features. Rates for a ten-day cruise on this ship are the same in every category as those on the other two ships: $2,590 to $3,340 for suites and mini-suites, $2,015 to $2,590 for outside cabins, and $1,545 to $1,985 for inside quarters. Single travelers pay a 50% surcharge, and all fares include round-trip air transportation. Those who don't need air transportation to the departure port can take $250 off the fare.

On this and on its other ships, Sitmar has instituted a $200-per-person Early Booking Discount, available if you book a trip three months before your chosen departure date.

Port charges average $30 to $50, depending on the itinerary, but range from $25 to $75.

FAIRMAJESTY: A 1,470-passenger ship, the *FairMajesty* measures in at 62,500 tons, and is 13 decks high and three football fields in length. Among the special features of the new craft are a fancy forward observation lounge at the top of the ship, a three-story atrium lobby and shopping gallery, and the cruise industry's first in-pool bar.

It will have 14 suites, 36 mini-suites, 510 outside cabins, and 165 inside staterooms. Cabins are equipped with a video system that does everything but talk to you: you press buttons on it to order shore excursions, wine, room service, even a wake-up call. Twin beds convert to doubles and there's color television, four music channels, picture windows, refrigerators, and outdoor terraces in suites and mini-suites.

On board this new ship you can prowl a shopping arcade, sip a glass of wine at the wine bar, go for an espresso, cappuccino, or a pastry sin at the demitasse bar. To work it off there's a health and beauty center with an exercise room, Nautilus equipment, an aerobics area, sauna, and massage tables.

Evenings, the ship's showy shows take place in a two-level showroom while dining occurs under a two-story ceiling in a restaurant seating 800. For less formal consumption there's an indoor-outdoor buffet restaurant serving lunch, snacks, and dinner. Naturally, Sitmar's trademark pizzeria will be whipping up made-to-order pizzas all day long and well into the night.

A domed observation lounge offers a 270° view of passing scenery, while a card room, library, and cinema offer quieter pursuits.

There are two outdoor swimming pools on board, one with a swim-up bar, the other surrounded by four Jacuzzis and a waterfall.

Sitmar's emphasis on young sailors translates here to a teen and youth center and a childrens' pool.

29. SUN LINE CRUISES

Contact: Sun Lines, One Rockefeller Plaza, Suite 315, New York, NY 10020 (tel. 212/397-6400, or toll free 800/468-6400).

Cruising Grounds: Caribbean, Mexico's Yucatán Peninsula, South America (including the Amazon River and various Brazilian, Argentinian, and Uruguayan ports), Mediterranean and Black Seas.

Itineraries: *Stella Solaris* —

IN WINTER: Fort Lauderdale – Key West – Cozumel – Grand Cayman – Ocho Ríos – Port Limón – San Blas Islands – Panama Canal – Balboa – Guayaquil *or* Guayaquil – Costa Rica – Acapulco – Zihuatanejo – Cabo San Lucas – Los Angeles or reverse; followed by an around–South America cruise from Los Angeles or Guayaquil as follows: Guayaquil – Callao – Coquimbo – Valparaíso – Puerto Montt – Cape Pilar – Dungeness – Usuaia – Cape Horn – Puerto Madryn – Montevideo – Buenos Aires – Punta del Este – Puerto Madryn – Montevideo – Santos – Rio de Janeiro – Salvador da Bahía – Belém – Barbados – Martinique – St. Thomas – Port Everglades.

IN SUMMER: Mediterranean cruises, including Greek islands, Egypt, and Israel.

Stella Oceanis —

IN WINTER: St. Croix – St. Barthélemy – Palm Island – Trinidad – Carriacou – Grenada – Iles des Saintes – Nevis – St. Kitts – St. Croix *or* St. Croix – St. Maarten – Mustique – Barbados – Bequia – St. Vincent – Antigua – Virgin Gorda – Tortola – St. Croix.

IN SUMMER: Greek Island and Turkey cruises.

Sun Line Cruises can trace its history back to the Aegean where warm waters and sunny islands have been luring adventuresome cruisers since the Phoenicians began touring here. But romantic and ethereally beautiful as those islands are, they are somewhat less interesting when visited on cargo boats, which are to cruises what cheap old hotels are to motoring trips: just a way to get there.

That's about how Greek entrepreneur Alex Keusseoglou sized it up in the early 1960s when he decided to do something about the quality of life on the Mediterranean Sea. Figuring it couldn't hurt to add a little elegance to Med voyages, Keusseoglou set out to create a cruise line of his own. He had plenty of background to give him a clue on how to go about this gargantuan task: he'd been a founder of Home Lines and helped develop that company into a major force in transatlantic cruising.

Beginning in 1960 with a vessel named *Stella Maris,* which sailed on Aegean cruises, Keusseoglou soon had two ships, the second called *Stella Solaris I*. As time went on both those vessels were replaced with two new ships called the *Stella Maris II*, which became part of the line in 1965, and the *Stella Oceanis*, which joined the company two years later. And in 1973 the *Stella Solaris*, a new ship, became the pride, joy, and largest vessel in the Sun Line fleet.

Sun Line is still managed by the Keusseoglou family, which tends to all the details right down to the décor of the ship (coordinated by Isabella Keusseoglou, widow of the line's founder).

Sun Line likes to call itself the "elite fleet" of the travel world, and it's certainly true that the line's three ships sail to glamorous places and are themselves good-looking ladies.

Largest of the three is the far-from-massive 18,000-ton *Stella Solaris*, which carries just 620 passengers and 330 staffers off to much-loved Caribbean ports and exotic destinations in South America most of the winter, with stops at dozens of fascinating ports in the Caribbean and on the Amazon River. In spring she sails to Europe for stops in Turkey, Egypt, and Israel.

North Americans don't see much of these ships, although the *Stella Solaris* often makes Fort Lauderdale's Port Everglades her winter home, sailing from there to the Caribbean and South America.

Meanwhile her much smaller sister ship, the 5,500-ton *Stella Oceanis*, spends the winter cruising from St. Croix through the Caribbean to some most unusual South American ports. She drops anchor in Bequia, Carriacou, Tortola, Grenada, Mustique, Guadeloupe, and St. Kitts, among other Caribbean islands on 7- or 14-day round-trip journeys.

Stella Maris II, yacht-like at a mere 3,500 tons, sails in summer on Greek island and Mediterranean itineraries that take its 186 passengers from Venice to Nice via Corfu, Costa Smeralda, Elba, and Portofino.

Activities

Ports are important to this cruise line, which offers you many on every cruise. Those port visits fill almost every day on many cruises, so when you do have a day at sea it's probably not a round of activity you'll be seeking but a nice quiet place in the sun.

Because its ships visit quite unusual ports, the line goes out of its way to make those ports a memorable and educational experience. Lecturers of considerable reknown, including such luminaries as an Amazon explorer and authorities from the Costeau Society, are aboard to offer enrichment programs and to accompany passengers on shore tours. It's a nice touch and one much appreciated by fans of this line.

At night, however, the ship sizzles with zappy singers, a Greek choir, dancers, and comedians, or dances to the music of an orchestra. Occasionally a concert pianist will turn up to turn passengers on to the music of Beethoven. More often a mariachi band or reggae dancers will come aboard to dazzle and amuse, since the *Stella Solaris* likes you to have a cultural taste of the countries you visit.

A special feature of this Greek line, of course, is a Greek Night, when the staff offers you ouzo and Greek wines at cocktail hour, then entertains you at dinner and later with Greek folkloric dancing, winding up finally in the disco where they'll teach you the syrtaki.

You can dress up if you like for the ship's masquerade evening. On other nights the ship celebrates French Night, Ladies' Night, Caribbean Night, and finally, throws a farewell banquet.

For quiet evenings there's music in the piano bar or dancing on deck.

Special pasta lovers alert! At midnight there's a spaghetti party.

If you miss that one, fear not. In addition to the usual wide variety of cruise-ship eating opportunities, this line can always come up with a feta-cheese-laden Greek salad, souvlaki, or moussaka. For those without sin in their souls, Sun Line has added special menu selections conforming to low-cholesterol, low-sodium, and low-fat guidelines.

On the *Stella Oceanis,* too, port visits are a very important part of a cruise, so on-board activities are less frenetic and jam-packed than on some ships. In fact on some cruises you are in port every single day of the journey so that leaves very little time for arts-and-crafts classes or nutty contests.

You can, of course, see a movie, visit any of several sipping spots on board, play cards or read in the library and card rooms, get some exercise in the ship's swimming pool or in the gym.

Nighttime activities begin with before-dinner cocktails, work their way through a leisurely dinner, and then move into the ship's lounges where shows are similar to those aboard the *Stella Solaris.* Take a look at what's going on there and expect to see more of the same on this ship.

STELLA SOLARIS: Enter the massive reception area in the *Stella Solaris* and you'll know that there are some good reasons why this ship is so popular. Undoubtedly, this handsome craft has much to recommend it.

Public Rooms

First, it has a certain old-world elegance. From decks named after gems—ruby, emerald, sapphire—to a big cinema decorated in gray velvet to a below-stairs disco outfitted in leather and featuring a steel dance floor, the 18,000-ton *Stella Solaris* is a ship at once cozy and contemporary.

Although not a particularly large ship—just 18,000 tons and carrying 620 passengers—the *Stella Solaris* has such an open airiness you often feel as if you're on a much larger craft.

The Main Lounge is a sweeping bilevel room with long expanses of glass and raised seating along the sides of the room. Front and center, a glowing parquet dance floor provides a focal point for a handsome tranquil room. An ornate open wall cordons off an adjoining lounge and bar where you can watch the sun setting over the stern through a bank of glistening windows. Leather banquettes add a contemporary touch to a room decorated in subtle orange and brown tones.

Up on the Lido Deck, the Lido Bar is a popular retreat for sunseekers who spend their days draped around the ship's eye-catching figure-eight, double-circle blue mosaic swimming pool. It's built that way to help keep down the wave action in the pool as the ship plows through the water.

On the Solaris Deck is the ship's dining room, a tranquil spot decorated in a soothing blue-and-white theme.

When you see how well you eat on this ship, you may want to be introduced to the gymnasium, the saunas, and the massage room. The *Stella Solaris* provides quite a nice environment in which to huff and puff: carpets throughout, a big shiny set of chromed weights, rowing machines, mats, incline boards, bicycles, the lot.

Built for cooler climes, the *Stella Solaris* sports one of those covered promenade decks that can't help but remind you of old movies in which passengers sat sipping tea, their knees neatly covered with an afghan as they crossed the North Atlantic. (Just what you'd be doing with an afghan in the Caribbean is difficult to say, but the image is seductive anyway.)

Just around the corner from the purser's desk on the Solaris Deck is a handsome shopping area with wide windows displaying everything from showy caftans to pre-Columbian replica jewelry.

Beauty salons and barbershops seem to be the most neglected area on most ships, but not here—these are very classy operations, clean and shiny with marble floors.

Up top on the Boat Deck there's a comfortable reading and card room, and down on Golden Deck there's a special playroom for children.

Down on the main deck, which on this ship is beneath the ship's seven passenger decks, is that slinky gray-and-silver discothèque, and on the Sapphire Deck is the ship's big cinema. And there is a Monte Carlo Casino aboard of course.

Cabins

Cabins come in all sizes and shapes, but have one unusual feature: more expensive quarters have closed-circuit television sets in them, but there are hookups in every room so you can bring your own portable if you're a real television fan.

On this ship the cabins are down a short passageway that leads off the main thoroughfares of the vessel. All the ship's quarters are reasonably spacious, usually with twin beds, a couple of chairs, sometimes even a couch and coffee table. Large dressers and closets give you ample room to stow your belongings, and many of them have a special corner for storing your bed pillows during the day when you're using the beds as a seating area. All rooms have private baths.

Sun Line keeps it reasonably simple with cabin price categories. There are 11—Categories 1 through 11.

If you're really going first class, deluxe suites B6 and B8 are especially handsome quarters, the former smartly outfitted in a beige-and-brown diamond pattern and twin beds almost hidden from the sitting area. There's lots of storage space: a full dresser, three full closets. Suite B8 on the Boat Deck is decorated in soothing shades of deep burgundy, and similar quarters, suite B2, in deep blue and white. The main allure of B2 is its location all alone on a hallway, making it very private indeed.

A 14-day Galápagos Islands cruise in one of those elegant Category 1 suites, which feature two twin beds or a double bed and both tub and shower in the bathroom, plus a spacious separate sitting area, will cost $5,595 to $6,550 per person.

Moving down the price list, there are four categories of outside double cabins, all with two lower beds and private bath, of course. Categories 4, 5, 6, and 7 range in price from $4,250 to $4,885 per person for the 14-day cruise.

The remaining cabins—Categories 8, 9, 10, and 11—are all inside quarters. Inside cabins, of course, are smaller, but they are still roomy. Cabin R53 and its counterparts in Category 9 look comfortable. The top-priced accommodations among those inside selections have two lower and two upper beds while standard inside rooms have two lower beds. Fares in these cabins are $3,220 to $4,090 per person, depending on size and location.

Category 8 cabins are quite spacious, with shower only in the baths, two lower and one upper bunk, and two full-length closets. Cabin R69 is an attractive example of this category.

That works out to a daily rate beginning at $230 per person, rising in the more expensive cabins to $303 or $349 per person a day, higher for suites.

A third person sharing a cabin pays the minimum fare for that cruise, while children 2 to 12 occupying a third or fourth berth in the same cabin pay 50% of the minimum rate, $30 a day for those under 2.

Single occupants of a superior or standard double cabin pay 150% of the fare for that cabin, 200% in suites.

You must also budget $65 additional for port charges on the 14-day cruise, more on longer voyages, to a high of $120 for a 28-day journey.

STELLA OCEANIS: A much smaller ship, the *Stella Oceanis* is just 5,500 tons and carries 300 passengers, half that number of staff. On a ship this small you'll feel almost as if you're on a big yacht. Although we've never been on the *Stella Oceanis,* friends have praised the intimate feeling of this small ship.

Public Rooms

Greek history and culture play a big part in the theme aboard this ship, so learn your mythology.

You'll be dining, for instance, in the Aphrodite Dining Room, which seats 200 and is decorated in gold and blue. On the Oceanis Deck just outside the restaurant you can amuse yourself in a small casino or shop in a boutique with some interesting Greek creations for sale.

Entertainment takes place in the ship's Minos Lounge, which is big enough for all 300 passengers. A tiny club at the back of the Minos Lounge makes a good spot for quiet post-prandial sipping.

For more eventful evenings, head for the Plaka Taverna, which becomes the ship's disco at night.

Cabins

There are eight grades of cabins on board this small vessel, numbered Category 1 through 8, with the highest numbers the most expensive quarters on board.

A fascinating cruise available on the *Stella Oceanis* is a ten-day Greek island trip. The following prices are for one of these ten-day sojourns.

If you opt for a deluxe outside suite with two beds and sitting room, you'll pay $2,145 per person for the trip.

In outside cabins you pay $1,880 to $2,015 per person.

Categories 6, 7, and 8 are inside cabins with two trim lower or upper and lower beds. The cost in one of those is $1,690 to $1,880 per person for the ten-day cruise.

Third- and fourth-person prices are the same aboard the *Stella Oceanis* as aboard the *Stella Solaris*—minimum fare for the cruise. Children under 12 pay 50% of the minimum rate when occupying a cabin with two adults paying full fare.

Single travelers also pay the same aboard both ships, 150% to 200% of the fare for single occupancy of a double cabin.

Per diem rates run from a minimum of $169 per person to a high of $215.

30. WINDSTAR SAIL CRUISES

Contact: Windstar Sail Cruises, 7205 Corporate Center Dr., Miami, FL 33126 (tel. 305/592-8008, or toll free 800/258-7245, 800/341-7245 in Florida).

Cruising Grounds: Caribbean, Mediterranean, Tahiti.

Itineraries: *Wind Star*—Martinique – Pigeon Island – Mustique – Tobago Cays – Barbados – Bequia – Palm Island – Martinique, year round.

Wind Song—Papeete – Huahine – Tahaa – Raiatea – Bora Bora – Moorea – Papeete, year round.

Wind Spirit—

IN SUMMER AND FALL: Monte Carlo – Antibes – St. Tropez – Corsica – Elba – Livorno – Portofino – Monte Carlo.

IN WINTER AND SPRING: St. Thomas – St. John – St. Maarten – Prickley Pear Cays – St. Barthélemy – Virgin Gorda – Jost Van Dyke – St. Thomas.

If you dream of sliding through silvery waters, wind whipping through the sails, here comes Windstar Sail Cruises to bring your fantasy to life.

Quite a departure from every other cruise ship afloat, this new line has something new in ships: a cruise ship with sails!

Claiming to have built the longest sail ships ever, the line has set out to combine the best of two worlds—sailboats and cruise ships.

WIND STAR / WIND SPIRIT:
What they came up with is a fleet of sailing craft 440 feet long—and that's *quite* a lengthy tale—with six sails rising 185 feet above the sea. You won't, however, see an intrepid sailor clambering up into the rigging to furl a sail—on Windstar ships that's all done by computer!

For those curious types who need to know how this computer business works, here's as much as we know. Wind speed and direction, movement of the water and of the vessel, and the given course of the craft are all poured into the ship's computers. There the constant stream of data is calculated and turned into sailing commands transmitted to hydraulic winches that control the stand of the booms and the furl of the 21,500 square feet of sail.

The *Wind Star*'s six sails can be furled in two minutes, and if the captain differs with the computer he can just override it and sail with his own human skills. To back it all up, there are three diesel-electric engines that can propel the ship when required.

Computers also control the hydraulic pumps of the anti-heeling tanks, limiting the angle of heel to a maximum of 6°.

On board this sailing ship are 74 cabins, each with an ocean view and some comforts you'll never find on your neighbor's weekend sailer: a video cassette recorder, color television, radio, and mini-bar in your cabin, for openers.

Activities

Lest you think someone's going to call on you to help reef a mainsail, rest easy. There are, of course, engines as well as sails, and a staff of 89 to see to the furling and to the care and feeding of 148 passengers.

Those 148 will be living in considerable luxury, complete with beauty salon, two lounges, a disco, boutique, library, gymnasium, sauna, swimming pool, piano bar, and casino, plus plenty of deck space on which to acquire the perfect tan.

If all those sails stir a latent desire to get out there and try a little jibbing yourself, Windstar has a whole fleet of sailboats and windsurfing boards, and can even get you parasailing, waterskiing, scuba-diving, and deep-sea fishing.

You'll find a Norwegian crew at the helm and Europeans on the staff. You're also likely to find quite a French touch in the galley—the line's president is a quite charming Frenchman, Jean-Claude Potier, who left cuisine-conscious Paquet Cruises to join this new venture.

With such a small number of passengers, the ship has another advantage: everyone dines between 8 and 10 p.m.—no set hours, dining companions, or tables.

Because it has a shallow draft—just 13 feet—the ships can sneak into harbors denied the big-bruiser cruisers. That's why you'll find them in such idyllic spots as Bequia, a tropical-dream island accessible only by sea; lovely St. Lucia; and Mustique, stomping ground of England's Princess Margaret and Mick Jagger—not necessarily together.

Golf and tennis can be arranged at some stops, and at Palm Island you can get a look at a coral reef and a ship that sank on it.

Public Rooms

In keeping with its posh ports and its matching price tags, Windstar Sail Cruises runs some very classy sailing ships. Goodness, they even *look* elegant, their tall sails unfurling in perfect symmetry as these grown-like-Topsy yachts surge through the sea.

Insides are every bit as sleek as outsides: colorful but tasteful paintings, subtly handsome furnishings—even tasteful coverings featuring reproductions of famous paintings or photographs or drawings of historic ships.

Wood, particularly burls, is much in evidence, mixed with soft-hued fabrics often sparked by touches of brilliant color, and with leather and other natural fabrics.

In the ship's dining room and lounge you dine in easy view of the sea and of passing islands visible through tall windows. An unusual glass-enclosed and skylit veranda top deck is a delightful spot for quiet contemplation of sky and sea.

Back on the aft deck sun lovers will find the requisite swimming pool, a saltwater splasher, and down one deck is the open-air launching platform from which you can board small sailboats, windsurfers, or motorized inflatable boats for yet another kind of day at sea.

For fitness enthusiasts, there's a sauna and gymnasium, the toils of which can be erased in a beauty salon and barbershop.

Those whose idea of a dream vacation is an armload of good books and a warm place to read them can ease up to the library where both books and videotapes offer less strenuous diversion.

Later, there's dining among vivid colors on cuisine that owes much to the French but calls frequently upon unusual local treats, tropical accents, and popular light cuisine.

Top that off with a visit to the piano bar or a stop in the ship's nightclub, where you can dance beneath the stars on a glass-domed dance floor.

Cabins

On these ships you'll never have to face the inside-outside cabin decision. Here every cabin is an outside cabin, and each is exactly alike so there's no oneupsmanship.

Quite contemporary, the ships' cabins show careful thought given to design as well as to color, something that cannot always be said about modern cruise ships. Storage space, for instance, is tucked in behind handsome wood paneling. Soft colors are offset by unexpectedly colorful, but quite pleasant, paintings and touches of color. Bathrooms are Scandinavian-sleek with showers that can be stationary or hand-held, and their bright whiteness is often sparked with towels in rainbow hues. Another thoughtful touch: a hairdryer in every bathroom.

Designed as they are for the first-class traveler, these cabins come complete with color televisions, a video cassette player (with a well-stocked video cassette library also on board), radio, mini-bar stocked with all the requisite goodies, and direct-dial ship-to-shore telephones. Twin beds can be converted to a queen-size sleeper in every cabin, and for midnight munchers there's a cabin steward on duty around the clock to provide late-night snacks or early-morning continental breakfast.

On each sailing all cabins are the same price, but those prices differ by season —lowest in summer, highest in winter—ranging from $2,495 to $2,895 per person for a seven-day cruise, a per diem rate of $356 to $413 per person.

To those costs must be added air fares ranging from $300 to $400 on Caribbean cruises.

A third person sharing a cabin pays $575 to $720.

31. WORLD EXPLORER CRUISES

Contact: World Explorer Cruises, 555 Montgomery St., San Francisco, CA 94111 (tel. 415/391-9262, or toll free 800/854-3835).
Cruising Grounds: Alaska.

Itinerary: *Universe*—
IN SUMMER: Vancouver – Wrangell – Juneau – Skagway – Glacier Bay – Columbia Glacier – Valdez – Anchorage – Sitka – Ketchikan – Victoria – Vancouver *or* Vancouver – Wrangell – Juneau – Skagway – Haines – Columbia Glacier – Anchorage – Sitka – Ketchikan – Victoria – Vancouver.

In these pages you've read about floating hotels and love boats, mini-cruisers and maxi-yachts. Now it's time to meet a floating university campus!

Step right up and say hello to the 18,100-ton S.S. *Universe,* one and only craft of World Explorer Cruises.

We're going to go out on a limb here and *guarantee* you that no ship afloat has a larger library—and we mean that literally! How, after all, could you beat 11,000 volumes?

What's going on here? Well, half the year this ship is chartered to the University of Pittsburgh, which uses it as a floating campus for its Institute of Shipboard Education's Semester-at-Sea. (Where were semesters like that when we were in college?) If you missed that floating-semester era, you are about to get another chance.

In late May the ship arrives at Vancouver where it spends the summer cruising glacial Alaska waters on quite reasonably priced 14-day cruises. Of the ships sailing on 14-day Alaska cruises, this is the only one cruising 14 days from Vancouver, allowing you to see more of Alaskan waters than do cruises from San Francisco or Los Angeles.

UNIVERSE: Formerly the S.S. *Atlantic,* this American-built ship went into service in 1959, and was bought by this cruise line in 1977 and refurbished throughout in 1987.

Activities

Aboard you will find 550 passengers intent on learning more, indeed as much as possible, about the lands they are visiting. To help them do that, the line brings lecturers on board for detailed discussions of the art, literature, and cultures of the people you'll be meeting at ports you visit.

You may hear an art expert lecturing on ceremonial art of the Mekoryuk or an oceanographer explaining how the Tongans trick an octopus into leaping at their lures. Anthropologists outline the possible meanings of petroglyphs and naturalists will explain the importance of the walrus to native Alaskans.

You'll find historians, political scientists, even musicians aboard to introduce you to the places you're visiting, offering you a firm foundation of knowledge on which to create your own cultural exchange with those you meet.

While these are not stuffy events, they're definitely meant for the person who wants more than the superficial cruise experience, the more sophisticated traveler with a strong interest in a cruise as an educational experience.

Line executives unabashedly admit that this is not an elegant luxury ship, adding that they consider the ship a "value cruise."

Cabins and public areas are spacious but not elegant, they point out, "and you won't find people wearing furs and diamonds." You will find many retired professional people, teachers, educators, people still active physically and mentally, and in search of an improvement in both.

All is not seminars, of course. Evenings there may be a classical guitarist or pianist performing in a quiet lounge, or a sing-along going strong in the piano bar.

In keeping with the general atmosphere of the cruises, masquerade parties aboard are more likely to feature historic characters than pregnant nuns or big-bellied male hula dancers. Entertainment runs more toward quiet evenings of dance music and conversation than frenetic disco sessions.

As one line executive put it: "We offer a lot more steak and a lot less sizzle. We wine and dine and entertain, but don't serve flaming desserts or have Broadway revues."

Public Rooms

You'll find plenty of entertainment aboard, and plenty of places for it. For openers, there are seven decks, five lounges, a nightclub, bar, 200-seat theater, and glass-enclosed promenade deck.

Up in the North Star Lounge on the Boat Deck a piano is the focal point of a bright room flanked by the small bar. Not far away is another small lounging area, outfitted with banquettes, comfortable chairs, and low tables.

Down a deck, on the Promenade Deck, there's always dancing in the Commodore Lounge or quiet talks in the Denali Room or Alyeska Room.

Just off the open deck at the stern you'll find the ship's big Mandarin Lounge, where an orchestra provides dance music for terpsichoreans who whirl on the big rectangular dance floor. The Commodore bar here is a favorite gathering spot, and has some cozy nooks and crannies for conversations with new friends.

Down on the main deck is the ship's dining room, a bilevel room lined with tables for four. Here you can dine on a wide range of American favorites, or try some new gustatory adventures created by the Chinese chefs aboard. Although the cruise staff is American, all the crew is Chinese and Filipino, so you can be sure you'll get an opportunity to try some "different" Oriental specialties.

In the theater you can see some top films, and in the lounges, variety shows, passenger talent shows, and entertainment by the cruise staff keep things hopping. There are some rousing bridge tournaments aboard too.

Naturally, you'll find gift and beauty shops on board, and way up top there's even a special room for the youngsters. Not to mention a hospital and that monstrous library, which, as a line executive pointed out to us, is bigger than the library of many a small town!

Cabins

All accommodations on board have private baths and are quite spacious, as you would expect on a ship of this age and type. All are carpeted and feature simple furnishings, usually including a dresser/desk, a chair or two, and closet space. Following that recent renovation, all the cabins are decorated in soft and pretty earth colors.

Twelve price categories range from A through K, with an extra BB category tossed in to cover outside double cabins. All Alaskan cruises are 14-day trips.

Let's look at the prices for a 14-day Alaska cruise in peak season.

The top-of-the-line accommodations are deluxe cabins with two lower beds, a tub bath, shower, loads of space, and a long mirrored dresser. For that the cost is $3,395 per person for a 14-day cruise.

Moving down in price a bit, outside staterooms with two lower beds are

$3,295 per person, and outside double cabins with similar accoutrements cost $3,195 per person for a 14-day cruise.

Three mid-priced categories of outside cabins—Categories D, E, and F—differ a little in size but have about the same general look to them, many including a couple of easy chairs and two beds with really quite a lot of space in between. For one of those you will pay $2,595 to $2,995 per person.

If you think you'll be happy with an inside cabin, you'll find them on the Upper, Main, and Promenade Decks, the latter sharing a deck with some quite high-priced quarters. Depending on what you ask for and what you pay, there will be either two lower beds or an upper and lower berth in these inside cabins. The price for one with two lower beds is $2,595 per person for a two-week cruise, dropping to $2,295 to $2,395 per person for cabins with upper and lower berths.

The rock-bottom price aboard is $2,095 per person for the two-week cruise. (Elevators do not connect to this floor, but you can catch one on the next floor up.)

Single travelers have a choice of a roomy outside single cabin in Category C for $3,095 or an inside single cabin for $2,595.

Third or fourth persons sharing a cabin are $595 per person for the Alaskan sojourn, and you'll also need to budget port charges of $35 per person.

On a per-person per diem basis, those figures work out to a low of $150 and a top price of $243. For Alaskan waters these are quite reasonable per diem rates. Line execs claim they're *the* lowest for Alaska sailings.

One May sailing is $200 cheaper in every category.

CHAPTER VI

FARE WEATHERING: BOOKING YOUR TICKET

□ □ □

1. WORKING WITH A TRAVEL AGENT
2. BOOKING YOUR TICKET
3. CANCELLATIONS
4. DINING, MAIL, SPECIAL PLANS
5. DOCUMENTATION

So now you have picked a ship, chosen a price category, pulled out your checkbook, and you're all set to commit yourself to a week as Captain Cook—or Captain Hook!
So now what?
If you haven't done it already, now is the time to see a travel agent. All along here we've been touting these travel agent people, and for very good reason: they can help you and they won't charge you a penny for doing so.

1. WORKING WITH A TRAVEL AGENT

As surprising as it sounds, travel agents tell us that there are still many people who don't really know what travel agents are or what they do, and who are afraid they'll have to pay for an agent's help in booking tickets.
If you're not altogether sure just what an agent is, let it be known that travel agents' services are free. They will do all the work, share all their considerable knowledge, and probably even send you flowers or a bottle of wine when you book a cruise.
How do they earn money? Simple. Just like real-estate agents, they are paid by the seller, in this case the cruise line, which pays them 10% to 15% of the cost of your ticket for having sent the line your business. Before you begin thinking that travel agents must be millionaires, figure that they must subtract all the costs of a business from their commissions, which doesn't leave many millionaires.
Many agents pay dues to belong to a group called the American Society of Travel Agents. Like any trade organization, ASTA offers its members educational

seminars and lobbying services. An ASTA logo on the agency door or advertising at least means that that agency is serious about its business. Other trade organizations include the Association of Retail Travel Agents (ARTA) and the Institute of Certified Travel Agents (ICTA), which confers a degree, Certified Travel Counselor (CTC), on agents who have been in business for five years and have completed many hours of required training courses.

While membership in any of those groups does not guarantee a good agent, it gives you a place to start looking. From there on, your personal assessment of an agent's talents and personality will help you decide if you want to do business with that agent or agency.

We really do advise you to seek an agent's help in booking a cruise. They have all the latest information on renovations, good and bad cabins, itineraries, and best of all, special price deals. What's more, they usually know the cruise lines' reservation agents and sales representatives well and will solicit their help on your behalf. That's especially nice if you have special problems or requests on a cruise.

Let's just say that travel agents are your business mom (or dad). They'll do their best to see that everything goes perfectly for you.

When you talk to your travel agent, don't be shy. Tell them how much money you have to spend. Holding back on that information is like refusing to tell your doctor where it hurts. As good business people and smart travelers, they may try to "sell up," that is, suggest that you pay a little more for a cruise than you'd planned. If you absolutely can't afford any more, stick by your guns. If you can, listen to their reasoning. It's based on experience, both personal and through reports from other clients.

While you're unburdening your financial soul, tell them something about yourself and your companion, if you have one. Do you like to meet lots of new people and socialize with them or are you happier keeping to yourself? How fussy are you about your living quarters? Do you like things contemporary or antique? What kind of entertainment do you like?

Good agents will ask you many questions like that in an attempt to narrow down the numbers of ships they think you will enjoy. They know, after all, that if *you* aren't happy, you'll see to it that *they* aren't happy!

Which brings us to the final point in working with a travel agent: don't blame them if some shipboard employee was rude or the line couldn't find your ticket or some other major or minor calamity occurred. They are in the unenviable position of promising a product that will be delivered, but having no control over the successful delivery of that promised product. If you do have service or other problems with a ship, tell—but don't berate—your travel agent.

If you insist on booking your own tickets, you can do so by contacting the line and following their instructions. Booking specifics usually are detailed on the back of a line or ship brochure too. Note, however, that some lines book *only* through travel agents.

2. BOOKING YOUR TICKET

When you've settled on a cruise and a cabin, you'll be asked to give the line a deposit, which varies from a set amount to a percentage of the total cost of each ticket. Your deposit will be confirmed by the cruise line and your cabin will be assigned, but you may get no specific cabin number until embarkation.

If you are determined to have a certain cabin, you can request it by number. Most lines will do all they can to give you the cabin you want—the more you pay for the ticket, the better chance there is that you'll get what you want. Money talks here as everywhere.

Travel agents can be really invaluable to those who want a specific cabin. In this industry, as in all industries, it's not what you know but *who* you know that counts. Travel agents know where to go with special requests, and their buying clout makes shipping lines eager to honor their requests.

You will be asked to pay the remaining amount at some time before a departure. Once again, when you must pay the full amount to reserve the cabin varies from line to line.

GROUP BOOKINGS: All lines sell at reduced rates to groups of 10, 15, or more, and many offer travel agents a free "tour conductor" cabin for every group they book. Agents often don't use the tour conductor cabin and pass the savings along to the group. Discounts for groups are usually 10% to 15% of the total, and each cruise line decides for itself how many people comprise a "group." If you are traveling with several other couples, read the ship's brochure information on group bookings and ask an agent how much you might be able to save.

Agents may also be able to team you up with a group the agency is booking on a certain ship. Ask about that possibility. Unlike group travel on the ground, ship groups are not herded about as a group and, of course, you have individual cabins.

MONEY-SAVING TIPS: Wherever money is changing hands, there are ways to secure a bargain.

Booking as far in advance as possible is one of the best ways to save money for two reasons: (1) cruise lines often offer a discount for early bookings (the definition of "early" varies); and (2) the least expensive cabins—and strangely enough, the most expensive quarters—are the first to be sold.

Another money-saving trick: Some lines will accept bookings known as "to be assigned," or TBA, at minimum or average rates. Such an arrangement stipulates that you will be given a cabin at least as good as the price category you paid. If you have paid a minimum rate and those cabins are all sold at the departure time, you will be "upgraded," as they say, and given a cabin in a higher price category. We've heard of some really lucky souls who have sailed in suites at the minimum rate! That's very rare, however, so don't be too optimistic. Do, however, ask about TBA arrangements on the line you're interested in sailing.

Single passengers have a similar opportunity. On ships that offer you the option of sharing a cabin—and that's almost all ships—you can ask your travel agent to specify that you will book only on a per-person double basis. If the line agrees and is unable to find someone to share your quarters, you pay only the per-person double rate instead of the 50% to 100% supplement required of single travelers occupying a double cabin by themselves.

One line, Norwegian Cruise Line, has a "Sea Saver" program in which you choose the cabin, they choose the ship. Designed to help NCL spread the passenger load over its sizable fleet, the program offers you bargain prices if you're willing to go on any cruise offered. Other lines may be working out a similar program even as you read. Look at travel ads in the newspaper and ask a travel agent about possible money-saving plans. Carnival Cruise Lines sometimes offers a similar program called "Super C Saver."

A real gambler (so some real gamblers tell us) can take cash in hand on the day he wants to sail, or perhaps just a few days before, walk up to the booking desk, and tell them that he wants to go on a cruise and has just this much money to spend.

Naturally, the amount you offer must be in the ballpark of at least the minimum price aboard—cruise operators are not idiots. If a line is hungry and sailing emptier than it would like, however, there's a possibility you could get a nice cabin for the minimum price or less. We can't tell you if this rumor is true since no one will admit to it, but if you're very flexible—and prepared for rejection—it might be worth a try. Very risky though.

LOOK AT YOUR TICKET: Not only is it fun to hold that paper promise of tomorrow's pleasures in your hand and meditate on the fun ahead, it's vital to check it to make sure everything is right. In this heavily mechanized world mistakes seem to occur with more, instead of the promised less, frequency. So when you get your tickets, take a close look at them.

It's going to sound stupid for us to tell you to look at the name of the ship you're sailing on, but we've been told that many people who arrive at the bustling Port of Miami don't know what ship they've booked! Be sure you know the name of the ship, and that you have indeed been booked on the one you requested.

A ticket is a valid contract between you and the cruise line. They must fulfill their obligations and you must fulfill yours. That means it would be wise for you to read the ticket or passage contract accompanying it to see what your cancellation responsibilities and expectations are and what will happen if you fail to sail or if you leave a cruise before it's over.

You'll also find in that contract the details of your fare, luggage restrictions (if there are any), line policy on cabin changes, information on what to do with money and valuables, details of what the line will do for you if it is forced to cancel or shorten a cruise, and warnings about illegal substances or dangerous items.

That brings up the matter of the line's cancellation of a cruise. Ships are, after all, mechanical creatures. Occasionally something major breaks down and the line is forced to cancel a cruise. In recent years ships have cancelled cruises when air conditioning broke down (who would want to cruise the Caribbean without it?) and when a ship struck a submerged object and was damaged, among other incidents.

Cruise lines have bent over backward to be fair in those instances by offering disappointed passengers everything from a free hotel room for the night to future cruises at enormous discounts.

Let's hope nothing goes awry before or during your cruise, but if it does, rest easy. The line will try very hard to ameliorate your disappointment. After all, they want you to come back and sail with them again.

3. CANCELLATIONS

If you must cancel, do so as soon as you know you're not going to be able to go on the cruise. Cancellation charges vary widely, but most lines look kindly on refunds if you cancel more than 30 days before the scheduled date of departure. If there are medical reasons for your cancellation, ask your doctor for a brief note. That will also help you get your money refunded.

As your sailing date approaches, it becomes more difficult to secure a full refund, but you can usually get a partial refund. Amounts vary from line to line.

If you miss the boat, you miss the boat. Don't expect to get your money back. Unlike planes, cruise lines can't count on overbooking and can't take standbys. Anyway, they promised *you* the space and kept it for you, so it's only fair that if you don't show up or cancel soon enough for them to sell the cabin to someone else, you are the one who should suffer.

Read the cancellation rules on the back of the ship's brochure and don't expect them to grant you any special favors, although if there are compelling reasons why you cannot go, your travel agent may be able to help you get all or some of your money back.

Travel agents and others also sell trip insurance. For a small fee, the insurance company will cover your losses if you should be forced to cancel. If you have any reason to believe you might have to cancel, this inexpensive insurance is well worth the cost.

Travel insurance covering any medical costs you might incur on a trip also is available. If you're going on a long cruise and/or have any medical problems, purchase of this kind of insurance is wise. Check your existing medical insurance policy, however. You may already be covered.

4. DINING, MAIL, SPECIAL PLANS

Once you've made a decision on line and price, it's time to think beyond the ticket to those wondrous moments known as meals. Just to reinforce what we've said elsewhere in this guide: all your meals and all your snacks—everything you consume on the ship—is included in the cost of your ticket. When you finish dinner or lunch or any other meal, you get up from the table and leave. No tipping, no cashiers, nothing.

Isn't that a pleasant thought?

Before you book your tickets, however, you might give some thought to your dining room seating arrangements. All large ships have tables for four or six, and many have tables for two or eight or ten as well.

If you like to meet people, you'll probably want to dine at a large table, while honeymooners may want only each other for company.

You can request a table for two, four, or whatever at the time you book. Dining room stewards and the maître d'hôtel will do their best to assign you to the kind of table you specify.

There is another consideration too: the hour at which you want to dine. On very small ships or very elegant ones, you will find only one seating so no decision is necessary. On large vessels, however, you will find two seatings at all or two of the three meals.

You can find a more detailed discussion of dining aboard in Chapter IX, so look that over, decide when and with how much company you would like to dine, and make your requests at the time you book the tickets. Late seatings are the most popular, by the way, so if you prefer to eat about 8 p.m. (as opposed to early seating at 6 or 6:30 p.m.), get in your bid for that seating now.

If you're going on a long cruise, you can have mail delivered to you at various ports. Now is the time to peruse the brochure and/or ask your agent or the line for the port addresses to which your friends and relatives can write.

If you want anything special aboard, now is also the time to indicate what those special needs might be. We are talking now about details on facilities for the handicapped; special diets (kosher, vegetarian, salt-free, oil-free, sugar-free, etc.); and any medical needs you might have or anticipate.

5. DOCUMENTATION

If you're visiting countries that require a passport or a visa, you will need to have those papers. A travel agent or the cruise line can tell you what, if any, papers are necessary.

No passport is necessary for cruises to the Bahamas, most Caribbean islands, Mexico, Canada, Hawaii, or Alaska (exotic as they are, those last two destinations are U.S. states, remember?), but it's always wise to have some proof of citizenship with you. Driver's licenses are not proof of citizenship, but a birth certificate, voter registration card, or citizenship papers are acceptable proof that you are indeed who and what you say you are. The exceptions in the Caribbean are the French *departements* Martinique and Guadeloupe. If you do not get a visa in advance from a French consulate, you must present a passport or other proof of citizenship (plus a photograph) at the airport.

SPECIAL PLANS / DOCUMENTATION □ 325

If you're sailing to Mexico, you may need a Mexican Tourist Card, available through a travel agent or from the Mexican Consulate prior to departure.

We carry our passports in our wallets all the time. They are small enough not to take up too much space, and it never hurts to have it with you. Who knows when someone may offer to fly you to Tahiti for the afternoon (although, sadly, that hasn't happened to us yet).

Passports are, of course, then very best proof of citizenship of all. Take yours along. If you don't have a passport, write to the U.S. Immigration Service and they will send you the necessary forms to apply for one.

On some cruises to South America, a visa is required. When you book one of those cruises (Sun Line Cruises, Conard, Royal Viking, and Epirotiki Lines make several South American visits, for instance), the line may ask you to send them your passport and they will secure a visa for you. Travel agents also perform these services.

If you're sailing to some far-away port, you'd be well advised to ask a travel agent or the line what, if any, inoculations might be required. While smallpox vaccinations are no longer required in North or South American waters, malaria inoculations are sometime suggested in some areas, and other shots may be necessary or suggested if an outbreak of some illness has occurred there recently. If shots are necessary, take them *before* you go so you have time to recover from any swelling or other adverse reaction.

CHAPTER VII

SURELY YOU DIDN'T FORGET THE . . . : WHAT TO PACK

□ □ □

1. SHOES
2. DAYTIME WEAR
3. JEWELRY
4. EVENING WEAR
5. RAIN AND GLACIER WEAR
6. LAUNDRY FACILITES
7. OTHER THINGS TO PACK

The very word "cruise" conjures up visions of bejeweled ladies and handsome gentlemen fluttering off to dinner in floating organza dresses and white wing collars, dancing under the stars, gazing out to sea as balmy breezes ruffle their hair and moonlight glitters overhead.

Is it true? Yes . . . and no.

All that glamour can be there if you want it, or can be radically modified if the idea of a starched shirt and bow tie sends you into a paroxysm of panic.

In days of yore when people dressed formally for dinner at *home,* a cruise was an extension and expansion of that formality, a place to see and be seen in your finest. In those days of high tea and higher society, only the very wealthy could afford to take a sea trip. In these socially leveled days, cruises are available to a wide range of pocketbooks, the majority of which have no necessity to own paste copies of their jewels, for they don't own jewels.

Cruises have changed with the times and these days are much more informal events. Now one or two dashing evening outfits will be fine. On most ships, gentlemen, those outfits need not include a tuxedo or dinner jacket. A business suit, preferably a dark one, will do nicely.

It is interesting to note here that cruise line execs tell us the one thing that most quickly sells women on the idea of taking a cruise is anticipation of dressing up for formal evenings and for dinner. Conversely, or perversely, that is the single point they say is most likely to discourage the gentlemen of the species. C'mon, guys, shape up and ship out—you'll love it.

Okay, so let's get down to it. Just what should you pack and how much of it?

1. SHOES

Let's start at the bottom—your feet. Footwear can include rubber-soled shoes of any kind ranging from flip-flops to low-heeled sandals. If it rains or if there's water splashed on the decks, surfaces are often slippery, so don't plan on too many Miss America appearances in bathing suit and three-inch heels.

Lots of stairs—and we do mean lots—will make you happy to see those low heels too. Shoes, comfortable ones, are a very important ingredient in your cruise wardrobe. Many ports you visit won't have fancy sidewalks, and will be dusty in dry heat, muddy and sloppy in the rain. With that in mind, don't pack a raft of fancy new shoes for port visits either.

You'll also find that although you can take taxis, if you elect to walk from the ship to town or back again, the hike can be a long one. Add a couple of hours of shopping and sightseeing to that and whew! Comfortable shoes make it fun. Uncomfortable ones make it a level of Dante's Hell.

Joggers should pack their running shoes and outfits. Nearly every ship has made some concession to this national fad and now either has a running track or an outline of how many times around Promenade Deck is a mile. Some lines, Norwegian Cruise Line, for example, has an on-shore running session when the ship is in port, and will even provide you with a map of the best running spots ashore. That same jogging outfit can be used in the gymnasium, one of which now appears on most vessels.

2. DAYTIME WEAR

By day, T-shirts and shorts, bathing suits and cover-ups, low-heeled sandals and casual shoes will keep you chic. Do take something to cover your bathing suit when you're taking short cuts through the public rooms or having lunch on deck.

It's quite amazing how many times you can change outfits in a day if you're a real clothes horse. One outfit for breakfast, a swimsuit for sunning until lunch, another outfit for lunch and some afternoon games or port visits, still another outfit for dinner and dancing later.

Of course, you don't *have* to change for all those occasions, but you may very well find yourself doing so. Salt air is everywhere and does leave you feeling a bit sticky. In combination with hot sunshine . . . well.

If you've ever seen the March and April department store ads, you'll have an idea what they're selling as "cruise wear." Colorful is a prime ingredient: bright reds, plenty of white, marine blue, sunny yellow, apple green.

Very brief shorts or skirts are fine on shipboard—if you have the body to wear them—but are frowned on in some ports, notably Haiti, the Dominican Republic, and some parts of Mexico. Limit those scanty little nothings to the Sun Deck and don't wear them ashore.

Scarves are a necessity if you like to keep your hair in place. All but the tightest hats get blown off in the breeze. They're all right for port visits, however.

Don't forget your sunglasses. Or your prescription glasses. Two pairs. There's nothing as disconcerting as losing your glasses on a vacation and needing someone to read the menu for you.

3. JEWELRY

You'd be well advised not to wear very showy and/or expensive jewelry in port. Many of the places you visit have high levels of poverty and it seems gauche somehow to flaunt scads of gold chains in front of people who are working hard to sell a string of shell beads for a quarter.

Some consideration should also be given to what a relative of ours calls the Eleventh Commandment: Thou shalt not tempt!

If you have beautiful jewelry and feel downright naked without it, of course, bring it along, but keep it in the ship's safe when you're not wearing it, and wear it on board, not in port.

4. EVENING WEAR

At night, ships come alive. Big beautiful lounges that seem a little sleepy by day turn into glitter palaces. Your ship's dining room will gleam with silver and crystal, linens starched to wooden stiffness, and napkins folded into pretty fans or angular geometric shapes.

About this time the company begins to glitter as well. The captain and his officers roam in spotless white coats and gold braid, while passengers turn out in all colors of the rainbow.

Some ships are more formal than others, as we've pointed out in several parts of this guide. In general those include any ship that is sailing on cruises longer than seven days. Specifically, you'll find a more formal atmosphere on the *QE2,* Royal Viking Line ships, Cunard's *Vistaford, Sagafjord,* and *Sea Goddesses,* Holland America Line / Westours' *Rotterdam,* Sun Line Cruises' *Stella Solaris* and *Stella Oceanis,* and Royal Caribbean Cruise Line ships that cruise for more than a week. Let's just sum that up with: the more expensive the cruise, the more formal the atmosphere.

On three- and four-day cruise ships, life is very, very informal so pack very dressy clothes only if you like the idea of getting dressed up for dinner. On most of these short cruises you won't see black tie at all, and sometimes you'll hardly see anything fancier than a sport jacket.

On your first night out and your last night aboard, you need not dress up for dinner. First night is always casual, a sensible tradition since most people have just flown or driven to the port and clothes are not yet unpacked and pressed. On your last night aboard, the theory is that your bags will be packed in preparation for the next morning's debarkation so you wear the clothes you'll be wearing for the journey home.

From there on each line differs, but on all ships dinner is the high point of the day. Men are requested to wear jacket and tie after 6 p.m. on most ships, although on many the absence of a tie is forgiven. For the ladies, this is the time to break out the silks and the satins, the chiffons and the high heels.

On a seven-day cruise you'll have two to four formal nights aboard, depending on how many days you spend in port. After a day spent in port, dinner is usually not a formal night.

Among the events that are always formal are the captain's cocktail party and dinner and an event known as the Gala Farewell Banquet, scheduled near the end of the cruise.

Each day you'll receive a ship's newspaper alerting you to the activities of the day and outlining the formality of the evening. Formal, informal, and casual will be explained in that news sheet. "Formal" generally refers to tuxedo or fancy evening jacket for men, long or short dressy dresses for women; "informal" is dark suit for men, long or short dressy dresses for women; and "casual" is no jacket or tie for men, and good-looking slacks or jeans or casual evening wear for women.

Many ships have theme evenings like country and western nights, and on those occasions your jeans and red kerchiefs, ten-gallon hats and sombreros are perfectly acceptable at dinner. Other specialty nights include masquerade eve-

WHAT TO PACK □ 329

Royal Caribbean Cruise Line, Inc.

DAILY CRUISE COMPASS

M.S. Song of Norway

Wednesday

CAPTAIN OSTEN ANDREASSEN – MASTER

WELCOME TO ST. THOMAS, U.S. VIRGIN ISLANDS !!

Approximately	7:00 a.m.	M/S "SONG OF NORWAY" is due to arrive at Charlotte Amalie, St. Thomas.
8:00 a.m.	9:45 a.m.	TOUR OFFICE IS OPEN – MAIN DECK, Purser's Square.
8:15 a.m.	9:45 a.m.	THE MORNING CITY AND ISLAND TOUR – Leaves from "B" Deck, Forward.
8:30 a.m.	9:45 a.m.	THE CORAL WORLD TOUR – Leaves from "B" Deck, Gangway
	9:00 a.m.	The V. I. DIVING SCHOOL TOUR – Meet on "B" Deck
	9:00 a.m.	THE SEA SAFARI TOUR – meets at Purser's Square
	9:30 a.m.	THE V. I. DIVING SCHOOL SNORKEL TOUR – Meet on "B" Deck Forward.
	1:00 p.m.	THE SEA SAFARI TOUR – is departing. Please gather at Purser's Square – Main Deck.
	1:00 p.m.	AFTERNOON SCUBA TOUR DEPARTS – "B" Deck Forward
	1:15 p.m.	THE KON TIKI BOAT TOUR DEPARTS – Please meet in the "South Pacific Lounge".
	1:15 p.m.	ST. THOMAS – ST JOHN ISLAND TOUR – Please meet in the "My Fair Lady Lounge".
	1:30 p.m.	AFTERNOON SNORKEL TOUR departs "B" Deck Forward.
	2:30 p.m.	MOVIE – "THE CHAMP" – Starring Jon Voight and Faye Dunaway. Rated "PG". Ends 4:31 p.m. in the "South Pacific Lounge".
	5:30 p.m.	ALL PASSENGERS ARE REQUESTED TO BE ABOARD NO LATER THAN ONE HALF HOUR PRIOR TO SAILING.
5:30 p.m.	6:30 p.m.	Departure Music & Limbo Contest – Sun Deck, Poolside. (Weather Permitting).
5:30 p.m.	6:30 p.m.	Supplies, ideas, and suggestions for all PIRATES in the "My Fair Lady Lounge", Port Side.
	6:00 p.m.	THE M/S "SONG OF NORWAY" sails promptly for Miami Florida, (1,039 Nautical Miles).
7:00 p.m.	8:15 p.m.	CASH BINGO for passengers on SECOND SITTING – In the "South Pacific Lounge".
7:30 p.m.	8:30 p.m.	Supplies, ideas, and suggestions for all PIRATES in the "My Fair Lady Lounge". Port Side.
7:30 p.m.	10:30 p.m.	Popular Dance Music – "My Fair Lady Lounge".
8:30 p.m.	9:45 p.m.	CASH BINGO for passengers on MAIN SITTING – In the "South Pacific Lounge".
9:30 p.m.	12:30 p.m.	Popular Dance Music and Disco – In the "Lounge of the Midnight Sun".
9:45 p.m.	10:30 p.m.	Official Hanging of all Pirates in the "My Fair Lady Lounge".
	10:00 p.m.	MOVIE – "IN-LAWS" – Starring Peter Falk and Alan Arkin. Rated "PG". Ends 11:43 p.m. in the "South Pacific Lounge".
	10:30 p.m.	"PIRATES PARADE" – All hands fall in for the Biggest Ball of all – "THE PIRATES PARTY". Dancing, Fun, Prizes, & Surprises for all hands! In the "My Fair Lady Lounge" and the "Lounge of the Midnight Sun".
	Midnight	Floor Show – Night Club.
12:15 a.m.	1:00 a.m.	Dance Music in the "My Fair Lady Lounge".
12:30 a.m.	1:15 a.m.	The Pirates Parade to the "Lounge of the Midnight Sun" – and the PIRATES PARTY continues. Hidden treasure can be found.
1:15 a.m.	3:00 a.m.	Popular Music and Disco. In the Night Club.

nings, pastel night, Oriental night, pink or blue night, at which the line would like you to dress in those colors.

Don't fail to read your cruise newspaper. Everything you want to know about what to wear is in there.

Except on the most formal ships, gentlemen need bring truly formal wear —the tuxedos and wing collars—only if they enjoy wearing them. Dark suits are now considered *de rigueur* on most ships. Many modern fellows are wearing, particularly in summer, formal pleated shirts with light or dark suits, a bow tie, even a cummerbund, in place of the traditional tuxedo or white dinner jacket. In winter, velvet smoking jackets have a contemporary look.

Long dresses have suffered a bit of a decline in recent years, but many people drag them out of the back of the wardrobe and bring them along on a cruise. If you have a lovely long dress you'd like to wear, bring it along. In warm climates and warm months of the year, some pretty candy-striped long cotton dresses and those long crinkled-cotton dresses seem particularly appropriate. Short cocktail dresses and evening suits with silk or lacy blouses are always appropriate.

Silky or lightweight wool shawls are easy to pack and very convenient for cool evenings.

When you're planning your wardrobe, keep two things in mind: (1) travel irons are frowned on or downright forbidden on many ships, and shipboard do-it-yourself pressing facilities are limited and often antiquated, not ideal for fragile fabrics; and (2) storage space on modern cruise ships is, shall we say, compact. Older ships have much more closet space, but even there you've got to find some place to stick all those suitcases.

Suitcases, by the way, can often be stashed away under the bed, but if you've really overdone it and can't find another single inch in which to stuff the Samsonite, ask your cabin steward if he can find a place to store the beast. Stewards are ingenious.

Try to keep your wardrobe as coordinated as possible so you can make several different outfits from a minimal number of matching pieces.

5. RAIN AND GLACIER WEAR

Out on the briny blue, evenings are a bit cooler than on shore. Although the temperature may be in the 70s (let's keep our fingers crossed), that constant breeze from the movement of the ship will make a shawl or sweater a welcome sight. Air conditioning on ships can be very, very good too, so plan on some kind of wrap for evening.

In Alaskan waters you'll definitely want a sweater and/or jacket for evening, and something similar for daytime visits to glaciers. If you have a fur jacket or stole, you could certainly wear it on many Alaskan and some transatlantic cruises. Furs on Caribbean voyages? No.

Raincoats and umbrellas always seem to be back at the ship when it rains on land so we just don't bother. One of those little pleated rainhats some company is always giving away to advertise itself is usually enough to keep you dry until you can run to the nearest shelter spot. Windbreakers are convenient.

If you're very organized, plastic raincoats that fold up into little squares you can stick in a pocket or purse are clever and very convenient to carry along without fuss. Getting them back into that little square is quite another matter, however. (How *do* those things work anyway?)

Some very small ships, by the way, have a luggage limit, so if you're planning on traveling on one of the coastal sailing vessels, check the line's brochures for luggage restrictions.

Now that didn't hurt did it? Go ahead, pack it in and get out there and dazzle 'em.

6. LAUNDRY FACILITIES

Dry-cleaning facilities are not available on most ships, although many offer laundry service for a small charge.

As cruises become more popular, some ships are beginning to add small laundromats on board, either coin operated or free. You might have to have your own soap, however, so if you've discovered a laundromat listed in the ship's brochure, pack a small box of soap.

Don't figure you're going to do what you did on your last European trip: hang all those clothes around the room on inflatable hangers with towels underneath to catch the water. There simply is no space in most cabins to hang up even your small washable items. Pack enough to last the voyage or plan to send your things to the ship's laundry. Your steward will give you a bag to pack them in, take them away, and bring them back.

So good are the laundries on some ships that they garner top praise from frequent cruise travelers. Some travelers claim the *Rotterdam*'s laundry is so skilled that they bring their dirty clothes on board with them just to be able to send them to the ship's laundry!

7. OTHER THINGS TO PACK

Man (and woman) does not live by clothes alone. There are other things you should pack for your glorious adventure.

What? Well, for openers, a camera. If you like swimming, diving, and snorkeling, and plan to do lots of that on your trip, you might consider a waterproof camera. At least consider waterproof housings into which a camera fits. Tell your local camera store what you want to photograph and they can help you get outfitted with film and camera for some sensational shots that will be quite different from the pictures everyone else aboard is taking.

If you're strictly a snapshot-taker, Polaroids let you know immediately whether your magic moment has been successfully captured on film. Some of the new small cameras that fit in a pocket can be very convenient to carry around on port visits as well as on board the ship.

To dwell on that diving business for just a moment, if you're planning on learning or perfecting your snorkeling or scuba-diving, don't forget to take whatever equipment you need. Some equipment is available on board, but it's nice to have your own, which will fit you better and have all the features *you* consider important.

You can join in organized diving expeditions on most ships or head-off with a companion—no diving alone, for safety's sake—to find your own no-traffic reef to explore. There are quite a lot of diving possibilities on most cruises, so even if you've never tried it before, sink a few bucks into snorkeling gear and get out there and look!

Binoculars may sound like a hassle, and they are on land trips, but at sea you can stow them in your room without difficulty. They're great for getting a good look at the shoreline as the ship enters or leaves port, for a closeup look at a whale or dolphin or sea bird, and for spotting promising bikinis.

A tote bag to carry beach gear, camera, and things you buy ashore is worth its weight.

If your idea of a marvelous time is hour after endless hour with a fascinating story, stock up on books. Books are available on many ships, but selections are sometimes quite limited. There are, of course, bookstores in ports, but if you're visiting foreign ports most of what those bookstores sell will be written in that foreign language. Take your own or figure on heading for the ship's library the minute the ship leaves the dock.

With all the modern emphasis on fun and sun, many ship's libraries are woefully inadequate and open seemingly only for 20 minutes right in the middle of lunch. Scholars, arise and protest—but don't plan on finding much of a library aboard. Some ships' libraries, by the way, ask you to leave a $5 or $10 deposit to ensure that you'll return the book at the end of the voyage.

Which brings up another very important take-along: money. Although many ships now tally your bills as you sail and permit you to settle the whole thing at once at the end of the voyage, some don't. Most ships want to see cash or traveler's checks in payment of bar charges and for items from the gift shops. Many ships accept credit cards, but not all. Once again, the ship's brochures will indicate what form of payment is accepted on board and when.

Ships visiting countries in which foreign currency is required will have a bank on board to perform currency exchange for you. Once again, they want to see cash or traveler's checks, and usually are not prepared to advance you money on the strength of your credit card.

You may also need money for some special services like massages, beauty salon and barbershop services, special spa services like facials or manicures. On some ships, although very few, there is a small charge (about $5 a week) for use of a deck chair. All ships we know of also charge for skeet shooting, about $2 to pay for the clay pigeons on which you test your shooting skills.

If you take any kind of medication regularly, get your prescriptions filled before you go. Ships do not carry or dispense special prescriptions, and the difficulties of getting a prescription filled in a foreign country are virtually insurmountable. Pack more than enough medication to last the voyage and then some, in case you spill or lose it. There's nothing more frustrating than spending a day in port chasing around trying to get a prescription filled.

Basic medication like aspirin and sunburn relievers will be available on board or in port shops. You'll also find toothpaste, shaving cream, shampoos, and the like in shops on board.

Zip-lock plastic bags, big ones, always seem to come in handy, as do premoistened towelettes.

If you're a shopper, take an empty suitcase or totebag to pack your purchases.

Amateur archeologists should pack a tiny flashlight to illuminate caves and such.

CHAPTER VIII

GET ME TO THE PORT ON TIME: BON VOYAGE

▫ ▫ ▫

1. MIAMI / PORT OF MIAMI
2. FORT LAUDERDALE / PORT EVERGLADES
3. CAPE CANAVERAL / PORT CANAVERAL
4. TAMPA BAY / PORT OF TAMPA AND PORT OF ST. PETERSBURG
5. SAN JUAN / PORT OF SAN JUAN
6. NEW YORK / NEW YORK CITY PASSENGER SHIP TERMINAL
7. NEW ORLEANS / WHARVES
8. LOS ANGELES / PORT OF LOS ANGELES
9. SAN FRANCISCO / PORT OF SAN FRANCISCO
10. VANCOUVER / PORT OF VANCOUVER
11. GETTING YOUR LUGGAGE ABOARD
12. BON VOYAGE PARTIES
13. EXPLORING THE SHIP

That glorious day has arrived. You're going on a cruise and today's the day! Envious friends are all lined up to share the bubbly and watch you sail off into the sunset. Bags are all packed and checked and rechecked, tickets clutched, money counted, excitement mounting.
   Now what?
   Well, first you have to find the ship.

THE PORTS

   In North America the main embarkation ports are first Miami, the world's busiest cruise port, followed by Port Everglades, New York, San Juan, San Francisco, Los Angeles, Vancouver, Seattle, Cape Canaveral, and Tampa in Florida, not necessarily in that order. As you can imagine, we could go on and on here because you can get on ships in many places.

Far and away the largest number of passengers embark at the ports we've just mentioned though, and one has to call a halt to this somewhere. So if you're anticipating boarding a ship somewhere in the Chesapeake Bay or at Warren, R.I., or in Nassau to join one of several small coastal sailers, the cruise line will provide you with maps of their dock sites.

Let's take them one by one then, beginning with the largest cruise port, for a look at some of the details of getting there, staying overnight, parking, getting to the port by public transportation, and getting back to the plane or home when the cruise is over.

1. MIAMI / PORT OF MIAMI

Getting to Miami by plane is quite easy. This city has an international airport served by more than 60 airlines including every major carrier in the U.S., Canada, South America, and Europe—even British Airways' zippy supersonic Concorde!

So many cruise ships depart from Miami that airport personnel here are quite used to dealing with the needs of passengers. Your luggage will be handled efficiently and usually quickly. Thanks to a new rapid Customs clearance program you should be into and out of the airport within an hour, even if you're coming here from a foreign country.

There is another advantage in sailing from Miami. Such a gaggle of cruise ships dock here that the competition is downright snarling-viscious at times, meaning you can be sure you will find bargain rates.

Recent years have seen the birth of a concept known as "free air" or "air/sea" or "fly-free" programs designed to offer you free or very low-cost air fare from perhaps as many as 100 cities across the country and in Canada.

Each cruise line has its own air-fare deal, and most of them have free air fare to Miami. Somewhere along the way it's built into the cost, of course, but it's nice to know you don't have to pay a few hundred dollars more per person to fly to Miami to take a cruise. Your travel agent or the cruise line will be able to tell you all about the benefits of air/sea programs offered to Miami.

LINES SAILING FROM THE PORT OF MIAMI: More major cruise lines are based in Miami than in any other port on earth. These include the fleets of Royal Caribbean, Norwegian Cruise Line, Carnival, Commodore, Chandris, Dolphin, P&O/Princess, SeaEscape, and Admiral Cruise Line.

Miami is home to several fleets, so ships in those fleets have been assigned permanent docking spots, or as permanent as anything can be in this floating world. Here's a list of those pier assignments:

Piers 1 & 2:	*Norway* (both 1 & 2)
	Skyward
	Sunward II
Pier 3:	*Emerald Seas*
	Nordic Prince
	Pacific Princess
	Sun Princess (or Pier 6)
	Sun Viking (or Pier 6)

Pier 4:	*Dolphin*
	Sovereign of the Seas (both 4 & 5)
Pier 5:	*Song of America*
Pier 6:	*Scandinavian Sky*
Pier 8:	*Holiday*
Pier 9:	*Carnivale*
	Celebration
	Jubilee
Pier 10:	*Britanis*
	Caribe I
	Galileo

PRE- AND POST-CRUISE STOPOVERS: If you must take a plane that arrives a day before the ship sails in order not to miss the boat, some lines offer special overnight packages that will save you money. In fact you can spend several days in the sunshine of Miami at quite reasonable rates with a pre-cruise package. Ask a travel agent what's available.

If you're not taking advantage of a package rate but do plan to stay overnight, hotels near the Port of Miami include the comparatively inexpensive and recently renovated Marina Park, where prices are in the $60 to $80 range, moving up to the Everglades, Dupont Plaza, Inter-Continental, Sheraton Brickell, Hyatt, Marriott Biscayne Bay, and Omni, where rates will range up to about $125 to $150 double in high season. Some hotels may offer special pre-cruise rates for cruise passengers.

The **Greater Miami Convention and Visitors Bureau,** 4770 Biscayne Blvd., Penthouse A, Miami, FL 33137 (tel. 305/573-4300), can provide you with information on hotels, motels, and sightseeing in the area.

Our *Frommer's Dollarwise Florida* also provides valuable information on this area. Check it out.

SIGHTS: If you spend a few days in Miami before or after the cruise, you can visit lovely Key Biscayne, where beautiful beaches trim the highway and lush trees and vines will show you what tropical means.

Historic and posh Coconut Grove, the Greenwich Village of Miami, is now a top shopping spot too. Vizcaya, a huge Italianate mansion built by industrialist James Deering, is lushly beautiful.

Miami Seaquarium features a performing killer whale, and at the new uncaged MetroZoo animals roam free, separated from you and from each other by moats. Parrot Jungle or Monkey Jungle or Orchid Jungle are fun, and in Miami Beach the delightful art deco district on the south end of Miami Beach is a don't-miss for art lovers.

Bayside Marketplace, an airy, two-level oceanside marketplace lined with a wide spectrum of boutiques and restaurants, is a new don't-miss in Miami. It's easy walking distance from most of the cruise ships, but a free shuttle bus will also pick you up and whizz you over there if you don't want to walk.

You can also take a day trip to Orlando from Miami on special buses that go directly to Walt Disney World early in the morning and bring you back about midnight.

If you have a full day or more in the city, you can visit that fascinating primeval swamp known as the Everglades and take a ride on a speeding airboat that "floats" over the swamp waters.

GETTING TO THE PORT: The Port of Miami is located on Dodge Island, an island in Biscayne Bay between downtown Miami and the island of Miami Beach.

Red Top Limousine service (tel. 305/526-5764) is the cheapest way to get from the airport to downtown and Miami or Miami Beach hotels—$5 to $8. Taxi service like Yellow Cab (tel. 305/633-3333) from the airport to the downtown area or the port is $15 to $20; from downtown hotels to the port, about $5; from hotels on Miami Beach to the port, about $15. If you want to stay in less expensive Fort Lauderdale (about a 45-minute drive), you can get a limousine from there to the Miami Airport for about $12 per person, and then get a cab from there.

Metrobus service (tel. 305/638-6700) from the airport to downtown (taxi from there) and vice versa is Rte. 7 and costs $1 per person.

If you're driving to the port and leaving your car there while you're on a cruise, you'll pay in advance $3 a day. Parking is in an open lot (no covered parking), and there are security guards on duty at the port.

You get to the Port of Miami by car on I-95, exiting at the Port of Miami exit. At the exit, follow the signs to the Port, crossing over Biscayne Boulevard and, a block or so later, over Biscayne Bay.

At the port look for long narrow signs on which the names and pier numbers of the ships are listed and color coded. Follow the signs to the ship.

Most lines provide free transfers from the airport to the ship. Once again, your travel agent can tell you if such a transfer program is offered by the line on which you're sailing. If it is, you'll probably be transported to the ship by van or bus.

Greyhound buses stop in downtown Miami, and from there you'll have to take a cab, although very good walkers with very little luggage could hoof the mile or so distance to the ships.

Amtrak trains stop west of the city at the new train station, and you can get a cab or bus from there.

AT THE PORT: At the Port of Miami the terminal facilities are among the most modern in the nation. Each ship has its own enclosed, carpeted waiting area on the second floor of new concrete buildings. There's plenty of sitting on seating areas built along the sides of the rooms.

For that matter, there's even a jogging track, a picnic area, a football field, and a tennis area. (Officially they're for port employees, but no one will mind if you want to take a turn around the track while you're waiting for your ship.)

Porters will take your luggage right at the entrance to the terminal and see that it gets aboard the ship. There's next to no possibility that it could go astray and end up on some other ship because the next terminal down the line is a healthy block walk away!

Meanwhile you can take an escalator up to the comfortable second-floor waiting area where your tickets will be checked and your boarding pass issued.

2. FORT LAUDERDALE / PORT EVERGLADES

About 40 miles north of downtown Miami is Fort Lauderdale's Port Everglades, where several new terminals were completed in 1984. One of those is a knockout *trompe l'oeil* (French for fool-the-eye) building on which columns, arches, and windows are painted so cleverly they make a solid concrete wall look like a Mediterranean villa!

Port Everglades, the second-largest cruise-ship base in Florida and one of the top five in the world, is home to some very classy ships, in fact the classiest ships afloat, and brags about that at every chance.

Located in a quiet, posh community of higher-than-average per capita household income, the port has become increasingly alluring to cruise lines in recent years. That allure stems from its proximity to a comparatively small, hassle-free airport about a five-minute drive from the port, and to a seven-mile strip of palm-lined open beaches.

LINES SAILING FROM PORT EVERGLADES: When we say classy ships sail from here, we mean *classy* ships sail from here.

Start with Cunard's *Queen Elizabeth 2* and move beautifully on to Royal Viking Line, Cunard's *Sagafjord* and *Vistafjord*, Costa Cruises, Sun Line, Sitmar, P&O/Princess, Holland America / Westours, Clipper Cruise Line, and Royal Cruise Line.

Sitmar's *Fairwind*, Costa's *CostaRiviera*, and Carnival's *Mardi Gras* are based here year round, but the others make forays into the Caribbean or on transPanama cruises from this port all winter long.

PRE- AND POST-CRUISE STOPOVERS: Port Everglades is just a few minutes' drive from the main Fort Lauderdale beach area, so your choice of hotels ranges from very large, top-notch hotels like Pier 66, Marriott, Sheraton Yankee Clipper, or Yankee Trader, to small family-run properties a block or so west of the main beach highway, Rte. A1A.

Prices at those large hotels will run upward of $150 in high winter season, while prices at small properties a block or two off the beach like the Sea Château, Worthington, and Palace Bleu are about $50 a night double, half that in summer.

Taxi fares from that main beach area to the port are not likely to exceed $10 or so.

SIGHTS: Fort Lauderdale's pride and its selling point is its seven-mile beach, a glorious strip of sand trimmed with palm trees.

While you're here you can explore the city's hundreds of miles of canals—more than Venice!—aboard the *Jungle Queen*, a paddlewheel dinner/sightseeing boat, or a similar craft called the *Paddlewheel Queen*.

To get a look at the city's posh gas-lighted Las Olas Boulevard, take a ride on the Voyager Train. There's also a small but pretty historic district called Himmarshee Village, where the city's first hotel is still intact and operating as a small hands-on museum called the Discovery Center.

From Fort Lauderdale you can visit Walt Disney World on one-day or longer tours arranged by local tour companies, which also offer tours to the Everglades, Miami, and the Keys.

GETTING TO THE PORT: Most major airlines offer service to Fort Lauderdale / Hollywood International Airport, including American, Delta, Eastern, Continental, Midway, Northwest, Nordair, Piedmont, TWA, United, and USAir. Miami International Airport is about 25 miles away, $12 by airport limousine.

From Fort Lauderdale / Hollywood International Airport the taxi ride to Port Everglades will take about five minutes and costs about $8 to $10.

If you're driving to Port Everglades on the Florida State Turnpike, exit at the Fla. 84 interchange. If you're traveling on I-95, you should also exit at Fla. 84 and head east to the port, which begins at the eastern end of that highway.

You can park your car there for the duration of your cruise for $4 a day. Parking is outdoors in a locked and guarded area.

If you're coming to town by Greyhound bus or on an Amtrak train, you'll need to get a cab from the station. The taxi ride will cost about $10, perhaps less.

AT THE PORT: Port Everglades spent a bundle of money building two new terminals, the newest of which opened in 1983. Very contemporary buildings, these new bilevel terminals feature snackbars, lounges, and loads of comfortable chairs to sit in if you arrive before boarding begins on your ship. There are escalators so you don't have to climb stairs lugging your hand baggage. Plenty of porters see to it that your luggage gets safely onto the ship.

If you have to sit around and wait for boarding to begin, there could hardly be a more pleasant place to wait: goodlooking contemporary seating areas, food and drink, even a pretty glassed-in wall-full of rare shells on display. We've seen airline terminals that aren't this pleasant. Also, there are covered walkways to the ships too, so you don't get damp if it rains.

3. CAPE CANAVERAL / PORT CANAVERAL

This tiny port was strictly a "Port What?" until a few years ago when Scandinavian World Cruises (now called SeaEscape) began operating daily cruises to nowhere from here. Then other ships began making tentative forays into these Walt Disney World waters, and in 1984 a new cruise line with high hopes and a bright-red ship began sailing from Port Canaveral.

Now the port has embarked on an ambitious building program that port officials hope will make it one of Florida's premier ports in just a few years.

There are certain drawbacks: Orlando's airport, the nearest one, is about an hour's drive away, although that drive is on a major expressway, no traffic lights. It's also more than an hour's drive from the tourist centers that have grown up around Walt Disney World, and about a five-hour drive from the major metropolitan areas of southern Florida.

On the very positive side, it's comparatively easy to combine a cruise from this port with a trip to Walt Disney World's Magic Kingdom or EPCOT, but you will need to stay in the area at least a week to wedge in both activities.

LINES SAILING FROM PORT CANAVERAL: The biggest news in many a moon at Port Canaveral was the arrival of Premier Cruise Lines, a new cruise line operating the *Starship Royale* and *Starship Oceanic* on three- and four-night cruises from Port Canaveral to Nassau and a Bahamian Out Island. And SeaEscape's *Scandinavian Sky* sails on cruises to nowhere.

Other lines occasionally call at Port Canaveral.

PRE- AND POST-CRUISE STOPOVERS: Beach lovers ought to settle in at nearby Cocoa, a beach and surfers paradise, for a few days. Hotels and motels in the area are listed in a publication produced by the **Cocoa Chamber of Commerce,** 400 Fortenberry Rd., Merritt Island, FL 32952 (tel. 407/459-2200).

Those who want to meet the Mouse will head for any of hundreds of motels and hotels in the Orlando area. Prices there range from a low of about $35 or so to a high well into the $150 range. The full story on all there is to see and do in Orlando is available in another book we wrote, *Frommer's Orlando, Disney World, and EPCOT*.

It will take you an hour or more to get from the port to the Walt Disney World area. Information on hotels and motels near the park is available from the **Kissimmee–St. Cloud Visitor and Convention Bureau**, 1925 E. Spacecoast Pkwy. (P.O. Box 2007), Kissimmee, FL 32742 (tel. 407/847-5000, or toll free 800/327-9159, 800/432-9199 in Florida).

SIGHTS: We hardly need tell you at this point that the chief sight anywhere hereabouts is Walt Disney World's Magic Kingdom and EPCOT. But that certainly is not all there is to see.

Cape Canaveral's Spaceport USA, home of the astronauts and site of rocket launchings, is right here. If you time your cruise very carefully, you may even be able to go to sea to see a launch.

Over in Orlando, about an hour's drive away, you can also visit Sea World, where sweet Shamu, the killer whale, kisses pretty girls and toddlers; Boardwalk and Baseball, which has a baseball game going on every day of the year, plus rides, a Baseball Hall of Fame, and plenty of baseball-oriented activities; and Cypress Gardens, a serene setting for some daring exhibitions of waterskiing and high diving.

GETTING TO THE PORT: If you're coming to central Florida by plane, you'll fly to Orlando International Airport, a new airport with whooshing monorail transportation and the latest technology everywhere. Most major air carriers fly there.

Transportation from the airport to the port is a bit limited, but Premier and SeaEscape both operate buses from many parts of the state to the port and will book your transportation on one of those when you make your reservations.

Premier offers a package combining a cruise with a visit to Walt Disney World. That package includes hotel and a complimentary rental car. The line also books bus transportation for you when you buy your cruise tickets.

A limousine service operates from the airport to the ship, but you'd have to charter the car, an expensive proposition.

That leaves rental cars. You can rent a car from one of many companies operating in Orlando and drive to the port, parking the car there while you go on the cruise. That, however, means you'll be paying for a car that's just sitting there for several days while you're on the cruise. So you'd be wiser to use the cruise lines' free transportation from the airport to the port and back, then rent a car at the airport if you like. There are no rental-car facilities at Port Canaveral.

Many people who take this cruise live in Florida or have driven to the state in their own cars, which helps to account for the lack of transportation from airport to port. If you're one of those, you can drive to the port and park your car there while you go on the cruise. Parking rates are $3 a day at the lot for SeaEscape, $4 a day at Premier's parking facilities.

If you want to visit the wonders of Walt Disney World, you must make your way to a road called the Beeline Expressway (Fla. 528), which does indeed make a beeline across the state from Orlando to Port Canaveral. From other areas of the state you can take I-95 to the Cape Canaveral—A1A exits or I-75 from the northern parts of Florida to the Beeline and east on the Beeline.

AT THE PORT: Two of the three dome-topped terminal buildings (tel. 407/783-7831) here were acquired by the port from Walt Disney World and have a bit of a futuristic look. Inside these circular structures are just the bare essentials, not thrilling for long waits.

If you must wait a while, get in some beach time at nearby Jetty Park, where you'll find a campground, recreational facilities, concession stands, and showers. Now that's not bad!

Porters are available to take your luggage and see that it gets onto the ship.

Greyhound buses stop in Cocoa Beach, but you'll have to take a cab from the station to the port.

Amtrak trains stop in Kissimmee and in Orlando, but you'll need to rent a car to go from either of those stations across the state to the terminal at Port Canaveral.

4. TAMPA / PORT OF TAMPA AND PORT OF ST. PETERSBURG

Tampa is another newcomer port that pulled off its biggest coup in 1984 when it lured Holland America's brand-new liner, the *Nieuw Amsterdam,* to its piers.

Although the Tampa port area itself is huge, stretching for miles and miles, almost all of that is cargo area with only three passenger terminals, one of them constructed in 1982. Land has been purchased in downtown Tampa to provide another port in the area, but don't expect completion of that for years.

Nearby, small St. Petersburg is crowing over the arrival of the first cruise ship ever to offer scheduled service from this small port.

LINES SAILING FROM THE TAMPA BAY PORTS: Although Tampa would certainly welcome new cruise lines, at the moment it has only three ships: Regency Cruises' *Regent Sea;* Holland America's *Nieuw Amsterdam,* which docks at Berth 202; and Bermuda Star Line's *Veracruz,* which ties up at a pier known as the Garrison Cruiseship Terminal.

Meanwhile, in St. Petersburg, SeaEscape's *Scandinavian Saga* ties up at the city's pier at 1st Street and Eighth Avenue SE, just south of Bayfront Center. There's a serviceable terminal facility there with carpeting, seating, and a baggage area, but there are no restaurants in the terminal. Parking there costs $21 a week.

PRE- AND POST-CRUISE STOPOVERS: By Florida historic standards, Tampa is a rather old city and has some interesting historical sights, as well as some very contemporary amusements.

If you're thinking of staying over for a few days before or after your cruise, nearby hotels include the Hilton Tampa, Hyatt Regency Tampa, Harbour Island, and Days Inn Tampa, all of which are in the downtown area, about a $15 to $20 cab ride from the airport. It will cost you about $5 to $7 to get from downtown hotels to the cruise terminals.

Hotel rates in peak winter season will be in the $75 to $125 range, although hotels in other price ranges are available in the city. If you'd like information on hotels in the Tampa Bay area, contact the **Tampa/Hillsboro Convention and Visitors Association,** 100 S. Ashley Dr., Suite 850, Tampa, FL 33602 (tel. 813/228-7777).

There are many, many hotels of all sizes in the St. Petersburg–St. Petersburg Beach–Clearwater area. For information on them, contact the **Pinellas Tourist Development Council,** Newport Square, Suite 109A, 2333 E. Bay Dr., Clearwater, FL 33546 (tel. 813/530-6452).

Or check with *Frommer's Dollarwise Florida* for further information.

SIGHTS: Busch Gardens' Dark Continent is the Tampa Bay area's most famous sight and is an amusing way to spend a day. You'll find thrilling rides, several theme areas depicting parts of Africa in everything from shops to entertainment and food, wild animals roaming an open "veldt," and plenty of what made Busch famous.

History buffs should head for the University of Tampa, which occupies a historic hotel built by Henry Plante, a railroad kingpin on this coast. Built in the '20s, the structure's famous onion-shaped minarets can be seen from many parts of the downtown area.

Ybor City, once home to Cuban tobacco workers, is another intriguing historical site and home to several good restaurants and lots of interesting small shops.

St. Petersburg and the surrounding area, promoted as the Pinellas Suncoast, has beautiful beaches and a number of small but interesting attractions including gardens, a wax museum, and a bird sanctuary.

GETTING TO THE PORTS: Tampa's comparatively new international airport is still getting raves for its very contemporary facilities. So well organized is the airport that it's possible to get from plane to taxi in fewer than 700 steps and in just a few minutes. Most major U.S. airlines have flights to Tampa.

If you're driving here, you'll arrive on I-275, a branch of I-75 that stretches along the west coast of Florida; on I-4, which connects Tampa with Daytona through Orlando; or on I-75 from points north. Exit any of them at 21st Street South and follow that road until it merges with 22nd Street. Turn right on Maritime Boulevard and make the first left on Verger Boulevard. Verger will take you right by the Holland America terminal and, farther along, past the terminal for Regency Cruises.

To get to the *Veracruz* terminal, take Fla. Rte. 60 through downtown to the intersection of 13th Street and Kennedy Boulevard, where a huge sign will show you the way to Garrison Terminal.

Parking fees in an uncovered lot are $20 a week at the Holland America and Regency terminal, $4 a day at the *Veracruz*'s terminal.

Greyhound buses have terminals in downtown Tampa from which you will have to take a cab to the port.

Amtrak trains from the Northeast and from other parts of Florida stop in Tampa too.

To get to St. Petersburg, take I-275 or U.S. 92 across Tampa Bay from Tampa, then follow the signs to the city's pretty downtown Bayfront area. You'll find the port at 1st Street and Eighth Avenue SE.

AT THE PORT: Holland America Line / Westours' terminal at the Port of Tampa sports a nautical theme. You'll alight at a canopy-covered entrance where porters will see to your luggage. If you're a bit early, you can wait in an attractive building with lots of windows through which you can watch the activity in historic Tampa Bay, visited by pirates and explorers for more than 400 years.

Baggage-claims areas here feature colored stripes that correspond to colored arrows overhead, so it's quite easy to find your luggage when you return.

Smoky-gray carpets and blue-and-gray couches offer a pleasant place to wait, and there's a covered gangway to the ship so the weather's no problem.

Regency Cruises' terminal, located a mile south, is a great deal less impressive. It's just a converted cargo warehouse and has no facilities for waiting around or for anything else, so don't get there way ahead of time. There are no snackbars, lounges, or restaurants in the area, so bring your own snacks or diet.

SeaEscape's terminal is also new and is much closer to the downtown area. The line has offices at 1304 York St.—that's right at the dock—plus seating and basic facilities but no restaurant in the terminal building which is less than a block away.

5. SAN JUAN / PORT OF SAN JUAN

Lovely old San Juan has become almost as popular a starting point for cruises as it is an itinerary. There's a very good reason for that too: its location in the middle of the Caribbean Sea lets you explore, in a week or so, many island destinations that would take much longer to get to from Florida.

LINES SAILING FROM SAN JUAN: Ships that have settled here as home or frequent base include Cunard's *Countess* and *Princess*, Chandris's *The Victoria* and *Amerikanis*, Costa's *CarlaCosta* and *Daphne*, P&O/Princess Cruises' *Pacific Princess*, Carnival's *Festivale*, Norwegian Cruise Line's *Starward*, Exploration Cruise Lines' *Explorer Starship*, and Royal Caribbean Cruise Line's *Song of Norway*.

PRE- AND POST-CRUISE STOPOVERS: If you're taking a cruise from San Juan you'll surely want to spend some time exploring this old—and very new—city, and if you have time, the rest of this mountainous and very tropical island.

Several hotels have special overnight packages and transfer arrangements for cruise passengers. Rates at very large hotels will be in the $100-and-up range in peak season, but there are plenty of other accommodations in the city ranging from charming guesthouses to mid-priced hotels and sprawling resorts. To find out about hotels on the island, write to the **Puerto Rico Tourism Co.** at 1290 Avenue of the Americas, New York, NY 10019 (tel. 212/541-6630). Ask for a copy of "Qué Pasa?" a very informative brochure that will tell you what to see and do in San Juan and out on the island. We also recommend that you check *Frommer's Dollarwise Caribbean* for this and other ports of call in the Caribbean.

From San Juan International Airport, the ride to the port or to area hotels will take about 35 minutes and costs about $5 per person by airport limousine, the cheapest way to get there.

Taxi fare from the airport to downtown San Juan is about $10 to $15, less if you're staying closer to the airport.

Some cruise lines offer transfers by charter bus, and on cruise departure days the line will have a representative in the baggage-claim area. At the docks, you can get airline help from airline representatives stationed there.

SIGHTS: San Juan's port is located right in Old San Juan, the most picturesque part of the city and one of the best shopping areas as well.

You can spend days exploring among tiny lanes and pastel town houses with beautiful ornate wrought-iron balconies. A must-see is placid El Morro fortress. Other interesting sights: Pablo Casals Museum, the 400-year-old Dominican Convent, La Fortaleza (the oldest executive mansion in the Western Hemisphere), and El Convento, an old convent turned hotel.

GETTING THERE: American, TWA, and Eastern fly into Puerto Rico from many major cities in the U.S. San Juan's airport is a reasonably hassle-free spot, although parking there is chaotic, to put it mildly.

You can rent a car from a variety of all the usual major U.S. car-rental companies if you want to strike out across the island for a few days before or after a cruise. We recommend the trip.

AT THE PORT: San Juan's port is a really lovely place, open, clean, and well attended by taxi drivers who will want to take you on sightseeing tours. If you don't want to strike a deal with one of them, a simple "No, thanks, we're walking" will discourage them.

Piers in San Juan are equipped with bright and clean terminal buildings where you will find food, drinks, and small shops to keep you busy if you're waiting to board a ship. Escalators are available to get you up to the second-story gangways, but not all of the area is covered so if it's raining, you might have to dash a bit between the ship and the door to the terminal building.

You're right at the edge of Old San Juan, so if you're very early, walk around a bit or find a spot in one of dozens of nearby cafés and watch the passing parade. In San Juan that can be very colorful.

6. NEW YORK / NEW YORK CITY PASSENGER SHIP TERMINAL

The Big Apple's passenger ship terminal is a popular and often crowded place in summer when a number of cruise ships sail from here on trips to Bermuda or on transatlantic journeys.

One of the greatest cruising thrills you'll ever have is the one you'll see as you enter this harbor area: the majestic Statue of Liberty greeting you as she did many of our forebears.

LINES SAILING FROM NYC TERMINAL: In spring and summer you'll see the *QE2* steaming grandly in and out of this port, joined by smaller counterparts, Cunard's *Vistafjord* or *Sagafjord*, Royal Viking Line's ships, Chandris's *Amerikanis*, *Galileo*, and *Britanis*, Bermuda Star Line ships, and Royal Caribbean Cruise Line's *Nordic Prince*.

PRE- AND POST-CRUISE STOPOVERS: To be in New York and not take advantage of all the dining, entertainment, theater, museums, etc., of the nation's busiest city would be a shame indeed. If you can, spend a few days in the city before or after your cruise, and perhaps move on to New England if you have time.

Hotels in New York are easily in the $150- to $200-a-night range, although there are some budget spots in slightly lower brackets. Midtown hotels and those in the Central Park area are reasonably close to the port, about a $5 taxi ride away.

Taxi transportation from La Guardia or JFK International Airports to downtown hotels will run about $20 to $35; bus service from either airport is $6 to $8. Those coming in to Newark Airport can take an Olympia Trails bus (tel. 212/964-6233) to a downtown hotel for $5 one way.

From there to the port will cost you another $5 or so in cab fares.

SIGHTS: New York City's multitudes of sightseeing options are so numerous people have written hundreds of books about them! Certainly we can't tell you here all the things to see and do in New York, but top sights include the Empire State Building and the World Trade Center, the Statue of Liberty, Central Park, the United Nations, the Metropolitan Museum of Art, the Museum of Modern Art, Wall Street, Rockefeller Center, Greenwich Village, Lincoln Center. Check out *Frommer's New York* and/or *New York on $50 a Day* for best tips.

GETTING TO THE PORT: Every major airline in the world flies into New York City, either to La Guardia, the airport closest to Manhattan, or to John F. Kennedy International, or Newark International, about equidistant from the city.

New York has a nifty number (tel. toll free 800/AIR-RIDE) that gives you what must surely be every last detail on how to get to and from New York area airports to Manhattan.

From wherever you land, however, you'll need to take a cab to the Passenger Ship Terminal, about a $5 to $10 ride from most downtown locations.

Bus or bus-subway trips will cost you $5 to $8 from the airport to downtown locations or vice versa.

If you're driving, there are many ways to make your way to the port, which stretches from 48th to 55th Streets on Twelfth Avenue. A brochure available from the New York City Passenger Ship Terminal, Port Authority of New York and New Jersey, Marine Terminals Dept., 1 World Trade Center, New York, NY 10048 (tel. 212/765-7437), will detail how to reach the port area from the Henry Hudson Pkwy. (West Side Hwy.); the Holland, Lincoln, Queens Midtown, and Brooklyn Battery Tunnels; the Major Deegan Expressway (New York State Thruway); from northern New Jersey and Rockland County; and from the Triboro Bridge.

Open parking on the roof of the building is available for those who are seeing you off, using the automobile ramp at 55th Street and Twelfth Avenue. Long-term covered parking is available next to the terminal at Pier 94, and there's a free courtesy car to and from the terminal.

Enter the parking area adjacent to the automobile ramp at 55th Street and Twelfth Avenue. Write Kinney System, Inc., New York City Passenger Ship Terminal, 711 Twelfth Ave., New York, NY 10019 (tel. 212/757-4936), for reservations. The charge is $10 a day. In prime months like June and July when there are likely to be quite a number of ships in port, you would be well advised to reserve a parking space well ahead of time.

AT THE PORT: New Yorkers always see to their creature comforts, albeit varying degrees of that comfort. That means that at the ship terminal you'll find places to sit, places to eat and drink, and you'll have some very nice views of the ships while you're waiting to board.

Negotiating your way to the port can be a mind-boggling traffic experience, but once you're there you won't starve or die of thirst or be forced to stand up.

Porters are available to help you with your luggage.

To help you plan, the Port Authority has a number you can call to discover arrival and departure times of vessels: 212/765-7437.

7. NEW ORLEANS / WHARVES

New Orleans doesn't have a huge fleet of ships or flashy passenger-ship terminals, but it makes up in charm what it lacks in size.

There are just two passenger wharves here, one called the Poydras Street Wharf, the other called the Robin Street Wharf. At either one you are just blocks from the city's intriguing French Quarter.

LINES SAILING FROM NEW ORLEANS: Delta Queen Steamboat Co.'s two oldtimey sailing craft fit right into this antique and charming atmosphere. The *Delta Queen* and *Mississippi Queen* both sail from the new Robin Street Wharf on trips up the Mississippi River as far as Pennsylvania and even into Minnesota.

Bermuda Star Line sails its *Bermuda Queen* from New Orleans on week-long winter cruises to the western Caribbean and Yucatán Peninsula. And American Cruise Lines also is now operating the *New Orleans* on the river. Both Bermuda Star Line and American Cruise Lines sail from the Poydras Street Wharf.

PRE- AND POST-CRUISE STOPOVERS: One could hardly think of a lovelier place to get into the mood for a cruise up the lazy river. New Orlean's French Quarter, with its wrought-iron balconies and slow-talking, slow-walking ways, looks as if a Mississippi riverboat gambler might step out of one of the taverns any moment.

Hotels quite near the wharves include Bienville House Motor Hotel, Marriott Hotel, Monteleone Hotel, International Hotel, and New Orleans Hilton, which is the closest to Poydras Street Wharf. At these you will pay about $100 to $150 in the busiest seasons. Many other smaller hotels and guesthouses are available in New Orleans. You can get a list of those by writing the **New Orleans Tourist and Convention Commission,** 1520 Sugar Bowl Dr., New Orleans, LA 70112 (tel. 504/566-5011). Another excellent source is, of course, *Frommer's New Orleans.*

Taxis from the airport to the old section of the city will cost about $15 to $20 and take about 30 minutes.

SIGHTS: By day New Orleans offers narrow streets, lovely old restored homes, lacy wrought iron, and flower-filled courtyards. History lives here, and its address is Vieux Carré. You can discover it tucked away among the boutiques, streetside artists, and conventioneers in such pretty and historic places as Jackson Square, St. Louis Cathedral, Ursuline Convent, the Old Absinthe House. Walking-tour maps and other historical background materials are available from the Tourist Commission.

By night the city turns on its steamy and seamy side to provide you with some of the world's greatest jazz clubs, renowned Preservation Hall, and a raft of dives and nudity shows that are more fun hearing about from the hawking doormen than they are to attend.

GETTING TO THE PORT: Major air carriers across the nation will take you to the city's Moisant International Airport, about 15 miles from downtown New Orleans and the wharves.

Airport limousine transportation (tel. 504/464-0611) costs about $7 to the Hilton Hotel. From there you'll have to walk the final block or so to the International Cruise Ship Terminal at the wharf, so if you have quite a lot of luggage and want to be delivered right to the Poydras Street Wharf, you'll have to take a taxi from the airport or from the Hilton. Taxi fare from area hotels will be about $5 to the wharves, but from the airport will be about $20.

The Robin Street Wharf is about a mile upriver from the Poydras Street Wharf. Taxi prices will be similar.

Greyhound has a terminal in the city, but you'll have to take a cab from the bus terminal to the wharves. Amtrak has service from a number of points in the Midwest to New Orleans.

If you're driving into the city, you can reach the wharves by taking the Poydras Street exit from I-10 for the Poydras Street Wharf. You can park your car in the area at Rivergate Building or World Trade Center, 2 Canal St. (tel. 504/529-5708), for $5.50 a day. The Hilton Hotel, which is right at the wharf, also has parking.

Delta Queen Steamboat Co. is now docking at Robin Street Wharf, a new facility at the foot of Thalia Street. To reach it, drive down Magazine Street, turn left on Race Street to Tchoupitoulas Street, and left again on Celeste, which will take you to the river. Follow the signs from there to the Robin Street Wharf.

8. LOS ANGELES / PORT OF LOS ANGELES

Los Angeles has quite a busy port, and a growing one, now looking forward to the appearance of several new cruise ships. Popular for its weather and its proximity to the Mexican coastline, Los Angeles is another port city in which there is much to see and do.

LINES SAILING FROM THE PORT OF LOS ANGELES: Los Angeles has its fair share of cruise competition these days with two lines sailing sleek new ships from this port: P&O/Princess Cruises' *Royal Princess*, and Sitmar's *Fairsky*. Those join Carnival Cruise Lines' *Tropicale*, Admiral Cruise Line's *Azure Seas*, Sitmar Cruises' *Fairsea*, Cunard's *Princess*, and Royal Cruise Line and Royal Viking Line ships.

PRE- AND POST-CRUISE STOPOVERS: According to all the jokes, it's worth going to Los Angeles once in your life just to play in the traffic on the freeways! Traffic games notwithstanding, there are enough interesting things to do in this metropolis and in the general area to make a pleasant stop before or after a cruise. In this far-flung city, elevations range from sea level to 5,000 feet, and the inhabitants are every bit as diverse as the landscape.

If you're flying into the city or coming in from out of town, taxi fare to downtown hotels will cost $20 to $30.

Included among those downtown hotels are Westin Bonaventure, Sheraton, Hilton, Hyatt Regency, and Biltmore.

Information on the city and its hotels is available from the **Los Angeles Convention and Visitor Bureau**, 515 S. Figueroa St., Los Angeles, CA 90071 (tel. 213/624-7300). Or check out *Frommer's Los Angeles*—it's packed with valuable information.

Downtown hotels are about 25 miles from the port, so you'll have to figure about $30 to $40 to get to the port from downtown by taxi. The airport is about an hour's drive from the port. Airport vans take you to hotels, but you'll have to take a taxi or bus to the port. Long Beach has some hotels about a 15-minute drive from the port if you can arrange to fly into Long Beach Airport.

If you are really saving pennies, the Southern California Rapid Transit District (tel. 213/626-4455) can give you information on what buses to take from the airport to downtown and then (on another bus) to the port.

Amtrak goes into downtown Los Angeles, and Greyhound buses will bring you to the city too.

SIGHTS: More is new than is old in Los Angeles, but you can still see a little of the antiquity of this city on Olvera Street, at Old Mission church and Avila Adobe.

La Brea Tarpits will be of interest to archeology buffs, and Chinatown is fascinating to everyone for one reason or another.

In nearby Anaheim is Disneyland, and every bit as fantasyland as Disneyland is Hollywood.

What else? Marineland, restaurants, nightclubs, theater, the Rose Bowl, a zoo.

GETTING TO THE PORT: Like everything else in Los Angeles, getting to the port involves miles of travel—after you've found your way to Los Angeles.

Dozens of national and international air carriers land at Los Angeles International Airport, one of the nation's major gateways.

You are about to look at some very daunting taxi fares, but remember that nearly all lines now not only provide free or low-cost air fares, but they also meet and greet you at the airport and transport you to the ship on buses or vans. That means that unless you're arranging all your own transportation independent from the line—and that's always likely to cost you more—you won't need to find a cab or any other transportation. Just look for your friendly greeters who will probably be dressed in nautical uniforms and be hoisting a sign announcing what line they represent.

Taxi fares from downtown or the airport to the harbor area are about $30 to $40. You can also catch buses that will take you to the pier area for about $5. Kiosks outside each terminal area at the airport can give you information on what buses to take and the price.

Mini-van services operate an airport-harbor shuttle service too, and can be reached on a courtesy telephone located in the baggage pickup area of the airport. Call one of those, Super Shuttle, at 213/777-8000. The rate is $18 per person from airport to pier.

For information on transportation and other services provided by the Los Angeles Airport, call the airport referral system (tel. 213/646-5260).

If you're traveling to the port by car, drive south on the San Diego Freeway from the airport, or south on the Harbor Freeway from downtown, toward San Pedro or Wilmington. Berths 91 and 93 are now called the World Cruise Center and are used by all the cruise ships based here including Carnival, Cunard, Costa Princess, Norwegian Cruise Line, Sitmar, Royal Viking, and Admiral. It's located off Harbor Boulevard at Swinford Street.

Outdoor parking is available at Catalina Terminal, Harbor Boulevard at Swinford, in San Pedro, next to Berth 93 (tel. 213/548-4537), and costs $4 a day.

AT THE PORT: Los Angeles doesn't yet run a showplace port area, but it could be worse. Near Berth 93 is a cluster of shops and restaurants called Ports of Call Village, which features architectural elements of New England, Polynesia, and Cannery Row. It's about a mile from Berth 93. A cab will get you there for about $5.

Los Angeles' World Cruise Center is an ambitious project that, when completed, will be able to welcome five ships simultaneously at the refurbished Berths 93A and 93B and at Berth 91, a brand-new complex complete with shops and restaurants. There are to be 4,000 parking spaces at the site and a new traffic pattern that mimics the efficient one-way-street system in operation at Los Angeles Airport.

Los Angeles also is developing a region known as West Channel / Cabrillo Beach Recreational Complex, which by 1989 will sport a complex featuring beaches, marinas, restaurants, and a Doubletree Compri Hotel.

You'll find no food or beverage centers at the terminal, just basic seating areas, if you have to while away a few hours until your ship departs.

At Berth 93 you can begin your cruise experience without ever leaving shore—have lunch on the *Princess Louise,* a cruise ship-turned-restaurant! It's within easy walking distance of the pier.

9. SAN FRANCISCO / PORT OF SAN FRANCISCO

The best thing about San Francisco's harbor is that it's right in the middle of things. When you're standing at the harbor you're right on the city's Embarcadero, not far from Telegraph Hill, and not all that far from Chinatown and Nob

Hill, a quick trip away from Fisherman's Wharf. And if you want to get right down to it, not far from Alcatraz either!

LINES SAILING FROM SAN FRANCISCO: Many ships make a stop in San Francisco, but most of them are just passing through on their way to somewhere else. American Hawaii Cruises, although its ships sail almost solely in the Hawaiian Islands, is officially based in San Francisco. Others calling at this port include Cunard, Exploration Cruise Lines, Holland America Line / Westours, P&O / Princess Cruises, Royal Cruise Line, Royal Viking Line, Sitmar Cruises, and Admiral Cruises.

PRE- AND POST-CRUISE STOPOVERS: It's not so much one or two single sights that make San Francisco so intriguing, but the collage of all the sights in this hilly bayside city where the slopes seem to go straight up—and straight back down the other side.

Plenty of hotels in the downtown area offer you a wide variety of places to stay, ranging from small inns to huge hotels. Among the hotels nearest the port area is the Hyatt Regency, and in the Fisherman's Wharf area are the Sheraton, TraveLodge, Holiday Inn, Howard Johnson's, Ramada Inn, and San Francisco Marriott.

For more suggestions, contact the **San Francisco Chamber of Commerce,** 465 California St., San Francisco, CA 94103 (tel. 415/974-6900), or the **San Francisco Convention and Visitors Bureau,** 201 3rd St., San Francisco, CA 94103 (tel. 415/974-6900). Or check out *Frommer's San Francisco.*

SIGHTS: Put on your mountain-goat shoes and take to the hills in this up-and-down city. Better yet, see it by cable car. San Francisco without a cable car ride is . . . well, don't!

Chinatown is a fascinating mélange of sound, color, and scent, and is said to be the largest Chinese community in the world outside Asia.

The Golden Gate Bridge is a smashing sight, and so is Sausalito on the other side. Golden Gate Park will please open-space enthusiasts, and the Fisherman's Wharf waterfront area, where you catch the ship, is a must-do on every tourist's list.

Don't bother with the boat trips, though; you'll shortly be doing one of your own. Do bother with a little paper cone full of fresh seafood.

Other favored stopping spots: Seal Rocks, the Opera House, Wells Fargo Historical Collection, Cliff House.

GETTING TO THE PORT: All major airlines fly into San Francisco International Airport, and from there Airporter buses (tel. 415/673-2432) will take you to the downtown terminal at $4 for adults, $2 for children. A cab from there to the docks is $5 to $10; to the hotels, $20 to $25.

Amtrak trains run to Oakland and then buses transfer you to San Francisco.

Greyhound buses also have terminals in the city, but you'll have to take a cab from there to the pier.

If you're driving into town, you'll find Pier 35 at the foot of Bay Street where it meets Embarcadero. Off I-80 (the James Lick Freeway) or the Bay Bridge, take the Main Street exit to Mission Street and go north on the Embarcadero.

There is no parking on Pier 35, but you can park at Pier 45 after dropping off your luggage on Pier 35. Parking fees at San Francisco Parking Garages, 923 Folsom St. (tel. 415/495-3909), are $3 a night at this open lot. You can also park between Piers 31 and 33, where fees are $5.

AT THE PORT: Once you've found your way here, you'll discover a new $1.5-million terminal building, modern, with lots of windows and open space inside an old-fashioned transit shed. A two-story building, it features a downstairs Customs area and room upstairs for passengers. There are bars and restaurants in the neighborhood, but not in the terminal. That doesn't matter much, however—you're just minutes away from famous Fisherman's Wharf and in sight of Alcatraz!

10. VANCOUVER / PORT OF VANCOUVER

It's certainly not surprising that Vancouver has emerged as one of the most popular ports in North America, and the number one departure point for cruises to the glacial waters of Alaska.

There's water, water everywhere in these parts, and what isn't water is lovely pastoral countryside given to picket fences and privet hedges, shades of old England.

A spiffy new passenger terminal that may just be the world's most modern and complete cruise-ship terminal was opened in Vancouver with considerable fanfare on April 28, 1986, when Holland America Line / Westours sailed the first ship into the new dock.

That dock and the hotel, restaurants, boutiques, and convention center that go with it are all part of an expensive and expansive new facility called Canada Place. Architects who created this new marvel figured form should follow function, so they built it in marine style—the building looks just like a cruise ship, and even has "sails" flying from the top!

LINES SAILING FROM VANCOUVER: Ships from a number of lines call in here in the summer months. In fact you can catch an Alaska cruise from this port on almost any day of the week! Among the lines sailing from Vancouver in the summer months are Admiral, Cunard, Costa, Exploration, P&O / Princess, Holland America, Regency, Sitmar, World Explorer Cruises, and Royal Viking Line.

PRE- AND POST-CRUISE STOPOVERS: This is a city with spectacular scenery, and it knows just how to take advantage of it. As long as you're way up here on the edge of the world anyway, you really ought to spend a few days exploring this watery wonderland.

Hotels in the area are very near the harbor. You'll find such luxury hotels as the Pan Pacific, Four Seasons, Hotel Vancouver, Westin Bayshore, Holiday Inn Harbourside, Hotel Georgia, Sheraton Landmark, Granville Island Hotel, and Hyatt Regency just a short distance away and featuring prices in the $100 to $125 range (in U.S. dollars). Some of the hotels have some terrific bargains on weekends, so be sure to ask.

You can find out more about hotels in this city by writing or calling the **Greater Vancouver Travel Information Center,** 562 Burrard St., Vancouver, BC V6C 2J6 (tel. 604/683-2000).

You can also get the whole scoop on what to see and do in Vancouver and the rest of the dramatically beautiful Pacific Northwest—and where to stay and eat while you're doing it—in another book we've written: *Frommer's Dollarwise Northwest.* As long as you've come all the way for a cruise, don't miss this chance to visit snow-capped peaks and sapphire lakes, take fascinating ferry rides to chic little islands, get a look at some fancy furbelowed Victorian architecture—even go summer skiing!

SIGHTS: Vancouver's top sights seem to be places you go to look at the sights! For instance, Harbour Centre is a soaring tower where a glass skylift takes you up 40 floors to look at awesomely lovely scenery in every direction. Stanley Park, the park lover's paradise, has everything from a giant checkerboard to a miniature railroad.

A pride of the city is the renovated brick-lined Gastown district, where a steam clock plays Westminster chimes on steam whistles. Nearby is North America's second-largest Chinatown (San Francisco's is the largest).

The Capilano Suspension Bridge is a wonder indeed, dangling across a canyon like a steel spider web, and the city's Aquarium is *some* goldfish bowl—9,000 species of fish and a couple of white whales!

GETTING TO THE PORT: Air Canada offers service to this city and is backed by a host of other national and international airlines connecting Vancouver with U.S. West Coast cities and with the world.

From the airport you can take the Airport Bus (tel. 604/273-0071) for $6.50 (Canadian) to downtown hotels, and from there go by taxi to the harbor (about $10 Canadian). A taxi straight from the airport will cost about $20 Canadian.

Train service is available from points across Canada but not from Seattle. A cross-Canada Via Rail train from Québec City to Vancouver takes five nights and four days to cross the nation.

If you're coming from Seattle you must take a Greyhound bus from Seattle to Vancouver. It's a 3½-hour trip by express bus, an hour longer by regular motorcoach.

If you're coming here by car, you'll need to know that there are now two piers: Ballantyne Pier, the older facility; and Canada Place, the new cruise port. Although they're close together, it would be wise to be sure you know at which pier your ship is docking.

To get to Ballantyne Pier, take Kingsway, Burrard, or Seymour Street to Hastings Street, then proceed east to Heatley Street. To get to Canada Place, which is at the foot of Howe Street, go to the foot of Burrard Street, which will lead you right to it. If you come into town on Seymour Street, turn left on Hastings to Howe and right on Howe. If Kingsway's your route, follow it to Hastings and follow that to Howe.

There is underground parking in Canada Place ($7 a day), if it's not filled, and some parking in a waterfront parking lot, but at busy times—and that's most of the summer cruise season—don't count on that. There's also some concern about vandalism in that area, so be forewarned.

Covered storage parking is available at Imperial Parking at the airport (tel. 604/681-7311) for $7 a day. Canada Place Pier and Ballantyne Pier are a 20-minute drive by free shuttle bus.

AT THE PORT: Vancouver began construction on a new pier several years ago and had it all ready for cruise ships in the spring of 1986—not coincidentally, just in time for the city's Expo celebration.

Called Canada Place, this new facility is modeled after a ship, with multiple decks and billowing sails atop the structure. Inside, you'll find a new hotel, the Pan Pacific, a convention center, international trade center, several restaurants and snack facilities, and plenty of gift shops and boutiques. Outside are all the transportation facilities you need, from buses to taxis and the city's new mass-transit system.

One of the fastest-growing ports in this hemisphere, the Port of Vancouver spent $26 million on its part of Canada Place and has plenty to show for it. There will be plenty of people to show it *to* as well: in 1988 the city was expecting 350,000 cruise passengers to pass through the facility.

Meanwhile, however, some cruise passengers will be docking at Ballantyne Pier, which is really just a bundle of warehouses set up to get you on and off the ship with nothing fancy in between. Facilities are train-station-basic with only some simple seating areas and a small standup snackbar. It's not a place you'd want to hang around for long, so plan your arrival here accordingly.

GETTING ABOARD AND SETTLING IN

So you've gotten to the port city your ship will be sailing from, and you've managed to find the right pier. Perhaps you've even had a chance to see some of the local sights or get a bite to eat. But departure time is drawing near and you're eager to get aboard.

11. GETTING YOUR LUGGAGE ABOARD

The next step is to find a porter for your luggage. That won't be difficult. There are porters at the entrance to every port and they'll jump to attention to take your baggage.

There seems to be rather a lot of debate about how much you should tip this streetside porter who really only takes your luggage to a conveyor belt or to a crewman who then takes it on board. Some people seem to think you should tip these porters not at all, others say the usual $1 a bag or so is the correct thing to do.

As far as we're concerned, we have yet to meet the sturdy soul with nerve enough to ignore a porter. In fact a friend of ours, whose job is to plan and pay for convention arrangements, steadfastly refuses to let a hotel bill him in advance for porter services. No one, he says, can look a porter in the eye and fail to tip him—even if the tip has already been paid!

That leaves us at square one. Make your own decision to tip or not to tip, but do feel justified in tipping lightly.

12. BON VOYAGE PARTIES

No matter how unselfish you are, one of the high points of a cruise is sailing off into the sunset leaving envious friends behind! This rite of passage is known as a bon voyage party, an event that can be great fun for all concerned until the moment the "all ashore" sounds and nonsailors have to stand on the dock watching you sail away.

It once was easy to share your excitement with friends by throwing a blowout of a bon voyage party. In these security-conscious days, however, a rip-roaring sendoff by 50 or so of your closest friends is a bit more difficult, and in some cases impossible.

Sadly, most lines are no longer all that keen to welcome on board folks who aren't sailing on the ship. So just as airlines have restricted wellwishers' access to aircraft, ships have begun limiting or refusing boarding permission to guests.

To discover the policy of the ship on which you're sailing, ask your travel agent to check with the line—or check with it yourself. Some will permit you to bring friends on board prior to sailing time, others won't. Sometimes it depends what port you're sailing from: most lines don't permit visitors on ships sailing from New York, but do allow them on ships sailing from Miami.

To solve the problem simply, you might consider throwing your bon voyage party at home—or better yet, get a friend to have the party for you. Then everybody can pile into cars and drive you to the dock where they can wave lace handkerchiefs at you and you can toss confetti and streamers down on them.

If you discover that the line on which you're sailing permits you to bring visitors aboard, go ahead and arrange an on-board bon voyage party and watch the ship's crew go into action even before you sail. Most cruise lines will happily arrange all the details of your party for you—everything from a tray of bon voyage goodies to that golden bubbly—if you let them in on your plans far enough in advance.

Lines differ on their requirements, so the advance notice can range from 24 hours to 14 days. How elaborately they prepare for your party is an arrangement that must be worked out between you and the line too.

To get your friends on board for the party it will also be necessary to arrange for boarding passes for them. Once again, each cruise line has its own attitude toward boarding passes, some issuing them in advance, some on the day of sailing, some both ways, some not at all. Some have a limit on the number of guests you may have board too. Ask the line or a travel agent what the policy is on the ship you're sailing, then make your arrangements with friends.

Once you're well into your bon voyage party, keep an eye on the clock.

In answer to the question you're now mulling: No. If your friends don't get off the ship, they cannot sail with you. They will be taken off on the pilot boat or dumped unceremoniously ashore at the first stop, from whence they will have to foot the bill to get themselves home.

13. EXPLORING THE SHIP

Despite the "Love Boat" image, it's most unlikely that there will be a Julie Cruise Director standing at the gangplank to welcome you aboard. Generally, however, there will be someone there to tell you where your cabin is located and at least point out the direction in which you should begin looking.

On some lines your welcome may be a wondrous event. European lines, in particular, station a horde of room stewards at the entrance to the ship, outfit them in snappy uniforms and white gloves, and instruct them to meet you with a smile and brain in gear.

That white-glove service is a lovely welcoming touch that ought to be followed by all lines, but isn't. Some just leave you milling about looking for someone who knows what, if anything, is happening. So we can't make any blanket pronouncements on what kind of greeting you'll receive or how much help you'll get in locating your stateroom. If you don't find a welcoming committee, ask the nearest person for the purser's office and there you'll find some help.

After all you went through selecting the ship on which you're sailing, you will be familiar with the line's brochure. Somewhere in that brochure, or readily available from the line or travel agent, is a deck plan of the ship. It would be well to bring that on board with you. Locating your cabin will be much easier if you have one of these ship "maps."

After you've located your cabin and explored all its nooks and crannies, why not spend some before-departure time exploring the rest of the ship? The deck plan shows all the ship's public rooms and outlines all the facilities, so go have a look at them.

If you're hungry or thirsty after a long plane ride, you'll usually find a bar open on board. Some ships even serve a pre-departure buffet—free to you, a small charge for your guests. A band will probably be playing somewhere on the ship. Up on deck, crewmen will be distributing the streamers and confetti and paper horns you'll use to signal your departure.

As you board the ship or as you prepare to sail, you'll also find photographers taking your picture. These will be posted later in the cruise and you can buy one of them to record the magic of these moments in your scrapbook.

CHAPTER IX

LOOK OUT SCALE, HERE IT COMES: DINING AT SEA

□ □ □

1. MORNING TO NIGHT
2. SELECTING A TABLE AND A TIME
3. DRINKING, ROMANCING, AND BEHAVING YOURSELF
4. SPECIAL OCCASIONS

Talk about fat city! Morning food, noon food, evening food, midnight food, mid-morning bouillon, afternoon tea, and in-between nibblies!

Let's get it straight right up front here: this is no time to begin a diet. This is no time to *continue* a diet. This is, in fact, no time even to recognize the existence of the *word* "diet."

If there's one single thing about cruising that appeals to everyone, it's the thought of wonderful food presented nonstop for seven or ten gluttonous days.

1. MORNING TO NIGHT

All this glorious gorging gets started first thing in the morning. If you arise early, you'll find that the cooks have arisen even earlier to organize some kind of hunger appeteaser on deck to hold you until official breakfast hours begin.

Next comes breakfast in the dining room, where you can select from a menu every bit as long as the dinner menu: kippers, lox, bacon, bagels, muffins, fancy breads, sweet rolls, eggs cooked every way but Sunday, fruit-laden pancakes, butter-drenched waffles, even a steak if you like, toast, jellies, five or six kinds of juices, coffee, tea, milk, Bloody Marys, screwdrivers. You name it, someone will produce it.

Even as you eat, someone somewhere is preparing mid-morning bouillon to be presented about 10 a.m. so you should not starve before lunch. This intriguing custom stems from chilly transoceanic voyages where something warm mid-morning dispersed the chill. Some lines sailing in Alaskan waters serve hot mulled wine in mid-morning for just the same reason.

Then comes lunch, a four- or five-course event that can be as simple as a fresh fruit salad or as hearty as, say, turkey, mashed potatoes, gravy, cranberries, salad, biscuits, vegetables, and perhaps a couple of appetizers for starters. Dessert finale, of course.

On most ships, if you don't want to dine in the dining room for lunch you can roam up on deck, where you'll find a snackbar serving (still at no charge, of course) hamburgers, hot dogs, salads, perhaps lasagne or omelets. Some ships specialize in glamorous deck buffets with dozens of hot and cold selections elaborately presented outside so you don't miss a minute of sunshine.

That's it until dinner? Certainly not. Next comes another of the holdovers from the days of transoceanic voyages: afternoon tea. Not just tea, of course, but *tea,* including some kind of cake or cookies, sometimes even small sandwiches.

A few hours later and here comes dinner. Dinner is a major event on every ship, an event into which both crew and passengers throw themselves with fervor.

Many ships sponsor theme evenings at each or many of the dinners aboard. Waiters and busboys dress in costumes appropriate to whatever nationality's being saluted that night—Caribbean Night, America the Beautiful Night, French or Italian Night. On the menu you will find entree selections reflecting the night's theme—Kansas City beef on U.S. night, coq au vin on French night, conch chowder on Caribbean evenings—among six or eight other entree selections.

On some lines these theme evenings are carried out with all the pizzazz of a Cecil B. DeMille production. Crewmen gather somewhere before dessert and come marching into the room singing or accompanied by musicians. Often they carry flaming desserts high in the air, sometimes even balancing trays of liqueurs atop their heads while they dance around the room—Caribbean waiters are experts at that little trick.

What's more, you can have anything you want on the menu and as much as you want of it. If you're still hungry when you've finished the main course, just ask your waiter and he'll bring you another. Heaven for trenchermen!

If you do a little culinary adventuring and discover you don't like what you ordered, ask for something else. No one will frown at you, no one will be upset. Someone might ask you what was wrong with it, but they're only asking because they're trying to please all of the people all the time. When they don't, they want to know why so they can correct the mistake.

Surely that's the end of the food barrage, you say. We can see you're a slow learner. Of course that's not the end! A couple of hours into the evening, and here comes the midnight buffet! Every ship has something served at midnight or thereabouts, although some have more sumptuous repasts than others. Some even go so far as to present something again at about 3 a.m., bringing their daily meal count to eight!

Some lines moderate their daily midnight presentations, saving their strength to produce the really big show, the grand finale event that features massive ice carvings, whole landscapes created from wax or lard, huge sides of beef, ham, poultry, breads baked into fish or animal shapes and presented in woven baskets also made of bread—all very elaborately decorated and presented. You'll probably take dozens of photographs that will floor the folks back home, those poor starving creatures.

Even if you're an early-to-bed, it's worth it to stay up for the extravaganza midnight buffet display. It's downright stupefying in beauty and sumptuousness, not even to mention tempting to the tastebuds.

What you'll want to know is that none of this costs you a cent! You paid all your bills when you booked the cruise and there's no more paying to be done. Everything from that dawn repast to the bouillon to the full-fledged dinners is free.

Paradoxically, in these days of please-let-me-be-skinny prayers, cruise lines have discovered that some fitness fans are now actually turned *off* by the idea of a nonstop food parade. Cruise lines, however, are not a booming business for no reason. No sooner had they discovered this new traveler proclivity toward three spare meals a day than they began catering to it.

Now nearly every cruise line afloat has special menus for dieters, for cholesterol watchers, for fitness buffs, for anti-salt folks. Royal Cruise Line, in fact, pioneered the business of special gourmet menu selections created from the recommendations of the American Heart Association.

Fear not, chocoholics and Grand Marnier mousse makers. You'll still find plenty of sin on the menus.

Those among us who are cooks will sooner or later wonder just what it takes to feed all these stuffees. If you're interested in some of those phenomenal statistics the chef is calculating even as you munch, here's a look at what the chef aboard the *Norway*—whose weekly market bill is more than $100,000—has on his shopping list each voyage:

Eggs	65,880
Ice cream	540 gallons
Hamburger, hot dog buns	9,360
Bananas	2,520 lbs.
Oranges	3,600
Potatoes	14,700
Lettuce	2,520 heads
Tomatoes	3,000 lbs.
Onions	3,000 lbs.
Carrots	1,050 lbs.
Lobster	1,800 lbs.
Shrimp	1,650 lbs.
Bacon	1,650 lbs.
Coffee	1,155 lbs.

2. SELECTING A TABLE AND A TIME

Now that you've come back from the refrigerator (we saw you sneaking off, salivating), it's time to consider the details of dining aboard a cruise ship.

Ships' dining rooms are not usually large enough to accommodate the entire passenger complement at one time. After all, how many 1,000-person dining rooms have you ever seen?

DINING TIMES: To solve the problem, cruise lines have created a method of service known as "two seatings," sometimes also called sittings. That means that one group of passengers is assigned to dine at one time of the morning, afternoon, or evening, the remaining group entering the dining room about two hours later.

The earlier of the two times is called "first seating," the later event "second seating." On most ships, if you select first seating you'll have breakfast at 7 or 7:30 a.m., lunch at noon, and dinner at 6 or 6:30 p.m. Second-seating diners are usually served at 8:30 a.m., 1:30 p.m., and 8 or 8:30 p.m.

You don't have to worry about missing anything because the ship will see to it that all pre- and post-dinner entertainment is repeated for both groups of diners.

The best time to request a certain seating is when you book and/or pay for your tickets. Second seating is particularly popular and is generally completely booked well before the day of departure, so act accordingly.

On some small, posh lines—Cunard's *Sea Goddesses*, for instance—you can dine whenever you like during certain hours of the evening and sit with whomever you like.

SEATING ARRANGEMENTS:
Yes, the little matter of dining companions. Wonderful new friends for the Christmas card list? Or a problem of such delicacy a U.N. ambassador would be boggled?

Let's dig right in here and discuss some of the possible seating arrangements you might encounter—or request.

Let it be known from the onset that all lines will try hard to accommodate requests, but most stop short of guaranteeing you any certain seating arrangement. Many reveal your table to you only at departure time when you pick up your ticket, some post the number of your table in your cabin.

Our advice is to request a certain kind of table and a certain seating when you book your ticket, no matter what the line's policy. It may not work, but then again it may, and what have you got to lose?

Honeymoon couples or couples whose jobs give them little time together may want to take this opportunity to fraternize at dinner only with each other. If that's your case, seek out a ship with tables for two and try very hard to secure one of those for yourself. If you want a table for two, it is wise to make that request as soon as possible, ideally when you book your ticket. Most ships have few, some no, tables for two, so the earlier you reserve one of those, the more likely your wish will be granted.

On some lines you can even ask to be seated with tablemates of a certain age bracket. Some grandmotherly types love to yak it up with the younger set, and vice versa, some prefer the dining company of those of a similar age.

The maxim in shipboard dining is "Ask!" You may not get what you want, but every effort will be put forth to make you happy.

Some lines now also feature smoking and non-smoking sections in both dining rooms and cocktail lounges.

We've tried all kinds of table arrangements from tables for two up to tables for ten. Each has its own pleasures and drawbacks.

The drawback of a table for two is this: on cruise ships, particularly very large ones, meals tend to be a friendship-forming time. If you dine alone, you'll miss some of the fun of meeting others on board. On the positive side, you don't have to concern yourself with bad luck-of-the-draw that leaves you sharing a table with incompatible companions.

If you're traveling alone you'll probably enjoy being included in a larger table where you can get to know some other people aboard. A delightful Irish doctor we met on one cruise, however, sat at a table alone and informed us nicely but firmly that she preferred it that way. She was a pediatrician, so perhaps after a year full of nervous mothers her idea of a wonderful time was a plentitude of solitude. Yours may be too.

Next we come to tables for four. If you're traveling with another couple, tables for four are pleasant. If you're not, this kind of seating arrangement offers you the opportunity to meet two other people, usually a couple, with whom you may become friends. On the negative side of that coin, well, let's just hope you enjoy the company of that other couple.

Tables for six increase your chance of meeting dining companions whose friendship you will enjoy for your sojourn at sea, and perhaps for many years to come. Tables that size also decrease the possibility of boredom. With four or five personalities to choose from, surely one will be compatible.

Tables for eight always seem to end up as two tables for four, if for no other reason than it's difficult to talk over intervening diners.

Tables for ten are usually round, which means you can talk comfortably only with those on either side of you.

The best-laid plans do not always work perfectly in this world. It is possible you'll find yourself with table companions whose conversation is absolutely stultifying to you. We once joined a table where the evening's conversation began with a discussion of appropriate cleaning compounds for grass stains and moved thrillingly on to a lively discussion of sump pumps.

If that happens to you, you need not endure. Just have a word with the maître d'hôtel, explain the situation as nicely and as courteously as possible, and ask to have your table assignment changed. Be nice about it but don't be shy. Dining room chiefs have dealt with this problem hundreds of times (at least) and will do all they can to settle you in with compatible dining companions. In fact, even as you're asking to have your table changed, someone else is probably doing likewise, making the switch just that much easier.

Perhaps in response to some of the problems engendered by togetherness-dining, and certainly in response to traveler's demands for variety, some of the larger and newer ships afloat now have casual dining rooms open for all three meals and a midnight buffet. Some have a pizza parlor—Sitmar is famous for these—and some new ships even are testing a new idea: an intimate gourmet restaurant in which you pay a surcharge to dine, if you want to try it out. All of this means, of course, that you don't have to turn up in the dining room every night if you'd rather not.

Understand, too, that much as the maître d'hôtel may want to make you happy, if the ship is packed and everyone else is pleased with his luck in dining companions, you may not get what you want. In that event, we have no solution to your problem. Look upon it as a challenge . . . or a cross to bear.

3. DRINKING, ROMANCING, AND BEHAVING YOURSELF

We know you already do all these things well. Still, when in Rome, let's discover how the Romans do things. Here are a few tips to make you feel more secure about things you might view a bit timidly and/or wonder what happens if. . . .

SEDUCTION SCENES: You might have seen romantic *diner-pour-deux* scenes on the "Love Boat," but don't count on participating in a candlelight, in-cabin dining experience on *your* love boat.

Dining in your cabin is possible on some luxury ships. Even on some not-so-luxury ships, passengers with suites or the most expensive accommodations aboard can sometimes have a meal served in their room. Less-expensive craft, however, simply don't have the staff to offer that service successfully. Stewards are wonderful people, however. If you get a bad sunburn or twist your ankle or are otherwise too indisposed to go to the dining room for meals, they will see to it that you are fed and watered. They do that with such grace and ingenuity that you will want to take them home. (Sorry, they're not up for adoption.)

Many ships also offer snack service and/or basic beverage service in your cabin, often 24 hours a day.

SPECIAL DIETS: If you're on a special diet, by choice or by doctor's orders, don't be afraid your requirements will not be met on a cruise ship. These people can do anything.

They will in fact *do* anything, but they need a little advance notice so they can see to it that whatever you want is aboard in sufficient quantity to meet your needs.

On most ships you can request vegetarian meals, kosher meals, salt-free, sugar-free, fat-free—everything but calorie-free—meals. On the *QE2,* if you're paying top dollar for your accommodations you can even request some of the world's rarest edibles and, no surprise, they will be there on your table.

Tell your travel agent if you have special dietary needs or tell the line yourself, well in advance of sailing. Or both.

WINE AND THOU: People who like to have a cocktail before or with dinner will be happy to know that they need not change their habits on board a cruise ship. If you don't get dressed in time to have that drink in one of the lounges, just ask your waiter to bring you one, the same as you would in any restaurant.

If you like wine, you'll find extensive wine cellars on board many ships and at least a few wines aboard all ships. Cruise lines often display samples of the wines available in the ticketing area, so you can look over the selection even before you board the ship. You can purchase wine then too, and each night a gentleman will bring your wine to the table.

That gentleman is called the *sommelier* (pronounced "som-el-*yay*"). You will recognize him by the silver key or cup (it's called a *tastevin,* a wine taster) dangling from a heavy silver chain around his neck. He's in charge of the wine cellar and will take your wine order at the beginning of each meal and collect payment for it. (On most cruise lines there is a charge for wine, just as there is a charge for cocktails.)

Wine and liquor prices on ships are quite reasonable, however, generally less than you'd pay in a shoreside restaurant or bar. Figure $1.50 to $2 for a drink, another dollar or so for really fancy concoctions in special glasses.

Travel agents often send their clients a bottle of wine. If yours has done so, the sommelier will have a record of it and will bring the wine to you at dinner if it has not been sent directly to your cabin.

Yes, you tip the sommelier, about 15% of the cost of the wine, and you generally tip him when he serves it, not at the end of the voyage.

Some lines also have a worker who comes around after dinner with a cart full of after-dinner liqueurs. If you buy one of these, you pay him and tip him just as you would a bartender.

SAMPLING: To get an idea what treasures await, take a look at the sample menu we've reprinted here.

Just as ships have personalities, cooks aboard those ships have their specialties too. Lines born and bred in Scandinavia will naturally have a special affinity for fish prepared Scandinavian style, things like kippers, herring in cream sauce, cold fish dishes.

On Cunard's ships you'll find fish and chips with that sensational malt vinegar you just can't get in these parts (and without which fish and chips are pffft).

Greek vessels are sure to feature those feta-topped Greek salads and black olives, lots of lamb concoctions.

Sitmar's pizza is renowned, as is its pasta.

Norwegian Cruise Lines has some great chocolate-chip cookies, and often has fresh Norwegian salmon aboard. Royal Caribbean Cruise Lines does wonderful things with lobster and poultry selections.

Appetizer
    Fresh Fruit in Cup with Kirschwasser
    Smoked Sturgeon and Salmon with Onions and Capers
    Swiss Cheese Salad—Melon Wedge with Prosciutto Ham
    Chilled Celery and Carrot Sticks, Olives, Radishes

From the Tureens
    Beef Consommé with Vegetables
    Cream of Asparagus

Fish Dish
    Golden Fried Fillet of Red Snapper with Sauce Rémoulade
    Salad "Doria" (Potato Salad with Cucumbers)

Farinaceous
    Cannelloni All' Etrusca (with Chicken Livers)

Dinner Selection
    Broiled Sirloin Steak, Onion Rings, "Café de Paris" Butter
    Coq au Vin (French Specialty)—Young Chicken, braised in Burgundy
       with Onions, Mushrooms, and Bacon, flavored with Cognac.

Vegetables
    Glazed Baby Carrots, Parsley
    Broccoli with Hollandaise Sauce

Potatoes
    French Fried–Fluffy Mashed–Pilaf Rice
    Baked Idaho Potato with Sour Cream and Chives or Bacon Bits

---

Carnival's Italian dining room staff produces some very good dinners, and we once had outstanding steaks aboard one of these ships.

After years of reviewing restaurants for newspapers and magazines, we've discovered two maxims: (1) you won't find meals prepared exactly the same way twice by any chef; and (2) you won't find two people who can agree at any moment on the definition of "good." Food that didn't impress us might be just your style, while what we found wonderful may be too gussied, too simple, too lean, too fat, too *something* to please your palate.

You'll often find that a kitchen does some things extremely well. After you've been aboard a day or two you'll be able to spot those "bests." Waiters can

Your Low-Calorie Dish
  "The Executive Salad"
    Coleslaw on Crisp Lettuce, Chicory, Egg Wedges, Tuna Flakes, Cottage Cheese, Stuffed Peach, Radishes and Tomatoes, Green Goddess Dressing

From the Garden
  Lettuce–Tossed Green–Tomatoes–Cucumbers

Choice of Dressings
  Bleu Cheese–French–Russian–Oil and Vinegar

The Finale
  A Selection of International Cheeses from the Tray
  Melba Toast–Rye Crisp–Pumpernickel–Dutch Rusks

Sherbert
  Orange

Desserts
  Surprise de Meringue with Assorted French Fruit and Pistachio Ice Cream
  Cheesecake–Key Lime Pie
  Bavarois "Hawaii"–Fruit Jello
  Vanilla and Chocolate Ice Cream
  A Selection from our Pastry Cart

Fruits
  Fresh Fruit in Season from the Basket
  Calimyrna Figs and Dates–Stemginger in Syrup

Beverages
  Coffee–Tea–Ovaltine–Sanka–Maxwell House
  Fresh Milk–Cold Chocolate

---

be good guides to what's cooking exquisitely today.

It would be simple-minded at best to say that the food on every cruise ship is outstanding. You get what you pay for in most things, and that's pretty generally true afloat as well as ashore. Ships that charge more have larger staffs and can afford to pay for the best in chefdom.

You'll soon discover the specific skills of the chef aboard your ship and learn to order around those skills. If he's a dessert demon, ease off on the rest of the dinner and wait for that creamy-rich chocolate cake or the brandy-touched mousse or the cream puff swans. If he's terrific with sauces, stick to sauce-y selections.

THINGS YOUR MOTHER NEVER TAUGHT YOU: Few of us were born with a silver-enough spoon in our mouths to be positive what's socially correct in sailing situations. Here we come, to the rescue.

Every ship has its Captain's Cocktail Party or Welcome Aboard Gala or something similarly named. On that night, you appear in the lounge at the appointed hour and are greeted in a reception line by several officers.

As you move through the line you'll be asked your name and be passed from person to person until you reach the chief hostess, who will introduce you to the captain. The captain will shake hands with you, perhaps make a small joke, and at that moment a photographer will pop out of the shadows and record your smiles on film. You can buy the photograph in a day or so at the photo shop.

Another crewman will step forward to offer you a complimentary drink and some hors d'oeuvres. Dance music plays and the atmosphere is everything you always dreamed a cruise would be.

Later you go on to dinner, but unless you've paid top dollar for your cabin or are a celebrity of sorts, it is unlikely you will be asked to dine with the captain. Depending on how gregarious the captain is, he may or may not even be present in the dining room for meals. Some captains are visible every night of the voyage while others show up only for the Captain's Dinner and perhaps one other evening.

If you are intent on dining with the captain, you might discuss the matter with the maître d'hôtel who may be able to arrange it, but no guarantees.

If you are asked to dine with the captain one evening during your voyage, consider it an honor as well as a delightful experience, perhaps even the highlight of your trip. Captains aboard these huge cruise ships all seem born with a marvelous, twinkly sense of humor. Perhaps that's not really so surprising. Think what it takes to accept with equanimity the responsibility for a thousand or so passengers and at least that many personnel. He'd better have a sense of humor!

In any case, the captains we've met have been charming and not the least bit stuffy. One so loved the jokes of a Texas story-teller who dined with us that he dragged one of his colleagues up to the man's cabin one afternoon to have the story told over again. Another we know often sings the passengers awake with a morning song over the PA system and another "plays" the spoons!

So that invitees will feel a bit more comfortable at dinner with the captain, you'll usually receive a note asking you to meet with the top crew members and the captain in the lounge before dinner. Some small talk at that time helps break the ice for dinner conversation later. Top officers, and perhaps even the captain, may join you later to watch the show and share the evening's activities.

As for other socially acceptable things to do aboard ship: show up on time for meals. Your waiter won't censure you if you don't, but he's been working all day and is looking forward to his time off too. The later you show up, the longer is day lasts and the harder he has to work. Try to be in the dining room within 15 minutes of the appointed dining hour.

Nowhere is it written that you have to show up for every meal. If you can't face the thought of getting out of bed in time for breakfast, don't. There are no penalties for nonattendance.

If you'd like to have something that is not on the menu, ask for it. Within reasonable bounds, the staff is likely to be able to produce it at a moment's notice. If you want something quite complicated that's not on the menu, ask a day or so in advance.

If you try something you don't like, don't suffer in silence. Explain the problem to your waiter and he will do something to rectify it. You don't have to make a scene. Just explain the problem quietly and ask for another selection.

If you want seconds, don't fear that you'll suffer an Oliver Twistian fate. Just tell your waiter how wonderful it was and ask if you might try another helping.

On ships, as in many European dining rooms, you order your choices from the first several courses. Vegetables will all be listed on the menu but there's no need to choose among them. At the appropriate moment after your entree is served, a waiter will come around bearing the vegetables on a big silver platter. You can try all of them or none of them, or any combination in between.

4. SPECIAL OCCASIONS

If you're celebrating a new marriage, the anniversary of an old one, a birthday, the day you met, or nothing at all, the ship will be happy to provide you with a cake and all the usual special-occasion salutes. Just let someone in the dining room know about your request a day or so before you'd like to have the cake and trimmings presented.

If you'd like to have some new friends up to your cabin for a cocktail party, once again let someone know a day or so in advance and hors d'oeuvres will be provided at the appointed time. Nice way to live, eh?

CHAPTER X

SMALL SAILORS: CHILDREN AT SEA

□ □ □

1. WHAT WILL IT COST?
2. KIDS AND CABINS
3. KEEPING THEM BUSY
4. KID FOOD
5. ASHORE WITH THE SMALL FRY
6. IS IT WORTH IT?

Can you take the kids? In a word, yes. Should you take the kids? Why not? Once you get them on the ship you'll hardly see them again until it's time to get off.

That last statement depends, as you might imagine, on what ship you take. As the cost of cruises has dropped, ship travel has become infinitely more attractive for families who never thought they could afford such a thing.

Indeed, in days of yore you couldn't afford it, but now you'll find more and more families sailing happily together, adults having a wonderful time and youngsters having, if it's possible, an even better time.

1. WHAT WILL IT COST?

Competition has spawned a flurry of special price breaks for couples sharing their cabins with the kids. Watch the newspaper ads each spring and you'll see a raft of special price breaks for parents traveling with children on summer holidays. Sometimes these breaks also occur on school holidays at Christmas or Easter, but that's not as common. On many ships there are special price deals for children, offering them a 50% reduction on the minimum fare aboard or a set price that's very low indeed.

At what age a child stops being a child and becomes an adult varies from line to line, ranging from 12 through about 17. However, even if your youngsters are old enough to be considered adults, they'll only pay the low rate for a third or fourth passenger sharing a cabin. If you read the prices for each ship, in Chapter V you may have noted that rate can be very, very economical indeed. Some cruise lines have even been known to offer deals in which the children can sail with you for free, so long as they share your cabin.

To make matters even better, cruise lines are thrilled to get families aboard their ships. Cruises had for so long been associated with high prices that family travel by ship has been virtually unknown outside the Rockefeller clan. Cruise lines found penetration of that market extremely difficult, so when they are now able to lure those families aboard, they are very pleased.

To prove it, your room steward will often be very accommodating to the needs of families. If the ship is not crowded and you ask nicely, you may very well get a separate stateroom nearby for the youngsters. Now doesn't that sound lovely—for both you and them?

2. KIDS AND CABINS

Even if that doesn't work out and you have to share a cabin with the youngsters, things won't be as bad as you might think. Ships are very large creatures so neither you nor the kids are likely to be spending much time in your cabin.

Admittedly, sharing the cabin with the kids doesn't do a great deal for romance, but it's not very much different than sharing a room in a hotel or resort with them. We guarantee that you'll get awfully clever awfully fast. (We aren't going to amplify that.)

Your cabin, unless you spring for a suite with separate sitting area and couch that becomes a bed, will probably feature upper and lower berths. You would do well not to scrimp too much on the cost of the cabin, for the lowest price will often buy you the tightest quarters. Opt for a larger inside room than a smaller outside one, for instance, or move up a bit in price category if the line or a travel agent can assure you there will be more room in the cabin. Also, older ships usually have much larger cabins for the money than the brand-new pared-down cruisers.

On ships that feature rooms very similar in size, it's safe to go for the lowest-priced quarters, however. You won't buy anything but proximity to the main public areas when you pay the higher price, so you might as well tuck everyone away on a lower deck, save some money, and wear the kids out running up and down the stairs (you take the elevator and meet them).

There's no denying that quarters can get a bit tight, but you probably won't be spending too much time in them anyway. And as one cruise exec told us: "After you shut your eyes, it really doesn't matter what size the room is."

Consign the youngsters to the upper berths, unless there are compelling reasons not to do so. They'll love climbing the ladder up to bed each night, thus making even bedtime a terrific new experience. Well, you can bill it that way anyway. Good luck.

3. KEEPING THEM BUSY

How wonderful a time all the family has depends on how the cruise line feels about children. Some ships simply don't have facilities for children and are not keen on having the little angels aboard. If so, they say so, flat out, in their brochure.

Most moderately priced cruise lines, however, go all-out to welcome the kiddies and provide a round of entertainment for them that some *adults* envy!

We've met some terrific kids on board ships. You'll usually find them at the electronic games, where they'll gladly show you the benefits of youthful eye-hand coordination if you'll come up with a few quarters to keep the Pac-Man moving.

If you're lost, as you will surely be at first, just ask one of the youngsters to help you find your way. They know every corner of the ship by the time they've been on board for an hour, and will happily show you around the place.

If there's gossip aboard, the kids will know what it is. Crew members love the kids, tell them everything, and show them around, indeed spoil them to death at every opportunity.

In our descriptions of the ships we've tried to indicate ships with special facilities for children. Those facilities range from a small room with sandboxes and merry-go-round-like rides for children to the full-fledged children's center you'll find on Sitmar ships, where the youngsters even have a swimming pool designated just for them, a recreation room, the works!

In Sitmar's children's section of the ship, the recreation center for older youngsters is supplemented by a nursery for very young sailors. All of it is strictly off-limits for adults, a rule the youngsters adore.

Ships that cater to children show movies just for the youngsters and have counselors who oversee a full program of activities, sometimes both on board and on shore. Usually, however, you'll find children's counselors and a raft of planned children's activities only in the summer months when the line expects to see many more children aboard.

Games aboard ships include all kinds of board games, plus table tennis, shuffleboard, sometimes badminton or basketball. Kids love the evening Bingo games, and are often the "jockies" for the horse races.

Ships that feature special programs for children often organize those activities so they run simultaneously with adult programs, up to and including meals and after-dinner activities. Others see to the youngsters' needs only from early morning to about dinnertime. After that, you and they are on your own. Babysitters are available, but you pay for that service. Charges are quite reasonable, however.

4. KID FOOD

Ship food is well loved by children, who can eat their fill of hamburgers, hot dogs, and french fries on deck all day long, and need endure adult food only at dinner and sometimes not even then.

Holland America's *Westerdam* has an Italian ice-cream parlor for the youngsters and the greatest miniature disco afloat. Right next to the small dance floor and the video machines there's a nifty sitting area featuring a raised floor into which a hole has been cut so the kids can sit on the carpeted floor and dangle their feet down into the hole while they sip soft drinks.

You'll also discover that youngsters who consider jeans formal dress at home will take to dressing up for dinner like puppies take to water. One 5-year-old we met was so proud of his new suit and tie, his parents reported, that it was all they could do to keep him from wearing it all day long!

5. ASHORE WITH THE SMALL FRY

Special youth-oriented shore excursions are tailored just for children, with none of that boring shopping mom and dad want to do.

If you want to take the kids with you when you go ashore, be prepared to modify your walking and shopping to fit the energy and boredom level of children. There may be nothing worse in the world than dragging a squalling child around in the heat as you try desperately to find the right linen napkins for Aunt Millie. As you very well know from expeditions on your home turf, a bored child is given to crying, whining, racing off in all directions, and generally driving you crazy from disciplinary tactics or from worry.

On ships with lots of foreign crewmen or with visits to foreign ports, the youngsters will get a chance to learn a few words in another language either by design (classes) or by osmosis (chattering to the crew). You'll be amazed how rapidly the little ones begin rattling off foreign phrases *you* may have trouble wrapping your tongue around. If there are foreign children on board, as there often are, especially aboard ships that sail to a foreign country and permit debarkation there, you'll find the youngsters happily playing bilingually together in just a few hours. Amazing little devils!

As we mentioned, some lines even provide recreational activities for youngsters in port. Recreation directors, who are usually young and enthusiastic themselves, take the kids off on shore excursions designed to appeal to their interests: lots of swimming, roaming, and peeking and poking into places.

6. IS IT WORTH IT?

Indeed, it's well worth it. It costs you little more, sometimes nothing more, than you'd be paying anyway.

Taking the kids along can make for a touching and rewarding vacation. You won't feel guilty about leaving them at home with a babysitter or the grandparents, and you'll often get a thrill out of watching their wonderment at meeting new kinds of people and experiences.

Watching children staring wide-eyed as they're hoisted up onto the shoulder of a gold-braided, snappily uniformed, smiling captain (who's thinking of his own toddlers at home) may be one of your most poignant cruise memories.

CHAPTER XI

ONE CAN BE FUN: SINGLES AT SEA

□ □ □

1. WILL YOU BE LONELY?
2. PAYING THE PRICE
3. DELIVERY FROM DINING TRAUMAS
4. SHIPBOARD FRIENDS . . . AND ROMANCES

By now you have absorbed the vision: romantic nights, action-packed days, fascinating ports of call, and no fretting travel details to distress you. But can you go it alone or will this turn out to be seven days of lonely Saturday nights? You haven't been listening carefully enough.

Forget Saturday nights and absorb this picture. You're on board a floating hotel with all the amenities of any major resort, but with one very special feature no landlocked resort can boast: no one can pack up and leave town.

1. WILL YOU BE LONELY?

As a single person you have a captive audience of a thousand or so other passengers, among which you'll surely find a few who share your prejudices and your priorities.

What's more, cruise lines, well aware of the quantities of single people in the world, have dived into the world of matchmaking with all the fervor of a new escort service. One of the first announcements you'll hear aboard any ship is one telling you the time, place, and ambience of the singles' get-together. Hardly will the last mooring lines have been reeled in before the single travelers on board will be meeting somewhere to ID each other and get in on some tandem fun.

One cruise line, Royal Cruise Line, has even gone so far as to seek out good-looking unattached gentlemen with gregarious personalities. After careful screening, these lucky fellows are treated to a free cruise in exchange for their services as a fourth at bridge and as dance and conversation partners for unattached women. How's *that* for working hard to keep singles from being all alone at sea?

It goes further than that, of course. All lines will work hard to see to it that, single as you may be, you are not alone unless you wish to be.

Now you may not think anyone would be alone by choice, but we once met a delightful Irish doctor who told us a couple of weeks of companionship strictly by *choice* was her idea of heaven. She stuck to it too, sitting happily alone at a table for two, conversing when she chose, but declining companionship just as frequently as she welcomed it. Now that's an independent spirit!

You can be just as independent—one of the joys of singlehood—or you can mix happily with others on board, meeting new friends among both crew and passengers.

2. PAYING THE PRICE

It's sad but true that single travelers must often pay a premium for what some consider a singular blessedness. Little by little these extra charges are easing a bit, particularly in slow season, but they do still exist.

There are, of course, sound economic reasons, from the cruise line's point of view, for the 150%, 175%, or 200% fares levied on single travelers. If you're living alone in a cabin for two in prime selling time, the line is automatically losing one full fare. No one stays in business by losing money.

Some ships, Holland America Line / Westours' *Westerdam* is one, have cabins just for singles. These are a bit smaller than a double cabin naturally, but are quite comfortable for a single traveler.

On some lines you will pay more for these single cabins than you would if you were sharing a cabin for two. On other lines there is little or no price differential over the per-person, double-occupancy rate in that price category. On most ships, however, you will have to face a classic battle between budget and solitude. If you can afford privacy, you may find it worth the extra price. Or you may not. Many people enjoy having a roommate's companionship for the voyage, even if that companionship does not turn out to be a lifelong friendship.

If privacy is not vital to your enjoyment of the cruise, you can save some money by taking advantage of an offer made by nearly all cruise lines. Somewhere in the fine print of most ship brochures you'll find an offer by the line to team you up with one or more roommates with each of you paying half the rate for that cabin. If you don't see any mention of sharing arrangements, ask the line or a travel agent if the ship offers this kind of deal. That way both you and your roommate will pay the same price per person as a couple occupying those quarters.

Your roommate will be of the same sex and probably, but not definitely, in a similar age bracket. As with any grab-bag situation, you may or may not enjoy the company of your roommate. You will, however, have a companion for the first few ice-breaking hours, and that may be worth something to you.

If you don't like your newfound roomie, plan on spending plenty of time in the ship's public rooms because there's little or no chance that a room switch can be made.

If you really want to save money, some lines will offer you the opportunity to share a cabin for four with three other single travelers, each of you paying one-fourth of the total cost of the cabin. That kind of a deal can make passage quite reasonable, but has the usual drawbacks you'd expect in a cabin for four—less space, more chance for friction, crowded storage conditions.

We have known several adventuresome single travelers who have sailed off to Europe or Africa sharing a cabin way down in the recesses of the ship. They bought, quite inexpensively, a lifetime of memories. Everything has its price.

One, in fact, says she always books single space in a cabin for four, if she can, and has occasionally ended up alone in the cabin when the line failed to fill it. That pleasant offshoot can also happen when you book one of the share-a-cabin deals. It's all the luck of the game, however, and although it does often happen, particularly in slow seasons, there are no guarantees.

To make that kind of luck work for you, however, you must specify that you will book only on the per-person, double, basis. If the line takes your money under those conditions, it will try to find you a roommate, but if it fails to do so, you won't be charged any additional fee for the cabin class you booked.

A line need not accept your booking under these conditions, but many of them will do so, particularly during less busy seasons of the year. If they at first refuse, try presenting your case once again closer to the departure date when the line's chances of booking the cabin have become more remote. Don't bother to try any of these nifty plans at peak seasons like Christmas or New Year's, however.

If you do book a shared cabin and find yourself with three roommates, ask your steward if there might be an empty cabin somewhere that you, or you and one of the others from your room, might occupy since no one is using it. Don't get demanding about this or you'll get nowhere. Do explain the crowded conditions or perhaps wave a bit of green about (or at least imply the appearance of some later) in compensation for his efforts. After all, if he manages to find an empty cabin for you he'll have to clean and care for two cabins instead of one.

Interestingly, because there are more single women travelers than men, single men have a greater chance of paying to share a single cabin and then finding they won't have to adjust to the presence of a roommate.

Singles can often save money by working with a travel agent who is very active in selling group cruises. Sometimes these groups are "affinity" groups, which means that they belong to the same garden club, church, or organization. More often, the group is just a loose coalition created by the travel agent who has booked a cluster of cabins in a certain price category for a specified cruise or cruises. You can join either.

An organization called Single World (tel. toll free 800/223-6490) offers guaranteed share rates for singles that can run as low as $575 for a week's cruise!

Many travel agents now send out regular newsletters and announcements of upcoming cruises you can join. It's often possible to save quite a bit of money over the regular cruise price by joining one of these groups. Unlike land tours, cruise tour groups need not spend much or any time together, so you don't have to worry about being stuck with a group of garden freaks when you wouldn't know an aphid from an asparagus.

3. DELIVERY FROM DINING TRAUMAS

Any woman who has ever been single knows that one of life's worst moments can be the dinner hour when all the rest of the world seems to be couples. As if that isn't depressing enough, every one of us has met some haughty dining room host or hostess who has sneeringly led us to the table by the kitchen door where presumably we could depress only the chef with our single status. Sooner, rather than later, that sort of bad manners is disappearing, but the good news tonight is that you don't have to worry about anything like *that* on a cruise.

When you book your trip, simply tell your travel agent or the line that you want to be at a table for six or more, and explain that you'll be traveling by yourself. You'll find yourself welcomed in the dining room with the same quiet courtesy as everyone else aboard and shown to your table where introductions will begin. *Voilà!* Already you have met five potential companions.

If you'd prefer to sit in solitary splendor, you should have little trouble securing a place at a table for two. Most travelers like the experience of meeting new people on board, so tables for two may be available. On the opposite side of that coin, however, most ships have few tables for two, so the odds against your getting one increase.

Take a good look at the ship's deck plans too. Many of them indicate the kinds and locations of tables on board so you can select a table for two (in this case for one) that's near other larger tables, then join or not join in their fun.

You'll have to make your own decision about what you think of tables for four. You may find yourself the third party at a table with a couple. A fourth, probably also a single traveler, may be added to your table. Once again, if you make sure the ship's dining room staff knows you're traveling alone and don't particularly want to keep it that way, they'll make every effort to team you up with compatible companions.

Some lines, Carnival for one, will even make an effort to take your *age* preference in dining companions into consideration!

If you give your dining room companions a college try and find you aren't pleased with them, tell the maître d'hôtel or dining room captain your problem and ask for a change of companions. You are, after all, going to spend four or five hours a day with them. If it's humanly possible, the crew will try to accommodate you.

4. SHIPBOARD FRIENDS . . . AND ROMANCES

Once upon a time when one of us was single, that one took a weekend cruise, primarily, it must be admitted, to avoid a dateless weekend. What an avoidance! From the first dinner to debarkation it was a whirlwind weekend of laughter and dance that is remembered fondly to this day. On another occasion the voyage was a much longer but no less eventful one.

Perhaps the single most wonderful thing about a cruise ship is that you can wander into any of the piano bars, cocktail lounges, dining rooms, or decks, sit down and have a drink (or buy someone else one) without feeling like a lost gosling wandering into a den of foxes.

Everyone on board a ship is out to have a good time. You're all thrown together in a big unabandonable barrel, so you'll find everyone intent on making a great time of it. No one will draw any conclusions about a single man or woman in one of the ship's bars. In fact it's very likely that the couple beside you or a fellow down the bar or a couple of women two tables away will strike up a conversation about the best buys in the next port.

We were charmed by two young women who sent us over a drink one evening as an ice breaker. No special reason, just for fun. They, like the other passengers, were in high spirits on that first night aboard and were anxious to talk about their impressions of this ship as compared to several others they had sailed. Happenings like that are the rule rather than the exception on a cruise.

Some travelers begin making acquaintances very early on in the cruise, that is to say, before the ship leaves the harbor. They do that, crew members tell us, by being among the first to answer the boat drill call. You'll read more about boat drills in the Introduction, but for now you need only know that as the ship begins to leave the dock you'll be asked to don your lifejacket and get yourself to an assigned place on the ship where you will be instructed in safety procedures.

Get up to the assigned boat station early, experienced lookers tell us, and check out who's arriving. Fumble helplessly with the lifejacket in the immediate vicinity of someone interesting, and *violà!* introductions.

If you prefer somewhat more organized introductions, the singles party we talked about earlier will be occurring either just after the ship leaves port or after dinner that first night out. See what we mean about the ship's crew wanting you to have a good time? If you're not already too busy with new friends, go to the party. At least you'll get a look at some of the options.

There's another way to get a look at some of the possibilities: ogle the crew. Every ship has many good-looking men and women aboard. What's more, the peripatetic nature of their seagoing career means that many of them are single. That almost always excludes the captain, so perhaps you should avoid shooting quite that high. On the other hand several captains have told us stories about marrying ladies they met aboard ship. That is, after all, where the captain spends almost all his time.

On most ships, officers are permitted—in some cases, encouraged—to mix with the passengers but to maintain basic discretion in their activities. Sometimes there is only moderate, if any, discouragement of crew-passenger romances. If you do make friends with a crew member, you may very well spend some time in the crew's own lounges. Crew members are very good party-ers and have an uncanny ability to cram ten friends into their tiny cabins for a party. You can be sure you'll have a good time.

We'd say it's up to the crew member, not you, to know and follow the ship's rules on fraternization with passengers. With so many more single men and women in the world and so many of them opting for a cruise vacation, it seems to us a bit counterproductive to bar the crew from friendships with passengers. But then we're not running a cruise line.

Certainly there are few more romantic atmospheres in which to pursue and be pursued: moonlight and roses, starlight and champagne, lazy days and dancing nights.

Good hunting!

CHAPTER XII

MAL DE MER: IT'S NOT THE SIZE OF THE SHIP, IT'S THE MOTION OF THE OCEAN

□ □ □

1. CURES AND PREVENTIONS
2. IS THERE A DOCTOR IN THE HOUSE?
3. SPECIAL PROBLEMS

If you have never been to sea before (or only on troopships, and those don't count), your first question will be "Are cruises fun?" Your second question, delivered within seconds of the first, will, we predict, be "Will I get sick?"

Be encouraged by the news that modern ships are steadied to a faretheewell with huge stabilizers that shoot out like side fins and hold the ship steady in the water, keeping the roll to a minimum. In the ship's brochure are details describing the kind and amount of the ship's stabilizers. If you don't find that information, ask your travel agent to inquire.

Only a cock-eyed optimist would guarantee you won't suffer from that famous—and infamous—malady the French call *mal de mer*. Everybody is different and each inner ear reacts to motion in its own peculiar way. Some people can feel queasy in a Rolls-Royce, then cross the Atlantic in a hurricane and love every blustery minute of it. Others ride rollercoasters and ferris wheels with never a moment's fear, but panic when terra firma becomes unfirma.

We can't tell you just how you'll react, but we can tell you that it doesn't really matter. There are ways to be sure you'll have a lovely cruise, no matter what your reaction to motion.

1. CURES AND PREVENTIONS

Ask your physician for effective cures. There is a new motion-sickness cure available, which requires that a small circle called Transderm-Scop be attached to the skin behind your ear. This implantation, which doesn't hurt a bit, is an anti-motion-sickness drug that is time-released into your bloodstream. It isn't used for children, however, as it has not yet been determined to be safe for them. No one else need worry about it, however, particularly not pregnant women: the drug contained in Transderm-Scop was first used in a medication called "twilight sleep" given to women prior to delivery of a baby. In a few cases, however, the drug may have a mild hallucinatory effect or produce confusion, but that's quite rare.

In any drugstore you can buy over-the-counter anti-motion-sickness drugs. Dramamine is the best-known one, although there are now other brands as well. The drawback to these drugs is that the relaxant in them makes some people very drowsy. Better drowsy, however, than seasick, and you're not driving so why worry? Dramamine in fact has a similar history to Transderm-Scop: its ingredients were first used to combat morning sickness.

We know you're going to sneer and scoff at this next recommendation, but knowledge is power so we push fearlessly forward—ginger. Yes, some natural-foods fans insist, ginger can help you avoid seasickness. No, we don't know if there's any truth in it, but we do know that there are enough people convinced of the efficacy of ginger that the spice now appears in capsule form at drugstores.

One of us has a tummy shakey enough to act up at the *dock* and is, therefore, here to tell you two things: when it comes to seasickness, *anything* is worth a try; and the fun of a cruise is worth almost any risk, certainly one as tame as a thrummy tummy.

Something new in seasickness prevention appeared a couple of years ago: Sea-Band. Applying the principles of acupressure, these bands fit around the wrists and a button applies pressure at the Nei-Kuan point on the wrist. No medication is used and the bracelets can be used by anyone. Sea-Bands are distributed by Travel Accessories, P.O. Box 391162, Solon, OH 44139 (tel. 216/248-8432, or toll free 800/854-0601). A pair of bands is $15 and the company can send you a set for a small mailing charge.

What exactly causes seasickness nobody knows for certain. In general terms motion seems to affect the inner ear, which controls other parts of the body including your equilibrium. If that sensitive inner ear is disturbed by unfamiliar motion, you feel queasy.

If you have reason to suspect that you might be prone to motion sickness, try one of these preventatives. The key to the success of any of these remedies, doctors tell us, is to take it *before* sailing. Don't wait until you're feeling the butterflies to begin wondering how you should go about snaring them. You'll find plenty of anti-motion-sickness pills aboard any ship in the ship's drugstore and often in every lounge on board.

Once again, one of us is prone to this ailment and knows bitterly how miserable it can be. In a couple of all-too-memorable encounters with the *mal* of the *mer,* we've learned *absolutely* that you cannot drink your way to a cure. Whatever anyone tells you about a brandy or some champagne, don't.

On most cruises you won't find the water rough enough to cause you any problems. By far the majority of cruises in the Caribbean, Alaska, inland waterways, and along the Pacific coastline are operated, by design, in still waters.

It does occasionally happen, however, that the wind picks up and ruffles the waters, causing the ship to roll in the trough of the waves from side to side or to pitch forward and back. Pitch is easier to bear than roll. Transatlantic cruises are often rough too, particularly those that travel across the North Atlantic in early spring or late fall when the winds are brisk.

If you're suffering from seasickness, you may find some relief from its most immediate effects by getting yourself up on deck where you can see the horizon. People who get carsick if they read in a car but feel all right again if they look up at the horizon seem to do well with the up-on-deck cure. Believe us, you'll want to try anything without argument. We've found that the stabilizing effect of seeing the horizon often works so well that you are cured right at the start.

Yes, you say, but I can't stay up on deck all night. What happens when I go back inside? Well, chances are you'll feel queasy once again. Take a motion-sickness pill before you go up on deck and stay up there for a few hours after you start to feel better. Stay near the edge of the deck too.

Crew members often prescribe soda crackers and soup. Who knows where this old tradition started, but it seems to work for some sufferers.

It also often helps to take to your bunk and sleep it off. Cabins amid-ships and deep down in the ship have the least roll. If you're really worried, book one of these. Avoid quarters in the bow or as high up on the ship as the lifeboats.

If you're feeling horrible but hungry, don't try to make it to the dining room, where the roll may be worse and the sight and smell of food is . . . well, forget it. Explain your problem to the steward and ask him to bring some light meal to your cabin. He'll be glad to oblige.

There is this final consolation: you *will* get your sea legs after a bit (notice we're not saying how long "a bit" is) and begin to feel better on your own. Usually this only takes a day or two. By that time your body will have adjusted to the roll of the ship, so don't do anything to confuse it—for instance, don't try to eat at one meal enough to make up for all the meals you didn't eat. Dine lightly and give thanks.

One of the best antidotes to this sickness is to stay so busy you don't have time to think about it. That advice, we realize, is cold comfort when your stomach feels like Jell-O.

We don't think mal de mer will be a problem for you, but if you have doubts, ask your doctor about the behind-the-ear implant or take an anti-motion-sickness pill well before the ship sets sail.

Bon voyage!

2. IS THERE A DOCTOR IN THE HOUSE?

In a word, yes. Every large ship is required to have a doctor aboard, and some ships have a hospital nearly as big as one you might find in a small town!

On a recent visit to the *QE2*, we were amazed to be shown not only a handsomely decorated waiting room but a dentist's office, a complete pharmacy, 15 beds, a crew examining room, and a complete operating theater! Now *that* is prepared.

While there won't be such elaborate facilities on smaller cruise ships, there will be a doctor and a nurse on all but the tiniest inland cruisers. Even those will have someone on board with at least nurse's training. Those very small ships (100 or fewer passengers) also stop in port every evening and are rarely out of sight of land, so if you should need a doctor, the ship can get you to one quickly.

Ship's doctors are quite interesting people, as you might have guessed from watching "Love Boat." One we met had always dreamed of cruise-ship travel and spread the word around until he was finally selected to fill in for the ship's regular doctor during a vacation.

Ship's doctors are considered among the crew's top officers and will often be seen dining at the captain's table. That, of course, is the ideal way to meet the ship's doctor.

If, however, you must meet him or her by necessity, rest assured that you'll be getting good medical care. Most ship's doctors, however, say that about the most they ever see is a bad sunburn, a sprained something, or an occasional broken bone.

Speaking of sunburn, it's amazing how many people think they can take a pale epidermis that hasn't seen sun for months and stuff it right out there in the sunshine. They can—but they pay. In Caribbean or Mexican sunshine you will burn—and fast—so be smart and limit your sunbathing to 15 minutes the first day, adding an additional 15 minutes each day thereafter up to about an hour and a half on the seventh day.

Sunscreens are very effective products, and combined with a sensible sunning schedule can give you a nice tan that will look great back in your hometown —instead of a blotchy mess that flakes off behind you in little trails of peeling skin.

Handsome as the ship's doctor may be, meeting him when you're in major sunburn pain is not ideal. Be patient. Olympic-quality suntans are not acquired in a day.

If you're suffering from seasickness and don't seem to be improving as rapidly as you'd like, stop in to see the doctor. Doctors on board have regular hours, which usually will be announced in the ship's newspaper and will always be posted at the infirmary.

Some ships charge a small amount, usually $10 or less, for a visit to the doctor to have him sympathize with such things as sunburn or sea sickness. Others do not charge for that service. Like shoreside house calls, visits to your cabin and/or at night can cost about double that. Medication is sold to passengers at cost on some ships, and minor medication is distributed free on most.

No one wants to think about this, much less talk about it, but if you should need major medical help, the ship's doctor has contingency plans to care for you until the ship reaches the next port where you can be taken to a hospital, should that be necessary. From there, if necessary, you can be flown home.

Ships maintain close radio contact with the home port and with nearby ports, so close, in fact, that EKG readings can be reported instantly to heart specialists. In really rare emergencies helicopters can remove passengers from large ships.

Naturally, such a calamity would incur awesome expenses, so you would do well to check your medical coverage to be sure that you're covered for care in another country. Travel agents and insurance companies, including special travel-oriented insurance companies, can explain what special travel insurance is available to help protect you if you have medical problems far from home.

3. SPECIAL PROBLEMS

If you have or have had an illness that could cause a problem during your cruise, speak to the ship's doctor early on in the voyage.

Those whose illnesses are so incapacitating as to require confinement to a wheelchair may or may not be welcomed on certain ships. If you or a companion must use a wheelchair, you must tell the line in advance so they can outline wheelchair size requirements aboard. Some chairs are simply too wide for the ship and won't be able to negotiate passageways or cabins.

Some ships have gone out of their way to provide facilities for those with special medical problems. One recently installed kidney dialysis equipment on board so that those requiring that kind of treatment periodically could still go sailing.

Wheelchair travelers should also take a very close look at the ship's deck plans and give some thought to the presence or absence of elevators and the access, or lack of it, to public rooms. Some ships are more accessible for wheelchair travelers than others. In general, more modern ships have wider passageways, more elevators, and more provisions for all kinds of handicapped travelers.

You should also examine the itinerary and check to see if the ship docks at each port or anchors offshore, taking passengers into port by tender. Generally, wheelchair travelers cannot negotiate the tender's accessways and must stay on the ship. Obviously, you'd be wiser to pick a ship that pulls into a dock in each port.

Wheelchair travelers must, by the way, be accompanied by someone who can push the chair around, since ships do not carry enough personnel to permit assigning a crewman specifically to you.

If you require any kind of special diet, you must let the line know in advance so they can plan and prepare it for you each day. A travel agent can make those arrangements for you too.

If you have special medication, take it with you. Do not, repeat, *do not* count on being able to fill your prescription at some port of call. For the most part you'll be visiting foreign countries ill-prepared to deal with filling your prescription. At best it will cost you time and money for long-distance calls to your doctor. At worse you won't get the prescription filled.

Avoid all those problems by being sure you have enough medication (even better, twice as much as you need), bottled and packed separately so that if you lose one you'll have a backup bottle. Naturally, we aren't talking aspirin here, just medication that you must take regularly.

CHAPTER XIII

SEA TALK: SOUNDING LIKE A SAILOR

□ □ □

1. AHOY, BUOY, GET THAT HAND OFF THE FANTAIL
2. SHIP DESIGNATIONS
3. COUNTING STRIPES: CALLING A CAPTAIN A CAPTAIN

Goodness knows your mother said you sounded like one just before she washed your mouth out with soap, but that isn't exactly what we have in mind.

As you begin the first days of your seven years before the mast, you will hear people speaking in tongues, babbling on about "tendering"—no, they're not discussing an hour in the moonlight—or "heads," which have much to do with just the opposite. "All hands" is not one of those men your mother warned you about, and "abreast" is not what pops, er, instantly to mind.

If you hear some words that sound pretty risqué to you, it may just be some experienced swabbies talking sea talk. And it's nothing mom would disapprove of!

Quite a separate language from the one the rest of us speak, nautical talk is comparatively easy to learn. Before long you'll discover that "port" is not only something you drink but somewhere you look.

To give you a clue to what everyone's talking about on board, we've compiled a list of the most common nautical terms, carefully excluding some of those that really will make you sound like a sailor.

You'll notice that throughout the book we haven't indulged in a great deal of sea talk, figuring that total immersion in companionways, bulkheads, and screws will come soon enough.

1. AHOY, BUOY, GET THAT HAND OFF THE FANTAIL

abeam—at right angles to the keel, which runs from front to back down the center of the ship (see "keel"). Something may be said to be abeam of something else. Don't worry about this one; it's not very common anyway, and usually heard as a descriptive state about a ship or, sadly, about some bikini-clad lass as in "she's broad abeam."

aboard—on board, or on the ship.

SAILING TERMS □ 379

about—most commonly used in the phrase "to come about," meaning to turn the ship around.

above board—decks located above the waterline. The expression "to be above board" about something stems from ship talk.

abreast—this is a reference to a ship pulling alongside another vessel or a dock.

aft—toward the rear, or more properly, the stern, of the ship.

aground—to run a ship up onto a sand bar where it becomes stuck until floated off by high tides, an extremely rare occurrence on cruise ships, so relax.

ahoy—a call from one captain or crewman to another to hail the vessel. On modern ships calls are made quite quietly on powerful radios so don't look forward to hearing the captain screaming across the bay.

alleyway—a narrow hallway, or more correctly, passageway, of a ship.

all hands—everyone working on a ship, most often heard as "all hands report to. . . ."

amidships—in the middle of the ship halfway between front and back, or if you're beginning to catch on, between bow and stern.

anchor ball—a black ball hoisted in the forward section of the ship to show that the vessel is anchored.

anchor off—an anchor, of course, is what is used to hold the ship in place in the ocean. To "anchor off" is to drop the anchor offshore but close in because the docks are filled with ships or the ship has too deep a draft to enter the harbor. If the ship anchors off, passengers get to shore on boats called tenders.

ashore—on shore. You "go ashore" when the ship pulls into port, but one would hope you are not still "ashore" when it leaves.

astern—toward the rear or stern of the ship, sometimes referring to something actually behind the ship or in its wake.

athwart—across the width of the ship.

ballast—weight that ships used to carry to keep on an even keel when empty, it also refers to any weight on board. Stones were often used in early sailing ships to keep them steady until cargo was taken on board.

bar—a sandbar, created by tidal conditions and the thing upon which you run aground.

barge—a ship with a flat bottom usually used as a cargo carrier.

beacon—a beam of light on shore that serves as a landmark and directional signal.

beam—the width of the ship at the widest point, usually right through the middle. Ships with wider beams are said to be broad of beam.

bearing—the way the ship is headed, a compass direction like northeast, southwest, etc., expressed in degrees.

bells—a now largely abandoned way of telling time, bells were once sounded at half-hour intervals with one bell at 4:30 a.m., two bells at 5 a.m., three bells at 5:30 a.m., and so on to eight bells at 8 a.m., when the count began again with a bell at 8:30 a.m., two bells at 9 a.m., etc., until 12:30 p.m., when the count began once again, ending with eight bells at 4 p.m. So the eight bells you may have heard mentioned was 8 a.m., noon, 4 p.m., 8 p.m., or midnight. It's really only six bells that matters anyway: that's cocktail time!

below—on a deck lower than the main deck of the ship. To "go below" is to go to a lower deck, and sometimes refers to a crewman going off duty, as "I'm going below now."

berth—bed, what you'll call the thing you sleep on in your cabin, if you're a nautical purist. It also refers to the "bed" the vessel sleeps in when it's in port, that is, the dock or place the vessel is docked.

bon voyage—a French term meaning "good voyage" or "good trip," pronounced "bawn voy-adge."

bow—the front or foremost part of the ship, pronounced to rhyme with cow.

bridge—where the captain and navigational officers control and operate the ship. It's located above the passenger areas of the ship and contains complex navigational equipment. Most ships offer daily or regularly scheduled visits to the bridge. Go, you'll love it.

bulkhead—walls inside the ship between cabins or public areas, or walls built to strengthen the ship; partitions. Walls of your cabin are not walls but bulkheads.

bunkers—where fuel is stored.

buoy—a warning float or a marker, usually pronounced "boo-eee" but sometimes "boy."

cabin—if you can't figure this one out you're in trouble—it's your bedroom, also called a stateroom, although stateroom sometimes refers to accommodations larger than a cabin.

cable—heavy chains used to hold the ship's anchor.

cast off—to let go of the ship's lines in preparation for sailing.

charts—maps of the ocean showing depths, landmarks, sandbars.

class—years ago passengers traveled first class, cabin class, perhaps second, third, or tourist class on transoceanic voyages. Now almost all ships are one-class ships with the exception of the *Queen Elizabeth 2*, which has two classes, first and "transatlantic."

colors—the national flag flown on the ship.

companionway—interior stairways connecting decks.

course—the route the ship takes. The course is plotted these days by computers but once was "reckoned" on the location of moon and stars by night, charts (or maps of the ocean) and landmarks by day.

crow's nest—once the tiny cage high on the mast where a crewman was stationed to look for land; now any lookout, including a bar or observation lounge, high on the ship.

davits—steel structures to which the ship's lifeboats are hooked and from which they and the ship's tenders are launched; pronounced "*da*-vits."

deck—each floor, or story, of the ship.

disembark, debark—to get off the ship; used interchangeably.

dock—a pier, wharf, or quay, a place to tie up the ship; also used as a verb, to dock, meaning to come into port.

draft—sometimes spelled draught, the amount of water a ship needs to sail without allowing the bottom of the ship to touch the ocean floor. It is figured from the lowest point of the ship underwater to the waterline. Ships with a "deep draft" cannot go into shallow ports without running aground, but ships with a "shallow draft" can negotiate shallow-water areas to visit some less-frequented ports.

drill—any safety test or instruction session ordered by the captain. You will participate in a lifeboat drill as soon as you leave port; crewmen participate in their own fire drills, announced well ahead of time.

embark—to get on the ship, to board it.

fair wind—a tail wind, or wind blowing in the same direction as the ship is moving.

fantail—has nothing to do with feather dancers but refers instead to a part of the stern extending behind the stern post, an overhanging stern.

fathom—a measure used to determine water depth under the ship. One fathom is six feet. Depth is determined today by sophisticated sounding equipment.

flag of convenience—refers to registration of a ship in a country simply because that country offers the vessel lower tax rates and other levies. Popular flags of convenience include Liberia and Panama.

flags—crewmen run up flags as signals to other ships if the ship is in distress or under certain other conditions, for instance, when a ship's pilot is on board. Flag codes are international and are recognized in every country in the world. On freighters flags may indicate what cargo is carried on board. Flags are not flown at sea except in emergencies. A flag of registry showing what country the ship is registered in appears at the stern of the ship. A ship's destination flag appears at the bow of the ship.

fore, forward—referring to the front of the ship as opposed to the back or aft end.

free port—a port that is free from import taxes and hence can offer tax-free goods at a lower price. St. Thomas in the U.S. Virgin Islands is the most ballyhooed free port, but Freeport, Bahamas, Bermuda, and other islands also have tax breaks.

funnel—there is some debate about whether the smokestack at the top of the ship should be called a smokestack or a funnel. Either way, everyone will know what you mean.

galley—kitchen.

gangway—a bridge connecting the ship to the shore. After the ship docks, the crew will lower a gangway for you to walk ashore. When the ship leaves port the gangway is pulled back aboard. If you have not yet crossed the gangway and the ship's lines are being loosed, you had better go like gangbusters.

gross register tons—a size measurement by which ships are compared, although a somewhat controversial one. A gross register ton refers to 100 cubic feet of enclosed space on a ship.

hand—a crewman.

harbor master—the person in charge of harbor operations, ship dock assignments, etc.

hatchway—also known just as hatches, these are deck openings through which crewmen go to reach the "holds," which are places in which cargo and ship's supplies are stored.

head—toilet.

helm—the ship's steering equipment. To be "at the helm" is to be operating the ship, steering the course.

high seas—all the ocean beyond the territorial limits and waters not subject to the jurisdiction of any country.

hold—the ship's cargo area below decks. Steamer trunks used to be stored in the hold while passengers were on long transoceanic voyages.

hook—slang for the anchor. To drop the hook is to drop anchor.

house flag—the line's logo designating ownership of the ship; the ship's identification either on the funnel or on a flag.

hull—the outer structure of the ship, its "body."

Jacob's ladder—also simply called a ladder or accommodation ladder, and most often used by the pilot who comes aboard to advise the captain on port-departure maneuvers. It may also be used by passengers to board a tender.

Jones Act—this act, passed in 1886, prohibits foreign-registered ships from carrying passengers directly between U.S. ports, for instance between New York and Miami, without a stop at a foreign port. That's also why you cannot get on the ship in Miami and get off, to stay off, in Puerto Rico, although you can do that in the Virgin Islands, which is exempt from these regulations. U.S.-registered ships, however, are permitted to sail between American ports.

keel—the main structural member of a ship, running fore and aft along the bottom of the ship, the backbone of the ship to which all of the crosswise parts are attached. Expressions like "keel over," meaning to turn bottom up or fall over, and "on an even keel," meaning to be stable or steady, stem from this word.

knot—the nautical equivalent of miles per hour. A knot is one nautical mile—6,080.2 feet, about 1.15 land miles—per hour. A ship's speed is measured in knots, with most cruise ships capable of about 15 to 20 knots.

latitude—the distance north or south of the equator, expressed in degrees.

league—you've heard of *20,000 Leagues Under the Sea*? Well, multiply 20,000 times 3.45 nautical miles (that's how much a league is) and you'll find out how far Jules Verne's 20,000 leagues was.

leeward—the sheltered side of an island or the direction toward which the wind is blowing. In nautical circles the word is pronounced "loo-erd," and is the opposite of windward.

let go—no, no, silly, not that. Lines, the ship's ropes, are "let go" as the ship prepares to sail.

lifeboats—small boats you will see rimming an open deck and used to carry passengers in an emergency. The location of your lifeboat station is posted in your cabin. You'll learn how to get there and what to do there at the lifeboat drill—mandatory attendance, no shirkers.

lines—massive ropes that are used to tie the ship up to cleats on shore.

log—a diary maintained by the captain and the ship's officers detailing the weather, ship's course, navigation details, and in the old days, some pretty interesting personal material.

longitude—the distance east or west measured by the angle that the meridian through a specified place makes with the Prime Meridian, which runs through Greenwich, England. It's expressed in degrees, minutes, and seconds.

manifest—a list of the names of the ship's passengers, cargo, and crew.

master—used in reference as "the master," meaning the captain.

Mark Twain—a name taken by Mississippi River chronicler Samuel Clemens. It refers to a sounding or water measurement of two fathoms or 12 feet (see "fathoms").

moor—to hold a ship in place with cables at a pier or with an anchor. You do not "park" a boat, you moor it.

muster—a requested assembly of the passengers and/or crew. The phrase "to pass muster" stems from reviews of the troops or crew.

nautical mile—a nautical measurement of a mile, slightly longer than a land or statute mile (6,080.2 feet as compared to a land mile of 5,280 feet).

nautical timekeeping—at sea, as in the military, time is kept on a 24-hour basis beginning at 0001, which is 12:01 a.m., and moving along past 2 p.m. or 1400 hours, ending finally at midnight, 2400 hours.

navigable waters—water that is deep enough for the ship to pass through undamaged.

Old Man—slang meaning the captain. Like "skipper" it is less commonly heard on a cruise ship.

passageway—a hallway of the ship, usually a major thoroughfare through the vessel.

pilot—a specially trained and licensed captain who temporarily takes command of the ship to maneuver it into or out of a harbor or in difficult waters. As you are sailing out of port, when the ship is safely under way, you may see the pilot climb down a Jacob's ladder and jump into a small craft called a pilot boat.

pitch—the forward-backward rise and fall of a ship in rough water, and the opposite of "roll," which refers to the sideward rolling motion of the ship. Roll is said to be more conducive to seasickness than pitch, a detail for which you will have little concern if you are suffering from either pitch or roll or both.

port—the left side of the ship as you face forward, that is, face the bow of the ship. You can remember which is port and which is starboard by remembering that both the word "port" and the word "left" have four letters.

quarters—crew living space.

quay—another word for dock or wharf. It's pronounced "key" and is an excellent word to use in the ship's Scrabble contest.

rail—railings running alongside the open decks of the ship to keep you from falling overboard and to provide you with something on which to lean as you gaze out to sea or into each other's eyes.

registry, country of registry—the country in which the ship's certificate of ownership is registered. The national flag of the ship's country of registry will fly from the stern of the vessel.

roll—a side-to-side motion of the ship in rough water, and the opposite of its forward-backward motion, called pitch.

running lights—colored lights required on all vessels, including small boats, at night so other ships can spot the craft and determine its size and course. Red lights appear on the port side of a vessel, green ones on the starboard side.

safety at sea laws—laws governing standards that must be met by ships embarking passengers in U.S. ports (see the Introduction).

screw—calm down, this is just another name for the ship's propeller.

scuppers—draining holes below the rails.

scuttle—a small opening or hatchway in the deck or side of the ship or valve in the bottom of a ship. Sailing ships were once scuttled by opening these valves, called sea cocks, or by putting holes in the bottom. Scuttle butt, referring to gossip, arose from scuttled butt, a cask of water around which people gathered and, of course, gossiped.

she—ships are called she, despite what feminists may think of the appellation. No one knows the derivation of this female reference, but theories relating to capriciousness, expense, and need for delicate handling are among the explanations you will hear. Our favorite is: ships are called "she" because her rigging is worth more than her hull. In more serious circles, it is believed to have stemmed from the grammatical gender of early French translations.

ship to shore—radio communication with land now frequently accomplished by using satellite telephone communications.

sister ships—ships built on the same design, or sometimes two ships owned and operated by the same line.

skipper—a slang word denoting the captain of the ship, although on cruise ships the captain is more often known as the master, or simply the captain.

sounding—measurements taken of water depth (see "fathoms").

stabilizers—retractable side pieces that extend into the water from the sides of the ship enabling it to sail more evenly in rough water.

starboard—the right side of the ship as you face the bow or forward end of the ship; the opposite of port.

stateroom—a bedroom or cabin, although sometimes used to mean accommodations grander than a cabin.

stern—the rear of the ship, the aft end.

stowaway—an unpaid passenger illegally on board.

swell—not as pleasant as it sounds. A swell is a big wave that rolls without breaking.

tender—nothing to do with romance, a tender is a launch used to ferry you ashore in ports at which the ship must anchor offshore. Usually quite a large boat, the tender has also spawned a verb form: to tender into or out of port.

under way—the ship that has "weighed anchor" and set sail is "under way" or "making way."

wake—the track left by a vessel as it cuts through the water. Look for it at the stern of the boat, the white path behind the ship.

waterline—a line painted on the hull, or side, of the ship to indicate the level to which the water rises on the ship at various loads.

weigh anchor—to pull the anchor from the bottom and prepare to sail; also a command prior to sailing.

wharfinger—we know you're going to think we're making this up but we're not. Perhaps, however, somebody is putting us on. Either way, the term, which refers to the man in charge at a wharf, is alleged to have derived from early sailing days when the man in charge went out on the wharf and pointed his finger at the place an incoming vessel should dock, hence wharfinger. Listen, do *you* know it's not true?

windward—on the side exposed to the wind, or in reference to the direction from which the wind is blowing. Waters are rougher on the windward side of land than they are on the leeward side.

the writer—no, it's not us, it's the purser's secretary.

yardarm—on old sailing vessels the yardarm was the tapering horizontal arm of a mast and was used to judge time passage by shadow and also to hang offenders as "Hang 'im from the yardarm, matey." When the sun is over the yardarm became a term for the time of the setting sun or . . . cocktail hour.

yaw—to steer wildly out of course in rough water, as in the ship "yawed."

2. SHIP DESIGNATIONS

Just as people have Mr., Mrs., Ms., Master, or Mlle before their names, ships have titles too. Ships' titles, however, are determined by the way the vessel is powered. Here is a list of ship prefaces:

H.M.S.	Her (or His) Majesty's Ship (British)
M.S.	Motor Ship
M.T.S.	Motor Turbine Ship
M.V.	Motor Vessel
T.S.S.	Turbine Steamship
S.S.	Steamship
U.S.S.	United States Ship

3. COUNTING STRIPES: CALLING A CAPTAIN A CAPTAIN

You will see some handsome, snappy-looking officers striding about the ship, so perhaps now is the time to discover who is who.

That gentleman with the most gold stripes or bars on his shoulder epaulet is the captain. Depending on the line, the captain may have one wide bar and three smaller ones or just four bars, plus a loop or diamond shape. He's in charge of everything, absolutely *everything*, but sorry, he cannot marry you anymore. He can, of course, be married *to* you—good luck!

Staff captains are the second in command and have four stripes on their epaulets. A chief officer has three bars, and a first officer, two bars.

Engineers in charge of the ship's engine room rank from chief with four stripes down through chief engineer junior with 3½ stripes, first engineer with three stripes, and second engineer with two. On many lines the engineers' epaulets also will have a propellor or something that looks like one.

A chief purser, as the word suggests, is in charge of the ship's purse, a kind of office manager overseeing money, information, safety deposit boxes, a good person to know. His or her insignia will be three bars, followed by 2½ for the first purser, two stripes for the second purser, and one stripe for junior purser. A leaflike mark or a star shape may also appear on the epaulet of purser staff.

The chief radio officer will have three stripes, the first radio officer two. Each of those officers may have something suggesting radio waves on their epaulets.

The hotel manager for the ship is in charge of all the cabin services, and the food and beverage service as well. Hotel managers have four stripes. Working with them are food and beverage managers.

The chief of all the entertainment staff is the person known as the cruise director, responsible for all passenger entertainment on board and in ports of call. Cruise directors are the people you'll get to know best on the ship because you'll see the entertainment staff every day.

Electricians have three stripes for chief, 2½ for first, and two for second electrician, plus some electrical-looking wavy lines on their shoulder boards.

Your ship's doctor will have three or four stripes on the epaulet too.

Somewhere on board you will find a guide to officer identification. Ask the purser's staff where it is.

CHAPTER XIV

IS IT POSSIBLE A WEEK IS ONLY SEVEN DAYS?: HOME AGAIN

□ □ □

1. PACKING UP
2. CUSTOMS
3. GETTING YOUR LUGGAGE AND GETTING OFF

No matter how long or how short the cruise, there comes that poignant moment when you realize that when you wake in the morning it will be all over. Just as that first booming blast of the ship's great whistle thrilled you right to your toes, the final Farewell Banquet, sumptuous and fun though it was, was a sobering event.

Sure you're glad to be back home, but, oh, wasn't it wonderful when we went up on deck in the moonlight and watched the ship steaming through the water, its wake a gleaming diamond-tipped spray of foamy whiteness streaming out behind us? And remember the day we all hired that funny little taxi driver who kept calling you "boss" and saluting? And did you get Natalie and Dorothy's address? Wouldn't it be fun if we could stop to see them the next time we're near there?

Memories, already in the making even before the ship has pulled into port. Memories made in perhaps only a few days but made to last a lifetime.

Yes, a cruise *is* a wondrous experience, full of the wonder of nature and the wonder of man's ability to adapt to it and alter it—day after day of new foods, new friends, new experiences, new ideas.

There is something about the sea that is humbling, that can change you forever. Its vast, unending horizons put you in your place with crushing rapidity. Its ever-changing moods, frivolous as a coquette, are just as fascinating. You will return changed, unnoticeably perhaps, but irrevocably.

Return, however, you must.

Let us deal with that bittersweet moment when you return once again to familiar places.

1. PACKING UP

On your last night at sea, be it after 3 days or 30, you will dress casually for dinner on the premise that you have already packed your finest.

It would be a good idea at least to begin that packing on the final afternoon or evening aboard. In the wee hours of the morning your steward will pick up your luggage, which you'll leave outside your cabin door. He will send it off to join everyone else's baggage at a central collection point and crewmen will lug it off the ship when it docks.

Anything you haven't put outside your door for collection by the steward you'll have to carry off yourself. It is unlikely, if not downright out of the question, that you'll find anyone to help you. When the ship docks, cabin stewards are busy cleaning cabins for the next cruise so they can have some time off in port. Most other crewmen are working somewhere around the ship or are already off it, headed for a little well-earned relaxation.

When, ever the efficient soul, you put your suitcase outside the door for removal by the steward, remember to leave *out* the clothes you'll need to get off the ship in the morning! Silly as that may sound, tales are rife of organized, but not very bright, travelers racing about the ship in a towel, crying over packed—and now gone to the docks—luggage. You'll hear a couple of the more amusing stories from your cruise director at the debarkation talk. So keep out your toiletries kit and some clothes when you're packing up the night before arrival back in port.

If you discover, as you no doubt will, that you bought reams of stuff that won't fit in the suitcase, ask your cabin steward for help. These fellows can often roust out a carton and some string somewhere and you'll be in business.

Before you leave your cabin for the last time, look around carefully, under the beds and in the drawers. Items you have left behind will be kept for a month or so in the company's offices, but it's just another hassle to go pick them up or arrange for delivery. If you do find you've left something behind, however, write to the line.

In your cabin you'll find baggage tags and the necessary Customs declaration forms. If you don't find them, ask the cabin steward to bring you what you need.

Fill out the luggage tags and attach them to your baggage. Many ships color-code your baggage, matching the colorful tags to colored stripes on the ground or colored signs. When you get off the ship you just locate your color area and look for your baggage in that section. Some use alphabetical designations.

If you've taken a hanging garment bag on board and don't find it piled up with the other luggage, don't panic. Crewmen often unsnap hanging bags and hang them from the bar of a trolley to help minimize wrinkling. Look around and see if there's one of those trolley-with-bar things set up somewhere in the luggage-collection area.

If you have looked very carefully absolutely everywhere (including places it shouldn't be, like other color codes or letters) and still can't find your belongings, go back on board and explain the problem to the purser or to any visible crewman. Your belongings will turn up eventually and, in fact, will rarely be misplaced.

2. CUSTOMS

We've had a little fun with headlines in this book but we're being very serious at this point. Customs is not snicker material. In fact the very words "Customs officials" strike fear and dread in the hearts of the intrepid.

It need not be so, unless, of course, you're bringing back something you know the ladies and gentlemen of U.S. Customs Service will find disappointing at best, criminal at worst.

When you figure that many of these Customs officials have been rummaging through dirty laundry and poking into purses for years, it seems reasonable to assume that they know we all have a little larceny in our hearts. They really don't care much, we wouldn't think, about the $1.50 you spent over your quota, but they certainly do care if you're cheating the government out of hundreds of dollars of duty or bringing in some substances they'd much rather not see.

There is every indication, too, that by now they have a pretty good idea how to spot someone who's contemplating illegalities.

For most travelers, Customs clearance at the end of a cruise is marvelously simple, much easier than similar clearance at airports. It wouldn't hurt, however, to put your purchases on the top of your luggage or pack them separately. That way, if you are questioned by officials, you can point out what you bought without tearing up hours of packing. Keep your receipts too, if you feel there might be any question about the cost of your purchases.

In most cases you'll pick up your luggage, hand your declaration card to a Customs officer who will simply stack it with some others, and you'll go blithely off to your transportation. Sometimes there is a closer inspection of luggage, and a consequent delay, especially if you've visited a country known for the care and feeding of marijuana or cocaine fields (like Jamaica or Colombia) or a country famous for its precious gemstones (Colombia or Brazil).

Customs declarations must be filled out by every passenger, although couples can fill out one for both of them, and include any accompanying children in it too.

You can now make an oral declaration if you have not purchased more than $400 worth of items per person ($800 if you've visited the U.S. Virgin Islands), so there's no need to fill in the back of the form, which suggests you should write down every straw basket or piñata you purchased.

Customs officers are most interested in expensive items like cameras, liquor, gemstones, expensive china or silver, and really don't care much about your simpler purchases unless they're concealing illegal substances or there are enough of those purchases for you to go into the import-export business.

On the matter of illegal substances: *don't*.

If you have purchased more than the $400 or $800 limit per person, you are required to declare in writing the amount of your purchases above the allotted maximum. Remember that *each* traveler gets that allotment, not just one of you, so you will declare only the amount that exceeds the *total* exemption.

Here are the basic exemptions on which you pay no duty: $400 worth of purchases per adult or child; a fifth of liquor per person over 21; any item made in the U.S. no matter where it is purchased; 100 cigars (but no Cuban ones); one carton of cigarettes per adult. If you are on a ship that has stopped in the U.S. Virgin Islands, your exemptions double to $800 per person, plus a gallon of liquor, five cartons of cigarettes, and 100 cigars for each person over 21, plus one extra bottle each of locally made rum.

Each day you are away, you can also send home duty free, as gifts, items valued at up to $50 ($100 in the U.S. Virgin Islands). A gift of that value can be sent by each person each day, but be sure to mark the package "unsolicited gift" and indicate the contents and value of the item on the outside of the package. Shops in the islands will know how to handle these gifts. Just remember to tell the kids they are absolutely *not* to open any packages until Christmas.

If you buy more than these allotted amounts, you pay 10% duty (5% from the U.S. Virgin Islands) on the excess above your exemption up to $1,000, a higher percentage after that. Many people buy more than the allotted quota of liquor, finding it cheaper to buy in the islands even with the additional duties.

Other things you can bring in duty free are: original works of art, antiques at least 100 years old, any items made in U.S. territories like the U.S. Virgin Islands, American Samoa, or Guam.

In 1976 the United States put into effect a program called the Generalized System of Preferences (GSP) to help developing countries improve their lot through exports. Under that system you may bring back duty-free products from more than 100 third-world nations. These products range from loose semiprecious stones to shell products, toys, binoculars, cameras, earthen tableware or stoneware, china figurines, wood or plastic furniture, furs, ivory, unset jade, music boxes, musical instruments, cultured or imitation pearls loose or temporarily strung without clasp, perfume, silver, electric shavers, ski equipment, unset stones except emeralds and diamonds, wood products.

If you're thinking about buying any of these in quantity, it would be wise to contact the U.S. Customs Service, 1301 Constitution Ave. NW, Washington, DC 20229 (tel. 202/566-8195). Ask for their booklets entitled "GSP & the Traveler" and "Customs Hints—Know Before You Go."

If you're thinking of buying ivory, skins, furs, or animal-related products, contact the U.S. Fish and Wildlife Service, Department of the Interior, C Street between 18th and 19th Streets NW, Washington, DC 20240 (tel. 202/343-1100).

If you're planning to stock up on Christmas presents and expensive purchases, it would be a good idea to do some comparison shopping at home before you leave on your cruise so you will know when a bargain really is a bargain.

If you are bringing any fruit, vegetables, plants, seeds, flowers, meats, or pets into the country, they must meet U.S. Department of Agriculture requirements for entry. You should contact the Department of Agriculture to find out what it takes to meet the requirements with any plants you are planning to bring back. Rules vary widely. If you can bear to pass up that stuff, *do*. You'll save yourself a lot of red tape.

Generally, Customs inspectors will just confiscate fruit and vegetable products, so don't bother bringing the remnants of your ship fruit basket off the ship. Those apples or oranges will cost you a lot more trouble and Customs inspections than they're worth.

Certain materials like Haitian goatskins, products made from the fur of endangered species, and ivory and tortoise-shell items have been banned at various times. Cruise directors may know what's legal to bring home these days, but one of the U.S. Customs Service booklets is the only really reliable guide.

Canadian Customs have been known to be particularly hard on Canadians returning home from abroad. At last count, Canadians were permitted to bring home only $150 in goods purchased abroad, plus one liter of liquor for each person and one carton of cigarettes for each person over 16. For any amount over those quotas you are required to pay duty and taxes. If you are Canadian and planning to buy quite a lot of items on a trip, you should check details of duties and taxes with Customs officers to determine just what the duties, which can be as high as 25%, will be.

3. GETTING YOUR LUGGAGE AND GETTING OFF

You would do well to attend the cruise director's little talk on the day or evening before the cruise ends. You will be briefed then on all the details of Customs clearance and baggage pickup, and given some good tips on car rental, bus transportation, and transfers to airplanes.

Once again, get off the ship with only luggage you can easily carry yourself. You may have to walk some long corridors to get to the gangway, and from there it may be a bit of a distance to the luggage pickup area. There's no need to carry your baggage with you, so don't.

After the ship has docked and Customs inspectors have cleared the vessel, you will be permitted to debark. There will be announcements over the ship's public address system to guide you in your debarkation. You'll be asked to await the "all ashore" announcement in one of the ship's public rooms, and not to crowd the corridors. You would be wise to follow that advice. If you don't, you'll find yourself sitting on the floor with people stepping over you, or standing up for perhaps an hour or more.

Figure that Customs clearance of a vessel will take at least an hour and more often two hours, and it might take you 15 minutes or so to pick up your luggage and go through Customs. Don't tell friends or relatives who are coming to pick you up to be at the ship the moment it docks. They'll just have to stand around and wait.

After you've turned in your Customs declaration card to the officer at the gate, you can hail a cab, find a bus or limousine service or your car, and head home. Some terminals have rental cars available right there. At others you'll need to call a rental-car company to pick you up or get to the company's office yourself. That information, too, will have been given to you by the cruise director at his debarkation talk.

Air/sea passenger arrangements and airport transfers also will be announced by the cruise director, so don't miss that talk.

CHAPTER XV

TAKING A SLOW BOAT: FREIGHTER TRAVEL

□ □ □

The very first thing you pack for a freighter trip is patience. You'll need it on these meandering trips that may not leave when they say they're going to leave, or go where they say they're going to go, or stop where they say they're going to stop, or get anywhere when they say they're going to get there.

That's no critical remark, just the facts. These are, after all, cargo ships first and passenger carriers second. When the captain has a chance to pick up some cargo, it gets picked up whether or not that means an extra two days in port or a stop at some unscheduled dock.

That devil-may-care capriciousness is just what appeals to many a starry-eyed freighter bum intent on steaming across the ocean for 25 or 50 or even 75 days. To go on one of these journeys you must have unlimited vacation time and be in no hurry to meet any schedules. That, of course, is the beauty of it all.

You get on the ship and never know just where you might end up next, although there will certainly be at least a rough itinerary.

If you have always wondered, sometimes longingly, what it must be like to sail a tramp steamer to veiled Casablanca or rough-and-ready Marseille or intrigue-fancying Venice, a freighter may be your kind of paradise.

Sadly, the era of the true tramp steamer is gone. True tramps just kind of hung around the oceans until they found cargo to transfer to another port. These days that kind of hanging around is too expensive, so the tramps are an endangered species.

Nor will you find tramp-steamer conditions in this day and age. Most of these ships are small in passenger-carrying terms, but most offer excellent, if not downright luxurious quarters, both in public areas and in cabins.

Sadly, we haven't had the time to sail a freighter yet, but the dream of doing so lingers. We have read numerous reports and talked to several people who have sailed the freighters of the world to come up with some general information for you on what to expect and where to find out more about this kind of cruise travel.

We've read accounts, for instance, of freighter cabins that were, as one writer put it, "embarrassingly spacious—by no means can I tell friends that I roughed it across the Atlantic." Included in that cabin were two wood-framed beds, a six-foot couch, two lounge chairs, a coffee table, a large bureau, spacious closets, a sink and medicine cabinet, and an ocean view!

Cabin and dining room service is good and may even border on elegant, although the food is likely to be simple basic fare, nutritious and appealing but not nouvelle cuisine.

People say getting to know the officers and crew well is one of the most enjoyable parts of a freighter journey. Quite believable: just hearing about their unusual careers should fill many days of conversations.

You won't find dancing girls and deck tennis, crafts classes or hula competitions aboard a freighter either, unless one of the other passengers becomes a teacher! On these vessels you are left pretty much to your own devices so you end up in marathon bridge or Scrabble games, trivia competitions, reading books, or just lying in the sun watching the ocean roll by.

Top names in freighter travel and information on how to reach them include:

Polish Ocean Lines (from New York, Wilmington, and Baltimore to France and Holland), Gdynia America Line, 39 Broadway, New York, NY 10006 (tel. 212/952-1280).

Lykes Brothers (from Galveston, Houston, and New Orleans to Africa and the Mediterranean), 300 Poydras St., New Orleans, LA 70130 (tel. 504/523-6611).

American President Lines (from West Coast ports to the Orient/Pacific or Southeast Asia), 1950 Franklin St., Oakland, CA 94612 (tel. 415/271-8148).

Ivaran Lines (from Houston to South America), One Exchange Plaza, New York, NY 10305 (tel. 212/809-1220).

A number of freighter lines are booked by one company, **Freighter World Cruises**, 180 S. Lake Ave., Suite 335, Pasadena, CA 91101 (tel. 818/449-3106). We recently met George Henck, board chairman of that company, who spoke at a national travel agents meeting on the subject of freighters to a rapt audience.

Henck's photographs and descriptions of the many ships booked by his company confirmed our impression that this is indeed a pleasant way to travel if you have lots of time.

Often, accommodations aboard freighters are two-room suites—some even have two bathrooms!—most luxuriously togged out.

As Henck frankly pointed out, however, service is much more limited aboard these vessels. A steward will keep your quarters cleaned but you can forget dinner in your cabin and room service.

Henck is quite an authority on freighter travel, which by the way is a favorite getaway for some celebrities (including Alex Haley, author of *Roots*). He and his employees can give you very detailed information on these sailing ships and will send you a packet of information that, at the very least, will provide a Wish Book for your coffee table.

Among the lines booked by Freighter World Cruises are **Adriatic/Australia/New Zealand Line, Cast Line, CMB, Columbus Line, Chilean Line, Egon Oldendorff Line, Mineral Shipping, and Yugoslav Great Lakes Lines.**

Freighter travel, Henck said, costs about $100 a day per person, a very reasonable per diem rate as you have already discovered from our discussions and descriptions in Chapter V. Some freighters charge a bit less than that too.

For a most complete description of the lines he handles and other lines' offerings as well, we'd recommend a chat with Mr. Henck, who also happens to be quite a nice man with a droll sense of humor.

We recently got a look at the newest of Ivaran Lines' cargo ships and were quite overwhelmed at the luxury of this craft. A brand-new ship, the line's *Americana* can rival any passenger ship afloat in snappily elegant décor.

Chrome glitters everywhere aboard this ship, which also sports soft gray leather couches, tall windows seemingly everywhere, light-wood trims, a very handsome dark-green bar with a flashy piano front and center, and an airy and elegantly appointed dining room with plenty of windows. In chrome-trimmed hallways are some handsome sketches you'll find quite bawdily amusing if you move in for a close look.

To top off all this chic contemporary style, cabins are quite large. Double cabins feature a sitting area separate from the sleeping area, single cabins are plenty big enough for a single traveler, and for high-rollers there's an owner's suite that will knock your socks off, whether or not you're wearing any.

We couldn't find a single creature comfort missing here: there's a beauty/barbershop, a gym full of shiny new equipment, a sundeck with swimming pool and two Jacuzzis, sauna, and massage room. And all that's on a freighter!

This new ship carries just 108 passengers, making it small for a cruise ship but large for a passenger-carrying cargo ship, which usually has not more than a dozen passengers on board.

In 1988 Ivaran's *Americana* began sailing on 46- and 48-day round trips from New York to Buenos Aires and back. As with any long itinerary, shorter segments of the trip can be booked.

Here's the itinerary: New York – Baltimore – Norfolk – Charleston (or Savannah) – Jacksonville – Miami – Rio de Janeiro – Santos – Buenos Aires – Montevideo – Rio Grande do Sul – Paranagua (or Itajai) – Santos – Rio de Janeiro – Ilheus (or Salvador) – Fortaleza – New York. You spend 26 of the cruise's 48 days at sea, so take plenty of diversionary material.

As you can see, you can board the ship in several U.S. ports on the way south, but the ship does not stop at any U.S. port on its return voyage to New York.

Fares for this 48-day dream cruise, which naturally attracts travelers with both time and money (translate: usually older passengers), range from $7,200 to $8,400 for singles to $9,000 to $10,500 for double cabins and $16,800 for a suite. In 1988 the line offered a 25% reduction on those fares for passengers booking a round-trip cruise from New York or Miami to Buenos Aires, returning to New York.

Ivaran operates two other passenger-carrying cargo vessels, the *Santa Fe* and the *Salvador*, both of which have accommodations for only 12 passengers.

Most passenger-carrying freighter operations carry no more than 12 passengers. If they take more passengers than that, the line must provide a doctor, more staff members, and additional lifesaving gear, so they solve the problem in the simplest of ways: they limit the passengers to 12.

That means, of course, that you'll probably need to book a freighter trip early to be sure you're included on this small list.

To find out what ship is going where, you can become a member of a freighter travel club or subscribe to one of several publications that outline freighter schedules. Among the freighter travel clubs in operation are **Freighter Travel Club of America**, P.O. Box 12693, Salem, OR 97309, or **Trav-L-Tips Freighter Travel Association**, 163-09 Depot Rd., Flushing, NY 11358 (tel. 718/939-2400).

Freighter Travel Club provides you with a monthly newsletter, *Freighter Travel News*, which contains accounts of freighter experiences, a few ads, and news about freighter travel.

Trav-L-Tips publishes a bimonthly 32-page illustrated account of freighter and budget travel written by members who have been on freighter trips, and a supplementary *Budget Travel News* publication plus booking services. Price of membership is $30 a year, with occasional discount offers of $15 annual membership.

You can also write for a copy of a publication published twice a year that lists scheduled freighter trips. It's called *Ford's Freighter Travel Guide*, and you can get one by writing to the guide at P.O. Box 505, Woodland Hills, CA 91365 (tel. 818/347-1677) or ordering it at a bookstore.

Official Airlines Guides also publishes a *World Wide Cruise and Shipline Guide*, issued six times a year at a cost of $81. You can reach the company at 2000

Clearwater Dr., Oak Brook, IL 60521 (tel. toll free 800/323-3537, 800/942-1888 in Illinois).

Dress on freighters is much more casual than on scheduled cruise vessels. You will need sport and informal clothes with perhaps a few more elaborate outfits for port evenings.

Take lots of books, puzzles, crocheting, or whatever kind of amusements you prefer, for there will be few aboard. You may also have to bring your own liquor aboard some ships that do not provide it.

Bone up on ports before you go because there won't be any cruise director to help you find out where to go and what to see.

Don't wonder if you'll be invited to dine with the captain: you'll see him every night at dinner because you'll be eating with all the crew, usually early—about 8 a.m. for breakfast, noon for lunch, and 5 or 6 p.m. for dinner.

You'll have plenty of chances to learn foreign languages, so take advantage of your time with the crew to get them to teach you whatever language or, more likely, languages they speak.

Throw away your watch and calendar the first day aboard.

Tip about 5% of your cruise price distributed equally to your stateroom and dining room steward or stewardess on the last day of your trip, weekly on long trips.

Make sure all extra charges are clearly understood when you buy your ticket. There is usually no extra charge if a ship spends extra days in port or at sea.

Ask before you buy your ticket for a list of definite stopover ports and tentative dockings. Container ships spend less time in ports, so if you want to travel on land a bit, noncontainerized ships are a better idea.

Make sure you've gotten the definitive word on departure time from an officer of the ship *before* you go on a shore exploration trip. Then be back on time.

Pack a washable wardrobe that can be dunked in a sink and washed by hand. Some ships have washing machines, but don't count on it.

On Ivaran freighter cruises you can expect to pay costs per day that range from $150 to a high of about $187. That's less than most scheduled cruises, but as we've pointed out, there are plenty of differences.

The main one, once again, is the amount of time you can expect to travel: from a minimum of about 14 days to perhaps 90 or more. A trip from Milwaukee to Israel, for instance, lasts 60 days. Another trip departing from New Orleans takes you to Holland in 14 days, and one around-the-world cruise from Los Angeles spent 132 days at sea.

Don't tell *us* you aren't tempted.

CHAPTER XVI

WHAT'S GOING WHERE: SHIP SCHEDULES

□ □ □

1. Alaska
2. The Bahamas
3. Bermuda
4. Cruises to Nowhere
5. Caribbean
6. Hawaii / Tahiti / The Orient / Southeast Asia / South Pacific
7. Mexico
8. Mediterranean Sea and Europe
9. Mississippi River
10. Northeastern U.S. / Canada / Chesapeake Bay / Inland Waterways
11. Panama Canal
12. South America
13. Transatlantic and World Cruises
14. Caribbean Island-by-Island Port Calls

First, let it be remembered that we are talking about floating ships here, not stationary hotels. These capricious floating resorts *move,* so all it takes for a cruise line to change its image, its market, and its appeal is to pull up anchor and move its ship or ships to another cruising ground.

As competition gets meaner and meaner in this growing part of the travel industry, you'll see ships changing their schedules and their ports of call more frequently. That's already happening.

We mention all this so you don't get angry at us when you find a ship you want to sail and then discover that sailing plans have changed. We're working with the most up-to-date information available straight from the cruise lines themselves—but no guarantees.

Many ships maintain a steady winter schedule traveling, for instance, from San Juan to the Caribbean, moving in summer to Alaska. To get from San Juan to Alaska the ship makes what is called a "positioning cruise." Various segments of that cruise, say, San Juan to Acapulco or Los Angeles, Los Angeles to Vancouver, or San Francisco to Vancouver, may be sold. The same holds true in reverse when the ship moves back to its winter schedule. We have referred to some of those cruises in this listing. Lines or a travel agent will be able to supply you with the dates and details of positioning cruises.

To be sure exactly what's happening to "your" ship, check with the line or with a travel agent.

Cruises are wonderful just *because* they move at an unhurried pace, but in these days of assault-by-information, it's sometimes nice to do and see things quickly. Figuring that lots of you will select a ship because it goes to ports you want to visit, we've compiled a list of the major cruising grounds and what ships visit them.

Itineraries for visits to such still-exotic places as Alaska can be expected to remain constant, for now. But in the Caribbean—whew! Here in the world's most popular cruising ground, cruise lines seem to be as busy as Columbus—they're "discovering" a new island every day!

What's more, those islands are such an intriguing melting-pot mix of sights and heritages—Dutch, French, Spanish, British, and sundry combinations of the above—that it seems all of us have a Caribbean dream spot we've been hoping to visit someday.

To help you figure out what ship is going to your dream vacation haven, we've included a roster of favorite Caribbean islands, listing the ships that visit them. You'll find a similar list under each of the island descriptions in Chapter I.

Now don't get discouraged. It's really quite easy. Anyway, life could be worse: *you* could be the one compiling these lists!

1. ALASKA

Cunard Princess—Cunard Line. 7 days.
Daphne—Costa Cruises. 7 days.
Explorer Starship—Exploration Cruise Lines. 7 days.
Fair Majesty—Sitmar Cruises. 7 and 14 days.
Fairsea—Sitmar Cruises. 7 days.
Glacier Bay Explorer—Exploration Cruise Lines. 7 days.
Great Rivers Explorer—Exploration Cruise Lines. 7 days.
Island Princess—P&O/Princess Cruises. 7 days.
Nieuw Amsterdam—Holland America Line / Westours. 7 days.
Noordam—Holland America Line / Westours. 7 days.
North Star—Exploration Cruise Lines. 7 days.
Pacific Northwest Explorer—Exploration Cruise Lines. 7 days.
Regent Star—Regency Cruises. 7 days.
Rotterdam—Holland America Line / Westours. 7 days.
Royal Princess—P&O/Princess Cruises. 10 days.
Royal Viking Sea—Royal Viking Line. 11 days.
Sagafjord—Cunard Line. 10 and 11 days.
Sea Princess—P&O/Princess Cruises. 7 days.
Stardancer—Admiral Cruise Line. 7 days.
Sun Princess—P&O/Princess Cruises. 7 days.
Universe—World Explorer Cruises. 14 days.

2. THE BAHAMAS
Britanis—Chandris Fantasy Cruises. 2 to 5 days.
Carnivale—Carnival Cruise Lines. 3 and 4 days.
Discovery I—Discovery Cruises. 1 day.
Dolphin—Dolphin Cruises. 3 and 4 days.
Emerald Seas—Admiral Cruise Line. 3 and 4 days.
Fairsky—Sitmar Cruises. 10 days.
Galileo—Chandris Fantasy Cruises. 2 and 5 days.
Jubilee—Carnival Cruise Lines. 7 days.
Mardi Gras—Carnival Cruise Lines. 3 and 4 days.
Noordam—Holland America Line / Westours. 7 days.
Rotterdam—Holland America Line / Westours. 7 days.
Scandinavian Star—SeaEscape. 1 day.
Scandinavian Sun—SeaEscape. 1 day.
Starship Oceanic—Premier Cruise Lines. 3 and 4 days.
Starship Royale—Premier Cruise Lines. 3 and 4 days.
Sunward II—Norwegian Cruise Line. 3 and 4 days.
Viking Princess—Crown Cruise Line. 1 day.
Westerdam—Holland America Line / Westours. 7 days.

3. BERMUDA
Amerikanis—Chandris Fantasy Cruises. 7 days.
Atlantic—Holland America Line / Westours. Projected; itinerary not announced.
Bermuda Queen—Bermuda Star Line. 7 days.
Nordic Prince—Royal Caribbean Cruise Line. 7 days.

4. CRUISES TO NOWHERE
Discovery I—Discovery Cruises. 1 day.
Scandinavian Saga—SeaEscape. 1 day.
Scandinavian Sky—SeaEscape. 1 day.
Viking Princess—Crown Cruise Line. 1 day.

5. CARIBBEAN
Amerikanis—Chandris Fantasy Cruises. 7 days.
Atlantic—Holland America Line / Westours. Projected; itinerary not announced.
The Azur—Chandris Fantasy Cruises. 7 days.
Britanis—Chandris Fantasy Cruises. 7 days.
Caribe I—Commodore Cruise Line. 7 days.
CarlaCosta—Costa Cruises. 7 days.
Celebration—Carnival Cruise Lines. 7 days.
Colonial Explorer—Exploration Cruise Line. 7 days.
CostaRiviera—Costa Cruises. 7 days.
Caribbean Prince—American Canadian Caribbean Line. 12 days.
Crown Odyssey—Royal Cruise Line. 14 and 18 days.
Cunard Countess—Cunard Line. 7 days.
Cunard Princess—Cunard Line. 7 to 17 days.
Daphne—Costa Cruises. 7 days.
Explorer Starship—Exploration Cruise Lines. 7 days.
Fair Majesty—Sitmar Cruises. 10 days.
Fairsky—Sitmar Cruises. 10 days.
Festivale—Carnival Cruise Lines. 7 days.
Future Seas—Admiral Cruise Line. Projected; 10 days.

Island Princess—P&O/Princess Cruises. 7 days.
Nantucket Clipper—Clipper Cruise Line. 7 days.
Newport Clipper—Clipper Cruise Line. 7 days.
New Shoreham—American Canadian Caribbean Line. 12 days.
Noordam—Holland America Line / Westours. 7 days.
Nordic Prince—Royal Caribbean Cruise Line. 8 and 10 days.
Norway—Norwegian Cruise Line. 7 days.
Ocean Islander—Ocean Cruise Lines. 7 days.
Ocean Princess—Ocean Cruise Lines. 10 days.
Pacific Princess—P&O/Princess Cruises. 7 days.
Regent Sea—Regency Cruises. 7 days.
Regent Sun—Regency Cruises. Projected; itinerary not announced.
Rotterdam—Holland America Line / Westours. 7 days.
Royal Viking Sky—Royal Viking Line. 12 and 15 days.
Royal Viking Sun—Royal Viking Line. 13 to 15 days.
Sagafjord—Cunard Line. 7 to 101 days.
Sea Goddess I—Cunard Line. 7 days.
Seaward—Norwegian Cruise Line. 7 days.
Skyward—Norwegian Cruise Line. 7 days.
Song of America—Royal Caribbean Cruise Line. 7 days.
Song of Norway—Royal Caribbean Cruise Line. 7 days.
Sovereign of the Seas—Royal Caribbean Cruise Line. 7 days.
Starward—Norwegian Cruise Line. 7 days.
Stella Oceanis—Sun Line Cruises. 7 and 14 days.
Stella Solaris—Sun Line Cruises. 15 days.
Sun Viking—Royal Caribbean Cruise Line. 7 days.
The Victoria—Chandris Fantasy Cruises. 7 days.
Vistafjord—Cunard Line. 7 to 20 days.
Westerdam—Holland America Line / Westours. 7 days.
Wind Spirit—Windstar Sail Cruises. 7 days.
Wind Star—Windstar Sail Cruises. 7 days.
World Renaissance—Epirotiki Lines. 14 days.
Yorktown Clipper—Clipper Cruise Line. 7 days.

6. HAWAII / TAHITI / THE ORIENT / SOUTHEAST ASIA / SOUTH PACIFIC

Constitution—American Hawaii Cruises. 7 days.
Crown Odyssey—Royal Cruise Line. 14 and 16 days.
Fairsea—Sitmar Cruises. 12 to 16 days.
Fairwind—Sitmar Cruises. 12 to 16 days.
Golden Odyssey—Royal Cruise Line. 7 to 12 days.
Independence—American Hawaii Cruises. 7 days.
Majestic Tahiti Explorer—Exploration Cruise Lines. 7 days.
Ocean Pearl—Ocean Cruise Lines. 11 to 15 days.
Royal Viking Sea—Royal Viking Line. 12 to 23 and 26 days.
Sagafjord—Cunard Line. 10 and 11 days.
Sea Goddess II—Cunard Line. 14 days.
Sea Princess—P&O/Princess Cruises. 14 days.
Wind Song—Windstar Sail Cruises. 7 days.

7. MEXICO

Caribbean Coast
Bermuda Queen—Bermuda Star Line. 7 days.

SHIP SCHEDULES □ **399**

Britanis—Chandris Fantasy Cruises. 7 days.
Crown Odyssey—Royal Cruise Line. 9 days.
Cunard Princess—Cunard Line. 7 to 17 days.
FairMajesty—Sitmar Cruises. 10 days.
Fairsea—Sitmar Cruises. 7 days.
Fairsky—Sitmar Cruises. 10 days.
Fairwind—Sitmar Cruises. 7 days.
Galileo—Chandris Fantasy Cruises. 5 days.
Holiday—Carnival Cruise Lines. 7 days.
Jubilee—Carnival Cruise Lines. 7 days.
New Shoreham—American Canadian Caribbean Line. 12 days.
Nieuw Amsterdam—Holland America Line / Westours. 7 days.
Regent Sea—Regency Cruises. 7 days.
Royal Princess—P&O/Princess Cruises. 10 to 14 days.
Royal Viking Sky—Royal Viking Line. 12 to 15 days.
Royal Viking Sun—Royal Viking Line. 12 to 18 days.
Sagafjord—Cunard Line. 14 to 17 days.
Scandinavian Saga—SeaEscape. 3 days.
Seaward—Norwegian Cruise Line. 7 days.
Skyward—Norwegian Cruise Line. 7 days.
Song of America—Royal Caribbean Cruise Line. 7 days.
Sun Viking—Royal Caribbean Cruise Line. 7 days.
Veracruz—Bermuda Star Line. 5 days.
Westerdam—Holland America Line / Westours. 7 days.

West Coast
Azure Seas—Admiral Cruise Line. 3 and 4 days.
Bermuda Star—Bermuda Star Line. 7 days.
Crown Odyssey—Royal Cruise Line. 9 days.
Cunard Princess—Cunard Line. 7 to 17 days.
Fairsea—Sitmar Cruises. 7 days.
Fairwind—Sitmar Cruises. 7 days.
New Shoreham—American Canadian Caribbean Line. 12 days.
North Star—Exploration Cruise Lines. 7 days.
Royal Princess—P&O/Princess Cruises. 10 to 14 days.
Royal Viking Sun—Royal Viking Line. 12 to 18 days.
Sagafjord—Cunard Line. 14 to 17 days.
Southward—Norwegian Cruise Line. 3 and 4 days.
Stardancer—Admiral Cruises. 7 days.
Stella Solaris—Sun Line Cruises. 14 days.
Sun Princess—P&O/Princess Cruises. 7 days.
Tropicale—Carnival Cruise Lines. 7 days.

8. MEDITERRANEAN SEA AND EUROPE
The Azur—Chandris Fantasy Cruises. 7 to 16 days.
Crown Odyssey—Royal Cruise Line. 13 days.
Ocean Islander—Ocean Cruise Lines. 7 days.
Ocean Princess—Ocean Cruise Lines. 7 to 12 days.
Pacific Princess—P&O/Princess Cruises. 12 to 14 days.
Pegasus—Epirotiki Lines. 3 and 4 days.
Romanza—Chandris Fantasy Cruises. 7 days.
Royal Viking Sky—Royal Viking Line. 9 to 22 days.
Royal Viking Sun—Royal Viking Line. 9 to 22 days.
Sea Goddess I—Cunard Line. 6 days.

400 □ DOLLARWISE GUIDE TO CRUISES
Sea Goddess II—Cunard Line. 7 to 11 days.
Stella Maris—Sun Line Cruises. 3 to 7 days.
Stella Oceanis—Sun Line Cruises. 3 and 4 days.
Stella Solaris—Sun Line Cruises. 7 and 14 days.
Vistafjord—Cunard Line. 8 to 15 days.
Wind Spirit—Windstar Sail Cruises. 7 to 10 days.

9. MISSISSIPPI RIVER
Delta Queen—Delta Queen Steamship Co. 2 to 12 days.
Mississippi Queen—Delta Queen Steamship Co. 2 to 12 days.
New Orleans—American Cruise Lines. 7 days.

10. NORTHEASTERN U.S. / CANADA / CHESAPEAKE BAY / INLAND WATERWAYS
Bermuda Star—Bermuda Star Line. 7 days.
Caribbean Prince—American Canadian Caribbean Line. 12 days.
Charleston—American Cruise Lines. 7 to 14 days.
Colonial Explorer—Exploration Cruise Line. 6 days.
Crown Odyssey—Royal Cruise LIne. 7 and 14 days.
Fairsky—Sitmar Cruises. 9 days.
Glacier Bay Explorer—Exploration Cruise Lines. 3 days.
Nantucket Clipper—Clipper Cruise Line. 7 to 14 days.
Newport Clipper—Clipper Cruise Line. 7 to 14 days.
New Orleans—American Cruise Lines. 10 to 14 days.
New Shoreham II—American Canadian Caribbean Line. 12 days.
Royal Viking Sun—Royal Viking Line. 7 days.
Sagafjord—Cunard Line. 10 days.
Savannah—American Cruise Lines. 7 to 14 days.
Yorktown Clipper—Clipper Cruise Line. 7 to 14 days.

11. PANAMA CANAL
Britanis—Chandris Fantasy Cruises. 7 days.
Crown Odyssey—Royal Cruise Line. 14 to 18 days.
Explorer Starship—Exploration Cruise Lines. 15 days.
Great Rivers Explorer—Exploration Cruise Lines. 5 days.
Regent Sea—Regency Cruises. 7 days.
Regent Star—Regency Cruises. 7 days.
Regent Sun—Regency Cruises. Projected; itinerary not announced.
Royal Viking Sky—Royal Viking Line. 13 to 18 days.
Royal Viking Sun—Royal Viking Line. 13 to 18 days.
Stella Solaris—Sun Line Cruises. 15 days.

12. SOUTH AMERICA
Atlantic—Holland America Line / Westours. Projected; itinerary not announced.
Britanis—Chandris Fantasy Cruises. 47 days.
CarlaCosta—Costa Cruises. 7 days.
Crown Odyssey—Royal Cruise Line. 14 to 18 days.
Cunard Countess—Cunard Line. 7 days.
Cunard Princess—Cunard Line. 7 to 11 days.
Fairsky—Sitmar Cruises. 10 and 14 days.
Fairwind—Sitmar Cruises. 14 days.
Ocean Islander—Ocean Cruise Lines. 7 days.

Ocean Princess—Ocean Cruise Lines. 10 to 14 days.
Queen Elizabeth 2—Cunard Line. 60 days.
Pegasus—Epirotiki Lines. 22 days.
Regent Sun—Regency Cruises. Projected; itinerary not announced.
Rotterdam—Holland America Line / Westours. 7 days.
Royal Viking Sky—Royal Viking Line. 12 and 15 days.
Royal Viking Sun—Royal Viking Line. 13 to 15 days.
Stella Solaris—Sun Line Cruises. 15 days.
The Victoria—Chandris Fantasy Cruises. 7 days.
World Renaissance—Epirotiki Lines. 14 days.

13. TRANSATLANTIC AND WORLD CRUISES

TRANSATLANTIC CRUISES: Only Cunard's famous *QE2* offers regularly scheduled transatlantic service, traversing the Atlantic from about May to November.

However, all lines sailing in North American waters in the winter and moving to the Mediterranean in the summer must, by geographic necessity, sail on a transatlantic cruise in spring and in fall to get the ship into position to begin its seasonal schedule. Transatlantic cruises vary in length from 8 to 30 days, depending on ports of embarkation and debarkation. Most stop in the Caribbean and Africa, then move on to Mediterranean ports or to England.

Among the lines that usually schedule a transatlantic crossing from March to May or from September to November are the following:

Cunard—*Vistafjord, Sea Goddess I, Sea Goddess II,* and *Sagafjord.*
Epirotiki Lines—*Jason, Jupiter,* and *World Renaissance.*
Ocean Cruise Lines—*Ocean Princess* and *Ocean Islander.*
P&O/Princess Cruises—*Pacific Princess.*
Royal Cruise Line—*Crown Odyssey* and *Golden Odyssey.*
Royal Viking Line—*Royal Viking Sea, Royal Viking Sky,* and *Royal Viking Sun.*
Sitmar—*Fairwind.*
Sun Line Cruises—*Stella Solaris* and *Stella Oceanis.*

WORLD CRUISES: World cruises, those ultimate-dream vacations toward which we all are working, have long been an endangered species for the simplest of reasons: there simply are not throngs of travelers around who can budget $20,000 for this year's vacation. Knowing that, cruise lines have split those fabulous around-the-world-in-80-days cruises into many smaller, more fiscally negotiable sojourns. Try one—you can always *say* you were on the *QE2's* world cruise. Who will know you got off after the first eight days?

World cruises usually begin in January after the cruise lines have milked the most they can out of Christmas/New Year's sailings. For that reason, several world cruises begin in or stop in Fort Lauderdale, following the sun west through the Panama Canal and on to South America, the Orient, the South Pacific, and Southeast Asia, winding up in early spring somewhere near the Suez Canal and the Mediterranean, heading back to the U.S. from there or spending the summer in Europe. Those stuff-fantasies-are-made-of cruises range in length from 80 to 100 days.

Just to get you dreaming, here's a sample itinerary followed one year by the *QE2.* This one was a perverse reverse on the usual westbound trip, circumnavigating the globe by first traveling west, then east:

Fort Lauderdale – Playa del Carmen – Cancún – Limón – Panama Canal – Balboa – Callao – Valparaiso – Puerto Montt – Straits of Magellan – Montevideo – São Paulo – Rio de Janeiro – Cape Town – Durban – Mombasa – Mahe Island – Karachi – Bombay – Colombo – Penang – Singapore – Bangkok – Hong Kong – Keelung – Pusan – Kagoshima – Yokohama – Honolulu – Maui – San Francisco – Los Angeles – Acapulco – Panama Canal – Cristobál – Cartagena – Kingston – Port au Prince – Fort Lauderdale.

Not every line that sends a ship on a world cruise does so every year, but here's a look at those lines that have scheduled a world cruise in years past or are likely to be pencilling one in for upcoming seasons:

Costa Cruises—*Danae.*
Cunard Line—*QE2, Vistafjord,* and *Sagafjord.*
Royal Viking Line—*Royal Viking Sky* and *Royal Viking Sea.*

14. CARIBBEAN ISLAND-BY-ISLAND PORT CALLS

Antigua/Barbuda
Amerikanis—Chandris Fantasy Cruises
Atlantic—Holland America Line / Westours
Caribbean Prince—American Canadian Caribbean Line
Crown Odyssey—Royal Cruise Line
Cunard Countess—Cunard Line
Daphne—Costa Cruises
FairMajesty—Sitmar Cruises
Fairsky—Sitmar Cruises
Nantucket Clipper—Clipper Cruise Line
New Shoreham—American Canadian Caribbean Line
Nordic Prince—Royal Caribbean Cruise Line
Pacific Princess—P&O/Princess Cruises
Sagafjord—Cunard Line
Sea Goddess I—Cunard Line
Song of Norway—Royal Caribbean Cruise Line
Stella Oceanis—Sun Lines
Starward—Norwegian Cruise Line
Vistafjord—Cunard Line

Aruba
Britanis—Chandris Fantasy Cruises
Crown Odyssey—Royal Cruise Line
Ocean Princess—Ocean Cruise Lines
Sagafjord—Cunard Line
Vistafjord—Cunard Line

Bahamas
Britanis—Chandris Fantasy Cruises
Carnivale—Carnival Cruise Lines
Dolphin—Dolphin Cruise Line
Emerald Seas—Admiral Cruise Line
FairMajesty—Sitmar Cruises
Fairsky—Sitmar Cruises

SHIP SCHEDULES: CARIBBEAN PORTS □ 403

Galileo—Chandris Fantasy Cruises
Jubilee—Carnival Cruise Lines
Mardi Gras—Carnival Cruise Lines
Noordam—Holland America Line / Westours
Rotterdam—Holland American Line / Westours
Sagafjord—Cunard Line
Scandinavian Star—SeaEscape
Scandinavian Sun—SeaEscape
Starship Oceanic—Premier Cruise Lines
Starship Royale—Premier Cruise Lines
Sunward II—Norwegian Cruise Line
Vistafjord—Cunard Line

Barbados
The Azur—Chandris Fantasy Cruises
Crown Odyssey—Royal Cruise Line
Cunard Countess—Cunard Line
Daphne—Costa Cruises
Explorer Starship—Exploration Cruise Lines
FairMajesty—Sitmar Cruises
Fairsky—Sitmar Cruises
Festivale—Carnival Cruise Lines
Nordic Prince—Royal Caribbean Cruise Line
Ocean Islander—Ocean Cruise Lines
Pacific Princess—P&O/Princess Cruises
Royal Viking Sky—Royal Viking Line
Royal Viking Sun—Royal Viking Line
Sagafjord—Cunard Line
Sea Goddess I—Cunard Line
Song of Norway—Royal Caribbean Cruise Line
Stella Oceanis—Sun Line Cruises
Starward—Norwegian Cruise Line
Vistafjord—Cunard Line
Wind Star—Windstar Sail Cruises

Cayman Islands
Cunard Princess—Cunard Line
FairMajesty—Sitmar Cruises
Fairsky—Sitmar Cruises
Seaward—Norwegian Cruise Line
Regent Sea—Regency Cruises
Song of America—Royal Caribbean Cruise Line
Sun Viking—Royal Caribbean Cruise Lines
Skyward—Norwegian Cruise Line
Stella Solaris—Sun Line Cruises
Westerdam—Holland America Line / Westours

Curaçao
Crown Odyssey—Royal Cruise Line
CarlaCosta—Costa Cruises
Explorer Starship—Exploration Cruise Lines
Rotterdam—Holland American Line / Westours
The Victoria—Chandris Fantasy Cruises

Dominica
- **The Azur**—Chandris Fantasy Cruises
- **New Shoreham**—American Canadian Caribbean Line

Dominican Republic
- **Caribe I**—Commodore Cruise Line
- **Crown Odyssey**—Royal Cruise Line
- **Sagafjord**—Cunard Line
- **Vistafjord**—Cunard Line

Grenada
- **CarlaCosta**—Costa Cruises
- **Crown Odyssey**—Royal Cruise Line
- **Cunard Countess**—Cunard Line
- **New Shoreham**—American Canadian Caribbean Line
- **Rotterdam**—Holland American Line / Westours
- **Sagafjord**—Cunard Line
- **Skyward**—Norwegian Cruise Line
- **Stella Oceanis**—Sun Line Cruises
- **The Victoria**—Chandris Fantasy Cruises
- **Vistafjord**—Cunard Line
- **Wind Star**—Windstar Sail Cruises

Guadeloupe
- **Cunard Countess**—Cunard Line
- **New Shoreham**—American Canadian Caribbean Line
- **Sagafjord**—Cunard Line

Haiti
- **Song of America**—Royal Caribbean Cruise Line
- **Sovereign of the Seas**—Royal Caribbean Cruise Line
- **Sun Viking**—Royal Caribbean Cruise Line
- **Vistafjord**—Cunard Line

Jamaica
- **Britanis**—Chandris Fantasy Cruises
- **Crown Odyssey**—Royal Cruise Line
- **Cunard Princess**—Cunard Line
- **FairMajesty**—Sitmar Cruises
- **Fairsky**—Sitmar Cruises
- **Regent Sea**—Regency Cruises
- **Sagafjord**—Cunard Line
- **Seaward**—Norwegian Cruise Line
- **Skyward**—Norwegian Cruise Line
- **Song of America**—Royal Caribbean Cruise Line
- **Stella Solaris**—Sun Line Cruises
- **Sun Viking**—Royal Caribbean Cruise Line
- **Vistafjord**—Cunard Line
- **Westerdam**—Holland America Line / Westours

Martinique / Mayreau / Devil's Island / French West Indies
- **The Azur**—Chandris Fantasy Cruises
- **CarlaCosta**—Costa Cruises

SHIP SCHEDULES: CARIBBEAN PORTS □ 405

Crown Odyssey—Royal Cruise Line
Cunard Countess—Cunard Line
Daphne—Costa Cruises
Explorer Starship—Exploration Cruise Lines
FairMajesty—Sitmar Cruises
Fairsky—Sitmar Cruises
Festivale—Carnival Cruise Lines
Island Princess—P&O/Princess Cruises
New Shoreham—American Canadian Caribbean Line
Nordic Prince—Royal Caribbean Cruise Line
Ocean Islander—Ocean Cruise Lines
Ocean Princess—Ocean Cruise Lines
Pacific Princess—P&O/Princess Cruises
Rotterdam—Holland American Line / Westours
Royal Viking Sky—Royal Viking Line
Royal Viking Sun—Royal Viking Line
Sagafjord—Cunard Line
Sea Goddess I—Cunard Line
Song of Norway—Royal Caribbean Cruise Line
Starward—Norwegian Cruise Line
Stella Oceanis—Sun Line Cruises
The Victoria—Chandris Fantasy Cruises
Vistafjord—Cunard Line
Wind Star—Windstar Cruises

Puerto Rico

The Azur—Chandris Fantasy Cruises
Caribe I—Commodore Cruise Line
CarlaCosta—Costa Cruises
Celebration—Carnival Cruise Lines
Crown Odyssey—Royal Cruise Line
Cunard Countess—Cunard Line
Daphne—Costa Cruises
Explorer Starship—Exploration Cruise Lines
Festivale—Carnival Cruise Lines
Island Princess—P&O/Princess Cruises
Noordam—Holland American Line / Westours
Ocean Islander—Ocean Cruise Lines
Pacific Princess—P&O/Princess Cruises
Sagafjord—Cunard Line
Skyward—Norwegian Cruise Line
Song of Norway—Royal Caribbean Cruise Line
Sovereign of the Seas—Royal Caribbean Cruise Line
Starward—Norwegian Cruise Line
The Victoria—Chandris Fantasy Cruises
Vistafjord—Cunard Line
Westerdam—Holland America Line / Westours

St. Kitts / Nevis / Anguilla

The Azur—Chandris Fantasy Cruises
Caribbean Prince—American Canadian Caribbean Line
Explorer Starship—Exploration Cruise Lines
Nantucket Clipper—Clipper Cruise Line

Sagafjord—Cunard Line
Stella Oceanis—Sun Line Cruises
Vistafjord—Cunard Line

St. Lucia
Cunard Countess—Cunard Line
Daphne—Costa Cruises
Explorer Starship—Exploration Cruise Lines
New Shoreham—American Canadian Caribbean Line
Ocean Islander—Ocean Cruise Lines
Sagafjord—Cunard Line
Sea Goddess I—Cunard Line
Skyward—Norwegian Cruise Line
Vistafjord—Cunard Line

St. Maarten / St. Martin / St. Barthélemy
Caribbean Prince—American Canadian Caribbean Line
Celebration—Carnival Cruise Lines
Crown Odyssey—Royal Cruise Line
Cunard Countess—Cunard Line
Daphne—Costa Cruises
Explorer Starship—Exploration Cruise Lines
Festivale—Carnival Cruise Lines
Island Princess—P&O/Princess Cruises
Nantucket Clipper—Clipper Cruise Line
Nordic Prince—Royal Caribbean Cruise Line
Norway—Norwegian Cruise Line
Pacific Princess—P&O/Princess Cruises
Sagafjord—Cunard Line
Sea Goddess I—Cunard Line
Skyward—Norwegian Cruise Line
Song of Norway—Royal Caribbean Cruise Line
Starward—Norwegian Cruise Line
Stella Oceanis—Sun Line Cruises
Vistafjord—Cunard Line
Westerdam—Holland America Line / Westours
Wind Spirit—Windstar Sail Cruises

St. Vincent / Grenadines
The Azur—Chandris Fantasy Cruises
Explorer Starship—Exploration Cruise Lines
Island Princess—P&O/Princess Cruises
New Shoreham—American Canadian Caribbean Line
Ocean Islander—Ocean Cruise Lines
Sagafjord—Cunard Line
Sea Goddess I—Cunard Line
Stella Oceanis—Sun Line Cruises
Vistafjord—Cunard Line
Wind Star—Windstar Sail Cruises

Trinidad / Tobago
Ocean Islander—Ocean Cruise Lines
Ocean Princess—Ocean Cruise Lines

Stella Oceanis—Sun Line Cruises
Wind Star—Windstar Sail Cruises

U.S. Virgin Islands
The Azur—Chandris Fantasy Cruises
Caribbean Prince—American Canadian Caribbean Line
Caribe I—Commodore Cruise Line
CarlaCosta—Costa Cruises
Celebration—Carnival Cruise Lines
Colonial Explorer—Exploration Cruise Lines
CostaRiviera—Costa Cruises
Crown Odyssey—Royal Cruise Line
Cunard Countess—Cunard Line
Daphne—Costa Cruises
Explorer Starship—Exploration Cruise Lines
FairMajesty—Sitmar Cruises
Fairsky—Sitmar Cruises
Festivale—Carnival Cruise Lines
Island Princess—P&O/Princess Cruises
Nantucket Clipper—Clipper Cruise Line
Newport Clipper—Clipper Cruise Line
Noordam—Holland American Line / Westours
Nordic Prince—Royal Caribbean Cruise Line
Norway—Norwegian Cruise Line
Pacific Princess—P&O/Princess Cruises
Rotterdam—Holland American Line / Westours
Royal Viking Sky—Royal Viking Line
Royal Viking Sun—Royal Viking Line
Sagafjord—Cunard Line
Sea Goddess I—Cunard Line
Skyward—Norwegian Cruise Line
Song of Norway—Royal Caribbean Cruise Line
Sovereign of the Seas—Royal Caribbean Cruise Line
Starward—Norwegian Cruise Line
Stella Oceanis—Sun Line Cruises
Vistafjord—Cunard Line
Westerdam—Holland America Line / Westours
Wind Spirit—Windstar Sail Cruises
Yorktown Clipper—Clipper Cruise Line

British Virgin Islands
Caribbean Prince—American Canadian Caribbean Line
Colonial Explorer—Exploration Cruise Lines
Cunard Countess—Cunard Line
Explorer Starship—Exploration Cruise Lines
Nantucket Clipper—Clipper Cruise Line
Newport Clipper—Clipper Cruise Line
Noordam—Holland American Line / Westours
Sagafjord—Cunard Line
Sea Goddess I—Cunard Line
Stella Oceanis—Sun Line Cruises
Vistafjord—Cunard Line
Wind Spirit—Windstar Sail Cruises
Yorktown Clipper—Clipper Cruise Line

APPENDIX

MATCHING SHIPS AND LINES

□ □ □

The following list is a "quickie" guide to which ships belong to which line, so that you'll know where in Chapter V to look for more information about any given ship.

Amerikanis	Chandris Fantasy Cruises
Atlantic	Holland America Line / Westours
Azure Seas	Admiral Cruise Line
Azur	Chandris Fantasy Cruises
Bermuda Star	Bermuda Star Line
Bermuda Queen	Bermuda Star Line
Britanis	Chandris Fantasy Cruises
Caribbean Prince	American Canadian Caribbean Line
Caribe I	Commodore Cruise Line
CarlaCosta	Costa Cruises
Carnivale	Carnival Cruise Lines
Celebration	Carnival Cruise Lines
Charleston	American Cruise Lines
Colonial Explorer	Exploration Cruise Lines
Constitution	American Hawaii Cruises
CostaRiviera	Costa Cruises
Crown Odyssey	Royal Cruise Line
Cunard Countess	Cunard Line
Cunard Princess	Cunard Line
Daphne	Costa Cruises
Delta Queen	Delta Queen Steamship Co.
Discovery I	Discovery Cruises
Dolphin	Dolphin Cruise Line
Emerald Seas	Admiral Cruise Line
Explorer Starship	Exploration Cruise Lines
FairMajesty	Sitmar Cruises
Fairsea	Sitmar Cruises
Fairsky	Sitmar Cruises
Fairwind	Sitmar Cruises
Festivale	Carnival Cruise Lines
Future Seas	Admiral Cruise Line
Galileo	Chandris Fantasy Cruises
Glacier Bay Explorer	Exploration Cruise Lines
Golden Odyssey	Royal Cruise Line
Great Rivers Explorer	Exploration Cruise Lines
Holiday	Carnival Cruise Lines

MATCHING SHIPS & LINES □ 409

Ship	Line
Independence	American Hawaii Cruises
Island Princess	P&O/Princess Cruises
Jubilee	Carnival Cruise Lines
Majestic Tahiti Explorer	Exploration Cruise Lines
Mardi Gras	Carnival Cruise Lines
Mississippi Queen	Delta Queen Steamboat Co.
Nantucket Clipper	Clipper Cruise Line
New Orleans	American Cruise Lines
New Shoreham II	American Canadian Caribbean Line
Newport Clipper	Clipper Cruise Line
Nieuw Amsterdam	Holland America Line / Westours
Noordam	Holland America Line / Westours
Nordic Prince	Royal Caribbean Cruise Line
North Star	Exploration Cruise Lines
Norway	Norwegian Cruise Line
Ocean Islander	Ocean Cruise Lines
Ocean Pearl	Ocean Cruise Lines
Ocean Princess	Ocean Cruise Lines
Pacific Northwest Explorer	Exploration Cruise Lines
Pacific Princess	P&O/Princess Cruises
Pegasus	Epirotiki Lines
Queen Elizabeth 2	Cunard Line
Regent Sea	Regency Cruises
Regent Star	Regency Cruises
Regent Sun	Regency Cruises
Romanza	Chandris Fantasy Cruises
Rotterdam	Holland America Line / Westours
Royal Princess	P&O/Princess Cruises
Royal Viking Sea	Royal Viking Line
Royal Viking Sky	Royal Viking Line
Royal Viking Sun	Royal Viking Line
Sagafjord	Cunard Line
Savannah	American Cruise Lines
Scandinavian Saga	SeaEscape
Scandinavian Sky	SeaEscape
Scandinavian Star	SeaEscape
Scandinavian Sun	SeaEscape
Sea Goddess I	Cunard Line
Sea Goddess II	Cunard Line
Sea Princess	P&O/Princess Cruises
Seaward	Norwegian Cruise Line
Skyward	Norwegian Cruise Line
Song of America	Royal Caribbean Cruise Line
Song of Norway	Royal Caribbean Cruise Line
Southward	Norwegian Cruise Line
Sovereign of the Seas	Royal Caribbean Cruise Line
Stardancer	Admiral Cruise Line
Starship Oceanic	Premier Cruise Lines
Starship Royale	Premier Cruise Lines
Starward	Norwegian Cruise Line
Stella Oceanis	Sun Line Cruises
Stella Solaris	Sun Line Cruises
Sun Princess	P&O/Princess Cruises
Sun Viking	Royal Caribbean Cruise Line

Sunward II	Norwegian Cruise Line
The Victoria	Chandris Fantasy Cruises
Tropicale	Carnival Cruise Lines
Universe	World Explorer Cruises
Veracruz	Bermuda Star Line
Viking Princess	Crown Cruise Line
Vistafjord	Cunard Line
Westerdam	Holland America Line / Westours
Wind Song	Windstar Sail Cruises
Wind Spirit	Windstar Sail Cruises
Wind Star	Windstar Sail Cruises
World Renaissance	Epirotiki Lines
Yorktown Clipper	Clipper Cruise Line

Index

Acapulco, **86–7**, 186, 187, 218, 219, 261, 262, 291, 310
Admiral Cruise Lines, 121, 123, **133–41**, 334, 349, 396, 397, 399, 402, 408, 409
Admiralty Island, 26
Adriatic/Australia/New Zealand Line, 392
Air/sea packages, 113–14
Alaska Fest (Anchorage), 28
Alaska/Northwest Passage, **19–29**, 178, 186, 218, 223, 261, 271, 295, 303, 317, 396–7; Anchorage, 28–9; clothing to pack for, 330; Glacier Bay, 27–8; Juneau, 25–6; Ketchikan, 23–4; map, 21; Misty Fjords National Monument, 23; most popular attractions, 22; Skagway, 26–7; Vancouver, British Columbia, 22–3
Alaska State Museum (Juneau), 26
Alaska Zoo (Anchorage), 28
Alcazar de Colón (Dominican Republic), 49
All-Alaska Logging Championships (Sitka), 25
Alter do Chao, 106, 211, 303
Amazon River, **105–7**, 211, 250, 303, 310
Amelia Island, 144, 145
American Canadian Caribbean Line, **141–4**, 397–9, 402, 404–9
American Cruise Lines, 121, **144–8**, 345, 400, 408, 409
American Hawaii Cruises, **148–51**, 398, 408, 409
American President Lines, 392
American Society of Travel Agents (ASTA), 320–1
Amerikanis, 35, 96, 168, 169–70, 342, 343, 392, 393, 397, 402, 408
Anchorage, **28–9**, 187, 218, 271, 303, 304, 317
Anegada (British Virgin Islands), 78, 141
Anguilla, **56–8**, 141, 173, 405–6
Annandale Falls (Grenada), 50
Annapolis (Maryland), 101, 173
Anse Bertrand (Guadeloupe), 52
Antigua, **34–5**, 141, 168, 173, 178, 186, 187, 237, 261, 278, 279, 291, 303, 310, 402
Antigua Rum Distillery, 35
Arawak hieroglyphs (Aruba), 37

Arawak rock carvings (Guadeloupe), 52
Archeological Museum (St. Vincent), 70
Ardastra Gardens (Bahamas), 42
Argonaut, 212
Arts and Crafts Center (Mazatlán), 83
Aruba, **35–7**, 168, 187, 250, 262, 271, 291, 402
Asa Wright Nature Center (Trinidad), 72
Association of Retail Travel Agents (ARTA), 231
Astoria, 218
Atlantic, 35, 104, 223, 224, **231–4**, 397, 400, 402, 408
Atlas, 212
Auckland, 262, 304
Azur, 40, 47, 58, 63, 66, 71, 77, 168, 172, 397, 399, **403–8**
Azure Seas, 81, 123, 133, 134, **136–7**, 346, 399, 408

Bahamas, the, **40–2**, 133, 141, 155, 167, 178, 185, 207, 208, 237, 256, 301, 397, 402–3
Bahamian Out Island, 208, 256
Bahamian Private Island, 133, 223
Balboa, 186, 218, 310
Bali, 187, 251, 262, 291
Baltic Sea, 250, 304
Baltimore, 101, 144, 145, 173
Bangkok, 251, 262, 291
Bar Harbor, 96, 144, 173, 291, 295, 303
Barbados, **37–40**, 155, 168, 178, 186, 187, 219, 237, 251, 261, 278, 279, 291, 295, 303, 310, 314, 403
Barbados Museum, 39
Barbancourt (Jane) Distillery (Haiti), 55
Barbuda, **34–5**, 141, 402
Barrier Reef Islands, 141
Barrouallie (St. Vincent), 70
Basse-Terre (Guadeloupe), 52
Basseterre (St. Kitts), 57
Bathrooms, 127
Bath (Maine), 145, 173
Baths, the (British Virgin Islands), 78
Baton Rouge, 90–1, 144, 203
Bay of Islands, 262
Beaches: Aruba, 37; Bahamas, 42; Bermuda, 94; Caracas, 104; Cartagena, 105; Caribbean Islands, 33; Cayman Islands, 44; Grenada, 50; Guadeloupe, 52; Jamaica, 59; Mexican

Note: **boldface** page numbers indicate principal references.

Riviera/Yucatán Peninsula, 82–7; Trinidad, 72; U.S. Virgin Islands, 76
Beaufort, 101, 173
Beijing, 251, 262
Beds, 127
Belém, 106, 250, 310
Belize, 141
Bequia, 70, 168, 212, 219, 251, 310, 314
Bermuda, 93–6, 151, 167, 168, 186, 187, 278, 397
Bermuda Queen, 89, 96, 151–2, 153–5, 345, 397, 398
Bermuda Star, 82, 99, 151, 152, 153–5, 399, 400, 408
Bermuda Star Line, 151–5, 340, 343, 345, 397–400, 408, 410
Blackbeard Tower (U.S. Virgin Islands), 76
Black Sea, 168, 310
Block Island, 141, 144
Bluebeard's Castle (U.S. Virgin Islands), 76
Blue Grotto Dolphins (Bermuda), 95
Blue Lagoon (Jamaica), 61
Blue Mountains (Jamaica), 58
Boca do Valerio, 106, 211, 303
Bolivarian Museum (Caracas), 103
Bon voyage parties, 351–2
Bonaventure Island, 151, 303
Bonneville Lock, 218
Booking tickets, 320–5; cancellations, 323–4; by groups, 322; money-saving tips, 322–3; travel agents, 320–1
Books, 332
Boothbay Harbor, 144, 173
Bora Bora, 218, 262, 291, 303, 304, 314
Borneo, 262
Boston, 96, 144, 145, 173, 187, 295
Botanic gardens: Caracas, 103; St. Vincent, 70; Trinidad, 72; U.S. Virgin Islands, 77
Bovedas (Cartagena), 105
Breves, 106, 211
Brimmer Hall Estate (Jamaica), 60
Brimstone Hill Fortress (St. Kitts), 57
Brisbane, 262
Britanis, 37, 42, 61, 89, 102, 105, 168, 169–70, 335, 343, 397, 399, 400, 402, 404, 408
British Virgin Islands, 77–9, 407
Brochures, cruise, 8–10
Brunei, 251
Budget Travel News, 393
Buenos Aires, 212, 250, 295, 310
Bullfights (Mexican Riviera/Yucatán Peninsula), 83, 86
Burlington (Iowa), 92

Cabin selection, 124–32; bathrooms, 127; beds, 127; deck plans, 128–9; electrical outlets, 127, 130; inside vs. outside cabins, 131; kids and, 365; location, 130–1; sharing a cabin and, 131–2; size of cabin, 126–7
Cabo San Lucas, 81–2, 133, 151, 155, 218, 219, 261, 304, 310
Cairo (Illinois), 91–2
Caldera, 291
Callao, 310
Cambridge (Maryland), 144, 145
Camden (Maine), 173
Canada, 96–9, 400; Customs, 389; *see also* Northeast Passage/U.S. East Coast
Cancellations, 323–4
Cancún, 87–9
Canton, 251, 262
Cape Cod, 295
Cape Horn, 310
Cape Canaveral (Port Canaveral), 144, 145, 256, 301; as embarkation port, 338–40
Cape Pilar, 310
Cap-Haïtien, 56
Capri, 187
Captains: dining and socializing with, 360–1; insignia of, 384–5
Caracas, 103–4, 168, 178, 186, 223, 250, 291
Carbet Peak (Martinique), 62
Careenage (Barbados), 38
Caribbean Islands, 29–79, 141, 155, 167, 173, 175, 178, 185–7, 211, 218, 223, 237, 250, 261, 271, 278, 295, 303, 310, 314, 397–8; Antigua (and Barbuda), 34–5; Aruba, 35–7; the Bahamas (Nassau and Freeport), 40–2; Barbados, 37–40; British Virgin Islands, 77–9; Cayman Islands, 43–4; Curaçao, 44–5; Dominica, 46–7; Dominican Republic, 47–9; Grenada, 49–51; Guadeloupe (and Îles-des-Saintes), 51–3; Haiti, 53–6; island by island port calls, 402–7; Jamaica, 58–61; map, 30–1; Martinique, 61–3; Puerto Rico, 63–6; St. Kitts, Nevis, and Anguilla, 56–8; St. Lucia, 66–7; St. Maarten/St. Martin (and St. Barthélemy), 67–9; St. Vincent (and Grenadines), 69–71; Trinidad and Tobago, 71–3; U.S. Virgin Islands, 73–7
Caribbean Prince, 35, 51, 58, 69, 77, 79, 99, 141–2, 142–4, 397, 400, 402, 405–8
Caribe I, 49, 66, 77, 175, 176–8, 335, 397, 404, 405, 407, 408
Carib Rock (St. Vincent), 70

INDEX □ 413

Carib's Leap (Grenada), 50
CarlaCosta, 46, 51, 63, 66, 77, 104, 178, 179–81, 342, 397, 400, 403–5, 407, 408
Carnival Cruise Lines, 120, 121, 123, 155–67, 334, 342, 346, 397, 399, 402, 403, 405–10
Carnivale, 42, 155, 156, 157–9, 335, 397, 399, 402, 408
Caroni Bird Sanctuary (Trinidad), 72
Carriacou, 310
Carriage Museum (Bermuda), 95
Cartagena (Colombia), 104–5, 168, 187, 262, 271, 272, 291
Catalina Island, 133, 237
Casa Blanca (Puerto Rico), 64
Casa de Bastidas (Dominican Republic), 49
Casa de los Contrafuertes (Puerto Rico), 64
Casa Natal (Caracas), 103
Casinos: Bahamas, 40; Caribbean Islands, 33
Cast Line, 392
Castries (St. Lucia), 66
Caves of Nonsuch (Jamaica), 61
Cayman Islands, 43–4, 223, 303, 403
Cayman Turtle Farm, 44
Celebration, 66, 69, 77, 155, 157, 161–4, 335, 397, 405–8
Central Market (Trinidad), 72
Centre d'Art (Haiti), 54
Centro Comercial Chacaito (Caracas), 104
Chandris Fantasy Cruises, 121, 167–72, 334, 342, 343, 397–410
Changing of the Guard: Bahamas, 42; Barbados, 39
Chapel-by-the-Lake (Juneau), 26
Charleston (Nevis), 57
Charleston (ship), 99, 101, 144–6, 146–7, 400, 408
Charleston (South Carolina), 101, 144, 145, 173
Charlotte Amalie (U.S. Virgin Islands), 74–5
Charlottetown, 187, 295
Chattanooga, 93, 203
Chesapeake Bay, 101, 400
Chichén-Itzá (Cancún), 88
Children, 84, 123, 364–7; cabins and, 365; cost of bringing, 364–5; food for, 366; keeping them busy, 365–6; shore excursions with, 366–7
Chilean Line, 392
China, 250, 295
Chobolobo Mansion (Curaçao), 46
Christiansted (St. Croix), 76
Christmas Island, 291, 304
Christoffel National Park (Curaçao), 46

Ciboa, the (Dominican Republic), 48
Cincinnati, 203
Ciudad Guayana, 251
Clarence House (Antigua), 35
Clarkston (Oregon), 218
Clipper Cruise Lines, 121, 173–5, 337, 398, 400, 402, 405–7, 409, 410
Clock Monument (Cayman Islands), 44
CMB, 392
Cocoa Beach (Florida), 338
College Fjord, 186, 261, 262
Colón, 101, 218
Colonial Art Museum (Caracas), 103
Colonial Explorer, 77, 79, 218, 219, 220–1, 397, 400, 407, 408
Columbia Glacier, 186, 261, 262, 271, 303, 304, 317
Columbia Gorge, 218
Columbus Line, 92
Commodore Cruise Line, 175–8, 334, 397, 404, 405, 407, 408
Companhia Paraense de Turismo Paratúr (Belém), 107
Constitution, 121, 148–9, 149–51, 398, 408
Cooper Island, 141
Coral World (U.S. Virgin Islands), 75
Corfu, 187
Cornwall Beach (Jamaica), 59
Corsica, 314
Costa Cruises, 120, 123, 178–85, 337, 342, 349, 396, 397, 400, 402–8
Costa Rica, 186, 187, 219, 271, 272, 310
CostaRiviera, 77, 178, 181–4, 337, 397, 407, 408
Cost of cruises, 108–18, 120; air/sea packages and, 113–14; children and, 364–5; comparing, 109–11; discounts and, 111–13; flexibility and, 111; fly-free programs and, 113–114; onboard expenses, 117–18; seasonal variation in, 111; shore excursions and, 115–17; tipping and, 114–15
Coward (Noël), home of (Jamaica), 60
Cozumél, 89, 141, 151, 155, 168, 186, 187, 223, 237, 271, 278, 279, 295, 303, 310
Credit cards, 118, 332
Creek Street (Ketchikan), 24
Crew, nationality of, 120
Crisfield, 101
Crow Creek Mine (Anchorage), 29
Crown Cruise Line, 185–6, 397, 410
Crown House (U.S. Virgin Islands), 75
Crown Odyssey, 35, 37, 40, 46, 49, 51, 61, 63, 66, 69, 77, 84, 86, 87, 99, 102, 105, 291, 292, 294–5, 397–408
Cruise Lines International Association

(CLIA), 7
Cruise Passenger Center (Barbados), 39
Cruise Passengers Club International, 11
Cruises: history of, 3–6; information on, 7–12; long vs. short, 123–4; popularity of, 6–7; reasons for going on, 2–3; selecting, 119–24
Cruises to nowhere, 185, 207, 301, 397
Cruise Travel (magazine), 11
Cumberland River, 203
Cunard Countess, 35, 40, 51, 53, 63, 66, 67, 77, 79, 104, 121, 123, 186, 189, **194–6**, 342, 397, 400, 402–8
Cunard Line, 121, **186–202**, 328, 337, 342, 343, 346, 349, 396–410
Cunard Princess, 23, 24, 26, 27, 29, **44**, 61, 89, 121, 123, 186, 189, **196–7**, 342, 346, 396, 397, 399, 400, 403, 404, 408
Curaçao, **44–6**, 168, 178, 219, 223, 262, 291, 403
Curaçao Museum, 46
Customs, 387–9

Dalian, 251, 262
Danae, 178–9, 402
Daphne, 23, 24, 26, 27, 35, 40, 63, 66, 67, 69, 77, 178–9, **184–5**, 342, 396, 397, 402, 403, 405–8
Darien Jungle, 218
Darwin, 262
Davidson Glacier, 178
Debarkation, 389–90
Deck plans, 9, 128–9
Delta Queen, 93, 121, 203–4, **204–6**, 344, 400, 408
Delta Queen Steamboat Co., **202–7**, 344–6, 400, 408, 409
Denali National Park and Preserve (Alaska), 29
Deshaise (Guadeloupe), 52
Devil's Island, 212, 250, 295, 303, 404–5
De Tempel Theatre (Curaçao), 45
Diamond Rock (Martinique), 63
Diets, special, 358–9
Dining at sea, 354–63; with the captain, 360–1; in-cabin, 358; meals and food served, 354–6; sample menu, 359–60; seating arrangements, 324, 357–8; singles, 370–1; special diets, 358–9; special occasions, 363; times for meals, 356–7; wine and liquor, 359
Discounts, 111–13
Discovery Cruises, **207–8**, 397, 408
Discovery I, 397, 408
Diving: Cayman Islands, 44; Dominica, 47; equipment to take, 331
Doctor's Beach (Jamaica), 59

Documentation, 324–5
Dolphin, 42, 123, 208–9, **209–11**, 335, 397, 402, 408
Dolphin Cruise Line, 123, **208–11**, 334, 397, 402
Dominica, 46–7, 141, 168, 404
Dominican Convent (Puerto Rico), 64
Dominican Republic, 47–9, 404
Dougaldston Estate (Grenada), 50
Drake's Seat (U.S. Virgin Islands), 76
Drax Hall (Barbados), 39
Dry-cleaning facilities, 331
Dubrovnik, 187
Dubuque, 92
Dungeness, 310
Dunn's River Falls (Jamaica), 60

Eaglecrest, 26
East Coast, U.S.: *see* Northeast Passage/U.S. East Coast
Egon Oldendorff Line, 392
Egypt, 168, 310
Elba, 314
Electrical outlets, 127, 130
El Mirador (Mazatlán), 83
El Morro (Puerto Rico), 64–5
Emancipation Park (U.S. Virgin Islands), 75
Embarkation ports, 333–51; Cape Kennedy (Port Canaveral), 338–40; Fort Lauderdale (Port Everglades), 336–8; Los Angeles, 346–7; Miami (Port of Miami), 334–6; New Orleans, 344–6; New York (New York City Passenger Ship Terminal), 343–4; San Francisco, 347–9; San Juan (Puerto Rico), 342–3; Tampa (Port of Tampa and Port of St. Petersburg), 340–2; Vancouver, 349–51
Emerald Seas, 42, 123, 133, 134, **135–6**, 334, 397, 402, 408
Emilio Goeldi Museum (Belém), 107
Endicott Arm Fjord, 178
English Harbour (Antigua), 35
Enseñada, **81**, 133, 237
Entertainment, 120
Epirotiki Lines, 121, **211–18**, 398, 399, 401, 409, 410
Evansville (Indiana), 93
Evening wear, packing, 328, 330
Excursions, shore, 115–17; with children, 366–7
Exploration Cruise Line, **218–22**, 342, 349, 396–400, 403, 405–9
Explorer Starship, 24, 26, 27, 29, 40, 46, 58, 63, 66, 67, 69, 71, 77, 79, 102, 218–19, **221–2**, 342, 396, 397, 400, 403, 405–8

FairMajesty, 23, 24, 26, 27, 29, 35, 40, 42,

INDEX □ **415**

44, 61, 63, 77, 89, 303, 304, 309–10, 396, 397, 399, 402–5, 407, 408
Fairsea, 23, 24, 26, 27, 29, 82–84, 89, 303–4, 305–8, 346, 396, 398, 399, 408
Fairsky, 35, 40, 42, 44, 61, 63, 77, 89, 99, 101, 107, 303, 304, 308–9, 346, 397, 399, 400, 402–5, 407, 408
Fairwind, 82, 83, 84, 87, 99, 107, 304, 305–8, 337, 398–401, 408
Fall River, 151
Falls of Baleine (St. Vincent), 70
Fellow passengers, 122–3
Fern Gully (Jamaica), 60
Festivale, 40, 63, 66, 69, 77, 155–7, 159–61, 342, 397, 403, 405–8
Fiesta Yacht Cruise (Mazatlán), 82
Fiji, 262, 303
Fishing, Mexican Riviera/Yucatán Peninsula, 82–3
Floating Schooner Markets (Curaçao), 45–6
Florianopolis, 250
Florida Keys, 144, 145, 151, 168, 237, 310
Fly-free programs, 113–14
Ford's Freighter Travel Guide, 393
Fort Amsterdam (Curaçao), 46
Fort Berkley (Antigua), 35
Fort Charlotte (Bahamas), 42
Fort Charlotte (St. Vincent), 69–70
Fort Christian (U.S. Virgin Islands), 75
Fort Desaix (Martinique), 62
Fort Frederick (Grenada), 50
Fort George (Grenada), 50
Fort George (Trinidad), 72
Fort Lauderdale (Florida), 144, 145, 155, 178, 186, 187, 208, 223, 295, 301, 303, 310; as embarkation port, 336–8
Fort Myers (Florida), 144
Fort Pierce (Florida), 144, 145
Fort St-Louis (Martinique), 62
Fort San Felipe (Dominican Republic), 48
Fort San José (Cartagena), 105
Fort San Sebastian (Cartagena), 105
Fort Tartenson (Martinique), 62
Fort Zoutman (Aruba), 36
Fortaleza, 250, 295, 303
Frederick Lutheran Church (U.S. Virgin Islands), 75
Frederiksted (St. Croix), 76
Freeport/Lucaya, 40–2, 133, 155, 185, 208, 237, 301
Freighter travel, 391–4
Freighter Travel Club of America, 113, 393
Freighter Travel News, 393

Freighter World Cruises, 392
French Cloister (Bahamas), 42
French West Indies, 404–5
Future Seas, 134, 141, 397, 408

Gaillard Cut, 101
Galena (Illinois), 92
Galileo, 42, 89, 168, 169–70, 335, 343, 397, 399, 403, 408
Gallipolis (Ohio), 93
Garden of the Groves (Bahamas), 42
Gardens of Atherny (Jamaica), 61
Gaspé Peninsula, 98, 151
Gastown (Vancouver), 23
Gatun Lake, 101, 271, 272
Gemstones: Amazon River, 106; Cartagena, 105
Gestemani Barrio (Cartagena), 105
Gibbs Hill Lighthouse (Bermuda), 95
Gibraltar, 187
Glacier Bay Explorer, 24–7, 218, 219, 220–1, 396, 400, 408
Glacier Bay National Monument, 27–8, 218, 223, 261, 262, 317
Glacier wear, 330
Glossary of sailing terms, 378–84
Gold Creek Salmon Bake (Juneau), 26
Golden Odyssey, 291, 292, 293–4, 398, 401, 408
Goldmining area (Alaska), 28
Gold Rush Cemetery (Skagway), 27
Golf courses, Caribbean Islands, 33
Government House (Bahamas), 42
Government House (Barbados), 39
Government House (U.S. Virgin Islands), 75
Grand Anse (Guadeloupe), 52
Grand Case, 141
Grand Cayman, 155, 186, 187, 223, 237, 271, 278, 279, 310
Great Britain, 295
Great Rivers Explorer, 24, 25, 26, 27, 102, 218, 219, 220–1, 396, 400, 408
Great Stirrup Cay, 237
Greece, 168, 187, 211, 212, 310
Greenport (Connecticut), 144, 145
Greenwood Great House (Jamaica), 59
Grenada, 49–51, 141, 168, 178, 186, 187, 212, 219, 223, 237, 291, 295, 310, 404
Grenadines, the, 70, 141, 187, 218–19, 406
Gros Piton (St. Lucia), 66
Group bookings, 322
Guadalupe, Church of (Puerto Vallarta), 84
Guadeloupe (and Îles-des-Saintes), 51–3, 141, 168, 186, 187, 212, 310, 404
Gustavia, 68

Haddam (Connecticut), 144, 145
Haines (Alaska), 133, 218, 295, 317
Haiti, 53–6, 278, 279, 404
Halifax, 96, 98, 151, 187, 291, 295, 303
Halifax River, 144, 145
Hamilton (Bermuda), 95, 278
Handicapped, travel for the, 376–7
Hannibal (Missouri), 92
Harrison's Cave (Barbados), 39
Hawaiian Islands, 148, 187, 291, 398
Hell (Cayman Islands), 44
Hermes, 212
High divers (Acapulco), 87
Hiking: Barbados, 40; Puerto Rico, 63
Hilo, 148, 187, 304
Hilton Head Island, 101, 144, 145, 173
Hiroshima, 262
Historic buildings and sites: Barbados, 40; Caribbean Islands, 33; Cartagena, 105; Jamaica, 59; Nevis, 57; South America, 103; U.S. Virgin Islands, 77
Holiday, 89, 155, **161–4**, 335, 399
Holland American Line/Westours, 123, 222–37, 328, 337, 340, 341, 349, 369, 396–410
Homeric, 42; see also *Westerdam*
Hong Kong, 251, 262, 291
Honolulu, 148, 187, 291, 304
Hotels: Anchorage, 29; Los Angeles, 346; Miami, 335; New Orleans, 345; New York, 343; San Francisco, 348; San Juan (Puerto Rico), 342; Tampa/St. Petersburg, 340; Vancouver, 349
Houmas House (New Orleans), 90, 203
House of Assembly (Barbados), 39
Huahine, 218, 314
Hubbard Glacier, 186, 218, 303, 304

Îles-des-Saintes, 51–3, 187, 310
Independence, 121, 148–9, **149–51**, 398, 409
Indonesia, 250, 251
Inland waterways, **99–101**, 144, 400
Inoculations, 325
Institute of Certified Travel Agents (ICTA), 231
International Bazaar (Bahamas), 42
Iron Market (Haiti), 55
Isabel de Torres (Dominican Republic), 48
Isla Cedros, 219
Island Princess, 23, 24, 26, 27, 29, 63, 66, 69, 71, 77, 121, 261, 263, **265–9**, 396, 398, 405–7, 409
Israel, 168, 310
Ivaran Lines, 392, 393
Ixtapa, 85–6, 218, 261

Jacksonville, 144, 145
Jakarta, 187, 251
Jamaica, 58–61, 303, 404
Jason, 212, 213, 401
Jewelry, packing, 327–8
Jogging, 327
Jost Van Dyke (British Virgin Islands), 78, 79, 141, 187, 218, 315
Jubilee, 42, 155, 157, **161–4**, 335, 397, 399, 403, 409
Juneau, 25–6, 133, 178, 186, 187, 218, 261, 262, 271, 295, 303, 304, 317
Jupiter, 212, 401

Kauai, 148, 187
Kennewick (Oregon), 218
Kenscoff (Haiti), 54
Ketchikan, 23–4, 133, 178, 186, 187, 218, 223, 261, 262, 271, 295, 303, 304, 317
Key West, 151, 168, 237, 310
King's Square (Bermuda), 95
Kingston (Jamaica), 59
Kingston (New York), 144, 145
Klondike Gold Rush National Park, 27
Kobe, 251, 262
Kock (Jan) House (Curaçao), 46
Kona, 148
Kuala Lumpur, 187, 251

La Atarazana (Dominican Republic), 49
La Audiencia Beach (Manzanillo), 84
Labadee (Haiti), 53
La Boca de Reloj (Cartagena), 104
La Citadelle (Haiti), 56
La Fortaleza (Puerto Rico), 64
La Guaira, 103–4
Lahaina, 187, 304
Lake Gatun, 101, 271, 272
Lake Okeechobee, 144
La Paz, 218
La Pie de la Cuesta (Acapulco), 86
La Popa Monastery (Cartagena), 105
La Savane (Martinique), 62
La Soufrière (St. Vincent), 70
Laundry facilities, 331
La Vista (Acapulco), 87
Learnington caves (Bermuda), 95
Le Conte Glacier, 218
Le Grand Banc (Haiti), 55
Lewiston (Maine), 218
Libraries, ships', 332
Library Schoelcher (Martinique), 62
Lisbon, 187
Little Stirrup Cay, 134
Livorno, 314
Locke (California), 218
LoLoLai Festival (Puerto Rico), 65
Los Angeles, 133, 155, 237, 261, 291,

INDEX □ 417

304, 310; as embarkation port, 346-7
Los Arcos (Cabo San Lucas), 82
Louisville, 93
Lucaya: *see* Freeport/Lucaya
Luggage: getting aboard, 351; getting your (at end of cruise), 389
Lykes Brothers, 392

McNary Lock, 218
Madeira, 187
Madison (Indiana), 93
Magens Bay (U.S. Virgin Islands), 76
Mail delivery, 324
Majestic Tahiti Explorer, 218, 219, **220-1,** 398, 409
Malacca, 187
Malaysia, 250, 251
Mal de mer: *See* Seasickness
Malecon (Mazatlán), 83
Manaus, 106, 211, 250, 303
Manila, 251, 262, 291
Manzanillo, **84-5,** 218
Maps: British Virgin Islands, 78; Dominica, 47; East Coast inland waterways, 100; New England, 99; Northeast Passage, 97; U.S. Virgin Islands, 77
Maracas Beach (Trinidad), 72
Mar del Plata, 212
Mardi Gras, 42, 155, 156, **164-6,** 337, 397, 403, 409
Marigot (St. Maarten), 68
Marigot Bay (St. Lucia), 66
Maritime Museum (Bermuda), **94-5**
Marron, the (Haiti), 55
Martha's Vineyard, 96, 141, 144, 151, 173
Martinique, **61-3,** 141, 155, 168, 178, 186, 187, 218, 223, 237, 251, 261, 262, 278, 279, 291, 295, 303, 310, 314, 404-5
Mataha Island, 251
Maui, 148, 187, 291
Mayreau (West Indies), 261, 404-5
Mazatlán, **82-3,** 133, 151, 155, 218, 261, 304
Medical problems, 373-7
Medication, packing, 332
Mediterranean Sea, 167, 168, 187, 211, 250, 251, 261, 291, 295, 304, 310, 314, 399-400
Memphis (Tennessee), 91, 144, 203
Mendenhall Glacier, 25-6
Mérida, 223
Mesopotamia Valley (St. Vincent), 70
Metlakatla, 24
Mexican Riviera/Yucatán Peninsula, **79-89,** 151, 155, 167, 186, 218,

223, 237, 261, 271, 278, 291, 301, 303, 310, 398-9; Acapulco, 86-7; Cabo San Lucas, 81-2; Cancún, 87-9; Cozumél, 89; currency, 80; Enseñada, 81; Manzanillo, 84-5; Mazatlán, 82-3; Puerto Vallarta, 83-4; Zihuatanejo/Ixtapa, 85-6
Mexican Tourist Card, 325
Miami, 133, 155, 168, 175, 208, 237, 261, 278, 279, 291, 301; as embarkation port, 334-6
Mikve-Israel Emanuel Synagogue (Curaçao), 45
Mineral Shipping, 392
Minneapolis/St. Paul, 92
Mississippi and Ohio Rivers, **89-93,** 144-8, 202-7, 400
Mississippi Queen, 93, 121, 203-4, 206-7, 344, 400, 409
Misty Fjords National Monument, **23,** 218, 261, 262
Moment's Notice, 112
Money, how much to take, 332
Monte Carlo, 187, 314
Montego Bay (Jamaica), 59, 168, 186, 187, 271, 272
Montevideo, 212, 310
Mont Pélée (Martinique), 62
Montréal, 98-9, 141, 151, 187, 291, 295, 303
Montserrat, 173
Moorea, 218, 262, 291, 303, 304, 314
Morne Fortune (St. Lucia), 66
Morne Trois Pitons National Park (Dominica), 47
Morocco, 187
Mountain Top (U.S. Virgin Islands), 76
Mount Avila (Caracas), 103
Mount McKinley (Alaska), 29
Mount Sage (British Virgin Islands), 78
Mount Soufrière (St. Lucia), 66
Mulatas Islands, 102
Mullins Mill (Barbados), 39
Municipal Marketplace (Puerto Vallarta), 84
Musé Départmentale de la Martinique (Martinique), 62
Musée d'Art Haïtien du College St-Pierre (Port-au-Prince), 54
Musée Volcanologique (Martinique), 63
Mustique, 71, 187, 251, 310, 314
Mystic, 144

Nantucket, 96, 144, 173
Nantucket Clipper, 35, 58, 69, 77, 79, 99, 101, 173, **173-5,** 398, 400, 402, 405-7, 409
Nashville, 203
Nassau, **40-2,** 133, 155, 168, 178, 187,

203, 208, 223, 237, 256, 303
Natchez, 91, 144, 203
Nationality of crew, 120
National Museum and Art Gallery (Trinidad), 72
National Palace (Haiti), 55
Nauvoo (Illinois), 92
Nawiliwili, 187
Nelson's Dockyard (Antigua), 35
Neptune, 212, 213
Nevis, **56–8**, 187, 310, 405–6
New Archangel Russian Dancers (Sitka), 25
New Bedford, 144, 173
New Caledonia, 304
New Harmony (Indiana), 93
New London, 144
New Orleans, 90, 144, 151, 203, 345; as embarkation port, 344–6
New Orleans (ship), 93, 101, **144–6**, 147–8, 400, 409
Newport (Rhode Island), **96**, 141, 144, 151, 173, 187, 295, 303
Newport Clipper, 77, 79, 99, 101, 173, 173–5, 398, 400, 407, 409
New Shoreham, 398, 399, 402, 404–6
New Shoreham II, 35, 47, 51, 53, 63, 67, 71, 89, 99, 141–2, **142–4**, 400, 409
New York City, 141, 144, 145, 151, 168, 186, 187, 278, 291, 295, 303; as embarkation port, 343–4
Nieuw Amsterdam, 23–6, 89, 223, 224, 225–9, 340, 396, 399
99 Steps (U.S. Virgin Islands), 75
Noordam, 23–6, 42, 66, 77, 79, 218, 219, 220–1, 396–8, 403, 405, 407, 409
Nordic Prince, 35, 40, 63, 69, 77, 96, 278–80, **288–90**, 334, 343, 397, 398, 402, 403, 405–7, 409
Norfolk, 144, 145
Norman Island, 218
Northeast Passage/U.S. East Coast, 96–9, 141, 144, 151, 173, 218, 295, 400
North Star, 24–7, 82, 84–7, 218, 219, 220–1, 396, 399, 409
Norway, 69, 77, 237–9, **240–3**, 334, 398, 406, 407, 409
Norwegian Cruise Line, 121, 123, 237–50, 334, 342, 397–9, 402–7, 409, 410
Nova Scotia, 187, 303
Nude swimming, Guadeloupe, 52–3

Ocean Cruise Lines, **250–6**, 398–402, 405, 409
Ocean Islander, 40, 63, 66, 67, 71, 73, 104, 251–2, **252–4**, 398–401, 403, 405, 406, 409
Oceanos, 212

Ocean Pearl, 251, 398, 409
Ocean Princess, 37, 63, 73, **104**, 250–2, 254–6, 398, 399, 401, 402, 405, 406, 409
Ocho Rios (Jamaica), 59–60
Officers' insignia, 384–5
Official Airlines Guides, 393–4
Ohio and Mississippi Rivers, **89–93**, 144–8, 202–7, 400
Okeechobee, Lake, 144
Open House Program (Barbados), 39–40
Orpheus, 212
Oxford (Maryland), 101, 144, 145

Pablo Casals Museum (Puerto Rico), 64
Pacific Northwest Explorer, 24–7, 218, 219, 220–1, 396, 409
Pacific Princess, 35, 40, 63, 66, 69, 77, 121, 261, 263, **265–9**, 334, 342, 398, 399, 401–3, 405–7, 409
Packing, 326–32; daytime wear, 327; at end of cruise, 387; evening wear, 328, 330; jewelry, 327–8; rain and glacier wear, 330; shoes, 327
Palace of the Inquisition (Cartagena), 104
Palais de Sans Souci (Haiti), 56
Palancar Reef (Cozumél), 89
Pall Mall Square (St. Kitts), 57
Palm Beach (Florida), 99, 185
Panama Canal, **101–2**, 167, 168, 178, 186, 218, 219, 261, 262, 271, 291, 295, 303, 310, 400
Panama City, 218, 262
P&O/Princess Cruises, 123, **261–71**, 334, 337, 342, 346, 349, 396, 398, 399, 401–3, 405–7, 409
Papeete, 218, 262, 291, 314
Paradise Beach (Bahamas), 42
Parliament Square (Bahamas), 42
Parque Bolívar (Cartagena), 104
Parque Centenario (Cartagena), 105
Parties: bon voyage, 351–2; welcome aboard, 360
Pasco, 218
Passports, 324, 325
Pearl Islands, 218
Pedro's Castle (Cayman Islands), 44
Pegasus, 212, 214–15, **217–18**, 399, 401, 409
Penang, 187
Percé, 151
Peter Island (British Virgin Islands), 78, 141, 173, 187, 219
Petersburg, 218
Pétionville (Haiti), 54
Petit Piton (St. Lucia), 66
Philadelphia, 151
Philipsburg (St. Maarten), 67

INDEX □ 419

Pico Duarte (Dominican Republic), 48
Pigeon Island (St. Lucia), 66, 314
Pittsburgh, 93, 203
Placentia, 141
Playa Azul (Manzanillo), 84
Playa del Carmen, 151, 155, 168, 186, 223, 237, 271, 278, 279, 295
Playa del Sol (Puerto Vallarta), 83
Playa Langosta (Acapulco), 86
Plaza Bolívar (Caracas), 103
Plaza de Artesanías (Acapulco), 87
Plaza de la Merced (Cartagena), 104
Plymouth, 144
Pointe-á-Pitre (Guadeloupe), 52
Pointe de la Grande Vigie (Guadeloupe), 52
Point Saline (Grenada), 50
Polish Ocean Lines, 392
Port Antonio (Jamaica), 60
Port Canaveral (Cape Canaveral), 256, 301; as embarkation port, 338-40
Porte d'Enfer (Guadeloupe), 52
Port Everglades, 310; as embarkation port, 336-8; *see also* Fort Lauderdale
Port Jefferson, 144, 145
Portland (Oregon), 218
Port Limón, 310
Portofino, 187, 314
Port-of-Spain (Trinidad), 72
Ports (of call), 121-2; *see also* Embarkation ports; *and specific ports of call*
Portsmouth, 145, 173
Prairie du Chien (Wisconsin), 92
Premier Cruise Lines, 256-61, 338, 397, 403, 409
Prescott, 141
Prickley Pear Cays, 315
Prince Edward Island, 98, 303
Prince of Wales Island, 218
Prince Rupert (B.C.), 218
Print Shop (Bermuda), 95
Prospect Plantation (Jamaica), 60
Provincetown, 173
Puerto Madryn, 310
Puerto Montt, 310
Puerto Plata, 48, 175
Puerto Rico, 63-6, 405
Puerto Vallarta, 83-4, 133, 151, 155, 218, 219, 261, 291, 304
Punta del Este, 212, 250, 310
Pusan, 251, 262

Qingdao, 251
Qinhuangdao, 251
Québec, 187, 291, 295
Québec City, 98, 141, 151, 303
Queen Elizabeth II, 186-9, **189-94**, 328, 337, 375, 401-2, 409
Queen Emma Pontoon Bridge (Curaçao), 45

Queen's Park Savannah (Trinidad), 72
Queen's Royal College (Trinidad), 72
Queen's Staircase (Bahamas), 42
Quinta Caracas (Caracas), 103

Rafting, Jamaica, 59, 60
Raiatea, 218, 314
Rainbow Glacier, 178
Rain forest: Dominica, 47; Grenada, 50; Guadeloupe, 52
Rainwear, packing, 330
Rand Memorial Nature Center (Bahamas), 42
Red Dog Saloon (Juneau), 26
Red House (Trinidad), 72
Red Onion (Skagway), 27
Regency Cruises, 271-8, 340, 341, 349, 396, 398-401, 403, 404, 409
Regent Sea, 44, 61, 89, 102, 105, 271, 272-5, 340, 398-400, 403, 404, 409
Regent Star, 23-7, 29, 102, 105, 271, 272, 275-6, 396, 400, 409
Regent Sun, 102, 105, 272, 276-8, 398, 400, 401, 409
Returning home, 386-90
Revolcadero (Acapulco), 86
Richland, 218
Rio de Janeiro, 212, 250, 295, 303, 310
Rio Grande River (Jamaica), 60
Ripley (Ohio), 93
Road Town (British Virgin Islands), 78
Rockland, 145
Romanza, 168, *172,* 399, 409
Rose Hall Great House (Jamaica), 59
Rotterdam, 23-6, 42, 46, 51, 63, 77, 104, 223, 224, **229-31,** 328, 396-8, 401, 403-5, 407, 409
Royal Caribbean Cruise Line, 121, 278-91, 328, 334, 342, 343, 397, 402-7, 409
Royal Cruise Line, 121, 291-5, 337, 346, 368, 397, 398-408
Royal Princess, 23, 26, 89, 262, **263-5,** 346, 396, 399, 409
Royal Viking Line, 121, 295-301, 328, 337, 343, 346, 349, 396, 398-401, 403, 407, 409
Royal Viking Sea, 23-7, 295, 296, 298-300, 396, 398, 401, 402, 409
Royal Viking Sky, 40, 63, 77, 105, 295, 296, 298-300, 398-403, 405, 407, 409
Royal Viking Sun, 40, 63, 77, 89, 99, 105, 295, 296, **300-1,** 398, 399, 401, 403, 405, 407, 409

Saba, 141
Sabalo Beach (Mazatlán), 82

Sacramento, 218
Sacramento River, 218
Sacré-Coeur de Balata Cathedral (Martinique), 62
Safety at sea, 7-8
Sagafjord, 23-7, 29, 35, 37, 40, 42, 49, 51, 53, 58, 61, 63, 66, 67, 69, 71, 77, 79, 89, 99, 187-9, 197-9, 328, 337, 343, 396, 398-407, 409
Saguenay Fjord, 151, 291
Saguenay River, 98, 141, 303
Sailing terms glossary, 378-84
St. Augustine (Florida), 99, 144, 145
St. Barthélemy, 67-9, 141, 173, 187, 219, 291, 310, 315, 406
St. Christopher: *see* St. Kitts
St. Croix, 76-7, 141, 173, 178, 187, 218, 219, 237, 291, 303, 310
St. Eustatius, 173
St. Francisville, 91, 203
St. George (Bermuda), 95, 278
St. George Botanical Gardens (U.S. Virgin Islands), 77
St. George's (Grenada), 50
St. George's Anglican Church (St. Kitts), 57
St. John (U.S. Virgin Islands), 77, 141, 173, 175, 187, 218, 237, 315
St. John's Cathedral (Antigua), 35
St. John's Church (Nevis), 57
St. Johns River, 144
St. Kitts (St. Christopher), **56-8**, 141, 168, 173, 187, 218, 237, 310, 405-6
St. Lawrence River, 98
St. Louis (Missouri), 203
St. Louis Roman Catholic Cathedral (Martinique), 62
St. Lucia, 66-7, 141, 168, 178, 186, 187, 219, 237, 251, 406
St. Maarten/St. Martin, 67-9, 141, 155, 168, 173, 178, 186, 187, 219, 223, 237, 261, 262, 278, 279, 291, 310, 315, 406
St. Mary's Catholic Church (St. Vincent), 70
St. Mary's City, 173
St. Michaels (Maryland), 101, 144, 145, 173
St. Michael's Cathedral (Sitka), 25
St. Nicholas Abbey (Barbados), 39
St. Nicholas Russian Orthodox Church (Juneau), 26
St. Paul, 203
St. Peter's Church (Bermuda), 95
St. Petersburg, 301: as embarkation port, 340-2
St-Pierre (Martinique), 63
St. Simons Island, 99-101, 144, 145, 173
St. Thomas (U.S. Virgin Islands), 74, 141, 155, 168, 173, 175, 178, 186, 187, 218, 223, 237, 261, 262, 278, 279, 291, 295, 303, 310, 315
St-Trinité Cathedral (Haiti), 55
St. Tropez, 187, 314
St. Vincent, 69-71, 141, 187, 310, 406
Salt Island, 141, 218
Salvador (Bahía), 250, 295, 303, 310
Salvador (ship), 393
San Blas, 218, 310
San Blas Islands, 102, 168, 218, 272, 295
Sand Cay Reef (Haiti), 55
San Diego, 133, 151, 187, 219, 237
San Felipe Fortress (Cartagena), 105
San Fernando Castle (Cartagena), 105
San Francisco, 218, 295; as embarkation port, 347-9
San Francisco do Sul, 212
San Joaquin River, 218
San Juan (Puerto Rico), 155, 168, 175, 178, 186, 187, 218, 219, 223, 237, 261, 262, 279, 291, 295, 303; as embarkation port, 342-3
San Juan Cathedral (Puerto Rico), 64
San Juan Gate (Puerto Rico), 64
San Pedrito (Manzanillo), 84
San Pedro Claver, Church of (Cartagena), 104
Santa Fe, 393
Santa María la Menor, Cathedral of (Dominican Republic), 49
Santarém, 106, 211, 303
Santo Domingo (Dominican Republic), 48, 187, 291
Santo Domingo Church and Convent (Cartagena), 104
Santos, 212, 250, 310
Santo Tomas Winery (Enseñada), 81
Sausalito, 218
Savane de Petrifications (Martinique), 63
Savannah (Georgia), 144, 173
Savannah (ship), 99, 101, 144-6, **146-7**, 400, 409
Scandinavia, 250, 291, 295
Scandinavian Saga, 89, 301, 302, **302-3**, 340, 397, 399
Scandinavian Sky, 301, 302, **302-3**, 335, 338, 397, 409
Scandinavian Star, 42, 301, 302, **302-3**, 397, 403, 409
Scandinavian Sun, 42, 301, 302, **302-3**, 397, 403, 409
Scenic drives: British Virgin Islands, 79; U.S. Virgin Islands, 77
Schooner Harbor (Aruba), 36
Scuba-diving: *see* Diving
Sea-Band, 374
SeaEscape, 123-4, **301-3**, 334, 338, 340, 397, 399, 403, 409

Sea Gardens (Bermuda), 94–5
Sea Goddess I, 35, 40, 63, 67, 69, 71, 77, 79, 187, 188, **202**, 398, 399, 401–3, 405–7, 409
Sea Goddess II, 187, 188, **202**, 328, 398, 400, 401, 409
Sea Princess, 23, 24, 26, 27, 262, 396, 398, 409
Seasickness, 373–5
Seating arrangements, dining, 324, 357–8
Seattle, 295
Seaward, 44, 61, 89, 237–9, **248–50**, 398, 399, 403, 404, 409
Selecting a cruise, 119–24
Semarang, 291
Sessions House (Bermuda), 95
Seward, 187, 262
Shanghai, 251, 262
Sharing a cabin, 131–2; with children, 365
Shaw Park Gardens (Jamaica), 60
Sheldon Jackson Museum (Sitka), 25
Ship(s): debarking from, 389–90; designations for, 384; exploring the, 352–3; freighter, 391–4; registration, 8; visits to, 11
Shoes, packing, 327
Shore excursions, 115–17
Shrine of St. Therese (Juneau), 26
Sign Great House (Jamaica), 59
Singapore, 187, 251, 262, 291
Singles, 368–72; dining, 370–1; friends and romances, 371–2; roommates for, 369–70
Sitka, **24–5**, 187, 218, 223, 271, 295, 317
Sitka Historical National Park, 25
Sitmar Cruises, 120, 123, **303–10**, 337, 346, 349, 396–405, 407, 408
Skagway, 26–7, 133, 178, 186, 187, 218, 261, 262, 271, 295, 303, 304, 317
Skindiving: *see* Diving
Skyline Highway (Trinidad), 72
Skyride Restaurant (Anchorage), 28
Skyward, 44, 51, 61, 66, 67, 69, 77, 89, 89, 237, 239, **243–4**, 334, 398, 399, 403–7, 409
Somers' Wharf (Bermuda), 95
Somerset Falls (Jamaica), 60–1
Sommelier, 359
Song of America, 44, 56, 61, 89, 278–80, **286–8**, 335, 398, 399, 403, 404, 409
Song of Norway, 35, 40, 63, 66, 69, 77, 279, 280, **284–6**, 342, 398, 402, 403, 405–7, 409
Soufrière (Guadeloupe), 52
South America, **102–7**, 167, 168, 178, 187, 211, 295, 310, 400–1; Amazon River, 105–7; Caracas/La Guaira, Venezuela, 103–4; Cartagena (Colombia), 104–5
Southeast Asia, 187, 398
South Florida Cruises, 112
Southampton (England), 186
South Pacific, 261, 291, 295, 398
Southward, 81, 237, 239, **246–7**, 399, 409
Sovereign of the Seas, 56, 66, 77, 335, 398, 404, 405, 407, 409
Soviet Union, 250
Spain, 187
Spur of the Moment, 112
StandBuys, 112
Stardancer, 23, 24, 26, 27, 82–4, 133, **138–41**, 396, 399, 409
Starship Oceanic, 42, 256–7, **259–61**, 338, 397, 403, 409
Starship Royale, 42, 256–7, **258–9**, 338, 397, 403, 409
Starward, 35, 40, 63, 66, 69, 77, 237–9, **247–8**, 342, 398, 402, 403, 405–7, 409
Steamship Historical Society of America, 11
Stella Maris II, 311
Stella Oceanis, 35, 40, 51, 58, 63, 69, 71, 73, 77, 79, **310–12**, **314**, 328, 400–7, 409
Stella Solaris, 44, 61, 82, 86, 87, 102, 310, 311, **312–13**, 328, 398–401, 403, 404, 409
Stockton, 218
Straw market: Jamaica, 60; Nassau, 41–2
Sulfur Springs (Dominica), 47
Sunburn, 375–6
Sun Line Cruises, 121, **310–14**, 328, 337, 398–407
Sun Princess, 23, 24, 26, 27, 82–4, 86, 87, 121, 123, 261, 263, **269–71**, 334, 396, 399, 409
Sun Viking, 44, 56, 61, 89, 279, 280, **290–1**, 334, 398, 399, 403, 404, 409
Sunward II, 42, 237–9, **244–6**, 334, 397, 403, 410
Sydney, 151, 262, 295, 304

Tadoussac, 141
Tahaa, 218, 314
Tahiti, 303, 304, 314, 398
Taku Lodge (Juneau), 26
Tampa, 151, 223, 271; as embarkation port, 340–2
Taormina, 187
TBA ("to be assigned") bookings, 322
Teatro Amazonas (Manaus), 106
Tenerife, 187
Tennessee River, 203

Tickets, booking, 320-5; cancellations, 323-4; by groups, 322; money-saving tips, 322-3; travel agents, 320-1
Tipping, 114-15; the sommelier, 359
Titusville (Florida), 99
Tlingit, 20
Tobago, 71-3, 212, 250, 251, 406-7
Tobago Cays, 314
"To be assigned" (TBA) bookings, 322
Tonga, 262
Tortola (British Virgin Islands), 78, 141, 173, 186, 187, 218, 223, 310
Totem Bright Park (Ketchikan), 24
Totem Heritage Cultural Center (Ketchikan), 24
Tower of the Clock (Cartagena), 104
Tracy Arm (Alaska), 186, 218
Trafalgar Falls (Dominica), 47
Trafalgar Square (Barbados), 38-9
Trail of '98 Museum (Skagway), 27
Transatlantic cruises, 186, 401
Transderm-Scop, 373-4
Travel agents, 7; booking tickets with, 320-1; cost of cruises and, 109
Travel clubs, 113
Traveltips Cruise & Freighter Travel Assn., 113
Trav-L-Tips Freighter Travel Association, 393
Trinidad and Tobago, 71-3, 212, 295, 303, 310, 406-7, 409
Trois-Îlets (Martinique), 62
Tropicale, 82, 83, 84, 155-7, 166-7, 346, 399, 410
Troy, 141
Tucker (President Henry) House (Bermuda), 95
Tulúm (Cancún), 88, 141
Turkey, 168, 310

U.S. Virgin Islands, 73-7, 407; *see also* St. Croix; St. John; St. Thomas
Universe, 23-7, 29, 317, **317-19**, 396, 410
University City (Caracas), 103
Usuaia, 310

Valdez, 187, 262, 310, 317
Vancouver:
Vancouver, British Columbia, 22-3, 133, 178, 186, 187, 223, 261, 262, 271, 295, 303, 304, 317; as embarkation port, 349-51
Venice, 168, 187
Veracruz, 89, 151, 152, **152-3**, 340, 399, 410
Vero Beach (Florida), 99
Vero-Peso Market (Belém), 107

Vicksburg, 91, 144, 203
Victoria, The, 46, 51, 63, 66, 104, 168, 169-70, 317, 342, 398, 401, 403-5, 410
Viking Princess, 185, **185-6**, 397, 410
Virgin Gorda (British Virgin Islands), 78, 79, 141, 173, 187, 218, 219, 310, 315
Virgin Islands: *see* British Virgin Islands; U.S. Virgin Islands
Virgin Islands National Park, 77
Visas, 324, 325
Visits to ships, 11
Vistafjord, 35, 37, 40, 42, 49, 51, 56, 58, 61, 63, 66, 67, 69, 71, 77, 79, 187-9, 199-202, 328, 337, 343, 398, 400-7, 410
Volcanoes (St. Vincent), 70
Voodoo (Haiti), 56

Wabasha (Minnesota), 92
Walt Disney World, 339
Warren (Canada), 141
Washington, D.C., 173
Waterfalls: Jamaica, 60-1; St. Vincent, 70; U.S. Virgin Islands, 77
Water Tower (Bahamas), 42
West Coast, U.S., 218
West Point, 144, 145
Westerdam, 44, 61, 66, 69, 77, 223-5, 234-7, 366, 397-9, 403-7, 410
Whampoa, 251
Wheelchair travel, 376-7
Whim Great House (U.S. Virgin Islands), 77
Whitehall Mansion (Trinidad), 72
White Pass & Yukon Railway, 27
White River (Jamaica), 60
Whitsunday Island, 262, 304
Whittier, 186
Wildlife preserves or sanctuaries: Trinidad, 72
William III Tower (Aruba), 36
Williamsburg, 101, 144, 145
Wind Song, 314, 398, 410
Wind Spirit, 69, 77, 79, 314-15, 315-16, 398, 400, 406, 407, 410
Wind Star, 40, 51, 63, 71, 73, 314, 315-16, 398, 403-7, 410
Windstar Sail Cruises, **314-16**, 398, 400, 403, 404, 405, 406, 407, 410
Windward Highway (St. Vincent), 70
World cruises, 401-2
World Explorer Cruises, **317-19**, 349, 396, 410
World Ocean & Cruise Liner Society, 113
World Renaissance, 107, 211-12, 214-15, **215-17**, 398, 401, 410

World Wide Cruise and Shipline Guide, 393
Worldwide Discount Travel, 112
Wrangell, 178, 218, 317

Yakutat Bay, 186, 218
Yantai, 251
Yelapa Beach (Puerta Vallarta), 84

Yorktown, 101, 144, 145, 173
Yorktown Clipper, 77, 79, 99, 101, 173–5, 398, 400, 407, 410
Yugoslav Great Lakes Line, 392
Yugoslavia, 168

Zihuatanejo, 85–6, 218, 261, 291, 310

NOW!
ARTHUR FROMMER LAUNCHES HIS SECOND TRAVEL REVOLUTION with

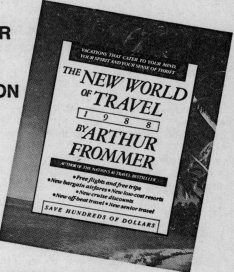

The New World of Travel

The hottest news and latest trends in travel today—heretofore the closely guarded secrets of the travel trade—are revealed in this new sourcebook by the dean of American travel. Here, collected in one book that is updated every year, are the most exciting, challenging, and money-saving ideas in travel today.

You'll find out about hundreds of alternative new modes of travel—and the many organizations that sponsor them—that will lead you to vacations that cater to your mind, your spirit, and your sense of thrift.

Learn how to fly for free as an air courier; travel for free as a tour escort; live for free on a hospitality exchange; add earnings as a part-time travel agent; pay less for air tickets, cruises, and hotels; enhance your life through cooperative camping, political tours, and adventure trips; change your life at utopian communities, low-cost spas, and yoga retreats; pursue low-cost studies and language training; travel comfortably while single or over 60; sail on passenger freighters; and vacation in the cheapest places on earth.

And in every yearly edition, Arthur Frommer spotlights the 10 GREATEST TRAVEL VALUES for the coming year. 384 pages, large–format with many, many illustrations. All for $12.95!

ORDER NOW
TURN TO THE LAST PAGE OF THIS BOOK FOR ORDER FORM.

NOW, SAVE MONEY ON ALL YOUR TRAVELS!
Join Frommer's™ Dollarwise® Travel Club

Saving money while traveling is never a simple matter, which is why, over 27 years ago, the **Dollarwise Travel Club** was formed. Actually, the idea came from readers of the Frommer publications who felt that such an organization could bring financial benefits, continuing travel information, and a sense of community to economy-minded travelers all over the world.

In keeping with the money-saving concept, the annual membership fee is low—$18 (U.S. residents) or $20 U.S. (Canadian, Mexican, and foreign residents)—and is immediately exceeded by the value of your benefits which include:

1. The latest edition of any TWO of the books listed on the following pages.
2. A copy of any Frommer City Guide.
3. An annual subscription to an 8-page quarterly newspaper *The Dollarwise Traveler* which keeps you up-to-date on fastbreaking developments in good-value travel in all parts of the world—bringing you the kind of information you'd have to pay over $35 a year to obtain elsewhere. This consumer-conscious publication also includes the following columns:

   Hospitality Exchange—members all over the world who are willing to provide hospitality to other members as they pass through their home cities.

   Share-a-Trip—requests from members for travel companions who can share costs and help avoid the burdensome single supplement.

   Readers Ask . . . Readers Reply—travel questions from members to which other members reply with authentic firsthand information.

4. Your personal membership card which entitles you to purchase through the club all Frommer publications for a third to a half off their regular retail prices during the term of your membership.

So why not join this hardy band of international Dollarwise travelers now and participate in its exchange of information and hospitality? Simply send $18 (U.S. residents) or $20 U.S. (Canadian, Mexican, and other foreign residents) along with your name and address to: Frommer's Dollarwise Travel Club, Inc., Gulf + Western Building, One Gulf + Western Plaza, New York, NY 10023. Remember to specify which *two* of the books in section (1) and which *one* in section (2) above you wish to receive in your initial package of member's benefits. Or tear out the next page, check off your choices, and send the page to us with your membership fee.

FROMMER BOOKS
PRENTICE HALL PRESS
ONE GULF + WESTERN PLAZA
NEW YORK, NY 10023

Date_____

Friends:
Please send me the books checked below:

FROMMER'S™ $-A-DAY® GUIDES

(In-depth guides to sightseeing and low-cost tourist accommodations and facilities.)

☐ Europe on $30 a Day...................$14.95	☐ New Zealand on $40 a Day.............$11.95
☐ Australia on $30 a Day $12.95	☐ New York on $50 a Day................$10.95
☐ Eastern Europe on $25 a Day...........$10.95	☐ Scandinavia on $50 a Day $10.95
☐ England on $40 a Day..................$11.95	☐ Scotland and Wales on $40 a Day........$11.95
☐ Greece on $30 a Day...................$11.95	☐ South America on $30 a Day $10.95
☐ Hawaii on $50 a Day...................$13.95	☐ Spain and Morocco (plus the Canary Is.)
☐ India on $25 a Day $10.95	on $40 a Day........................$13.95
☐ Ireland on $30 a Day...................$10.95	☐ Turkey on $25 a Day $10.95
☐ Israel on $30 & $35 a Day $11.95	☐ Washington, D.C., & Historic Va. on
☐ Mexico (plus Belize & Guatemala)	$40 a Day..........................$11.95
on $25 a Day.......................$13.95	

FROMMER'S™ DOLLARWISE® GUIDES

(Guides to sightseeing and tourist accommodations and facilities from budget to deluxe, with emphasis on the medium-priced.)

☐ Alaska $12.95	☐ Cruises (incl. Alask, Carib, Mex, Hawaii,
☐ Austria & Hungary $14.95	Panama, Canada, & US)...............$14.95
☐ Belgium, Holland, Luxembourg.........$11.95	☐ California & Las Vegas................$14.95
☐ Brazil (avail. Nov. 1988)...............$14.95	☐ Florida $11.95
☐ Egypt.............................$11.95	☐ Mid-Atlantic States...................$12.95
☐ France $14.95	☐ New England......................$12.95
☐ England & Scotland....................$14.95	☐ New York State....................$12.95
☐ Germany..........................$12.95	☐ Northwest........................$11.95
☐ Italy $14.95	☐ Skiing in Europe....................$14.95
☐ Japan & Hong Kong..................$13.95	☐ Skiing USA—East...................$11.95
☐ Portugal, Madeira, & the Azores.........$12.95	☐ Skiing USA—West..................$11.95
☐ South Pacific $12.95	☐ Southeast & New Orleans $11.95
☐ Switzerland & Liechtenstein $12.95	☐ Southwest........................$14.95
☐ Bermuda & The Bahamas..............$11.95	☐ Texas $11.95
☐ Canada...........................$12.95	☐ USA (avail. Feb. 1989)................$15.95
☐ Caribbean........................$13.95	

FROMMER'S™ TOURING GUIDES

(Color illustrated guides that include walking tours, cultural & historic sites, and other vital travel information.)

☐ Australia...........................$9.95	☐ Paris..............................$8.95
☐ Egypt.............................$8.95	☐ Thailand...........................$9.95
☐ Florence...........................$8.95	☐ Venice $8.95
☐ London............................$8.95	

TURN PAGE FOR ADDITONAL BOOKS AND ORDER FORM.

FROMMER'S™ CITY GUIDES

(Pocket-size guides to sightseeing and tourist accommodations and facilities in all price ranges.)

☐ Amsterdam/Holland $5.95	☐ Montreal/Quebec City $5.95
☐ Athens........................$5.95	☐ New Orleans.......................$5.95
☐ Atlantic City/Cape May $5.95	☐ New York........................$5.95
☐ Boston........................$5.95	☐ Orlando/Disney World/EPCOT...........$5.95
☐ Cancún/Cozumel/Yucatán $5.95	☐ Paris..........................$5.95
☐ Dublin/Ireland....................$5.95	☐ Philadelphia $5.95
☐ Hawaii $5.95	☐ Rio (avail. Nov. 1988) $5.95
☐ Las Vegas $5.95	☐ Rome.........................$5.95
☐ Lisbon/Madrid/Costa del Sol $5.95	☐ San Francisco....................$5.95
☐ London.......................$5.95	☐ Santa Fe/Taos (avail. Dec. 1988) $5.95
☐ Los Angeles....................$5.95	☐ Sydney $5.95
☐ Mexico City/Acapulco $5.95	☐ Washington, D.C...................$5.95
☐ Minneapolis/St. Paul $5.95	

SPECIAL EDITIONS

☐ A Shopper's Guide to the Caribbean $12.95	☐ Motorist's Phrase Book (Fr/Ger/Sp) $4.95
☐ Beat the High Cost of Travel.............$6.95	☐ Paris Rendez-Vous....................$10.95
☐ Bed & Breakfast—N. America $8.95	☐ Swap and Go (Home Exchanging) $10.95
☐ Guide to Honeymoon Destinations	☐ The Candy Apple (NY for Kids) $11.95
(US, Canada, Mexico, & Carib) $12.95	☐ Travel Diary and Record Book............$5.95
☐ Manhattan's Outdoor Sculpture..........$15.95	☐ Where to Stay USA (Loding from $3
	to $30 a night).....................$10.95

☐ Marilyn Wood's Wonderful Weekends (NY, Conn, Mass, RI, Vt, NH, NJ, Del,Pa)................$11.95
☐ The New World of Travel (Annual sourcebook by Arthur Frommer previewing: new travel trends, new modes of travel, and the latest cost-cutting strategies for savvy travelers)..................$12.95

SERIOUS SHOPPER'S GUIDES

(Illustrated guides listing hundreds of stores, conveniently organized alphabetically by category)

☐ Italy..........................$15.95	☐ Los Angeles......................$14.95
☐ London.......................$15.95	☐ Paris..........................$15.95

GAULT MILLAU

(The only guides that distinguish the truly
superlative from the merely overrated.)

☐ The Best of Chicago (avail. Feb. 1989) $15.95	☐ The Best of New England (avail. Feb. 1989)...$15.95
☐ The Best of France (avail. Feb. 1989) $15.95	☐ The Best of New York................$15.95
☐ The Best of Italy (avail. Feb. 1989).........$15.95	☐ The Best of San Francisco..............$15.95
☐ The Best of Los Angeles................$15.95	☐ The Best of Washington, D.C............$15.95

ORDER NOW!

In U.S. include $1.50 shipping UPS for 1st book; 50¢ ea. add'l book. Outside U.S. $2 and 50¢, respectively.

Allow four to six weeks for delivery in U.S., longer outside U.S.

Enclosed is my check or money order for $_____

NAME _____

ADDRESS _____

CITY _____ STATE _____ ZIP _____